Sex and Reason

RICHARD A. POSNER

Sex and Reason

HARVARD UNIVERSITY PRESS

CAMBRIDGE, MASSACHUSETTS LONDON, ENGLAND 1992

Library of Congress Cataloging-in-Publication Data

Posner, Richard A.
Sex and reason / Richard A. Posner.
p.   cm.
Includes bibliographical references and index.
ISBN 0-674-80279-9 (alk. paper)
1. Sex—Economic aspects.   2. Sex customs.   I. Title.
HQ16.P67   1992
306.7—dc20   91-30700
CIP

CONTENTS

Sex and Reason

> Pleasures are an impediment to rational delib-
> eration, and the more so the more pleasurable
> they are, such as the pleasures of sex—it is
> impossible to think about anything while ab-
> sorbed in them.
>
> ARISTOTLE, *Nicomachean Ethics*

Introduction

Anyone in our society who wants to write about sex without being accused of prurient interest had better explain what the source of his interest in the subject is. In my case it is the belated discovery that judges know next to nothing about the subject beyond their own personal experience, which is limited, perhaps more so than average, because people with irregular sex lives are pretty much (not entirely, of course) screened out of the judiciary— especially the federal judiciary, with its elaborate preappointment investiga- tions by the FBI and other bodies. This screening, along with the gap, for which the screening is in part responsible, in judges' systematic knowledge of sex, is a residue of the nation's puritan—more broadly of its Christian— heritage. Another residue is the large body of laws regulating sex which judges are called on to interpret and apply, and sometimes asked to invalidate.

Two events, occurring at the time that I was casting about for a topic for the Rosenthal Lectures at Northwestern University, set me on the research path that has culminated in this book. The first was an attempt to plug one of many embarrassing gaps in my education by reading Plato's *Symposium*. I knew it was about love, but that was all I knew. I was surprised to discover that it was a defense, and as one can imagine a highly interesting and articulate one, of homosexual love.[1] It had never occurred to me that the greatest figure in the history of philosophy, or for that matter any other respectable figure in the history of thought, had attempted such a thing. It dawned on me that the discussion of the topic in the opinions in *Bowers v. Hardwick* (the decision in which the Supreme Court in 1986 upheld the constitutionality of state laws criminalizing homosexual sodomy)[2] was superficial, although that did not

---

1. That is not all it is. Martha C. Nussbaum, *The Fragility of Goodness: Luck and Ethics in Greek Tragedy and Philosophy*, ch. 6 (1986). But it is an important part. Homosexual love figures largely in the *Phaedrus* as well, but as something taken for granted, not examined.

2. 487 U.S. 186 (1986).

mean the decision was incorrect. The second event was the decision of my own court to hear en banc (that is, before the entire court rather than, as is customary, a three-judge panel drawn randomly from the court's membership) a case involving the constitutionality of a state statute that had been interpreted to forbid striptease dancers to strip to the buff.[3] Unusually for our court, the case generated six opinions covering fifty-three dense pages in the *Federal Reporter*. (The decision by the Supreme Court, reversing our 7–4 decision by a 5–4 vote, generated four opinions—none of which commanded the support of a majority of the justices.) It will be apparent to anyone who takes the trouble to read these opinions that nudity and the erotic are emotional topics even to middle-aged and elderly judges and also that the dominant judicial, and I would say legal, attitude toward the study of sex is that "I know what I like" and therefore research is superfluous.

I disagree. Because of the reticence that, though diminishing, still characterizes public discussion of sex in our culture, Americans tend not to be well informed about the subject. Of course, everyone who is or has ever been sexually active, and many people who have not, know something about sex. But that something is not enough to provide a solid basis for judgments of social policy, and such judgments are inescapable in our law. The reticence I have mentioned is an obstacle to research as well. Yet despite it there is a vast multidisciplinary literature on sex, a literature to which medicine, biology, sociobiology, psychiatry, psychology, sociology, economics, jurisprudence, theology, philosophy, history, classics, anthropology, demography—even geography and literary criticism—have all contributed. Much of this literature is genuinely scientific, and much that is not is nevertheless highly informative. One of my goals is to summarize its principal findings, as far as they bear on law, in a form accessible to the legal profession. The timeliness of such an effort requires little comment in view of the stress that has been placed on the already badly strained American legal system by such phenomena (many of them interrelated) as the AIDS epidemic; the abortion controversy; the homosexual rights movement (which is pressing for the repeal of sodomy laws, for allowing homosexuals to marry and to adopt children, and for eliminating discrimination against homosexuals by the armed forces and other employers); the sexual revolution of which homosexual advocacy is one component and rampant illegitimacy another; the moral majority's counterrevolution; surrogate motherhood; the controversy over federal funding of erotic art; and the concerns forcefully expressed by feminists about marital and date rape, sexual harassment in the workplace, sexual abuse of children, and pornography.

My larger ambition is to present a theory of sexuality that both explains

3. Miller v. Civil City of South Bend, 904 F.2d 1081 (7th Cir. 1990) (en banc), reversed under the name Barnes v. Glen Theatre, Inc., 111 S. Ct. 2456 (1991).

the principal regularities in the practice of sex and in its social, including legal, regulation and points the way toward reforms in that regulation—thus a theory at once positive (descriptive) and normative (ethical). Students of sexuality recognize and deplore the lack of a rigorous and comprehensive scientific theory of human sexual behavior,[4] but, perhaps misled by Aristotle's dictum that furnishes the epigraph for this introduction, have not sought assistance in theories of rational choice. I try to cure that oversight. Functional, secular, instrumental, utilitarian, the theory that I present relies heavily on economic analysis, heretofore applied rarely to issues of sexuality though often to related issues of nonmarket behavior, including marriage, the family, and family law.[5] I shall call it the economic theory of sexuality.

On the positive side, the theory asserts the paramountcy of rational choice in volitional human behavior, which sexual behavior is. But it does not deny that sexual desire, including gender preference, is rooted in our biological nature, and so it does not deny the intense emotionality of the sexual act or quarrel with Aristotle's dictum. On the normative side, the theory is a libertarian—not to be confused with either libertine or modern liberal—theory of sexual regulation. Libertarianism—or, as it is sometimes called, classical liberalism—the philosophy of John Stuart Mill's *On Liberty*, can be summed up in seven words: "Your rights end where his nose begins." Government interference with adult consensual activities is unjustified unless it can be shown to be necessary for the protection of the liberty or property of other persons.

The economic theory is merely the latest in an endless procession of theories of sexuality: Thomist, feminist, Marxist, sociobiological, Freudian, constructionist—the list goes on and on. But I shall argue that the economic theory incorporates, integrates, and transcends the perspectives, insights, and findings of the other theories of sexuality that can fairly be described as either scientific or social scientific. The uncompromising, the truly unassimilable rival of the economic theory—deserving of the most careful consideration not only because of its intrinsic merits but also because it reflects the beliefs of most of the people in our society—is not scientific or social scientific; it is a heterogeneous cluster of moral theories. These theories, the work of Catholic theologians such as Thomas Aquinas, Catholic philosophers such as Elizabeth Anscombe, lawyers such as James Fitzjames Stephen and Patrick Devlin, neoconservatives such as Irving Kristol, and philosophers of liberalism from Immanuel Kant to Joel Feinberg and Ronald Dworkin, are not convergent—

4. See, for example, Paul R. Abramson, "Sexual Science: Emerging Discipline or Oxymoron?" 27 *Journal of Sex Research* 147 (1990).

5. No longer are explicit markets the sole domain of economics. For discussion and references, see my book *The Problems of Jurisprudence* 367–370 (1990). On the economics of marriage and the family, see Gary S. Becker's magisterial economic study *A Treatise on the Family* (enlarged ed. 1991). For an introduction to the economic analysis of family law, see my *Economic Analysis of Law,* ch. 5 (3d ed. 1986). None of these works contains an index reference to sex.

far from it. But they are at one in regarding moral and religious beliefs that are irreducible to genuine social interests or practical incentives as the key to both understanding and judging sexual practices and norms. This makes them incompatible with the broadly scientific outlook that informs the approaches I seek to recast in the mold of economics—incompatible even though John Stuart Mill is a patron saint of both liberalism and utilitarianism.

An approximation to a scientific, nonmoral outlook on sexuality is highly influential today in northern Europe, especially Sweden, Denmark, and the Netherlands, as well as in Japan and other areas of East Asia. The outlook has a weaker grip in southern Europe, but it is resisted most strongly by a diverse group of nations that includes the United States, Ireland, South Africa, Cuba, Saudi Arabia, and Iran. The pattern of acceptance and rejection is itself a challenge to the positive side of my theory. One is not surprised that a government should repress freedom in both the economic (narrowly conceived) and sexual spheres, as in Cuba (a reflection of the orthodox communist position since Stalin's day), or permit it in both spheres, as in Japan. But why Swedes should have more freedom in matters of sex than Americans but less economic freedom is a considerable puzzle, although I shall attempt an explanation.

Neither my theory nor its rivals are about sex *tout court*. They are about the social, including the legal, implications of sex—hence my frequent use of the term sexuality, implying concern with attitudes and customs as well as with practices. It is well known that laws punishing socially disfavored sexual behavior, with the partial exception of those regulating coercive sex, such as rape and the seduction of young children, are rarely enforced with even minimum effectiveness. Mostly they are dead letters, yet efforts to repeal them are resisted vigorously. We shall therefore have to consider the social function of the unenforced or radically underenforced law, as well as the relation—a staple in the discussion of sex laws, many of which are concerned with consensual and hence seemingly harmless although morally offensive conduct—between law and morals.

So: fact (background, history), theory, and regulation (legal and other) are the successive focuses of this book. But a more specific enumeration of its aims may be helpful.

First, to bring to the attention of the legal profession the rich multidisciplinary literature on sexuality—and to shame my colleagues in the profession for ignoring it.

Second, to demonstrate the feasibility and fruitfulness of an economic approach to the subject—more broadly of a functional approach in which insights are borrowed from a variety of fields but in which economics, the science of rational human behavior, provides the organizing perspective. The effort may seem quixotic, for it is a commonplace that sexual passion belongs to the domain of the irrational; but it is a false commonplace. One does not will sexual appetite—but one does not will hunger either. The former fact no more excludes the possibility of an economics of sexuality than the latter excludes the possibility of an economics of agriculture.

My third aim is to expound a specific economic theory of sexuality, and as part of that project to derive hypotheses from the theory and confront them with data both quantitative and qualitative. All theories are tentative, a theory as novel as the economic theory of sexuality especially so. Nevertheless, I believe that much of the variance among different eras, cultures, social classes, races, and the sexes themselves in behavior, attitudes, customs, and laws concerning such aspects of sexuality as premarital sex, homosexuality, polygamy, prostitution, rape, contraception, abortion, infanticide, pornography, public nudity, and child sexual abuse can be explained, and changes in them predicted, by reference to the handful of variables that the theory identifies as likely to be significant. The principal variables are the occupational profile of women and—a related but not identical factor—women's economic independence, plus urbanization, income, the sex ratio, and scientific and technological advances relating to the control of fertility and to the care of mothers and infants. There are causal relations among these variables as well, which I shall discuss from time to time.

The reader may be primed by mention of economic theory to expect a book bristling with mathematical formulas and forbidding jargon. That is not the character of this book. I do not question the value of formal theory,[6] but the theory expounded in this book is informal and nontechnical. Yet it has considerable explanatory and suggestive power. It can illuminate questions about human sexuality such as why the morality of modern Sweden is different from that of medieval Europe and why both are different from that of ancient Greece; why Roman women were sexually freer than Greek women and Victorian women were less free sexually than women in eighteenth-century England; how income and wealth affect sexual morality differently; why cities are traditionally believed to be centers of vice; why an increase in the effectiveness of contraceptive methods results in a higher frequency of coitus; why black men in the United States are less likely than white men either to undergo voluntary sterilization or to use condoms; why the nature of the sexual services offered by prostitutes has changed since the Middle Ages; why marital rape is increasingly a crime; and why in some societies a homosexual tends to be thought of primarily as a person who has a strong preference for same-sex relations whereas in others he is thought of as a "normal" person who commits unnatural acts because of lust or other wickedness.

Explanatory power is only one test of a theory's fruitfulness. Another is its

---

6. Powerfully defended—with significant reservations—by a leading mathematical economist, Gerard Debreu, in his article "The Mathematization of Economic Theory," 81 *American Economic Review* 1 (1991).

power to generate counterintuitive (hence novel, nontrivial, nonobvious) hypotheses that can be tested empirically and that do not flunk the test. A number of such hypotheses are proposed in this book (the qualification "other things remaining unchanged" should be understood with respect to each of them), including these:

- The AIDS epidemic, by making homosexual activity unavoidably more costly—whether through the greater cost of AIDS or the lesser cost of switching to safe sex—has reduced the amount of that activity, not just the amount of unsafe sex. It has also reduced the number of illegitimate births and increased the number of legitimate ones.

- Effeminate heterosexual men, handsome heterosexual men, and "macho" heterosexual men have, on average, more homosexual experience than noneffeminate, nonhandsome, and nonmacho heterosexual men.

- If a city, having attracted a large number of homosexuals, stops growing, the percentage of homosexuals will continue to increase.

- Homosexuality, but not (female) prostitution, is more likely to be approved or tolerated in a polygamous society than in a monogamous one.

- A larger fraction of female than of male homosexual activity is opportunistic or situational rather than driven by a strong preference for same-sex over opposite-sex relations.

- An opportunistic male homosexual will prefer boys to men, a "real" homosexual men to boys.

- The percentage of Roman Catholic priests who are homosexual has risen since the Middle Ages.

- Black men are less likely to rape or to abuse children sexually than white men are.

- The external costs of venereal diseases are lower than those of other infectious diseases.

- In Sweden the increase in women's market earnings has generated an even larger increase in women's full income—the sum of their own market earnings and of contributions in cash and services from men.

- The incidence of adultery relative to fornication has declined over time.

- Polygamy, de jure or de facto, will be found in a society of noncompanionate marriage; monogamy, in a society of companionate marriage; and monogamy with an admixture of de facto polygamy, in modern Western nations, where marriage is companionate but many women have children outside of marriage because they are no longer dependent on men.

• Clitoridectomy (removal of the clitoris) and infibulation (sewing up the entrance to the vagina) are more common in a polygamous than in a monogamous society.

• Both a sexually repressive society and a permissive one will have a lower incidence of rape than a society in which repressive and permissive attitudes toward sex are mingled.

• Recent technological advances in reproduction, such as artificial insemination and in vitro fertilization, have increased the full income of women relative to men.

My fourth aim is to use social scientific knowledge of sexuality, including the knowledge generated by economic analysis, as a foundation for proposing reforms in law and public policy. Although I make some concrete suggestions for reform, the emphasis throughout the book is on positive (descriptive) rather than normative (prescriptive) analysis. Sound reform depends on knowledge to a degree that lawyers do not always appreciate. We shall see that the Supreme Court's decisions on sexual privacy are not only poorly reasoned but poorly informed.

My remaining aims are to demonstrate the inadequacy of conventional legal and moral reasoning in dealing with complex, emotion-laden social phenomena such as sexuality; to illuminate general issues concerning the nature, causes, consequences, and justification of laws and of morals; and to contribute to the blurring of the lines that separate academic disciplines.

A WORD MORE on organization. Part I presents essential background of a historical, anthropological, and sociological character. Its three chapters take up the history of scholarship on sexuality, the variance (historical and cross-cultural) in human sexual customs and regulations, and the laws regulating sex. To help find the pattern in those laws, I develop in Chapter 3 an index of relative sex-law severity by comparing a nation's or a state's punishments for the principal sex offenses to its punishments for other offenses.

Part II describes and tests the economic theory of sexuality and compares it with the principal moral theories of the subject. I begin, however, with the biology of sex (Chapter 4). I do this to mark off the biological or determined from the rational or chosen (in a sense to be explained), the latter being the domain of economic theory, and also to note the parallels between the biological and economic approaches to the subject. I see biology as explaining the drives and preferences that establish the perceived benefits of different sexual practices to different people. Although nothing essential to the economic analysis depends on whether these drives and preferences are indeed determined by our genes or whether instead, as some social constructionists believe, they are cultural artifacts, my own view is that an integrated biological-economic theory of sex (call it the bioeconomic theory, with the economic component the one emphasized in this book) is the most promising theory of the subject that we are likely to have for some time. Chapters 5 and 6 develop the positive side of the economic theory, emphasizing the role of what I call the effective sex ratio, urbanization, and women's occupational profile in explaining the extent of sexual liberality in a society. Chapter 7 presents the normative side of the economic theory and also considers the political economy of sex regulation, that is, the political forces that sometimes guide the regulation of sexuality into the optimal path laid out in that chapter and sometimes deflect it from that path. Chapters 5 through 7 are the theoretical core of the book.

A number of applications of the economic theory are set out in Part II, and several are then examined in depth in Part III; these more detailed examinations (which emphasize regulatory issues) reveal new strengths, but also limitations, of the economic approach. Economic analysis cannot, for example, solve the moral issue of abortion; but it can help to clarify it. The order of chapters in Part III may seem random, but it is not. To lay the groundwork for a discussion of the judicial response to the sexual revolution (the subject of Chapter 12), I must explore (in Chapters 9 through 11) the regulatory questions raised by contraception, abortion, and homosexuality, for these are the principal subjects of the Supreme Court's sexual privacy cases. The last two chapters take up discrete but important areas of sexual regulation. Chapter 14 is about coercive sex, mainly rape and the sexual abuse of children. Chapter 15, a mirror image of Chapters 9 and 10, discusses not, as those chapters do, efforts through contraception and abortion to divorce sex from reproduction, but efforts through adoption and artificial insemination to divorce reproduction from sex. Such efforts drag in their wake significant ethical as well as economic issues.

The danger in using either the brief chapter descriptions just tendered or the table of contents with its chapter titles and subtitles as a guide to the book is that a number of topics are not confined to the particular chapter or subchapter the title of which mentions them. Homosexuality, for example, is discussed—from a historical, biological, economic, legal, and family-law angle (homosexual adoption)—in a number of chapters besides Chapter 11 ("Homosexuality"). Polygamy enters in Chapter 5 as well as in Chapter 9, abortion in Chapters 5 and 12 as well as 10, rape in Chapters 4, 5, 7, 13, and 14. Moral theories of sex figure prominently in Chapters 10 and 13 as well as in Chapter 8. Prostitution appears in a number of chapters. Theoretical issues crop up in Part III as well as Part II, regulatory issues in Part II as well as Part III. More than in many books, the index is an essential reference tool.

A word about the boundaries of my subject and specifically its relation to the study of the family on the one hand and of population on the other. As demonstrated by Gary Becker's book on the family (cited in note 5), it is possible to analyze the family without explicit consideration of sex. Of course, sex is in the background, because a basic function of the family is procreation, and, at least until recently, procreation required sexual intercourse.[7] Discussions of marriage cannot avoid topics such as impotence and adultery. Similarly, discussions of fertility by demographers cannot avoid topics such as contraception that are central to the study of human sexuality. And, on the other side, it is impossible to consider sex as a *social* phenomenon, as I do in this book, without bringing in the family and fertility, since so much regulation of sex is concerned with preserving and strengthening the family, or at least particular kinds of family, and some of that regulation has been explicitly concerned with the consequences for population. Nevertheless, the family, fertility, and sexuality are distinct even though overlapping subjects. It makes a difference whether one is interested in the family as such, the growth (or decline) of population as such, or sexual relationships as such. To the student of the family, homosexuality is of peripheral interest; Becker's book contains but two brief mentions of the topic. To the demographers, the regulation of homosexuality is evidently of no interest, for the only mentions I have seen of the topic in discussions of population—apart from a very fleeting mention by Malthus (see Chapter 1)—are by Aristotle and Heinrich Himmler. But to the student of sexual relationships, homosexuality is of central importance; indeed, it is the subject of the vastest literature in the domain of sexology, as scholarly (and sometimes not so scholarly) writing about sex is called. Similarly, prostitution is of some interest from the standpoint of family and demographic studies, but not much; yet as a significant and much-regulated form of sexual relationship it is of major interest to the student of sexuality. An even clearer example is pornography: a topic of considerable interest to the student of sex but of virtually no interest to the student of the family and, I am sure, of absolutely no interest to the student of demography.

But there is much overlap among the three areas of inquiry. Polygamy illustrates this point. The polygamous organization of families is a focus of Becker's book. But the rejection of polygamy by Christian societies (with a few exceptions, of which the best known is Mormon society in the nineteenth century) is a notable example of the Christian effort to confine sexual activity to monogamous marriages, so it receives attention in this book as well. I am hugely indebted to Becker and other economists whose studies of the family and fertility have provided me with essential tools for the economic study of sexuality, but I emphasize that these are separate inquiries. Moreover, my analysis is not exclusively economic. It draws heavily on other disciplines.

Because sex is not a fully respectable subject for public discussion in the United States (at the same time it permeates the popular media, and for that

7. Although successful artificial insemination of humans goes back to the eighteenth century, the procedure was rare until this century—in fact is still quite rare. See Chapter 15.

matter high-brow art and literature as well), anyone who writes about it is apt to be thought a little off. That was Kinsey's fate certainly. Yet the subject is not only rich in analytical and historical interest but also—as is almost too obvious to mention—of enormous practical significance, and this quite apart from its traditional and now declining importance to the future of the human race. A major source of human pleasures and pains (the latter including death long before AIDS came on the scene), of human institutions, of political controversy, perhaps even of the growth and decline of nations, it deserves our best intellectual efforts.

The History of Sexuality

Theoretical Sexology

THERE IS SEXUAL behavior, having to do mainly with excitation of the sexual organs. There is sexuality, as we may (following Foucault) term the social attitudes that make sex problematic, self-conscious, rather than just "natural" or biological. And there is systematic, analytic thinking about sex and sexuality. The last is the domain of sexology, the body of multidisciplinary inquiries into sex and sexuality, and the subject of this chapter. More precisely *theoretical* sexology, as distinct from the practical science of treating problems of sexual dysfunction. When I speak of sexology in this book, I mean the theoretical, not the practical, branch.[1]

The Development of the Field

Plato's *Symposium* is the first reflective discussion of sex that has come down to us. To be more precise, the *Symposium* is an examination of *eros;* but this means sexual love and desire as distinct from love generally, which is *philia.* So the *Symposium* is the first document of sexology, and it is also the first entry in a disappointing branch of philosophy: the philosophy of the erotic.

1. A somewhat dated but still highly worthwhile survey is John H. Gagnon and William Simon, *Sexual Conduct: The Social Sources of Human Sexuality* (1973). A more recent survey, rather too polemical for my taste but highly readable, is Jeffrey Weeks, *Sexuality and Its Discontents: Meanings, Myths and Modern Sexualities* (1985). On the evolution of what I call theoretical sexology, see—from two very different angles—Paul Robinson, *The Modernization of Sex: Havelock Ellis, Alfred Kinsey, William Masters, and Virginia Johnson* (1976), and Michel Foucault, *The History of Sexuality,* vol. 1, *An Introduction* (1978). There are a number of excellent textbooks, such as William H. Masters, Virginia E. Johnson, and Robert C. Kolodny, *Human Sexuality* (2d ed. 1985), and Albert Richard Allgeier and Elizabeth A. Rice, *Sexual Interactions* (2d ed. 1988), and many fine anthologies, such as *Theories of Human Sexuality* (James H. Geer and William T. O'Donohue eds. 1987). Scholarly journals devoted to the subject include *Archives of Sexual Behavior, Journal of Sex Research,* and *Journal of the History of Sexuality.*

Only a handful of philosophers have made significant (yet, even then, for the most part either minor or deeply flawed) contributions to sexology. In addition to Plato and Foucault, the list includes Aristotle, Hume, Kant, Bentham, Schopenhauer, Nietzsche, Russell, and Marcuse.[2] Admittedly the brevity of this list is a result in part of my implicitly defining philosophy narrowly. A more latitudinarian definition would bring in not only Freud but also the great Catholic theologians who have discussed sex, in particular Paul, Augustine, and Aquinas, together with some jurisprudential writing on the legal regulation of sexual morality. Yet however broadly philosophy is defined, the entire body of philosophic speculation about sex is deeply inadequate, although general moral and (especially) analytic philosophy have useful contributions to make to the subject. Both points will be amplified in due course.

The *Symposium* deals with two principal topics: the relative merits of heterosexual and homosexual love, and the relation between (erotic) love and other goods, such as knowledge. Neither discussion has much contemporary analytic interest, but the first is relevant to understanding the Greek concept of homosexuality, a concept of cardinal importance in the theory of sexuality. I shall examine that concept in subsequent chapters, so let me leave the *Symposium* and point out the rising note of asceticism in the subsequent Platonic dialogues, culminating in *Laws*. That a man's principal emotional relationships with others should be with other men, not women—a central tenet of the *Symposium*—is not challenged in *Laws*; but the physical consummation of such relationships, already questioned by Socrates in the *Symposium*, is now (as indeed earlier, in the *Republic*) forbidden. It is in Plato that we first encounter the idea that sexual pleasure is a questionable good for human beings, perhaps even a downright bad; the (related) attempt to distinguish between love and sex and between "natural" and "unnatural," procreative and sterile, sex; and the classification of homosexuality as one of the "unnatural" kinds because it is sterile. The ascetic approach, amplified in the writings of the Stoic philosophers of Greece and Rome and converging with a concern about deviant sexuality sporadically expressed in the Old Testament, forms the background to the distinctive Christian approach to sexuality that begins with Paul's Epistle to the Romans in the generation after Jesus Christ,

---

2. For a brief survey of the history of philosophical writing about sex, see the editors' introduction to *Philosophy and Sex* (Robert Baker and Frederick Elliston eds. 1984), an anthology of philosophical essays on sex. Another anthology, this one consisting of very brief excerpts, is *Sexual Love and Western Morality: A Philosophical Anthology* (D. P. Verene ed. 1972). Irving Singer's three-volume history of the philosophy of love, *The Nature of Love* (2d ed. 1984–1987), discusses most of the philosophical literature on sex. Other book-length treatments include Singer, *The Goals of Human Sexuality* (1973); Russell Vanoy, *Sex without Love: A Philosophical Exploration* (1980); and Michael Ruse, *Homosexuality: A Philosophical Inquiry* (1988). The dearth of philosophical writing on sex is discussed and deplored in W. M. Alexander, "Philosophers Have Avoided Sex," 72 *Diogenes* 56 (1970).

continues in the influential writings of Augustine, and culminates in Aquinas, whose thirteenth-century analysis of sexuality remains authoritative for devout Roman Catholics.[3]

The difference between, on the one hand, the Christian approach to sexuality, foreshadowed by *Laws* and by the Stoic philosophers, although not by the behavior and attitudes actually prevailing among the Greeks and the Romans, and, on the other hand, the "pagan" approach of the Greeks in the generations before Plato is the difference between a naturalistic conception of man and a theistic conception. The former, which the modern scientist and secularist shares with the ancient Greeks, regards man—implicitly in the ancient Greek view, explicitly in the modern view—as a predator whose large brain has made possible language, culture, society, morals, and the other distinctive features of humanity. It would hardly occur to people having this view to regard the possession by human beings of sexual organs and the desires associated with that possession as somehow questionable. That sexual passions might be dangerous, distracting, even socially disruptive must be acknowledged by anyone having even a nodding acquaintance with the world. But these facts do not raise profound or distinctive moral or aesthetic issues.

Suppose, however, that you believe with the Christians (also with the Jews and the Muslims, but traditionally Christians have worried the most about sexuality) that man was created in the image of God the all-good and all-powerful and all-knowing, with the result that man's physical and behavioral resemblance to animals marks a declension from the original conception rather than the base from which we have ascended a certain distance by dint of intelligence. The involuntary physical spasms characteristic of, even to a great extent defining of, sex; the intense emotions that precede and accompany those spasms; the proximity of the sexual organs to those of defecation; and the striking, if in some ways superficial, resemblance of human sexual behavior to that of other animals have made sex seem to many thoughtful observers in the Christian tradition part of our animal nature rather than part of our divine nature: part, that is, of the declension. It is only a small step to the view that sex is, at best, a necessary evil (necessary to the survival of the human race, and some early Christians thought that the survival of the race was too high a price to pay); to the correlative view that nonprocreative sex, like gluttony, is an unqualified evil; and—when that evil, that animality, is stressed rather

3. On this evolution, see, besides the works by Foucault and Noonan cited later in this chapter, A. W. Price, *Love and Friendship in Plato and Aristotle* (1989), esp. Appendix 2 ("Plato's Sexual Morality"); K. J. Dover, *Greek Homosexuality* (2d ed. 1989); John Boswell, *Christianity, Social Tolerance, and Homosexuality: Gay People in Western Europe from the Beginning of the Christian Era to the Fourteenth Century* (1980); Peter Brown, *The Body and Society: Men, Women and Sexual Renunciation in Early Christianity* (1988); James A. Brundage, *Law, Sex, and Christian Society in Medieval Europe* (1987).

than the necessity—to the glorification of celibacy and virginity as holier states than marriage.

If the sexual ethics taught by medieval Catholic theologians such as Aquinas were very severe, the practice was different. Concubinage, prostitution, adultery, fornication, and homosexuality flourished—even, in the case of concubinage and homosexuality, among the clergy—with little interference from church or state. (Aquinas even tried to justify prostitution as a safety valve.) This division between theory and practice enabled the Protestant theologians of the Reformation on the one hand to teach that there was no essential baseness in marital sex and on the other to denounce the Roman Catholic Church for the licentiousness of its clergy and votaries. When the Puritans came to power in England, Geneva, Holland, New England, and elsewhere, they repressed extramarital sexual activity, including fornication, adultery, concubinage, homosexuality, and prostitution, with a vigor unknown in Catholic states. So although the Catholic theologians were more severe than the Protestants in theory, the Protestant (especially Puritan) theocrats were more severe in practice. The combination can make for highly repressive sexual regulation, as we see today in parts of our own country, which is unusual in having both a Puritan heritage and a large Catholic population.

Between the Reformation and the eighteenth century there were few interesting contributions to sexology. The gradual although irregular decline in sexual repression—a decline anticipated in the celebration of the nude in Renaissance art and marked by landmarks such as the abolition of the crime of sodomy (when committed in private by consenting adults) by France in 1791 and the dismantling of many Puritan sex laws in Great Britain and the American states—went largely unremarked by the scholarly community of the day, although de Sade and Diderot can be seen as important celebrators of that decline.

The situation changed dramatically in the nineteenth century. Victorian prudery, which came to dominate middle-class thinking in the United States and the Protestant states of the European Continent as well as in Great Britain, was encouraged, systematized, and defended in a growing literature that pronounced sex dangerous on scientific, specifically medical and eugenic, grounds, as distinguished from the older theological grounds. Child sexuality, for example, previously considered humorous or even cute rather than either significant for the child's development or potentially ominous for society as a whole, was reconceived as a menace to the child and, through the child, to the race. That most characteristic expression of child sexuality, masturbation, having previously been largely ignored outside of theological circles, was "discovered" by Victorian science to cause feeble-mindedness, insanity, criminality, impotence, homosexuality, early death, sterility, and (when not sterility) deformed offspring. The disapproval of masturbation was not new. For orthodox Catholics it has always been a mortal sin because it is a form of nonmarital, nonprocreative, and therefore "disordered" sex. Indeed, since it is less like marital, procreative sex than rape is (rape, after all, can produce a child), it is, in traditional Catholic thought, the worse sin.[4] Victorian sexology was not primarily interested in sin. Its objection to masturbation was medical in the first instance and moral only insofar as a practice that could debilitate the entire race necessarily raised broader concerns than the health of the individual child.

Other strands of nineteenth-century thought contributed to Victorian sexology.

1. The spread of literacy and a decline in the costs of printing placed pornographic literature for the first time within the reach of the lower classes, awakening concern in the governing class over the possible impact of pornography on sexual behavior and family values.

2. The teachings of Malthus, in combination with the rise of nationalism and the advent of mass conscript armies (whose efficacy was demonstrated by France's Revolutionary and Napoleonic armies), made a nation's population, theretofore rather taken for granted, an issue of public policy. Malthus' focus was on overpopulation—what a modern economist would call the negative externalities of population. But political emphasis shifted quickly to the positive externalities, particularly military power, well illustrated by the decline in the French birth rate (apparently owing largely to contraception) relative to the German and, as the difference worked its way through the age distribution, by the correlative shift in military and political primacy from France to Germany.

3. Malthus influenced Darwin, whose theory of natural selection brought the eugenic and geopolitical implications of sexual behavior to center stage. Hume, Kant, and Schopenhauer anticipated the sociobiology of sex (see Chapter 4).

4. The growth of liberalism made the regulation of morals problematic for the first time. Jeremy Bentham wrote, but did not publish, an essay attacking the criminalizing of homosexuality,[5] while Mill's *On Liberty* implied the undesirability of such regulations, and by doing so sparked efforts by James Fitzjames Stephen and others to justify them. The "law and morals" literature, in which a primary concern is the propriety of using law to promote the dominant sexual morality, had been born.

5. Cutting against liberalism was the discovery by medical science, reversing a millennium of orthodox belief, that a woman can conceive without having

---

4. As noted by Aquinas in *Summa Theologica* II–II, Q. cliv, art. XII. On similar grounds some medieval theologians considered anal intercourse with one's wife a worse sin than vaginal intercourse with one's mother. Danielle Jacquart and Claude Thomasset, *Sexuality and Medicine in the Middle Ages* 89 (1988).

5. "An Essay on 'Paederasty,'" in *Philosophy and Sex*, note 2 above, at 353 (first published in 1978!).

an orgasm. The discovery reinforced the age-old "double standard," both directly, by encouraging the devaluation of female sexual pleasure, and indirectly, by making the relation of male and female to orgasm asymmetrical; men and women were not as sexually alike as previously believed.

As a result of these movements in scientific and social thought, sex and sexuality became, perhaps more than at any other time since the early Christian era, matters of self-conscious study and reflection. The rudiments of sexology were in place. With Richard von Krafft-Ebing, author of *Psychopathia Sexualis* (first published in 1886), and in the next generation Havelock Ellis, Sigmund Freud, and Magnus Hirschfeld, the field came of age and forked into the two branches that continue to dominate and divide it. One, which I shall call the speculative and which is well illustrated by Krafft-Ebing and Freud, is interested in the causes, nature, and consequences of sexual behavior and attitudes, which it explores through psychiatric case studies and other laboratory-type research projects that generate experimental data for hypothesis testing. The other, the descriptive or atheoretically empirical, which sees the reticence and taboos about sex that characterize Judeo-Christian civilization as the main, or at least first, obstacle to the understanding of sexuality and to the reform of the laws and social practices regulating it, undertakes the daunting task of collecting comprehensive data about actual sexual practices in the world outside the psychiatrist's office or the psychologist's laboratory. (Straddling the two approaches is field research in the anthropology of sex, most famously by Bronislaw Malinowski and Margaret Mead.) Ellis and Hirschfeld are the great names among the pioneers of this branch of sexology. Ellis had theoretical pretensions, but in the history of the field he is significant chiefly for the energy with which he collected data concerning sexual practices the world over. Hirschfeld, the methodological predecessor of Alfred Kinsey, collected, through thousands of interviews and interview records, vast information about homosexual and other sexual behavior in Germany and other European countries. But Hirschfeld had the misfortune to be a Jewish homosexual. The Nazis destroyed his archives as one of their first orders of business when they came to power.

The descriptive branch of sexology is the simpler, so let me start my consideration of the modern scholarly scene with it. The central figure is Kinsey. A zoologist at Indiana University who had made his name as a student of insects in the years before the Second World War, Kinsey was picked by the university authorities to head up the newly created Institute for Sex Research in part because his scientific credentials and the regularity of his personal life seemed likely to deflect (but in the end did not) the derision with which Americans were bound to greet any ambitious project for the study of sex. His goal for the institute was to interview in depth 100,000 Americans concerning their sexual behavior and attitudes, as well as their age, race, and other characteristics with which such behavior and attitudes might be correlated. He died before reaching this ambitious goal. The two great studies that the institute published under his direction, in 1948 and 1953, respectively— *Sexual Behavior in the Human Male* and *Sexual Behavior in the Human Female*—were based on a total of 11,000 interviews. Although large, the sample was not random, or even representative, being heavily skewed toward young, white, college-educated midwesterners; nor was there any way to verify—or at least no steps were taken to verify—the accuracy of the answers given interviewers. Kinsey's method of sampling, and other aspects of his methodology, drew some withering criticisms.[6] Nevertheless, the Kinsey studies, when their limitations are understood and respected, are a vast mine of useful information, have been repeatedly corroborated by other studies, and appear to be generally accurate, at least for the sample interviewed, because of the extraordinary lengths to which the interviewers went to elicit truthful answers.

At least for the sample interviewed: that is the critical qualification. The problem is not so much the unrepresentativeness of the sample, for in projecting the sample results to the population from which it was drawn, one can make adjustments for known discrepancies between the sample and the population. The problem is that Kinsey had no means of compelling people to participate in his surveys, and we cannot be confident that the average person who was not willing to participate had the same sex life as the average person who was. It is plausible that the most straitlaced people would be least likely to participate in a sex survey, and if so the Kinsey reports may exaggerate the degree of irregular sexual behavior in the United States population during the period covered by the studies. But this distortion would not affect any of the conclusions of my analysis.

The two Kinsey reports remain the high-water mark of descriptive sexology, dwarfing as they do all other such studies in both sample size and interviewing depth. The Institute for Sex Research survived Kinsey (it is now called the Kinsey Institute for Research in Sex, Gender, and Reproduction) and has conducted other valuable studies, as have other research groups, but not on the same scale or with the same impact on popular and professional thought. The National Opinion Research Center of the University of Chicago is seeking $18 million to conduct the most ambitious survey of sexual behavior since the Kinsey reports themselves. The survey is to be of a representative sample of 20,000 Americans.

6. See, in particular, W. Allen Wallis, "Statistics of the Kinsey Report," 248 *Journal of the American Statistical Association* 463 (1949); Lewis M. Terman, "Kinsey's 'Sexual Behavior in the Human Male': Some Comments and Criticisms," 45 *Psychological Bulletin* 443 (1948). For a more favorable view of Kinsey's methodology, see William G. Cochran, Frederick Mosteller, and John W. Tukey, *Statistical Problems of the Kinsey Report on Sexual Behavior in the Human Male: A Report of the American Statistical Association Committee to Advise the National Research Council Committee for Research in Problems of Sex* (1954).

Speculative sexology did not begin with Krafft-Ebing and Freud. It had begun with Hippocrates (and other Greek physicians) and Aristotle, in the fifth and fourth centuries B.C., and had proceeded slowly. Sperm and ovum were not discovered until the seventeenth century; until then it was believed either that women emitted semen in sexual intercourse just like men—the "modern" view at the time—or, in the older view (dramatized, for example, in Aeschylus' *Eumenides*), that (male) semen was the equivalent of the fertilized seed in plants and the womb the equivalent of the soil in which the seed is planted, nurtured, and grown. At a time when women were thought to emit semen (essential to conception) in intercourse, it was natural to suppose that the female orgasm was as essential to conception as the male, and hence that female sexual pleasure, although always thought problematic by men for reasons explored in subsequent chapters, was important to more than female happiness and hence could not be discounted and repressed entirely. The discovery of the actual mechanism of fertilization showed that the female orgasm was inessential to procreation, and thus set the stage for the devaluing of female sexual pleasure, a salient element of Victorian sexual values. Such are the curious by-products of scientific progress.

The biology of sex remains a leading field within sexology. In addition to experimental biology, with its studies of nerves and hormones and other biochemical machinery, and zoological studies of primate and other animal sexual behavior, a new and controversial extension of evolutionary biology— sociobiology, which seeks genetic explanations for social behavior and institutions—has advanced striking hypotheses concerning aspects of human sexuality such as courting, the double standard, polygamy, and homosexual preference.[7] The last of these may appear wholly resistant to genetic explanations, because, on casual reflection at least, it seems antithetical to survival of the species. But, as we shall see in Chapter 4, there is a respectable argument in support of a genetic basis for such preference.

Another offshoot of traditional biology is the use, most famously by William Masters and Virginia Johnson,[8] of research into the biology of sex to treat sexual dysfunctions. The theoretical interest of this therapy is in the primacy it assigns to the clitoris as the center of female sexual excitement (as evidenced, for example, by the much greater density of nerve endings in the clitoris

---

7. The pioneering figures are William Hamilton and Robert Trivers. The best single book on the sociobiology of sex, as far as I am able to judge, is Donald Symons, *The Evolution of Human Sexuality* (1979). The large critical literature on sociobiology is well represented by Philip Kitcher, *Vaulting Ambition: Sociobiology and the Quest for Human Nature* (1985); for rebuttal, see Richard D. Alexander, *The Biology of Moral Systems* (1987). On primate sexuality, see, for example, Barbara B. Smuts, "Sexual Competition and Mate Choice," in *Primate Societies* 385 (Barbara B. Smuts et al. eds. 1986).

8. Notably in their first book, William H. Masters and Virginia E. Johnson, *Human Sexual Response* (1966).

compared to the vagina) and the finding that sexual intercourse is a clumsy method of bringing the clitoris to orgasm compared to simple manual stimulation. The implication, as radical feminists have not been slow to point out, is that vaginal intercourse, and lesbian simulacra of intercourse such as the penetration of the vagina by an artificial penis, may be inessential to female sexual satisfaction—and, given artificial insemination, intercourse is clearly inessential to procreation. The possibility is opened up of decoupling female sexuality entirely from intercourse with men or even from being modeled on intercourse with men (the use of the artificial penis), thereby freeing women from their traditional dependence on their oppressors, as some feminists consider men to be. Yet we shall see that there are feminists who regard artificial reproduction as a threat to women's freedom.

Contemporary feminism has contributed to sexology in other ways as well. To feminists we owe the renewed concern with pornography as a possible inciter to rape and instiller of male contempt for women and the increased attention to sexual harassment in the workplace, to the costs of forbidding abortion, to the sometimes tepid enforcement of the laws against rape and against the sexual abuse (whether violent or seductive, incestuous or nonincestuous) of children, to the astonishing frequency of these practices (especially sexual abuse of female children), and to gaps in the coverage of rape law.[9] (One gap that has attracted particular attention is the traditional though now disappearing refusal to consider marital rape a crime.) Feminists have attacked and defended prostitution, attacked and defended surrogate motherhood contracts, questioned the new reproductive technologies, questioned biological theories of sex, and promoted social constructionism.

Like sexology itself, feminism is multidisciplinary. Feminists use the methods of biology, sociology, history, philosophy, anthropology, psychology, and other fields of study to illuminate issues of concern to women, including sexual issues. Of course, within each of these fields there is also a good deal of sexual research that is not guided by feminist concerns. Within psychology and psychiatry the principal focus is on departures from the statistical norm (or deviance, a term I use without pejorative connotations). Among these are homosexuality, including pederasty; transsexuality; incestuous and other seduction of young children; rape (some perhaps incited by certain forms of pornography, especially that stressing violence); voyeurism; exhibitionism; intercourse with animals; and fetishism. Freud remains the big name, but his role in sexology is easily misunderstood. In the popular mind Freud is the man who thought everything came down to sex, and infantile sexuality at that, as well as being the inventor of a therapy for neurotics. What is true is that by

9. See, for example, Catharine A. MacKinnon, *Feminism Unmodified: Discourses on Life and Law* (1987); MacKinnon, "Reflections on Sex Equality under Law," 100 *Yale Law Journal* 1281 (1991); Linda Brookover Bourque, *Defining Rape* (1989).

placing sexuality at the center of psychology, he contributed to the erosion of Victorian reticence at the same time that his insistence on the centrality of sex to human development epitomized the Victorian conviction that sexuality was a deep problem requiring medical and political management. But Freud's actual writings about sexual practices and problems are few,[10] and his influence on scientific sexology lies less in the specific theories—most of which either are unsupported or have been disproved[11]—sketched in those writings than in his emphasis on the importance of early childhood, and in particular the behavior of the parents toward the child, in the development of personality, including sexual preference. Child development remains the focus of psychological and psychiatric investigations of sex. For example, whereas biologists see the key to understanding homosexuality in hormones and genes, most psychologists and psychiatrists see it in the young child's relationship with his parents and in other features of the child's social environment.

The normative dimensions of Freud's writings about sex have also been both influential and controversial. In his view, which despite the gulf in premises and terminology resembles that of the Catholic Church, there is only one form of mature human sexuality: vaginal intercourse within the framework of a stable monogamous marriage. The achievement of mature sexuality requires the repression of the polymorphous perversity characteristic of the infant—an eroticism incestuous, narcissistic, onanistic, oral, anal. Adults who masturbate, who are homosexual, or who otherwise fail to channel their sexuality exclusively into vaginal intercourse in marriage are thus victims of arrested development. So are women who require clitoral stimulation to achieve orgasm. It is true that the proper channel is insufficient to bank the sexual impulse fully, but in the mature individual the overflow is sublimated, that is, redirected into creative activity in the arts, science, politics, business, religion, and other nonsexual activities. Repression takes its toll on the individual psyche, but a necessary toll. Repression is civilization.

Herbert Marcuse, in *Eros and Civilization*,[12] turns Freud on his head. He

10. Sigmund Freud, *Three Essays on the Theory of Sexuality* (James Strachey trans. 1949); Freud, *Sexuality and the Psychology of Love* (Philip Rieff ed. 1963), a volume in the Collier Books edition of *The Collected Papers of Sigmund Freud*.

11. For penetrating criticism of Freud's sexual theories, and of the scientific claims of psychoanalysis generally, see Richard C. Friedman, *Male Homosexuality: A Contemporary Psychoanalytic Perspective*, ch. 19 (1988), esp. 229–236. Friedman's criticisms carry particular weight because he is himself a psychoanalyst—as is Robert J. Stoller, who criticizes psychoanalytic theories of homosexuality in his book *Observing the Erotic Imagination*, ch. 9 (1985). In like vein Adolf Grünbaum, *The Foundations of Psychoanalysis: A Philosophical Critique* 278 (1984), while rejecting Karl Popper's contention that psychoanalysis is a pseudoscience, concludes that most of its hypotheses are unsupported.

12. Herbert Marcuse, *Eros and Civilization: A Philosophical Inquiry into Freud* (1955). The political and economic absurdities (as they now appear to be) in *Eros and Civilization*, and in its follow-up volume, *One-Dimensional Man: Studies in the Ideology of Advanced Industrial*

agrees with Freud at the descriptive level about the stages of human sexual development, the role of repression, and even the indispensability of repression to civilization; he merely reverses the sign. For unlike Freud, he believes that civilization is bad and should be overthrown. It would be a very good thing, therefore, if the polymorphous perversity of the infant were not repressed in the adult but instead were allowed to flourish; sexual revolution would be the harbinger of political revolution. In these propositions one glimpses not only the revolutionary infant of Romantic poetry, such as the six-year-old "seer blest" of Wordsworth's immortality ode,[13] but also the idea, most famously expressed in *Nineteen Eighty-Four,* that sexual love endangers totalitarian order.

Social Constructionism (with a Glance at Gender Disorders)

The philosophical side of speculative sexology culminates in Michel Foucault, whose multivolume *History of Sexuality,* left unfinished at his death in 1984, is a remarkable fusion of philosophy and intellectual history.[14] Foucault was a "social constructionist" in the tradition of Nietzsche and the American pragmatists, and his most audacious contention, but one that reverberates throughout contemporary sexology, is that sexuality itself is a social construction. How can that be? one asks. Sexual desire, sexual preference are facts of our biological nature; surely the differences between men's and women's sexual organs, and between the sexual preferences of homosexuals and heterosexuals, are "real" differences, not social artifacts. Foucault did not deny that there are biological differences between men and women, or that there are deep-seated differences among people in sexual preference—that some men, for example, prefer men to women as sexual objects, and some women prefer women to men. His point was rather that the significance attached to these differences is social, cultural, and alterable rather than, as we tend unreflectively to believe, natural, inherent, immutable. The difference between being left-handed and being right-handed is a biological difference, but it is no longer a significant social difference because we have come to believe that

Society (1964), should not be allowed to obscure the many interesting things that Marcuse has to say about sex and about art.

13. Laurence Goldstein, *Ruins and Empire: The Evolution of a Theme in Augustan and Romantic Literature,* ch. 11 (1977) ("The Wordsworthian Child").

14. Four volumes were completed, of which only the first three have as yet been translated into English (all by Robert Hurley). In addition to the *Introduction,* note 1 above, they are *The Use of Pleasure* (1985) and *The Care of the Self* (1986). Those for whom Foucault is a symbol of postmodernist obscurantism will be happy to discover that his books on sexuality, brilliantly translated by Hurley, are entirely lucid.

it does not matter whether one is more comfortable writing with one's left hand or with one's right hand. No more, argued Foucault, need society distinguish between male and female sexuality (Masters and Johnson again), or between homosexuals and heterosexuals. To the ancient Greeks, and to a lesser extent the modern Greeks and other heirs of Mediterranean civilization, the male sex drive, as expressed in phallic penetration, is more important than the sex object. The criterion of manliness is that one be the penetrator, not the penetrated. What one penetrates—whether a vagina or a male or female anus—is of secondary importance, just as whether one is right- or left-handed is secondary to whether one is able to write at all.[15] It is not surprising that the Greeks had no words for homosexuality; they were not much interested in whether persons copulating were of the same sex or different sexes. The broader point is that the Greeks did not *moralize* sex; the idea that sexuality is a moral category is invention, not discovery. Neither did they medicalize or psychologize sex; that was left for the Victorians to do.

Foucault's work relativizes the concepts of sexual deviance, inversion, normality, abnormality. It teaches that sexual norms, and more radically the perceptual and other cognitive distinctions that we make in regard to sex, do not come from nature but instead express the values of influential social groups (political, professional, whatever); that such norms therefore differ in different societies and change over time within the same society; that they are not always or essentially *moral* norms—indeed, ultimately they are political. The affinity to Marcuse (whom apparently Foucault had not read) is unmistakable. Marcuse also believed that sexuality was a political, an ideological, category, not found but made.

⌐Foucault, Freud, and Marcuse merge in Salvatore Cucchiari, who argues that the earliest human beings formed a "bisexual horde": "Anatomical differences between proto-men and proto-women are not cognized."[16] For Cucchiari, as for many other radical feminists (not all of whom are women), the division of humankind into two sexes—or "genders," a term borrowed from

15. This insight was not novel with Foucault. It had long been a commonplace in discussions of Greek sexuality, and had been emphasized in Dover's book, note 3 above, first published before, and cited in, Foucault's *History*. Here is how Freud had put it: "The most striking distinction between the erotic life of antiquity and our own no doubt lies in the fact that the ancients laid the stress upon the instinct itself, whereas we emphasize its object. The ancients glorified the instinct and were prepared on its account to honour even an inferior object; while we despise the instinctual activity in itself, and find excuses for it only in the merits of the object." "The Sexual Aberrations," in *Three Essays on the Theory of Sexuality*, note 10 above, at 13, 28 n. 1. The more radical idea that homosexuality itself is a social construct was not original with Foucault either; it was proposed in Mary McIntosh, "The Homosexual Role," 16 *Social Problems* 182 (1968).

16. "The Gender Revolution and the Transition from Bisexual Horde to Patrilocal Band: The Origins of Gender Hierarchy," in *Sexual Meanings: The Cultural Construction of Gender and Sexuality* 31, 45 (Sherry G. Ortner and Harriet Whiteheads eds. 1981). See also id. at 48–49.

grammar to designate the sexes viewed as social rather than biological classes—is as arbitrary as Americans' insistence, as he believes it to be, on dividing the people of the United States into two races.[17]

Constructionist students of sexuality are fascinated by transvestism and by transsexuality (gender dysphoria),[18] cases (of unknown etiology) in which sex and gender diverge. The transvestite wants to wear women's clothes, use women's cosmetics, and adopt feminine—indeed, stereotypically feminine—mannerisms, though usually only on a part-time basis. But he is content with having male genitals; and although many transvestites are homosexual or bisexual, most are heterosexual. Transsexuals are different. The transsexual, who can be of either sex, feels trapped in the wrong body. The male transsexual wants to be a female, the female a male. Both will have their genitals altered accordingly. The male will have his penis and testicles removed, a vagina constructed from penile tissue (a well-constructed vagina of this kind apparently can fool a gynecologist in a superficial examination),[19] and silicone breasts implanted, and he will take estrogen, the female sex hormone. Some male transsexuals, after their conversion to females, marry men. The female transsexual will have a double mastectomy, and perhaps be fitted with a penile prosthesis.

As constructionists point out, the phenomenon of transvestism exists because society—not biology, certainly—insists that men and women dress differently. "If men could wear dresses there would be no transvestism, as we now understand the category."[20] More particularly, society insists that men not dress up as women. There is much less disapproval of women's wearing men's clothes, although it was one of the grounds on which Joan of Arc was executed, in accordance with Deuteronomy's impartial condemnation as abominations of men's wearing women's clothes and women's wearing men's clothes. There is also much less female transvestism in the deeper sense of dressing as a man in order to assume a subjectively male identity.[21] The horror

17. Id. at 53–54.

18. Annie Woodhouse, *Fantastic Women: Sex, Gender and Transvestism* (1989); Richard F. Docter, *Transvestites and Transsexuals: Toward a Theory of Cross-Gender Behavior* (1988); Anne Bolin, *In Search of Eve: Transsexual Rites of Passage* (1988); Suzanne J. Kessler and Wendy McKenna, *Gender: An Ethnomethodological Approach,* chs. 3, 5 (1978); Deborah Heller Feinbloom, *Transvestites and Transsexuals: Mixed Views* (1976); Vern L. Bullough, "Transsexualism in History," 4 *Archives of Sexual Behavior* 561 (1975); Serena Nanda, "The Hijras of India: A Preliminary Report," 3 *Medicine and Law* 59 (1984).

19. Kessler and McKenna, note 18 above, at 130.

20. Id. at 120.

21. Docter, note 18 above, at 39–40. Traditionally, female transvestism was a form of disguise motivated by practical ends, such as committing crimes without being detected, or joining the army, or accompanying one's husband to places forbidden to women, or—perhaps especially—

of transvestism—for that is the feeling it inspires in most Americans—is, on the constructionist view, related to the horror of hermaphroditism and to the persisting strong antipathy to homosexuality, especially when the (male) homosexual, by either effeminate or "hypermasculine" mannerisms, appears to be masquerading as something he is not.[22] The sorting of all persons into male and female and the pairing of persons by opposite sex are fundamental elements of our construction or mediation of reality, and the violation of the pattern is felt as unnatural, transgressive.

Maybe; but there is another possibility. It is that the shock value of transvestism and of effeminate or hypermasculine male homosexuality is related to our deep-seated anxiety about disguises. To maneuver effectively in the world, we need to assume that people and things have stable identities. The idea that someone might change his identity by changing his clothes violates this assumption. The method is too facile. It is inconsistent with stable expectations. It is as if an old man could pass himself off as young just by dressing like a child.

Admittedly this hypothesis fails to account for the insistence by parents and physicians on assigning a hermaphroditic infant to one or the other gender and on using surgery and hormone treatments to efface, as far as possible, any trace of the other gender.[23] Primitive societies, in contrast, often are willing to recognize the possibility of three rather than two sexes, the third being the hybrid sex, hermaphrodites. The difference may be that the only choice for the primitive society is between killing the hermaphroditic infant and finding some social niche for it to fill.[24] We do not have a social niche for hermaphrodites, and in addition we can intervene surgically to correct what, given our social organization, is indeed an anomalous condition.

To constructionists, transsexualism is the most dramatic illustration of society's insistence that sex (organs) and gender (public classification of a person as belonging to one sex or the other) coincide. "Since genitals can now be changed, gender identity can now be seen as the less flexible criterion."[25] Instead of society following biology, biology follows society. This is constructionism made literal. But is it a correct description? Most Americans do not

---

conducting a lesbian affair without being detected. Rudolf M. Dekker and Lotte C. van de Pol, *The Tradition of Female Transvestism in Early Modern Europe* (1989), esp. 55–63.

22. Mary Riege Laner and Roy H. Laner, "Personal Style or Sexual Preference: Why Gay Men Are Disliked," in *Homosexuality in International Perspective* 78, 88 (Joseph Harry and Man Singh Das eds. 1980).

23. Arnold Davidson, "Sex and the Emergence of Sexuality," in *Forms of Desire: Sexual Orientation and the Social Constructionist Controversy* 89, 93–95 (Edward Stein ed. 1990).

24. Clifford Geertz, "Common Sense as a Cultural System," in Geertz, *Local Knowledge: Further Essays in Interpretive Anthropology* 73, 80–84 (1983).

25. Laner and Laner, note 22 above, at 88.

consider, say, a male transsexual, even following conversion, to be a woman. The transsexual may fool them, as might a female impersonator or a transvestite. But if they were apprised of the facts, they would say, this is not really a woman; this is a man who has undergone surgical and hormonal therapy to make him look and feel like a woman.[26]

Yet if my analysis of transvestism is correct, we should expect the converted transsexual to engender less shock than the transvestite. (I believe this is true.) Transsexual conversion, requiring as it does surgical and hormonal treatments, is not facile impersonation. It is painful, time-consuming, expensive—and irreversible. Transsexualism does not imply that we can change our sexual identity by changing our clothes.

I called *The History of Sexuality* history as well as philosophy. Impelled partly by the exhaustion of traditional topics in political, military, and diplomatic history, and partly by a dawning realization that these topics tend systematically to exclude women and minorities because of the traditional political weakness of these groups, historians in recent years have switched their emphasis to social history. This has been an auspicious change from the standpoint of sexology. A thorough knowledge of the history of sexual practices and attitudes is an essential foundation for the understanding of their present state. To take but one example, one cannot, or at least should not, feel entirely comfortable either in condemnation or condonation of homosexuality without an accurate understanding of the attitudes of the ancient Greeks and Romans and of how and why those attitudes changed in the Christian era. Foucault's great work on sexuality drew heavily on the work of social historians, such as his fellow Frenchmen Philippe Ariès and Jean-Louis Flandrin, and on classical scholars.[27]

26. Whether a converted transsexual is entitled to claim the legal rights of the sex that he or she has converted to was left open in Ulane v. Eastern Airlines, Inc., 742 F.2d 1081 (7th Cir. 1984). The decision holds that an airline did not violate Title VII of the Civil Rights Act of 1964, 42 U.S.C. §2000—which forbids, among other forms of discrimination, sex discrimination—when it fired a transsexual pilot. The airline did not fire the pilot because he had become a woman, but because he had what the airline regarded as a psychiatric disorder. Transsexuals are not a third sex protected by the laws against sex discrimination.

27. Illustrative of historical sexology are Jacques Rossiaud, *Medieval Prostitution* (1988); *Unauthorized Sexual Behavior during the Enlightenment,* the May 1985 special issue of *Eighteenth Century Life* 9 (n.s.) (Robert P. Maccubbin ed.); and volumes 1 and 2 (*Education of the Senses* [1984] and *The Tender Passion* [1986]) of Peter Gay's social history *The Bourgeois Experience: Victoria to Freud.* See also the references in note 3 above, and the review essay by Eli Coleman, "Expanding the Boundaries of Sex Research," 27 *Journal of Sex Research* 473 (1990). Because of traditional Western reticence about sex, imaginative literature is a potentially important source of information about sexual behavior and attitudes, and one to which literary scholars, particularly of feminist or historicist bent (or both), are beginning to turn. For a notable example, see Lisa Jardine, *Still Harping on Daughters: Women and Drama in the Age of Shakespeare* (2d ed. 1989), esp. ch. 1 ("'As Boys and Women Are for the Most Part Cattle of This Colour': Female Roles and Elizabethan Eroticism").

The use of the constructionist approach by a professional historian is illustrated by Thomas Laqueur's book *Making Sex*.[28] Its thesis, to which I alluded in discussing the discovery of sperm and ovum, is that until the nineteenth century, Western thought adhered to a "one-sex" theory of sexuality, then for reasons that were ideological rather than scientific switched to a "two-sex" theory. In the one-sex theory women's sexual organs were the male sexual organs, only inside out, the vagina, for example, was an inside-out penis. Women ejaculated, like men; like men they had to reach orgasm in order to ejaculate; and the ejaculate was semen, essential for conception just as male semen is. In the two-sex theory the female sexual organs are viewed as completely different from the male, and one consequence is that women, far from having to reach orgasm in order to conceive, have no proper physical or psychological need for sexual pleasure; sexual desire in women is pathological. That something like the one-sex theory was popular, even dominant, until the nineteenth century is powerfully argued and probably true, although Laqueur's own quotations from Aristotle, the most influential of sexologists in medieval and Renaissance as well as ancient thought, shows that Aristotle was a two-sex man.[29]

That the two-sex theory, with the idea of female sexual anesthesia that it permits, held sway in the nineteenth century is probably true as well—but not that the switch in theories was due to ideological rather than scientific change. Laqueur is correct that until this century the details of conception were not sufficiently well understood to dispel *all* doubt that female orgasm was inessential. But irrefutable proof is not a sine qua non of nonideological scientific change. The one-sex theory had long had its doubters;[30] it was contrary to experience. The wonder is not that it was discarded but that it persisted as long as it did. Laqueur's inability to come up with an ideological explanation for the change in theory leaves the scientific explanation—the one-sex theory was discarded because it appeared to be, and in fact was, false—in possession of the field.

Laqueur is nonchalant about this failure. In this he shows a fondness for discontinuity that is one of the hallmarks of social constructionism—most famously in Thomas Kuhn's philosophy of science but conspicuous in Foucault

28. Thomas Laqueur, *Making Sex: Body and Gender from the Greeks to Freud* (1990).

29. Id. at 47–48. See Aristotle, *Generation of Animals*, bk. IV, ch. 1. As I noted earlier, many Greeks believed that the woman played no germinating role in conception at all, but was merely an incubator. Greek theories of reproduction are summarized in Angus McLaren, *A History of Contraception: From Antiquity to the Present Day* 17–22 (1990).

30. The first edition of *Aristotle's Mâster-Piece* (1690), a popular treatise on sex, stated—as most women and many men must long have known—that women did not have to reach orgasm in order to conceive. Roy Porter, "'The Secrets of Generation Display'd: *Aristotle's Master-Piece* in Eighteenth-Century England," in *Unauthorized Sexual Behavior during the Enlightenment*, note 27 above, at 1, 9.

as well. That fondness is also reflected in the suggestion that Greek "homosexuality" was so different from what we understand by the term today that we should not use the same word.[31] If we want to speak of the Greek and modern versions in the same breath, we should use a term like "same-sex contacts." The constructionists regard the issue as ontological; I regard it as terminological. It would indeed be a mistake to think that if one says that homosexuality was common in ancient Athens, this implies that Athens must have had a homosexual subculture such as we observe today in New York City, San Francisco, and Amsterdam. I mean homosexuality broadly and trust to context to disambiguate.

There may be little at stake in the debate between social constructionists and essentialists. The extreme positions have deservedly few adherents. On the one hand, no one except Cucchiari and a few other radical feminists believes that human sexual drive and preference are purely social artifacts—that heterosexuality, for example, is the invention of patriarchy. The proposition is not only deeply counterintuitive but also contrary to the biological and anthropological evidence. Freud, who believed that we are born bisexual and that infants are polymorphously perverse, did not think it a mere social contingency that our parents guide us (or most of us) into heterosexual channels. On the other hand, no one really believes that human sexual behavior is invariant to incentives, norms, and other features of the social environment, and is therefore constant across societies; plainly it is not. Almost all students of sexuality, therefore, are—and for good reasons—both essentialist and constructionist, though in different mixtures. Homosexuality does mean something rather different in ancient Athens and modern Amsterdam, but not completely different, because in both societies there were (are) persons who felt an erotic attraction to, and engaged in unequivocally sexual relations with, members of the same sex as themselves. The economic approach that dominates this book is more constructionist than a purely biological theory would be, but more essentialist than an approach which denies that there have always been some men who preferred sex with other men to sex with women, a far greater number of men who preferred sex with women to sex with other men, and in this group of men a fair number quick to substitute a man or (preferably) a boy for a woman if women were unavail-

31. See, for example, David M. Halperin, "One Hundred Years of Homosexuality," in Halperin, *One Hundred Years of Homosexuality and Other Essays on Greek Love* 15 (1990), a model Foucauldian essay. The contrary position is well argued in John Boswell, "Revolutions, Universals, and Sexual Categories," in *Hidden from History: Reclaiming the Gay and Lesbian Past* 17 (Martin Bauml Duberman, Martha Vicinus, and George Chauncey, Jr., eds. 1989), and in James Weinrich, "Reality or Social Construction?" in *Forms of Desire: Sexual Orientation and the Social Constructionist Controversy*, note 23 above, at 175. The book in which Weinrich's essay appears is a debate, and a very worthwhile one, on the constructionist hypothesis applied to sex.

able. The first group dominates the homosexual subculture of today; the last group dominated "Greek love" (which should really be called Athenian love, because we know little about the sexual customs of the other Greek city-states). Provided we are aware of this difference, we shall not get into trouble if we call Greek love homosexual.

The economic approach differs from the familiar constructionist approaches in assigning less weight to power, exploitation, malice, ignorance, accident, and ideology as causes of human behavior and more to incentives, opportunities, constraints, and social function. (This is partly a methodological consequence; concepts such as power, exploitation, and ideology are not concepts in economics.) The difference is not trivial. To show that a practice serves a social function does not make it good in an ethical sense but does suggest that it may be difficult to change. Left-leaning constructionists—and that is the posture of most constructionists today—are not comfortable with the idea that institutions, customs, laws, and other features of the social world might be rational, and specifically might be durable adaptations to deep, though not necessarily innate or genetic, human capacities, drives, needs, and interests. They prefer to think that the existing social pattern is fluid, contingent, plastic, because sustained by a ruling class, or by an ideology, or by some absurd misunderstanding, which might be swept away in a social or intellectual revolution that would turn the pattern inside out. (I mentioned Laqueur's fondness for discontinuities.) They dislike the functional outlook that economics shares not only with evolutionary biology but also with influential schools of political science, sociology, and anthropology, because that outlook is implicitly antiutopian.

Other Threads in the Multidisciplinary Tapestry

In allocating so much space to social constructionism, I do not mean to belittle conventional social science—to which, indeed, my own approach has a closer affinity. Some historians are social constructionists; many are not. Many sociologists are social constructionists,[32] but some are not. Although Kinsey was a zoologist, not a sociologist, the Kinsey reports, especially when viewed as a contribution to theory rather than as a mere amassing of uninterpreted data, are conventionally and I think accurately viewed as contributions to the sociology of sex, as is the subsequent research output of the Institute for Sex Research. Based on that favorite modern sociological research tool, the survey,

32. See, for example, Jeffrey Weeks, *Sexuality* (1986); William Simon and John H. Gagnon, "Sexual Scripts: Permanence and Change," 15 *Archives of Sexual Behavior* 97 (1986); Leonore Tiefer, "Social Constructivism and the Study of Human Sexuality," in *Sex and Gender* 70 (Phillip Shaver and Clyde Hendrick eds. 1987).

the Kinsey reports tabulate the incidence of various sexual practices and relate them to such variables of traditional interest to sociologists as religion, ethnicity, gender, education, and social class (indeed, one of the analytically most interesting findings in the reports is the systematic differences in sexual practices and attitudes between members of the upper middle class and the lower middle class). Other sociological studies have focused on such specialized topics in sexology as the existence and character of homosexual subcultures, the organization and staffing of prostitution, the sexual revolution in America (the clearest manifestation of which has been a vast increase in this century in the frequency of premarital intercourse), racial differences in sexual behavior, the characteristics of sexual offenders, and the enforcement of sex laws. Leading names here are Kingsley Davis and Paul Gebhard, although there are many other notable contributors to this literature.

Closely allied to the sociology of sex is the anthropology of sex, that is, the systematic description and analysis of the sexual practices of tribal and other technologically primitive non-Western cultures.[33] Also closely allied to the sociology of sex is demography, the study of changes in the size and composition of human populations. Prominent in the causality of those changes are, alongside changes in mortality and in immigration and emigration, changes in fertility. On its descriptive side demography is a branch of statistics, but on its theoretical side it is a branch of sociology, of history, and, as we are about to see, of economics.

I have left for last two branches of modern sexology that are particularly relevant to this book, the legal and the economic. Both remain nascent. It is true that one of the classics of sexology, John Noonan's authoritative history of Catholic doctrine on contraception,[34] was written by a lawyer. But it is a book of intellectual and religious history. It is about law only in the extended sense in which Catholic doctrine is "law" for believers, and it does not employ legal reasoning. Works of legal sexology properly so called fall into three principal categories. One is the contributions by H. L. A. Hart, Patrick Devlin, and others to the debate over whether law ought to regulate sexual and other

33. A useful review essay is William H. Davenport, "The Anthropological Approach," in *Theories of Sexuality,* note 1 above, at 197; a comprehensive literature review is D. L. Davis and R. G. Whitten, "The Cross-Cultural Study of Human Sexuality," 16 *Annual Review of Anthropology* 69 (1987); and an enduring classic is Bronislaw Malinowski, *The Sexual Life of Savages in North-Western Melanesia* (1929). Gilbert Herdt's research into ritual homosexuality in New Guinea is illustrative of anthropological research that I discuss in this book.

34. John T. Noonan, Jr., *Contraception: A History of Its Treatment by the Catholic Theologians and Canonists* (enlarged ed. 1986). The enlargement consists of the addition of an appendix to the otherwise unchanged first edition published in 1965. Noonan, formerly a professor of law at the University of California, Berkeley, is now a judge of the United States Court of Appeals for the Ninth Circuit. Another notable work of his is "An Almost Absolute Value in History," in *The Morality of Abortion: Legal and Historical Perspectives* (Noonan ed. 1970).

morals and not just behavior demonstrably harmful to other persons. The second, vast in extent but narrow, overwhelmingly polemical, and highly repetitious, is concerned with whether the Constitution of the United States, in the name of a "right to privacy" that the Supreme Court has held to be implicit in various provisions of that document, should ever be used to invalidate laws that regulate sexual behavior and its consequences, including abortion. The clauses in the First Amendment protecting freedom of speech and of the press enter here as well, insofar as the corpus of sex law includes statutes regulating pornography and other sexually expressive writing, speech, and display.

What is remarkable about these two categories of legal sexology is how little there is in them about sex. The contributors are for the most part interested in broad issues of moral principle or legal doctrine to which specific questions of sexual regulation are relevant chiefly as examples, rather than in theories of and empirical findings on sexual behaviors and attitudes.[35] Implicitly constructionist, much of this literature belittles biological sex differences, which leads the writers to regard legal distinctions built on those differences as presumptively arbitrary.

The third category consists of feminist writings on rape, sexual harassment, sexual abuse of children, lesbians' rights, abortion, and pornography.[36] The leader is Catharine MacKinnon, whose writings on sexual harassment in the workplace and on pornography as an instrument of male dominance have been particularly influential.[37] Her position is extreme. "To be about to be raped is to be gender female in the process of going about life as usual . . . Just to get through another day, women must spend an incredible amount of time, life, and energy cowed, fearful, and colonized, trying to figure out how not to be next on the list."[38] MacKinnon fears that "sexuality has become the fascism of contemporary America and we are moving into the last days

---

35. Notable exceptions are David A. J. Richards, "Commercial Sex and the Rights of the Person: A Moral Argument for the Decriminalization of Prostitution," 127 *University of Pennsylvania Law Review* 1195 (1979), a deeply learned study of prostitution; and Thomas C. Grey, "Eros, Civilization and the Burger Court," 43 *Law and Contemporary Problems* 83 (Summer 1980), an imaginative effort to relate the Supreme Court's "sexual privacy" cases (which I discuss in Chapter 12) to different models of sexuality. There is a useful descriptive literature on sex law illustrated by John F. Decker, *Prostitution: Regulation and Control* (1979), and Tony Honoré, *Sex Law in England* (1978). And works on family and criminal law sometimes touch on sexual matters.

36. Illustrative is Deborah L. Rhode, *Justice and Gender: Sex Discrimination and the Law,* ch. 10 (1989).

37. Catharine A. MacKinnon, *Sexual Harassment of Working Women: A Case of Sex Discrimination* (1979); MacKinnon, *Feminism Unmodified,* note 9 above, pt. 3.

38. *Feminism Unmodified,* note 9 above, at 7.

of Weimar."[39] She believes that *Playboy* magazine is to women what the *Protocols of the Elders of Zion* is to Jews. She seems to have bought into Adrienne Rich's position—the reductio ad absurdum of social constructionism applied to sex—that heterosexuality is itself a male invention and imposition,[40] for she writes that "the major distinction between intercourse (normal) and rape (abnormal) is that the normal happens so often that one can't get anyone to see anything wrong with it."[41]

It would be a mistake, though, to dismiss MacKinnon's work and that of other radical feminists. There may be nuggets of truth in the mountains of hyperbole. In particular we shall consider in Chapter 13 the validity of MacKinnon's claim, developed in conjunction with Andrea Dworkin, that pornography, even—perhaps especially—in its "soft core" *Playboy* version, fosters the intimidation and subordination of women.

When we turn from law to economics, we turn to a field whose contributions to sexology are to an even larger extent potential rather than actual. It is true that economists have made major contributions to the study of population and the family. Malthus was an influential economist and one of the founders of demography. Two famous Swedish economists, Kurt Wicksell and Gunnar Myrdal (the latter in collaboration with his wife, Alva Myrdal, a psychologist), made important contributions to Swedish family-planning policies.[42] And we shall meet in later chapters the contemporary economist-

---

39. Id. at 15. Yet a study conducted by the Justice Department's Bureau of Justice Statistics finds that the incidence of rape and attempted rape decreased by nearly a third from 1973 to 1987. Tamar Lewin, "Women Found to Be Frequent Victims of Assaults by Intimates," *New York Times,* January 17, 1991, A12. Despite the title, the article reports not only the decrease in rape and attempted rape but also that women are less frequent victims of violent crime than men are, and that, overall, violent crime against women did not rise over the period covered by the study.

40. Adrienne Rich, "Compulsory Heterosexuality and Lesbian Existence," 5 *Signs: Journal of Women in Culture and Society* 631 (1980). Cucchiari's theory of the bisexual horde is cut from the same cloth.

41. Catharine A. MacKinnon, "A Feminist/Political Approach: 'Pleasure under Patriarchy,'" in *Theories of Human Sexuality,* note 1 above, at 65, 84–85.

42. Allan Carlson, *The Swedish Experiment in Family Politics: The Myrdals and the Interwar Population Crisis* (1990); David Popenoe, *Disturbing the Nest: Family Change and Decline in Modern Societies* 106–117 (1988). Carlson, at 7–8, discusses Wicksell's advocacy of lifting the then (1880s) ban on contraceptives. The character of the Myrdals' writings on demography, the family, and the role of women is well illustrated by Alva Myrdal, *Nation and Family: The Swedish Experiment in Democratic Family and Population Policy* (1941). The Myrdals held the view, which in retrospect appears not only erroneous but absurd, that socialism was necessary to prevent the Swedish population (or that of any other industrialized country) from declining. That view was stated in extreme form by two admirers of the Myrdals. "So long as men, twisting, turning, fighting and rotting in an economic society, in which they are saturated with class thinking, are forced to compete with one another so long will they refuse to reproduce themselves

demographer Joseph Spengler and also discuss the demographic contributions of the economist Gary Becker.[43] Becker is also the leading contributor to the growing economic literature on the family.[44] Nevertheless, the body of economic writing that can be said to be "about" sex is small. Apart from occasional mentions in the demographic and family literatures, I have found a handful of studies of contraception and abortion,[45] a study of the demand

---

... Capitalism is a biological failure." Richard Titmuss and Kathleen Titmuss, *Parents Revolt: A Study of the Declining Birth-Rate in Acquisitive Societies* 116 (1942).

43. Illustrative works in the contemporary economic analysis of demographic issues are Gary S. Becker, "An Economic Analysis of Fertility," in Becker, *The Economic Approach to Human Behavior* 171 (1976); Becker and Robert J. Barro, "A Reformulation of the Economic Theory of Fertility," 103 *Quarterly Journal of Economics* 1 (1988); Becker and Kevin M. Murphy, "The Family and the State," 31 *Journal of Law and Economics* 1 (1988); T. Paul Schultz, *Economics of Population* (1981); David Friedman, *Laissez-Faire in Population: The Least Bad Solution* (1972); Paul A. David and Warren C. Sanderson, "Rudimentary Contraceptive Methods and the American Transition to Marital Fertility Control, 1855–1915," in *Long-Term Factors in American Economic Growth* 307 (Stanley L. Engerman and Robert E. Gallman eds. 1986); Robert J. Willis, "A New Approach to the Economic Theory of Fertility Behavior," 81 *Journal of Political Economy* S14 (1973); Ronald Demos Lee, "Target Fertility, Contraception, and Aggregate Rates: Toward a Formal Synthesis," 14 *Demography* 455 (1977). The articles by Becker and Barro and Becker and Murphy are reprinted in Becker, *A Treatise on the Family* (enlarged ed. 1991), at 155 and 362, respectively. For a summary of economic demography, see W. Keith Bryant, *The Economic Organization of the Household*, ch. 7 (1990).

44. A literature illustrated by Becker's *Treatise*, note 43 above, by Marc Nerlove, Assaf Razin, and Efraim Sadka, *Household and Economy: Welfare Economics of Endogenous Fertility* (1987) (a book that like Becker's straddles family economics and demography), and by Becker, Elisabeth M. Landes, and Robert T. Michael, "An Economic Analysis of Marital Instability," 85 *Journal of Political Economy* 1141 (1977). For a summary, see David D. Friedman, *Price Theory: An Intermediate Text*, ch. 20 (1986). For applications to law, see my books *The Economics of Justice* 184–192 (1981), and *Economic Analysis of Law*, ch. 5 (3d ed. 1986), and my articles "The Regulation of the Market in Adoptions," 67 *Boston University Law Review* 59 (1987), and "The Ethics and Economics of Enforcing Contracts of Surrogate Motherhood," 5 *Journal of Contemporary Health Law and Policy* 21 (1989); also Lloyd Cohen, "Marriage, Divorce, and Quasi Rents; Or, 'I Gave Him the Best Years of My Life,'" 16 *Journal of Legal Studies* 267 (1987), and Michael J. Trebilcock, "Commodification" 29–61 (University of Toronto Faculty of Law, January 28, 1991).

45. Robert T. Michael, "Education and the Derived Demand for Children," 81 *Journal of Political Economy* S128, S140–S161 (1973); Michael, "Why Did the U.S. Divorce Rate Double within a Decade?" 6 *Research in Population Economics: A Research Annual* 367 (1988); Michael and Robert J. Willis, "Contraception and Fertility: Household Production under Uncertainty," in *Household Production and Consumption* 27 (Nestor E. Terleckyj ed. 1975); Timothy A. Deyak and V. Kerry Smith, "The Economic Value of Statute Reform: The Case of Liberalized Abortion," 84 *Journal of Political Economy* 83 (1976); Stephen P. Coelen and Robert J. McIntyre, "An Econometric Model of Pronatalist and Abortion Policies," 86 *Journal of Political Economy* 1077 (1978); Mark R. Rosenzweig and Daniel A. Seiver, "Education and Contraceptive Choice: A Conditional Demand Framework," 23 *International Economic Review* 171 (1982); Arleen Leibowitz, Marvin Eisen, and Winston K. Chow, "An Economic Model of Teenage Pregnancy

for engagement rings that touches on premarital sex,[46] a paper on the economic organization of Japanese prostitution,[47] and a brief discussion of sex as an "inferior good" (anticipating a point I make in Chapter 5) in a book on the economics of time.[48] Most of the studies of abortion, moreover, are only peripherally about sex. The promisingly titled "An Economic Model of Teenage Pregnancy Decision-Making," for example, takes as given the decision to become sexually active.[49] The even more promisingly titled "The Political Economy of Sexuality" turns out to be a Marxist screed on "surplus orgasm."[50]

Because neither of the main economic literatures that relate to reproduction—the literatures on the family and on population—emphasizes the actual process used for producing new human beings, in neither are questions central to an economic analysis of sex asked, such as how changes in costs and benefits affect the relative frequency of different types of sexual acts (for example, heterosexual versus homosexual), different forms of sexual commerce (for example, prostitution versus concubinage), and the feasibility and desirability of different types of sexual regulation. The family is assumed to be a device for producing and rearing children, not for channeling sex drives. The sexual character of reproduction is assumed, but analysis would be unchanged if people had no sex drive and made babies exclusively by artificial insemination. The rate of population growth is understood to depend in part on such things as contraception and abortion, but these are not emphasized.

Malthus, to be sure, thought the reason we are in danger of producing more children than can be fed is that we like sex. That is why (he thought) a reduction in the cost of children would lead inevitably to an increase in the population,[51] and an increase in that cost either to later marriage with premarital abstinence or to "vice"—"promiscuous intercourse, unnatural pas-

---

Decision-Making," 23 *Demography* 67 (1986); Theodore Joyce, "The Impact of Induced Abortion on Black and White Birth Outcomes in the United States," 24 *Demography* 229 (1987); Marshall H. Medoff, "An Economic Analysis of the Demand for Abortions," 26 *Economic Inquiry* 353 (1988); Michael Grossman and Theodore J. Joyce, "Unobservables, Pregnancy Resolutions, and Birth Weight Production Functions in New York City," 98 *Journal of Political Economy* 983 (1990).

46. Margaret F. Brinig, "Rings and Promises," 6 *Journal of Law, Economics & Organization* 203 (1990).

47. J. Mark Ramseyer, "Indentured Prostitution in Japan: Credible Commitments in the Commercial Sex Industry," 7 *Journal of Law, Economics & Organization* 89 (1991).

48. Staffan Burenstam Linder, *The Harried Leisure Class* 83–89 (1970).

49. Liebowitz, Eisen, and Chow, note 45 above, at 75.

50. Rhonda Gottlieb, "The Political Economy of Sexuality," 16 *Review of Radical Political Economics* 143, 147 (1984).

51. *An Essay on the Principle of Population*, ch. 5 (1798).

sions, violations of the marriage bed, and improper arts to prevent the consequences of irregular connexions."[52] By "improper arts" Malthus meant the use of contraception in nonmarital intercourse, and by "unnatural passions" he probably meant homosexuality, which, he remarks, is said to be a method of contraceptive intercourse in Turkey.[53] It is something of a paradox that, concerned as he was with overpopulation, he rejected "family planning"—that is, the use of contraceptives, or even periodic abstinence, in marriage. He thought the only proper method of contraception was late marriage, with abstinence till then. His ground was religious: fecundity was God's challenge to our power of self-control.

Malthus' interest in the sexual dimension of the family and population is exceptional among economists. Abstracting from sex, economic analysis of marriage has treated the marital household much like any other small firm, leading to such remarks as "the approach to marital dissolution developed here should also prove useful in analyzing the dissolution (implicit as well as explicit) of contracts of indefinite duration between employees and employers, business partners, friends, etc."[54] I do not doubt that this is so; but by emphasizing what distinguishes marriage from other forms of partnership I hope to enrich the economics of the family as well as to explain variance over time and across cultures in sexual behavior and customs. Yet while placing the economic approach in the forefront of the analysis, I have tried to be as eclectic as the universe of modern sexology that this chapter has sketched. Sexuality is the multidisciplinary subject par excellence.

52. *An Essay on the Principle of Population* 16 (6th ed. 1826).
53. Id. at 186.
54. Becker, Landes, and Michael, note 44 above, at 1185.

C H A P T E R   T W O

Autres Temps, Autres Moeurs

THE VARIETY of sexual customs across time and cultures is bewildering.[1] Homosexuality (including pederasty), prostitution, pornography, rape—even of children—seduction, adultery, fornication, concubinage, bigamy, digamy (remarriage following widowhood or widowerhood), contraception, abortion, infanticide, foreplay, pedophilia, masturbation, transvestism, the surgical removal of the clitoris, and a variety of other practices have evoked in different societies or in the same society at different times emotions ranging from loathing and horror to indifference to outright encouragement. Not all of these are sexual practices, strictly speaking. Infanticide certainly is not. But, like abortion and contraception, it is a practice designed to reduce the costs of sex and is therefore within the domain of sexuality. In fact it has important affinities with abortion, as we shall see.

This chapter seeks to convey a sense of the variety of sexual customs but always with a view toward identifying patterns that, together with the patterns in the legal treatment of sexuality discussed in the next chapter, I will eventually endeavor to explain.

The History of Western Sexual Mores

I divide my discussion of sexual customs into two parts. The first, and much the longer, is about the sexual customs of the West, from ancient Greece to

1. For glimpses, see Wainwright Churchill, *Homosexual Behavior among Males: A Cross-Cultural and Cross-Species Investigation* (1967); David F. Greenberg, *The Construction of Homosexuality* (1988); Suzanne G. Frayser, *Varieties of Sexual Experience: An Anthropological Perspective on Human Sexuality* (1985); David D. Gilmore, *Manhood in the Making: Cultural Concepts of Masculinity* (1990); John E. Williams and Deborah L. West, *Measuring Sex Stereotypes: A Thirty-Nation Study*, ch. 10 (1982); Gwen J. Broude and Sarah J. Greene, "Cross-Cultural Codes on Twenty Sexual Attitudes and Practices," 15 *Ethnology: An International Journal of Culture and Social Anthropology* 409 (1976).

modern North America, Europe, and South America. Here the major divisions (which plainly do not exhaust the subject) are ancient Greece and Rome; the orthodox Judeo-Christian religious tradition; the undermining of that tradition by the Reformation and the Enlightenment; the Victorian era in Great Britain and America; the sexual revolution of the twentieth century; and the situation today. The second part of the chapter is about the sexual customs of the non-Western world, including not only Islam and the modern societies of Asia (with particular reference to Japan, India, and the societies of southeast Asia) but also primitive cultures the world over.

The vastness of the subject and the amount of detail encompassed by it should be obvious. Nor should it come as a surprise that the relevant scholarly literature is staggering in its immensity. The sociologist, the anthropologist, the classicist, the theologian, and the social historian will be distressed by the superficiality of the coverage in this chapter. But my objective is not to give exact or exhaustive description; it is to begin to provide data for the theoretical analysis in Part II. Some of the topics brushed lightly in this chapter are examined in greater depth in Part III as well.

Ancient Greece and Rome

Without further apologies I turn to the sexual customs of ancient Greece and Rome.[2] Civilization did not begin with the Greeks, of course. But our knowl-

---

2. For helpful treatments on which I have drawn, see K. J. Dover, *Greek Homosexuality* (2d ed. 1989); Dover, *Greek Popular Morality in the Time of Plato and Aristotle* 205–216 (1974); Dover, "Classical Greek Attitudes to Sexual Behaviour," 6 *Arethusa* 59 (1973); Michel Foucault, *The Use of Pleasure* (Robert Hurley trans. 1985) (vol. 2 of *The History of Sexuality*); Foucault, *The Care of the Self* (Hurley trans. 1986) (vol. 3 of *The History of Sexuality*); Roger Just, *Women in Athenian Law and Life* (1989), esp. chs. 6 and 7; David M. Schaps, *Economic Rights of Women in Ancient Greece* (1979); Mark Golden, *Children and Childhood in Classical Athens* (1990); David M. Halperin, *One Hundred Years of Homosexuality and Other Essays on Greek Love* (1990); Greenberg, note 1 above, at 141–160; David Cohen, *Law, Sexuality and Society: The Enforcement of Morality in Classical Athens* (1991); L. P. Wilkinson, "Classical Approaches: I. Population & Family Planning," 50 *Encounter* 22 (April 1978); Wilkinson, "Classical Approaches: II. Women's Liberation," 50 *Encounter* 25 (May 1978); Eva Cantarella, *Pandora's Daughters: The Role and Status of Women in Greek and Roman Antiquity* (1987); Giulia Sissa, *Greek Virginity* (1990); John J. Winkler, *The Constraints of Desire: The Anthropology of Sex and Gender in Ancient Greece* (1990); Paul Veyne, "The Roman Empire," in *A History of Private Life*, vol. 1, *From Pagan Rome to Byzantium* 33–49, 204 (Paul Veyne ed. 1987); Veyne, "Homosexuality in Ancient Rome," in *Western Sexuality: Practice and Precept in Past and Present Times* 40 (Philippe Ariès and André Béjin eds. 1985); John Boswell, *Christianity, Social Tolerance, and Homosexuality: Gay People in Western Europe from the Beginning of the Christian Era to the Fourteenth Century*, ch. 3 (1980) ("Rome: The Foundation"). Wilkinson's articles are republished in his book *Classical Attitudes to Modern Issues* (1979).

edge of the sexual customs of earlier societies is quite limited[3]—and remember that I do not aspire to exhaustiveness. Even with regard to the Greeks, our knowledge is limited. Relatively little is known about Greek sexual customs before the fifth century B.C. or about those customs outside Athens. And what we do know, even about Athenian customs, is based largely on literary and philosophical sources and on vase paintings. The point of view expressed in such works may be that of an intellectual and artistic subculture rather than that of society as a whole.

With these caveats, and the further one that what follows depicts tendencies and ignores many exceptions, it is nonetheless possible to reconstruct a good deal of the ancient Greek attitude toward sex. That attitude is permissive by comparison to Jewish, Christian, and Victorian standards, except in regard to women of the citizen class. Ancient Greece had a technically monogamous, misogynistic culture and, for "respectable" women—that is, women of citizen families—a firmly entrenched double standard that enjoined on them but not on men premarital virginity and marital fidelity. (It is characteristic of early societies that adultery is an offense—and a very serious one—only against a husband, not against a wife.) Women were considered markedly inferior to men in intellect and character and were barred from school, the ownership of land, and participation in the political life of the state. Marriages were arranged—marriage was in fact a contract between the husband-to-be and the father of the bride-to-be. Even the woman's role in reproduction was disparaged; a popular view was that (male) semen was the human seed (our word *semen* is derived from the Greek word for "seed") and the womb merely the soil in which it grew.[4] Rationalizing the frequent resemblance of children to

3. The major exceptions are the Judaic society depicted in the Old Testament, of which more shortly, and some of the other civilizations of the ancient Near East, on which see, for example, G. R. Driver and John C. Miles, *The Babylonian Laws*, vol. 1, *Legal Commentary*, ch. 4 (1952); Driver and Miles, *The Assyrian Laws* 36–118, 126–271 (1975); J. J. Finkelstein, "Sex Offenses in Sumerian Laws," 86 *Journal of the American Oriental Society* 355 (1966); Martha T. Roth, "'She Will Die by the Iron Dagger': Adultery and Neo-Babylonian Marriage," 31 *Journal of the Economic and Social History of the Orient* 186 (1988); Amélie Kuhrt, "Non-Royal Women in the Late Babylonian Period: A Survey," in *Women's Earliest Records: From Ancient Egypt and Western Asia* 215 (Barbara S. Lesko ed. 1989); Jonathan R. Ziskind, "Legal Rules on Incest in the Ancient Near East," 35 *Revue internationale des droits de l'antiquité* 3d. ser. 79 (1988). The sexual laws and customs that these studies depict are broadly similar to those of the Old Testament (there are also numerous parallels to Greek and Roman law; see, for example, Roth at 195), except that they are much less condemnatory of homosexuality. J. Bottéro and H. Petschow, "Homosexualität," in *Reallexicon der Assyriologie und Vorderasiatischen Archäologie*, vol. 4, 459 (1975); Driver and Miles, *The Assyrian Laws* at 71; Vern L. Bullough, "Attitudes toward Deviant Sex in Ancient Mesopotamia," 7 *Journal of Sex Research* 184 (1971). For an introduction to the sexual customs of the ancient Chinese, see Barrington Moore, Jr., *Privacy: Studies in Social and Cultural History* 152–156 (1984).

4. On the political status of women in ancient Athens, see Gregory Vlastos, "Was Plato a Feminist?" *Times Literary Supplement*, March 17–23, 1989, 276. The misogyny of the ancient

their mothers was easy, given the ancient and durable belief in the heritability of acquired characteristics and life experiences, as in the story of Jacob and Laban, in which the ewe's sight of rods at the moment of conception caused her to give birth to striped lambs.[5]

Partly because of their lack of education, partly because of the large difference in the ages of the spouses in the typical marriage—the woman (girl, rather) would be in her teens and the man in his late twenties or thirties—and partly because of the general male attitude of disdain for women, Greek women were not considered fit companions for men; they did not even take their meals with their husbands. For these reasons, too, the upbringing of male children of preschool age was entrusted to male tutors, and, needless to say, schools (the *gymnasia*) were for boys only. For the same reasons, plus concern with maintaining the premarital chastity of their daughters and the marital fidelity of their wives, Greek men believed that their women should be confined to the home except for religious and other special occasions. No doubt, as Cohen and others (see note 4) stress, social practice deviated from official male ideology. We should not suppose that Greek women were literally sequestered, any more than modern Islamic women are; yet sequestration remains an apt term with which to contrast the status of ancient Greek women with that of women in northern Europe, and North America, today.

The social life of ancient Greek men was passed either with other men or with the high-class prostitutes (socially, artistically, even intellectually more accomplished than respectable women) known as *hetairai* (female "companions").[6] Apart from the duty of economic support, a husband's legal obligation to his wife was limited to having sexual intercourse with her a few times a month and not installing another woman in his house. Beyond that he was free to seek sexual pleasure anywhere he pleased except with another citizen's wife or daughter. He might take a concubine, implying the provision of

---

Greeks is exhaustively treated in Cantarella, note 2 above, chs. 2–6. But Just, Cohen, and Schaps (all note 2 above) point out that the official ideology of female seclusion and subordination was not fully descriptive of actual social practice; the Athenian woman's practical status—her command over resources, the respect in which she was held, and so forth—was higher than her official status.

5. Martin Luther reported that in his home town, when he was a boy, "a beautiful and virtuous matron gave birth to a dormouse" because while pregnant she was startled by the sight and sound of a dormouse upon which someone had hung a bell. "Lectures on Genesis," in 5 *Luther's Works* 381 (Jaroslav Pelikan and Walter A. Hansen eds. 1968).

6. For a vivid picture of the martial roles in a traditional Mediterranean family, see Naguib Mahfouz's novel *Palace Walk* (1990); and for scholarly description, Fatima Mernissi, *Beyond the Veil: Male-Female Dynamics in a Modern Muslim Society* (1975). The sequestration of women in traditional Muslim society—also well described in *Separate Worlds: Studies of Purdah in South Asia* (Hanna Papanek and Gail Minault eds. 1982)—has many parallels to the ancient Greek treatment of women, as emphasized by Cohen, note 2 above.

support in exchange for exclusive sexual rights, but with the relationship terminable at the will of either party and creating no legal obligations on the part of the man toward either the woman or any children born of the union.[7] He might patronize any of the numerous male or female prostitutes, use sexually any of his own slaves, male or female, or seduce adolescent *gymnasium* boys. Children of both sexes frequently were sex objects, too; there was no distinct concept of child abuse, although sexual abuse of a citizen's child, like seduction of a citizen's wife or daughter, was sanctionable. Athens and other Greek city-states had large populations of slaves and resident aliens, and they had few sexual rights.

Greece appears to have been overpopulated, a hypothesis that is supported by the heavy emigration of Greeks to other parts of the Mediterranean region. Large families were not prized. Abortion and, especially, infanticide—particularly but not exclusively female infanticide—were practiced widely, and for the most part without reproach, although Aristotle thought abortion wrong after the fetus had assumed a recognizably human form, and the Hippocratic oath forbade physicians to perform abortions. The killing of deformed or sickly babies of either sex not only was allowed but was the norm. Marriage was not a sacrament, and either spouse could obtain a divorce without difficulty, although a divorced wife was entitled to support from the interest on her dowry; so in effect the husband held the dowry in trust for his wife. Plato proposed to abolish marriage among the ruling class of his utopian Republic and require the members of that class to engage in eugenic breeding.

The Greeks were not reticent about sexual matters. Many of their vase paintings, including the most artistic, and a number of their surviving works of literature, particularly the comedies of Aristophanes, are obscene even by today's standards. Aphrodite, the goddess of sexual love, was of course worshiped openly, and every Athenian home had a statue of Hermes, with his penis erect, before its front door. The Greeks tolerated practices that are considered heinous crimes today, including pederasty; indeed, apart from incest (remember Oedipus), bigamy, and interferences with what amounted to a citizen's property rights in the chastity of his women, there was little

---

7. A word on concubinage, a term that recurs throughout this book. It implies, as the text indicates, a relationship that is of some although indefinite duration, often with the expectation of children (on both counts it is different from prostitution and "affairs"), and in which the man has exclusive sexual rights to the woman with no corresponding obligation of fidelity to her on his part. It can be either a marriage supplement, as in the discussion in the text, or a marriage substitute, as was common, for example, in the Middle Ages. Either way it is a sort of quasi-marriage; the children may or may not be legitimate. For a good discussion, see Jack Goody, *Production and Reproduction: A Comparative Study of the Domestic Domain,* ch. 5 (1976) ("Concubines and Co-Wives: The Structure of Roles in Africa and Eurasia"). Its modern counterpart, as a marriage substitute, goes by the name cohabitation.

concept of sexual wrongdoing. Male nudity was not shameful; although men normally went about clothed, they wrestled, and engaged in other athletic contests, in the nude. Dancing girls performed stripteases.[8] Gods and goddesses were represented nude in statuary and were believed to lead active sex lives. Zeus was an adulterer, a rapist, and a pederast, though not too much should be made of this, since the Greek view of their deities appears to have been that they were less, rather than more, moral than human beings. This is one of the things that marks the Greek outlook as naturalistic.

The best-known example of Greek sexual permissiveness concerns male homosexuality, more specifically pederasty in the sense of sexual desire of adult men for adolescent boys (and thus to be distinguished from homosexual pedophilia, the sexual desire of adult men for boys who have not yet reached adolescence). It would be a mistake to suppose that homosexuality was considered unproblematic. Aristophanes' comedies are replete with jokes, which do not seem good-natured, at the expense of homosexuals. Fellatio and lesbianism were disapproved, and the "passive" sodomite—he who was sodomized rather than sodomizing—was despised. All men were expected to marry in order to have an heir; and although it was understood that some men preferred males to females as sexual objects, it was not supposed that anyone had an *exclusively* homosexual preference, and there was no homosexual subculture. Plato and Socrates appear to have approved of homosexual desire but to have wanted it to remain unconsummated. Although homosexual relations were not criminal, a man who had been a boy prostitute was disqualified from holding public office or addressing the Athenian assembly.

The overall position seems to have been roughly this.[9] Men, especially young men, were assumed to have an overmastering desire for sexual release. This desire, defining as it was of manhood, the central virtue of humankind, was good, and it was more important that it be satisfied than that it be confined to particular objects. Before he married—and remember that marriage was late for men—a man of the citizen class (the only men in whom Greek sexology took an interest) might masturbate, might inseminate a slave or a prostitute, might take a concubine; but one thing he could not do was have a sexual, or indeed any, relationship with a girl or woman of his own class. There was a substitute, however: the *gymnasium* boys. These were members of the citizen class, and so the social equals of their seducers and on that account likely to be more fascinating, challenging, even alluring than slaves or prostitutes. They were not sequestered, and until they reached physical maturity somewhat

8. Vern L. Bullough, *The History of Prostitution* 35 (1964).

9. The discussion that follows draws heavily on Dover, Foucault, and Halperin, note 2 above; and on Just, note 2 above, at 146–148. See also Sarah B. Pomeroy, *Goddesses, Whores, Wives, and Slaves: Women in Classical Antiquity,* ch. 5 (1975).

resembled teenage (that is, nubile) girls. Here then was an additional sexual, and perhaps the principal *romantic,* outlet for a bachelor, which, along with masturbation and intercourse with slaves and prostitutes, would serve as a stopgap until he married.

But there was a problem. These boys, of the same social class as the seducers, were the future citizens of the state. Correlative with the strong approbation of male thrust and with the misogynistic character of Greek culture was the disapprobation, as remarked in Chapter 1, of playing the "insertee" role in sexual intercourse. The difference in the social valuation of the two roles was unproblematic when the penetrator was a male citizen and the penetrated a slave of either sex or a (free) woman, for then the social superior was penetrating the social inferior. But what if the penetrated was a proto-citizen, a *gymnasium* boy? This problem was handled in several ways. First, when the boy became a man, he ceased to be considered a proper sexual object. One could think of a boy as the social inferior of the seducer, thus preserving the hierarchical character of sexual relations, but not a man. Second, the class of seducers was confined as a matter of social propriety to young, unmarried men. Married men were not to seduce boys. Third, anal intercourse, though undoubtedly common, was disapproved in favor of interfemoral intercourse, that is, ejaculating between the boy's thighs (this position is depicted in many vase paintings), with both the man and the boy standing. This posture was thought to weaken the analogy between boy—a proto-man—and woman, who was irremediably inferior. Fourth, some thinkers promoted *chaste* pederasty. The man would be erotically attracted to boys—that was fine—but would restrain himself from giving physical expression to his love. This is Socrates' position in the *Symposium.* But it is probably a mistake to attribute this view to anxiety about homosexuality, as distinct from anxiety about sexuality in general, an anxiety that leads to the idea that sexual pleasure is bad and sex should be confined to procreation. On this view homosexuality is merely one of a number of sexual practices that are bad because nonprocreative and therefore self-indulgent.

Greek tolerance for homosexuality did not extend to lesbianism, which the Greeks thought unnatural and revolting; nor, for reasons that are unclear, to oral intercourse, although, if we may judge from vase paintings, anal intercourse was a common and unremarkable practice in heterosexual as well as homosexual relations (we shall see that this is a recurrent feature of Mediterranean culture). The Greeks' antipathy to lesbianism can be understood as a corollary of their phallocentrism. Normal sexuality for the Greeks placed male desire at center stage, leaving no room for sexual activity lacking a male participant. Homosexual relations between adult citizens were also disapproved, as I have mentioned, because they cast a citizen in the unseemly role (for a citizen) of being an insertee. This may be another reason for Socrates' advocacy of chaste homoerotic relations in the *Symposium,* a work that, surprisingly for the Greeks, emphasizes adult homosexuality rather than pederasty.

Although most of our knowledge about Greek attitudes toward homosexuality comes from Athenian sources, Athens appears not to have been remarkable among Greek states in its tolerance, even encouragement, of pederasty. Crete and Boeotia had the reputation of being even more pederastic than Athens. Sparta was remarkable among the Greek states for having, or at least for being believed to have, no cult of female chastity. This and other Spartan gestures in the direction of female equality are reflected in the utopian proposals in Plato's *Republic.*

The Roman sexual culture was similar to the Greek in being highly permissive by traditional Christian—even by modern American—standards; and since Gibbon it has been commonplace to blame the decline and fall of the Roman Empire in part at least on the Romans' licentiousness, although Gibbon himself did not do so. Most of the emperors led sexually disordered lives—some, such as Nero, dramatically so. There was not, it is true, the same cult of pederasty as in Greece. This may be related to the fact that Roman women were neither as sequestered as women in Greece—indeed, Roman matrons appear to have had a considerable and frequently indulged taste for adultery—nor as disvalued as companions for men, for they were permitted to raise their male children.[10] But pederasty was common and unremarkable. For example, Hadrian, a highly regarded emperor, had a public affair with the boy Antinous, and after Antinous died, Hadrian had him deified and worshiped extensively.

Infanticide was common and approved in Rome, since large families were considered a disaster and effective methods of contraception were unknown. Abortion was also an authorized method of birth control, provided the husband, who had exclusive rights over his children, consented. The condonation of abortion was inevitable; people who do not balk at infanticide will hardly do so at abortion. Rather than being killed outright, however, most unwanted children were either put up for adoption or abandoned. So infanticide could not have been quite so unproblematic a practice as I have suggested. Adoption was more common than in modern society, and money often changed hands. Indeed, children were virtually a commodity. A family might put up its second child for adoption, and then if its first child died adopt a replacement. Most abandoned children died, but some were picked up by passersby and might be raised as child prostitutes. Prostitution, both male and female, was extremely common (as was concubinage), as it had been in Greece as well,[11]

10. Pomeroy, note 9 above, ch. 8; Beryl Rawson, "The Roman Family," in *The Family in Ancient Rome: New Perspectives* 27 (Rawson ed. 1986).

11. Fernando Henriques, *Stews and Strumpets: A Survey of Prostitution,* vol. 1, *Primitive,*

and public bathhouses were a common locus of sexual activity (including prostitution), beginning a tradition that would culminate in the homosexual bathhouses of New York and San Francisco. Women appeared on the stage, as actresses and dancers, often in the nude and sometimes performing sexual acts. Actresses were considered the moral equivalent of prostitutes.

Gibbon's idea that sexual puritanism in the Roman Republic gave way to sexual license in the empire appears to be the reverse of the truth, although evidence for the republican period is scanty. Three facets of a trend against sexual permissiveness can be discerned in the imperial period. First, belated concern with the very low Roman birth rate led to proposals and occasional unenforced decrees intended to encourage marital fertility. Second, the body-soul dualism and sexual asceticism introduced by Plato and elaborated by the Stoics became in some quarters a frank hostility toward the body and all its works, foremost among them sex. Third, a notion of companionate marriage, nascent in Greek writings from Xenophon's *Oeconomicus* onward, made considerable headway in theory, and perhaps also (unlike asceticism) in practice.[12]

The concept of companionate marriage plays an important role in this book, so let me pause to define it. The term signifies marriage between at least approximate equals, based on mutual respect and affection, and involving close and continuous association in child rearing, household management, and other activities, rather than merely the occasional copulation that was the principal contact between spouses in the typical Greek marriage. The equality and companionship envisaged in such a marriage are in tension with the traditional double standard, if only because the husband is expected to refocus his affective energies within rather than outside the home. The idea of companionate marriage implies the injection of feeling and sentiment into a relationship dominated up to then by considerations of male sexual desire, financial arrangements, and heirship.

The Era of Catholic Hegemony

In the fourth century after Christ, Christianity became the official religion of the Roman Empire. Although Christianity is a syncretic religion, and Platonic and Stoic ideas about the human body in general and about sexuality in particular, including the idea of companionate marriage, greatly influenced what we have come to think of as the Christian attitude toward sex, the

---

Classical and Oriental, chs. 2, 3 (1961); John F. Decker, *Prostitution: Regulation and Control* 32–38 (1979).

12. This movement is emphasized by Foucault, *The Care of the Self,* note 2 above, esp. 72–80, 228–232. See also Veyne, "The Roman Empire," note 2 above, at 36–37.

contrast between that attitude as formulated by the early Church and the dominant sexual customs of the pagan empire is sharp enough.[13] Almost all that is distinctive in that attitude can be derived from the essential although not original ethical move made by Christianity (for Christianity got it from Judaism), which was to conceive of man—and woman too—as having been created in the image of God and thus of having a quasi-divine dignity. Immediately infanticide and even abortion—even, though more remotely, contraception—become deeply problematic. A child is created in the image of God. To kill it, whether outside or inside the womb, even to prevent it from being created in the first place by contracepting it, is to mistreat profoundly a semidivine person, or at least a semidivine proto-person. The thinking here is similar to the thinking that led to the outlawing of gladiatorial combat.

That is not all. To suppose that man is created in the image of God is to make the body and everything pertaining to it questionable. It is hardly to be supposed that people are physically *identical* to God—for God is all-powerful, immortal, flawless, a stranger to eating and defecating and ejaculating. Man is a degenerate version of God, the degeneracy consisting not only in pride and envy and other spiritual flaws but also in the possession of a body that is prone not just to decay but to every sort of shame and indignity. The body, male or female, should be clothed, ideally at all times; for it is a shameful thing, a thing to be concealed, not flaunted in the manner of the Greeks and Romans. And bodily activities should be confined to those that are necessary. So one may eat, but only enough to keep healthy. One may engage in sexual intercourse, but only to preserve the human race. Since not every fertile adult need be sexually active to preserve the race from extinction, even lifelong virginity, male or female, can be thought a nobler state than marriage because it involves more restraint of bodily impulse; it is therefore a proper qualification for clerical (originally just high clerical) office. Nonprocreative sex, ranging from masturbation to sodomy to contraceptive intercourse and possibly even to sex with one's infertile spouse, is out; it is necessary for nothing except sexual release, and sexual release is not necessary, since people can live without it. Well, perhaps not completely: men who have no (other) sexual outlet will have involuntary nocturnal emissions. But this is merely proof of original sin, which indeed, Augustine argued, is transmitted from generation

13. On the views of the early Church on sex, see Peter Brown, *The Body and Society: Men, Women and Sexual Renunciation in Early Christianity* (1988), and R. A. Markus, *The End of Ancient Christianity*, chs. 4–5 (1990). On the evolution of Catholic sexual doctrine, see John T. Noonan, Jr., *Contraception: A History of Its Treatment by the Catholic Theologians and Canonists* (enlarged ed. 1986). And on the subject matter of this section of the chapter generally, see James A. Brundage, *Law, Sex, and Christian Society in Medieval Europe* (1987), and Georges Duby, *The Knight the Lady and the Priest: The Making of Modern Marriage in Medieval France* (1983).

to generation in the very act of conception. Nonmarital sex is sinful even when procreative, because God has ordained marriage as the exclusive channel for licit sexual activity. But even in marital sex, positions and caresses designed to enhance sexual pleasure are sinful, for such pleasure is unnecessary beyond the bare minimum required to produce penetration and ejaculation (although when women were widely believed to ejaculate semen essential for conception, the minimum pleasure in question was that of women as well as of men). Since it is the nature of man as distinct from beast to conform his bodily functions to his rational needs, the illicit forms of sexual activity are not merely wrong; they are unnatural.

Despite its emphasis on a common humanity, organized Christianity did not propose to abolish all human hierarchies. Among those to be preserved was the authority of men over women. But despite its fulminations against woman the temptress and the devil's helper, Christianity seems to have been, on balance, more solicitous of women's interests than the pagan religions had been.[14] By praising celibacy, the Church gave women other options besides marriage. The Church also democratized marriage by eliminating barriers based on class or status. Even slaves could marry, as they could not do under Roman law. In forbidding divorce, the Church protected married women against being cast off by husbands who had tired of them—and losing their children in the process, since, under both Greek and Roman law, in the event of divorce the children remained with their father.[15] And by insisting that marriage should be consensual—that a man or woman should be free to reject the family's choice of mate—the Church not only promoted companionate marriage but made indissoluble marriage more tolerable than it would have been in a system in which one's spouse was selected for, rather than by, one.[16]

Like the proscription of nonmarital sex, divorceless marriage had potential benefits for children, by making it more likely that they would have the assistance and protection of two parents. Compared to paganism, then, Christianity was pro-child, just as it was pro-woman; but in neither case consistently, and this apart from the gulf between aspiration and achievement in grafting a new sexual morality onto the pagan cultures to which Christianity succeeded. (For example, it took the Church centuries to impose its view that

14. For a balanced discussion of the early Church's "feminism," see Ben Witherington III, *Women in the Earliest Churches* (1988); for the fulminations, see Cantarella, note 2 above, at 169–170; A. W. Richard Sipe, *A Secret World: Sexuality and the Search for Celibacy* 40, 45–46 (1990).

15. Pomeroy, note 9 above, at 65, 169; Rawson, note 10 above, at 35.

16. The Church's promotion of spousal choice may also have been designed to weaken the great families, which were rival power centers to the Church. John T. Noonan, Jr., "Marriage in the Middle Ages: I—Power to Choose," 4 *Viator: Medieval and Renaissance Studies* 419 (1973); Jack Goody, *The Development of the Family and Marriage in Europe* (1983).

marital choice should be uncoerced and divorce forbidden.)[17] In proscribing contraception and abortion, the Church probably increased the death rate of women as well as the risk that a poor family would have too many children, too fast, to support. Some might starve outright; the others might find their life prospects gravely impaired by the poverty of their upbringing; and their mothers were placed at high risk by repeated pregnancies. The Church was aware of these problems, but its only solution was to counsel abstinence after the family had reached its target number of children. (Contrary to myth, it was never the official policy of the Church to maximize the birth rate in order to increase the number of souls, the better to glorify God.) This was not realistic counsel in an age of high infant mortality, but then the uncertainties of medieval contraception and the medical dangers of medieval abortion were such that tolerating these practices might not have alleviated the plight of families significantly.

I said that the Christians got the idea of man's having been created in God's image from the Jews; yet the Jews, with the exception of fringe sects such as the Essenes, never embraced asceticism. Neither were they as permissive as the Greeks and Romans. It is true that the traditional interpretation of the punishment of Sodom and Gomorrah as being for homosexuality and that of Onan for practicing coitus interruptus—more broadly for ejaculating outside the vagina, a practice that includes masturbation and homosexual intercourse as well as coitus interruptus—can be questioned. The alternative interpretations are that the people of Sodom and Gomorrah were punished for violating the norms of hospitality and that Onan was punished for disobeying his father's order to impregnate the widow of Onan's brother.[18] (The duty of an unmarried man to marry his brother's widow—levirate marriage—remains a part of Orthodox Judaism.) But Leviticus condemns male homosexuality; fornication is denounced throughout the Old Testament; and there is a strong nudity taboo in Judaism.[19] Polygamy and concubinage are approved, it is

17. Brundage, note 13 above, at 242–244 (1987); also Roderick Phillips, *Putting Asunder: A History of Divorce in Western Society,* ch. 1 (1988).

18. The leading revisionist account of the Bible's references to "unnatural" sex is Boswell, note 2 above, ch. 4; for criticism, see Bruce A. Williams, "Homosexuality and Christianity: A Review Discussion," 46 *The Thomist: A Speculative Quarterly Review* 609 (1982). The ambiguous misconduct of the men of Sodom continues to infect the term *sodomy.* The commonest meaning is anal intercourse, whether homosexual or heterosexual, and it is the meaning that the term usually bore in the English common law crime of sodomy, although as punishments moderated in the nineteenth century, the crime (also known as "buggery" and "the crime against nature") expanded to take in some additional homosexual sex acts. American statutes often define sodomy to include fellatio and cunnilingus as well as anal intercourse. The statutes generally are written to apply regardless of the sex of the participants but often are interpreted to apply only to homosexual activity.

19. On Jewish sexual customs and attitudes, see Louis M. Epstein, *Sex Laws and Customs in Judaism* 25–31 (1948); Epstein, *Marriage Laws in the Bible and the Talmud* (1942); Moore,

true—we remember Solomon, with his hundreds of wives and concubines. Western Jews practiced polygamy until about A.D. 1000, Eastern Jews until well into the twentieth century. Nevertheless, the traditional Jewish attitude toward sex was more regulative than the Greek and Roman attitude, yet without disapproval of sexual pleasure. Celibacy was considered an inferior state to marriage, not, as in early Christianity (and in Roman Catholicism to this day), a superior state. The asceticism of Christianity is a legacy not of its Jewish but of its Platonic and Stoic roots. The Gospels evince little interest in sexual issues and do not even indicate whether Jesus married, although they report his making an approving reference to celibacy, and of course the tradition is that he did not marry.[20] The distinctively Christian attitude toward sex was fashioned primarily by Paul, in the generation after Christ, and, centuries later, by Augustine.

Sexual practice in the Christian era was altogether more lax than theory prescribed, the gap between theory and practice that one expects in dealing with so imperative a feature of human nature as the sex instinct being widened by a confluence of factors. A remarkably open scientific literature on sex circulated side by side with the theological.[21] Most priests were illiterate and poorly informed about the nuances of Church doctrine.[22] They were often advised by Church authorities not to interrogate the flock too closely about sexual activity lest the interrogation plant ideas (this continues to be a common

---

note 3 above, at 206–216; David M. Feldman, *Marital Relations, Birth Control, and Abortion in Jewish Law* (1968). On the Jewish condemnation of homosexuality, see Epstein, *Sex Laws and Customs in Judaism* at 134–138.

20. Some Christian theologians, however, have thought that Jesus must have been married because most Jews were. Geoffrey Parrinder, "A Theological Approach," in *Theories of Human Sexuality* 21, 28 (James H. Geer and William T. O'Donohue eds. 1987).

21. Helen Rodnite Lemay, "Human Sexuality in Twelfth- through Fifteenth-Century Scientific Writings," in Vern L. Bullough and James Brundage, *Sexual Practices & the Medieval Church* 187 (1982). See also Danielle Jacquart and Claude Thomasset, *Sexuality and Medicine in the Middle Ages*, ch. 3 (1988).

22. On the various aspects of medieval sexuality discussed here, see Bullough and Brundage, note 21 above; John Boswell, "Homosexuality and Religious Life: A Historical Approach," in *Homosexuality in the Priesthood and the Religious Life* 3 (Jeannine Gramick ed. 1989); André Burguière, "The Charivari and Religious Repression in France during the Ancien Régime," in *Family and Sexuality in French History* 84 (Robert Wheaton and Tamara K. Hareven eds. 1980); Natalie Zemon Davis, "The Reasons of Misrule: Youth Groups and Charivaris in Sixteenth-Century France," 50 *Past & Present* 41, 52–54 (1971); Jean-Louis Flandrin, *Families in Former Times: Kinship, Household and Sexuality* (1979); Flandrin, "Repression and Change in the Sexual Life of Young People in Medieval and Early Modern Times," in *Family and Sexuality in French History* at 27; Jacques Rossiaud, *Medieval Prostitution* (1988); Guido Ruggiero, *The Boundaries of Eros: Sex Crime and Sexuality in Renaissance Venice* (1985); Julius Kirshner and Anthony Molho, "The Dowry Fund and the Marriage Market in Early *Quattrocento* Florence," 50 *Journal of Modern History* 403 (1978); David Herlihy, *Medieval Households* (1985).

objection to conducting surveys of people's sexual experiences). Many priests feared driving their parishioners from the confessional if they reproved them too vigorously for deeply rooted practices. And the doctrine of "good faith" counseled the priest not to enlighten his parishioners about the sinfulness of a sexual practice that they believed to be innocent if they were likely to persist in the practice, since in that event the only consequence of enlightenment would be to throw them into a state of mortal sin.

Among the discrepancies between the theory and the practice of sex during the period of Roman Catholic hegemony were these:

First, cohabitation flourished; many peasant couples simply did not bother getting married.

Second, most marriages were arranged by parents, often with scant or even no regard for the preferences of the prospective spouses. In part this may have been due to pressure exerted by the Church in favor of early marriage as a means of minimizing immoral activity, for the younger the spouses, the less able they were to make sensible choices for themselves.

Third, until the twelfth century the Church did not feel strong enough to ban marriage among the lower clergy; after the ban took effect, many priests took concubines.

Fourth, homosexuality appears to have been common among the clergy, and the Church often protected homosexual priests against the secular authorities who wanted to prosecute them.

Fifth, prostitution flourished. A major reason was that there were hordes of bachelors. This phenomenon was caused by, among other things, the persistence of female infanticide, which generated a surplus of males; the high cost of raising children, which made marriage costly if the wife could not continue working; and the high death rate of women in childbirth—as a result of which a man of wealth would often have a sequence of wives. This serial polygamy, by bringing older men into competition with younger men for young women, reduced the supply of women to poorer men, giving rise to charivari demonstrations in which bachelors harassed widowers who remarried. In one sample of medieval Venetian marriages, approximately 50 percent lasted nine years, 25 percent eighteen years, and 10 percent twenty-seven years[23]—this in a society that did not recognize divorce.

From the Reformation to Victoria

The official teachings of the Church in matters of sex made demands on the average man and woman that were unrealistic. And since the Church authorities, as distinct from Church intellectuals such as Aquinas, were supremely realistic, the Church laid itself open to accusations of hypocrisy that the

23. Ruggiero, note 22 above, at 170 n. 8.

Protestant reformers led by Luther and Calvin were not slow to make. The Reformation attacked Catholic sex theory as too severe and Catholic sex practice as too lax. Clergy, the reformers said, should be allowed, indeed encouraged, to marry, in order to avoid the temptation to engage in fornication and sodomy that mandatory celibacy created. And if even priests and bishops should marry, this must mean that sexual activity was not as shameful as Catholic theology painted it, provided that it was confined to marriage—more rigorously than the Catholics had attempted to do. Fornication, adultery, and sodomy should, therefore, be severely punished and prostitution outlawed. Even the theaters should be closed (and they were, during Cromwell's reign) because of the historically well-grounded belief that actresses were not chaste. It is true that as a consequence of this belief women had not been allowed to perform on the English stage even before the Puritans took power. But since the Puritans did not approve of the Elizabethan and Jacobean practice of using boys to play women's roles—they considered this "transvestism" a solicitation to homosexuality—the only alternative was to shut down the theaters.

The Stuart Restoration ushered in a long period of liberalization in sexual attitudes, coupled with a continuation of the trend toward companionate marriage that is one of the distinctive features of northern European culture.[24] Adultery and fornication were decriminalized. Sodomy remained, as it had long been, a capital offense, but prosecution languished, and a homosexual subculture appeared—for the first time in England—in eighteenth-century London.[25] Prostitution flourished once again. Pornography circulated widely. The illegitimate birth rate soared.

There were parallel liberalizing developments on the Continent, notably in France, which during the Revolution decriminalized sodomy committed in private between consenting adults. The Code Napoléon confirmed this abolition and spread it to the lands that Napoleon conquered. It was not rescinded when the Bourbons were restored, and it became the pattern in Continental Europe, with the notable exception of Prussia. Yet there was considerable harassment of French homosexuals by the police throughout the nineteenth century on grounds of public indecency, corruption of minors, and aggressive solicitation.[26] The analogy is to the sporadic harassment of prostitutes by

24. Lawrence Stone, *The Family, Sex and Marriage in England 1500–1800*, chs. 8, 10–13 (1977); Peter Laslett, *Family Life and Illicit Love in Earlier Generations: Essays in Historical Sociology* 39–43 (1977).

25. Randolph Trumbach, "Sodomitical Subcultures, Sodomitical Roles, and the Gender Revolution of the Eighteenth Century: The Recent Historiography," in *Unauthorized Sexual Behavior during the Enlightenment,* the May 1985 special issue of *Eighteenth Century Life,* vol. 9 (n.s.) (Robert P. Maccubbin ed.).

26. Alain Corbin, "Backstage," in *A History of Private Life,* vol. 4, *From the Fires of Revolution to the Great War* 451, 642–643 (Michelle Perot ed. 1990); Antony Copley, *Sexual*

police in France and other European countries in which prostitution is not criminal. Prussia, however, continued to criminalize sodomy and other coital acts between homosexuals—which meant, however, that mutual masturbation was not punishable. When the German Empire was formed under Prussian leadership in 1871, the Prussian law became paragraph 175 of the new German criminal code. The law was dormant until the Nazis embarked on their antihomosexual program, described later in this chapter. The Nazis broadened the law to cover noncoital as well as coital acts between homosexuals, and in 1942 made infractions punishable by death.[27]

During the Revolutionary period France became the first Western country since pagan times in which, as far as is known, married couples began to practice contraception on a wide scale—initially in the form of coitus interruptus, which remained until relatively recently the favorite French form of contraception. The anticlericalism of the Revolutionary period contributed to the erosion of Catholic sexual doctrine in France, but that erosion did not cease when the Bourbons were restored, and as a result the French birth rate began to fall decades before the British and German rates did.

Perhaps because of the deep enmity between England and France during the Revolutionary and Napoleonic eras, French sexual liberalization produced a reaction in England, evidenced by a surge in executions for sodomy. In 1806 more people were executed for sodomy in England than for murder, although only a handful of persons were executed for either crime.[28] The spread of pornography among the lower classes as the cost of books fell also aroused concern among the governing class. But behind the turn away from permissiveness that marked the Victorian period in England and all other English-speaking countries, including the United States, and to a lesser extent in Continental nations such as Germany, were deeper forces of a political and epistemic character.[29] Reflecting the scientific advances (but also mistakes) and

Moralities in France, 1780–1980: New Ideas on the Family, Divorce, and Homosexuality: An Essay on Moral Change 99–103 (1989).

27. Richard Plant, *The Pink Triangle: The Nazi War against Homosexuals* 30–33, 110, 219 (1986).

28. Jeffrey Weeks, *Sex, Politics and Society: The Regulation of Sexuality since 1800* 100 (1981). On English persecution of homosexuals in the Georgian period, see the fascinating account in Louis Crompton, *Byron and Greek Love: Homophobia in 19th-Century England*, chs. 1, 7 (1985); also A. D. Harvey, "Prosecutions for Sodomy in England at the Beginning of the Nineteenth Century," 21 *Historical Journal* 939 (1978), and Arthur N. Gilbert, "Sexual Deviance and Disaster during the Napoleonic Wars," 9 *Albion* 98 (1977).

29. As emphasized by Michel Foucault, *The History of Sexuality*, vol. 1, *An Introduction* (Robert Hurley trans. 1978). For good discussions of the emergence and character of Victorian sexual morality, see John R. Gillis, *For Better, for Worse: British Marriages, 1600 to the Present*, chs. 7 and 8 (1985); Peter Gay, *The Bourgeois Experience: Victoria to Freud*, vol. 1, *Education of the Senses* (1984), and vol. 2, *The Tender Passion* (1986); Weeks, note 28 above.

nationalistic passions of the period, these forces sparked anxiety over the interrelated issues of personal health and national power. Almost for the first time since Sparta, the production of an adequate number of reasonably fit offspring to maintain the vitality of a nation came to be seen as a variable that society could and should influence. There was a renewed effort to channel sexual activity into marriage in order to encourage the procreation of numerous well-cared-for children; the effort was fostered by dawning recognition of the extraordinary prevalence of venereal disease. A traditional, almost universal, superstition that ejaculation weakens men led not only to medical recommendations for limiting sexual intercourse to once or at most twice a month, but also to severe measures to prevent children from masturbating. These efforts were fostered by a new awareness of childhood as a distinct phase of life, in contrast to the earlier view of children as simply small adults: a distinct phase and ideally a sexless one. For the first time, efforts were made to shield children from sexual knowledge[30]—and women also. With the belief that female orgasm was necessary to conception overthrown, and with it any social interest in encouraging female sexual pleasure, a feasible method of discouraging illicit sex was to keep women and children in the dark as far as possible concerning their sexual potential. The result was a pervasive reticence in sexual matters, a virtual embargo on the public discussion of sex.

The upshot of all this was a return, at least at the theoretical level, to an almost Augustinian asceticism. But the grounds were hygienic rather than religious. This is seen in the example of masturbation, which preoccupied Victorian sexology.[31] To Catholic theologians, masturbation was just another example of extravaginal ejaculation, and hence of unnatural sex. To the Victorians it was a symptom of a serious psychiatric disorder. Interviews with sex criminals and other sexual deviants revealed that most had masturbated,

---

30. Compare the true story of one Mlle. de Bouillon, a six-year-old living at the French court in the seventeenth century. One day the ladies of the court "play a joke on her: they try to persuade the young lady that she is pregnant. The little girl denies it. She defends herself. It is absolutely impossible, she says, and they argue back and forth. But then one day on waking up she finds a newborn child in her bed. She is amazed; and she says in her innocence, 'So this has happened only to the Holy Virgin and me; for I did not feel any pain.' Her words are passed round, and now the little affair becomes a diversion for the whole court. The child receives visits, as is customary on such occasions. The Queen herself comes to console her and to offer herself as godmother to the baby. And the game goes further: the little girl is pressed to say who is the father of the child. Finally, after a period of strenuous reflection, she reaches the conclusion that it can only be the King or the Count de Guiche, since they are the only two men who have given her a kiss. Nobody takes this joke amiss. It falls entirely within the existing standard. No one sees in it a danger to the adaptation of the child to this standard, or to her spiritual purity." Norbert Elias, *The Civilizing Process,* vol. 1, *The History of Manners* 178–179 (1978).

31. Corbin, note 26 above, at 494–496. Actually the medical evils of masturbation had been "discovered" in the eighteenth century. Peter Wagner, *Eros Revived: Erotica of the Enlightenment in England and America* 16–21 (1988).

and this made it plausible to suppose that masturbation encouraged sex crimes and deviance (compare the modern argument that, because most sex criminals are avid consumers of pornography, pornography must cause sex crime). Theories to explain the correlation between masturbation and deviance were not difficult to excogitate, an example being Krafft-Ebing's theory that masturbation causes homosexuality by fixating a boy on the male genitals.[32] Masturbation provided a convenient explanation for all sorts of other disorders, especially congenital ones, such as mental retardation and epilepsy.

The psychologizing of sexual deviance in the nineteenth century reflected the rise of scientific thinking. Where once homosexual acts had been thought the product of a vicious choice and had been bracketed with other criminal expressions of a depraved will, in particular treason and heresy, increasingly they came to be thought a manifestation of mental illness. Freud took a less moralistic and more tolerant view of sexual deviation than his predecessors in the psychology of sex, such as Krafft-Ebing, had done. But, like them—indeed, more emphatically than they—he taught that sexual behavior was the product of deep psychic forces. In fact, finding in the sexual fantasies of infancy the keys to human personality and social institutions, he made sex fundamental to issues of personal identity and social interaction.

Twentieth-Century Trends

From something taken rather for granted in the eighteenth century, sex by the end of the nineteenth and beginning of the twentieth century had become, as insistently as in the early Christian era, a matter for troubled, self-conscious reflection: an issue. Against this background the First World War, both by weakening established authority generally and by bringing women into the urban workplace on a large scale for the first time, ushered in what is popularly but also accurately called the sexual revolution. The effect of the war should not be exaggerated. Well before then the official medico-politico-religious position against contraception was widely flouted.[33] The war coincided with—it did not bring about—such relevant technical and social changes as the widespread availability of cheap and effective contraceptives, both male and female; the decline of religious authority; and the decline in infant mortality, which, coupled with a decreasing desire for large families, liberated women

32. A theory resuscitated in C. A. Tripp, *The Homosexual Matrix* 83–84 (1975), which points to evidence that homosexuals begin masturbating earlier than heterosexuals. But homosexuality and early masturbation could be effects of whatever it is that causes homosexuality, rather than homosexuality's being the consequence of masturbation. Moreover, one expects a homosexual male to be more attracted to male genitals, including his own, than a heterosexual male would be.

33. J. A. Banks, *Prosperity and Parenthood: A Study of Family Planning among the Victorian Middle Classes* (1954).

from a life of continual pregnancy and from the submissiveness to male authority entailed by so debilitating and vulnerable a state.

The causal relationships are complex, and it is not until Chapter 5 that I shall begin trying to sort them out. All that is important here is to point out that between about 1920 and 1980 there were dramatic changes in sexual mores, both in the United States and in most other Western countries.[34] Among the changes are these:

- The incidence of premarital intercourse rose steeply, especially among women. No longer are most women virgins when they marry. This is true even after correction is made for changes in the age of marriage.

- Legalized abortion and sex education increased, and restrictions on the distribution of contraceptives, even to minors, dwindled.

- The marriage rate fell.

- The divorce rate skyrocketed, and with it cohabitation in lieu of, as well as in preparation for, marriage. With nonmarital sex so utterly common-place, the word *fornication,* with its strong pejorative connotation, has virtually passed out of the language.

34. For general discussions, see John D'Emilio and Estelle B. Freedman, *Intimate Matters: A History of Sexuality in America* (1988); Frayser, note 1 above, ch. 6; *Contemporary Marriage: Comparative Perspectives on a Changing Institution* (Kingsley Davis ed. 1985); Michael Gordon, "From an Unfortunate Necessity to a Cult of Mutual Orgasm: Sex in American Marital Education Literature, 1830–1940," in *The Sociology of Sex: An Introductory Reader* 59 (James M. Henslin and Edward Sagarin eds., rev. ed. 1978); Christina Simmons, "Modern Sexuality and the Myth of Victorian Repression," in *Passion and Power: Sexuality in History* 157 (Kathy Peiss and Christina Simmons eds. 1989).

For careful statistical studies substantiating the changes in sexual behavior described in the text and thereby confirming the findings in the original Kinsey studies, see National Research Council, Committee on AIDS Research and the Behavioral, Social, and Statistical Sciences, *AIDS: Sexual Behavior and Intravenous Drug Use,* ch. 2 (Charles F. Turner, Heather G. Miller, and Lincoln E. Moses eds. 1989), esp. 88–113; Richard G. Niemi, John Mueller, and Tom W. Smith, *Trends in Public Opinion: A Compendium of Survey Data* 191–213 (1989); Theodore Caplow et al., *Middletown Families: Fifty Years of Change and Continuity,* ch. 8 (1982); Larry L. Bumpass and James A. Sweet, "National Estimates of Cohabitation," 26 *Demography* 615 (1989); Sandra L. Hofferth, Joan R. Kahn, and Wendy Baldwin, "Premarital Sexual Activity among U.S. Teenage Women over the Past Three Decades," 19 *Family Planning Perspectives* 46 (1987); Norval D. Glenn and Charles N. Weaver, "Attitudes toward Premarital, Extramarital, and Homosexual Relations in the U.S. in the 1970s," 15 *Journal of Sex Research* 108 (1979); John H. Gagnon and William Simon, "The Sexual Scripting of Oral Genital Contacts," 16 *Archives of Sexual Behavior* 1, 21–23 (1987); Charles W. Hobart, "Changes in Courtship and Cohabitation in Canada, 1968–1977," in *Love and Attraction: An International Conference* 359 (Mark Cook and Glenn Wilson eds. 1979); Ulrich Clement, Gunter Schmidt, and Margret Kruse, "Changes in Sex Differences in Sexual Behavior: A Replication of a Study on West German Students (1966–1981)," 13 *Archives of Sexual Behavior* 99 (1984). For a good summary, see Milton Diamond and Arno Karlen, *Sexual Decisions* 198–200 (1980).

• The average age of first intercourse has fallen dramatically for both sexes, but particularly for women.

• The rates of teenage pregnancy and illegitimate births have both soared, but the increase in the illegitimate-birth rate has been more than offset by a decline in the legitimate-birth rate, resulting in a net decline in the overall birth rate.

• With most "respectable" girls and women no longer averse to premarital sex, prostitution has diminished.

• Pornography of the grossest sort circulates widely with little interference from the law.

• Social tolerance for noncoercive deviant sexual acts, such as heterosexual sodomy between spouses and homosexual activity between consenting adults, has increased to the point where these acts have been decriminalized in many nations and in many states of the United States. Even where they remain prohibited, efforts at enforcement are perfunctory at best, and the prohibited behavior may actually be flaunted.

Although careful students of public attitudes object to popular exaggerations of the extent to which we Americans are losing our sexual inhibitions and our belief in monogamy, they do not deny the aptness of the metaphor "sexual revolution" or the decline of monogamous behavior. They do, however, emphasize various eddies, particularly since the specter of AIDS began to stalk the world in the 1980s.[35]

I am speaking of a broad multinational trend, and this aggregation conceals significant differences in the timing and extent of change across countries, in the current situation in them, and in variations among subcultures in heterogeneous nations such as the United States.[36] At the forward edge of the sexual revolution are the Scandinavian countries, particularly Sweden and Denmark, followed closely by the other western European countries (in particular the Netherlands),[37] with the cardinal exception of Ireland. The sexual permissiveness of the Scandinavians appears to have deep roots. The medieval Norse culture was more permissive than the general European sexual culture

35. Tom W. Smith, "The Polls—A Report: The Sexual Revolution?" 54 *Public Opinion Quarterly* 415 (1990); Andrew M. Greeley, Robert T. Michael, and Tom W. Smith, "A Most Monogamous People: Americans and Their Sexual Partners," 27 *Society* 36 (July/August 1990).

36. For helpful discussions with interesting data, see Eleanore B. Luckey and Gilbert D. Nass, "A Comparison of Sexual Attitudes and Behavior in an International Sample," 31 *Journal of Marriage and the Family* 364 (1969); Harold T. Christensen and Christina F. Gregg, "Changing Sex Norms in America and Scandinavia," 32 *Journal of Marriage and the Family* 616 (1970).

37. See, for example, Barbara Meil Hobson, *Uneasy Virtue: The Politics of Prostitution and the American Reform Tradition* 225–232 (1987), discussing Dutch policy toward prostitution.

of the time,[38] and it has long been a Scandinavian custom to regard betrothal rather than marriage as the starting gate for full sexual relations between a couple,[39] even to the point of regarding marriage as an appropriate ceremony for welcoming the birth of a child to the betrothed couple.[40] The relaxation of laws forbidding abortion began in Sweden and Denmark in the 1930s, and by 1970 the sexual revolution was virtually complete in those countries.[41] Premarital virginity was no longer prized, or teenage sexuality frowned on, the girl's home being the preferred site for teenage intercourse. Cohabitation was considered an acceptable substitute for marriage, and welfare benefits for mothers were generous and unrelated to whether the mother was married or not.[42] By 1983 more than 40 percent of all births in Sweden were illegitimate.[43] Abortion had been available virtually on demand, and at insignificant cost, in Sweden since 1975, yet the rate of teenage pregnancy was low, probably because of intensive and effective sex education at home and in school, from a very early age, with heavy emphasis on contraception; and the easy avail-

38. Neil Elliott, *Sensuality in Scandinavia,* chs. 2–3 (1970); Roberta Frank, "Marriage in Twelfth- and Thirteenth-Century Iceland," 4 *Viator: Medieval and Renaissance Studies* 473, 474, 478, 481 (1973).

39. Thomas D. Eliot et al., *Norway's Families: Trends, Problems, Programs* 227 (1960); Robert T. Anderson and Gallatin Anderson, "Sexual Behavior and Urbanization in a Danish Village," 16 *Southwestern Journal of Anthropology* 93, 101 (1960); Helge Brunborg, "Cohabitation without Marriage in Norway" 24 (Central Bureau of Statistics, Oslo, March 29, 1979).

40. Peter Laslett, "Introduction: Comparing Illegitimacy over Time and between Cultures," in *Bastardy and Its Comparative History: Studies in the History of Illegitimacy and Marital Nonconformism in Britain, France, Germany, Sweden, North America, Jamaica and Japan* 1, 56 (Peter Laslett, Karla Oosterveen, and Richard M. Smith eds. 1980); Allan Carlson, *The Swedish Experiment in Family Politics: The Myrdals and the Interwar Population Crisis* 142 (1990).

41. Birgitta Linnér, *Sex and Society in Sweden* (1967); Ira L. Reiss, "Sexual Customs and Gender Roles in Sweden and America: An Analysis and Interpretation," 1 *Research in the Interweave of Social Roles: Women and Men: A Research Annual* 191 (1980); Annika Baude, "Public Policy and Changing Family Patterns in Sweden 1930–1977," in *Sex Roles and Social Policy: A Complex Social Science Equation* 145 (Jean Lipman-Blumen and Jessie Bernard eds. 1979); Elise F. Jones et al., *Teenage Pregnancy in Industrialized Countries: A Study Sponsored by the Alan Guttmacher Institute,* ch. 8 (1986); Richard F. Tomasson, *Sweden: Prototype of Modern Society,* ch. 6 (1970); Charles F. Westoff, "Perspective on Nuptiality and Fertility," in *Below-Replacement Fertility in Industrial Societies: Causes, Consequences, Policies* 155, 167–168 (Kingsley Davis et al. eds. 1986); Erik Manniche, *The Family in Denmark* (1985); and the two articles cited in note 36 above. The best recent treatment of the general question of the family and sex in Sweden is David Popenoe's book *Disturbing the Nest: Family Change and Decline in Modern Societies* (1988), which, despite its title, is mainly about Sweden.

42. Indeed, it is many years since illegitimacy carried any legal disabilities in Sweden. Linnér, note 41 above, at 34. The very term is an anachronism as applied to Sweden.

43. Jean Bourgeois-Pichat, "The Unprecedented Shortage of Births in Europe," in *Below-Replacement Fertility in Industrial Societies,* note 41 above, at 3, 15 (tab. 5). This was more than twice the U.S. rate.

ability of both male and female contraceptives to young people.[44] Sex crimes were narrowly defined (for example, marriage to an aunt was not considered incest), and maximum punishments were low, for example, two years in prison for incestuous relations with a child. Homosexual intercourse between consenting adults was not criminal, homosexuals were not excluded from the armed forces or from other occupations, and the level of social tolerance of homosexuals was high.[45] Recently Denmark, which in the 1960s had taken the bold step of lifting all restrictions on the sale of pornography, passed a law authorizing "registered partnership," whereby a same-sex couple can opt into all the provisions of the marriage code other than those relating to the custody of children. In Sweden cohabitation is a recognized legal status the chief incident of which is an even division of marital property upon separation, and it is a status available to homosexual as well as heterosexual couples.

The divorce rate is high in the Scandinavian countries and the birth rate low, but these are phenomena typical of developed countries today. Indeed, what once seemed the exceptional permissiveness of Scandinavian sexual culture is now fairly characteristic of western Europe as a whole, including nations such as Italy and France that are formally Catholic, although traditional Catholic anxieties about sexual pleasure have apparently left traces in Italian sexual attitudes.[46] Even the Irish Republic, where until recently the traditional Catholic disapproval of sexual pleasure held full sway, with such concomitants as horror of nudity, widespread celibacy, and the full panoply of legal restrictions on unnatural sex, is moving toward conjunction with the other western European nations. Age of marriage has fallen, as has the percentage of men and women who are single; the illegitimacy rate has risen, contraceptives are widely used, and even abortion—banned in Ireland itself but available by a short trip to England—is becoming common.[47]

Germany and eastern Europe require separate consideration. Although the German sexual culture of today is quite similar to the Scandinavian, with the notable exception that an abortion is more difficult to obtain, the history of

44. On abortion in Sweden, see Mary Ann Glendon, *Abortion and Divorce in Western Law* 22–23 (1987). On sex education and its effects, see Ronald J. Goldman and Juliette D. G. Goldman, "Children's Perceptions of Length of Gestation Period, the Birth Exit, and Birth Necessity Explanations: A Cross-National Study of Australian, English, North American and Swedish Children," 14 *Journal of Biosocial Science* 109, 119–120 (1982).

45. Thomas Fitzgerald, "Gay Self-Help Groups in Sweden and Finland," 10 *International Review of Modern Sociology* 191, 195 (1980).

46. Giovanni Caletti, "Report of the Sexual Behavior of a Selected Group of People," in *Medical Sexology* 144 (Romano Forleo and Willy Pasini eds. 1978).

47. Compare Finola Kennedy, *Family, Economy and Government in Ireland* 28 (tab. 2.3), 31 (tab. 2.4), 41–42 (1989), with John C. Messenger, "Sex and Repression in an Irish Folk Community," in *Human Sexual Behavior: Variations in the Ethnographic Spectrum* 3 (Donald S. Marshall and Robert C. Suggs eds. 1971).

German sexual attitudes in this century is distinctive. In no other country did the First World War precipitate so dramatic a liberalization of sexual attitudes. Berlin in the 1920s was a symbol of sexual freedom in much the same way that New York, San Francisco, and Amsterdam were in the 1960s, or that Paris had been in the nineteenth century. The Nazis in their rise to power campaigned from time to time against the sexual degeneracy of the capital, but this was a muted theme, in part because of the prominence of known homosexuals such as Ernst Röhm in Hitler's entourage. After the purge of Röhm and the rise of Himmler, a eugenicist and homophobe, a distinctive Nazi sexual culture emerged.[48] It combined intense hostility to male homosexuals—a hostility unusual in non-Christian societies, and Nazi ideology was ostentatiously anti-Christian—tens of thousands of whom may have died in concentration camps,[49] and to miscegenation (notably sexual intercourse between Germans and Jews), with efforts to boost the birth rate by encouraging not only early marriage and large families but also the production of "racially pure" children by unmarried women and the sterilization of the genetically unfit. Apart from the failure to take any measures to repress lesbianism, the program can be seen as a coherent effort to promote the Nazi goal of creating a large master race. The program was of course abandoned after the war, although the Nazi-strengthened law criminalizing homosexual acts between consenting adults was not repealed until 1967 in East Germany and 1969 in West Germany.

The communist countries experienced their own vicissitudes in sexual attitudes. The Soviet Union began by making divorce and abortion available on demand and indeed experimenting with the abolition of the family and conventional sexuality morality altogether.[50] But under Stalin severe punishments were instituted for homosexuality and abortion, divorce was made more difficult to obtain, and erotic art and literature were suppressed.[51]

48. Erwin J. Haeberle, "Swastika, Pink Triangle and Yellow Star—The Destruction of Sexology and the Persecution of Homosexuals in Nazi Germany," 17 *Journal of Sex Research* 270 (1981); Hans Peter Bleuel, *Sex and Society in Nazi Germany* (1973); Heinz Heger, *The Men with the Pink Triangle* (1980); Frank Rector, *The Nazi Extermination of Homosexuals* (1981); Plant, note 27 above; James Woycke, *Birth Control in Germany 1871–1933* 153–155 (1988).

49. This is the estimate of Heger, note 48 above, at 14. There are no reliable data, and there is no basis at all for the occasional assertions by homosexual rights advocates that hundreds of thousands of homosexuals were killed. Rector, note 48 above, at 113–116, says that as many as 500,000 may have been killed, but he offers no substantiation whatsoever. Plant, note 27 above, at 154, estimates that between 5,000 and 15,000 were killed—and Haeberle, note 48 above, at 281, says that between 5,000 and 15,000 were sent to concentration camps, implying that fewer died. There were no laws against lesbianism. And apparently the Nazis did not punish homosexuality among the peoples whom they conquered, believing that those peoples would be weakened by homosexuality, a result the Nazis desired.

50. Mikhail Stern, *Sex in the USSR* 7–36 (1980).

51. Id., passim. See also Henry P. David, "Abortion and Family Planning in the Soviet Union:

Hostility to homosexuality became a leitmotif of communist policy, culminating in a campaign of persecution waged by Castro against Cuban homosexuals in the 1960s and 1970s.[52] Communist strictures on abortion eventually were relaxed, to the point where abortion not only was available on demand but became a principal method of birth control in the Soviet Union and other communist states. Concerned, however, with falling birth rates in the decades after the Second World War, these states (for which social engineering was more than a metaphor) made occasional efforts to reverse the trend not only by providing financial incentives for mothers but also by restricting abortion. Romania's ban on abortion and on the manufacture and importation of contraceptives, which began in the 1960s, caused a sharp rise in the birth rate. But it was only temporary, and the downward trend resumed.[53]

The English-speaking world has its own distinctive modern history of sexual mores. The conviction of Oscar Wilde for homosexual acts, followed by his imprisonment for two years, occurred at the turn of the century, at a time when homosexual relations between consenting adults had long been decriminalized, de jure or de facto, on the Continent. It symbolizes the stubborn puritanical streak in Anglo-Saxon society, that is, the society of Great Britain and its former colonies. Today, however, that streak is for the most part visible only in the United States and Australia.[54] England decriminalized sodomy in 1967, although it continues to bar homosexuals from the armed forces. Today the English sexual scene is similar to that of the other European, especially northern European, nations. The cult of virginity has vanished, abortion and contraceptives are freely available and frequently availed of, the illegitimate-birth rate is high, pornography is widely available, and there is a good deal of nudity on television and in newspapers. As in the rest of western Europe prostitution is not illegal as such, although pimping and brothel keeping are.

The United States

The heterogeneity of the United States, coupled with the decentralization of policy responsibility in a federal system, makes for a complex tapestry. During the colonial period, and not only in Puritan New England, the impression is

---

Public Policies and Private Behavior," 6 *Journal of Biosocial Science* 417 (1974), a more scholarly though also more limited treatment of Soviet sexual customs than Stern's book.

52. Allen Young, *Gays under the Cuban Revolution* (1981). See also Stern, note 50 above, ch. 16.

53. William Moskoff, "Pronatalist Policies in Romania," 28 *Economic Development and Cultural Change* 597 (1980).

54. On Australia, see Denise Thompson, *Flaws in the Social Fabric: Homosexuals and Society in Sydney* 169–170 (1985); Michael W. Ross, "Actual and Anticipated Societal Reaction to Homosexuality and Adjustment in Two Societies," 21 *Journal of Sex Research* 40 (1985).

of a society rather more straitlaced than that of England,[55] though not consistently; for example, there were no executions for sodomy in America after the seventeenth century.[56] The sexual liberality of eighteenth-century England was primarily a phenomenon of a sophisticated urban upper class that had few representatives in America. (We shall see in Chapter 5 that the traditional association of aristocracy with licentiousness is plausible.) And the New England states retained in full force the sexual laws that, with the exception of capital punishment for sodomy, England had jettisoned at the Restoration. In those states adultery, fornication, bestiality, and sodomy were all severely though sporadically punished. Despite a shortage of women in America during the colonial period, prostitution and homosexuality appear to have been uncommon; this appearance may of course attest to the severity of the laws against these practices. Nor was that severity limited to the New England states; it was, in fact, especially great in the South.[57]

If England in the eighteenth century was more permissive than the United States, the nineteenth century reversed the pattern—at first. The United States was strongly influenced by Victorian sexology, but not as strongly as England. American women were less sheltered and more forthright than English women. There was relatively little anxiety about homosexuality; there were few prosecutions, and no executions after independence.[58] (England was still executing homosexuals in 1830.) The temporary shortage of women during the great waves of immigration fostered prostitution on a large scale in the cities.

After the Civil War, a reaction set in. This was the era of Comstockery and the Purity Crusade, which tried to suppress pornography, abortion, contraception, and prostitution. The fruits of this campaign included state and local laws against prostitution and abortion and federal laws against the importation of contraceptives, the mailing of obscene books and other matter, and the interstate traffic in prostitutes (forbidden in the Mann Act, enacted in 1910). These developments coexisted with, and by no means smothered, the early flames of the sexual revolution, which included a vigorous birth control movement.[59] Yet they were portents of an eventual divergence, now plainly

55. D'Emilio and Freedman, note 34 above, ch. 2; Vern L. Bullough, *Sexual Variance in Society and History,* ch. 17 (1976).

56. D'Emilio and Freedman, note 34 above, at 30.

57. Louis Crompton, "Homosexuals and the Death Penalty in Colonial America," 1 *Journal of Homosexuality* 277, 287–288 (1976). On the enforcement of sex laws in New England, see Roger Thompson, *Sex in Middlesex: Popular Mores in a Massachusetts County, 1649–1699* (1986); Edmund S. Morgan, "The Puritans and Sex," 15 *New England Quarterly: An Historical Review of New England Life and Letters* 591 (1942).

58. Crompton, note 57 above, at 285–288.

59. On the Comstock and birth control movements, see Linda Gordon, *Woman's Body, Woman's Right: A Social History of Birth Control in America* (1976); C. Thomas Dienes, *Law, Politics, and Birth Control,* chs. 1, 3 (1972).

visible, between English and American sexual mores; for although England had its own purity movement, closely parallel in time and scope to that in the United States, it was less intense.[60]

The essential difference today between the United States and England, more broadly the United States and Europe, in matters of sex is this. In part because of the extraordinarily varied origins of its people and in part because of its federalist system of government, the United States is more heterogeneous than any European nation; it may even be—with its large Asian, black, and Hispanic populations—more heterogeneous than all of northern Europe combined, despite that region's greater linguistic diversity. The heterogeneity of the United States extends to fundamental dimensions of culture, including sexual mores. Much of the population—northern European in origin, secular in outlook, educated, urban, prosperous—has the sexual mores of modern northern Europeans. These people are untroubled by premarital sexuality and unpersuaded (whether or not they are Catholic) by official Church doctrine in matters of sex. They affirm the propriety of birth control and of female sexual pleasure and are generally tolerant of teenage sex, cohabitation, divorce, abortion, homosexuality, masturbation, nudity, and most forms of pornography. They are more concerned about censorship and repression than about promiscuity, save as promiscuity may spread disease—in particular, of course, AIDS.

Over against this group is an alliance of two like-minded sexually conservative groups and a third that stands a little apart. The first group consists of the diminishing number of American Catholics who subscribe to the offical sexual doctrines of the Roman Catholic Church. The second consists of Mormons and other fundamentalist or otherwise religiously conservative Protestants (plus Orthodox Jews) who hold, for the most part, traditional Reformation and Jewish views of sex, and who thus, although they are untroubled by sexual pleasure as such or (here departing from tradition) by the use of contraception by a married couple, strongly disapprove of nonmarital sex, including homosexuality, and consider most abortions infanticide. A third group, consisting of political and social conservatives with no particular religious commitment, associates sexual freedom with radicalism and anarchy, or simply disapproves of it as a novelty. Those who are, on whatever ground, sexually conservative, disapprove of female promiscuity more strongly than male but male homosexuality more strongly than female. The emphasis on female chastity reflects the traditional double standard, which is correlated with the traditional view of "woman's place."

This does not complete the mosaic. Many American men, regardless of their ethnic antecedents, remain in the grip of the macho sexual ethic, which I shall

60. For a good discussion of the English movement, see Judith R. Walkowitz, *Prostitution and Victorian Society: Women, Class, and the State* (1980).

describe in a moment. Finally, the radical feminist movement finds rape, pornography, sexual harassment in the workplace, discrimination against lesbians, and male sexual abuse of female children to be methods, pervasively employed, by which men maintain dominance over women. The movement has pressed for stricter laws against these practices. Some adherents have advocated the separation of the sexes, urging women to seek companionship and sexual pleasure in lesbian unions, and to raise children (obtained through adoption or artificial insemination) in lesbian households.

The Kinsey reports created a precedent for surveying Americans about their sexual practices and attitudes, and as a result those practices and attitudes are the most studied of any group's. Let me summarize the recurrent findings.[61] First, in confirmation of my previous observation about the nation's cultural heterogeneity, significant differences in sexual behavior and especially attitudes are found to be correlated with differences in social variables, such as religiosity, income, education, and urbanization.[62] Religiously observant Americans, whether Catholic, Protestant, or Jewish, are more conservative both in their sexual attitudes and, to a lesser extent, in their sexual behavior than nonbelievers or casual believers. Liberalism in matters of sex is positively correlated not only with lack of religiosity but also with youth, with education, with early exposure to sex, with political liberalism, with living in a large city, and with growing up in a small family.[63] Of course, many of these factors are correlated with one another and with religiosity, making ascriptions of causality difficult. There are interesting correlations between sexual behavior and social class, itself a function largely of income and education. Masturbation

61. See, besides the Kinsey reports themselves, Alfred D. Klassen, Colin J. Williams, and Eugene E. Levitt, *Sex and Morality in the U.S.: An Empirical Inquiry under the Auspices of the Kinsey Institute* (Herbert J. O'Gorman ed. 1989) (belatedly published results of a careful survey of 3,000 Americans, conducted in 1970); Arland Thornton and Donald Camburn, "The Influence of the Family on Premarital Sexual Attitudes and Behavior," 24 *Demography* 323 (1987); John De Lamater and Patricia MacCorquodale, *Premarital Sexuality: Attitudes, Relationships, Behavior* (1979); Seward Hiltner, "Sex Patterns and Culture," in *Sexual Behavior in American Society: An Appraisal of the First Two Kinsey Reports* 175 (Jerome Himelhoch and Sylvia Fleis Fava eds. 1955); Robert J. Havighurst, "Cultural Factors in Sex Expression," in *Sexual Behavior in American Society* at 191; Andrew M. Greeley, *Religious Change in America* 90–93 (1989); Tom W. Smith, "Classifying Protestant Denominations," 31 *Review of Religious Research* 225, 240–241 and tabs. 6 and 7 (1990); and studies cited in notes 34 through 36 above.

62. See, besides sources cited in note 61 above, Alfred C. Kinsey, Wardell B. Pomeroy, and Clyde E. Martin, *Sexual Behavior in the Human Male*, ch. 13 (1948); James E. Smith, "A Familistic Religion in a Modern Society," in *Contemporary Marriage*, note 34 above, at 273 (Mormon sexual mores).

63. A 1989 Gallup Poll illustrates two of these points. Asked whether homosexual relations between consenting adults should be legal, 61 percent of respondents aged 18 to 29 answered yes compared to only 32 percent of those 50 and older, and 61 percent of the college graduates answered yes compared to only 32 percent of those who had not completed high school. Gallup Report no. 289, October 1989, 13.

and foreplay are more common among upper-class than among lower-class people, whereas average age of first intercourse is higher in the former group, and frequency of intercourse at early ages is lower.

Americans as a whole do not have notably liberal attitudes toward sex. There is, for example, very broad disapproval of homosexuality, and not merely or primarily in reaction to the AIDS epidemic. The percentage of Americans who believe that sexual relations between two adults of the same sex are "always wrong" has varied only between 70 and 75 percent since 1980; its low point since 1973 was 67 percent in 1974 and 1976.[64] Yet far fewer than 70 percent of the population are religious conservatives. Other survey figures confirm—despite the extraordinary incidence of teenage pregnancy in America, the pervasive sexual innuendo in popular culture, and the high visibility of the homosexual rights movement—the impression of a population whose *attitudes,* at least, in matters sexual remain quite conservative: 46 percent of the population think that it is "wrong" for a man and a woman to have sex before marriage, 63 percent that pornography leads to a breakdown in morals, and 60 percent that it leads to rape; 37 percent disapprove of offering sex education in schools to children in grades four through eight.[65] Consistent with the last point, Americans are not well informed about sex. For example, more than 25 percent believed (at least in 1970) that most homosexuals could be "converted" to heterosexuality by sexually skilled women.[66] Many teenage American girls harbor myths about sex such as that a girl cannot become pregnant the first time she has intercourse, and many American men believe that the size of a man's penis is proportional to his height, that large penises facilitate female orgasm, and that the ratio of the length of a limp penis to that of an erect one is constant across men.

The tenacity of our Puritan heritage, which has discouraged free, frank, objective, informed, and public discussion of sex, is apparent in these data. Perhaps what sets us apart is that no other country except Switzerland—also a stronghold of conservative sexual attitudes[67]—has both a large Catholic population and a Puritan background.

The macho sex ethic, another thread in the American sexual tapestry, has finally to be examined. That ethic is most succinctly described as self-conscious, competitive masculinity. It implies a high awareness of oneself as importantly, fundamentally different from, and superior to, a woman, and a striving to demonstrate masculinity by sexual conquests and by aggressively—

64. Smith, note 35 above, at 424.

65. Id. at 422, 426–427, 429. Some attitudes are liberal, however: for example, 76 percent believe that public high schools should offer sex education and 85 percent that birth control information should be available to teenagers. Id. at 429–430.

66. Klassen et al., note 61 above, at 170 (tab. 7-2).

67. Popenoe, note 41 above, at 262–270.

if necessary violently—protecting one's own women (wife, girlfriend, or daughter) from the sexual advances of other men. It has been contended that machismo, whether blatant or muted, is a nearly universal characteristic of human society and is necessary for male self-respect and achievement.[68] However that may be, there is no doubt that it is a common element in many cultures.[69] Machismo is most familiar to us as an element of traditional Mediterranean culture, with its swagger and misogyny and male solidarity, its sequestered females and jealous males, the sexual culture not only of Greece, Italy, and Spain but also of North Africa and Latin America. It exists in its purest form in Spain, which has given us not only the word itself but also the legend of Don Juan. Variants are found, as we shall see, among certain African tribes and in parts of Polynesia. The macho style has a considerable influence in the United States, and one by no means limited to men of Mediterranean heritage.[70] The contrast between the macho sexual culture and the sexual culture of modern northern Europeans and highly educated Americans is sharp, these being groups in which most men mute the outward signs of masculine aggressiveness and in which women enjoy considerable freedom.

Machismo illustrates the extraordinary tenacity of sexual customs, for the macho style is essentially that of ancient Greece and Rome,[71] and it has managed to survive two millennia of contrary teachings (often backed by law) by the Catholic Church. I remarked at the beginning of this chapter the phallocentric character of the ancient Greek sexual culture. A feminist might wish to point out that virtually all societies have been phallocentric in the sense of being dominated by men and inclined to disvalue the work of women. But I am using the word more literally. The Greeks believed not only that male sexual desire and performance were all-important but also, a corollary by no means drawn in all male-dominated societies, that this desire and performance were more important than the object on which they were exercised. We do not find in today's macho societies the cult of pederasty, but we also do not find the traditional Anglo-Saxon abhorrence of anal intercourse.[72]

---

68. These are the principal themes in Gilmore, note 1 above.

69. For a good discussion, see Lee Rainwater, "Marital Sexuality in Four Cultures of Poverty," 26 *Journal of Marriage and the Family* 457 (1964).

70. See, for example, George Austin Chauncey, Jr., "Gay New York: Urban Culture and the Making of a Gay Male World, 1890–1940" 77–97 (Ph.D. diss., Yale University, 1989). The culture of "wolves" and "lambs" that Chauncey describes in New York's Bowery district at the turn of the century bears a family resemblance to ancient Greek pederasty as well as to homosexual activity in modern American prisons. In fact, in all three cultures the same terms—"wolf" and "lamb"—are applied to the penetrator and the penetratee, respectively.

71. Churchill, note 1 above, at 167–169. Cohen, note 2 above, stresses the continuity between the macho sexual culture of ancient Greece and that of other Mediterranean societies.

72. For a good discussion, see Frederick L. Whitam and Robin M. Mathy, *Male Homosex-*

A man who always takes the penetrating role is a "real" man, not a homosexual, and this whether or not he penetrates vaginas or the male or female anus. If he engages in both vaginal intercourse and homosexual sodomy (provided he is always the penetrator), he is not a homosexual or bisexual but simply a man of strong desires who naturally and appropriately is not fastidious about the object on which he gratifies those desires.[73] A man who allows himself to be penetrated, or a man who, regardless of his sexual tastes, has an effeminate manner, is despised. Yet he is not feared and will not be punished,[74] or even harassed, because he is thought of not as a monster—a member of a third sex—but rather as a kind of woman,[75] a that-which-is-penetrated, and because he provides a secondary outlet for real men.

So we have the paradox, to be explored in subsequent chapters, that macho cultures are on the whole more tolerant of sexual deviance than otherwise more sexually liberal Anglo-Saxon societies. A further puzzle to be explored is that, until recently, members of Mediterranean societies were apt to deny that there were any homosexuals among them.

The Sexual Mores of Non-Western Cultures

I want to leave the Western world now and speak briefly and with alarming superficiality about the sexual mores of the vast non-Western world, past and present.[76] Non-Western is largely a synonym for non-Christian, and, with the

uality in Four Societies: Brazil, Guatemala, the Philippines, and the United States 132–135 (1986); also Stanley Brandes, "Like Wounded Stags: Male Sexual Ideology in an Andalusian Town," in Sexual Meanings: The Cultural Construction of Gender and Sexuality 216, 233–234 (Sherry B. Ortner and Harriet Whitehead eds. 1981); Richard G. Parker, Bodies, Pleasures, and Passions: Sexual Culture in Contemporary Brazil 46–47 (1991).

73. On the popularity of anal intercourse, heterosexual as well as homosexual, in Latin cultures, see, for example, Nancy M. Flowers, "The Spread of AIDS in Brazil," in AIDS: AASA Symposia Papers 1988 159 (Ruth Kulstad ed. 1988).

74. Most Latin American countries, like the Latin countries of the Mediterranean, took their cue from the Code Napoléon and did not criminalize sodomy. Whitam and Mathy, note 72 above, at 131.

75. Tripp, note 32 above, at 134–136. See also Kari Ellen Gade, "Homosexuality and Rape of Males in Old Norse Law and Literature," 58 Scandinavian Studies 124, 132–135 (1986). For a striking example in this country of the macho male who regards the boyish, passive men whom he penetrates as "women," see David M. Halperin, "One Hundred Years of Homosexuality," in Halperin, note 2 above, at 15, 38–39, describing Jack Abbott (the murderer befriended by Norman Mailer), whose French counterpart in this respect (and others) is Jean Genet.

76. For helpful surveys, see Frayser, note 1 above; Broude and Greene, also note 1 above; Barry D. Adams, "Age, Structure, and Sexuality: Reflections on the Anthropological Evidence on Homosexual Relations," in Anthropology and Homosexual Behavior 19 (Evelyn Blackwood ed. 1986); and two older but still useful works, Clellan Stearns Ford, "A Comparative Study of

doubtful exception of Islam and the erratic exception of communism, no major religion or ideology has been as sexually repressive as Christianity. Islam, which adopted the Levitican prohibitions, prescribes severe punishments for nudity, pornography, adultery, and fornication. Muslim states such as Iran and Saudi Arabia that enforce religious law thus are highly repressive by modern Western standards. But the qualification "modern" must be emphasized. Muslim societies have traditionally been more tolerant of homosexuality than Christian societies,[77] and that is the least of their differences. Islam is not dubious about sexual pleasure, is not puritanical or Victorian, and, like Judaism (which it resembles in matters of sex), places a negative valuation on celibacy. Not only are Muslims permitted four wives, but concubinage is a recognized status, temporary marriages are permitted (though only among Shiite Muslims), and the husband can divorce at will. Mohammed himself had many wives, and heaven is a place of sensual pleasures. Islam has always permitted contraception and been tolerant of abortion.[78]

Many non-Western cultures seem positively licentious by Western standards; this is a traditional ground on which Westerners have pronounced themselves more civilized. The Hindu religion celebrates sexual technique and erotic dancing, and as a result much Indian religious art is obscene by Western standards. Although Samoa was not in fact the paradise of adolescent free love described by Margaret Mead,[79] Polynesian societies such as Samoa *are* striking in their departure from Western sexual norms.[80] For example, the

---

Human Reproduction" (Yale University Publications in Anthropology no. 32, 1945), and George Ryley Scott, *Far Eastern Sex Life: An Anthropological, Ethnological and Sociological Study of the Love Relations, Marriage Rites and Home Life of the Oriental Peoples* (1943) (marital and sexual customs of China and Japan).

77. Parker Rossman, *Sexual Experience between Men and Boys: Exploring the Pederast Underground* 116–124 (1976); Mernissi, note 6 above, at 53; Vincent Crapanzano, *Tuhami: Portrait of a Moroccan* 34, 48, 109–110 (1980).

78. Mernissi, note 6 above; Jamal J. Nasir, *The Status of Women under Islamic Law and under Modern Islamic Legislation* (1990); Madelain Farah, "Introduction," in *Marriage and Sexuality in Islam: A Translation of al-Ghazali's Book on the Etiquette of Marriage from the Ihya'* 3 (Farah ed. 1984); Abul A'La Maududi, *Purdah and the Status of Woman in Islam* (1972); Shahla Haeri, *Law of Desire: Temporary Marriage in Shi'i Iran* 49–72 (1989); B. F. Musallam, *Sex and Society in Islam: Birth Control before the Nineteenth Century* (1983); Soraya Altorki, *Women in Saudi Arabia: Behavior among the Elite* (1986), esp. ch. 5. Male and even female masturbation was not considered sinful. *Sex and Society in Islam* at 33–34.

79. Derek Freeman, *Margaret Mead and Samoa: The Making and Unmaking of an Anthropological Myth*, ch. 16 (1983), discussing Mead's famous book *Coming of Age in Samoa* (1928).

80. "Consider Marshall's data on sexual behavior in Mangaia, a southern Cook Island in central Polynesia, where all women are said to orgasm during intercourse. At the age of 13 or 14 Mangaian boys undergo superincision [the making of a longitudinal slit in the foreskin], and at this time are instructed in sexual matters by the superincision expert. The expert emphasizes techniques of coitus, cunnilingus, kissing and sucking the breasts, and bringing the partner to

Sambia, a tribe in New Guinea, have made a form of pederasty mandatory. All adolescent boys are assigned adult male lovers whom the boys fellate; the ingestion of adult semen is believed to be necessary to male maturation.[81] The belief resembles one of the Greek rationales for pederasty: that it helps bond men and boys and by doing so helps the boys grow into men. At the same time, and very much in the macho tradition, the Sambia deny the existence of any other form of homosexuality—hence of what *we* think of as homosexuality (lifelong, strongly homosexual preference)—in their society.

In Southeast Asia generally, whether or not a society actually encourages homosexuality, it is almost certain to tolerate it with fewer misgivings than even liberal Western societies. The Philippines, for example, presumably despite rather than because of Spanish and American influences, is highly tolerant of homosexuals.[82] The Spanish Conquistadors found that homosexual sodomy was practiced openly in many American Indian tribes, and this shocking discovery helped the Spanish rationalize their genocidal treatment of the Indians. In a number of Indian tribes, North American as well as South and Central American, effeminate homosexuals—*berdaches* is the term anthropologists apply to them—are honored, even privileged members of society.[83]

---

several orgasms before the male allows himself to ejaculate. According to Marshall, Mangaian knowledge of sexual anatomy probably is more extensive than that of most European physicians. Two weeks after superincision there is a 'practical exercise' in intercourse with an older, experienced woman. She coaches the neophyte in applying the information he has acquired from the superincision expert, especially the techniques of delaying and timing ejaculation so that he orgasms simultaneously with his partner." Donald Symons, *The Evolution of Human Sexuality* 85 (1979).

81. Gilbert H. Herdt, *Guardians of the Flutes: Idioms of Masculinity* (1981); Gilmore, note 1 above, ch. 7. The "Sambia" (a pseudonym that Professor Herdt gave the tribe that he studied, to protect its privacy) are not alone in this. In addition to the other tribal societies in New Guinea examined in Herdt, "Ritualized Homosexual Behavior in the Male Cults of Melanesia, 1862– 1983: An Introduction," in *Ritualized Homosexuality in Melanesia* 1 (Herdt ed. 1984), equally striking parallels to the Greek cult of pederasty can be found in several African tribal societies (see E. E. Evans-Pritchard, *The Azande: History and Political Institutions* 183, 199–200 [1971], for an example), as well as in traditional Chinese, and especially in Thai and Japanese, society. Bret Hinsch, *Passions of the Cut Sleeve: The Male Homosexual Tradition in China* 10–11 (1990); Peter A. Jackson, *Male Homosexuality in Thailand: An Interpretation of Contemporary Thai Sources* 216, 230 (1989); Paul Gordon Schalow, "Male Love in Early Modern Japan: A Literary Depiction of 'Youth,'" in *Hidden from History: Reclaiming the Gay and Lesbian Past* 118 (Martin Bauml Duberman, Martha Vicinus, and George Chauncey, Jr., eds. 1989); Ian Buruma, *Behind the Mask: On Sexual Demons, Sacred Mothers, Transvestites, Gangsters, Drifters and Other Japanese Cultural Heroes* 127–129 (1984). Cf. Jan Bremmer, "An Enigmatic Indo-European Rite: Paederasty," 13 *Arethusa* 279 (1980); J. Bottéro and H. Petschow, note 3 above, at 462 (pederasty in the ancient Near East).

82. Whitam and Mathy, note 72 above, at 144–156.

83. Walter L. Williams, *The Spirit and the Flesh: Sexual Diversity in American Indian Culture* (1986); Harriet Whitehead, "The Bow and the Burden Strap: A New Look at Institutionalized

Hermaphrodites, too, in some primitive cultures.[84] Polygamy, in the form of polygyny, or plural wives (polyandry—plural husbands—is extremely rare), is so common in non-Western societies that it can fairly be regarded as the norm.

Of particular interest, in light of the common Western belief that the sexual freedom of technologically primitive and other non-Western cultures is a consequence or even a cause of their backwardness, is the sexual culture of Japan,[85] a nation as technologically advanced as any in the world. Japan has not escaped Western influence even in the area of sex. Its prohibition of prostitution in 1958 was a gesture of ingratiation toward its protector, the United States. But the essential culture of Japan is indigenous, and conforms to the generalization that non-Christian societies are not as anxious about sex as Christian ones. Despite formal prohibitions, which continue on the books, prostitution flourishes in Japan along with other forms of nonmarital sex with little social disapproval. Homosexuality is treated tolerantly,[86] and pornography—dominated by scenes of rape and bondage—is sold openly wherever newspapers or magazines are sold. Abortion and contraception are not restricted (except that the pill is banned on health grounds), and although teenage sex is common and illegitimacy is taken in stride, the rate of both teenage births and illegitimate births is very low, as is the divorce rate. The overall birth rate is very low, too—indeed, well below replacement. And the nudity taboo is weaker than in the West.[87] The parallels to ancient Greece are unmistakable.

Homosexuality in Native North America," in *Sexual Meanings,* note 72 above, at 80. Cf. Anne Bolin, *In Search of Eve: Transsexual Rites of Passage* 189–192 (1988) (examples from non-Indian cultures).

84. Clifford Geertz, "Common Sense as a Cultural System," in Geertz, *Local Knowledge: Further Essays in Interpretive Anthropology* 73, 80–84 (1983).

85. On which see Joy Hendry, "Japan: Culture versus Industrialization as Determinant of Marital Patterns," in *Contemporary Marriage,* note 34 above, at 197, esp. 215; Buruma, note 81 above, at 58–62, 100, 127–129; Samuel H. Preston, "The Decline of Fertility in Non-European Industrialized Countries," in *Below-Replacement Fertility in Industrial Societies,* note 41 above, at 26; Shigemi Kono, "Comment," in *Below-Replacement Fertility* at 171.

86. "Homosexuality has never been treated as a criminal deviation or a sickness. It is a part of life, little discussed, and perfectly permissible if the rules of social propriety—getting married for instance—are observed." Buruma, note 81 above, at 127. See the works cited in note 81 for parallels between traditional Japanese and ancient Greek attitudes toward pederasty.

87. Scott, note 76 above, ch. 13. On the relaxed attitude of the Japanese toward erotic literature, see id. at 189–190, and bear in mind that Scott was writing about Japanese customs of nearly half a century ago.

Sexuality and Law

THE DIVERSITY in sexual customs that was discussed in the preceding chapter is mirrored by diversity in the legal treatment of sexual behavior—most strikingly, of course, in Islamic societies, where the criminal law is drawn directly from religious law. Yet in most societies it is a distorting mirror in this sense: it is not the case that every sexual practice that is contrary to the mores of a society is made punishable by the laws of that society and that every sexual practice not contrary to those mores is permitted. The ancient Greeks, for example, regarded incest with horror, but did not (as far as we know) make it a crime. They considered lesbianism obscene, disgusting, but did not make it a crime either. Indeed, although almost everywhere abhorred, lesbianism has rarely been criminalized. The English common law, which meted out savage punishments to sodomites, did not punish lesbian relations at all; neither did German law during the Nazi regime. Prostitution has generally been disapproved of in Western societies but usually not punished—and this as a matter of law, not just of practice. And even though traditional Catholic doctrine considered masturbation a worse sin than rape, masturbation was never made a crime, though rape was.

These are exceptions (to be explained, as far as possible, in subsequent chapters). In general, the most important of a society's sexual customs will be reflected in law, though not necessarily in law that is enforced; and so the severity of punishment provides an index of the fear and loathing that a particular sexual practice inspires. The retention on the statute books of laws that are unenforced, such as the laws in many states of the United States today forbidding adultery and fornication, may reflect the views of only a small minority of the population—or even sheer inertia. Moreover, one reason for punishing a crime heavily is that the probability of catching the criminal is low, and it is a reason independent of the gravity of the offense. But most crimes are difficult to detect in this sense, because most criminals take pains to elude capture; and retributive considerations strongly influence the design of criminal codes. On both counts we should expect punishment to be at least roughly proportional to the perceived gravity of the crime.

The sexual tolerance of ancient Greek and Roman, and modern Scandinavian, societies does seem to be reflected in the punishments, or lack thereof, for what in other societies—and even in those same societies—was or is regarded as deviant behavior. Apart from certain civil disabilities attached to a Greek citizen who had been a prostitute in his youth,[1] and capital punishment for raping the wife or daughter of a citizen—conduct condemned not for any sexual impropriety as such (since the rape of a slave or an alien was not a crime) but because it infringed the property rights of male citizens, the husband or father as the case might be—very little that modern Americans consider morally questionable in the realm of sex and procreation was punishable: not abortion, infanticide, prostitution, fornication, adultery, sodomy (homosexual or heterosexual), pederasty, public nudity, public indecency, pornography, or even the sexual abuse of small children. Rape was not a crime unless the victim had reached or was approaching pubescence, and there was no crime of seducing a minor.[2] It is true that the Greeks and Romans punished, or rather allowed the husband to punish, the wife who committed adultery (and the man who committed adultery with her) or who obtained an abortion against her husband's will, but these were offenses against the property rights that a husband had in his wife and children.

We should not confine our attention to criminal and other punitive laws; they are not the only types of law that affect sexual behavior. Of particular relevance is the law of marriage and divorce, but here again the picture in classical antiquity is one of laxity by our standards. Although incestuous marriages were forbidden, incestuous relations as such were not. The minimum age of marriage was low (12 for girls in Roman law), and it is unlikely that as a practical matter the woman's consent was required. The husband's marital obligation was limited to economic support and occasional intercourse. He could divorce the wife at will, and if he did she had no further claims on him or his property, or on the children of the marriage; so, in effect, he could also abandon her at will, without obligation other than to return her dowry (if any) or to support her out of it. Although polygamy was forbidden, concubinage was not, and thus a man could in effect have several wives, the only difference between marriage and concubinage being that the

1. A male prostitute, since only men were citizens. As in virtually all other cultures, the customers of male prostitutes were men, not women.

2. David Cohen, whose book *Law, Sexuality and Society: The Enforcement of Morals in Classical Athens* (1991), is the fullest account of ancient Greek sex law, believes that the seduction of a citizen's young daughter would have been considered the crime of *hubris*, but Mark Golden, *Children and Childhood in Classical Athens* 58 (1990), argues the contrary. And Cohen does state that "there are no 'sexual offenses,' in the modern sense, in Athenian law." *Law, Sexuality and Society* at 123.

concubine's children had no right of inheritance from the father unless he chose to recognize them as his legitimate children.

The modern Scandinavian scene[3] is not identical, although it may appear so to an American of conventional sexual and family mores. Abortion, though not formally available on demand, as it is for American women during the first trimester of pregnancy—and, in practice, often much later—by virtue of the Supreme Court's decision (currently undergoing rapid erosion) in *Roe v. Wade,* is subject to few restrictions. As a practical matter it is *more* available than in the United States, owing to the legal restrictions in this country on the public funding of abortions and the reluctance of most American hospitals to perform them (see Chapter 10). Prostitution is not a crime in Sweden, although aggressive solicitation and brothel keeping are, nor is the sale of pornography, nor consensual homosexual relations between adults. Fornication is not a crime either, and children born out of wedlock have all the rights of "legitimate" children; indeed they *are* legitimate children. Incest, rape, and seduction of a minor are crimes, but the punishments are light. In Sweden, for example, the maximum prison sentence for rape is only six years, unless the rapist inflicted a serious injury or otherwise behaved with especial brutality, in which event the maximum rises to ten years. The maximum sentence for sexual intercourse with a child under the age of 15 (the age of consent) is only four years, and for father-daughter incest two years; for sibling incest the maximum punishment falls to one year. The schedule of punishments is almost identical in Denmark.

All these sentences are low by American standards, but we must consider the possibility that they reflect a generally lenient attitude toward criminals rather than a special tolerance for sexual misconduct. Although the maximum sentence in Sweden for murder, kidnapping, or arson in a heavily populated area is life in prison, the maximum for grand larceny and robbery is only six years, and for nonaggravated arson eight—and these are much lower than the corresponding maximum punishments in the United States. This relative lenity need not reflect a more tolerant view of crime; I doubt that Swedes are less disapproving of criminal activity than Americans are; it could just reflect the ease of catching criminals in a small and homogeneous society. That is why it is important, in gauging different national attitudes toward sex crime, to

3. On which see, for example, Lena Johnsson, "Law and Fertility in Sweden," in *Law and Fertility in Europe: A Study of Legislation Directly or Indirectly Affecting Fertility in Europe,* vol. 2, 544 (Maurice Kirk, Massimo Livi Bacci, and Egon Szabady eds. 1975); Norman Bishop, "Crime and Crime Control in Scandinavia 1976–80," 21, 24–28 (Norman Bishop ed., Scandinavian Research Council for Criminology (1980); Patrik Törnudd, "Crime Trends in Finland 1950–1977," 28 (Research Institute of Legal Policy, Helsinki, 1978). My discussion ignores the differences among Scandinavian sex laws. Sweden, Denmark, and Iceland are more liberal than Norway and Finland.

adjust for differences in the general severity of a nation's criminal code, as I shall try to do shortly.

The period in between the culture of classical antiquity and that of modern Scandinavia was dominated by Christian sexual ethics, which shaped the law of sex in the West. Much of that law was administered not by secular but by ecclesiastical courts, which imposed distinctive sanctions, such as penance and excommunication, that may have had less actual effect on behavior than the clergy believed.[4] Except in theocratic societies (such as Calvinist Geneva), ecclesiastical courts did not impose the death penalty; but the most feared sexual offenses, notably sodomy, were made secular offenses as well so that the death penalty could be—and was—imposed.[5] Laws inspired by Christian sexual doctrine were on the whole stricter than the population (especially the rural population), and even the lower clergy, believed reasonable. This was especially so with regard to fornication, and the result was that the law against it was only laxly enforced.[6] This has been a characteristic of sex law throughout history. Most sexual behavior takes place in private and is consensual rather than coercive, and therefore "victimless," and laws punishing private conduct are difficult to enforce in the best of circumstances and doubly so if there is no complaining witness. Especially if the will to enforce is weak because the conduct is not regarded as deeply threatening, laws punishing victimless crimes committed in private are unlikely to be enforced effectively unless the forbidden conduct is flaunted—an important qualification to which I shall return.

Before turning to the modern United States, where comparison with other countries is complicated by the fact that most sex crimes are made such by state rather than by federal law, I want to compare the situation in Sweden and Denmark with that in some of the other developed nations. England is, at least superficially, the most severe. For sodomy committed upon a woman, a boy under the age of 16, or an animal, the maximum punishment is life imprisonment. Sodomy between consenting men both of whom are at least 21 years old is not a crime (although, remarkably, consensual sodomy between

---

4. See, for example, Ralph Houlbrooke, *Church Courts and the People during the English Reformation 1520–1570,* ch. 3 (1979); F. G. Emmison, *Elizabethan Life: Morals and the Church Courts,* ch. 1 (1973); E. William Monter, "Women in Calvinist Geneva (1550–1800)," 6 *Signs: Journal of Women in Culture and Society* 189, 190–198 (1980).

5. See, besides references in Chapter 2, E. William Monter, "Sodomy and Heresy in Early Modern Switzerland," 6 *Journal of Homosexuality* 41 (1981).

6. See references in note 4 above; also J. A. Sharpe, *Crime in Seventeenth-Century England,* ch. 5 (1983); G. R. Quaife, *Wanton Wenches and Wayward Wives: Peasants and Illicit Sex in Early Seventeenth Century England* (1979), e.g. 179, 245. The situation appears to have been different in New England: there even the law against fornication was vigorously enforced. Roger Thompson, *Sex in Middlesex: Popular Mores in a Massachusetts County, 1649–1699* 31–33 (1986).

two adults, one of whom is a woman, is).[7] But should one of them be 21 or over and the other under 21, the maximum punishment is five years in prison even if there is consent. The maximum punishment for rape is life imprisonment. That is also the maximum punishment for statutory rape of a girl under 13; if she is 13 or older but not 16 (the age of consent), the maximum punishment falls to two years. For incest the maximum punishment is seven years. But the severity of these punishments could bespeak merely the greater severity of the English criminal code in general compared to the Swedish. For example, in England life imprisonment is the maximum punishment not only for murder and kidnapping but also for arson (whether or not aggravated), for robbery, and for aggravated burglary, and the maximum for larceny is ten years. Of course this comparison cannot explain the separate punishment of homosexual acts and the criminalizing of heterosexual sodomy and of bestiality. Moreover, the sale of pornography is criminal in England but not in Sweden.

France, like England, has a severe criminal code. Simple arson is punishable by up to life imprisonment, and the maximum punishments for the various forms of larceny are very severe as well, but sodomy as such is not a crime. Homosexual acts committed upon a person under 21 are criminal, as in England, but the maximum punishment is three years rather than five. The maximum punishment for rape is twenty years, and for statutory rape where the victim is under 15 ten years, unless the victim is the defendant's child, in which event the maximum rises to twenty years.

One can make an index of the severity of a nation's sex crime code by dividing the punishment for sex crimes by the punishment for the principal nonsex crimes. I have done this in Table 1, where to the nations already discussed I have added Japan, Germany, and Italy. The ratio in the bottom row is the sum of the first three rows divided by the sum of the next three. To make life imprisonment commensurable with a term of years, I deem a sentence of life imprisonment equivalent to thirty years. Where the jurisdiction distinguishes between an ordinary and an aggravated version of the offense, I use the ordinary version; and in the case of grand larceny I use the lowest degree of the offense. Since offenses are often defined differently in different jurisdictions, the comparisons are only approximate.

Table 1 suggests that the difference in the criminal laws of sexually permissive and sexually restrictive cultures lies not in the severity with which sex crimes are punished but in the decision as to what conduct to criminalize. Sweden criminalizes less sexual conduct than England does; but once the difference in the severity of punishment is adjusted to reflect different penal philosophies for the culture as a whole, we see that Sweden punishes its sex

7. In re Harris, 55 Crim. App. 290 (1971), upheld an eighteen-month prison sentence for consensual sodomy between a man and a woman.

Table 1 Index of severity of nations' sex crime codes

Crime	Maximum prison sentence (years) in—					
	England	France	Italy	Japan	Sweden	Germany
Rape	30	20	10	15	6	15
Statutory rape	16[a]	10	10	15	4	10
Incest[b]	7	20	6.5	N.A.[c]	2	3
Arson	30	30	7	15	8	10
Robbery	30	30	10	15	6	15
Larceny	10	10	3	10	2	5
Ratio	0.76	0.71	1.33	1.13	0.75	0.93

a. Average of life imprisonment if victim is under 13, and two years if she is over 13 but under 16.

b. Excluding between siblings.

c. In computing the ratio for Japan, I have assumed arbitrarily that the punishment for incest is the same as that for rape and statutory rape. I have not been able to discover the punishment for incest.

crimes approximately as severely as England does. It is of course possible that the more narrowly a society defines forbidden sexual behavior, the more severely it will punish that behavior; the decision to define the scope of the prohibition narrowly suggests that only the most serious forms of sexual misconduct will be penalized. But this suggestion is inconsistent with the figures for societies such as France, Italy, and Germany, which are less permissive in matters of sex than Sweden is.

Table 2 is a parallel table for eleven U.S. states, selected (before examination of their sex crime statutes) to provide regional diversity. The far right-hand column in this table corresponds to the bottom row in the previous one.

Like Table 1, Table 2 indicates that the severity with which a state punishes sex crimes is highly correlated with the severity with which it punishes nonsex crimes. For example, although California and Illinois punish sex crimes lightly relative to most of the other states in the table, and Georgia punishes them the most heavily relative to the other states, the severity with which Georgia punishes such crimes *relative to nonsex crimes* is lower than in the case of either California or Illinois.

Treating my eleven states as a composite of U.S. sex crime law (without weighting them by population, as might be a better procedure) and my six foreign countries as a composite of the sex laws of other developed nations,

Table 2   Severity of sex crime codes, selected U.S. states

State	Maximum prison sentence (years) for—						
	Rape	Statutory rape	Incest	Arson	Robbery	Larceny	Ratio
New York	25	7[a]	4	15	25	4	0.82
California	8	1	30	6	6	1	3.00
Illinois	15	7	15	7	7	5	1.95
Massachusetts	20	30	20	20	30	5	1.27
Texas	20	20	10	20	20	20	0.83
Florida	30	15	5	30	15	15	0.83
Georgia	30	30	20	20	20	10	1.60
Minnesota	25	25	10	20	10	10	1.50
Pennsylvania	20	10	10	10	20	7	1.03
Nevada	30	30	10	15	15	10	1.75
Ohio	10	10	10	10	15	5	1.00

a. Victim under the age of 14.

Table 3   International comparison of sex crime laws

Crime	Maximum prison sentence (years)	
	U.S.	Foreign
Rape	18	16
Statutory rape	16	11
Incest	10	7
Arson	14	17
Robbery	14	18
Larceny	8	7
Ratio (sex/nonsex)	1.41	0.94

we can compare the U.S. and foreign indices of severity. This is done in Table 3.

Table 3 shows that American law tends to punish sex crimes, especially statutory rape and incest, more heavily than the foreign nations in my sample do but nonsex crimes less heavily. The result is a striking difference in the relative severity with which sex and nonsex crimes are punished in the sample of U.S. states compared to the sample of foreign nations. The comparison, limited as it is to a nonrandom sample of American and foreign jurisdictions and to maximum as distinct from average penalties (with no consideration of the likelihood of punishment or the amount of time actually served for those who are punished),[8] and further hobbled by the lack of standardization in the definition of the offenses that I have labeled rape, statutory rape, incest, and so forth, must be interpreted with great caution. But insofar as it is valid, it suggests that Americans take sex crime more seriously than the citizens of other developed countries do.

This conclusion is strengthened if we consider precisely what conduct is criminalized. Here there are a number of important differences between the U.S. and foreign samples. The age of consent tends to be higher in the United States—sometimes as high as 18, compared to 15 or 16 in Europe. All but four of the states in my sample make sodomy a crime even between consenting adults, although in three of the other states the courts have, by statutory or

---

8. In fact the prosecution of sex crimes has diminished in the United States since the 1950s, and incarceration for sex crimes other than rape or incest has become rare. Roy Walmsley and Karen White, *Sexual Offences, Consent and Sentencing* (1979).

constitutional interpretation, rendered the sodomy law unenforceable. Maximum punishments range as high as twenty years, whereas in none of the nations in the foreign sample (with the partial exception of England) is sodomy between consenting adults even a crime. Five of the eleven states in my sample make adultery a crime, and four of these make fornication a crime as well. Enforcement, of course, is rare; but in contrast to the five states (almost one-half of my U.S. sample), only two of the six nations in the foreign sample (France and Italy) make adultery a crime, and none makes fornication a crime. Furthermore, prostitution is illegal throughout the United States, except in a few counties in Nevada, a state that has made the legality of prostitution a matter of local option.[9] And a federal law, the Mann Act (of which more presently), is directed primarily at prostitution.

With all the limitations of my study acknowledged, it remains difficult to resist the conclusion that the United States criminalizes more sexual conduct than other developed countries do and punishes the sexual conduct that it criminalizes in common with those countries more severely, relative to the punishment of nonsex crimes. The disparity would be even greater were it not for the unique role of American courts as a buffer between legislatures and the citizenry. It is by virtue of the Supreme Court's decision in *Roe v. Wade* that all of America has a liberal policy on abortion; and it is by virtue of the Court's decisions applying the First Amendment to pornography that "soft core" pornography is legal in all states. All this is well known; what is less well known is the role of the courts in taking the sting out of sexually restrictive legislation through interpretation.[10]

One example will suffice. Among the fruits of the purity movement of the late nineteenth century was the Comstock Act, passed in 1873, a federal statute that forbade (among other things) the importation of "any article whatever for the prevention of contraception."[11] The language could not have been clearer. But in the 1930s a distinguished panel of federal judges, in an opinion by Judge Augustus Hand (cousin of Learned Hand, who was also a member of the panel), held that the prohibition did not apply to the importation of contraceptives (they happened to be diaphragms) by a physician for

9. John F. Decker, *Prostitution: Regulation and Control*, ch. 3 (1979). Foreign controls on prostitution are described id., ch. 4. Prostitution as such is not a crime in Western European nations, although procuring and aggressive solicitation are, except that in Germany there still are licensed brothels.

10. C. Thomas Dienes, *Law, Politics, and Birth Control*, ch. 4 (1972); Comment, "The History and Future of the Legal Battle over Birth Control," 49 *Cornell Law Quarterly* 275, 283–285 (1964).

11. This is actually the language of a later redaction, section 305(a) of the Tariff Act of 1930, 19 U.S.C. §1305(a), but it is materially the same as section 3 of the original Comstock Act of 1873, 17 Stat. 598.

use in her practice.[12] It applied only to the importation of contraceptives for an "immoral" purpose.[13] The physician testified that she prescribed the contraceptives "in cases where it would not be desirable for a patient to undertake a pregnancy," but apparently not just in cases where the patient's health, physical or mental, would be endangered by a pregnancy.[14]

Learned Hand concurred in his cousin's opinion with evident reluctance, commenting: "There seems to me substantial reason for saying that contra-conceptives were meant to be forbidden, whether or not prescribed by physicians, and that no lawful use of them was contemplated. Many people have changed their minds about such matters in sixty years, but the act forbids the same conduct now as then; a statute stands until public feeling gets enough momentum to change it, which may be long after a majority would repeal it, if a poll were taken."[15] Still, he did concur, in major part because his court had in an earlier case imposed a similar interpretation on the provision of the Comstock Act forbidding the mailing of contraceptives. His cousin made the same technical point in the majority opinion, and another: the statute also forbade the importation of articles intended for "producing *unlawful* abortion" (my emphasis), implying that an abortifacient used where the mother's health was endangered by the pregnancy would be acceptable. On what rational basis could a contraceptive intended for the identical purpose be forbidden? But the use upheld by the opinion was not so circumscribed. The majority opinion also, and I think crucially, said: "We are satisfied that this statute . . . embraced only such articles as Congress would have denounced as immoral if it had understood all the conditions under which they were to be used."[16] Perhaps for "Congress" should be read "we enlightened judges." (Congress repealed the Comstock Act in 1971.)

The other great legal monument to the purity movement, the Mann Act, did not receive a similarly flexible interpretation. The statute forbade transporting women across state lines for "immoral purpose[s],"[17] a term not defined. The act's official name, until its recent amendment, was the White Slave Traffic Act, a reference to the interstate and international traffic in female prostitutes; and the main, perhaps the only, purpose of the act was to punish the transporting across state lines of prostitutes and of women hired or coerced to be prostitutes. Yet long after criminal laws against adultery and fornication had ceased to be taken seriously in most states, the Supreme Court held that the statute forbade transporting a woman who was not the wife of

12. United States v. One Package, 86 F.2d 737 (2d Cir. 1936).
13. Id. at 739.
14. Id. at 738.
15. Id. at 740.
16. Id. at 739.
17. 18 U.S.C. §2421 (as it read before being amended in 1986).

the defendant across state lines for purposes of sex, even though prostitution was not involved.[18] The interpretive issue became moot when Congress overhauled the act in 1986. The title was changed to Transportation for Illegal Sexual Activity and Related Crimes,[19] and the act is no longer limited to transporting women. Most important, "immoral purpose" was dropped; the act now forbids transporting any individual in interstate or foreign commerce "with intent that such individual engage in prostitution, or in any sexual activity for which any person can be charged with a criminal offense."[20]

Because American courts are freewheeling interpreters of statutes as well as executors of conveniently vague constitutional doctrines, the pressure to modify or repeal obsolete laws is relaxed, and hence those laws may give a misleading impression of current legislative opinion. Yet even after the Supreme Court declined to give the Mann Act a modernized interpretation, the act remained on the books, unmodified, for many years. Had it not been for *Roe v. Wade,* no doubt the gradual movement toward liberalizing the states' abortion laws, a movement well in train when *Roe* was decided, would have brought us nearer to the liberal European model than we have come; nearer—but, considering the ferocity of the antiabortion countermovement, a gap would have remained. American legislators, including members of the federal legislature, reflecting the views of their constituents, are more conservative in their attitudes about sex than their counterparts in other developed countries, even—as is apparent from Table 2—in such liberal states as California, New York, and Minnesota (the last with a large Scandinavian population). Indeed, two of these three states (New York and Minnesota) have criminal laws on their books forbidding even *heterosexual* sodomy between consenting adults (though so does England).

The underenforcement of laws forbidding sexual misconduct makes it tempting to argue that they have so little practical impact as to vitiate the normal incentives for eliminating legislative anachronisms. It might even be argued that the jurisdiction that was the laxest in enforcing its criminal sex laws might have the most severe such laws; the pressure for updating would be weakest in that jurisdiction. But this is an oversimplification. Even when no active efforts (comparable to the "sting" operations used against drug rings and public corruption) are made to enforce victimless crimes, such as consensual sodomy and statutory rape, or crimes with inarticulate or reluctant

18. Caminetti v. United States, 242 U.S. 470 (1917); see also Cleveland v. United States, 329 U.S. 14 (1946). I questioned the continued vitality of this interpretation, in light of changed standards of sexual morality, in United States v. Wolf, 787 F.2d 1094, 1100–1 (7th Cir. 1986), shortly before the act was amended. See also the dissenting opinion in Cleveland v. United States at 24–29.

19. 18 U.S.C. ch. 117.

20. 18 U.S.C. §2421. But this leaves *Caminetti* intact in states that still criminalize adultery or fornication.

victims (many victims of child sexual abuse and of rape), criminal law can suppress the public, organized, institutional manifestations of the forbidden practice. Laws forbidding homosexual conduct have rarely been enforced with much energy, yet they probably delayed the emergence of a homosexual subculture and by doing so probably reduced the amount of homosexual activity, perhaps considerably. Even today, when these laws are not enforced against consenting adults acting in private, their mere existence and the fact that they have been held to be constitutional strengthen the arguments of persons and institutions (such as the U.S. Department of Defense) that wish to impose disabilities on homosexuals. Laws forbidding abortion, even when lackadaisically enforced, drive reputable physicians out of the abortion business, and by making abortion either a dangerous operation or one that can be obtained only by incurring substantial travel expenses raise the cost and reduce the number of abortions, although, as we shall see in Chapter 7, the magnitude of these effects is easily exaggerated. Even the American sex law most widely viewed as completely absurd—Connecticut's law, invalidated by the U.S. Supreme Court in 1965, criminalizing the use of contraceptives even by married persons—was, as we shall also see in that chapter, effective in closing all the birth-control clinics in the state, and as a consequence may well have increased the number of unwanted births. So even if many sex crime laws lack bite, the impact of a society's criminal code of sexual conduct need not be negligible.

A word, finally, on the civil remedies, other than divorce or loss of custody over children, that the Anglo-American common law provides or provided for sexual offenses.[21] Rape, mainly when forcible but sometimes when involving no force but only grave deception (for example, concealment of venereal disease or impersonation of the woman's husband or lover), is a form of battery, and the victim can sue her assailant for damages, both compensatory and punitive. The tort of alienation of affections, now abolished in many states, is a civil remedy primarily for adultery, although it is not actually limited to the disruption of a sexual relationship. The tort of criminal conversation, also abolished in many states, is targeted squarely on adultery: it provides a remedy against a spouse's lover. The tort of seduction allows an unmarried woman (formerly her father or other guardian), usually but not always a virgin, to obtain damages from her seducer, provided that he made misrepresentations to obtain her consent to sex. This tort, abolished in most states, overlaps the right to bring suit for breach of a promise to marry, a type of suit (now also widely abolished) ordinarily brought by a woman induced to consent to premarital sex by a promise of marriage.

Because the defendants in these domestic-relations tort suits rarely have

---

21. *Prosser and Keeton on the Law of Torts* 917–923, 926–930 (W. Page Keeton et al. eds., 5th ed. 1984).

substantial assets out of which to pay a judgment, such suits are not a very effective remedy. As soon as divorce on the ground of adultery was allowed, the adultery torts began to wither; and as virginity lost its value, the tort of seduction, too, and the closely related action for breach of promise, came in most quarters to be thought more trouble than they were worth. Their deterrent effect, which was never great, is today swamped by the costs and uncertainties that they impose on the judicial system.

PART TWO

A Theory of Sexuality

The Biology of Sex

THE CHAPTERS in Part II are the most theoretical in the book. In them I try to strip away the moral and emotional overtones, the preconceptions, the myths, the customary attitudes that make it difficult for people in our society, however well educated, to treat sex, and its regulation by law or social custom, as subjects of dispassionate scientific study. I propose the concept of *morally indifferent sex*. Suppose we were as matter-of-fact about sex as we are about eating or driving. Sex would nevertheless be an issue of public concern. There are all sorts of public regulations of food, and of driving as well, because these activities can impose (most obviously in the case of driving) costs on third parties. But the question *what* regulations of these activities—these activities that, compared to sex, are for us morally so indifferent, emotionally so uncharged—are appropriate can be framed, quite satisfactorily for the most part, in functional (which largely means nowadays in economic) terms. We can compare the costs and benefits of alternative regulations of agriculture or restaurants or the taxi industry or traffic safety and determine on that basis which ones should be adopted. When a regulation flunks the cost-benefit test yet is adopted anyway, we can appeal to a rich theory of public choice to explain the divergence between the optimal and the actual. I shall try to do the same things for sex. Of course, this undertaking assumes that sexual behavior is rational, in the sense not necessarily of conscious but of well adapted to the actor's ends, for in economic analysis regulation is viewed as a matter of altering incentives through sanctions viewed as prices. Responding appropriately to incentives, whether consciously or not, is rational; so animals are rational as well as people. I shall argue that sexual behavior is rational in this nonmentalist sense.

Whenever one tries to apply functional, means-end, rational—in other words, economic—theory to nonmarket behavior (not that there are no explicit markets, notably prostitution, in the area of sex), howls of protest are heard. It is said that economics works only for the analysis of markets, that applied to other areas it misses the point, or at best simply relabels familiar insights in an impenetrable jargon; that it is dehumanizing, ideological, complacent, imperialistic, reactionary; that it is at once obvious and obviously wrong, and immoral to boot. These charges, which amount to a wholesale rejection of one of the most exciting areas of social science today, are answered at length elsewhere, and no purpose would be served by repeating the answers here.[1] Anyway the proof of the pudding is in the eating. By the end of this book the reader will be able to judge for himself or herself whether my attempt to apply economic analysis to sex and its regulation has been fruitful.

But I do want to make a couple of methodological points. First, what the hostile critic is apt to deride as "relabeling" is, potentially at least, a constructive effort to impose a uniform—and, I think the reader will find, a simple and nontechnical—vocabulary upon what are, after all, the same phenomena, only discussed by a bewildering variety of disciplines each with its own specialized vocabulary. This relabeling is a stage in the project—a major endeavor of this book—of finding unity in diversity. While apt to be derided as "reductionism," that endeavor is the worthy scientific quest for parsimonious explanations of seemingly unrelated phenomena. (The bad reductionism, a product of ontological confusion, is looking for an explanation in the wrong place, for example, trying to explain Rembrandt's art by the chemical formula of his paints.) I claim that much of the variance in sexual behavior and customs across cultures and eras is explained by a handful of factors, such as the sex ratio (which is far more variable than usually assumed), the extent of urbanization, and, above all, the changing occupational role of women. That changing role is, in turn, a function of infant mortality, the value of children, the technology of contraception, the existence of labor-saving devices in household production (ranging from baby bottles to dishwashers), and the degree to which well-remunerated work not requiring great physical strength or stamina is available in the economy. All these are things that reduce the costs to women (including opportunity costs, that is, the costs of forgoing other productive activities such as household work) of working in the market.

But explanation, or even theory, is not the only—and I would say not the major—project of science. The major project is to add to human knowledge that can be used to gain control over the natural and social environment. Theory viewed in this light is a source of testable hypotheses: when intuitive hypotheses flunk their tests or counterintuitive ones pass them, human knowledge is enlarged. A particular emphasis of my theoretical discussion is on counterintuitive hypotheses (some listed in the Introduction) that the theory generates and that empirical data could but do not refute.

My second methodological point leads directly to the main business of this chapter, which is to introduce the reader to some fundamental propositions concerning the biology of sex. For it might seem that an economic analysis

1. Richard A. Posner, *The Problems of Jurisprudence*, ch. 12 (1990).

of sex, to be worth doing, must explain *everything* about sex—including preference and performance—as being willed, chosen. That would be absurd.[2] But it is not in fact a requirement. The economist, in analyzing rational choice (economics, in the sense used in this book, *is* the analysis of rational choice, or more precisely a body of useful terms and techniques for analyzing rational choice), understands that choice is constrained by circumstances that may have nothing to do with economics. An economic analysis of clothing and shelter does not ignore climate—does not suppose, for example, that the preference of inhabitants of northern climes for housing that keeps out the cold is itself a choice to be analyzed by economics. The preference is treated as a given, and the focus of the economic analysis is on the costs and benefits of alternative methods of satisfying the preference.

There are important givens in the economic analysis of sex as well. The sex drive itself is one of them. There is reason to believe that it is given by our biology and perhaps also by our development, that is, by the influences that play on us as we grow from infancy to adulthood (the field of developmental psychology). Likewise, the range of possible and potentially desired sex acts is determined to a large extent by biological and developmental factors. But the object of the sex drive—whether it shall be male or female, or perhaps a fetish, and which male or female (or fetish) it shall be—is partly a given, partly a choice. For (I shall argue) while a person's preference among the possible sexual objects (male, female, or whatever), if costs are the same, is given, not chosen, the decision to engage in a particular sex *act*, that is, to act on a preference (whether it involves a more or a less preferred sexual object) in light of all pertinent costs and benefits, is a matter of choice.

To locate the line between the determined and the chosen aspects of sexual behavior will require an examination of the biology of sex,[3] under which

2. Although it is an element of the traditional Christian view of homosexuality—that one chooses to be a homosexual the same way one chooses to be a traitor. Nowadays, Catholics and many other Christians, though not fundamentalist Protestants, distinguish between homosexual preference (not chosen, hence not sinful) and homosexual acts (chosen and thus sinful). A few Christian denominations, such as the Quakers, no longer consider even homosexual *acts* sinful.

3. For helpful treatments, see Donald Symons, *The Evolution of Human Sexuality* (1979); Symons, "An Evolutionary Approach: Can Darwin's View of Life Shed Light on Human Sexuality?" in *Theories of Human Sexuality* 91 (James H. Geer and William T. O'Donohue eds. 1987); Glenn Wilson, *Love and Instinct: An Evolutionary Account of Human Sexuality* (1983); Raymond E. Goodman, "Genetic and Hormonal Factors in Human Sexuality: Evolutionary and Developmental Perspectives," in *Variant Sexuality: Research and Theory* 21 (Glenn D. Wilson ed. 1987); Wilson, "The Ethological Approach to Sexual Deviation," in *Variant Sexuality* at 84; Jane B. Lancaster, "Sex and Gender in Evolutionary Perspective," in *Human Sexuality: A Comparative and Developmental Perspective* 51 (Herant A. Katchadourian ed. 1979); Richard D. Alexander, "Sexuality and Sociality in Humans and Other Primates," in *Human Sexuality* at 81; Robin Fox, "The Conditions of Sexual Evolution," in *Western Sexuality: Practice and Precept in Past and Present Times* 1 (Philippe Ariès and André Béjin eds. 1985); William Irons, "Human Female Reproductive Strategies," in *Social Behavior of Female Vertebrates* 169 (Samuel K. Wasser ed. 1983); Robert L. Burgess and Patricia Draper, "The Explanation of Family Violence: The

rubric I include the pertinent aspects of developmental psychology. That excursus is the subject of this chapter; the next introduces the economic model.

I anticipate two misunderstandings. The first is that I subscribe to a naive distinction between determinism and freedom, regarding the former as the domain of biology and the latter as that of economics. In fact, the model of economic man is as deterministic as the biological model; rational man goes where the balance of costs and benefits inclines. Nor are the determinants fundamentally different; biological opportunities and constraints are easily reformulated in terms of benefits and costs. The difference is only that economic analysis brings into the picture types of benefit and cost that are cultural, hence local, and hence explanatory of the extraordinary *variety* of sexual customs and attitudes in our biologically uniform species.

Second, the reader is apt to assume that the biological theory of sex is foundational to the economic theory. It is not. I doubt that everything about sex is cultural rather than biological, but if I am wrong, my economic analysis would not be affected; indeed, its domain might actually be enlarged. The reason for bringing the biology of sex into the picture is that it is an important theory in its own right (and I am trying to be eclectic), that (a related point) it generates some hypotheses that other theories do not, that there are illuminating analytical parallels between the biological and the economic approaches, and that the two approaches are mutually reinforcing and may in combination constitute a more powerful theory than either by itself.

The Biological Basis and Character of "Normal" Sex

To begin with, why sex?[4] It greatly complicates reproduction to require the cooperation of two creatures to create a third. Mitosis or some other form of

Role of Biological, Behavioral, and Cultural Selection," in *Family Violence* 59, 74–80 (Lloyd Ohlin and Michael Tonry eds. 1989); Steven J. C. Gaulin and Alice Schlegel, "Paternal Confidence and Paternal Investment: A Cross Cultural Test of a Sociobiological Hypothesis," 1 *Ethology and Sociobiology* 301 (1980); Mildred Dickemann, "Paternal Confidence and Dowry Competition: A Biocultural Analysis of Purdah," in *Natural Selection and Social Behavior: Recent Research and New Theory* 417 (Richard D. Alexander and Donald W. Tinkle eds. 1981); Laura L. Betzig, *Despotism and Differential Reproduction: A Darwinian View of History*, ch. 4 (1986).

The leading student of the application of evolutionary biology to law is John H. Beckstrom. See, for example, his book *Evolutionary Jurisprudence: Prospects and Limitations on the Use of Modern Darwinism throughout the Legal Process* (1989). My academic colleague Richard A. Epstein has also made interesting forays into evolutionary biology. See, for example, his articles "The Utilitarian Foundations of Natural Law," 12 *Harvard Journal of Law and Public Policy* 713 (1989), and "The Varieties of Self-Interest," 8 *Social Philosophy & Policy* 102 (1990). But he has not discussed the regulation of sexuality. Nor is sexuality a focus of Beckstrom's work, although he has some interesting suggestions for applying biological insight to the control of rape and child sexual abuse.

4. A persistent puzzle in evolutionary biology. George C. Williams, *Sex and Evolution* 129–

cloning would be much simpler. The most plausible answer, though not one that all evolutionary biologists accept, is that sexual reproduction increases the probability that a species will survive. It does this in two ways. First, a genetic vulnerability is less likely to be shared by creatures that do not have identical genes than by those that do, and sexual reproduction increases genetic diversity; the genes are reshuffled every generation. In terms of perpetuating the species, sexual reproduction is a low-risk strategy analogous to that of an investor who holds a diversified portfolio of securities so that a disaster to one company or even to an entire industry will not wipe him out. Low risk—not necessarily high return. But (and this is the second point in favor of sexual reproduction) there may be high return too. Recombination of genes creates progeny with different qualities. It makes the population more varied, creating a wider field for natural selection to operate on. It thus speeds up evolution, and by doing so confers a competitive advantage over the slower-changing cloned species.

The differentiation of progeny also facilitates the filling of all available niches in social or ecological space. A family whose members are by virtue of genetic differences suited for different tasks will have an easier time finding useful work for all in the same locality than if by virtue of being genetically identical they all do the same thing. This may confer an advantage in the struggle for survival if family support is important to survival, although there is a downside: a greater danger of incest, and a loss of geographic diversification, if the entire family lives in one spot.

These are arguments not for two sexes as such but for more than one sex. Requiring more than two sexes for reproduction, however, would increase sexual transaction costs enormously.

The next question is, why sexual differentiation? Why are there males and females rather than just hermaphrodites, as in some animal species? Reproduction would be vastly simplified if each of us had both sets of functioning sex organs, just as the maintenance of electrical service is made easier by the fact that an electrician carries in his toolbox both plugs and sockets. One answer is that the necessity of endowing each human embryo with two sets of different sex organs would complicate the process by which a human being develops out of a fertilized cell. The length of gestation and infancy, already considerable in humans because of the complexity of the organism, would have to be even greater in order to accommodate additional complexity. This would make human communities more vulnerable.

Another and more interesting answer is that sexual differentiation facilitates specialization in essential human tasks, such as defense and reproduction, the

139 (1975); Harris Bernstein, Frederic A. Hopf, and Richard E. Michod, "The Evolution of Sex: DNA Repair Hypothesis," in *The Sociobiology of Sexual and Reproductive Strategies* 3 (Anne E. Rasa, Christian Vogel, and Eckart Voland eds. 1989).

latter broadly defined to include the rearing of offspring; and the broad definition is proper because reproduction fails of its purpose if offspring do not live long enough to repeat the reproductive cycle. Just by virtue of *not* having female sex organs a man does not have to worry about being incapacitated by pregnancy. He can specialize full-time in physically demanding activities, such as hunting and defense, that were essential to survival in the era in which human beings reached their present state of evolution,[5] and that pregnancy interferes with. Nor need he be endowed with such requisites of the female role as broad hips (important to surviving childbirth, before cesarean section) and breasts—attributes that would interfere with running or throwing. By contrast a woman, by virtue of not having male sex organs, with their incredible fecundity, and not having to devote herself to hunting or defense because the community contains specialists in those activities—men—has both incentive and opportunity to specialize in reproduction, an activity to which the male, in the male-female division of labor that I am sketching, devotes less time. Pregnancy and lactation, time-consuming activities essential to reproduction that are performed by women and not by men, illustrate the female specialization in reproduction.

The difference between the male and female sexual organs dictates in turn different, although complementary, optimal sexual strategies for the two sexes. (*Optimal* here means, of course, from an evolutionary standpoint—the standpoint of spreading one's genes—because a strategy that was not optimal in that sense would tend to be weeded out by natural selection. And *strategy* carries with it no implication of *conscious* strategizing. It is a metaphor for the suiting of means to end; in this it resembles the economist's concept of rationality.[6]) The male cultivates the extensive margin, the female the intensive. The male has a vast potential reproductive capacity because his only absolutely indispensable role in reproduction is to inseminate the female, a task of minutes (minutes, not seconds, to include the time necessary for erection and penetration), and because he can play the role with great frequency without substantial sperm depletion. The reproductive capacity of the individual female is so much more limited—twenty children a lifetime was a realistic maximum before in vitro fertilization (which, in principle, would enable a woman to have a child every time she ovulated by implanting the fertilized ovum in another woman's uterus)—that a male cannot realize his full reproductive potential with a single sex partner. The man who wants to father hundreds of children must practice some form of polygyny,[7] and must have,

---

5. "This hunting and gathering way of life is the only stable, persistent adaptation humans have ever achieved." Symons, *The Evolution of Human Sexuality,* note 3 above, at 35.

6. Posner, note 1 above, at 169–170.

7. *Polygyny,* which means many wives, is so much the commoner form of polygamy (many

therefore, a taste for variety in sexual partners. A person who indulges such a taste is called, in our society, promiscuous. We should expect many men to be promiscuous, in taste if not in action.

A woman who wants to maximize her reproductive success must be charier of her sexual favors than a man. She must try to make every pregnancy count: every pregnancy, ideally, must have a reasonable probability of producing a child that will survive to adulthood. So, especially in the evolutionary period, when life was precarious, a woman had to be intensely concerned about the quality of her mate as a potential father. (Would he stick around after impregnating her? Had he the willingness and the ability to protect her and her offspring?) She had in a word to be choosy—choosier than a man—if she was to have reasonable confidence in the survival of her children to reproductive age. A taste for variety in sexual partners would tend, therefore, to reduce a woman's inclusive reproductive success (inclusive, that is, of her offspring's reproductive success). Since a powerful sex drive would probably stimulate a taste for sexual variety, or at least make it more difficult to adhere to a strategy of being choosy about one's sexual partners, it is plausible to expect natural selection against a powerful sex drive in women. Promiscuity is not completely riskless to a man, because it puts him into a competition with other men that can end violently; and we shall examine a case in which it is advantageous to the woman. But, in general, it is riskier for the woman, not only because it could cause her to be undiscriminating among suitors but also because a man would be reluctant to extend protection to a woman who was likely to end up carrying other men's children.

There is much evidence that women do in fact have (on average, of course, not in every case) a weaker sex drive than men.[8] For example, lesbian couples have intercourse less frequently, on average, than heterosexual couples do, while male homosexual couples have intercourse more frequently than heterosexual couples do. Even in societies in which women are prosperous and independent (modern Scandinavia, for example), and therefore could easily

---

spouses) that I shall often use the two words interchangeably. Polyandry (many husbands) is rare, but we shall encounter an example in the next chapter.

8. Donald Symons and Bruce Ellis, "Human Male-Female Differences in Sexual Desire," in *The Sociobiology of Sexual and Reproductive Strategies*, note 4 above, at 131, and studies cited there; Douglas T. Kenrick and Melanie R. Trost, "A Biosocial Theory of Heterosexual Relationships," in *Females, Males, and Sexuality: Theories and Research* 59, 81 (Kathryn Kelley ed. 1987); Wilson, *Love and Instinct*, note 3 above, at 3 and ch. 6; Alfred C. Kinsey et al., *Sexual Behavior in the Human Female* 458 and ch. 6 (1953); John F. Decker, *Prostitution: Regulation and Control* 311 (1979). The qualification "on average" is vital in comparing men and women. Much invidious discrimination is due to a failure to recognize that the distributions of two groups may overlap even if the means of the distributions are different. Some women have a stronger sex drive than some men, just as some women are taller and heavier than some men and some men are more loyal and nurturant than some women.

afford to patronize prostitutes, there is no demand for prostitutes of either sex to service women. Of course, this may be due in part to the fact that, since men are naturally promiscuous, they bid the price that women must pay for sex down to zero. But this is consistent with my main point, which is that men *are* naturally more promiscuous than women.

Some feminists believe that the greater sex drive of men than of women is a cultural phenomenon, but their evidence is weak. Laurie Shrage[9] offers as her single piece of evidence a study that found—surprisingly enough, I admit—that men as well as women of the Dani tribe of New Guinea observe a period of four to six years of sexual abstinence after the birth of a child.[10] The study is a little misleading because the required abstinence is limited to sex between the parents; there is no rule against their having sex with other people. And whereas Dani boys like to make drawings of female sexual organs, Dani girls do not make erotic drawings.[11] Nevertheless, Dani men do seem to have an unusually weak sex drive, for men. But all that this may prove is that the sex drive of either sex can be blunted by social circumstances. Evidently that of women is more easily blunted, for there is no counterpart in Dani culture to the sexual anesthesia that Victorian culture imposed on many women.

Mary Jane Sherfey goes further than Shrage and argues that if not repressed by men, women would have the stronger sex drive.[12] Her principal evidence is that women, unlike men, can have repeated orgasms without a pause between each. But capacity for orgasms and desire for them are two different things.[13]

Biology also provides a more persuasive explanation than culture for the fact that men are far more likely than women to be aroused by seeing the sex organs of a member of the other sex or a depiction of those organs.[14] Re-

9. "Should Feminists Oppose Prostitution?" 99 *Ethics* 347, 353–354 (1989).

10. Karl G. Heider, "Dani Sexuality: A Low Energy System," 11 (n.s.) *Man: The Journal of the Royal Anthropological Institute* 188 (1976).

11. Symons, *The Evolution of Human Sexuality*, note 3 above, at 176–177.

12. *The Nature and Evolution of Female Sexuality* 112 (1966).

13. For other criticism of Sherfey, see Symons, *The Evolution of Human Sexuality*, note 3 above, at 91–92.

14. Id., ch. 6, marshals the evidence for this proposition. See also Symons and Ellis, note 8 above, at 143; Wilson, "The Ethological Approach to Sexual Deviation," note 3 above, at 101; Jennifer C. Jones and David H. Barlow, "Self-Reported Frequency of Sexual Urges, Fantasies, and Masturbatory Fantasies in Heterosexual Males and Females," 19 *Archives of Sexual Behavior* 269 (1990); Berl Kutschinsky, *Studies on Pornography and Sex Crimes in Denmark* 47–48, 50 (1970); F. M. Christensen, *Pornography: The Other Side* 4 (1990); Symons, "An Evolutionary Approach," note 3 above, at 102–106 (distinguishing male striptease shows directed at women from female striptease shows directed at men). Indeed, whereas a woman's displaying her sexual organs to a man will ordinarily be read by a man as an invitation, a similar display by a man is likely to be read by a woman as a threat. Symons, *The Evolution of Human Sexuality*, note 3

sponsiveness to such visual stimuli ensures that the male will not miss an opportunity to impregnate a female, and the taking of such opportunities is necessary to maximize the male's reproductive success. But as random mating is no part of the female's optimal sexual strategy, it would be contrary to her interests to be sexually aroused by the sight of male sex organs. We expect her to be aroused by cues related to the male's likely ability to protect her and her offspring.

Thus the different survival strategies of the two sexes are reflected not only in physical differences (such as in hips and breasts) that are in addition to the differences between the male and female sex organs themselves, but in psychological differences as well. Apart from those directly related to sex, the female's primary role in child care may result in a selection in favor of females who are nurturant and loyal,[15] while the male's primary role in hunting and fighting may result in a selection in favor of males who are bold and aggressive.[16] Male competition for females may lead in the same direction. The incentive for such competition lies not only in the fact that one male can exploit the full reproductive capacity of many females, but also in the fact that females vary in their apparent reproductive fitness. The sexual attractiveness of women is correlated with female fertility. Most men find healthy-looking women of childbearing years more attractive sexually than women who are either younger or older, or who appear to be unhealthy. This has been true in all known human societies. (The apparent universality[17] of these and other sexual attitudes implied by the biological model, such as that women in choosing men place less weight on physical attractiveness and chastity than men in choosing women, provides the principal empirical ground for prefer-

---

above, at 181. Male striptease and pornography for women are described in Barbara Ehrenreich, Elizabeth Hess, and Gloria Jacobs, *Re-Making Love: The Feminization of Sex* 111–117 (1986).

15. That women are more caring, nurturant, in a word altruistic than men is the thesis of Carol Gilligan, *In a Different Voice: Psychological Theory and Women's Development* (1982). She takes no position on whether this difference is genetic.

16. "Stereotypes of males as aggressive and females as nurturant, however distorting and however limited, have some empirical claim." Carol Gilligan and Grant Wiggins, "The Origins of Morality in Early Childhood Relationships," in *The Emergence of Morality in Young Children* 278 (Jerome Kagan and Sharon Lamb eds. 1987). I cite supporting evidence in Posner, note 1 above, at 411 n. 30; see also Douglas T. Kenrick, "Gender, Genes, and the Social Environment: A Biosocial Interactionist Perspective," in *Sex and Gender* 14, 15 (Phillip Shaver and Clyde Hendrick eds. 1987). The proposition that genetically driven psychological differences between men and women, for example in regard to propensity for risk taking, have occupational and other social implications beyond the realm of sexuality and the family is argued in Epstein, "The Varieties of Self-Interest," note 3 above. I take no position on this issue.

17. David M. Buss, "Sex Differences in Human Mate Preferences: Evolutionary Hypotheses Tested in 37 Cultures," 12 *Behavioral and Brain Sciences* 1 (1989); Gwen J. Broude, "Extramarital Sex Norms in Cross-Cultural Perspective," 15 *Behavior Science Research* 181 (1980).

ring that model to one in which all sexual behaviors are deemed socially constructed.) And most men find "shapely" women more attractive sexually than other women. The shape in "shapely" is given by the hips and breasts, which played an important role in successful reproduction before the era of cesarean section and bottle-feeding. For example, capacity for breast-feeding is positively (although not strongly) correlated with size of breasts.[18] The greater emphasis placed by men than by women on the visual appearance of members of the other sex may reflect not only a difference in the taste for variety of sex partners but also the fact that change in shape, and therefore in appearance, is the principal outward sign of female pubescence, whereas the principal outward sign of male pubescence is the change in the pitch of the voice.

The male who can monopolize a number of fertile females—that is, can exclude other males from sexual access to them so that he can be confident that his women's children are his—is maximizing his genetic fitness, provided he can protect his offspring. A female thus faces a trade-off between a weak male who will devote all his protective resources to her and her (their) off-spring, and a strong male who, by virtue of having a plurality of mates, will devote only part of his resources to the protection of a particular female and her offspring—but a part that may be larger, in absolute terms, than the whole of the weak male's resources. The less the male's investment in protecting one of his families decreases his investment in protecting the others, and the more his wives are able to cooperate fruitfully among themselves, for example in child rearing, the more likely is a female to prefer a polygamous mate to a monogamous one.[19]

The enormous reproductive potential of the male, and his resulting drive for multiple partners, may seem more a disruptive than a constructive element in genetic fitness. But consider: the pace of evolution is accelerated when an outstanding male, whose qualities are due at least in part to his genetic endowment, can impregnate a large number of females. The analogy is to an efficient seller, who by expanding his market share can spread the benefits of his superior efficiency far wider than if he were limited to dealing with his existing customers. In addition, the male's promiscuity reduces the danger of incest. The male is not content with one sexual partner, who may happen to be a close relative; and the more sexual partners he has, the less likely are all or most of them to be his close relatives, since a person has only a limited

---

18. F. E. Hytten, "Clinical and Chemical Studies in Human Lactation—VI. The Functional Capacity of the Breast," 1 *British Medical Journal* 912, 914 (1954).

19. Stuart A. Altmann, Stephen S. Wagner, and Sarah Lenington, "Two Models for the Evolution of Polygyny," 2 *Behavioral Ecology and Sociobiology* 397 (1977). On the operation of these factors among nonhuman primates, see Linda Marie Fedigan, *Primate Paradigms: Sex Roles and Social Bonds* 240, 254 (1982).

number of close relatives. Another natural safeguard against incest, although one limited to sibling incest, is that persons raised together from early childhood rarely find each other sexually attractive. It has been conjectured that the mechanism of this repulsion is genetic. I discuss this issue, and the genetic harms of incest, in Chapter 7.

Note the inverse relation between the optimal male parental investment and both male and female promiscuity. If a father's support and protection are vital to the survival of his children to reproductive age, a man will have a powerful incentive to concentrate his reproductive energies on one or a very small number of women, whom he will watch like a hawk to make sure they are bearing his children, lest he waste costly protective efforts perpetuating another man's genes. And a woman, as I have already emphasized, will have a strong incentive to screen her suitors for those who have the willingness and the ability to ensure the survival of her children—carrying her genes, of course, as well as her mate's—to reproductive age. But if the optimal paternal investment is low—it could be zero, or even negative (that is, the father's presence might actually endanger the child)—then a man's best sexual strategy is promiscuity. A woman's, too. She may as well have sex as early and often as possible, provided only that her lover is strong and healthy, which argues the possession of good genes. She need not worry whether he is apt to be a faithful and effective protector of her or of her offspring. A man, however, will have an incentive to try to curb a woman's promiscuity in order to establish secure paternity. A society of promiscuous males is one in which, because optimal paternal investment is low, each male has an incentive to impregnate many women. This is a formula for male rivalry to establish exclusive sexual rights over as many women as possible: in a word, for polygyny.

So we expect less polygyny the higher the optimal parental investment, but not necessarily zero polygyny. If the optimal amount of polygyny is positive, however, one may wonder why the number of male and female births is so close to equal. Why are there not more female births to provide mates for all men when some men have more than one mate? (In fact there are more *male* births than female, but the surplus is just large enough to compensate for the greater vulnerability of male children to death through disease or accident.)[20] The answer may lie in the difficulty of imagining an evolutionary mechanism for attaining a persistent imbalance.[21] Every human being has one male and one female parent. So if there are (say) more females than males, the average female must have fewer children than the average male. Then on average an

20. Goodman, note 3 above, at 29.

21. R. A Fisher, *The Genetical Theory of Natural Selection* 158–160 (1929); David O. Conover and David A. Van Voorhees, "Evolution of a Balanced Sex Ratio by Frequency-Dependent Selection in a Fish," 250 *Science* 1556 (1990).

individual who has a daughter will have fewer grandchildren than an individual who has a son, and genes that predispose individuals to have daughters will therefore become rare compared to genes that predispose individuals to have sons. This process will reduce the percentage of females in the population until it equals the percentage of males. (The sexes can be reversed without altering the result.) The argument assumes, however, that the resources required to produce an adult male or female offspring are the same. If they are not, then individuals genetically predisposed to produce more offspring of the more common but also "cheaper" sex could make up for having fewer grandchildren per child by producing more children.

Even if an unequal sex ratio could be an equilibrium—and I have just suggested why it might be, though presumably only for a species with greater sexual dimorphism (that is, differences between the sexes in size, weight, and other characteristics bearing on the resources necessary to produce a child and raise it to adulthood) than is characteristic of the human species—it might not be optimal. If children require paternal protection, polygyny can flourish only where there is substantial inequality of resources among men, a condition that may not have been common during the evolutionary period of human prehistory. Without that inequality no man may be able to protect more than one woman and her offspring. This might seem to imply the desirability of a higher number of male than of female births in order to maximize parental protection. The danger here is excessive competition among males for females; males would dissipate their energies to the detriment of the survival of the community. We shall consider shortly how, given polygyny, which creates in effect a surplus of males, such excessive competition is avoided. It might not be avoidable if the surplus were even larger because more males were born than females. And it might especially not have been avoidable under the conditions in which human beings lived during the evolutionary period, before there was an elaborate social machinery for managing aggression.

I want to emphasize the progeny-protective role of the human male, who is so different in this respect from, say, the tomcat. The protracted vulnerability of the human infant compared with other infants, and of the pregnant woman and nursing mother compared to other pregnant and nursing animals, makes it vital to have mechanisms for inducing men to stick around after insemination and even after—even long after—birth, in order to protect the female, fetus, infant, and child; mechanisms, in other words, to limit promiscuity. A male who just happens to have a genetic propensity for such sticking around will have an advantage in the struggle of the genes to survive, at least if he does not jeopardize his safety and that of his family by doing so, and, perhaps, if he does not forgo *all* opportunities to impregnate females other than his wife or wives. That is, the optimal male strategy may be a mixed one—protection of one or several females, promiscuous insemination of others. Or maybe there are different strategies, depending on other endowments—a stay-at-home strategy for some men, a promiscuous one for others. The second strategy implies, incidentally, a preference for adultery over fornication. If you can impregnate a man's wife without his knowing it, the man will protect the resulting child as if it were his own; the natural father will not have to expend his own resources to ensure the child's survival. This is the cuckoo's strategy and the origin of the word *cuckold*.

The character of female sexuality encourages the man to stay around. Unlike other mammals, the human female is available for sex not only during the few days a month that she is fertile but throughout the month. And since nature has encouraged reproduction by making sex a continual desire of men, the satisfaction of which is intensely pleasurable independent of any procreative motive, the male is continually rewarded by the female for staying with her after conception has taken place—indeed, after the child is born, which is a time when the woman and her offspring have particular need for protection. Thus the fact that human beings have sex far more frequently—and it might seem wastefully—than other primates is a consequence of the greater vulnerability of the human infant compared to other primate offspring.[22]

Since conception and gestation take place within the female body, hidden from the male's view, he must monitor her activities in order to have warranted confidence that she is pregnant with his child rather than with some other man's. Here is an additional incentive for the father to stick around, not only before the birth of his child but afterward—for that after period is the before period of his next child. Here too lies the biological explanation for male sexual jealousy and for the fact that it is more intense than female sexual jealousy.[23] Male sexual jealousy is adaptive because it reduces the probability that a man will assist in replicating the genes of another man to whom he is not related.

Bronislaw Malinowski's famous study of Melanesian sexual beliefs and practices provides evidence that sexual jealousy really does have a genetic rather than a purely cultural explanation. The tribe that he studied did not

22. John Hurrell Crook, "Sexual Selection, Dimorphism, and Social Organization in the Primates," in *Sexual Selection and the Descent of Man 1871–1971* 231, 247–254 (Bernard Campbell ed. 1972), argues that many of the distinctive physical characteristics of human males and females are designed to facilitate pair bonding through frequent and pleasurable coitus.

23. Martin Daly, Margo Wilson, and Suzanne J. Weghorst, "Male Sexual Jealousy," 3 *Ethology and Sociobiology* 11 (1982); Symons, *The Evolution of Human Sexuality*, note 3 above, at 244–246; Symons, "An Evolutionary Approach," note 3 above, at 117. Gregory L. White and Paul E. Mullen, in their book *Jealousy: Theory, Research, and Clinical Strategies*, ch. 3 (1989), esp. 127–128, while skeptical of sociobiological theories of jealousy, acknowledge that men are more sexually jealous than women; the woman's jealousy focuses on threats to the overall relationship rather than to the exclusivity of her sexual rights. This implies, incidentally, that women will on average be more jealous in a society of easy divorce, since in such a society the marital relationship is more fragile and therefore more likely to be endangered by the husband's adultery.

believe in physiological paternity; they thought the only function of sexual intercourse was to enlarge the vagina so that spirits could implant the fetus in the womb. Nevertheless, men were as jealous, and adultery was as strongly—sometimes violently—reprobated, as in societies in which the male role in procreation is understood.[24]

A phenomenon that can also be traced ultimately to the vulnerability of the human infant is sexual love, which differs from sexual desire in that it finds a particular person uniquely attractive, desirable.[25] Love thus provides a stronger cement for a durable, though not necessarily permanent, relationship in which the male will protect the female and their offspring than the sexual impulse alone would do.[26]

The Biology of "Deviant" Sex

Thus far I have been discussing "normal" sex—vaginal intercourse designed either to produce offspring or to reward the male for protecting offspring already produced—and the institutions of normal sex, such as courting and marriage (whether monogamous or polygamous), that come into being in order to facilitate procreation. In dealing with a subject as central to the survival of species as procreative and "procreative-protective" sex,[27] and especially to the survival of *our* species—for it is the complexity of the human organism that lies at the root of the special features of human sexuality—we should not be surprised to find cogent explanations based on evolutionary biology. But much sex seems not to be even indirectly procreative; think of masturbation, homosexuality, voyeurism, exhibitionism, seduction of young children, and fetishism. What role does biology (it need not of course be evolutionary biology), or perhaps developmental psychology, play in these phenomena?

The common threads in the different forms of deviant sexuality are two. The first is that they are much more common among men than among

24. Malinowski, *The Sexual Life of Savages in North-Western Melanesia* 179–195, 459 (1929).

25. For an interesting discussion, see Robert Nozick, *The Examined Life: Philosophical Meditations,* ch. 8 (1989).

26. As emphasized in Robert H. Frank, *Passions within Reason: The Strategic Role of the Emotions* 196–199 (1988).

27. By that clumsy term I mean to denote vaginal intercourse that rewards the male for staying with the female, and by doing so increases the likelihood that the female will survive to the end of her fertile years and that her children will survive till they reach their fertile years and beyond, so that *their* children will survive to adulthood too. Note that anal and oral sex, when heterosexual, can be procreative-protective, hence not "deviant" as I use that term here.

women.[28] The second is that they involve little or no interaction with adult consenting members of the other sex. The threads are entwined. The over-mastering male sex drive incites a competition among men for women and may result in the assertion by the more powerful men of exclusive rights to a disproportionate number of women, leaving the remaining men to compete for an inadequate supply. What is needed is a safety valve or valves to enable male sexual desires to be satisfied when females are unavailable to particular men as sex objects. Masturbation, homosexual sex acts, fetishism, and voyeurism are such safety valves. These practices are not "unnatural," at least in a biological sense; rather, they are peripheral to procreative sexuality. In a society in which half of the men had exclusive sexual rights to all the women there could be nothing unnatural in the fact that the remaining men, instead of being asexual, engaged in masturbation, homosexuality, and other forms of nonvaginal sex. Another reason for not considering such practices unnatural is that, provided that every woman of childbearing years is allocated to a man, the fact that some or even many men do not procreate will not limit the birth rate; so male deviance poses little threat to the survival of the community or of the race.

It is otherwise with female deviance. Women who shun men cause a reduction in the birth rate, that rate being limited by the number of wombs, not by the number of penises; so in the evolutionary era, when there was no artificial insemination, lesbian preference would have tended to be selected out. That is one reason to expect deviance to be less frequent among women than it is among men. Another reason is simply that the stronger male sex drive requires more spillways. A third is that the creation of the male sex organs in the fetus is a more complicated process than the creation of the female sex organs, so there is a greater likelihood of something going wrong. Lesbianism is indeed less common than male homosexuality (Chapter 11), although it may have been underestimated in former times, when many women were coerced into marriage regardless of their sexual preference.

Even in a monogamous society deviant sexual practices can be expected, especially among men. Unless there is instantaneous search and perfect sorting, there will always be some males who lack sex partners. Their condition is analogous to that of the unemployed in a prosperous but not frictionless free-market system. Boys who have just reached sexual maturity are like young persons of either sex entering the job market for the first time. Corresponding to the permanently unemployed are those males who for one reason or another are unattractive to females. They may have particular difficulty in gaining access to females of childbearing years, since those are the females for whom there is the most competition among males, and since older males are effective

---

28. Pierre Flor-Henry, "Cerebral Aspects of Sexual Deviation," in *Variant Sexuality*, note 3 above, at 49, 54–55.

competitors for young women. The existence of sexual outlets that do not involve heterosexual intercourse mitigates the ferocity of competition among men for women and by doing so economizes on the resources expended in that competition. It thus becomes easy to understand why masturbation is more common among males than among females and why it is concentrated in (though of course not limited to) pubescent males. Males have a more urgent sex drive than females, young males have less access to sexual partners than young females do, and the "waste" of sperm in masturbation does not reduce a man's fertility.

The difficulty is in explaining a genetic tendency to forms of sexuality that actually impede fertility. The male who is content with masturbation or with homosexuality is unlikely to reproduce, so we can expect natural selection against such contentment. In fact, few males are content with masturbation; it is a stopgap, a temporary rather than a permanent substitute for intercourse. This is true of some homosexuality as well. Many men who, in our society at least, are apt to be classified as homosexuals (not always by themselves, however) consider an adolescent boy or a young man an acceptable albeit inferior substitute for a young woman when young women are scarce, for example in prisons and on naval vessels. The tendency to consider young women and boys interchangeable is illustrated by the robustly "masculine" adventure stories of John Buchan (author, most famously, of *Prester John* and *The Thirty-Nine Steps*). In *Mr. Standfast,* where the hero of the principal stories, Richard Hannay, at last falls in love, his inamorata is repeatedly compared to a boy. Upon first seeing her he remarks, "I stared after her as she walked across the lawn, and I remember noticing that she moved with the free grace of an athletic boy."[29] Later he realizes that he—who till then "had been as careless of women as any monk"—had fallen in love with a "young girl with a cloud of gold hair and the strong, slim grace of a boy."[30] "I remember the way she laughed and flung back her head like a gallant boy"; "I loved to watch her, when the servants had gone, with her elbows on the table like a schoolboy."[31]

Just as men who prefer women may at times nevertheless have sexual relations with men, so men who prefer men may at times have sexual relations with women, either because men are unavailable (perhaps because homosexual relations are severely punished) or because the desire to have children compensates for the reduced pleasure of the sexual experience itself. Very few men, even among those who have a strong preference for homosexual over heterosexual relations, are incapable of erection and ejaculation in heterosex-

29. John Buchan, *Mr. Standfast* 22 (1918).
30. Id. at 106.
31. Id. at 208, 252.

ual intercourse.[32] But the phenomenon of homosexual preference has still to be explained. The explanation may be a genetic one.[33] There is to begin with a good deal of genuinely homoerotic—not merely dominance-expressing—behavior among animals, especially, as we would expect, those (prominently including primates) living in polygamous societies, where there are not enough females to go around and therefore homosexuality provides a safety valve.[34] But the strongest evidence for a genetic basis of homosexuality comes from studies of human twins at least one of whom is homosexual.[35] Of the fifty-seven pairs of male identical twins that have been studied in which one twin was a homosexual, fifty pairs (88 percent) were concordant for homosexuality; that is, both twins were homosexual.[36] The significance of this figure depends, of course, on the incidence of homosexuality in the male population as a whole. But it is unlikely, as we shall see in Chapter 11, that it exceeds 4 percent, and it may well be less. For fraternal as distinct from identical twins (the former having, like ordinary siblings, approximately 50 percent rather than 100 percent of their genes in common), the concordance is no greater than among nonrelatives. Since most twins, identical or fraternal, are brought up in the same household, these figures are also evidence against a developmental theory of homosexuality—though not conclusive evidence, as we shall see shortly.

How could a gene for homosexuality have survived? For some men, the optimal strategy for spreading their genes may be to protect the offspring of their close relatives—with whom they share many of the same genes, so that the protecting relative is indirectly propagating his own genes by increasing the likelihood of the relative's surviving to reproductive age—rather than to

32. Marcel T. Saghir and Eli Robins, *Male and Female Homosexuality: A Comprehensive Investigation* 102 (1973).

33. For a careful survey of rival theories of homosexuality, see Michael Ruse, *Homosexuality: A Philosophical Inquiry* (1988).

34. R. H. Denniston, "Ambisexuality in Animals," in *Homosexual Behavior: A Modern Reappraisal* 25, 34–35 (Judd Marmor ed. 1980). See also Fedigan, note 19 above, at 142–143; Robin Fox, "In the Beginning: Aspects of Hominid Behavioral Evolution," in *Biosocial Man: Studies Related to the Interaction of Biological and Cultural Factors in Human Populations* 1, 8 (Don Brothwell ed. 1977). The rarity of lesbianism among animals (see Denniston at 31, 33) is further support for a sociobiological theory of sexuality.

35. *Twins and Homosexuality: A Casebook* (Geoff Puterbaugh ed. 1990). At best suggestive is the failure of treatment strategies—and many have been tried—to alter homosexual orientation. Richard Green, "The Immutability of (Homo)sexual Orientation: Behavioral Science Implications for a Constitutional (Legal) Analysis," 16 *Journal of Psychiatry & Law* 537, 555–568 (1988). The reason it is only suggestive is that the orientation could be congenital without being hereditary. Maybe the wires accidentally get crossed at birth in some more or less stable percentage of newborns, especially boys because of the greater complexity of the male reproductive system.

36. Geoff Puterbaugh, "Introduction," in *Twins and Homosexuality*, note 35 above, at xi, xiii.

form a strong, or perhaps any, attachment to a woman.[37] A family that has a gene that predisposes some (not all, of course) of its members to homosexuality may outcompete families who do not in the struggle for genetic survival. Against this, however, it has been argued that homosexual kin may dissipate their resources in homosexual sex activities, and that the strong antipathy of most parents toward a child's turning out to be homosexual suggests that homosexuality rarely if ever promotes inclusive fitness.[38] Also, the parallel genetic explanation for lesbianism is weak, because in the evolutionary period, which apparently was characterized by a high degree of interpersonal violence,[39] to have additional male protectors may well have done more for a child's chances of survival than to have additional female protectors. It is no surprise that the twin evidence does not support a genetic theory of lesbianism.[40]

Withal, the genetic explanation of male homosexuality has a definite plausibility, as well as the support of the twin studies. The hostile or distant father, and the effeminate of "sissified" child, form a characteristic though not universal dyad in the personal history of male homosexuals. In a noteworthy study Richard Green, rather than relying on the recollections of adult homosexuals (which might well be unreliable, for a homosexual rejected by his father when his homosexuality became known might retroject the rejection to his childhood), followed over a period of fifteen years a group of boys who had at an early age exhibited pronounced gender nonconformity, and a control group who had not. Three-fourths of the "sissies" grew up to be homosexual or bisexual, compared to only one out of the fifty-six boys in the control group.[41] The explanation? Suppose that because of some congenital hormonal

37. James D. Weinrich, "A New Sociobiological Theory of Homosexuality Applicable to Societies with Universal Marriage," 8 *Ethology and Sociobiology* 37 (1987).

38. Robert Trivers, *Social Evolution* 198 (1985). For other criticisms of genetic explanations of homosexuality, see Douglas J. Futuyma and Stephen J. Risch, "Sexual Orientation, Sociobiology, and Evolution," 9 *Journal of Homosexuality* 157 (1984). "Inclusive fitness" refers to the survival not of a particular individual (a person's survival is unlikely to be affected much by the number of grandchildren he has) but of a particular gene, which will be replicated in a number of related individuals, such as a man and his grandchildren.

39. Symons, *The Evolution of Human Sexuality,* note 3 above, ch. 5.

40. Elke D. Eckert et al., "Homosexuality in Monozygotic Twins Reared Apart," in *Twins and Homosexuality: A Casebook,* note 35 above, at 123, find no twin concordance among female homosexuals, which leads the authors to conjecture that lesbianism may be an acquired rather than an inherited trait. But the sample of female twins was very small (four pairs).

41. *The "Sissy Boy Syndrome" and the Development of Homosexuality* (1987). (But see id. at 384 for qualification of the second finding.) For other evidence that childhood gender nonconformity is a good predictor of both male and female homosexuality, see Alan P. Bell, Martin S. Weinberg, and Sue Kiefer Hammersmith, *Sexual Preference: Its Development in Men and Women* 188–189 (1981). Of course, the fact that most gender nonconformists grow up to be homosexuals does not imply that most homosexuals were gender nonconformists as children.

abnormality[42] a small percentage of male children are born somewhat deficient in characteristic male attributes such as boldness and aggressiveness (or they may simply be small and weak), and the deficiency will make them when mature relatively unattractive to women, although as yet no one is aware of this. The father is repelled by the boy's effeminacy, his "sissiness,"[43] and the boy reacts to this rejection by transferring his affections to, and seeking a role model in, his mother. She may welcome this and treat him as a girl; there is conjecture, though little evidence, that she will be more likely to do this if she already has several children. At all events he increasingly thinks of himself in other than typically male terms. At puberty he finds himself indeed unattractive to girls, and this reinforces his aversion to modeling himself on his father. Eventually he discovers that men are his preferred sex objects.[44]

This narrative of the creation of a homosexual blends psychological, developmental, hormonal, and genetic themes, but the genetic is primary. The hormonal abnormality that is conjectured to increase the likelihood of homosexual preference has not been eliminated by evolution because a homosexual, even though he is likely to have fewer children than his heterosexual siblings and perhaps no children at all, has as a result more time and resources to devote to the protection of his nephews and nieces. Some indirect evidence is the prevalence in polygamous human societies of sororal polygyny, that is, a marriage between a man and two or more sisters. Sisters who assist one another in child rearing are not merely exchanging services; they are directly assisting children with whom they have genes in common.[45] The analogy to a male homosexual's assisting with the rearing of his brother's children is straightforward.

The father's and mother's reactions (which may well be genetically programmed) to the incipient homosexual child steer him into a homosexual life pattern compatible with his innate tendencies so that he will not expend excessive resources on a fruitless effort to compete for women.[46] Some evidence that the parents' role is primarily reactive rather than causal is that twins only one of whom became homosexual recall having been treated

---

42. For which there is some though not much evidence. Goodman, note 3 above, at 36–38.

43. Although I have used "effeminacy" and "sissiness" interchangeably, prehomosexual boys are less likely to exhibit cross-gender behavior—for example, wearing girls' clothes—than simply an absence of conventional masculine behaviors. Stewart L. Hockenberry and Robert E. Billingham, "Sexual Orientation and Boyhood Gender Conformity: Development of the Boyhood Gender Conformity Scale (BGCS)," 16 *Archives of Sexual Behavior* 475, 485 (1987).

44. A parallel in animal societies is discussed in Denniston, note 34 above, at 37–38.

45. Gordon D. Jensen, "Human Sociobiology," in *Medical Sexology* 106, 109 (Romano Forleo and Willy Pasini eds. 1978).

46. Richard C. Friedman, *Male Homosexuality: A Contemporary Psychoanalytic Perspective* 63 (1988). See also id., ch. 5, on the general issue of reactive versus causal theories of the characteristic tensions between male homosexuals and their fathers.

differently by their father—the homosexual coldly and distantly, the hetero-sexual not.

Since uncles no longer play a vital role in the care of their nephews, maybe the gene that predisposes some families to produce a homosexual now and then will eventually be weeded out. And as families become smaller, the genetic rationale for homosexuality diminishes. We can expect parental steering of children toward heterosexuality to be stronger the fewer the children. An only child, to take the extreme case, will have no sibling's child to play protecting uncle to. (This analysis implies that a child is more likely to turn out to be homosexual the more older siblings he has, but the data do not bear this out.)[47] A further point, stressed in the next chapter, is that homosexuals are less likely to marry, and hence to reproduce, in a system of companionate marriage, now dominant in the developed world. On all three counts we should expect a gradual diminution of homosexual preference in human society. But the trend could easily be halted by developments in artificial reproduction, of which cloning would of course be the most dramatic.

Other accounts of homosexuality give more weight to parental and social influence than to genetic and hormonal factors. For example, the fact that boys in ancient Greece were brought up by male slaves rather than by their mothers, or that they wrestled naked, is sometimes offered as the (or a) reason for the apparent prevalence of homosexuality in that culture.[48] In a similar vein one might argue that the more like men women become in dress, hairstyle, cosmetics, gait, and career, the more readily men will substitute other men for women as sex objects. But against this it can be argued that the cultural homosexualization we are witnessing today, in which the traditional differ-ences between the sexes in appearance, attitudes, and activities are eroding, makes it easier for men of homosexual inclination to substitute women for men as their sex partners. And against the raised-by-male-slaves hypothesis can be set the view that what drives men in macho societies to homosexuality is the smothering love that mothers in such a society are apt to lavish on their sons.[49] The mother seeks with her son the emotional closeness denied her by her husband, and this makes it difficult for the son to transfer his love to another woman. Not only do the arguments cancel one another out, but it is unclear whether they relate to homosexual preference or to the opportunistic homosexuality of heterosexuals who as young men in macho societies lack easy access to women.

Then there is the common-sense view that our preferences tend to be formed

47. Bell, Weinberg, and Hammersmith, note 41 above, at 70.
48. Sigmund Freud, "The Transformations of Puberty," in Freud, *Three Essays on the Theory of Sexuality* 96 (James Strachey trans. 1949); David F. Greenberg, *The Construction of Homosexuality* 143 (1988).
49. Ira L. Reiss, *Journey into Sexuality: An Exploratory Voyage* 159–161 (1986).

in childhood, the period for most of us of our greatest happiness. So a boy seduced (not raped) by a man might be expected to seek similar encounters as an adult. In addition there are the related concepts of acquired tastes, addiction, and learning by doing—so the more homosexual experiences one had as a child or as an adolescent, it might seem, the more one would tend to enjoy homosexual relations as an adult. The evidence is against these hypotheses.[50] Some of the strongest evidence is indirect. If having homosexual relations as a boy predisposes one to adult homosexuality, how is it that, as we shall see in Chapter 11, tolerant societies apparently have no more "real" homosexuals—that is, persons with a predominant homosexual preference—than repressive societies do? And why is it that among the Sambians, who make pederasty mandatory, adult homosexuality is exceedingly rare?[51] The ancient Athenians who tolerated, perhaps even encouraged, pederasty may have been incorrect in believing that homosexual relations between adult men were rare, but there is no indication that the incidence of such relations was higher than it is in our society, which anathematizes pederasty.

Further conjectures about the relative weight of nature and culture in the creation of homosexual preference are discussed in Chapter 11. But it is important to emphasize here the distinction between the homosexual who prefers men to women as sex objects and the opportunistic or situational homosexual who prefers women but, perhaps by virtue of having an unusually strong sex drive, will accept male substitutes in a pinch—and a shortage of available women was endemic in ancient Greece among the citizen class, and has been in other Mediterranean and Latin cultures as well.

Although many people in our society group the two types together in an undifferentiated category of "homosexuals," they are different from a scientific standpoint. This is true even though there is a continuum between people who have an exclusive preference in matters of sex for persons of the opposite sex and those who have an exclusive preference for persons of the same sex. Kinsey created a scale of 0 to 6, with 0 representing people with an exclusively heterosexual preference and 6 representing people with an exclusively homosexual preference, and 3, thus, representing those indifferent between the sexes—the perfect bisexual.[52] (The word *bisexual* is sometimes used to denote

50. Bell, Weinberg, and Hammersmith, note 41 above, at 101; and references in Chapters 11 and 14 of this book. The recent evidence of physical differences between the brains of homosexual and heterosexual men will, if confirmed by further research, strongly reinforce the view that homosexual preference is innate rather than cultural. See Ann Gibbons, "Is Homosexuality Biological?" 253 *Science* 956 (August 30, 1991), discussing the work of Simon LeVay (reported in LeVay, "A Difference in Hypothalamic Structure between Heterosexual and Homosexual Men," id. at 1034) and other brain researchers.

51. Robert J. Stoller, *Observing the Erotic Imagination*, ch. 6 (1985) (chapter co-authored with Gilbert H. Herdt).

52. Alfred C. Kinsey, Wardell B. Pomeroy, and Clyde E. Martin, *Sexual Behavior in the Human Male* 638–641 (1948).

what I am calling the opportunistic homosexual, but that is a confusing usage.) A man who is a Kinsey 1 has a strong but not an exclusive preference for women but will substitute a man in a pinch, and a man who is a Kinsey 5 has a strong but not an exclusive preference for men but will substitute a woman in a pinch. We would expect opportunistic homosexuals to be drawn from the ranks of the 1s and the 2s and married homosexuals from the ranks of the 4s and the 5s. A 3 would make his choice on exclusively personal grounds—preferring an attractive male to a slightly less attractive female but an attractive female to a slightly less attractive male.

Given some substitutability between same-sex and opposite-sex relations—given, that is, that we are not all either Kinsey 0s or Kinsey 6s—societies could vary in the amount of homosexual activity even if homosexual preference were innate, as I suspect it is. Ancient Greece may have had more "homosexuals," in the sense common in our society, than we do, and yet the distribution of Greek men along the Kinsey scale may have been identical to that of modern American men.

The study of homosexuality is important not only in its own right but also for the light that it sheds on the question of the different sexual strategies of men and women.[53] The relative sexual activity of male homosexuals, heterosexuals, and lesbians has already been mentioned. Then there is the common observation that homosexual men and heterosexual women are better dressed than either heterosexual men or homosexual women. Since men are sexually more aroused by visual cues than women are, we expect both men who are sexually interested in men, and women who are sexually interested in men, to dress better than either men who are sexually interested in women or women who are sexually interested in women.

The idea of deviant sexuality—or better, because less charged with normative significance, "substitute" or "peripheral" sexuality—as a safety valve for men whose access to women is for one or another reason obstructed points to a commonality among exhibitionism, pedophilia (sexual desire for prepubescent children), and rape. For the repulsive man, the pathologically shy man, the man who for whatever reason finds it difficult or impossible to form a sexual relationship with a consenting adult, these practices provide a substitute method of sexual gratification. The exhibitionist does not negotiate with the woman to whom he exposes himself; the pedophile "negotiates" with children too young to give informed consent; and the rapist forces himself upon his victim. It is no surprise that exhibitionists and pedophiles tend to be shy men and rapists unattractive,[54] for this implies, consistent with the theory

53. Symons, *The Evolution of Human Sexuality,* note 3 above, at 292–305.

54. Frank G. Bolton, Jr., Larry A. Morris, and Ann E. MacEachron, *Males at Risk: The Other Side of Child Sexual Abuse* 65–66 (1989); Wilson, "An Ethological Approach to Sexual Deviation," note 3 above, at 89; Lee Ellis, *Theories of Rape: Inquiries into the Causes of Sexual*

being explored here, that much rape and molestation is the situational or opportunistic response of men who are socially or sexually inadequate.[55]

But there is more to the sexual perversions (as forms of deviant sexuality that involve coercion or fraud may rightly be called, to express a disapproval that is uncontroversial) than a simple substituting away from consensual sex. Were that all that is involved, then in a society such as our own in which coercive sexuality, even in such relatively innocuous forms as exhibitionism, subjects the practitioner to criminal penalties, we would expect would-be perverts to frequent prostitutes rather than to risk imprisonment—especially since sex with a prostitute is a closer substitute for ordinary sexual intercourse (biologically it *is* ordinary intercourse) than the perversions are. No doubt there is some, perhaps much, of this substitution; and some people are too poor to afford prostitutes with a frequency commensurate with their sexual urges. But it is apparent that many people have deep-seated, indeed obsessive, preferences for deviant sexuality which they will act on even when the expected costs of punishment are high. While the polymorphousness or motility of male sexual preference makes evolutionary sense, as we have seen, the occasional *fixation* of that preference, especially on forms of sex that are neither directly nor indirectly procreative, does not.

One exception is homosexuality, which even when exclusive may be an evolutionarily optimal strategy for males who happen to be better suited to assisting their siblings in raising children than to forming their own families. Another exception may be rape. Given the female propensity to ration sexual access, we would expect natural selection in favor of some degree of male sexual aggressiveness (though not too much, for then female screening for genetic fitness would be circumvented). A reinforcing factor is that male aggressiveness has survival value because of its usefulness in activities such as hunting and defense, so that the allocation of females to aggressive men could promote genetic fitness. The tail of the distribution of aggressiveness may

---

Aggression 52–53 (1989); Linda Brookover Bourque, *Defining Rape* 63, 288–289 (1989); David Lester, *Unusual Sexual Behavior: The Standard Deviations* 212 (1975). See however, chs. 6 and 8 of *Erotic Preference, Gender Identity, and Aggression in Men: New Research Studies* (Ron Langevin ed. 1985), which question the extensive literature finding pedophiles to be characteristically shy. In describing rapists as "unattractive," I do not mean homely—that would not be a strong demerit in the eyes of most women—but deficient in elementary social skills, diseased, or otherwise of low value, actual or apparent, as potential mates.

55. Anne E. Pawlak, John R. Boulet, and John M. W. Bradford, "Discriminant Analysis of a Sexual-Functioning Inventory with Intrafamilial and Extrafamilial Child Molesters," 20 *Archives of Sexual Behavior* 27, 28–29 (1991). The fullest presentation of the evolutionary approach to understanding rape is Randy Thornhill and Nancy Wilmsen Thornhill, "Human Rape: An Evolutionary Analysis," 4 *Ethology and Sociobiology* 137 (1983).

contain men so aggressive sexually that they cannot be easily deterred from forcing themselves on women.

Conclusion and Critique

This chapter has set the stage for a rational-choice, or economic, theory of sex. Already, indeed, economic language has crept into the discussion. This should be no surprise. Evolutionary biology, the principal branch of biology discussed in this chapter, is a parallel mode of inquiry to economic analysis.[56] Both analyze rational behavior in the sense of the fitting of means to ends, the difference being that the rational maximizer in evolutionary theory is the gene, and in economic theory it is the individual or the firm. The difference is not trivial. The gene is, as it were, single-mindedly concerned with replicating itself in the relatives of the human being in whose cells it happens to find itself, while a rational human being balances the claims of the gene against other claims—feels the tug of the genes but does not always yield to the tug. Were it not for such balancing, the choice of many persons not to have children would be incomprehensible, except in the rare cases where that choice was motivated by a desire (not necessarily conscious, of course) to have more time and resources to devote to other fertile or potentially fertile relatives. Evolutionary biology explains tendencies in human sexual behavior; it does not explain the behavior itself.

Despite such disclaimers, efforts to explain human social, including sexual, behavior in biological terms have proved immensely controversial. Sociobiology (= social biology, the biology of social interactions) is a fighting word, especially when applied to human as distinct from animal or plant behavior. There are two levels of controversy. One is scientific. Propositions about evolution, because they concern events buried in the remote past, cannot be

56. As illustrated by the economist Gary S. Becker's use of economic theory to explain the family behavior of nonhuman species, in his book *A Treatise on the Family*, ch. 9 (enlarged ed. 1991); by the economist Armen A. Alchian's use of evolutionary theory to explain competition, in his article "The Basis of Some Recent Advances in the Theory of Management of the Firm," 14 *Journal of Industrial Economics* 30 (1965); by the economist David D. Friedman's reformulation in economic terms of R. A. Fisher's explanation of sex ratios, in *Price Theory: An Intermediate Text* 16–18 (1986); by the heavy use of economic terms in discussions of evolutionary biology, a use well illustrated by Marion Blute, "Reply" (to comments on her article, cited in note 58 below, "The Sociobiology of Sex and Sexes Today"), 25 *Current Anthropology* 207, 210 (1984); and by actual borrowings of economic theory by biologists. For a list of those borrowings, see Jack Hirshleifer, "Economics from a Biological Viewpoint," 20 *Journal of Law and Economics* 1, 5 (1977), and for a notable example, see Michael T. Ghiselin, *The Economy of Nature and the Evolution of Sex* (1974). The reciprocal borrowing of economics from sociobiology is illustrated by Arthur M. Diamond, Jr., and Luis Locay, "Investment in Sister's Children as Behavior towards Risk," 27 *Journal of Economic Inquiry* 719 (1989).

confirmed or disproved experimentally. This lends a conjectural air to genetic explanations, especially in the social sphere, because the supposed genes for social behavior—a complex of genes for homosexuality (or for parental reaction to the incipiently homosexual child), a complex for altruism, for loyalty, and so forth—have not been found. A further difficulty is that since the social genes, as one might call them, are believed merely to create behavioral propensities, it is difficult to test sociobiological hypotheses; if people do not behave as the theory predicts, this may be not because the theory is false but because they have resisted the genetic tug. Furthermore, the genes are easy to fool in an environment that contains features which did not exist in human prehistory. We do not see men breaking down the doors of sperm banks in their eagerness to spread their genes or forgoing contraceptive intercourse. Despite all this, it would be a mistake to write off sociobiology as fake science,[57] just as it would be a mistake to write off on similar grounds paleontology, cosmology, and economics.

The second level of controversy is political. Sociobiology seems to place beyond the possibility of social reform all sorts of unjust institutions—most significantly for present purposes the double standard and the subordination of women—by positing a genetic basis for these institutions.[58] The appearance (for which popularizers of sociobiology must shoulder some of the blame)[59] is misleading, so we need not pause to consider the propriety of insisting that science be politically correct. Sociobiology identifies influences on behavior, not determinants of it. If the genes incline women to pursue a more conservative sexual strategy than men, nevertheless we shall see that in cultures where women are not dependent on men, many women resist the genetic inclination and abandon the conservative strategy. Many social customs plausibly rooted in the conservative female sexual strategy posited by the sociobiologists—coyness, the fashion for high heels (symbolizing the woman's limited mobility, hence the unlikelihood that she will stray from her man), requiring the man to pay the costs of a date (which screens out the inadequate

57. For good treatments of the scientific status of sociobiology, see Michael Ruse, *Sociobiology: Sense or Nonsense?* (2d ed. 1985); Florian von Schilcher and Neil Tennant, *Philosophy, Evolution and Human Nature,* ch. 2 (1984); Robert L. Simon, "The Sociobiology Muddle," 92 *Ethics* 327 (1982); Richard D. Alexander, *The Biology of Moral Systems* (1987). Alexander (at 5–6) complains about the word *sociobiology* because it erroneously suggests a discontinuity with mainstream evolutionary biology. The only novelty in the sociobiological approach is the concept of inclusive fitness, a concept wholly compatible with the basic assumptions of evolutionary biology.

58. It is no surprise, therefore, that some of the most astute critiques of sociobiology are by feminists. An example is Marion Blute, "The Sociobiology of Sex and Sexes Today," 25 *Current Anthropology* 193 (1984).

59. As pointed out in Symons, *The Evolution of Human Sexuality,* note 3 above, e.g. at 42–43.

provider), and so forth—are rapidly going by the board. Moreover, the only secure part of sociobiology, as far as differences between men and women are concerned, is the part that argues for differences in sexual strategy. To extrapolate to differences in educability or in vocational aptitudes—to suppose, for example, that because the female sexual strategy is more conservative than the male, women are less likely to take business risks than men—is to embark on a sea of conjecture.

I am prepared to defend the sociobiology of sex against its detractors, yet most of the analysis in this book would be unaffected if sociobiology were completely overthrown. That men and women have traditionally pursued different sexual strategies, that these are related to the different reproductive capacities of the two sexes, and that sexual attractiveness is related to reproductive fitness were all recognized before Darwin.[60] Whether these behaviors are themselves genetically rooted or are merely social responses to the elementary physical facts—it is fact, not theory, that the average man has a greater reproductive capacity than the average woman, although it is characteristic of social constructionists to equivocate regarding the line between the biological and the cultural in sex[61]—is a detail from the standpoint of economic analysis. It is not an unimportant detail; it bears on the likely rapidity and completeness with which sexual behavior and customs will adapt to changes in social conditions, beliefs, and the like, and on our expectations concerning the universality or localness of specific sexual behaviors or dispositions such as homosexuality. But the reader need not accept sociobiology to find the main arguments of this book persuasive.

60. As well illustrated by Hume's discussion of chastity and modesty, in *A Treatise of Human Nature*, bk. 3, pt. 2, § 12, and by Schopenhauer's essay on sex, "The Metaphysics of Sexual Love," in *The World as Will and Representation*, vol. 2, 531 (1958), esp. 542. See also Kant's insightful discussion of the sibling incest taboo, in *Lectures on Ethics* 168 (Louis Infield trans. 1930).

61. For an illustration, see Leonore Tiefer, "Social Constructionism and the Study of Human Sexuality," in *Sex and Gender*, note 16 above, at 70.

Sex and Rationality

THIS CHAPTER and the next present a positive economic theory of sexual behavior, showing how the type and frequency of different sexual practices, as distinct from the sex drive and sexual preference (inclination, orientation), can be interpreted as rational responses to opportunities and constraints. The model of rational sexual behavior emphasizes the varied goals of sex, the costs of sexual search, and the nature of marriage—whether companionate or noncompanionate—as critical determinants of sexual practices and attitudes, along with urbanization and, above all, the occupational and financial situation of women. Chapter 7 proposes a normative economic theory from which the pattern of regulation that would be optimal if sex were a morally indifferent subject can be deduced.

The Benefits of Sex

Let us begin by considering the ends that sex serves and then the means of serving those ends, that is, the practices themselves. The ends fall into three groups, which I shall call *procreative, hedonistic,* and *sociable.* The first is obvious. The second has two cells. One is relief from the urgency of sexual desire; the analogy is to scratching an itch, or to drinking water when one is thirsty. The other is *ars erotica,* the deliberate cultivation of the faculty of sexual pleasure; the analogy is to cultivating a taste for fine music or fine wine.

The third group of sexual ends, the sociable, is the least obvious. It refers to the use of sex to construct or reinforce relationships with other people, such as spouses or friends. The Roman Catholic concept of the "marital debt" (the obligation of each spouse to submit to the other's request for sexual intercourse) fits nicely here. The relationships can be explicitly commercial; thus the ends pursued by the prostitute fall into my category of sociability.

Many sexual relationships that are not classified as prostitution nevertheless contain a strong commercial element: for example, marriage for money. But an exchange need not be commercial to be economic. Marriage is a relationship of exchange that can be modeled in economic terms even if neither spouse's motives are crassly pecuniary, or indeed pecuniary at all. The idea of male friendship spilling over into a (homo)sexual relationship that in turn cements the friendship is an element of the ancient Greek theory of homosexuality; it is visible, for example, in Plato's *Symposium*.

The element of sociability is fundamental to an understanding of the sexual differences between companionate and noncompanionate marriage. (For the sake of simplicity, I treat companionateness as a dichotomous variable; actually it is a continuous one.) In noncompanionate marriage, husband and wife are virtual strangers from an emotional standpoint, and the sexual relationship between them is no more rewarding than that between strangers. For the husband, therefore, prostitutes, concubines, casual mistresses, and even (in particular circumstances to be explored) adolescent boys may offer good substitutes for marital sex, as lovers may for the wife. We are led to predict that noncompanionate marriage will foster extramarital sex on the part of both spouses, coupled with strenuous efforts by husbands—motivated either by instinctual jealousy or by conscious concern lest the children they support not be their own—to prevent wives from engaging in extramarital sex. Means to this end include physical sequestration of wives, disparagement of female sexuality, and the mutilation of the female sex organs in order to diminish women's capacity for, and hence incentive to seek, sexual pleasure.[1]

In companionate marriage, marital sex is invested with affective elements, thereby creating "socioemotional closeness and exchange" rather than just "psychophysiological pleasure and relief."[2] These elements have the effect on many men of making extramarital sex either an inferior substitute for marital sex (or at least no longer a superior one) or a more costly one, because the wife in a companionate marriage is more likely to be jealous and therefore the husband must devote resources to concealing his philanderings. Even if some extramarital sexual relationships—for example, keeping a mistress, as

1. Lee Rainwater, "Marital Sexuality in Four Cultures of Poverty," 26 *Journal of Marriage and the Family* 457 (1964), is an exemplary study of the operation of noncompanionate marriage. Also very much to the point is Fatima Mernissi, *Beyond the Veil: Male-Female Dynamics in a Modern Muslim Society* (1975). And cf. David Cohen, *Law, Sexuality and Society: The Enforcement of Morals in Classical Athens* 169–170 (1991). Clitoridectomy, by the way, is not merely an African tribal practice; Victorian doctors resorted to it (and sometimes even to the removal of the ovaries) as a last-ditch cure for female masturbation. Susan S. M. Edwards, *Female Sexuality and the Law: A Study of Constructs of Female Sexuality as They Inform Statute and Legal Procedure* 87–90 (1981).

2. Lee Rainwater, "Some Aspects of Lower-Class Sexual Behavior," in *Studies in Human Sexual Behavior: The American Scene* 177, 182–183 (Ailon Shiloh ed. 1970).

distinct from patronizing prostitutes—have the same affective value as marital sex, they are costly in time and other resources, quite apart from costs of concealment, compared to the now inferior alternative of a casual liaison with a prostitute or the equivalent.

I discuss only in passing another possible motive for sex, one stressed in the feminist literature, the literature on homosexuality among primates, and the literature on prison homosexuality, and that is the assertion of dominance by the penetrator over the penetrated.[3] This is frequently adduced as a motive for heterosexual and homosexual sodomy, for rape, and in some versions of radical feminist thought even for ostensibly consensual vaginal intercourse. The issue of dominance is examined in later chapters. But mention of primate sex is pertinent here in suggesting a possible genetic basis for the sociability dimension of human sexuality. Sex cements the bond between mates and by doing so helps ensure that the male will stay around to protect the female and her offspring from hunger and predation. But we must be careful. In one respect the bond is closer if the female enjoys sex than if she is indifferent; there is more mutuality of affection. In another respect, however, it is weaker, because once awakened to the possibility of sexual pleasure, the female is more susceptible to the advances of other males. Knowing this, her mate becomes suspicious, jealous, watchful, constraining; and mutuality of affection is undermined. Considerations such as these have led to questioning whether the female orgasm, and more broadly the continuous sexual availability of the human female, are actually adaptive.[4]

Let us now match the varieties of possible sexual practice to the ends just identified as being served by sex. It should be apparent that the means are not interchangeable; some are better suited to one end than to another. For example, noncontraceptive vaginal intercourse is well suited to the end of procreation, but, unless a large number of children are desired, not so well suited to the pursuit of sexual pleasure: an unwanted child is a heavy tax to pay for the pleasures of sex. Noncontraceptive vaginal intercourse may also, and for the same reason, undermine sex as the glue of a marital relationship; control over reproduction may, indeed, be essential to companionate marriage.[5] For those to whom sex is merely a matter of scratching an itch, masturbation should be an excellent substitute for intercourse because it is so much cheaper in terms of time, exposure to disease, and other dimensions of cost. Homosexual intercourse is worthless for producing children and is inferior from a pleasure standpoint for persons who prefer heterosexual sex,

---

3. See, for an example, Alan J. Davis, "Sexual Assaults in the Philadelphia Prison System and Sheriff's Vans," id. at 330. Cf. Cohen, note 1 above, at 186–187.

4. Donald Symons, *The Evolution of Human Sexuality*, chs. 3–4 (1979).

5. Angus McLaren and Arlene Tigar McLaren, *The Bedroom and the State: The Changing Practices and Politics of Contraception and Abortion in Canada, 1880–1980* 26–27 (1986).

but even for them it may score high on cementing relationships and do okay as a method for scratching the sexual itch. It may even serve the end of pleasure if persons of the opposite sex are unavailable; its suitability in this regard will vary depending on one's place on the Kinsey scale.

The role of substitution among sexual practices is illustrated by the changes in the behavior of homosexuals that have occurred in the wake of the AIDS epidemic. Homosexuals have responded to the increased cost of unshielded anal intercourse with multiple sex partners by reducing the number of their partners, increasing the use of condoms, and substituting fellatio and other practices that are less likely than anal intercourse to spread AIDS.[6] This example shows that even though sexual preference is not chosen, the area for rational choice in sexual practices is a large one. And substitution is not limited to practices but also includes the substitution of sexual objects (for example, a sexual partner of the opposite sex for one of the same sex), of nonsexual for sexual activities, and of various transactional forms, such as rape, concubinage, and prostitution.

"Safe sex" is not a perfect substitute for unsafe sex; if it were, it would have been universal among homosexuals before the AIDS epidemic, because unsafe sex was known to carry a high risk of contracting other venereal diseases.[7] Since safe sex is not a perfect substitute, I hypothesize that the AIDS epidemic, by making homosexual activity unavoidably more costly (whether through the greater cost of contracting AIDS or the lesser cost of switching to safe sex), has reduced the amount of that activity. One might expect the effect to be especially dramatic among those men whom I termed in the preceding chapter "opportunistic" homosexuals. Since the benefits of homo-sexual activity are less to them than to "real" homosexuals, they should respond more to an increase in the costs of the activity. But that is provided

---

6. Heather G. Miller et al., *AIDS: The Second Decade* 82–83 (1990); Marshall H. Becker and Jill G. Joseph, "AIDS and Behavioral Change to Reduce Risk: A Review," 78 *American Journal of Public Health* 394 (1988); Ron D. Stall, Thomas J. Coates, and Colleen Hoff, "Behavioral Risk Reduction for HIV Infection among Gay and Bisexual Men," 43 *American Psychologist* 878 (1988); National Research Council, Committee on AIDS Research and the Behavioral, Social, and Statistical Sciences, *AIDS: Sexual Behavior and Intravenous Drug Use* 132, 134–136 (Charles F. Turner, Heather G. Miller, and Lincoln E. Moses eds. 1989); Dennis Altman, "AIDS and the Reconceptualization of Homosexuality," in Altman et al., *Homosexuality, Which Homosexuality? International Conference on Gay and Lesbian Studies* 35, 44 (1989); R. W. Connell and Susan Kippax, "Sexuality in the AIDS Crisis: Patterns of Sexual Practice and Pleasure in a Sample of Australian Gay and Bisexual Men," 27 *Journal of Sex Research* 167 (1990). Protective measures are less common in cities in which the incidence of AIDS is low; see Miller et al. at 83; John S. Moran et al., "Increase in Condom Sales Following AIDS Education and Publicity, United States," 80 *American Journal of Public Health* 807 (1990). This is not surprising from an economic standpoint, since the expected cost of unsafe sex is lower in those cities.

7. See Chapter 6. For direct evidence that many homosexuals regard safe sex as more costly because less pleasurable than unsafe sex, see Miller et al., note 6 above, at 110.

the increase in costs for them is the same. It may be smaller. The riskiest behavior with respect to AIDS is *receptive* anal sex; opportunistic heterosexuals usually are penetrators.

I also hypothesize that the AIDS epidemic will result in a reduction in the number of illegitimate births. A condom serves two functions: contraception and disease prevention. Because AIDS can be spread through vaginal as well as anal intercourse, and the danger of infection is dramatically reduced by the use of a condom, the epidemic has increased the benefits of using condoms to heterosexuals as well as to homosexuals. We can therefore expect the use of condoms in heterosexual intercourse to increase,[8] and, as a by-product, the incidence of noncontraceptive vaginal intercourse to decline. The number of legitimate births will probably not fall significantly, since the vast majority of married couples in this country already use contraceptives except when pregnancy is desired. Indeed, the number of legitimate births may well rise. Since marital sex is safer than nonmarital sex, AIDS increases the benefits of marriage, and married persons are more likely to produce children than unmarried persons are. AIDS may therefore cause the *fraction* of illegitimate births to fall even faster than the *number* of such births. By like reasoning we should expect the incidence of AIDS to be higher the more society subsidizes illegitimate births by welfare programs such as Aid to Families with Dependent Children, for such subsidies reduce the benefits of contraceptive intercourse and therefore can be expected to reduce the use of condoms. All these predictions assume, of course, that other relevant variables are held constant.

In relating the various sexual practices, viewed as means to ends, to the ends that I have enumerated, I have been analyzing the *benefits* of the practices. To have a homosexual preference is to perceive homosexual intercourse as conferring greater benefits, in terms of pleasure and perhaps also sociability, than heterosexual intercourse would. A person who wants children will derive greater benefit from noncontraceptive than from contraceptive vaginal intercourse. The benefits of sex may be private or social, depending on society's attitude toward the ends that the practices serve.

The Costs of Sex

There are, of course, differences in the costs as well as the benefits of various sexual practices; and these differences are a particular focus of my analysis.

8. For evidence it has increased, see Jacqueline Darroch Forrest and Susheela Singh, "The Sexual and Reproductive Behavior of American Women, 1982–1988," 22 *Family Planning Perspectives* 206, 213 (1990). For other examples of heterosexuals' response to AIDS, see Gina Kolata, "Drop in Casual Sex Tied to AIDS Peril," *New York Times*, May 15, 1991, A12; Michael R. Kagay, "Fear of Aids has Altered Behavior, Poll Shows," *New York Times*, June 18, 1991, B5.

For example, noncontraceptive vaginal intercourse by a fertile couple is expensive or not, depending on whether children are desired and, if not, whether effective methods of contraception are available at reasonable cost. If few children are desired but contraception is uncertain, we can expect, as Malthus predicted, an increase in the age at marriage and a reduction (quite apart from age at marriage) in the frequency of intercourse.[9] The latter effect has probably been offset in recent times by increases in the efficacy, safety, and comfort of contraception, resulting in a net reduction in the cost of sexual intercourse, notwithstanding the reduced demand for children, and hence in an increase in the amount of intercourse—a prediction that the data confirm.[10] Likewise, we can expect that sterilization is more likely to be the contraceptive method of choice the older a person is and the more children he or she has, because these characteristics raise the cost (or reduce the benefits) of having more children and hence reduce the costs of permanent infertility. This prediction is also confirmed.[11]

As these examples suggest, the balance of private costs and private benefits determines the relative frequency of different sexual practices. Since that balance is bound to differ among societies, and within societies at different periods, the relative frequency of the different sexual practices will vary significantly across societies and periods. Institutional arrangements, such as punishment, will affect the balance of private costs and private benefits and hence the frequency of different practices, but for now I abstract from punishment and even social censure.

The tendency to think of sex in terms of biological or psychological compulsion rather than of rational choice makes it important to emphasize the substitutability of sexual practices as means towards the various ends of sex. Here are more examples.

1. Masturbation is more common among middle-class than among lower-class youths (see Chapter 2, and also note 70 in the present chapter) because the average age of first sexual intercourse is higher for the former.

2. Petting to orgasm and early marriage are more common in religious societies that discourage premarital intercourse than in permissive societies in

9. For empirical support, see Paul A. David and Warren C. Sanderson, "Rudimentary Contraceptive Methods and the American Transition to Marital Fertility Control, 1855–1915," in *Long-Term Factors in American Economic Growth* 307, 335–338 (Stanley L. Engerman and Robert E. Gallman eds. 1986).

10. Charles F. Westoff, "Coital Frequency and Contraception," 6 *Family Planning Perspectives* 136 (Summer 1974); Westoff and Norman B. Ryder, *The Contraceptive Revolution* 67–70 (1977); James Trussell and Westoff, "Contraceptive Practice and Trends in Coital Frequency," 12 *Family Planning Perspectives* 246 (September/October 1980). Cf. Ronald Demos Lee, "Target Fertility, Contraception, and Aggregate Rates: Toward a Formal Synthesis," 14 *Demography* 455, 465–466 (1977).

11. Westoff and Ryder, note 10 above, at 117–118, 128.

which such intercourse is common.[12] People in the permissive societies may even consider "heavy petting" immoral and themselves the moral exemplars. They probably wonder at teenage girls who submit to anal intercourse in order to preserve their virginity, a practice not unknown in this country and particularly common in South America (see Chapter 6).

3. One of the better-documented findings in the empirical literature on homosexuality is that the proportion of male homosexuals who marry is higher the more intolerant the society is of homosexuals.[13] Intolerance makes the practice of homosexuality more costly, so there is substitution in favor of a heterosexual alternative. Moreover, the value of marriage as a way of concealing homosexual activity is greater the less tolerant the society is and hence the greater the benefit of such concealment. On this view, heterosexual marriage could actually be a complement (in the economic sense of the term, discussed later in this chapter) to homosexuality as well as a substitute for it.

But it would be simplistic to conclude that the marriage rate for male homosexuals will always and everywhere be low in tolerant societies. The cost of homosexuality (or of being exposed as a homosexual) is not the only consideration; the cost to the homosexual of heterosexual marriage must also be considered. In some tolerant societies, notably that of ancient Greece, marriage was cheap for a homosexual. He was not required to associate intimately with his wife save for occasional sexual intercourse. True, there were also strong social pressures to marry, and lifelong bachelors were looked upon with suspicion—not because they were thought to be homosexuals, however, but because they were shirking a social duty. These social pressures, and the suspicion of older bachelors, may just have reflected the ease with which a homosexual could marry. He really would be an oddball if he forwent marriage, for he would be giving up the chance to have children and gaining nothing in return. Greek-style noncompanionate marriage was not a substitute for homosexual relations, so little time and emotional investment did it require; the homosexual was not forced to choose. It is in the tolerant society in which companionate marriage is the norm that we should expect the proportion of male homosexuals who marry to be low; modern Sweden is an example.

In considering substitutability in matters of sex, we must be careful not to confine analysis to the substitution of one sexual practice for another. This would imply unrealistically that the total amount of sexual activity of an individual and even a community is a constant. Abstinence, implying the

12. Harold T. Christensen, "Scandinavian and American Sex Norms: Some Comparisons with Sociological Implications," 22 *Journal of Social Issues* 60, 72 (April 1966). The specific comparison is between Utah, home of the Mormons, and Denmark.

13. Michael W. Ross, *The Married Homosexual Man: A Psychological Study* 110–111 and tab. 11.1 (1983). For example, the percentage of male homosexuals in the United States who marry is roughly twice as high as in Sweden.

substitution of nonsexual for sexual activity, is a possible response to an increase in the costs, or decrease in the benefits, of sex. This is implicit in the earlier point that an increase in the effectiveness of contraceptive methods results in a higher frequency of coitus; and recall that Malthus believed that the high cost of children resulted in delayed marriage, often with sexual abstinence until then. The stronger a person's sex drive, and the more varied the possible sources of sexual satisfaction, the less likely is abstinence to be the response to an increase in costs or a reduction in benefits of a preferred sexual practice. Improvements in contraception, by reducing the principal cost of heterosexual intercourse, have also reduced the benefits of abstinence.

My emphasis on substitution is likely to be resisted on the ground that it makes all sexual and indeed familial relationships appear commercial in character and by doing so distorts their actual character. It may seem to imply, for example, that in a legal system such as ours that permits divorce, every happily married man and woman must always be in the market for a better spouse. But that is not in fact an implication. We saw in the preceding chapter that love can be given a precise economic meaning that excludes such implausible hypotheses: it is a preoccupation with the unique particulars of another person, particulars for which there is, by definition, no substitute to be found in any other person. This is why extramarital sex is often a poor substitute for marital sex in companionate marriage. Rational choice and economic decision making are not synonyms for commercial exchange.

Love illustrates the difference between a bioeconomic and a purely economic approach to sex. The idea of the loved one as unique is an aspect of the bonding or imprinting observed in animal as well as human settings and illustrated by the mutual bonding of mother and infant in a variety of species. A purely economic analysis would emphasize such factors as the high costs of search for a new mate, the costs of separation to children and, through altruism, to the parents, and the benefits to one's reputation of adhering to commitments. None of these factors, however, explains the emotional character of the love bond. Their significance is in making possible prediction of how durable the bond will prove in various circumstances.

Love, then, is natural in a fairly literal sense; where culture enters is in deflecting, sublimating, erasing, or otherwise controlling love. If choice of spouse is important to the families of prospective spouses, the families will try to channel or if necessary override the development of love.[14] Since love is more important in companionate than in noncompanionate marriage, one can predict that the greater the power of families in a society, the weaker the institution of companionate marriage will be.

Two types of erotic love should be distinguished. One—headlong, passionate, romantic, and usually brief (call it infatuation)—is likely to disrupt a

14. William J. Goode, "The Theoretical Importance of Love," 24 *American Sociological Review* 38 (1959).

system of companionate marriage both by impeding rational marital search and by making spouses susceptible to adulterous temptations after any infatuation between them has faded. It is fairly harmless in noncompanionate marriage: the marriage is likely to have been arranged by the spouses' families; the husband is not expected to be faithful; and the wife is likely to be under continuous surveillance. The other type of erotic love is that which accompanies, reinforces, and is reinforced by a relationship characterized by emotional intimacy, shared values, and constant companionship.

Although noneconomists may believe that I overemphasize the substitutability of sexual practices, sexual objects, and sexual transactional forms, economists may believe that I underestimate sexual substitutability by distinguishing so sharply between sexual acts and sexual preferences. Consider the analogy of smoking. A person might give up smoking because of concern over his health yet retain an undiminished desire to smoke; he would be like a homosexual who was deterred by fear of punishment or disease from engaging in any homosexual acts. But most smokers, after a period of abstinence, lose their taste for smoking; their preference changes in line with their behavior. It is an empirical question whether sexual preference (of heterosexuals as well as homosexuals) is more like smoking or more like being left- or right-handed. A left-handed person can force himself to write with his right hand, but he never feels comfortable doing so. Evidence discussed in Chapter 4 and elaborated in later chapters has persuaded me that sexual preference is far closer to "handedness" than to smoking.

The Kinsey scale, however, may seem to imply substitutability of preference as well as of act. Although for clarity of exposition I frequently divide the world into heterosexuals and homosexuals, Kinsey was surely correct that many people have both heterosexual and homosexual preferences; indeed, the fact that some people of predominantly heterosexual preference are willing to substitute a homosexual sex act in a pinch (and vice versa) could be thought to *mean* that they have some degree of homosexual taste or inclination. I accept the Kinsey scale as a useful way of expressing the distribution of heterosexual and homosexual preferences, but I believe that one's position on the scale is exceedingly resistant to social influence. The position determines how likely one is to substitute a homosexual for a heterosexual sex act, but does not imply that one can be shifted from that position to even an adjacent one. In behavior one might move from a 6 to a 0; in preference one will remain a 6.

The Centrality of Search Costs

The different *types* of cost that sex involves, and the major factors that bear on these costs, have now to be considered. One is the cost of search.[15] It is

15. The subject of an enormous literature in economics, some of it concerned with marital

zero for masturbation, considered as a solitary activity, which is why it is the cheapest of sexual practices. (The qualification is important: "mutual masturbation," heterosexual or homosexual, is a form of nonvaginal intercourse, and its search costs are positive.) I do not mean that (solitary) masturbation is, necessarily, costless *tout court*. Apart from the trivial time costs, there are, if the practice is socially disapproved, costs of concealment and often of guilt.

The economic theory of search may help explain the curious but well-confirmed finding that marriages in which the spouses cohabited with each other before marriage are no more stable than marriages in which they did not, even after correction is made for other differences between the cohabitators and the noncohabitators.[16] The reason may be that couples that need more information about each other delay marriage and use cohabitation to generate that information, while couples that already have the necessary information skip that preliminary. The two types of couple may nevertheless have the same amount of information when they marry. If premarital cohabitation is forbidden or discouraged, however, the first set of couples will experience higher costs of marital search, and as a result make somewhat less satisfactory marriages.

Search costs explain why, among prostitutes, streetwalkers provide the lowest quality of sexual services and call girls the highest.[17] Streetwalkers, as distinct from bar girls, prostitutes who work in brothels or in massage parlors or for escort services, and, particularly, call girls, impose virtually no search costs on potential customers, and as a result minimize the full cost of their services. If search costs are relatively invariant to quality of service, they will be a larger percentage of the full cost the lower the quality, and hence the lower the other costs, of the service, and so there will be more reluctance to bear them when quality is low and more willingness when it is high. The analogy is to transportation costs. High-value goods are shipped a greater distance than low-value ones because shipping costs have a smaller effect on the final price of the former. Men will incur considerable search costs for a call girl—and even higher ones, of course, for a mistress or a wife—but few or none for the lowest quality of sexual services, which therefore are provided

---

search analogized to job search in the employment market. See, besides Becker's work cited in Chapter 1, Dale Mortensen, "Matching: Finding a Partner for Life or Otherwise," 94 *American Journal of Sociology* S215 (1988); Michael C. Keeley, "The Economics of Family Formation," 15 *Economic Inquiry* 238 (1977). For a lucid introduction to the economics of search, see George J. Stigler, *The Theory of Price* 1–5 and ch. 14 (4th ed. 1987).

16. See, for example, Alfred DeMaris and Gerald R. Leslie, "Cohabitation with the Future Spouse: Its Influence upon Marital Satisfaction and Communication," 46 *Journal of Marriage and the Family* 77 (1984).

17. For a good description of the structure of the market in prostitution in the United States today, see Miller et al., note 6 above, at 263–269.

by streetwalkers, the zero-search-cost prostitutes. Analogously, the lowest-quality goods are consumed at home, not shipped at all.

Search costs are positive for any type of interactive sexual activity, and sometimes they are, for all practice purposes, infinite. In a well-run prison, the cost of finding a sexual partner of the opposite sex may approach infinity. But is this really a search cost? One might suppose that if the (male) prisoner *knows* there are no women in the prison, his cost of heterosexual search will be zero—not infinite. But if "search" is understood to include not only looking for a match but also making it, the second characterization—infinite search cost—is more accurate.

Not all prisons are well run. A prisoner can try to bribe a guard to bring in a woman; he can try to break out of the prison; he can try to assault a female employee. Some prisons even allow conjugal visits. Nevertheless, the cost of heterosexual search, and hence of heterosexual sex, is much higher for prisoners than for free persons, and we can therefore expect homosexual relations to be more common within prisons than outside them, even if the distribution of homosexual preference among prisoners is identical to that among free persons.[18] In like vein we can surmise that the rise of monasticism in the early Christian period was a factor in the preoccupation of theologians with masturbation and homosexuality.

The prison example can be generalized. Consider a hypothetical man who sets a value of 20 on sex with a woman of average attractiveness and a value of 2 on sex with a male substitute—perhaps an effeminate male or a male made up to resemble a woman. (I intend these valuations to reflect all alternative uses of a man's time other than those involving a sexual relationship.) If the cost of sex with a woman is 30 and with a man only 1, our hypothetical man will prefer sex with the man rather than with the woman, even though his strong preference for women over men as sexual partners marks him as heterosexual. He might make this substitution even if he could have sex with some women at a cost lower than the benefits. Suppose he could have sex with a woman he valued at only 1 at a cost between 0 and 1; he would still prefer sex with the man. Of course, a man of even stronger heterosexual preference might set a value of 0 on sex with another man. But we know that many men will accept a man as a sexual partner even though they greatly prefer (equivalent) women to men.

Generalizing further, we can assume that our hypothetical man has a downward-sloping demand curve for heterosexual sex acts. It slopes down-

---

18. On the incidence of homosexuality in prisons, see Richard Tewksbury, "Measures of Sexual Behavior in an Ohio Prison," 74 *Sociology and Social Research* 34 (1989); D. J. West, *Homosexuality Re-Examined* 233–240 (1977); C. A. Tripp, *The Homosexual Matrix* 222n. (1975); Mikhail Stern, *Sex in the USSR* 217 (1980); Shakuntala Devi, *The World of Homosexuals*, ch. 8 (1977); Davis, note 3 above. Whether the distribution of homosexual preference is the same within prisons as outside them is considered in the next chapter.

ward not only because there is diminishing marginal utility of sex, but also because the male taste for sexual variety implies that homosexual sex acts become better substitutes for heterosexual sex acts the more sated with the latter a man becomes. The higher the cost of heterosexual sex, the more the man will substitute other activities—some of them nonsexual, such as watching television, others sexual, such as masturbation, or being fellated in a restroom encounter.

The more attractive someone is to a given class of potential sexual partners, the lower his costs of search for such partners will be; he will not have to search as far to find a partner whom he likes and who likes him. We would therefore expect unattractive men to patronize prostitutes more than attractive men do, and effeminate men—even if they are heterosexual—to engage in more homosexual activity, on average, than noneffeminate men, if we assume that effeminate men are on average less attractive to women than more masculine men are.

The suggestion that effeminate men who are no more homosexual in *preference* than other men will nevertheless engage on average in more homosexual *behavior* is sufficiently counterintuitive to warrant elaboration. Its plausibility hinges on the meaning of effeminacy. The term crops up constantly in discussions of male homosexuality, and is resisted by homosexuals because it is pejorative (although I do not use it pejoratively) and because by comparing male homosexuals to women it assimilates them to what is still the subordinate sex in our society; feminists would say that this is *why* the term is pejorative. The term is also vague, and for my purposes that is a more serious concern. C. A. Tripp, however, has offered a typology of effeminacies: "nelly," "swish," "blasé," "camp."[19] Roughly these mean, respectively, feminine, a masculine caricature of feminine, regal (like a fashion model), highly affected. Tripp was writing in the mid-1970s, and today one might wish to add a fifth type: boyish, androgynous, a Peter Pan. He was writing about homosexuals, but some heterosexual males fit into one of the five types I have described.

As one moves along the spectrum from the conventionally masculine to the effeminate, the percentage of men who are homosexual rises, and if women are not sure which effeminate men are heterosexual, they will tend to apply a discount factor to all such men—especially in the age of AIDS—with the result that the average effeminate (but heterosexual) man will incur higher costs of heterosexual search than other heterosexual men.[20] He will have to

19. Tripp, note 18 above, at 177–190.
20. For some evidence that most women do in fact prefer masculine-appearing men, see Paul J. Lavrakas, "Female Preferences for Male Physiques," 9 *Journal of Research in Personality* 324, 329, 331 (1975); Edward K. Sadalla, Douglas T. Kenrick, and Beth Vershure, "Dominance and Heterosexual Attraction," 52 *Journal of Personality and Social Psychology* 730 (1987); Michael R. Cunningham, Anita P. Barbee, and Carolyn L. Pike, "What Do Women Want? Facialmetric

look longer and harder to find a woman with whom to have a marital or other sexual relationship, and this will increase the likelihood of his substituting a man. The analogy is to two persons who have the same degree of preference for vanilla over chocolate ice cream, and therefore—if the prices are the same—eat more vanilla than chocolate, and in the same proportions. If the price of vanilla to the first person rises, he will buy less vanilla and more chocolate than the second person even though his preference for vanilla is intense.

To avoid any misunderstanding, let me emphasize that I am speaking in marginal terms. I do not suggest that every effeminate heterosexual engages in some homosexual behavior, but only that, given two groups of men of identically motile sexual preference, one group being more effeminate than the other, there will be more homosexual activity in the first group.

A further implication is that handsome heterosexual men will, on average, engage in more homosexual activity than men who are not handsome. We know from the preceding chapter that men tend to find good looks more sexually arousing than women do.[21] This is true of homosexual men as well.[22] Hence a handsome man will be relatively more attractive to homosexual men than to women. As a result, the costs of homosexual sex to the handsome man will be lower relative to his costs of heterosexual sex than they are to homely men. By the same token, homely women should have relatively better lesbian than heterosexual opportunities because women tend to place less value on good looks in a sexual partner than men do.

Still another implication is that, given two heterosexual men, the one with the stronger sex drive is likely to engage in more homosexual activity than the one with the weaker drive. By stronger and weaker I mean a greater or lesser demand for sex, in the economic sense in which A's demand for some good is greater than B's if at any given price A will buy more of the good than B will; only in the present context price includes time, risk of disease, and other nonpecuniary costs. The stronger a man's sex drive, it is plausible to speculate, the broader the range of sexual stimuli to which he will respond.[23]

Assessment of Multiple Motives in the Perception of Male Facial Physical Attractiveness," 59 *Journal of Personality and Social Psychology* 61, 68–70 (1990).

21. For additional evidence, not related to biological theory, see Jeffrey S. Nevid, "Sex Differences in Factors of Romantic Attraction," 11 *Sex Roles* 401 (1984), and studies cited there.

22. Judith A. Howard, Philip Blumstein, and Pepper Schwartz, "Social or Evolutionary Theories? Some Observations on Preferences in Human Mate Selection," 53 *Journal of Personality and Social Psychology* 194, 196–197 and tab. 2 (1987).

23. Glenn D. Wilson, "The Ethological Approach to Sexual Deviation," in *Variant Sexuality: Research and Theory* 84, 92–93 (Wilson ed. 1987). This may explain the positive correlation noted in Richard S. Randall, *Freedom and Taboo: Pornography and the Politics of a Self Divided* 101–104 (1989), between consumption of pornography and sexual experience.

A pretty boy may leave the tepid heterosexual cold but provide an acceptable albeit not ideal outlet for the sex drive of the superheated heterosexual.[24] It is like a passion for apples. The passionate apple eater is more likely to consider a slightly wormy or overripe apple an acceptable substitute for an orange than the person whose enthusiasm for apples is more measured. Replace apples with sex and oranges with television and the point should be clear. The superheated heterosexual may not be able to find enough women to satisfy his sexual desires and, faced with a choice between masturbation and boys, may choose boys.

What may seem to cut the other way is that if the heterosexual with the strongest sex drive is also the one most attractive to women, his costs of heterosexual search will be lower, and this may balance his more intense demand for sex. But between two noneffeminate men, the one with the stronger sex drive may be *less* attractive to women.[25] He is likelier to seek multiple sex partners, thereby reducing the amount of protection that he can offer to any one of his partners and her children. And if he is thus less attractive to women, this will further reduce his costs of homosexual sex relative to heterosexual sex.

There is only a superficial paradox in suggesting that the average woman may find both effeminate men and highly sexed men less attractive than other men. These are both extreme types—the first failing to emit unambiguous signals of heterosexual preference and competence, the second signaling an intensity of sexual desire likely to undermine his commitment to the woman. Both disadvantages have been amplified by the AIDS epidemic.

The fact that homosexual preference and homosexual behavior are only loosely correlated helps explain a curious dualism in popular thinking about

24. On the use of boys by heterosexual men as female substitutes, see, for example, Randolph Trumbach, "Sodomitical Assaults, Gender Role and Sexual Development in Eighteenth-Century London," in *The Pursuit of Sodomy: Male Homosexuality in Renaissance and Enlightenment Europe* 407 (Kent Gerard and Gert Hekma eds. 1989); George Austin Chauncey, Jr., "Gay New York: Urban Culture and the Making of a Gay Male World, 1890–1940" 77–97 (Ph.D. diss., Yale University, 1989); Alan Bray, *Homosexuality in Renaissance England* 78 (1982); James M. Saslow, "Homosexuality in the Renaissance: Behavior, Identity, and Artistic Expression," in *Hidden from History: Reclaiming the Gay and Lesbian Past* 90, 92 (Martin Bauml Duberman, Martha Vicinus, and George Chauncey, Jr., eds. 1989); Mernissi, note 1 above, at 53; William H. Davenport, "An Anthropological Approach," in *Theories of Human Sexuality* 197, 232 (James H. Geer and William T. O'Donohue eds. 1987). On residential boys' schools as hotbeds of homosexuality, see John Chandos, *Boys Together: English Public Schools 1800–1864* 307–311 (1984); Vern Bullough and Bonnie Bullough, "Homosexuality in Nineteenth-Century English Public Schools," in *Homosexuality in International Perspective* 123 (Joseph Harry and Man Singh Das eds. 1980). Evidence that opportunistic homosexuals indeed have a stronger sex drive than either exclusive homosexuals or exclusive heterosexuals is noted in Glenn Wilson, *Love and Instinct* 197, 199 (1981).

25. For some evidence, see Sadalla, Kenrick, and Vershure, note 20 above, at 737.

homosexuality. In sexually permissive societies a homosexual tends to be thought of primarily as a person who has a strong preference for same-sex relations, while in sexually repressive societies the very concept of homosexual preference is weak or absent, and a homosexual is likely to be thought of as a heterosexual who commits unnatural acts because of lust or other wickedness. The explanation is as follows. In permissive societies, heterosexuals have plenty of opportunities for heterosexual intercourse.[26] Opportunistic homosexuality—the homosexuality of heterosexuals—is therefore rare. At the same time, homosexuals are free to associate with one another—and do so, to reduce costs of search—forming visible homosexual subcultures from which heterosexuals learn that there is such a thing as homosexual preference. In repressive societies, homosexuals are under strong pressure to conceal their preference (as by marriage), and homosexual subcultures either do not form or are clandestine. Both factors retard awareness of homosexual preference, sometimes among homosexuals themselves. At the same time, the sequestration of unmarried young women that is characteristic of sexually repressive societies reduces heterosexual opportunities and therefore promotes opportunistic homosexuality, with the result that homosexual activity in repressive societies tends to be dominated by opportunistic homosexuals. It is even possible that, being only an occasional participant in the market for homosexual activity, the opportunistic homosexual may be less skillful at concealment of such activity and hence more likely to be apprehended than a "real" homosexual would be.[27] In that event most persons punished for homosexual behavior in a repressive society may be heterosexuals, and the evil-will theory of homosexuality will have a definite plausibility. The perversity of such a punishment system (perverse from the standpoint of repressing homosexual preference) is enhanced when, as is common, the penetrator in homosexual sodomy is punished more heavily than the receptor[28]—even though the latter (if an adult) is more likely to be a "real" homosexual.

This discussion may explain why the word *homosexual* is of recent origin (it was coined in 1869) and also helps to rebut a predictable criticism of my suggestion that the highly sexed heterosexual is more likely to engage in homosexual acts than the less highly sexed (but noneffeminate) heterosexual. The criticism is that the self-identity of the highly sexed heterosexual is likely

26. This is provided, of course, that the society is permissive with respect to female as well as to male sexual activity. If there is a very strong double standard, meaning that the society is highly permissive with respect to male sexual activity and highly repressive with respect to female sexual activity, the analysis in the text is changed, as we shall see in Chapter 6.

27. Michael Schofield, *Sociological Aspects of Homosexuality: A Comparative Study of Three Types of Homosexuals* 148–149 (1965). But see Paul H. Gebhard et al., *Sex Offenders: An Analysis of Types* 357 (1965).

28. Guido Ruggiero, *The Boundaries of Eros: Sex Crime and Sexuality in Renaissance Venice*, ch. 6 (1985).

to be, if anything, more bound up with rejection of homosexuality than the self-identity of other men. Not necessarily. The experience of ancient Greece and modern South America alike is that, as Foucault and others have argued, homosexuality as a normative rather than a descriptive category is cultural rather than natural. If one is macho, one is indeed not a fairy, a poof, a faggot; but whether sodomizing boys is the act of a fairy, a poof, a faggot depends on cultural factors—such as the availability of young women of one's social class.

An important determinant of search costs is the extent of the market. It is not only important but fundamental; it can subsume both the prison example and the effeminacy example. It explains not only the obvious point that human sexual intercourse with animals is more common in rural than in urban areas but also the slightly less obvious point that incest, too, is more common in rural areas.[29] The larger the sample of potential sex partners of a given type, readily accessible to the searcher, the lower the costs of search. In the prison example, the accessible sample of potential sex partners of the opposite sex was assumed to be zero, and in the effeminacy example it was assumed to be smaller for effeminate than for noneffeminate men, while in the incest example the corresponding sample—the sample of accessible persons of the opposite sex who are not relatives—is smaller in rural than in urban areas.

Urbanization

It is when a particular type of sex partner is rare in the society as a whole that the search costs for that type of sex will be most strongly influenced by urbanization. Suppose that a village of one hundred persons contains a single homosexual. As long as he confines himself to the village, his search costs for a homosexual relationship will be infinite, unless other homosexuals visit the village. He can travel to other villages, but his search costs will still be high since they include the costs of travel. So even if homosexuals are initially no larger a fraction of city dwellers than of village dwellers, our homosexual villager will be likelier to find a homosexual partner at reasonable cost if he moves to a city. So he is apt to move. And as a result of the migration of homosexuals to cities, the percentage of homosexuals in cities will be higher than in rural areas, which will make cities even more attractive to homosexuals by further enlarging their market. Instead of one homosexual in a village of one hundred persons (1 percent), there may be 2,000 homosexuals in a city of 100,000 persons (2 percent). The dearth of large cities in colonial America may explain the widespread impression that in that period homosexuality was

29. Joseph Shepher, *Incest: A Biosocial View* 129 (1983); D. James Henderson, "Incest: A Synthesis of Data," in *Traumatic Abuse and Neglect of Children at Home* 423, 424 (Gertrude J. Williams and John Money eds. 1980); Neil Elliott, *Sensuality in Scandinavia* 211 (1970).

exceedingly rare here, compared to England.[30] A further point is that there is more privacy in the sense of anonymity in cities than in rural areas, and hence less likelihood that unlawful sexual acts will be detected, which reduces the expected costs of punishment.[31]

The effect of urbanization in increasing the sample over which a member of a sexual minority can search at low cost for a sexual partner is likely to be especially pronounced in the case of male homosexuality because, as I shall explore more fully in Chapter 11, male homosexuals rarely form permanent unions akin to old-fashioned marriage. If they did, the market for unattached homosexuals would be reduced, perhaps drastically, as homosexuals paired off and withdrew from that market. Since AIDS encourages this pairing, cities may become less attractive to homosexuals than they once were.

By facilitating the creation of markets for homosexual activity, urbanization affects not only the geographic distribution of such activity but also its amount. The village homosexual who has no potential male sex partners cannot be a practicing homosexual; when he moves to the city, he can be. Just as the creation of a market in a conventional good will lead to an increase in the supply of that good, so the creation of a market in homosexual relations will (with a qualification to be noted) increase the supply of homosexual acts. The total number of practicing homosexuals in a society will therefore increase with the rise of cities,[32] making homosexuality seem, and in a valid if partial sense be, a by-product of economic development and modernity. Even if a city, having attracted a large number of homosexuals, stops growing, homosexuals may continue to migrate to it, attracted by the large number of homosexuals already there; if so, the percentage of homosexuals will continue to rise. This is possible even if whatever factors have caused the city to stagnate operate as powerfully on homosexuals as on heterosexuals, because heterosexuals can be expected to leave the city at a faster rate than homosexuals since there is no sexual advantage in staying. The fact that the two cities that are generally considered the centers of homosexuality in the United States— New York and San Francisco—have long been stagnant in overall population is consistent with this analysis. Another bit of evidence is that the percentage of Catholic priests in the United States who are homosexual has apparently increased significantly since the 1960s,[33] a period during which the total number of Catholic priests in the nation has been level.[34] We shall see in the next chapter that the priesthood appears to be disproportionately homosexual.

---

30. David F. Greenberg, *The Construction of Homosexuality* 346 (1988).

31. Cf. Bray, note 24 above, at 43.

32. Alfred C. Kinsey, Wardell B. Pomeroy, and Clyde E. Martin, *Sexual Behavior in the Human Male* 455–459, 630–631 (1948).

33. A. W. Richard Sipe, *A Secret World: Sexuality and the Search for Celibacy* 107 (1990).

34. Id. at 7 (tab. 1.1).

I have said that urbanization increases the number of practicing homosexuals. It does not increase the number of persons with homosexual preference, and it may not even increase the number of homosexual acts. Opportunistic homosexuality should decrease with the rise of cities because the privacy of city life facilitates nonmarital heterosexual sex, including prostitution.[35] It is true that the costs of search for opportunistic homosexual contacts are lower. But I am assuming that these are second-best contacts, as they are for all "real" heterosexuals, though not for the relative handful of genuine bisexuals. If my analysis is correct, the precise sense in which urbanization fosters homosexuality is that it increases the total number of homosexual acts committed by "real" homosexuals.

The effect of urbanization on homosexuality explains how advocates of homosexual rights can make a credible, although almost certainly exaggerated, claim that 10 percent of the American population is homosexual. No one knows how many homosexuals there are in any society—the very concept of a "homosexual" is vague because of the equivocal status of act versus preference and because of the range of possible preferences. But we shall see in Chapter 11 that the best estimate of the percentage of adult males who have a strongly homosexual preference (thus excluding opportunistic homosexuals, most of whom consider themselves heterosexuals) is 3 to 4 percent, and of adult females 1 percent, for an average of 2 to 2.5 percent. Because homosexuals are concentrated in a handful of cities in which they are a significant fraction of the population, because our demographic impressions are shaped by mass media that are themselves concentrated in one of those cities (New York), and because the lingering taboo status of sex retards the dissemination of accurate information about sexual practices, the public is open to persuasion that there are many more homosexuals in the society as a whole than is really the case.

From an economic standpoint, prostitution is a parallel phenomenon to homosexuality. Consider a society in which there is a very large number of bachelors. This could be due to polygyny, a high cost of marriage, female infanticide, higher adult mortality among women than among men because

---

35. On the concentration of prostitutes in cities, see, for example, Mary Gibson, *Prostitution and the State in Italy, 1860–1915* 102–103 (1986); Richard J. Evans, "Prostitution, State and Society in Imperial Germany," 70 *Past & Present* 106 (1976). In addition to the greater privacy in cities, there is a larger number of transient males there, which increases the demand for prostitutes. A factor that might seem to cut the other way is that the sequestration of women is more costly in agrarian communities, because women are valuable as farm workers. See note 37 below and accompanying text; and K. J. Dover, *Greek Popular Morality in the Time of Plato and Aristotle* 98, 209 (1974). But sequestering women frees their husbands for sexual escapades outside the home. A society in which women are sequestered can therefore be licentious by our standards: consider the example of ancient Greece once again.

of high mortality in childbirth, or some combination of these factors. All but the first were present in medieval Europe, and so it is not surprising that a high percentage of young men were bachelors.[36] Why might marriage be costly? Suppose that in an era of limited contraceptive know-how, high infant mortality, and no bottle-feeding, a woman who married thereby disabled herself from pursuing remunerative work because of the burden of frequent pregnancies and of having to breast-feed the infants resulting from those pregnancies. In the Middle Ages, and indeed until much later, the disability was greater in towns and cities than in agricultural communities, where a woman could work close to home and on an intermittent basis.[37] If the wife cannot work, the husband's income will have to support not only himself but also her as well as their children, and this may be impossible unless his income is high or the woman comes to the marriage with a dowry.[38] A poor family may not be able to afford a dowry, however, in which event marriage may be out of the question for the man and, given a scarcity of high-income men, for the woman as well.

The high cost of marriage, coupled with the fact that women frequently died in childbirth, meant that a wealthy man might run through a series of young women—losing his first wife in childbirth, remarrying, losing that wife in childbirth, remarrying again. This was de facto polygyny, and, interestingly, was opposed, although not condemned, by the Church—and by young bachelors through the practice of charivari mentioned in Chapter 2. Like other forms of polygyny it was sustained by inequalities of wealth. As between two men otherwise alike, an older one with children by a previous marriage and a younger who has never been married, the younger man would pay more for a wife if both men had equal resources, since he would have a stronger desire

36. On the medieval dearth of women and its causes, see John Boswell, *The Kindness of Strangers: The Abandonment of Children in Western Europe from Late Antiquity to the Renaissance* 258, 409 n. 34 (1988); "Medieval Cemetery Patterns: Plague and Nonplague," in *Medieval Demography: Essays by Josiah C. Russell* 148 (1987); Marcia Guttentag and Paul F. Secord, *Too Many Women? The Sex Ratio Question* 54–55 (1983); David Herlihy, *The Social History of Italy and Western Europe, 700–1500: Collected Studies,* chs. 13, 14 (1978); Jacques Rossiaud, *Medieval Prostitution* 18 (1988).

37. Herlihy, note 36 above, ch. 13 at 16; Rae Lesser Blumberg, "A Paradigm for Predicting the Position of Women," in *Sex Roles and Social Policy: A Complex Social Science Equation* 113, 123 (Jean Lipman-Blumen and Jessie Bernard eds. 1979). Moreover, women are more valuable the more children are valued, and children tend to be highly valued in farming communities because they can do useful farm work from an early age. See, for example, Mark R. Rosenzweig, "The Demand for Children in Farm Households," 85 *Journal of Political Economy* 123 (1977).

38. On the operation of a dowry system, see Julius Kirshner and Anthony Molho, "The Dowry Fund and the Marriage Market in Early *Quattrocento* Florence," 50 *Journal of Modern History* 403 (1978).

both for a child (assuming that there is diminishing marginal utility of children as of other goods) and for sex (assuming, also realistically, that intensity of male sexual desire declines with age). But if the older man was wealthier, he might outbid the younger man even if he did not have as strong a desire to marry. The result would be another unhappy bachelor.

Enter prostitution. The existence of a large number of young bachelors creates a demand for paid sexual services in substitution for marital sex; the existence of a number of unmarried young women creates a supply. It might seem that if every bachelor were supporting a prostitute by paying for her services, there would be no cost savings compared to marriage. But the premise is incorrect, not only because the customer of the prostitute will not support the prostitute's child (and for this reason alone, a prostitute will take extreme measures to avoid becoming a mother), but also because each of the prostitute's customers pays only a small share of the costs of supporting her. Since the average prostitute has many more than one customer, there are fewer prostitutes than there are prostitutes' customers, and the cost of maintaining a woman is spread over a number of men, reducing the cost to each. A man who frequents prostitutes is not supporting a couple, let alone a family, but instead one man (himself) plus maybe a hundredth of a woman.

What we see here is de facto polyandry,[39] which in medieval times blotted up some of the surplus bachelors, and in doing so offset the serial polygyny just mentioned. Of course for bachelors whose sexual preference runs to men anyway, homosexuality may provide a cheaper as well as a more pleasurable substitute for marriage than patronizing female prostitutes. But they are related practices, and this may help explain their bracketing in the English debates over public policy toward sex. The famous Wolfenden report, for example, was a study of the laws against homosexuality *and* the laws regulating prostitution.[40] There is a more direct relationship, which incidentally supports the emphasis in this chapter on the substitutability of sexual practices: one does not have to go back to fourth-century B.C. Athens to find

39. "Enabling a small number of women to take care of the needs of a large number of men, it [prostitution] is the most convenient sexual outlet for armies and for the legions of strangers, perverts, and physically repulsive in our midst." Kingsley Davis, "Sexual Behavior," in *Contemporary Social Problems* 313, 351 (Robert K. Merton and Robert Nisbet eds., 3d ed. 1971). "A young man, lacking a legitimate wife, must satisfy himself with the devalued woman of the brothel . . . The disorder of fornication was allowed to young men to insure a superior order, the stability of the family." Madeleine Jeay, "Sexuality and Family in Fifteenth-Century France: Are Literary Sources a Mask or a Mirror?" 4 *Journal of Family History* 328, 340 (1979). Frontier societies, such as the nineteenth-century American West, also tend to be thick with prostitutes because of the high ratio of men to women. John F. Decker, *Prostitution: Regulation and Control* 59 (1979).

40. *Report of Committee on Homosexual Offenses and Prostitution*, Great Britain (U.S. ed. 1963).

heterosexuals who have considered a boy or a young man to be a tolerable substitute for a female prostitute.[41]

The demand for prostitution can be expected to be greater the lower the average wages of women *relative to* the average wages of men, for then men can easily afford to patronize prostitutes. This helps explain the extraordinary incidence of prostitution in modern Bangkok, where the prostitutes' principal customers are foreign tourists from countries in which wage levels are many times higher than those of rural Thai women.[42] Without international tourism, however, a society will encounter a problem in trying to use prostitution to cope with the problem of a surplus of bachelors. The more extreme the shortage of women, the higher their wages will be; therefore, the more bachelors there are, the fewer will be able to afford prostitutes. So we can expect that in a society in which the ratio of men to available women is high, opportunistic homosexuality as well as prostitution will be used to equilibrate the demand for and supply of sexual services. (Later, however, we shall consider an important qualification when the shortage of women is due to polygyny.) Other methods of coping with a surplus of bachelors are monasticism and eunuchism—the former a characteristic medieval technique of Roman Christians, the latter of Byzantine Christians and their Muslim successors. I discuss monasticism in the next chapter.

In describing prostitution as a substitute for marriage in a society that has a surplus of bachelors, I may seem to be overlooking a fundamental difference: the "mercenary" character of the prostitute's relationship with her customer. The difference is not fundamental. In a long-term relationship such as marriage, the participants can compensate each other for services performed by performing reciprocal services, so they need not bother with pricing each service, keeping books of account, and so forth. But in a spot-market relationship such as a transaction with a prostitute, arranging for reciprocal services is difficult. It is more efficient for the customer to pay in a medium that the prostitute can use to purchase services from others.

The percentage of men, especially heterosexual men, who are unmarried is lower in modern society than it was in the Middle Ages. Yet prostitution persists, though on a smaller scale. The decline is consistent with the economic model, both because demand should fall when the number of bachelors falls, since they value prostitution more than married men do, and because the

41. Chauncey, note 24 above, at 91–93.
42. Pasuk Phongpaichit, *From Peasant Girls to Bangkok Masseuses* 74–75 (1982). For an example from nineteenth-century America, see Christine Stansell, *City of Women: Sex and Class in New York, 1789–1860* 174–180 (1986). Marxists—generalizing, as it were, from these examples—were wont to say that the demand for prostitution comes from the bourgeoisie and the supply from the proletariat. But this is not quite accurate, as we are about to see.

supply of women for prostitution should fall as alternative job opportunities for women emerge.[43] We also expect—and we find[44]—that the demand for prostitution shifts toward the lower classes as the middle class moves (more rapidly than the lower classes)[45] toward companionate marriage. This is because prostitution is a poorer substitute for sex in companionate marriages than for sex in noncompanionate marriages.

That prostitution should persist at all may seem surprising in light of the sexual revolution, which has vastly increased the number of women available for casual liaisons. The economic model offers a possible explanation. Students of medieval prostitution have observed that the prostitutes of the time offered their customers "normal," ordinary sex; students of modern prostitution observe, confirming popular impression, that today's prostitutes specialize in "kinky" sex.[46] The reason may be that in the medieval period the principal customers of prostitutes were bachelors, whereas today, with the sharp decline in the number of heterosexual bachelors unable to form sexual relationships with unmarried women at reasonable cost, most customers of prostitutes are perforce married men.[47] Married men and men with steady girlfriends have all the "normal" sex they want, at home, more or less for free, and if these are companionate relationships, it is better sex than with prostitutes. Since prostitutes cannot underprice the wives or girlfriends, they have an incentive to differentiate their services—to offer something for which married men and men with steady girlfriends will pay because they do not have access to the identical service in the (free) home market.

---

43. Vern L. Bullough, *The History of Prostitution* 90 (1964). So it is no surprise that there is little prostitution in Sweden, even though it is not illegal. Decker, note 39 above, at 130–132. For there is considerable sexual freedom in Sweden, and, as we shall see in the next chapter, women's opportunities in the job market are probably better there than in any other country.

44. Theodore N. Ferdinand, "Sex Behavior and the American Class Structure," in *Studies in Human Sexual Behavior,* note 2 above, at 166, 174.

45. Rainwater, note 2 above.

46. Compare Rossiaud, note 36 above, ch. 8, and Leah Lydia Otis, *Prostitution in Medieval Society: The History of an Urban Institution in Languedoc* 100–104 (1985), with Richard Symanski, *The Immoral Landscape: Female Prostitution in Western Societies* 66–68 (1981), and Jennifer James, "Prostitutes and Prostitution," in *Deviants: Voluntary Actors in a Hostile World* 368, 402–409 (Edward Sagarin and Fred Montanino eds. 1977). James also emphasizes, much in the spirit of my analysis, the frequency of crippled men, impotent men, and travelers among a prostitute's customers—all being men with either permanently or temporarily high search costs in the market for "free" sex.

47. Rossiaud, note 36 above; Symanski, note 46 above, at 64, 73 (tab. 4.3); Decker, note 39 above, at 169, 218; David A. J. Richards, "Commercial Sex and the Rights of the Person: A Moral Argument for the Decriminalization of Prostitution," 127 *University of Pennsylvania Law Review* 1195, 1270 (1979). Rossiaud points out (at 39–41) that married men were forbidden to patronize the medieval brothels and that prostitutes described their relationships with their customers as "We are married for the night."

If cities attract prostitutes and homosexuals—if, moreover, as the economic theory of search suggests, *any* sort of minority sexual taste (any minority taste, period) will be better served in cities and therefore its practitioners will be attracted there—it becomes easy to understand why "vice" is traditionally regarded as an urban phenomenon and why the average urbanite has a more tolerant and permissive view of sex than the average nonurbanite.[48] People revolted by sexual excess or deviance (as it seems to them to be) will tend to leave cities, and their departure will reinforce the moral and attitudinal differences between city and country, more precisely between large cities and small towns,[49] in matters of sex. Within cities, moreover, groups of sexual deviants will tend to clump in order to reduce search costs. Hence "red light" districts will emerge even without zoning regulations and make deviants more conspicuous, reinforcing the cities' reputation for vice. Also, when the cost of marriage is higher in cities than in rural areas because married women in cities find it more difficult to get work, there will be not only more prostitution and opportunistic homosexuality but also more couples "living in sin," more abortion, more illegitimacy.[50]

Income and Wealth

Urbanization is one explanatory variable in the economic theory of sex; income is another. I have already noted the role of income in relation to the incidence of marriage. But there its effect is indirect; to the extent that poverty reduces the marriage rate, it increases the number of bachelors and so the demand for prostitution, and it also creates a supply of unmarried women to be prostitutes. Income may have a direct effect as well. Although a person who has more money can afford more of anything than a poorer person, including sex, some goods are what economists call inferior goods, meaning that an increase in consumers' income will—provided that price and quality remain the same—reduce the quantity of the good demanded. Sex may be an

48. For illustrative studies, see G. Edward Stephan and Douglas R. McMullin, "Tolerance of Sexual Nonconformity: City Size as a Situational and Early Learning Determinant," 47 *American Sociological Review* 411 (1982); Thomas C. Wilson, "Urbanism and Tolerance: A Test of Some Hypotheses Drawn from Wirth and Stouffer," 50 *American Sociological Review* 117 (1985); but see Mark Abrahamson and Valerie J. Carter, "Tolerance, Urbanism and Region," 51 *American Sociological Review* 287 (1986).

49. Not only are incest and bestiality more common in rural areas than in cities and women in farming communities less sequestered, but, as we are shortly to see, income may be negatively related to amount of sexual activity—and rural dwellers often have much lower incomes than city dwellers. For all these reasons sexual morals in the countryside, as distinct from small towns, may be lax by middle-class standards. G. R. Quaife, *Wanton Wenches and Wayward Wives: Peasants and Illicit Sex in Early Seventeenth Century England* 179, 245 (1979).

50. Cf. John R. Gillis, *For Better, for Worse: British Marriages, 1600 to the Present* 161–166 (1985).

inferior good.[51] It is time-intensive, because time is an important component of search and search an important component of sexual activity, and the cost of time rises with income earned from work.

This is far from a complete analysis, however. To begin with, sex is a leisure-time activity (it is not done during work), and leisure is usually assumed to be a superior good—people demand more of it as their incomes rise. Sex competes with other leisure activities, to be sure; but even if, because it is time-intensive, its share of the total time that people devote to leisure activities is falling, the absolute amount of sexual activity may be rising.

Prediction becomes easier if we distinguish between wealth and (earned) income. The demand for leisure, including sex, is an uncomplicated function of wealth, because the cost of time, and hence of sex, does not rise with wealth, as it does with earned income. A person who possesses wealth, perhaps through inheritance or past exertion, need not have high hourly earnings, and therefore need not incur high time costs to engage in sex. (Conversely, a very poor person may lack the health and energy required to be sexually active.) Since carrying on an adulterous liaison takes more time than patronizing prostitutes or obtaining sex from one's spouse, we can expect wealthy aristocratic men to choose adultery, concubinage, and simultaneous or serial polygyny over monogamy and prostitution, and bourgeois men to choose monogamy and (or) prostitution over adultery.

Other factors as well lead one to expect systematic differences in sexual behavior between wealthy and nonwealthy people—female as well as male. Noncompanionate marriage, particularly the form designed to cement political alliances or to shore up declining fortunes, is more desirable to wealthy people and aristocrats (who are more likely to be wealthy than commoners are) than to middle-class people—and noncompanionate marriage fosters extramarital intercourse.[52] Moreover, a wealthy man is more attractive to a variety of potential sex partners than an ordinary man is, so his costs of sexual search

51. Staffan Burenstam Linder, *The Harried Leisure Class* 83–89 (1970). A significant quali-fication should be noted: a person with extremely low wages may lack the wherewithal to conduct an active sex life. The general thesis of Linder's book—that modern people have less leisure, because their cost of time is high—is challenged, with specific reference to sleep, in Jeff E. Biddle and Daniel S. Hamermesh, "Sleep and the Allocation of Time," 98 *Journal of Political Economy* 922, 939 (1990). They point out that sleep may yield utility, in which event people may "buy" more of it (by giving up remunerative activities that would cut into their sleep) as their incomes rise even though the "price" of sleep (in alternative activities forgone) is rising too. In the text below I consider the parallel possibility in regard to sex.

52. "What was decisive [in aristocratic marriage] was the interest of a family, and beyond that—the class. We would shiver a little at the coldness, severity, and calculating clarity of such a noble concept of marriage as has ruled in every healthy aristocracy . . . Precisely this is why love as a passion—the great meaning of the word—was *invented* for the aristocratic world and in it, where constraint and privation were greatest." Friedrich Nietzsche, *The Will to Power* §732, at 388 (Walter Kaufmann and R. J. Hollingdale trans. 1968).

are actually lower even if his time is valuable. And an aristocratic woman, insofar as she has her own wealth, is less dependent on her husband than a middle-class wife and therefore less prone to comply with his desire that she be chaste.[53] The apparent proclivity of upper-class Roman women for adultery may have been related to the secure wealth these women possessed by virtue of Roman law governing dowry and inheritance, especially since this wealth was not an accumulation of the woman's "earned" income and hence did not imply a high value of the woman's time and therefore a high cost of amorous liaisons.[54]

This analysis may explain some of the tension between the middle class and the aristocracy that exploded in the English Revolution of 1640. Puritanism is a middle-class moral stance rather than an aristocratic one. The fact that the income of the middle class was rising in the seventeenth century would, if my analysis is correct, tend to increase the distance between the two classes in attitudes toward sex, because the rise in middle-class incomes would, by increasing the value of time for middle-class men, reinforce their puritanical values.

We can extend the analysis to the present and predict that young lawyers at high-pressure law firms will have fewer love affairs, and commit adultery less frequently, than persons who possess inherited wealth but have lower opportunity costs of time. More broadly, the ambiance of a highly competitive capitalist society will be less romantic, less given to sexual intrigue, leisurely courting, and elaborate flirtation, than that of a society in which average hourly wages are low, especially if wealth is less equally distributed in the static, traditional society than in the dynamic capitalist one. This point bears on the question, explored in Chapter 7, whether sexual morality has any macroeconomic effects.

It would be wrong to conclude, however, that as incomes in a society rise, sex must inevitably become less frequent or more hurried. Apart from the earlier point about leisure being a superior good, and the fact that sex is a positive function of health and that standards of health have improved, we must not ignore the fall in the costs (unrelated to time) of sex that has been brought about by improvements in contraception. We must not ignore quality either. Rising earned incomes cause the demand for time-intensive goods to fall if quality remains the same; but quality may not stay the same, because the demand for quality is itself a positive function of income. When people

53. Cf. Julian Pitt-Rivers, *The Fate of Schechem or The Politics of Sex: Essays in the Anthropology of the Mediterranean* 45–46 (1977).

54. Beryl Rawson, "The Roman Family," in *The Family in Ancient Rome: New Perspectives* 1, 19, 27 (Rawson ed. 1986); J. A. Crook, "Women in Roman Succession," in *The Family in Ancient Rome* at 58, 68–69; Suzanne Dixon, "Family Finances: Terentia and Tullia," in *The Family in Ancient Rome* at 93; Sarah B. Pomeroy, *Goddesses, Whores, Wives, and Slaves: Women in Classical Antiquity* 163, 181–182 (1975).

earn more, they do not just buy more cars, they buy better cars. Consider the case of children. The rearing of children is time-intensive, so as incomes rise, the average number of children falls. But the quality of children rises. That is, parents invest more in the care and education of their children. We might similarly expect that rising incomes would, other things being equal, reduce the amount of sexual activity in a society but increase its quality. This may be an important cause of the growth of companionate marriage.

The Effective Sex Ratio

Implicit in my emphasis on the costs of search is the importance of the effective sex ratio in explaining sexual customs. The sex ratio is the ratio of males to females in the population. By "effective" sex ratio I mean the ratio of males to *available* females. The higher the effective sex ratio, the higher the costs to men of heterosexual sex. Search costs are higher because it takes longer for each man to find a women who is not already spoken for; the analogy is to fishing in a pond that has very few fish. Moreover, the price of each woman is bid up because there are more demanders, and if price is not used to clear the market, we can expect queuing, illustrated by the long period of bachelorhood for most men in polygamous societies.

The difference between the pure sex ratio and the effective sex ratio can be dramatic. The sex ratio may be 1, but if half the women are the wives of one man, the effective sex ratio is 2, and there will be a tendency toward both desperate competition among men for wives and rebellion against the polygamist. That competition can be muted, however, and the stability of the polygamist's position enhanced, by the encouragement or at least toleration of prostitution and homosexuality, which provide safety valves for unmarried men.[55] One can predict, therefore, that these practices, and (for a reason about to be noted) perhaps especially homosexuality, will be more common, other things being equal, the more polygamy there is in a society. This hypothesis can be tested with data collected many years ago by Clellan Ford and Frank Beach on sexual practices, mainly in primitive societies.[56] In 53 of the 83

55. That a high ratio of males to females encourages male homosexual behavior has frequently been noted. See, for example, J. M. Carrier, "Homosexual Behavior in Cross-Cultural Perspective," in *Homosexual Behavior: A Modern Reappraisal* 100 (Judd Marmor ed. 1980). (One is therefore not surprised to discover that ancient Greece and Rome appear to have had a large and persistent surplus of males. Pomeroy, note 54 above, at 164–165, 227–228.) On the toleration of such behavior by old men eager to preserve polygyny, see Barry D. Adams, "Age, Structure, and Sexuality: Reflections on the Anthropological Evidence on Homosexual Relations," in *Anthropology and Homosexual Behavior* 19, 21–22 (Evelyn Blackwood ed. 1986). And on the demand for prostitution as a function of the sex ratio, see Decker, note 39 above, at 72.

56. Clellan S. Ford and Frank A. Beach, *Patterns of Sexual Behavior* 129 n. 1, 130 n. 2, 268–292 (1951). I have supplemented and in places corrected Ford and Beach's data with data from

societies for which the requisite data are reported—almost two-thirds—male homosexual activity is common or approved. But the percentage is lowest in the 10 societies that are strictly monogamous (50 percent), higher in the 30 societies in which polygamy is rare (60 percent), and highest in the 43 societies in which polygamy is common (70 percent). The order is as predicted, although a richer study would use finer distinctions among degrees of both polygamy and tolerance for homosexuality and would also control for other potential explanatory variables such as the sex ratio and the difference in average age of spouses at marriage (a proxy for whether marriage is companionate or noncompanionate).

One would also expect—and there is evidence of this as well—that polygamous households, and more generally any setting in which women are persistently deprived of male companionship, would foster opportunistic lesbianism, since a man with plural wives is likely to neglect some of them.[57] But the total amount of opportunistic lesbianism in a polygamous society might well be less than in a monogamous one, since there are fewer spinsters in the former and the average age of marriage for women is lower. This point helps explain, incidentally, why for men homosexuality may be the preferred safety valve to prostitution in a polygynous society. Prostitutes may be very expensive in such a society (unless it is a slave society and marriage with slaves is forbidden). By increasing the demand for females and thereby reducing the average age of women at marriage and the fraction of women who are unmarried, polygyny reduces the supply of women for prostitution. This can be expected to drive up the price and thus make substitutes more attractive.

We should not take a sex ratio of 1 for granted. Female infanticide has been common in many societies, and has sometimes led to a sharply skewed sex ratio,[58] which in turn skews the effective sex ratio. In America today black women significantly outnumber available black men. This is partly because of

the Human Relations Area Files. The findings reported in the text should be taken with more than a grain of salt, not only because of the failure to correct for other variables, but also because the ethnographic data frequently disagree about the proper characterization of a society's attitude toward homosexuality and (or) polygamy. Compare with Ford and Beach's characterizations John W. M. Whiting, "Effects of Climate on Certain Cultural Practices," in *Cultural Anthropology* 511 (Ward H. Goodenough ed. 1964), and Gwen J. Broude and Sarah J. Greene, "Cross-Cultural Codes on Twenty Sexual Attitudes and Practices," 15 *Ethnology: An International Journal of Cultural and Social Anthropology* 409 (1976).

57. Evelyn Blackwood, "Breaking the Mirror: The Construction of Lesbianism and the Anthropological Discourse on Homosexuality," in *Anthropology and Homosexual Behavior*, note 55 above, at 1, 11–13.

58. See, for example, Lloyd deMause, "The Evolution of Childhood," in *The History of Childhood* 1, 25–29 (deMause ed. 1974). I discuss infanticide in the last section of this chapter. When I say "skewed," I simply mean more or less than 1. In a *social* sense, a society that practices female infanticide regards a sex ratio of 1 as "skewed."

higher fetal and infant mortality of black than of white males, which is due in turn to the interaction of the tendency for pregnancy and neonatal care to be poor among blacks with the fact that male infants are more vulnerable than female ones; and partly because of the high death rate of black males from homicide and their high rate of imprisonment.[59] In addition, white women are more likely to date black men (and vice versa) than white men are to date black women.[60] Economic analysis predicts that with so favorable an effective sex ratio, black men (outside of prison) will be less likely than white men to engage in opportunistic homosexual behavior or to patronize prostitutes but more likely to have multiple sex partners, to be initiated into sex early, and to father illegitimate children, tendencies that make black men seem more promiscuous than white men.[61] In like vein, Mormon polygamy has been explained as a response to a surplus of women over men, caused by the absence of Mormon men on missionary work.[62]

59. The sex ratio for blacks between the ages of 25 and 44 is 0.87; for whites it is 1.01. U.S. Dept. of Commerce, Bureau of the Census, *Statistical Abstract of the United States 1987* 17 (1986) (tab. 18). Much of the difference, to be sure, may be due to the undercounting of young black males. Kristin A. Moore, Margaret C. Simms, and Charles L. Betsey, *Choice and Circumstance: Racial Differences in Adolescent Sexuality and Fertility* 112–114 (1986). But the sex ratio is only one determinant of the *effective* sex ratio. More than 3 percent of all black males are in jail or prison, while the corresponding percentage of black females is presumably much smaller, since fewer than 5 percent of state prisoners and fewer than 10 percent of jail inmates are female. U.S. Dept. of Commerce, Bureau of the Census, *Statistical Abstract of the United States 1990* 187 (1989) (tabs. 323, 325). Most prisoners, moreover, are young: for example, more than 90 percent of state prisoners are between 18 and 44 (more than 50 percent between 25 and 44); see 187 (tab. 325). For these and other reasons, there is little doubt that the effective sex ratio among American blacks is far below unity. Moore, Simms, and Betsey at 112–114; Osei-Mensah Aborampah, "Black Male-Female Relationships: Some Observations," 19 *Journal of Black Studies* 320, 321–322 (1989); Guttentag and Secord, note 36 above, ch. 8.

60. Martin S. Weinberg and Colin J. Williams, "Black Sexuality: A Test of Two Theories," 25 *Journal of Sex Research* 197, 214 (1988), and sources cited there. Whereas 63 percent of black-white marriages involve a black male and a white female, only 37 percent involve a white male and a black female. Guttentag and Secord, note 36 above, at 225 (tab. 8.8) (1970 data).

61. I have no evidence about opportunistic homosexuality among blacks or about black patronage of prostitutes. The other behavioral differences are well documented, however, and they persist even after such variables as education and income are controlled for. Guttentag and Secord, note 36 above, at 215–220; Moore, Simms, and Betsey, note 59 above; Weinberg and Williams, note 60 above; Sandra L. Hofferth, "Recent Trends in the Living Arrangements of Children: A Cohort Life Table Analysis," in *Family Demography: Methods and Their Application* 168 (John Bongaarts, Thomas K. Burch, and Kenneth W. Wachter eds. 1987); Thomas J. Espenshade, "The Recent Decline in American Marriage: Blacks and Whites in Comparative Perspective," in *Contemporary Marriage: Comparative Perspectives on a Changing Institution* 53 (Kingsley Davis ed. 1985); Ira L. Reiss, "Premarital Sexual Permissiveness among Negroes and Whites," 29 *American Sociological Review* 688 (1964).

62. William Lawrence Foster, "Between Two Worlds: The Origins of Shaker Celibacy, Oneida Community Complex Marriage, and Mormon Polygamy" 223–224 (Ph.D diss., University of Chicago, 1976).

Two other hypotheses generated by my theory are that black men commit fewer heterosexual rapes than white men, after allowance is made for other variables that explain differences in crime rates, because blacks have lower costs of heterosexual search than whites; and that black men are less prone to abuse children sexually than white men are. The first hypothesis can be tested with the aid of Isaac Ehrlich's regressions of crime rates on a variety of potentially explanatory variables, including race. It is not supported: the coefficient of the nonwhite variable is positive for rape, as it is for all the crimes in Ehrlich's study; it is, however, much smaller in the case of rape than in the case of any other crime against the person.[63] The second hypothesis (black men commit less child sexual abuse than white men) is supported by data showing that, at all income levels, blacks are indeed less likely to abuse children sexually than whites are.[64]

63. "Participation in Illegitimate Activities: An Economic Analysis," in *Essays in the Economics of Crime and Punishment* 68, 96–97, 100–101 (Gary S. Becker and William M. Landes eds. 1974) (tabs. 2–5). For example, in one of the regressions the coefficient for rape is 0.065 and for murder 0.542 (see 101 tab. 5—the data, incidentally, are for 1960), implying that a 1 percent increase in the number of blacks would result in an increase of more than half of 1 percent in the number of murders but only about one-fifteenth of 1 percent in the number of rapes. The crimes against the person in Ehrlich's study are, besides murder and rape, assault and robbery. Ehrlich classifies robbery as a crime against property, like larceny or auto theft, the other two crimes against property in his study, rather than as a crime against the person, like murder, assault, and rape. But actually it is the latter. Robbery is taking property from a person by threat or use of force. The coefficients on the nonwhite variable are low in the case of larceny and auto theft.

The qualification in the text—"after allowance is made for other variables that explain differences in crime rates"—is very important. Without such correction, the rape rate is far higher among blacks than among whites. In 1988 one third of all persons convicted of rape were black, although blacks were only 11 percent of the adult U.S. population. Patrick A. Langan and John M. Dawson, "Felony Sentences in State Courts, 1988" 4 (Bureau of Justice Statistics Bulletin, U.S. Dept. of Justice, December 1990) (tab. 5). (The percentage of blacks convicted was higher for *all* the offenses in the study, ranging up to 63 percent in the case of robbery. Illustrative of the need to correct for other variables is the fact that rape is often an incident to a nonsexual crime such as robbery or burglary. Diana Scully, *Understanding Sexual Violence: A Study of Convicted Rapists* 141–142 (1990). This implies that since blacks commit a disproportionate number of such crimes, their costs of raping are lower than the cost to whites. Another example of the need to distinguish between raw and interpreted data is that, despite my conjecture that opportunistic homosexuality is less common among black than among white males, the incidence of AIDS contracted through homosexual contact is twice as high per capita among black American than among white American males. "Centers for Disease Control Statistics," 4 *AIDS* 1307 (1990). But this is before correcting for other factors bearing on the incidence of homosexual-induced AIDS, such as knowledge about the disease, which may well be below average in the black community. Becker and Joseph, note 6 above, at 405–406.

64. U.S. Dept. of Health and Human Services, Office of Human Development Services, "Study Findings: National Study of the Incidence and Severity of Child Abuse and Neglect" 28–29 and fig. 6 (DHHS Publication no. (OHDS) 81–30325, September 1981). This study recognizes the possibility that child abuse is less frequently reported to the authorities by blacks than by whites

Marcia Guttentag and Paul Secord's book on sex ratios (note 36) is an ambitious effort to derive the implications of an imbalance in the sex ratio for sexual mores.[65] But it is weakened by the authors' lack of a cogent theory of human behavior. They speculate that lesbianism will be more common the lower the ratio of males to females and that men will tend to sequester women more the higher the ratio of males to females. The idea is that excess demand of men for women puts female chastity at greater risk by raising the "price" that unmarried men will pay for access to women, married or otherwise. These conjectures are congenial to economic analysis, but not the authors' overarching thesis that an imbalance in the sex ratio *dictates* the character of a society's sexual mores—repressive or at least straitlaced if there is a shortage of women, liberal or permissive if there is a shortage of men. The sex ratio is only one determinant of the relevant costs and benefits. Guttentag and Secord would be forced by the logic of their analysis to predict that the ancient Greeks and Orthodox Jews—both cultures with a persistent surplus of males[66]—had similar sexual mores, which they did not.

Nevertheless the sex ratio, in particular the effective sex ratio, is highly relevant to the economic analysis of sex and is especially pertinent to explaining differences between white and black sexual behavior that remain after correction for differences in income, education, and other nonracial variables. Besides the higher rate of black illegitimate births, the lower average age of sexual initiation of blacks, the higher average number of sexual partners per black male, and the lower incidence of child sexual abuse by blacks, black men are far less likely than white men to undergo voluntary sterilization or to use condoms; blacks are less likely to seek treatment for fertility problems than whites are; and black men are more disapproving of homosexuality than white men are.[67] Since black men are scarce and therefore have the upper

---

but concludes that correcting for this difference would not affect the study's conclusion. The possibility that rape is underreported in black communities must also be acknowledged.

65. See also Moore, Simms, and Betsey, note 59 above, at 136; David M. Heer and Amyra Grossbard-Schectman, "The Impact of the Female Marriage Squeeze and the Contraceptive Revolution on Sex Roles and the Women's Liberation Movement in the United States, 1960 to 1975," 43 *Journal of Marriage and the Family* 49 (1981); Grossbard-Schectman, "Marriage Squeezes and the Marriage Market," in *Contemporary Marriage,* note 61 above, at 375.

66. On Greece, see references in note 54 above. On Judaism, see Guttentag and Secord, note 36 above, at 42 and ch. 4.

67. Elizabeth Hervey Stephen, Ronald R. Rindfuss, and Frank D. Bean, "Racial Differences in Contraceptive Choice: Complexity and Implications," 25 *Demography* 53 (1988), esp. 67; Larry L. Bumpass, "The Risk of an Unwanted Birth: The Changing Context of Contraceptive Sterilization in the U.S.," 41 *Population Studies* 347, 350 (1987); Debra S. Kalmuss, "The Use of Infertility Services among Fertility-Impaired Couples," 24 *Demography* 575, 582–583 (1987); Gregory M. Herek and Eric K. Glunt, "AIDS-Related Attitudes in the United States: A Preliminary Conceptualization," 28 *Journal of Sex Research* 99, 111 (1991); Harlon L. Dalton, "AIDS in

hand in bargaining with black women, they can shift the burden of contraception to them. Since fertility problems more commonly afflict women than men, a man who has many women to choose among may decide to abandon a woman with whom he is failing to have children rather than cooperate in seeking a solution to the problem; indeed, a traditional rationale for polygyny is that it is a way of getting around female fertility problems without divorce and remarriage. And finally, the need for a homosexual safety valve is minimized in a community in which the ratio of men to women is low, so homosexuality is more likely to seem unnatural in such a community.

Religion and Education

A powerful variable explaining differences in sexual attitudes is, as I noted in Chapter 2, religiosity—though only in societies in which the dominant religions are hostile to particular sexual practices, as Christianity (particularly Roman Catholicism) and to a lesser extent Judaism and Islam are. Persons who believe that they face supernatural sanctions, or even just that they are displeasing God, by engaging in particular sexual practices are less likely to engage in them, or at least to express approval of them, than the irreligious. This may be one reason why better-educated people are more tolerant in sexual matters than less-educated people are, for educated people in our society are less likely to be religious.[68]

Another reason may be that educated people tend to be more aware of human sexual variety. They have heard of Freud and Margaret Mead, and maybe even of Malinowski. A person who knows that James I, Francis Bacon, Oscar Wilde, Henry James, Marcel Proust, Gertrude Stein, Virginia Woolf, John Maynard Keynes, E. M. Forster, Pyotr Ilich Tchaikovsky, George Santayana, T. E. Lawrence, Alan Turing, and Ludwig Wittgenstein were homosexuals, and that Sophocles, Socrates, Plato, Shakespeare, Christopher Marlowe, Alexander the Great, Julius Caesar, and Richard the Lion-Hearted may have been, is not so likely to believe that homosexuality is merely a ghastly blight.[69] Then too, as this list suggests, a number of the culture heroes of intellectuals have been homosexual—but they are not heroes to nonintellectuals. (For the nonintellectual, however, there are, among many other homo-

---

Blackface," 118 *Daedalus: Journal of the American Academy of Arts and Sciences* 205, 213 (1989).

68. See, for example, Gallup Report no. 259, April 1987, 11, 14.

69. Some of these illustrious figures, however, may have been opportunistic homosexuals (hence "really" heterosexual), or genuine bisexuals, rather than "real" homosexuals. Homosexual-rights advocates are apt to label famous persons homosexual on scanty evidence, but the *Encyclopedia of Homosexuality* (Wayne R. Dynes ed. 1990) reviews the evidence pro and con these labelings with appropriate caution. See under particular names.

sexuals who might be mentioned, William Tilden, Cole Porter, and Rock Hudson.) Differences between educated and uneducated people exist at the level of sexual behavior as well as of attitudes. For example, educated people have been said to masturbate more than the uneducated because their imaginative resources are greater, making fantasy sex a better substitute for real sex.[70]

Is religion an ultimate variable, or, as this brief discussion of education suggests may be possible, is it epiphenomenal? As we saw in Chapter 1, the basis in the text of the Old Testament and of the Gospels for the characteristic Christian attitudes toward sex is infirm. Sex was not a subject in the forefront of concern of either the Hebrew prophets or Jesus. There are the Levitical prohibitions against homosexuality and adultery, of course, but since Christianity abandoned many of the other Levitical prohibitions, the ones it retained could not have been retained under the compulsion of textual authority. Of course, text is not everything. Textual silences can be pregnant. From the fact that the Ten Commandments do not forbid incest we should not infer that the ancient Jews condoned the practice, just as we should not infer that by failing to specify the sex of the spouses the authors of a marriage statute intend to authorize homosexual marriage. Nevertheless, the Christian view of sex was invented—the decision to emphasize Jesus Christ's (apparent) celibacy, for example, was just that, a decision—and it is possible that the ends in view were practical. What those ends might be is a difficult question for economic analysis. I do not pretend to have a complete answer, but some elements of one, revolving around the role of the Church in promoting companionate marriage, will emerge in the next chapter.

Complementarity of Sexual Practices

One good is said to be a complement of another if a fall in the price of the first increases the quantity demanded of the second. An example of complementary goods in the area of sex is contraception and vaginal intercourse. If we think of the contraceptive "product" not as the physical good but as the service of preventing birth, thereby adjusting for improvements in the effec-

---

70. Morse Peckham, *Art and Pornography: An Experiment in Explanation* 166, 231 (1969). (Compare the discussion of pornography below.) A consistent but better-documented finding is that middle-class adolescents masturbate more than lower-class adolescents. See, besides references in Chapter 2, Robert J. Havighurst, "Cultural Factors in Sex Expression," in *Sexual Behavior in American Society: An Appraisal of the First Two Kinsey Reports* 191 (Jerome Himelhoch and Sylvia Fleis Fava eds. 1955). In addition to educational differences between the two groups, the average age of first intercourse is lower in the lower class. Finally, on the impact of education on the effective use of contraception, see Robert T. Michael, "Education and the Derived Demand for Children," 81 *Journal of Political Economy* S128, S140–S161 (1973).

tiveness as well as in the comfort and the nominal price of contraceptive devices, we will quickly realize that the cost of contraception has fallen by staggering amounts. That is why one would expect, other things being equal, the amount of vaginal intercourse to have risen—as it has (see note 10). Considerations of complementarity thus enable additional predictions to be made concerning the effect of social change or difference on sexual practices.

Abortion might seem to be a substitute for contraception, and it is, but it is also a complement to it. By backing up contraception, abortion reduces the costs of engaging in vaginal intercourse. If abortion is made very costly by legal regulations, then, since contraception is not 100 percent effective, a couple may be induced to substitute some method of nonvaginal intercourse (such as anal intercourse), or even to abstain. Conversely, if abortion is cheap, vaginal intercourse will be more frequent and, depending on people's knowledge of and the efficacy of contraceptive methods, may generate more unwanted pregnancies, not all of which will be aborted. This should help us to understand the combination of cheap contraceptives, frequent abortions, and yet a high rate of unwanted births in our society, although a more refined analysis will be presented in later chapters.

A related reason for believing that the number of abortions overstates the number of net live births lost as a result of abortion is that when used as a method of family planning in the sense of planning *for* a family, abortion may affect the timing more than the number of births. Since, in affecting the timing of births, abortion could result in an increase in the average quality of children, and since, as Chapter 7 will point out, modern people have a tendency (fostered by the decline in infant and child mortality) to substitute quality for quantity as a desired characteristic in children, we can understand why the force of the moral objections to abortion has weakened in recent decades. "The apparently paradoxical idea that birth control could be encouraged through an increased concern for children"[71] makes economic sense.

Like abortion, infanticide, when viewed, as it should be, as a method of family planning[72] rather than a species of motiveless malignancy, does not reduce the population by the number of infants killed. For in a poor society, the fewer children a woman has, the likelier they are to survive to adulthood.[73] This is true even when most or even all infants killed are girls, the "efficient"

71. André Burguière, "From Malthus to Max Weber: Belated Marriage and the Spirit of Enterprise," in *Family and Society: Selections from the Annales Economies, Sociétiés, Civilisations* 237, 239 (Robert Forster and Orest Ranum eds. 1976).

72. Clearly the dominant form of infanticide in the human species. See studies and references in *Infanticide: Comparative and Evolutionary Perspectives*, pt. 4 (Glenn Hausfater and Sarah Blaffer Hrdy eds. 1984).

73. For evidence from Japan, see Susan B. Hanley, "The Influence of Economic and Social Variables on Marriage and Fertility in Eighteenth and Nineteenth Century Japanese Villages," in *Population Patterns in the Past* 165, 176, 199 (Ronald Demos Lee ed. 1977).

form of infanticide because it limits the future growth of the population.[74] (Reducing the number of males need not reduce the number of children in the next generation, since one man can fertilize an indefinitely large number of women.) In a society in which women need dowries in order to marry, a couple may have to choose between killing one or more of its daughters and having few or even no grandchildren because the cost of raising all the daughters would prevent the family from dowering any of them. Hence—not today, of course, but in the radically different social conditions prevailing in earlier societies—a practice of female infanticide need no more bespeak hostility toward or a disvaluing of women than the thinning of trees in a forest signifies a dislike of trees.[75] It would be irrational from a genetic standpoint for a father to be indifferent to the procreative potential, and hence to the survival, of his daughters.

While contraception and abortion are complements as well as substitutes, infanticide and abortion are substitutes. Advocates of abortion rights do not like to view the relation between infanticide and abortion in this light, because infanticide is abhorred in our society. But the relationship is unmistakable, both being methods of preventing unwanted births after conception has occurred. If this is so, however, the question arises why the crueler method—infanticide—was until recently more common than abortion. The obvious answer is that until recently abortion was a dangerous procedure for a woman to undergo, but this answer is incomplete because until recently childbirth was also a dangerous procedure. The subtle answer is that if only female infants are unwanted and the sex of the fetus cannot be determined, abortion will kill on average twice as many infants as infanticide will, and only half those infants will be unwanted.

The interplay of substitutability and complementarity is further illustrated by the relation between contraception and prostitution. On the one hand, by reducing the probability that the prostitute will become pregnant, effective contraception reduces the cost of prostitution and therefore the price. On the other hand, by reducing the cost of marriage, contraception encourages early marriage, which reduces the demand for prostitution by providing more men with an alternative source of sexual gratification. Pornography is another good whose relation to sex combines elements of substitution and of complementarity. When used in conjunction with masturbation to create a closer fantasy substitute for sexual intercourse than masturbation alone would do,

74. Susan C. M. Scrimshaw, "Infanticide in Human Populations: Societal and Individual Concerns," in *Infanticide,* note 72 above, at 439, 454.

75. The Japanese word for infanticide, *mabiki,* is the same word used to denote the thinning out of plants. Hanley, note 73 above, at 176.

pornography operates as a substitute for intercourse and reduces the demand for it.[76] But when used to stimulate sexual desire, pornography may have the effect of increasing the amount of intercourse. The balance of these effects is the focal point of the debate over the role of pornography in rape, discussed in Chapter 13.

76. In this vein it has been argued that as pornography, formerly marketed only to men, becomes marketed more and more to women, women will masturbate more, leading in turn to a greater focus by women upon genital sexuality as distinct from the rather more diffuse sexual interest that has been characteristic of Western women. John H. Gagnon, "The Interaction of Gender Roles and Sexual Conduct," in *Human Sexuality: A Comparative and Developmental Perspective* 225, 242 (Herant A. Katchadourian ed. 1979). This is a typically constructionist hypothesis. The sociobiologist, in contrast, does not expect pornography, in the sense of erotic literature that emphasizes the depiction of sexual organs, ever to find a large market among women. The economist is neutral on the question.

The History of Sexuality from the Perspective of Economics

THIS CHAPTER elaborates the positive economic theory of sexuality with the aid of case studies that bring to the fore the role of companionate marriage and women's occupational profile as causes of change in sexual behavior and attitudes. The last section treats the causal relationship between the two highlighted factors themselves.

Greek Love and the Institutionalization of Pederasty

Among the citizen population in the Athens of Plato and Aristotle boys and girls were reared separately, and the boys attended school but the girls did not. Polygamy was forbidden but flourished informally as concubinage practiced by married men. For this and other reasons, including a shortage of women because of female infanticide, girls married young and the husband usually was considerably older than the wife. As a result of this age difference, the low average age of marriage for girls (about 16), the prevalence of arranged marriage, the practice of sequestering women, and the difference in educational attainments between the spouses, marriage was not companionate. Spouses were not good friends, united by bonds of love and trust and by shared interests, values, and experiences. They did not socialize together, did not even take meals together. And there was no expectation that the husband would be faithful to his wife—just that he would not bring his concubines into the marital home. Remember that one function of sex is to cement relationships. The thinner the relationship between husband and wife, the less demand there is for the cement of sex.

There is some exaggeration in this picture of sexual segregation, as we know from Chapter 2; in particular, "sequestration" should not be taken literally. But the picture is broadly accurate, and economics can explain four characteristics of it that may at first glance seem adventitious, or at least unrelated. These are universal marriage; a widespread toleration (almost, it seems, the institutionalization) of male homosexuality, usually involving a man of 25 to 30 and an adolescent boy; the idea of homosexual preference as a developmental phase for all males rather than as a permanent preference of some; and a corps of elite prostitutes—cultured, witty courtesans (*hetairai*)—as distinct from run-of-the-mill prostitutes, who were, however, also plentiful.

In a culture in which marriage is not companionate, men will seek affective ties outside the home,[1] either with other men of their own class or with women who, if not themselves of that class, specialize in providing companionship for them. Sex will sometimes, perhaps often, be used to cement these relationships; hence the homosexual relationships with citizen youths and the heterosexual relationships with tony courtesans. Yet the emergence of a distinct homosexual subculture, and even of a sharp awareness that there really are men whose sexual preference is homosexual (that is, who are not merely opportunistic homosexuals), will be retarded by the ease with which such men form and maintain noncompanionate marriages. The desire to have children appears to be as strong in homosexuals as in heterosexuals. But in a society in which women expect their husbands to be intimates rather than merely financial protectors and occasional inseminators, it is difficult for the homosexual man to make a success of marriage. Many try; few succeed.[2]

The difficulty is much less when marriages are noncompanionate. The wife does not expect the husband to be an intimate, to be faithful, to be attentive, and so forth; financial support and occasional intercourse are all that is expected; and, as I noted in Chapter 4, most homosexual men are capable of vaginal intercourse, although they do not find it highly pleasurable or emotionally satisfying. The fact that it was so easy to be a successful married man in ancient Greece and chase young men on the side made homosexuals seem less different from heterosexuals than in cultures of companionate marriage, such as our own. So much less different, indeed, as rarely to be remarked, in much the same way that we do not much remark left-handedness, because it has no significance for a person's social role. Prostitution was similarly unproblematic, since it did not threaten any essential feature of the marital relationship.

With women of the citizen class sequestered, and marriage for men occurring late, heterosexual men of the citizen class could expect to spend

---

1. See, for example, Richard G. Parker, *Bodies, Pleasures, and Passions: Sexual Culture in Contemporary Brazil* 32–34 (1991).

2. Marcel T. Saghir and Eli Robins, *Male and Female Homosexuality: A Comprehensive Investigation* 96–98 (1973). Some relatively successful such marriages are reported, however, in Catherine Whitney, *Uncommon Lives: Gay Men and Straight Women* (1990).

their years of maximum sexual energy as bachelors. In casting about for sexual substitutes for women, they frequently turned their eyes on adolescent boys. Why boys rather than men? Why boys rather than female prostitutes?

An adolescent boy is physically more like a young woman than is either an adult male, with his beard and deep voice, or a prepubescent boy, who is just a child; so we can expect the opportunistic homosexual—and many a bachelor whose access to females is highly restricted will become an opportunistic homosexual—to chase adolescent boys.[3] This is during his early manhood. He will move on to women (wife, *hetairai,* and concubines) when he reaches the age of marriage, implying acquisition of the financial resources required to support women.

Prostitutes and female slaves offered a low-cost alternative to boys, and one very frequently used. But, being from the lower classes, they were not perfect substitutes for the inaccessible citizen girls. Boys had the considerable disadvantage of not being girls but the advantage of being from the same social class as the girls whom young citizen men would have been romancing in a less sexually segregated society, and also of being educated, which even citizen girls were not. We need not assume that the advantages perfectly offset the disadvantage. Despite the prominence of pederasty in Greek literature and

3. Recall the references in the preceding chapter to boys as female substitutes; and see Parker Rossman, *Sexual Experience between Men and Boys: Exploring the Pederast Underground* 14, 16–17 (1976). Camille Paglia, *Sexual Personae: Art and Decadence from Nefertiti to Emily Dickinson* 109–125 (1990), following Freud, emphasizes the epicene quality of the Greek ideal of male beauty—small, largely hairless genitals, a shy, submissive glance, and so on: qualities of a girlish boy. Freud had said: "It is clear that in Greece, where the most masculine men were numbered among the inverts, what excited a man's love was not the masculine character of a boy, but his physical resemblance to a woman as well as his feminine mental qualities—his shyness, his modesty and his need for instruction and assistance. As soon as the boy became a man he ceased to be a sexual object for men." "The Sexual Aberrations," in *Three Essays on the Theory of Sexuality* 13, 22 (James Strachey trans. 1949). But we should not, as John Weightman suggests in "André Gide and the Homosexual Debate," 59 *American Scholar* 591, 595 (1990), worry about "what the [ancient Greek] women thought of this [i.e., pederasty], particularly the young girls, deprived of their male contemporaries between the ages of thirteen and twenty-three." These young girls were either sequestered in their parents' home or married to men over 23; the shortage of available girls is what made pederasty attractive to heterosexual young men. Which of course is not to say that *all* pederasts were or are heterosexuals. Indeed, in a society such as ours, in which young women are not sequestered, we would expect pederasty to be rare among heterosexuals. Yet even today it has been estimated that more than 50 percent of American pederasts are married (Rossman at 6), which is more than twice the percentage of (all) American male homosexuals who are married. Michael W. Ross, *The Married Homosexual Man: A Psychological Study* 110–111 and tab. 11.1 (1983). (These estimates are very rough.) Nor is it surprising that *all* the Africans in Rossman's sample were married. Rossman at 6. Noncompanionate marriage is more common in Africa than in the United States, and therefore it is easier for an African homosexual or a bisexual to marry than for an American homosexual or bisexual to do so.

art, its actual incidence is unknown, and it may well have been a minority taste even among young men of the citizen class.

Since the vast majority of men are heterosexuals, the tastes of the opportunistic homosexual will set the dominant tone for the culture as a whole if opportunistic homosexuality is widespread among the heterosexual population. Observers will conclude that transitory pederasty, as we may call it, is the dominant form of homosexuality in such a culture. Yet if my analysis is right, no matter how common transitory pederasty was, there is no reason to think that homosexual preference was more common in ancient Greece than it is in modern America.

The idea of pederasty as an approved or at least tolerated phase in the development of the male is not unique to ancient Greece, as we saw in Chapter 2; it is found in its most extreme form among the Sambia of New Guinea. To describe the ritual pederasty of the Sambians as opportunistic homosexuality will, I am sure, make Gilbert Herdt, the leading student of Sambian sexuality, wince. He believes Sambian pederasty to be a practice designed to create fearless warriors out of mamas' boys.[4] Maybe. But the linkage traced by Herdt in his distinguished study between ingesting semen and becoming self-confidently and aggressively masculine is intricate; let me suggest a simpler alternative. A warrior culture—the culture of ancient Greece as much as of Sambia—is one in which men of fighting age are frequently absent from home. Given male jealousy, there will be a felt need to separate women from men (other than their fathers and husbands) more effectively than if the fathers and husbands were continuously at hand to watch over them. This separation reduces the heterosexual opportunities of young men, creating a demand for substitutes that pederasty can satisfy. At the same time, by discouraging companionate marriage, the separation creates a climate of tolerance for homosexuality.

My alternative explanation to Herdt's could actually be complementary. The smothering affection of the Sambian mothers may reflect their segregated status, which as we know from my discussion of ancient Greek marriage can reduce the companionability of marriage and incite the wife to seek intense emotional relationships elsewhere—such as with her children (I am not suggesting an incestuous relationship)—if adultery is unavailable as an escape route. And intense maternal affection could conceivably complicate a boy's acquisition of martial attitudes. To survive as a warrior culture, the society might evolve a custom of taking the boy from his mother and reacculturating him in a homosocial setting. Heterosexual opportunities would be few in such a setting.

Not only is pederasty not synonymous with homosexuality; it is uncertain whether a "real" homosexual will find pederasty more attractive than will a

4. Gilbert H. Herdt, *Guardians of the Flutes: Idioms of Masculinity* 302–325 (1981).

heterosexual deprived of heterosexual opportunities. The opportunistic homosexual likes boys rather than men because they are a closer substitute for young women. A real homosexual does not find young women attractive—he is attracted to men (often, indeed, to heterosexual men)[5]—so why should he find a substitute for a young woman attractive? We must distinguish between boys (say, 13 to 15) and young men (say, 16 to 25). (Under 13 we are speaking of children—the domain of the pedophile, not the pederast. See Chapter 14.) Just as most heterosexual men find young women more attractive than older women, so most homosexual men find young men more attractive than older men. (This is evidence that, except with regard to the desired gender of their sexual partner, homosexual men are like other men rather than like women.) But most heterosexual men—I am not speaking of teenagers—are not strongly attracted to adolescent girls, and are attracted to adolescent boys only as the closest available substitute for young women; no more should we expect most homosexual men to be strongly attracted to adolescent boys. So we would expect the opportunistic homosexual to like boys but the real homosexual to like young men, though with overlap in the 16-to-17 age range. Consistent with this point is the fact that when homosexuals do pursue (younger) boys, it is often because there is too much competition for men; the boy is an inferior substitute to which the less attractive homosexual is driven.[6]

My suggestion that heterosexuals might pursue boys as avidly as (or even more avidly than) homosexuals would do may seem inconsistent with the fact that many homosexuals have an effeminate manner; presumably they are nevertheless attractive to other homosexuals, and if so why shouldn't boys be? This overlooks the costs of search. Even if a homosexual would prefer a "real" man as a sex partner, it would be harder for him to find a partner among heterosexual men than among homosexual men, and he may have to settle for an effeminate homosexual. This may not be his first choice and need not suggest that, because boys are less masculine than men, homosexuals must like boys.

Moreover, while many homosexuals go through an effeminate stage as young children, and many effeminate men are homosexual, it is uncertain whether effeminate men form a large fraction of homosexuals. True, many heterosexuals *believe* that most homosexuals are effeminate. But they believe this because effeminacy is observable and homosexual preference is not, and because a homosexual whose effeminacy makes him readily identifiable as such will find it more costly to "pass" as a heterosexual than the masculine homosexual will and therefore has less incentive to make an effort to conceal his homosexuality. Furthermore, homosexuals may adopt an effeminate man-

---

5. Jeffrey Weeks, *Sex, Politics and Society: The Regulation of Sexuality since 1800* 113 (1981).
6. Paul H. Gebhard et al., *Sex Offenders: An Analysis of Types* 321–322 (1965).

ner to signal their homosexuality. Men are readily recognizable as such to women, and women to men, because natural selection has made the differences between men and women in shape, gait, complexion, and voice salient. Male homosexuals are outwardly more like male heterosexuals than men are like women; recognition is therefore more difficult and is facilitated by the adoption of an identifiably "homosexual" manner. Effeminacy may be a device for reducing the costs of sexual search.

If my analysis of pederasty is correct, it suggests a certain futility, and ultimately even a certain incoherence, in the standard "conservative" view of sex that both reprobates pederasty and values female virginity. The less available young women are to satisfy male sexual desires, the greater will be the inclination of men to satisfy those desires with boys. Similarly, sexual conservatives in the Catholic tradition abhor both heterosexual (as well, of course, as homosexual) sodomy, and contraception and abortion, as "unnatural" practices. But if contraception and abortion are discouraged, the demand for heterosexual sodomy as a substitute for vaginal intercourse will rise, because sodomy is sterile.[7] Granted there is no inherent contradiction in wanting to repress both an activity and its substitute—for example, robbery and burglary. But it is a good deal easier to enforce abstinence from crime than abstinence from sex. Conservatives are supposed to be realistic about human nature. Since when has self-control been a dependable method of regulation? Was not Aquinas' condoning of prostitution (see Chapter 7) realistic for his time, and might not realism in our time dictate condonation of a broader range of noncanonical sexual practices?

Monasticism, Puritanism, and Christian Sex Ethics

I remarked in the preceding chapter on the high cost of marriage under conditions that were common in medieval life. That cost was bound to create a large population of bachelors, and did so, and since the Church forbade polygamy and tried to discourage concubinage, the high cost of marriage created a large population of spinsters as well. (The Church's ban on divorce would have had two offsetting effects: to increase the cost of marriage and thereby increase the number of persons who did not marry, but to reduce the number of persons unmarried as a result of the end of a marriage.) Monasteries—and the celibate priesthood more generally—and convents can be seen as institutions for siphoning off surplus bachelors and spinsters in order to reduce competition for the limited number of marital places. But it would be naive to suppose that the bachelors and spinsters channeled into monastic life were

7. For sodomy as a form of contraceptive heterosexual intercourse in a Catholic country, see Parker, note 1 above, at 128–129.

a random draw as far as sexual preferences and opportunities were concerned. A family that had a son who was sickly or homosexual might be expected to steer him into the priesthood because he would not be a particularly fit husband—especially since the Church tried to encourage companionate marriage—while if a daughter was sickly or homely, her family could be expected to steer her toward a convent.[8] An additional consideration in the latter case was that the dowry that a girl's family would have to offer in order to attract a suitable husband would be lower the more attractive and the more fit for childbearing a girl was.

A similar analysis may explain why homosexuality is more common aboard naval vessels than it is in army units.[9] Naval service is monastic in the sense that it involves not only close proximity to other males, true also of the other military services, but protracted deprivation of heterosexual opportunities even in peacetime, a deprivation obviously far less costly to homosexuals than to heterosexuals. Another reason for what appears to have been the extraordinary incidence of homosexual acts (not necessarily—or even, I would argue, probably—homosexual *preference*) in the British navy in the era of sail may have been that the crews included many boys, and these would be attractive to heterosexual males deprived of heterosexual outlets. Most of the cases reported by Arthur Gilbert (note 9) involved the sodomizing of boys by adult crew members. My analysis implies that both real and opportunistic homosexuality will be more common in navies than in other military services.

One of the charges leveled by the early Protestants against the Roman Catholic Church was that the monasteries were hotbeds of homosexuality. This charge may help explain why persecution of homosexuals continued in Protestant countries, albeit intermittently, after most Catholic countries had stopped persecuting them. No one knows how widespread homosexuality was in the medieval monasteries, but it would not be surprising if it was more common than in the society at large, simply because this is an expected characteristic of sexually segregated institutions.[10] The interesting point, how-

8. John Boswell, *The Kindness of Strangers: The Abandonment of Children in Western Europe from Late Antiquity to the Renaissance* 240–241 (1988).

9. Arthur N. Gilbert, "Buggery and the British Navy, 1700–1861," 10 *Journal of Social History* 72 (1976); C. A. Tripp, *The Homosexual Matrix* 222–227 (1975); Mikhail Stern, *Sex in the USSR* 217 (1980); Theodore R. Sarbin and Kenneth E. Karols, "Nonconforming Sexual Orientations and Military Suitability" B-2, B-3 (Defense Personnel Security Research and Education Center, Rep. no. PERS-TR-89-002, December 1988). George Austin Chauncey, Jr., "Gay New York: Urban Culture and the Making of a Gay Male World, 1890–1940" 77–97 (Ph.D. diss., Yale University, 1989), describes a Bowery demimonde in which seamen and immigrants, bereft of women, substituted boys and young men; and J. Dunbar Moodie, "Migrancy and Male Sexuality in South African Gold Mines," in Hidden from History: Reclaiming the Gay and Lesbian Past 411 (Martin Bauml Duberman, Martha Vicinus, and George Chauncey, Jr., eds. 1989), describes same-sex "mine marriages" between miners cut off from access to women.

10. For some evidence, see David F. Greenberg, *The Construction of Homosexuality* 283, 286

ever, is not that the monks, like other inmates of all-male institutions, were deprived of heterosexual outlets; that is obvious, and moreover is relevant to homosexual acts, not homosexual preference. The interesting point is that the selection of persons for the priesthood in general and monastery life in particular would tend (quite without the Church's intending or desiring such an outcome) to favor men who had relatively poor marital prospects; and homosexuals—real homosexuals—would be overrepresented among such men.[11] Consistent with this speculation is the fact that the Church was generally protective of homosexuals in its own ranks,[12] at the same time that its leading theologians were displaying a seemingly obsessive concern with homosexuality and masturbation. The concern may not really have been obsessive, given Catholic sexual doctrine, since homosexuality and masturbation are indeed more likely in celibate institutions than elsewhere.

All this would be of relatively little significance had the Church been able to enforce total sexual abstinence on its clergy. It was not. We may assume, nevertheless, that the level of sexual activity in monasteries was (and is) less than in the outside world. But we should expect a disproportionate fraction of such activity as did occur to have been homosexual—a larger fraction, indeed, than among Catholic clergy outside monasteries, since the latter would have had more heterosexual opportunities. It is the unrealism of expecting total abstinence that led not only the Protestant churches but also Judaism and Islam to encourage its clergy to marry, the effect of marriage being to reduce the benefits of nonmarital sex (including homosexuality) by providing a substitute.

Should we expect the percentage of homosexuals in the celibate clergy to be higher or lower today than in the Middle Ages? I should think higher,

---

(1988). The medieval Church was certainly concerned about the problem of clerical homosexuality. See, for example, Peter Damian, *Book of Gomorrah: An Eleventh-Century Treatise against Clerical Homosexual Practices* (Pierre J. Payer trans. 1982).

11. An alternative, but not inconsistent, hypothesis is that the rituals of the Roman Catholic Church were (and perhaps still are) particularly attractive to persons of homosexual preference. Cf. Peter Gay, *The Tender Passion* 236–237 (1986) (vol. 2 of *The Bourgeois Experience: Victoria to Freud*), discussing Cardinal Newman and the Anglo-Catholic movement. Such persons tend to be attracted, as we shall see in Chapter 11, to occupations that involve adornment, as well as to artistic and theatrical expression, and so they might find the splendor of traditional Catholic services—the rich clerical garb, the sonorous Latin intonation, the music, and the incense—more attractive than the average heterosexual would. Of course, even if this is true, the causality could be the opposite of what I have suggested: clerics of homosexual tendency may have influenced the design and elaboration of the liturgy.

12. Luiz Mott and Aroldo Assuncao, "Love's Labors Lost: Five Letters from a Seventeenth-Century Sodomite," in *The Pursuit of Sodomy: Male Homosexuality in Renaissance and Enlightenment Europe* 91, 99–100 (Kent Gerard and Gert Hekma eds. 1989); Guido Ruggiero, *The Boundaries of Eros: Sex Crime and Sexuality in Renaissance Venice* 141–144 (1985).

because heterosexual opportunities, marital and otherwise, are more numerous today, thereby reducing the relative attractiveness of the priesthood to heterosexuals. And precisely because those opportunities are so plentiful, bachelors who do not appear to be sexually active come under suspicion of being homosexuals unless they belong to the one profession that makes celibacy a condition of membership. The priesthood becomes a good place in which a homosexual can hide—particularly at a time when marriage has become a bad place to do so because it has become companionate and it is difficult for homosexuals to make a go of companionate marriage. Of course, if the Church took pains to screen out homosexual aspirants, it might counteract the self-selection of homosexuals for the priesthood. But the Church appears not to do this. It is not the "homophobic" institution that some advocates of homosexual rights depict it as. Decades ago the *New Catholic Encyclopedia* stated that the homosexual "needs a vocation of service to God and to men that the priest can help him to find . . . A homosexual is just as pleasing to God as a heterosexual, as long as he makes a sincere effort to control his deviate bent with the help of grace."[13] The sublimated homosexual has long been welcome in the priesthood.[14]

The hypothesis that the percentage of homosexuals in the Catholic clergy has risen cannot be tested directly. No one knows the percentage of homosexual priests either in the Middle Ages or today. All one can say is that it appears to be very high today. Granted we should give only limited credence to a 1989 finding that at least 50 percent of American Catholic priests and seminarians are homosexuals.[15] The methodology was deeply flawed. A mailing to a large number of Catholic priests yielded 101 responses by priests willing to acknowledge their homosexuality, and the 50 percent figure is based on their estimates of the number of priests who are homosexual. The essay-type responses to the questionnaire, which are quoted at length in the study, suggest that the respondents are a thoughtful group of men, unlikely to exaggerate deliberately. Yet no doubt there is unconscious exaggeration. How much? Leaders of the homosexual rights movement often use a figure of 10 percent for the fraction of the American population—both male and female—that is homosexual, a figure that, as we shall see in Chapter 11, may well be

13. "Homosexuality," in vol. 7 at 119 (1967). The *New Catholic Encyclopedia* bears the imprimatur of the Catholic archbishop of Washington, D.C.

14. Celibate homosexual love is discussed approvingly by Donald Goergen, a Catholic priest, in his book *The Sexual Celibate* 188–196 (1974). Roger Scruton, "Sexual Morality and the Liberal Consensus," in Scruton, *The Philosopher on Dover Beach: Essays* 261, 269 (1990), defends the prohibition of homosexual acts on the ground that it encourages homosexuals to join the priesthood and sublimate their homosexuality. He regards the sublimated homosexual as a natural for the priesthood.

15. James G. Wolf, "Homosexuality and Religious Ideology: A Report on Gay Catholic Priests in the United States," in *Gay Priests* 3, 60 (Wolf ed. 1989) (tab. 15).

a fourfold exaggeration. Suppose the homosexual priests' exaggeration is the same: still, if 12.5 percent of American Catholic priests are homosexual, this suggests that proportionately there are more than four times as many homosexual priests as there are homosexuals in the male population as a whole.

Another study, conducted by a married former priest who is a psychotherapist and based on treatment records of and interviews with more than 1,500 priests and sexual partners of priests, estimates that 20 percent of American priests have homosexual tendencies and that half of those 20 percent are (homo)sexually active.[16] Some other estimates are similar.[17] Some are higher: "Estimates of the proportion of Catholic priests who are gay run from 20 percent to as high as 40 percent."[18] The chairman of Notre Dame's theology department, writing in the distinguished Catholic magazine *Commonweal*, asked: "Do homosexual bishops give preference, consciously or not, to gay candidates for choice pastorates and diocesan positions?"[19] Estimates of the number of seminarians who are homosexual run as high as 70 percent.[20]

Three final points about homosexual clergy:

1. The more tolerant of homosexuals a society is, the smaller will be the fraction of priests who are homosexual, because the benefit in being able to allay suspicions arising from bachelorhood will be smaller. Moreover, tolerance is apt to bring with it awareness that many priests are homosexual, and the greater that awareness, the less effective the priesthood will be as a place to hide. This analysis implies that allowing priests to marry would reduce the number of homosexual priests at the same time that it increased the number of heterosexual ones.

2. The analysis in Chapter 5 of the effect of urbanization on homosexuality implies that the number of homosexual priests may continue to grow even

16. A. W. Richard Sipe, *A Secret World: Sexuality and the Search for Celibacy* 133 (1990).

17. Robert Nugent, "Homosexuality and Seminary Candidates," in *Homosexuality in the Priesthood and the Religious Life* 200, 203 (Jeannine Gramick ed. 1989); Andrew Greeley, "Bishops Paralyzed over Heavily Gay Priesthood," *National Catholic Reporter*, November 10, 1989, 13. Sipe, note 16 above, at 132, quotes some higher estimates. For a glimpse of clerical homosexuality in a major archdiocese, see Bill Kenkelen, "For Philly's Gay Priests, Life in the Shadows: Some Clergy Live Straight by Day and Gay by Night," *National Catholic Reporter*, October 5, 1990, 5.

18. Paul Wilkes, "The Hands That Would Shape Our Souls," 266 *Atlantic Monthly* 59, 80 (December 1990). See also Jason Berry, "Homosexuality in Priesthood Said to Run High," *National Catholic Reporter*, February 27, 1987, 1.

19. Richard P. McBrien, "Homosexuality & the Priesthood: Questions We Can't Keep in the Closet," *Commonweal*, June 19, 1987, 380.

20. Jason Berry, "Seminaries Seen to Spawn Gay Priesthood," *National Catholic Reporter*, March 6, 1987, 20. According to an article on AIDS testing for priests and seminarians (now common in the United States), the incidence of AIDS in the priesthood is at least twenty-seven times that in the general population. Rose Marie Arce and David Firestone, "Church Deals with AIDS—Among Priests," *New York Newsday*, September 16, 1990, 4 (news section).

though the total number of priests is level or even declining. "As many priests left active ministry, frequently to marry, the relative percentage of homosexuals in the clergy increased. As the relative percentage of homosexuals increased, it seems, more homosexuals were attracted to the Catholic all-male clerical life—precisely because the increased presence of homosexuals was apparent to other homosexuals."[21]

3. Because imprisonment is involuntary and a career in the priesthood is not, we should expect a higher fraction of priests than of prisoners to be homosexual. (Naval service, another example of a sexually segregated institution, sometimes is involuntary but more often is voluntary.) It is true that since the deprivation of heterosexual opportunities is less costly to a homosexual than to a heterosexual, the cost of prison should, other things being equal, be lower to homosexuals; hence the cost of crime should be lower to them; hence we should expect a disproportionate number of them to be in prison. But other things are not equal. Homosexuals may anticipate being mistreated by other inmates. (How many women would want to be thrown into male prisons?) And since homosexuals tend to be above average in education and income, characteristics negatively related to the propensity to commit crimes, any slight decrement in the costs of imprisonment and hence in deterrence is likely to be offset by an increment in the opportunity costs of crime, including the reduction in legitimate income that is brought about by being imprisoned. I know of no evidence that homosexuals form a disproportionate fraction of the male prison population, and let us assume they do not. They do appear to form a disproportionate fraction of the celibate clerical population. Nevertheless, the number of homosexual *acts* may well be less in a monastery, convent, seminary, or other Roman Catholic clerical community than in a prison of equal size, because the Church strongly disapproves of such acts. Thus economic analysis—so often criticized as reductive in a bad sense—suggests that two phenomena often grouped together indiscriminately as examples of homosexuality in all-male institutions are significantly different phenomena.

There may be another reason for the generally broader tolerance of homosexuality in Catholic than in Protestant cultures. The Catholic nations are for the most part in southern Europe and the Protestant nations in the north, and marriages in the northern nations in general, and England in particular—traditionally the society most hostile to homosexuals—are more likely to be companionate than marriages in the southern nations. England was the pioneer in companionate marriage,[22] although it did not invent the practice.

21. Berry, note 18 above, at 16.
22. Lawrence Stone, *The Family, Sex and Marriage in England 1500–1800* 543–545 (1977); Jean-Louis Flandrin, *Families in Former Times: Kinship, Household and Sexuality* 167–169 (1979); Niklas Luhmann, *Love as Passion: The Codification of Intimacy* 130–131 (1986);

There are strong hints of it in the Bible, beginning with the story of Adam and Eve,[23] and in the world of classical antiquity a movement in its favor had been urged by a number of intellectuals and had made progress during the Roman Empire. The hints, the movement, received the encouragement of the Church.[24] But noncompanionate marriage (often an arranged marriage between an adolescent girl and a much older man) remained common—probably dominant—for many centuries. Even today, macho attitudes, which celebrate the double standard and encourage the sequestration of girls and married women, belief in women's inferiority, and the ready substitution of adolescent boys for young women as sexual objects, undermine companionate marriage in the Latin cultures of the Mediterranean littoral and South America.

Companionate marriage and the abolition of monasteries (another legacy of the English Reformation) created pressure for the emergence of an overt homosexual subculture, which in turn created a sense of the homosexual as profoundly different from the heterosexual, a perception that invites hostility and discrimination. A traditional charge against homosexuals is that they are selfish, narcissistic, because unwilling to make the effort required to establish an intimate relationship with a woman. Such a charge would have little resonance in a society of noncompanionate marriage—a society in which no man tries to establish such a relationship with a woman. In this and other ways noncompanionate marriage fosters tolerant attitudes—even outright obliviousness[25]—toward homosexuality. Today the culture that most celebrates companionate marriage, in succession to England, is the United States; and it may be the Western nation least tolerant of homosexuals.

Homosexual activity is more likely to be punished in a society of companionate marriage than in one of noncompanionate marriage not only because

---

Roderick Phillips, *Putting Asunder: A History of Divorce in Western Society* 354–358 (1988); Edmund Leites, "The Duty to Desire: Love, Friendship, and Sexuality in Some Puritan Theories of Marriage," 15 *Journal of Social History* 383 (1982). On the contrasting situation in France, see William F. Edmiston, *Diderot and the Family: A Conflict of Nature and Law* 5–6 (1985); Charles Donahue, Jr., "The Canon Law on the Formation of Marriage and Social Practice in the Later Middle Ages," 8 *Journal of Family History* 144 (1983). Companionate marriage was a middle-class innovation, since the aristocracy was preoccupied with alliance marriages, which are noncompanionate, and the poor lacked the privacy and autonomy required to create and nurture a companionate relationship. John R. Gillis, *For Better, for Worse: British Marriages, 1600 to the Present* (1985), esp. 13–14.

23. Christopher N. L. Brooke, *The Medieval Idea of Marriage*, ch. 2 (1989).

24. Michael M. Sheehan, "Choice of Marriage Partner in the Middle Ages: Development and Mode of Application of a Theory of Marriage," 1 *Studies in Medieval and Renaissance History* 1 (1978), esp. 7–8.

25. Weeks, note 5 above, at 101–102; Antony Copley, *Sexual Moralities in France, 1780–1980: New Ideas on the Family, Divorce, and Homosexuality: An Essay on Moral Change*, ch. 1 (1989).

it is more anomalous in the former but also because it is more threatening. Even the predominantly heterosexual married man may be tempted at times by the pretty boy. The more society insists on male sexual restraint, the more concerned it will be with any form of nonmarital sexual activity. This may help explain what Chapter 5 described as an anomaly—that the penetrator in an act of sodomy was likely to be punished more heavily than the person penetrated, even though the latter is more likely to be the "real" homosexual. The real homosexual is indeed the greater anomaly in a society of companionate marriage because he is unfit for such marriage; but the opportunistic homosexual is the greater danger, for, as a heterosexual, he is an actual or potential partner in a companionate marriage.

Companionate marriage fosters puritanical attitudes generally, so we should not be surprised by the puritanical strain in the Anglo-American sexual culture. A husband's adultery becomes for the first time offensive, because it undermines love and trust and reduces the amount of time that he spends with his wife, which are elements of companionate but not of noncompanionate marriage. The patronizing of prostitutes by married men is a form of adultery, and so also becomes offensive. Moreover, as a male-female relationship signally lacking in love or trust—a relationship characterized, indeed, by the impersonality of a spot market—prostitution is incongruous in a society that has turned its back on the businesslike model of noncompanionate marriage. But because prostitution is a substitute for forms of extramarital sex that are more threatening to companionate marriage, and thus is a complement to as well as a substitute for such marriage, the effect of a social commitment to companionate marriage is not to condemn outright but to problematize what in a society of noncompanionate marriage would be an unproblematic institution.

Puritanism responds to the fundamental tension in companionate marriage, noted earlier, between encouraging and repressing female sexual pleasure. If it is repressed, which was the tendency of Catholic doctrine, the bonds of marriage fray. But they may also fray if it is encouraged, as women become more receptive to sexual opportunities outside of marriage and men therefore take redoubled steps to prevent adultery. The Islamic solution is to combine sequestration of married women and severe punishments for adultery with a positive view of female sexual pleasure: purdah rather than prudery. The Puritan solution substitutes for physical sequestration an emphasis on the inculcation of moral values. Like the Jews and Muslims, but unlike the Catholics before them or the Victorians after them, the Puritans did not systematically disparage female sexuality. They were not enthusiastic about it, but the important thing to them was to confine its expression to marriage. They did, however, reprobate passion (what I called in Chapter 5 infatuation), and this contributed to a striking contrast between English and French attitudes. The English saw passion as a spur to adultery and therefore as a threat to marriage. The French agreed in associating passion with adultery but were less troubled, because adultery is not as serious a danger to noncompanionate marriage as it is to companionate marriage, and the French lagged behind the English in moving from noncompanionate to companionate marriage (see note 22).

Christian sex ethics are related, via companionate marriage, to the status of women. If that status is very low—if women are deemed simple breeders and drudges, uneducated and uneducable—they will not seem fit to participate with men in a relationship, such as companionate marriage, that is built on love and trust. Christianity tried to raise the status of women above its level in the pagan societies of Greece and Rome. It did this in a number of ways. One—a particularly sharp break with the pagan past[26]—was the forbidding of infanticide, which had been directed mainly at female infants. (Yet we know from Chapter 5 that female infanticide, by reducing the number of women, may increase the welfare of the surviving women by making them scarce.) Another was the forbidding of divorce, which in Greek and Roman society had usually been divorce at the whim of the husband, and involved no alimony, resulting in the creation of a mass of destitute abandoned women.[27] Moreover, the husband kept the children, and the divorced wife did not even have visitation rights. It is true that if the wife had brought a dowry to the marriage, the husband was obliged to return it to her (or at least devote it to her support) if he divorced her without, and possibly even with, fault on her part.[28] But since few women had substantial dowries, it was only a thin upper crust of married women who enjoyed a secure status.

26. William L. Langer, "Infanticide: A Historical Survey," 1 *History of Childhood Quarterly: The Journal of Psychohistory* 353, 354–355 (1974). According to Donald Engels, "The Problem of Female Infanticide in the Greco-Roman World," 75 *Classical Philology* 112, 120 (1980), however, in classical antiquity "a rate of 10 percent of female births killed per year would be highly improbable, and the rate almost certainly never exceeded more than a few percent of female births in any era."

27. Today's no-fault divorce—effectively divorce at will—has had rather similar effects. "The major economic result of the divorce law revolution is the systematic impoverishment of divorced women and their children." Lenore J. Weitzman, *The Divorce Revolution: The Unexpected Social and Economic Consequences for Women and Children in America* xiv (1985). See also Lloyd Cohen, "Marriage, Divorce, and Quasi Rents; Or, 'I Gave Him the Best Years of My Life,' " 16 *Journal of Legal Studies* 267 (1987), esp. 277 and n. 30. Plus ça change, plus c'est la même chose.

28. Sarah B. Pomeroy, *Goddesses, Whores, Wives, and Slaves: Women in Classical Antiquity* 63 (1975); Roger Just, *Women in Athenian Law and Life* 73–74 (1989); David M. Schaps, *Economic Rights of Women in Ancient Greece*, ch. 6 (1979); Alan Watson, *The Law of Persons in the Later Roman Republic* 66 n. 3 (1967); W. W. Buckland, *A Textbook of Roman Law from Augustus to Justinian* 108–111 (2d ed. 1932); and references in Chapter 5, note 54. Compensation of a divorced wife is a fundamental feature of Jewish marriage law. Louis M. Epstein, *The Jewish Marriage Contract: A Study in the Status of the Woman in Jewish Law* (1927); Reuven Yaron, *Introduction to the Law of the Aramaic Papyri*, ch. 5 (1961). As under Greek and Roman law,

The Church further enhanced the status of women by encouraging men to regard them as sisters[29] rather than just as sex objects and breeders; by (a related point) making spinsterhood a thinkable and in fact highly respectable status, thus enlarging women's options; by forbidding the husband as well as the wife to commit adultery; and by requiring both spouses' consent to marriage while *not* requiring (as under Roman law) the consent of their fathers as well.[30]

Much of this program of legal and social reform remained, for centuries, aspiration rather than accomplishment;[31] much of it reflected and continued tendencies already visible in Roman culture; and it coexisted with a persistent and at times virulent hostility to women. But the measures I have described were, for their time, feminist measures, and the Church's efforts to encourage companionate marriage went hand in hand with them.

A woman who is interesting to her husband will also be interesting to other men—and more available to them, since sequestration is inconsistent with companionability. So the elevation of woman to fit companion for man must, if men are to be secure in their paternity, be accompanied by a general elevation of sexual morality, and more specifically by an increase in male sexual morality, since it is men who threaten a wife's chastity. On this view, the prudishness of Christian sex ethics (tempered by the condoning of prostitution as an essential safety valve for those bachelors who could not be absorbed into the priesthood) need not be regarded as a given in the analysis of the sexual policy of the Church. It may have been a consequence of

---

the husband was required to return the wife's dowry. Epstein at 196–197. But this assumes a dowry; any compensation upon divorce presupposes that the guilty spouse possesses or controls property. And while the husband could, under traditional Jewish law, divorce his wife at will, the wife could not divorce her husband on any ground. Epstein at 194–196, 200.

29. Pat Caplan, "Celibacy as a Solution? Mahatma Gandhi and *Brachmacharya*," in *The Cultural Construction of Sexuality* 271 (Caplan ed. 1987), describes a similar strategy used by Gandhi in an attempt to raise the status of Indian women.

30. Buckland, note 28 above, at 113; J. A. C. Thomas, *Textbook of Roman Law* 420–421 (1976); John T. Noonan, Jr., "Marriage in the Middle Ages: I—Power to Choose," 4 *Viator: Medieval and Renaissance Studies* 419 (1973); Brooke, note 23 above, at 129–130. Female celibacy, religious or secular, is a substitute for female infanticide. Mildred Dickemann, "Female Infanticide, Reproductive Strategies, and Social Stratification: A Preliminary Model," in *Evolutionary Biology and Human Social Behavior: An Anthropological Perspective* 321, 348–349, 353–357 (Napoleon A. Chagnon and William Irons eds. 1979). It reduces the expected dowry cost to parents and also reduces the rate of population increase.

31. A. H. M. Jones, *The Later Roman Empire 284–602: A Social Economic and Administrative Survey,* vol. 2, 970–979 (1964); Noonan, note 30 above; Charles Donahue, Jr., "The Policy of Alexander the Third's Consent Theory of Marriage," *Proceedings of the Fourth International Congress of Medieval Canon Law* 251 (Stephan Kuttner ed. 1976); Mary Ann Glendon, *The Transformation of Family Law: State, Law, and Family in the United States and Western Europe* 16–28 (1989).

companionate marriage, which in turn may have been a consequence of the Church's efforts to raise the status of women above its level in pagan society. Why the Church made such efforts is taken up briefly in the next chapter.

Swedish Permissiveness

If companionate marriage makes homosexuality for the first time highly problematic, how—to turn to my third case study, which incidentally will introduce us to the normative side of the economic analysis of sex—to explain the exceptional tolerance of homosexuality, and of other offenses to Christian sexual morality, in modern Sweden, and Scandinavia generally? The Scandinavian cultures are the antithesis of the macho—hence rather tolerant of homosexual behavior—cultures of southern Europe. Surely, few marriages in Sweden, to which I shall confine my discussion, are noncompanionate. If anything, educational and occupational parity between men and women, a parity more nearly achieved in Sweden, it appears, than in any other country, could be expected to make marriage more companionate, while at the same time reducing some of the more "businesslike" gains from marriage, such as division of labor and resulting specialization of task.

The first thing to note is the decline of religion in Sweden. A 1981 Gallup Poll asked people in fifteen nations (all European, except the United States, Japan, and South Africa) to rate, on a scale of 1 to 10, how important God was in their lives. Sweden ranked at the bottom, with a score of 3.99. Denmark was the second lowest, Japan the third lowest. The United States was second from the top after South Africa, with a score of 8.21, slightly higher than the Republic of Ireland.[32] The survey also inquired directly about belief in God, but for some reason only the Danish and not the Swedish response is reported. In contrast to the 71 percent of Americans who believe in God, only 26 percent of Danes do, and it seems unlikely that the Swedish percentage is higher.[33] If Christianity is fading in Sweden, we would not expect Christian

---

32. Gallup Report no. 236, May 1985, 50.

33. Id. at 53. See also Neil Elliott, *Sensuality in Scandinavia*, ch. 5 (1970); David Popenoe, *Disturbing the Nest: Family Change and Decline in Modern Societies* 138 (1988); Theodore Caplow, "Contrasting Trends in European and American Religion," 46 *Sociological Analysis* 101, 102 (1985); Lynn D. Nelson, "Religion and Foreign Aid Provision: A Comparative Analysis of Advanced Market Nations," 49 *Sociological Analysis* 49S, 54S (1988). As early as 1970 it was estimated that only 10 percent of Swedes attended church on Sunday, compared to almost 50 percent of Americans. Richard F. Tomasson, *Sweden: Prototype of Modern Society* 76 (1970). Tomasson reports that a survey conducted in 1968 placed Sweden at the very bottom in belief in God among Western nations. Tomasson at 78. Another European nation known for its liberal attitudes toward homosexuals—the Netherlands—has been said to have the largest percentage of "official nonbelievers" in the Western world. R. W. Ramsay, P. J. Heringa, and I. Boorsma, "A

objections to "unnatural" sexual practices to be highly influential. We would want to look elsewhere for the causes of Swedish sexual attitudes. The analogy is to usury laws in the United States. No one in this country believes any more that lending money at interest is a sin; that piece of traditional Christianity is dead; so we must look elsewhere—to interest-group politics, economic ignorance, or whatever—to explain the persistence of laws that place a ceiling on interest rates. Similarly, we must look elsewhere than to Christianity for reasons, if any, that might lead Swedes to disapprove of homosexuality and other deviant sexual practices or preferences. There have been ideologies of hostility to homosexuality that owed nothing to Christianity—notably Nazism—but none of them has any foothold in Sweden. Socialism and pacifism are strong in Sweden, but, with an important exception to be noted shortly, these ideologies do not appear to have a sexual-policy component.

We are left to speculate that Sweden probably does not attempt to suppress a particular form of sexual activity unless there is a practical reason to do so. To Swedes—unlike devout Catholics, for whom sex is a subject charged with profound moral significance—sex is much like eating or driving, activities that, subject to occasional deflection by interest-group pressures, a society regulates (whether directly through law or indirectly through social attitudes) only to the extent that they endanger third parties or give rise to other pragmatic or utilitarian grounds for regulation. It is difficult to find compelling practical reasons—even in the AIDS epidemic, as we shall see—for trying to stamp out homosexual relations between consenting adults (the definition of adult here is, of course, tricky) in a society such as that of modern Sweden. Conceivably there is a negative effect on the birth rate if society does not herd its homosexual men into marriage, if at the same time (a big if) heterosexual men are prevented from impregnating more than one woman apiece. But the effect must surely be trivial. I have never seen a demographic study that so much as considered the possibility that social attitudes toward homosexuality might measurably affect the birth rate.[34] Even the French, preoccupied as they were with their low birth rate and willing to blame it on everything from keeping poodles to riding bicycles,[35] did not think to blame it on homosexuality.[36] And, although the Swedish birth rate is very low, the birth rate in the United States is also very low, despite the fact that there is more hostility to homo-

---

Case Study: Homosexuality in the Netherlands," in *Understanding Homosexuality: Its Biological and Psychological Bases* 121, 123 (J. A. Loraine ed. 1974).

34. With the exception of Malthus' glancing reference to Turkish sodomy, which I remarked in Chapter 1.

35. Joseph J. Spengler, *France Faces Depopulation: Postlude Edition, 1936–1976* 135 n. 1 (1979).

36. In contrast, France did pass laws in the 1920s against contraception and abortion in order to increase the birth rate (id. at 127, 240 n. 48), as did communist Romania in the 1960s.

sexuality in this country. Moreover, Sweden can build up its population to any level it wants by reducing barriers to immigration (just as we can). Anyway there is no indication that Swedes want a larger population, or indeed view with dismay a possible fall in population.[37] But the deeper objection to the demographic argument is that Swedish women do not want to marry, or form any other type of sexual relationship, with homosexual men.

It is arguable that unless homosexuality is repressed, adolescent boys who are teetering on the edge of the homosexual precipice will be pushed over. The argument implies that societies that tolerate homosexuality have more homosexuals—real, not opportunistic, ones—than do intolerant societies. Since no one knows the homosexual population of any society, past or present, this hypothesis cannot be falsified. Nevertheless, there is no evidence to support. it. The formation of homosexual preference, at least in males, appears to be deeply rooted in genetic, hormonal, and (or) developmental factors unlikely to be offset by purely social influences.[38]

Finally there is the question of AIDS,[39] and of venereal disease more generally. Infectious disease is a standard example of the economist's concept of externality. If I refuse to be vaccinated against smallpox and later catch the disease, the costs of my refusal are not borne by me alone; they are also borne by those who catch smallpox from me. Hence vaccinating me will confer benefits that I may not take into account in deciding whether to be vaccinated, namely the benefits to other people. To force me to provide those benefits, society makes vaccination compulsory. Even before AIDS, venereal disease was far more common among homosexual than heterosexual men,[40] primarily because homosexual men tend to have far more sex partners.

---

37. Popenoe, note 33 above, at 150; C. Alison McIntosh, "Low Fertility and Liberal Democracy in Western Europe," 7 *Population and Development Review* 181, 184–187, 200–201 (1981). Before the Second World War, however, the declining birth rate in Sweden, as in other European countries, was considered worrisome. Allan Carlson, *The Swedish Experiment in Family Politics: The Myrdals and the Interwar Population Crisis* (1990).

38. See discussions in Chapters 4, 11, 14, and 15 of this volume.

39. For background, see John Mills and Henry Masur, "AIDS-Related Infections," 263 *Scientific American* 50 (August 1990); *AIDS: Etiology, Diagnosis, Treatment and Prevention* (Vincent T. DeVita, Samuel Hellman, and Steven A. Rosenberg eds. 1988). The financial dimension is well discussed in Henry T. Greely, "AIDS and the American Health Care Financing System," 51 *University of Pittsburgh Law Review* 73 (1989).

40. Alan P. Bell and Martin S. Weinberg, *Homosexualities: A Study of Diversity among Men and Women* 118 (1978); D. J. West, *Homosexuality Re-Examined* 228–233 (1977); A. J. King, "Homosexuality and Venereal Disease," in *Understanding Homosexuality*, note 33 above, at 187, 189–192; Arno Karlen, *Sexuality and Homosexuality: A New View* 197 (1971); Kingsley Davis, "Sexual Behavior," in *Contemporary Social Problems* 313, 358–359 (Robert K. Merton and Robert Nisbet eds., 3d ed. 1971). All these works predate the AIDS epidemic.

One should not jump to the conclusion that sexual promiscuity is inherently unhealthy. Although there was venereal disease in the ancient world, permissive societies such as Greece and

It might be argued that since the homosexual himself has a compelling self-interest in avoiding infection by a fatal disease, and since it is easy for him to reduce the danger of contracting AIDS from homosexual intercourse to a very low level by using a condom, the AIDS epidemic provides only a weak ground for attempts to limit the amount of homosexual activity. Indeed, it could be argued that AIDS provides a weaker ground for limiting homosexual activity than nonlethal venereal diseases do, because a lethal venereal disease gives a homosexual a stronger incentive to protect himself and by protecting himself to protect his partner (and his partner's other partners as well) than nonlethal venereal diseases such as syphilis (today) and gonorrhea do. A condom is more valuable to the user the deadlier the disease it prevents. Against this it can be argued that the homosexual who knows or strongly suspects that he is already HIV-positive has a much-reduced incentive to use a condom. True; but the incentive of his partner is not reduced, unless the partner is HIV-positive too—in which event unshielded sex between the two will not increase the incidence of AIDS significantly.

A further point of considerable theoretical interest is that, with the exceptions—not that they are unimportant—of persons who contract AIDS from their parents, or through a contaminated blood supply, or from persons who are unaware of or conceal the fact that they are carriers, AIDS, unlike the usual waterborne or airborne infectious disease, is spread through *voluntary* contact. Self-protection is therefore a more feasible preventive than in the case of other infectious diseases. This means that the element of externality that is the traditional economic justification for compulsory vaccination and other public health measures is attenuated in the case of venereal disease (though not eliminated, since self-protection is not costless). The curious implication is that the amount of such disease is likely to be closer to the economic optimum than in the case of diseases transmitted through the air or the water supply.

Even if we concede (as I think we must, given the sheer magnitude of the AIDS epidemic and the dangers that it poses to persons who do not knowingly assume the risk of being infected by the virus) that AIDS presents a compelling case for public intervention, it is by no means clear that the proper form of such intervention is to reinstate the Puritan sex ethic—if we assume, realistically, that this could not be done with 100 percent success. (If it could be, venereal disease would essentially disappear.) One effect of a revival that was

---

Rome seem not to have been ravaged by it, and the first fatal such disease—syphilis—did not appear in the Eastern Hemisphere until the end of the fifteenth century, having, in all probability (though not all scholars agree), been brought back to the Old World from the New by Columbus' sailors. Edgar Gregersen, *Sexual Practices: The Story of Human Sexuality* 305–306 (1983); Claude Quétel, *History of Syphilis,* ch. 2 (1990), esp. 38; Danielle Jacquart and Claude Thomasset, *Sexuality and Medicine in the Middle Ages* 177–178 (1988); Charles Clayton Dennie, *A History of Syphilis,* ch. 6 (1962).

only partially successful would be to reduce knowledge about sex, including knowledge about venereal disease and the use of condoms in preventing it. Another would be to discourage homosexuals from reporting venereal disease to public health authorities. A third might be, by discouraging voluntary nonmarital sex, to increase the amount of prostitution, and a fourth to encourage anal intercourse (which spreads the AIDS virus more readily than genital intercourse), a practice the demand for which is increased by the sequestering of young women (which fosters opportunistic homosexuality) and the restriction of access to contraceptives and abortion. A fifth effect would be to increase the fraction of male homosexuals who marry, thereby endangering women and children. A sixth would be to deflect energy and attention from practical measures of prevention and control to futile preaching of sexual abstinence. All but the last two factors have been found to be instrumental in the spread of AIDS,[41] and they are (along with the last two) more common in the United States than in Sweden—which has a much lower incidence of AIDS despite its greater sexual permissiveness.[42] A climate of sexual tolerance may actually retard rather than promote the spread of venereal diseases in general and AIDS in particular.

A larger point is that, terrible as the AIDS epidemic is, direct public regulation of sexual activity is unlikely to be the cost-justified response to it. If the heterosexual community were being ravished by some equally terrible venereal plague, no one would suggest that heterosexual intercourse should be banned and persons desiring children remitted to artificial insemination. Some might urge that people be encouraged to abstain from sex until marriage and then to refrain from all extramarital sex; but few would think it feasible, or even desirable in principle, to embody these desiderata in laws carrying sufficiently heavy sanctions, and enforced with sufficient energy, to eliminate nonmarital sex. Parallel regulation of the sexual activity of homosexuals seems no more feasible; and if it is correct that homosexuals cannot be converted into happy heterosexuals, then efforts to repress homosexual sex would, to the extent they were effective, impose enormous disutility on homosexuals.

41. See, for example, Nancy M. Flowers, "The Spread of AIDS in Rural Brazil," in *AIDS: AAAS Symposia Papers 1988* 159 (Ruth Kulstad ed. 1988); Richard G. Parker, "Sexual Culture and AIDS Education in Urban Brazil," id. at 169. (Anal intercourse is an old method of contraception. See, for example, James Woycke, *Birth Control in Germany, 1871–1933* 10–11 [1988].) The unusually high level of homosexual-induced AIDS among American blacks may be due to a lack of knowledge that is caused in part by the fact that homosexuality is even more of a taboo subject among blacks than among whites. Marshall H. Becker and Jill G. Joseph, "AIDS and Behavioral Change to Reduce Risk: A Review," 78 *American Journal of Public Health* 394, 405–406 (1988).

42. In 1987 there were 73 new cases of AIDS in Sweden. Appendix 1 to *AIDS: AAAS Symposia Papers*, note 41 above, at 412. The corresponding figure for the United States was 21,846. Id., appendix 2 at 416. The Swedish figure represents an incidence of fewer than 9 per million, compared to 89 per million for the United States.

Tolerance of homosexuals is only one feature that distinguishes the Swedish approach to sex from that of less permissive societies. There is no cult of virginity in Sweden, so no stigma is attached to premarital sexual intercourse even when engaged in by teenagers. For reasons that are thoroughly practical, the Swedes do not want unmarried teenage girls to have babies, but this is effectively discouraged by intensive sex education inside and outside the home and by widespread dissemination of female as well as male contraceptives to teenagers. These measures lower the cost of effective contraception, and the result is that although the average age of first sexual intercourse for girls is a year younger in Sweden than in the United States,[43] the rate of teenage pregnancy is little more than a third as high as in this country.[44] Hence the abortion rate is also much lower,[45] even though abortions are cheaper for Swedish women because many U.S. states, in part reflecting strictures in federal law, will not allow public funds to be used to pay for abortion.[46] By a combination of contraception and (some) abortions, the teenage birth rate in Sweden has been driven far below that in our own country.

This is not to say that the *nonmarital* birth rate, as distinct from the *teenage* birth rate, is low. It is very high—higher than in the United States. This is because marriage confers relatively few benefits on Swedish women. The extensive system of social welfare (including publicly financed day care, long and well-paid maternity leaves, and much else besides),[47] which does not distinguish between married and unmarried mothers, emancipates women from dependence on men. The taxpayer has in effect assumed the protective role formerly played by the husband. The high rate of nonmarital births in Sweden is a result of choice, not accident, as is indicated by the fact that the percentage of *unwanted* births is less than half what it is in the United States.[48]

Although Sweden is generally and correctly considered a more socialistic

43. Charles F. Westoff, "Perspectives on Nuptiality and Fertility," in *Below-Replacement Fertility in Industrial Societies: Causes, Consequences, Policies* 155, 168 (Kingsley Davis et al. eds. 1987).

44. Popenoe, note 33 above, at 290.

45. For example, for ages 15 to 19 the abortion rate in Sweden is 40 percent of what it is in the United States. Computed from Elise F. Jones et al., *Pregnancy, Contraception, and Family Planning Services in Industrialized Countries* 241 (1989) (app. B). The poverty of sex education in the United States is noted in id. at 110–113.

46. Id. at 96.

47. Popenoe, note 33 above, at 202–206; Siv Gustafsson, "Equal Opportunity Policies in Sweden," in *Sex Discrimination and Equal Opportunity: The Labor Market and Employment Policy* 132 (Günther Schmid and Renate Weitzel eds. 1984); Carolyn Teich Adams and Kathryn Teich Winston, *Mothers at Work: Public Policies in the United States, Sweden, and China* 50–54 (1980).

48. Jones et al., note 45 above, at 243 (app. B.).

society than the United States—and its far more extensive system of child welfare is one indication of the difference—it may in matters related to sex more nearly approximate a free-market society than the United States does. Sex in Sweden is for the most part a sphere of voluntary contracting, like the housing market in the United States, a market far more heavily regulated in Sweden. Sex in the United States is more heavily regulated than in Sweden through laws against sodomy, pornography, and the like, and through more severe punishments for sex crimes, noted in Chapter 3.

But the socialist component in Swedish sex policy should not be ignored. The system of child welfare is not a deliberate effort to alter sexual mores, but it could have that effect. In particular, it could lower the age of sexual initiation for Swedish girls, as well as the marriage rate. We expect the cult of female chastity to be stronger the bigger the role that men play in protecting women and children, since they will be reluctant to play that role unless confident that the children they are protecting are their own. If women do not need male protection for themselves and their children, they do not need to make this concession to male preference.[49] The cost to them of a freer, more active sex life is reduced. Biological differences stressed in Chapter 4 may prevent a complete erasure of the difference in the sexual attitudes of men and women, but the elimination of the social basis of that difference is bound to have some effect, perhaps a very large one.

We can observe parallel phenomena in poor black communities in the United States. Although our system of child welfare is chintzy by Swedish standards, it is reasonably generous for women living in poverty, because their earning capacities are highly limited. What is more, the men in these poor communities, in part because of their own poverty and in part because of the availability to them of multiple sex partners, tend not to be good providers. We should not be surprised that the rate of illegitimate births in these com-

---

49. As the sociologist James Coleman pointed out long ago. "Female Status and Premarital Sexual Codes," 72 *American Journal of Sociology* 217 (1966). For cross-cultural evidence that, indeed, the less significant the male as a family provider, the less restricted female sexual expression will be, see Kenneth W. Eckhardt, "Exchange Theory and Sexual Permissiveness," 6 *Behavior Science Notes; HRAF Quarterly Bulletin* 1, 9–10 (1971). Bear in mind that in Sweden maternity and child assistance is *not* channeled through the father; it goes directly to the mother and therefore emancipates her and her children from dependence on a man. Carlson, note 37 above, at 195, 197. Moreover, day-care fees are proportional to income and therefore, given that almost all Swedish women work, are higher for a married couple than for a single person. Jan Trost, "Married and Unmarried Cohabitation: The Case of Sweden, with Some Comparisons," in *Beyond the Nuclear Family Model: Cross-Cultural Perspectives* 189, 193 (Luis Lenero-Otero ed. 1977). And the filing of joint income tax returns, which in a highly progressive income tax system, such as that of Sweden, confers a tax advantage on married persons, was abolished in 1971. Carlson, note 37 above, at 201; Popenoe, note 33 above, at 148.

munities is comparable to the Swedish rate—in fact higher, perhaps because of the lower sex ratio.

But there is an important difference between Swedish and American welfare policies which helps explain the lower rate of teenage births in Sweden. Swedish maternity and child-care benefits are tied to the mother's employment, giving her an incentive to become established in the job market before having children, and thus raising the average age at which Swedish women start having children.[50] We do not build such an incentive into our welfare system.

That Aid to Families with Dependent Children and other welfare programs in this country that are available to unmarried women and their children (Medicaid is another such program), combined with a minimum wage law that restricts the employment opportunities of young men, foster promiscuity, illegitimacy, or both has long been a staple in the criticism of these programs.[51] The twist the present analysis gives is to perceive in this phenomenon not merely a lower cost of conception, and hence a lower cost of noncontraceptive intercourse, but an invitation to women to change their sexual strategy. In the economic analysis of sex, women surrender their sexual freedom to men not (or not only) out of altruism or biological predisposition, but in exchange for protection from men. If they do not need male protection—if the taxpayer has taken the man's place—they have less reason to surrender their freedom and share control of their children. If the economic role of the father is taken over by the state, "we must expect a complete breakdown of traditional morality, since there will no longer be any reason why a mother should wish the paternity of her child to be indubitable."[52]

50. Gustafsson, note 47 above, at 136; Günther Schmid, "The Political Economy of Labor Market Discrimination: A Theoretical and Comparative Analysis of Sex Discrimination," in *Sex Discrimination and Equal Opportunity,* note 47 above, at 264, 287–289 and tab. 5.

51. See, for example, Arleen Leibowitz, Marvin Eisen, and Winston K. Chow, *Decision-Making in Teenage Pregnancy: An Analysis of Choice* (1980), and Kristin A. Moore, Margaret C. Simms, and Charles L. Betsey, *Choice and Circumstance: Racial Differences in Adolescent Sexuality and Fertility* 110 (1986). There are doubters; see Sandra L. Hofferth, "The Effects of Programs and Policies on Adolescent Pregnancy and Childbearing," in *Risking the Future: Adolescent Sexuality, Pregnancy, and Childbearing,* vol. 2, *Working Papers and Statistical Appendixes* 207, 257–259 (Sandra L. Hofferth and Cheryl D. Hayes eds. 1987), and Daniel R. Vining, Jr., "Illegitimacy and Public Policy," 9 *Population and Development Review* 105 (1983). The fullest and most convincing case that these policies really do foster illegitimacy is presented in Michael S. Bernstam and Peter L. Swan, "The Production of Children as Claims on the State: A Comprehensive Labor Market Approach to Illegitimacy in the United States, 1960–1980" (Working Paper in Economics no. E-86-1, Hoover Institution of Stanford University, January 1986) (forthcoming in *Population and Development Review).* Apparently Hofferth was not aware of this study—and Vining could not have been.

52. Bertrand Russell, *Marriage and Morals* 9 (1929). The idea that the woman in effect offers guarantees of chastity in exchange for the man's protection for her and her (their) children is given a biological formulation in Susan M. Essock-Vitale and Michael T. McGuire, "What 70 Million Years Hath Wrought: Sexual Histories and Reproductive Success of a Random Sample

More than sexual freedom—more even than the control of children—is at stake here. The traditional female role, in which premarital virginity and marital chastity are so emphasized, is an impediment to women's educational and occupational, as well as their sexual, equality. That role entails physical or at least spiritual segregation of women. For the sake of chastity, women "have been kept artificially stupid and therefore uninteresting."[53]

The reader may question my bracketing of premarital virginity with marital chastity. It is obvious why a man should want his wife to be faithful; if she is not, the children she bears may not be his, and his reproductive strategy will be thwarted.[54] It is less obvious why he should want her to be a virgin at marriage. Of course, if she is not a virgin she may be pregnant by another man, but that concern could be dispelled by quarantining the bride for a couple of months before marriage. The point rather is that virginity is predictive of chastity. The woman who succumbed to temptation before marriage is more likely to succumb after than one who did not, and if she does, she may become pregnant by a man who is not her husband. At least, men may be primed to fear this behavior, for we know that in nature the female will sometimes have an incentive to cuckold her mate.[55] By demanding that his bride be a virgin, the man reduces the cost of monitoring her sexual behavior after marriage. One might even ascribe to the cult of virginity the function of enabling potentially promiscuous women to be identified, eliminated from the pool of marriageable women, and shunted into prostitution. But in a society in which the vast majority of women are sexually active before marriage, virginity is not a useful screening device, and the cult of virginity will disappear.

This analysis should help us to understand why prostitutes have usually been drawn from the ranks of women who lost their virginity before they reached marriageable age.[56] Some of these women may simply like sex with

---

of American Women," in *Human Reproductive Behavior: A Darwinian Perspective* 221, 229 (Laura Betzig, Monique Borgerhoff Mulder, and Paul Turke eds. 1988).

53. Russell, note 52 above, at 27. A point neither new nor male. See Mary Wollstonecraft, *A Vindication of the Rights of Woman* (1792).

54. There is nothing modern about this insight, either. See Just, note 28 above, at 67–68.

55. Current research into this question is well described in Natalie Angier, "Mating for Life? It's Not for the Birds or the Bees: Among Animals, Infidelity is Rife and Females Often Have the Wandering Eye," *New York Times,* August 21, 1990, B5.

56. Jennifer James and Peter Paul Vitaliano, "Multivariate Analysis of Entrance into Prostitution," in *Medical Sexology* 181 (Romano Forleo and Willy Pasini eds. 1978); Jacques Rossiaud, *Medieval Prostitution* 29–32 (1988). The fact that Muslim women appear to be disproportionately represented among Lebanese prostitutes has been ascribed in part to the fact that loss of virginity before marriage is a more serious transgression among Muslims than among Christians. Samir Khalaf, "Correlates of Prostitution: Some Popular Errors and Misconceptions," 4 *Journal of Sex Research* 147, 160 (1968).

many partners. But for most a more plausible explanation for their choice of career is that their opportunities in the marriage market have been reduced. We can expect that as premarital virginity becomes rarer, not only will prostitution become less common; prostitutes will be less distinct in background and attributes from other women.

In the combination found in poor black sections of our cities of a low ratio of men to women and a high rate of illegitimate births made possible by female independence from men, there is an echo of polygamy. The limiting factor in polygamy is the cost of supporting multiple wives, and is normally prohibitive if the wives do not work. But suppose that, while indeed not working, the wives are supported by the state. They are then like women in agricultural societies, who combine motherhood with agricultural labor that yields them real (not necessarily pecuniary) income. Polygamy is common in African tribal society in part because each wife of a polygamist works as well as breeds, thus reducing the cost to the polygamist.[57] The sexual freedom of Scandinavian women is sometimes explained by reference to the fact that the Scandinavian societies remained agrarian, and particularly fishing, societies until well after the rest of northern Europe had industrialized. In fishing communities in particular, wives are left on their own much of the time, shouldering greater responsibility for household management and therefore becoming more independent of men than women in other societies are.[58]

As the limiting case we can imagine a society in which women do all the work and the only male function is insemination; such a society would require very few men, except insofar as the society wished to preserve genetic diversity. Perhaps in our poorest black neighborhoods we are approaching this model of the dispensable male,[59] in which a few men impregnate many women because they do not have to support the women or their children in order to be reasonably assured that the children, or at least some substantial fraction of them, will survive to maturity. The women are as it were married to the state; their illegitimate children are, in an economic sense, the state's children. Where the analogy breaks down is with the suggestion that a few men monopolize most of the women. No doubt they would like to, or at least their

---

57. See references in Chapter 9. For a rigorous demonstration that the demand for polygamy is positively related to the value of women's contribution to family income, see Gary S. Becker, *A Treatise on the Family* 89–104 (enlarged ed. 1991).

58. Tomasson, note 33 above, at 193–194; Adams and Winston, note 47 above, at 112–113; Kingsley Davis, "Wives and Work: The Sex Role Revolution and Its Consequences," 10 *Population and Development Review* 397, 402–403 (1984).

59. On which see Clyde W. Franklin II, "Surviving the Institutional Decimation of Black Males: Causes, Consequences, and Intervention," in *The Making of Masculinities: The New Men's Studies* 155 (Harry Brod ed. 1987).

genes would like them to; but with polygamy forbidden and women emancipated, they cannot.

These examples are extreme but reflect a trend that is general. With the rise in women's job opportunities, the economic dependence of women on men has diminished. The result has been a change in the female sexual strategy. No longer is the male offer of protection as valuable to the female, so women are less willing to provide the commodity used to purchase that protection—female chastity. The decline of female chastity is, indeed, the most dramatic manifestation of the sexual revolution.[60]

How should men be expected to react to the shift in the female sexual strategy? That shift is potentially very costly to them. In the limit, it implies a world in which men do not know who their children are, let alone have any rights of access to them, the male's sole role in such a world being that of inseminator—and this without consideration of the additional opportunities for women to pursue an independent sexual strategy that are created by artificial insemination. One response might be a redistribution of resources within marriage: wives, quite apart from their market productivity, would receive a larger share of household income to compensate them for giving up their option of pursuing an independent reproductive strategy. Or the state might expand the custody rights of divorced or unmarried fathers, as indeed has happened in Sweden.[61] Note the interesting prediction of this analysis: women's full income—the sum of their own market earnings and of contributions in cash and services from men—can be expected to increase over time faster than their market income is increasing.

Four factors, however, cut the other way. First, we can expect that as women's income rises, courts will make lower awards of alimony in cases of divorce. It is no surprise that Swedish courts rarely award alimony.[62]

Second, for women living with men and enjoying a benefit from the man's income by virtue of joint consumption within the household, an increase in taxes on men's (as well as women's) incomes to pay for day care and other woman-oriented welfare programs will reduce women's consumption along with men's.[63]

Third, with the substitution of government for the father, we can expect government to assume regulatory functions within the household that were

---

60. John De Lamater and Patricia MacCorquodale, *Premarital Sexuality: Attitudes, Relationships, Behavior* 230 (1979); Carlson, note 37 above, at 200–203.

61. Tomasson, note 33 above, at 172; Adams and Winston, note 47 above, at 225.

62. Adams and Winston, note 47 above, at 225.

63. The economic interdependence of men and women, and the resulting difficulty of redistributing income from men to women, is the theme of my article "An Economic Analysis of Sex Discrimination Laws," 56 *University of Chicago Law Review* 1311 (1989).

formerly left to the family. This has famously occurred in Sweden, where the state vigorously enforces an elaborate set of children's rights against their parents.[64] Thus even such curiosities as Sweden's 1979 law against parents' spanking their children may have an economic rationale!

Fourth, fertility is a female asset, and as women switch the focus of their activities from the home to the market, the value of that asset diminishes. (The decline in Swedish alimony payments—my first point—is a minor symptom.) A man will "pay" a woman qua wife less the fewer the expected number of children of the marriage and the less secure the man's paternity is because the woman is not sequestered, either physically or emotionally. We cannot be certain that the increase in women's market income has exceeded the decrease in their implicit income as mothers, and therefore we cannot be certain that their full income is actually rising. The most thorough study of this question in the United States found that, between 1960 and 1986, women's economic well-being did not increase, relative to men's, at all.[65] Of course, many things were happening during this period besides a shift from childbearing and child rearing to market employment, such as the adoption of no-fault divorce without adequate provision for compensating the wife for the marital investment contributed by her work in the household. While the market income of American women was rising throughout this period, thus increasing the opportunity cost to them of childbearing and hence the amount a man who wanted a childbearing wife could have been required to pay in the form of a division in household consumption that favored the woman, there was no effective mechanism for preventing the husband from reneging on his implied bargain by abandoning the woman when the children were grown.[66] Apparently this has not happened in Sweden: the fact that Swedish women's postdivorce income is 90 percent of their predivorce income (far higher than in the United States)[67] is evidence that the market wage gains of Swedish women have not been offset as a result of perturbations caused by the high rate of family dissolution, as may well have happened in the United States.

Whether or not women's full income is rising as a result of the change in their occupational structure, that change predicts a continuing increase in

64. Adams and Winston, note 47 above, at 205–212; Popenoe, note 33 above, at 197–199, 216 n. 24.

65. Victor R. Fuchs, *Women's Quest for Economic Equality*, ch. 5 (1988), esp. 76. The fact that sexual freedom reduces a woman's value as a potential mother provides an economic explanation for the hostility of traditionalist women to abortion rights. Angus McLaren and Arlene Tigar McLaren, *The Bedroom and the State: The Changing Practices and Politics of Contraception and Abortion in Canada, 1880–1980* 68–69 (1986).

66. Weitzman, note 27 above; Glendon, note 31 above, at 86–91.

67. Popenoe, note 33 above, at 315. This is despite the fact that—is indeed no doubt a principal reason why—alimony is rarely awarded. Popenoe also cites some evidence that divorce is more costly to men in Sweden than to women, contrary to the American experience. Id. at 230.

their sexual freedom. In societies in which women's principal economic function is childbearing, the sequestration of women, whether physical or mental (for example, by their being denied an eduction), imposes little cost on men relative to the benefit of secure paternity.[68] But if women's economic function shifts in favor of occupations that involve work outside the home and travel, require eduction, and entail mingling with men, the cost of sequestration rises, so we expect less of it and therefore more sexual freedom for women. The relation between women's education and sequestration is illustrated by the fact that Muslim cultures, in which women tend to be sequestered, have an unusually low ratio of literate females to literate males.[69]

Economists have discussed the measures that principals take to prevent agents from shirking.[70] A wife who has a child by a man other than her husband is like a shirking agent. Physical surveillance of agents, as by making them employees and placing them under one roof where they can be watched by supervisors, is one method of preventing shirking; its analogy in the sexual market is physically sequestering wives. As the cost of surveillance rises, whether in the employment market or in the sexual market, the amount of surveillance can be expected to fall and the amount of shirking to rise.

Three Stages in the Evolution of Sexual Morality

I am now prepared to unravel the paradox noted at the outset of my discussion of Swedish sexual mores—the positive correlation of companionate marriage with sexual liberality in Swedish society, compared to the inverse correlation in medieval Europe.

If the woman's occupation is that of a simple breeder, companionate marriage is unlikely, and without it such "immoral" practices as prostitution, adultery, and homosexuality are likely to flourish. This is stage 1 in the evolution of sexual morality. If the woman's occupational role is enlarged to include that of child rearer and husband's companion, as well as breeder, companionate marriage is possible, and leads in turn to the condemnation of the "immoral" practices; they are more anomalous in conditions of companionate marriage, yield fewer benefits as safety valves, and endanger marriage

---

68. As emphasized in Fatima Mernissi, *Beyond the Veil: Male-Female Dynamics in a Modern Muslim Society* 53 (1975).

69. Nadia H. Youssef and Shirley Foster-Hartley, "Demographic Indicators of the Status of Women in Various Societies," in *Sex Roles and Social Policy: A Complex Social Science Equation* 83, 91 (Jean Lipman-Blumen and Jessie Bernard eds. 1979).

70. See, for example, Michael C. Jensen and William H. Meckling, "Theory of the Firm: Managerial Behavior, Agency Costs and Ownership Structure," 3 *Journal of Financial Economics* 305 (1976); *Principals and Agents: The Structure of Business* (John W. Pratt and Richard J. Zeckhauser eds. 1985).

more. This is stage 2, which in Western culture prevailed during the era of Roman Catholic hegemony and indeed until about the middle of the twentieth century.

The first two roles are strongly family oriented rather than market oriented, and considerations of secure paternity are foremost. But if the woman's role is further enlarged to include market employment, then while such marriages as there are will be companionate, there will be fewer marriages; other forms of sexual relationship will no longer seem quite so abnormal; and policies designed to foster premarital virginity and marital chastity for the sake of companionate marriage will lose much of their point. This process of role enlargement, which ushers in stage 3 in the evolution of sexual morality, has progressed further in Sweden than in any other country.[71] Almost three-fourths of Swedish women are employed outside the home, compared to fewer than 60 percent of American women, and the average wage of Swedish women is 90 percent of the average male wage, a third higher than in the United States.[72]

In stage 3, as in stage 1, and in contrast to stage 2, men enjoy almost complete sexual license. The difference between stages 1 and 3 is that in the latter, but not in the former, women do too. Therefore, if my analysis is correct, the sexually conservative retrenchment of the Victorian era should be associated with a reduction in the amount of female employment outside the home. It is.[73]

The loosening grip of Christianity in sexually liberal societies such as Sweden may thus be not the cause of these societies' sexual liberality but the

71. Eschel M. Rhoodie, *Discrimination against Women: A Global Survey of the Economic, Educational, Social and Political Status of Women* 167–186 (1989). While not disagreeing, Joyce Gelb, *Feminism and Politics: A Comparative Perspective* (1989), emphasizes persisting inequalities in such areas as housework and political influence. See, for example, 199–200.

72. Compare Rhoodie, note 71 above, at 167 (tab.19), 172 (tab. 22); Glen Cain, "Estimating the Impact of Labor Market Policies on Women: A Discussion of the Four-Country Studies on the Employment of Women," in *Sex Discrimination and Equal Opportunity,* note 47 above, at 249, 252; and June O'Neill, "Earnings Differentials: Empirical Evidence and Causes," id. at 69, 70 (tab. 1), with O'Neill, "Women & Wages," 1 *American Enterprise* 25, 26 (November– December 1990) (68 percent), and Louis Uchitelle, "Women's Push into Work Force Seems to Have Reached Plateau," *New York Times,* November 24, 1990, 1, 18. In the age group 25 to 44, 90 percent of Swedish women are employed, compared to 74 percent of American women. Uchitelle at 18. Again, Gelb, note 71 above, at 144–145, enters a disclaimer, pointing out that the wage comparisons are of full-time wage earners, and most Swedish women work part-time. See also Gustafsson, note 47 above, at 133. But if they do so by choice, they presumably are better off. Gelb, however, believes they are compelled to work part-time by the unwillingness of men to do their fair share of housework and child care. Gelb at ch. 5 ("Sweden: Feminism without Feminists?"). (Whether this is compulsion or choice could be debated.) Both Gelb and Gustafsson note the concentration of Swedish women in public-sector jobs, and other indications of possible occupational segregation.

73. Gillis, note 22 above, at 242–246.

consequence. People who reject Christian doctrine on sex as inapposite to their circumstances may reject the remainder of Christian doctrine as well— may cease to be believing as well as practicing Christians. Of course, another possibility is that the weakening of religious belief has undermined the sexual morality associated with that belief; nor are the two possibilities mutually exclusive. And while I am considering alternative hypotheses to the economic, I should remind the reader of the evidence in Chapter 2 that the sexual liberality of Scandinavian societies has deep historical roots. But this may reflect, as we have seen, differences in the occupational role of women in those societies compared to the other European societies of the time. More-over, it is uncertain just how distinctive the traditional Scandinavian sexual morality was. Engagement viewed either as a form of trial marriage to deter-mine whether the couple is fertile, or as the "real" beginning of marriage and so entitling the couple to have sexual relations, was not limited to Scandinavia; it was common, for example, in England in the eighteenth and nineteenth centuries.[74] In any event, by the 1950s the sexual morality of Sweden was similar to that of the United States.[75] The modern divergence began in the 1960s and is most cogently explained by economic analysis.

The underlying causes of the transition from stage 2 to stage 3 in the evolution of sexual morality are fairly plain. They are the decline in infant mortality, the decline in women's mortality in childbirth, the improvement in methods of contraception, and the growth of light employment, all factors working together to reduce the benefits and increase the costs (both private and social) of keeping women in the home. The underlying causes of the transition from stage 1 to stage 2—from woman as simple breeder to woman as child rearer and husband's companion—are more obscure. One possibility is that the decline of slavery, an institution which by the end of Charlemagne's reign had largely disappeared from western Europe, gave wives a bigger role in their husbands' households (recall that boys in ancient Greece were raised by male slaves), or in other words increased the costs of confining them in the extraordinarily limited role that they had played in a slave society. Of course, the possession of slaves or other servants, including wet nurses, could have the opposite effect—could free a woman to work outside the home; modern labor-saving devices and bottle-feeding, which are technological sur-rogates for domestic servants, have had this effect. But if women are prevented from working in the market, then an abundance of servants may, both by

74. Id. at 114–115, 126–127; Alan Macfarlane, *Marriage and Love in England: Modes of Reproduction 1300–1840* 305–307 (1986). See also Peter Laslett, *Family Life and Illicit Love in Earlier Generations: Essays in Historical Sociology* 12 (1977) (tab. 1.1). Some colonial American "bundling" was of this character as well. John D'Emilio and Estelle B. Freedman, *Intimate Matters: A History of Sexuality in America* 22 (1988).

75. Popenoe, note 33 above, at 132–134; Thomas D. Eliot et al., *Norway's Families: Trends, Problems, Programs* 223 (1960).

enabling women to raise more children and by shrinking their role as household producers, chain them all the more effectively to the home. This may explain the high birth rate and sequestered status of middle-class and upper-class white women in the antebellum South.[76]

My hypothesis concerning the effect of domestic slavery on sexual morality may appear to founder on the fact that Roman families had many slaves, too, including slave tutors,[77] and yet women had a higher, more responsible status in the Roman Empire than they did in Athens in the fifth and fourth centuries B.C. But while the wealthiest Roman families at the height of the empire undoubtedly had more slaves than the wealthiest Athenian citizens of the comparison period, it is unclear whether the *average* Roman citizen household has as many as three or four slaves, as did the average Athenian household.[78]

All that is clear is that Roman wives were less sequestered than Greek wives (some even had an education rather similar to that which Roman men received);[79] that they were sexually freer; and that companionate marriage made progress during the empire,[80] paving the way for the Christian embrace of the institution. Here are two other possible explanations: First, the ages of the spouses at marriage were generally closer in Roman than in Greek society.[81] This would have facilitated companionate marriage, placing pressure on sequestration. Second, Rome at its height was a wealthier society than Greece of the fifth and fourth centuries B.C., and it is about wealthy Roman women that we have the most information. A man who dowers his daughter generously wants to make sure—especially in a society that permits divorce at

---

76. Sally G. McMillen, *Motherhood in the Old South: Pregnancy, Childbirth, and Infant Rearing* (1990). That the presence of servants can reduce the power of women is remarked in another context by Julian Pitt-Rivers, *The Fate of Schechem or The Politics of Sex: Essays in the Anthropology of the Mediterranean* 39 (1977).

77. Pomeroy, note 28 above, at 169–170; Joseph Vogt, *Ancient Slavery and the Ideal of Man* 110–111 (1975). The importance of male "child minders" in Roman families is emphasized in Keith R. Bradley, *Discovering the Roman Family: Studies in Roman Social History*, ch. 3 (1991).

78. M. I. Finley, *Economy and Society in Ancient Greece* 102 (Brent D. Shaw and Richard P. Saller eds. 1982). Cf. W. K. Lacey, *The Family in Classical Greece* 137 (1968).

79. Pomeroy, note 28 above, at 169–170; Just, note 28 above, at 29; Vogt, note 77 above, at 111; Angus McLaren, *A History of Contraception: From Antiquity to the Present Day* 45 (1990).

80. McLaren, note 79 above, at 44, 55, 64–65.

81. Beryl Rawson, "The Roman Family," in *The Family in Ancient Rome: New Perspectives* 1, 21 (Beryl Rawson ed. 1986), states that a five-year difference in age at marriage was "probably most common." In Greece a ten-year or even fifteen-year difference appears to have been the norm. Just, note 23 above, at 151; Lacey, note 78 above, at 106–107; and other references in Chapter 2. Brent D. Shaw, "The Age of Roman Girls at Marriage: Some Reconsiderations," 77 *Journal of Roman Studies* 30, 43 (1987), estimates that the average spread was ten years, with the wife in her late teens or early twenties. Yet that would make her older than the average Greek bride (of the fifth and fourth centuries B.C.), and therefore more fit for a companionate marriage.

will—that the daughter's husband will not squander or make off with her dowry, which she may need in the event that he dies or divorces her. Roman law was highly protective of the interests of the wife and her father in her dowry,[82] and as a result the well-dowered woman had a degree of economic independence from her husband. This reduced the cost to her of sexual disobedience (of disobedience, period), just as if, like a modern woman, she had had good opportunities for employment outside the household.

I have assumed that changes in women's roles produce a movement to companionate marriage which in turn produces changes in sexual morality. But could not the changes in sexual morality come first and cause the movement to companionate marriage? Certainly. A society that disapproved of homosexuality, adultery, and abortion might encourage companionate marriage in order to reduce the demand for these goods (or rather bads). To some extent this is what happened; the Church encouraged companionate marriage in part to reduce adultery, which is more likely in a regime of noncompanionate marriage. And while it is true that the idea and to a limited extent the practice of companionate marriage preceded the invention and imposition of Christian sex ethics, the practice gained momentum during the Christian era, and the support of the Church may have been a key factor. In the next chapter I shall speculate on a possible economic reason for that support.

The connection between women's social position and a society's sexual morality helps explain the support of Gunnar and Alva Myrdal, prominent Swedish socialists, for the "deregulation" of the traditional family. Partly for unsound demographic reasons discussed in the next chapter, partly as a means of raising the standard of living of women and children as part of a broader program of reducing income inequalities in Swedish society, the Myrdals believed that women should be freed from dependence on men. The result of the program they helped create of making women independent[83] has been a change in Swedish women's marital and sexual strategy in favor of increased freedom. The freedom, though, is as much from traditional mores as from public regulation; and of course the former influence the latter, and, to a lesser extent, the latter influence the former. The combined effect is a big step toward the model of morally indifferent sex.

I have emphasized the impact of changes in the occupational role of women on women's sexual freedom, but there is an impact on men's sexual freedom too. (That is why I noted earlier, in passing, that the transition from stage 2 to stage 3 involves an expansion in the sexual freedom of men as well as of women—though for men it is merely a restoration of the freedom they enjoyed in stage 1.) To begin with, there have to be male partners for the (heterosexual)

82. See references in note 28 above and in Chapter 5, note 54.
83. Described in Annika Baude, "Public Policy and Changing Family Patterns in Sweden 1930–1977," in *Sex Roles and Social Policy,* note 69 above, at 145.

newly emancipated women, and so the cost of nonmarital sex to men falls. A subtler point is that the reduction in the gains of marriage that is a by-product of female emancipation is experienced by men as well as by women, so men have less incentive to avoid extramarital sexual activity, which might endanger the marriage. If, as I believe, conventional sexual morality is a function of companionate marriage, forces that weaken the marital bond or reduce the (companionate) marriage rate will foster departures from the conventional morality. In their different ways, neither ancient Athens nor modern Sweden was (is) a society dominated by a norm of companionate marriage: Athens because a rival norm, noncompanionate marriage, held sway; Sweden because the marriage rate is so low and the gains from marriage so limited.

The causal chain is intricate. For example, improvements in contraception reduce the cost of nonmarital sex to both men and women directly but also indirectly by reducing the female dependence on men that is fostered by a state of continual pregnancy and hence by reducing the female incentive to promise chastity in exchange for male support. But the relationship among the key variables—the occupational status of women, the strength of companionate marriage as an organizing principle of male-female relations, and the degree of sexual freedom in the society—seems clear. This is true even with respect to tolerance for male homosexuality, a marked feature of Swedish sexual attitudes and yet a matter that might appear to be neither of any interest to women nor related to their social role. The appearance is deceptive. Take social role first. Greater female independence reduces the marriage rate, and by doing so makes homosexuality less anomalous: with fewer marriages, the group least likely to marry does not stand out as much. Take women's interests next. Women do not want male homosexuals to be forced into the marriage market, where they will waste women's time and occasionally deceive them into an unrewarding marriage. And women recognize that hostility to homosexuality is bound up with a general hostility to nonmarital sex and hence threatens the sexual freedom of heterosexual as well as homosexual women. To the extent, moreover, that Christian sexual morality is regarded as a package, a breakdown in some of the components, such as the prohibitions against contraception, abortion, and fornication, may undermine the remaining ones. Finally, women want to be free to form lesbian relationships if they like, and what is sauce for the goose is sauce for the gander.

Mention of lesbianism is a reminder that homosexuality is not a unitary phenomenon. Partly because lesbianism is much less common than male homosexuality and partly because it is nearly invisible in traditional societies (not only have most women in those societies few options other than marriage, regardless of their sexual preference, but in addition lesbians have sex less frequently, and with fewer partners, than male homosexuals and therefore can conceal their homosexuality more easily), it has been of less social concern.[84] At a time when England forbade homosexual sodomy under penalty of death, it had no laws against lesbian activities.

But the more pertinent difference between male and female homosexuality is that the latter appears to be in more elastic supply than the former. Although the amount of male homosexual activity is likely to fluctuate with changes in the availability of women and with other determinants of the costs and benefits of homosexual versus heterosexual acts, lesbian activity is likely to be even more responsive to a shifting pattern of benefits and costs. For if it is true that the female sex drive is weaker than the male, it should follow that motives for sex other than release and pleasure, such as the motive of cementing relationships, should be stronger among women than among men. So if circumstances make it advantageous for women to form close relationships with other women rather than with men, they are more likely to switch their sexual interest to women than would men in the parallel situation be likely to switch their sexual interest to men;[85] the costs are lower. It is not surprising, therefore, that lesbianism is said to have declined as the sexual revolution has provided more heterosexual outlets for women,[86] that the promotion of lesbianism is a plank in the platform of some radical feminist groups, and that the incidence of lesbianism is extremely high among prostitutes and among striptease dancers,[87] both being in occupations in which it is difficult to form durable and rewarding relationships with men. In short, we expect opportunistic homosexuality to be more common among women than among men, at least relative to "real" homosexuality.

This suggestion may seem inconsistent with the argument in the preceding chapter that men with an unusually strong sex drive are more likely to engage in opportunistic homosexual activity than other men. But the inconsistency is

84. Judith C. Brown, "Lesbian Sexuality in Medieval and Early Modern Europe," in *Hidden from History,* note 9 above, at 69.

85. One lesbian has been quoted as saying that "if a partner or sexual situation has other desirable qualities it is possible to overlook the partner's sex." John H. Gagnon, "Gender Preference in Erotic Relations: The Kinsey Scale and Sexual Scripts," in *Homosexuality/Heterosexuality: Concepts of Sexual Orientation* 175, 195 (David McWhirter, Stephanie Sanders, and June Reinisch eds. 1990).

86. Mervin B. Freedman, "The Sexual Behavior of American College Women: An Empirical Study and an Historical Survey," in *Studies in Human Sexual Behavior: The American Scene* 135, 148 (Ailon Shiloh ed. 1970).

87. Jennifer James, "Prostitutes and Prostitution," in *Deviants: Voluntary Actors in a Hostile World* 368, 400 (Edward Sagarin and Fred Montanino eds. 1977); Copley, note 25 above, at 88; Karlen, note 40 above, at 251; Nanette T. Davis, "Prostitution: Identity, Career, and Legal-Economic Enterprises," in *The Sociology of Sex: An Introductory Reader* 195, 213–214 (James M. Henslin and Edward Sagarin eds., rev. ed. 1978); James K. Skipper, Jr., and Charles H. McCaghy, "Teasing, Flashing and Visual Sex: Stripping for a Living," in *The Sociology of Sex* at 171, 188–190; D. Lester, *Unusual Sexual Behavior: The Standard Deviations* 14–16 (1975).

only apparent. The difference in sex drives and sex strategies between men and women makes it easier for women to find heterosexual outlets than for men to do so, and therefore makes it unlikely that women would engage in lesbian activity because of an insufficiency of such outlets; certainly that could not be the motive of a prostitute. A final point is that the less intense the woman's need for sex, the stronger her bargaining position with men, for the less a man can compensate her simply by catering to her sexual desires.[88] We can begin to see the relationship between the anti(hetero)sex theme in some versions of feminist thought and the changing status of women.

THE LESSON of the Swedish experience is that the movement toward sexual permissiveness—the sexual revolution of the twentieth century—has been due ultimately to women. Not because their political power has grown, though it has, but probably as consequence rather than cause of their changing social and economic status, and not because (a persistent masculine myth and fear) women are more fiercely sexual than men (the opposite appears to be the case if by "sexual" we mean having a strong appetite for sex), but because traditional sexual morality is founded on women's dependence upon men. As that dependence lessens, the traditional morality weakens. The function of that morality is to protect the male's interest in warranted confidence that his children really are his biological issue. Women will cooperate in securing that interest only if they are compensated for doing so, as they were when they needed the protection of men in order to have children and when careers not involving children were closed to them. Women need and receive less male protection as their childbearing role diminishes and their market opportunities grow.

88. Donald Symons, *The Evolution of Human Sexuality* 262, 265 (1979).

Optimal Regulation of Sexuality

THE PRECEDING two chapters sought to discover the economic laws that shape sexual attitudes and behavior. But I began to sidle up to normative analysis in Chapter 6 by considering possible economic reasons, such as externalities, for social intervention in the sexual arena. That analysis has now to be elaborated. The focus will be on the question of what regulations are appropriate under a laissez-faire approach to sex—an approach that, by treating sex as morally indifferent, would limit sexual freedom only to the extent required by economic or other utilitarian considerations. I grant that economics, when viewed as a guide to social policy, and of course utilitarianism, are themselves moral theories. There is no escaping moral issues in normative analysis. But there is a difference between thinking of sex as charged with moral significance and thinking of it as just another source of regulatory issues in the libertarian or laissez-faire theory of the state.

Consideration of the normative issue—what limitations should be placed on sexual freedom from an economic standpoint—will require an examination of the actual effects of sexual regulations, since those effects are crucial to the costs and benefits of the regulations. And it will lead us to consider the political causes of sexual regulations in an attempt to explain why in our society the optimum and the actual regulation of sex do not coincide.

The Model of Morally Indifferent Sex Elaborated

It is difficult for people brought up in our society to imagine sex as a morally indifferent subject. Not that there haven't been distinguished advocates of such a position, for example, Bertrand Russell.[1] And not that the position lacks a distinguished lineage: it is essentially the position of the ancient Greeks

1. *Marriage and Morals* (1929).

and Romans.[2] Sweden too, as we saw in the preceding chapter; likewise Japan. But the ancient Greeks and Romans are too remote from most of us to provide a relevant precedent; Japan seems almost as remote culturally; there is little interest in or knowledge of Sweden in this country; and for his advocacy of what I call morally indifferent sex, Russell merely earned the reputation, in this country anyway, of being a "free love" nut. But morally indifferent sex is not free love. Few people in modern Western society consider eating (as long as it is not cannibalistic) an activity charged with moral significance, but everyone recognizes that it is an activity to be conducted with due regard for considerations of health, expense, time, and seemliness. Food disorders, such as bulimia and anorexia, are recognized; people are criticized for being too gluttonous or too fastidious; the gourmet is distinguished from the gourmand, cuisine from sustenance, healthy diets from unhealthy ones; there is a concept of good table manners. So while eating is not a moral subject except to vegetarians and to persons who adhere to religious dietary restrictions, neither is it a free-for-all; it is guided by aesthetic and prudential considerations. So would sex be in a society in which it was a morally indifferent subject.[3] An intelligent person understands that one is dealing with a strong desire that must be kept in place, not allowed to dominate or endanger one's life. It should not have required AIDS to teach this lesson. Not everyone is intelligent or self-controlled, however, and when a person engages in sexual acts that harm other persons without their explicit or implicit consent, there is a case for social intervention. It is that case that I want to explore.

Efforts to subvert a system of property rights by taking other people's property by force or fraud furnish the least controversial economic ground for intervening in markets. Although a deservedly esoteric literature cited in Chapter 14 argues that in special circumstances rape might be efficient (I argue that these circumstances are likely to be vanishingly rare), there is evidence that the average forcible rapist is in effect a sex thief, which makes the prohibition of forcible rape not only consistent with but entailed by a normative economic analysis of sex. The evidence includes the positive correlation between the incidence of rape and the average age of men at marriage and the negative correlation between the incidence of rape and participation in

2. Michel Foucault is eloquent on this subject, particularly in the second volume of his history of sexuality, *The Use of Pleasure* (1985). And David Cohen, in his book *Law, Sexuality and Society: The Enforcement of Morals in Classical Athens* 221–223 (1991), emphasizes that for the Greeks, sex was part of the private, not the public, sphere. Of course there is a private as well as a public or political morality, but when I speak of sex as a "morally indifferent" subject it is with reference to the public or political side of morality—the side that invites public intervention in (otherwise) private matters.

3. The analogy to food is noted in Russell, note 1 above, at 291. There are societies in which eating is charged with the sort of moral significance that sex is charged with in our society. Bronislaw Malinowski, *The Sexual Life of Savages in North-Western Melanesia* 441–443 (1929).

the labor force by young men.[4] The second correlation is particularly interesting. Men who do not work tend not to have the resources necessary to attract women and therefore have a greater incentive to bypass the market in sexual relationships.

The principal example of fraud in sex is the seduction of children, rightly prohibited even where force is absent. Yet the symmetry between the legal treatment of force and fraud in the sexual arena and their legal treatment in other markets is not complete. Only in recent years has marital rape been made criminal. Most rapes by trick, as distinct from forcible rapes, are still not criminal. We shall consider in Chapter 14 whether the traditional divergences can be justified on economic grounds (the first, excusing marital rape, probably not, the second, excusing most rapes by trick, perhaps).

I anticipate the objection that to treat rape as if it were a form of theft, and seduction of children as if it were a form of larceny by trick, makes rapists and child seducers seem "normal" men, and by doing so overlooks the pathological characteristics of many of the offenders. The objection confuses two groups. One consists of men who would commit rape and seduce children if there were no laws against these acts, as indeed there were not in ancient Greece and Rome unless the victim was a member of a citizen family, but who are deterred by the laws. Such men are, I imagine, for the most part quite normal. The other group consists of men who commit such acts even in societies such as ours that impose heavy criminal penalties for committing them and who in addition are caught. *This* group—the undeterred who are stupid enough to be caught—may well be dominated by psychologically disturbed or mentally deficient men.

The Externalities of Sex

Cheating

It is the externalities produced by adult, informed, consensual, although often nonmarital, nonvaginal sexual intercourse that make the normative analysis of sexual mores particularly interesting and challenging. An externality, as noted in the preceding chapter, is an effect (beneficial or harmful) that the person creating it will not take fully into account in deciding whether or how much to engage in the activity that produces it. Venereal disease is an obvious—though, as I explained in that chapter, an exaggerated—example, but

---

4. Kevin Howells, "Coercive Sexual Behaviour," in *The Psychology of Sexual Diversity* 115 (Kevin Howells ed. 1984); Isaac Ehrlich, "Participation in Illegitimate Activities: An Economic Analysis," in *Essays in the Economics of Crime and Punishment* 68, 104–106 and tab. 6 (Gary S. Becker and William M. Landes eds. 1974). Other evidence that rape is a substitute for voluntary sexual relations was mentioned in Chapter 4, and there is more in Chapter 14.

one unnecessary to elaborate upon here beyond the observation that concealing venereal disease from one's sexual partner is itself a serious form of sexual fraud, properly considered a legal wrong.[5] A subtler example is the increased cost of determining paternity in a society in which nonmarital vaginal intercourse is rampant. A man wants assurance that the child he is supporting is his own, and he is denied that assurance if his wife is adulterous. Therefore, were marriage a freely bargained relationship, virtually every prospective husband would insist on a clause in the marriage contract forbidding the wife to have intercourse with other men. Laws punishing female adultery (if only by giving the cuckolded husband a ground for divorce) can be understood to read this implied term into the marriage "contract" and to provide sanctions for violating it. Such laws thus reduce marital transaction costs.[6]

The wrong to the cuckolded husband is plain enough; the externality lies in the fact that the adulterous relationship, although voluntary between the parties to it, the adulterous wife and her lover, imposes costs on a third party, the husband: the expected costs both of supporting a child that the husband would not want to support if he knew the child's paternity and of losing the opportunity of fathering his own child. I call these, employing the standard economic terminology, *expected* costs because they will materialize only if the woman becomes pregnant; they are probabilistic rather than certain. Although they do not depend on the husband's discovering his wife's adultery, if he does discover it he will bear additional costs, emotional in character, as a consequence of jealousy.

Adultery by the husband is a lesser offense (in early law, no offense at all), because the main cost to the wife—in a noncompanionate marriage, at any rate—is merely some diminution in the resources available to support her and her children. (True, there is a greater risk that she will contract a venereal disease, but that is also a risk that the wife's adultery imposes on her husband.) It is therefore not infallible evidence of misogyny or of sex discrimination that the wife's adultery was traditionally considered a more serious offense than the husband's.[7] The costs are more nearly symmetrical, however, in a companionate marriage, because either party suffers a diminution in companionship when the other has a romantic liaison. This may explain not only the

5. Crowell v. Crowell, 180 N.C. 516, 105 S.E. 206 (1920). See Note, "Liability in Tort for the Sexual Transmission of Disease: Genital Herpes and the Law," 70 *Cornell Law Review* 101 (1984), advocating liability for negligently transmitting a disease sexually, as distinct from doing so with knowledge that one has the disease. It is that knowledge which, as in the *Crowell* case, makes sexual intercourse a species of the tort of battery.

6. Law's function of reducing transaction costs is a pervasive theme of economic analysis of law, on which see my book *Economic Analysis of Law* (3d ed. 1986), esp. pt. 2.

7. In France, for example, until 1975, when criminal penalties for adultery were abolished. Antony Copley, *Sexual Moralities in France, 1780–1980: New Ideas on the Family, Divorce, and Homosexuality: An Essay on Moral Change* 87 (1989).

historical novelty of Christianity's disapproval of male adultery—for remember that the Church encouraged companionate marriage—but also the erosion of the double standard in modern times and the fact that nowadays jealousy afflicts women about as much as men, although it is a less specifically sexual jealousy.[8] Yet it remains the case that, above and beyond the emotional costs of infidelity to the dishonored party, the costs in genetic fitness are greater to the husband than to the wife. The emotional costs may also be greater to the husband if sexual jealousy has a genetic root and is therefore more intense in men than in women, as I suggested in Chapter 4 is probably the case.

Suppose a cheap and infallible paternity test were invented (no doubt it will be). Then a man could easily discover with certainty whether the child his wife had just given birth to was his child. The genetic costs of adultery to him would fall, though not to zero because he would have lost an opportunity to father a child. They would fall because the test would deter some adultery (the deterrence would be of the wife's lover as well as of the wife, because the lover would be at risk of being ordered to support his illegitimate child) and also provide information that would enable the husband to get out of a marriage that was failing to produce children for him. The emotional costs to the husband, however, would fall little if at all. Those costs are triggered by the fact of adultery rather than by its procreative consequences. Human emotions are adapted to the conditions that prevailed during the evolutionary period of human prehistory, long before contraceptives and paternity tests. In that period, indignation at the fact of adultery was what was vital to a man's inclusive fitness, and it continues to be the usual male response to a wife's adultery.

There is another side to the secure-paternity coin. Merely because a man is justifiably confident that a particular child is his does not make it certain that he will want to support it. If there are alternative means of support, he may be more than happy to shirk his responsibility. Especially in a society in which a generous social safety net ensures the survival of children who have no father to support them, a man's optimal reproductive strategy may be to devote his limited resources to supporting his legitimate children while at the same time fathering illegitimate children whom he does not support at all— or even to devote all his reproductive resources to the nonmarital market, and shift the entire burden of supporting his children that would otherwise rest on him to the taxpayer. (Thus the social safety net stimulates nonmarital sexual activity by men as well as by women—another link between socialism and promiscuity.) Preventing, or more realistically limiting, this externalization of costs might require society to devote substantial resources to paternity

---

8. Kingsley Davis, "Sexual Behavior," in *Contemporary Social Problems* 313, 327 (Robert K. Merton and Robert Nisbet eds., 3d ed. 1971); Peter N. Stearns, *Jealousy: The Evolution of an Emotion in American History*, ch. 5 (1989); other references in Chapter 4.

litigation and to the enforcement of child-support orders, but the hypothetical infallible paternity test would economize on those resources and reduce the incidence of adultery.

This analysis suggests a possible economic rationale not only for laws against adultery but also for laws against prostitution, which can similarly be viewed as measures for the protection of children. The man who frequents prostitutes dissipates resources that he might otherwise devote to the support of his children. Of course, the fact that a law attempts to internalize an external cost does not make it an efficient law. The benefits of prostitution to the prostitute and her customers must be weighed against the costs to children. There are other costs in the picture, however: the costs to wives in companionate marriages, which are undermined by infidelity (a married man who patronizes a prostitute is an adulterer, and the prostitute is his paid accomplice in adultery), and the costs of venereal disease, which is spread more rapidly by persons who have large numbers of sex partners than by practicing monogamists. Efforts to curtail prostitution are therefore more likely the larger the fraction of marriages that are companionate, the higher the incidence and severity of venereal disease, and the higher the optimal paternal investment in child support.

All this assumes, however, that prostitution is only a substitute for marriage; it is also a complement. A man who is unsatisfied with the sexual aspects of his marriage may be driven to divorce his wife, or to support a mistress, if the alternative of patronizing prostitutes is closed to him; and the result is likely to be a greater diversion of resources from the support of his children. This is a traditional argument for regulating rather than prohibiting prostitution; it persuaded Augustine and Aquinas.[9] The only unequivocal "bad" of prostitution, then, is its tendency to spread venereal disease, and I am led to predict that the dominant factor in the extent of public intervention in prostitution will be the incidence and severity of such disease. There is some support for this prediction (see note 9).

Without going any further, we can see that adopting the model of morally indifferent sex would not necessarily confine public regulation to coercive

9. Mary Gibson, *Prostitution and the State in Italy, 1860–1915* 224 (1986); David A. J. Richards, "Commercial Sex and the Rights of the Person: A Moral Argument for the Decriminalization of Prostitution," 127 *University of Pennsylvania Law Review* 1195, 1211 (1979). Richards makes a powerful case for decriminalizing prostitution. Whether he would reexamine his case in light of the AIDS epidemic I do not know—but probably he would not (and should not). Apparently, very few people catch AIDS from prostitutes, despite the high incidence of AIDS among prostitutes, which is due to the fact that many of them are intravenous drug users. Heather G. Miller et al., *AIDS: The Second Decade*, ch. 4 (1990), esp. 262. Historically, campaigns against prostitution have been associated with rises in the incidence of venereal disease, as one would expect. John F. Decker, *Prostitution: Regulation and Control* 45–46 (1979); Judith R. Walkowitz, *Prostitution and Victorian Society: Women, Class, and the State* (1980), passim.

sexual acts such as rape and the sexual abuse of children. Libertarian and libertine are not synonyms after all.

Children

The external effects of sexual activity on children are probably the most important to consider. There are, speaking loosely, both microeconomic and macroeconomic effects, the first having to do with the welfare of children, the second with the size and quality of the population. Efforts to discourage teenagers from having children can, for example, be defended in terms of the relatively poor life prospects of such children. One might even argue that the child, if he could be consulted, would prefer to be born later, when his prospects for a happy, healthy, and prosperous life would be better. For the same reason, his brothers and sisters might also prefer that he be born later—when their parents would have ampler resources for all of them—or even not at all, so that there will be more for them.

Yet a society that discourages teenage childbearing, whether through encouraging contraception, permitting—even subsidizing—abortion, imposing punishments for fornication, fixing a high age of consent, or promoting an ideology of abstinence, may have a lower birth rate than a society that encourages it, and not merely shift the same number of pregnancies into subsequent years of women's fertile period. The contamination, as it were, of the issue of child welfare with that of the number of births complicates the normative economic analysis of sex enormously. How are we to count the welfare of people who, as a result of a public policy of discouraging teenage parenthood, are not just born later but are never born? We could elide the problem by confining the population whose preferences are considered in the normative analysis to living persons, thus excluding fetuses and potential human life generally. But from a normative standpoint this is an arbitrary cut-off, unless there is some ground for disregarding the welfare of people whom society wishes to prevent from being born. The only ground is a preference—itself arbitrary, unless I am exaggerating the indeterminacy of contemporary ethical discourse—for the slice of humankind that happens to be living today.

The last chapter of this book will glance at the suggestion by Gary Becker and Kevin Murphy for resolving the question whether additional births would be optimal by asking whether the unborn would be willing and able to compensate all those already born (in particular parents and siblings) for whatever costs the additional births would impose on them. The measurement problems are formidable; an additional and less obvious problem is that, unless actual compensation is paid (thus making the already born better off or at least no worse off), the validity of the suggestion depends on two assumptions: that the unborn are part of the community whose preferences are to be taken into account in fixing an optimal population policy, and that their lives "belong" to the already born, whom the unborn must therefore compensate in order to be permitted to live rather than being entitled to demand compensation from for being born later or for not being born at all. (Of course they might *want* to be born later, but this is uncertain.) These assumptions cannot be derived from economic theory or from any but highly controversial philosophical premises.

The implications of this analysis need not be thought pronatalist, however. If there is no solid basis for preferring the born over the unborn (or some unborn over other unborn), neither is there any solid basis for preferring the unborn over the born. Nor can we dispel these uncertainties by assuming that the interests of the various groups are harmonious, for they are not. We shall, for example, consider evidence in Chapter 10 that the practice of contraception and abortion leads to healthier, but fewer, infants.

The same problem of drawing the boundaries of the community arises if we ask whether there is a practical ground for trying to channel births into marriage. But we can minimize the problem in that setting by assuming, more plausibly than in the context of teenage pregnancy, that the principal effect of a strong policy in favor of marriage is to encourage people to marry, rather than merely encourage them to have fewer children. In fact, since young people rarely marry without wanting and expecting to have children, and since married people have more children on average than unmarried people do,[10] an increase in the marriage rate is more likely to increase than to decrease the birth rate. If we assume, therefore, that a promarital policy is not anti-natalist, but also assume (more questionably) that it is not pronatalist in the sense of substantially increasing the birth rate, the normative question becomes whether it is better for children to grow up in a home with two parents than in a home with only one. More precisely it is whether the benefits to the child from society's forcing procreation into the marital mold exceed the costs to the parents of their being constrained to a closer or more durable relationship with each other than they desire. The question of child welfare is thus isolated from that of the optimal birth rate. The former question should be answerable, and we shall examine some of the answers shortly. The Swedish answer is no, but many Swedes may not realize that their government's policies subsidize illegitimacy rather than leaving choice completely unfettered. The taxpayer pays a big share of the cost of raising a child, and by reducing the benefits of marriage to women, this subsidy makes procreation outside of marriage more attractive than it would be under pure free-market conditions, in which a

10. Susan M. Essock-Vitale and Michael T. McGuire, "What 70 Million Years Hath Wrought: Sexual Histories and Reproductive Success of a Random Sample of American Women," in *Human Reproductive Behavior: A Darwinian Perspective* 221, 228–230 (Laura Betzig, Monique Borgerhoff Mulder, and Paul Turke eds. 1988).

woman would have to support a child out of her own (or hers and a man's) pocket.

But have I really succeeded in framing the question whether encouraging marriage is a good thing in a way that makes it answerable? One of my assumptions was problematic: that a promarital policy will *not* increase the birth rate substantially. If this is incorrect, the impact on the welfare of the additional persons born must be factored into the analysis, and we are thrown back to a normative question that I said was intractable.

It might seem that if marriage were beneficial to children, the love that parents bear their children would suffice to channel procreation into marriage; the external costs of nonmarital sexual activity to children would be internalized to the parents' decision-making processes. This would be true if parents were selfless and therefore always made the decision affecting their children that maximized the children's welfare. It might be approximately true if one parent were totally altruistic toward his or her children—that is, valued the child's welfare as highly as the child itself would value it—because altruism would then determine the parent's choice of marital partner in the first place, the decision whether to divorce or on what terms and whether and whom to remarry, and all other decisions affecting the children's welfare. But in fact parents have their own interests, and though likely to be altruistic toward their children in the sense employed here (that their own welfare is a positive function of their children's welfare), are unlikely to be so altruistic that they give no weight to their own selfish interests, which will often diverge from their children's.[11] In other words, parents may not be the perfect guardians of their child, and this creates the possibility that social intervention designed to encourage marriage and discourage illegitimate births might increase social welfare. But it is only a possibility, and perhaps a small one except in cases of palpable parental abuse or neglect. In other cases, effective social intervention will be handicapped by the selfish interests of the persons who administer the welfare program, by those persons' ignorance of the needs and potential of other people's children, and, a variant of the first point, by their lack of altruism toward children to whom they are not related. The last point assumes that altruism is greater among kin than among nonkin—and certainly than among strangers. More than common sense supports the assumption: that altruism is greater toward persons (especially persons who are or will be fertile) who share one's genes is a fundamental implication of sociobiology.

11. On altruism within the family, see Gary S. Becker, *A Treatise on the Family* (enlarged ed. 1991). The welfare consequences of family altruism are stressed in Marc Nerlove, Assaf Razin, and Efraim Sadka, *Household and Economy: Welfare Economics of Endogenous Fertility* (1987), e.g. at 85–86. Some evidence that parental altruism is imperfect is the fact that parents underestimate the impact of divorce on their children. David Popenoe, *Disturbing the Nest: Family Change and Decline in Modern Societies* 315 (1988).

The Issue of Sex Education

If children benefit from growing up in a household that includes their father, sexual conservatives may be right that sex education is a bad thing. One effect of sex education is to bring sharply before the teenage mind the feasibility of engaging in sexual activity before marriage and to show teenagers, especially girls, how the risks of pregnancy and disease can be minimized by advance planning. In its latter aspect, sex education is education in contraception and in the prevention of disease; so, purveyed free of charge, it reduces the cost of sex for the teenager who in his or her ignorance might have overestimated the risks of pregnancy and disease. The Swedish experience suggests that the net effect of sex education is indeed to reduce the costs, and so increase the incidence, of premarital sex. And since premarital and marital sex are substitutes, an increase in the former should result in a reduction in the latter and, other things being equal, in a concomitant shift from legitimate to illegitimate births; again, that has been the Swedish experience. So the conservatives' correlation of sex education with promiscuity and the decline of family values is not as absurd as liberals believe.

That does not mean that conservatives are right to oppose sex education. Reducing the amount of premarital sexual activity is not the only effect of discouraging sex education. Another effect is to increase the incidence of pregnancy and venereal disease among the (smaller) population of teenagers who become sexually active without benefit of sex education. Again the Swedish experience is illuminating. Sweden has much lower rates of teenage pregnancy and venereal disease than the United States has, and these lower rates are (in part) benefits of sex education (we shall see additional evidence of this in Chapter 10); but it has a high ratio—higher than ours—of illegitimate to legitimate births, which is one of the costs of sex education. What weights to give these offsetting effects is uncertain. On the one hand, most illegitimate births in Sweden are to cohabiting couples rather than to women living by themselves, and cohabitation could in principle be as stable a relationship as marriage in a society with a high divorce rate. But usually it is not. Sweden probably has the highest rate of family dissolution in the developed world—when its divorce rate, slightly lower than the American, is combined with the very high rate at which cohabiting couples break up—and the highest rate of single-parent households in the developed world, higher even than ours.[12]

It becomes of vital importance to determine the benefit to a child of the father's being a member of the household. Remarkably, there is no research on this question in Sweden.[13] David Popenoe conjectures that the high inci-

12. Popenoe, note 1 above, at 173–174.
13. Id. at 314.

dence of juvenile delinquency in Sweden is related to the absence of the father,[14] but finds no other ill effects from Sweden's remarkable family structure.[15] Americans will be shocked. It is an article of faith among us that the social pathology of poor blacks is due to the absence of a guiding paternal hand. This belief is influenced by findings that divorce has bad effects on American children,[16] but the tensions that lead to the divorce rather than the divorce itself may be responsible. The Swedish divorce rate is lower than ours, and maybe split-ups of cohabiting couples are not as traumatic for the children as a divorce would be. While there is much evidence that illegitimate children in America have fainter prospects for a happy life than legitimate children do,[17] interpretation is complicated by the fact that illegitimacy in America is more prevalent among the poor.[18] One study finds that after correction is made for those factors, such as low income, which under American—but not under Swedish—social conditions are positively correlated with the father's absence from the household, the negative effects of fatherlessness on American children are not large.[19]

14. Id. at 318–319.

15. He points out, for example, that the rate of youth suicide in Sweden is only half that in Switzerland (id. at 317), which has a quite conservative sexual ethic. Id. at 262–270. Yet in a subsequent article, after remarking consistently with his book that "the clearest evidence of a problem is in the data on juvenile delinquency," Popenoe adds that "there is also much discussion and some hard data concerning a considerable increase in angst among Swedish youth, with such related problems as depression, suicide, and alcoholism." "Family Decline in the Swedish Welfare State," *Public Interest* 65, 76 (Winter 1991). "Hard data concerning . . . angst" is oxymoronic, and the remark about suicide is inconsistent with the data in Popenoe's book.

16. See, for example, the studies and references in *Impact of Divorce, Single Parenting, and Stepparenting on Children*, pt. 3 (E. Mavis Hetherington and Josephine D. Arasteh eds. 1988). And the bad effects are not mitigated—in some cases they are even aggravated—by remarriage. Nicholas Zill, "Behavior, Achievement, and Health Problems among Children in Stepfamilies: Findings from a National Survey of Child Health," id. at 325.

17. See, for example, Beth Berkov and June Sklar, "Does Illegitimacy Make a Difference? A Study of the Life Chances of Illegitimate Children in California," 2 *Population and Development Review* 201 (1976).

18. Id. at 208.

19. Elsa Ferri, *Growing Up in a One-Parent Family: A Long-Term Study of Child Development* 120, 134, 139 (1976). Needless to say, this single study should not be thought conclusive. Zill, note 16 above, at 363, found that while stepchildren in low-income families experience more behavior problems than stepchildren in moderate- and high-income families, the difference is small; a high income is not a complete anodyne for a broken home. Yet, much like Ferri, Verna M. Keith and Barbara Finlay in their article "The Impact of Parental Divorce on Children's Educational Attainment, Marital Timing, and Likelihood of Divorce," 50 *Journal of Marriage and the Family* 797 (1988), attribute the bad effects of divorce on children to the reduced economic and social resources available to the children of divorced parents, implying that in a society such as Sweden, in which divorce does not reduce the mother's income substantially, those effects will be small. See also Susan Maidment, *Child Custody and Divorce: The Law in Social Context* 161–176 (1984). Further support for the hypothesis that the principal effect of a

In evaluating these findings, keep in mind that the proper comparison is between the father on the one hand and the father substitute—the taxpayer and the welfare bureaucracy—on the other. The worse equipped by temperament or resources the father is to participate in the raising of his children, and the more generous and intelligent the provision of social services to the unwed mother and her children, the less need there is for public policy to discourage illegitimate births in order to reduce the percentage of children who are fatherless. The relevant social services are far more generous in Sweden than they are in the United States; this may be why the permissiveness of the Swedish sexual culture seems so much less destructive than ours. Of course, generous social services are costly; Swedes are far more heavily taxed than Americans, and most of their taxes go to support social services. Maybe the costs of sexual liberty are staggering to the Swedes after all, and just take a different form from those costs in our country.

This discussion shows that the evaluation of such policies as providing (or withholding) sex education for children and teenagers requires the identification, measurement, and comparison of a number of variables. These include the effect of sex education on promiscuity and through it on illegitimate births, the social costs of such births, the potentially offsetting effect of sex education on venereal disease and unwanted pregnancies and hence on unwanted (mainly illegitimate) births, the fiscal consequences of policies designed to mitigate untoward effects of unwanted births and of fatherlessness, and the incentive and other allocative effects of those fiscal measures.

The relations among variables can be subtle. For example, measures to improve fetal and neonatal health care among poor blacks might in the long run reduce rather than increase the number of illegitimate births, because we know from Chapter 5 that deficiencies in such care reduce the sex ratio and that a low sex ratio coupled with a social safety net raises the illegitimate birth rate. And if welfare benefits for the mothers of illegitimate children were not made less generous but merely conditioned in whole or in part on the woman's having established herself in employment (as in Sweden), the teenage pregnancy rate would fall because women would have an incentive to defer childbirth.

Population

I want to switch the focus now from the effect of sexual practices on individual children to their effect on population. Population has both a qualitative and

---

broken home on the children is to reduce the level of parental investment is found in Yochanan Peres and Rachel Pasternack, "The Importance of Marriage for Socialization: A Comparison of Achievements and Social Adjustment between Offspring of One- and Two-Parent Families in Israel," in *Contemporary Marriage: Comparative Perspectives on a Changing Institution* 157, 174–175 (Kingsley Davis ed. 1985).

a quantitative dimension, but I shall limit my analysis to the latter, deferring the former to the discussion of eugenics in the last chapter of the book.

The addition of one more person to the population can impose costs on the rest of society that the parents will not take into account because those costs are spread over the whole population, so that the parents bear only a minute and imperceptible share. If a society were very crowded, additional population could impose substantial costs in congestion or pollution. Concerns about overpopulation have fueled the family-planning movement in this country, although the concerns seem exaggerated.[20] Conversely, additional population might confer an external benefit.[21] Between the Franco-Prussian War and the Second World War, the French were concerned, and rightly so, that their low birth rate was weakening them militarily vis-à-vis the Germans.[22] But such a concern would not have led a rational French couple to have an additional child. The contribution made by that child, even if the child turned out to be male, to strengthening France militarily when he grew to adulthood would be realized only to an infinitesimal extent by the parents, while the cost of raising the child would be concentrated on them. Likewise an ancient Greek or Roman family contemplating female infanticide would not have been likely to consider the aggregate effect on the availability of wives for the family's own male children (who would face more competition in the marriage market if women were scarcer) and husbands for the family's surviving female children, let alone the effect on the availability of spouses for other families' children.

So there is a theoretical case for public intervention to assist in attaining an optimal population size and sex ratio. Such interventions have been common. In some Asian countries, for example, concerns about overpopulation have led in recent years to antinatalist polices that are draconian, while concerns with underpopulation in times past led many European nations to adopt such pronatalist policies as family allowances and prohibitions against abortion. Not only France but also Nazi Germany were vigorously pronatalist. One of the justifications that the Nazis offered for punishing homosexuality

20. As effectively argued in Julian L. Simon, *The Economics of Population Growth* (1977), and Simon, *The Ultimate Resource* (1981). But Simon carries as much ideological baggage as his adversaries, the "zero-population-growth" school, represented by Paul R. Ehrlich, *The Population Bomb* (1986), and I am skeptical of such facile claims as that an increase in population will reduce the costs of energy because "more people mean more imagination," hence more invention, hence more energy-saving devices. *The Economics of Population Growth* at 476.

21. For a careful analysis of both positive and negative population externalities, see Robert J. Willis, "Externalities and Population," in *Population Growth and Economic Development: Issues and Evidence* 661 (D. Gale Johnson and Ronald D. Lee eds. 1987).

22. Joseph J. Spengler, *France Faces Depopulation: Postlude Edition, 1936–1976* (1979); Michael S. Teitelbaum and Jay M. Winter, *The Fear of Population Decline* 17–30 (1985). Underpopulation has been a traditional concern of the Jewish people, which may explain the pronatalist character of their sexual ethics. David M. Feldman, *Marital Relations, Birth Control, and Abortion in Jewish Law* 51–53 (1968).

was that it reduced the birth rate. The argument was that the 2 million German deaths in the First World War plus the (crudely estimated and probably exaggerated) 2 million German male homosexuals added up to a deficit of 4 million fertile males, with disastrous implications for population. This was absurd. The limiting factor in the birth rate is not the number of males (unless that number falls to a minute fraction of the number of women) but the number of fertile wombs. The Nazis should have worried more about lesbians than about male homosexuals, but in fact imposed no penalties on lesbians.

At present, in the Western world anyway, it is difficult to justify the regulation of sexuality by reference to either the external benefits or the external costs of additional population. For one thing, the lesson of history is that the actual effects of either pronatalist or antinatalist policies on population tend to be negligible, at least when those policies are limited to financial incentives and disincentives, and often even when more direct methods of coercion are applied. Pronatalist policies are especially futile.[23] Subsidies have to be paid for in higher taxes, which may (depending on the form of the tax) induce more women to enter the job market, raising their opportunity costs of having children and thus reducing the birth rate. The larger the subsidy, the larger this effect. If the subsidy is kept low in order to minimize the effect on taxes, it is unlikely to induce many births, because the cost of the child to its parents will be high relative to the subsidy. Even huge subsidies may not do the trick. By 1938 France was spending 2 percent of its national income on family allowances and other pronatalist policies, with little effect.[24] It has been estimated that it would cost $380 billion in annual subsidies to raise the U.S. birth rate to the replacement level.[25]

But the more interesting point is that, despite much hysteria mongering on the question, underpopulation may not be a serious problem in the West, while overpopulation has become self-correcting (again, I am speaking only of the West). As regards the first half of this proposition, the growth of the technological element in war has greatly attenuated the relationship between

23. Jerome S. Legge, Jr., and John R. Alford, "Can Government Regulate Fertility? An Assessment of Pronatalist Policy in Eastern Europe," 39 *Western Political Quarterly* 709 (1986); William J. Serow, "Population and Other Responses to an Era of Sustained Low Fertility," 62 *Social Science Quarterly* 323, 327 (1981). Beginning in 1966, Romania tried to increase its birth rate by forbidding abortions and the manufacture or importation of contraceptives. After initially vigorous efforts at enforcement and a short-run increase in the birth rate, the program flopped, William Moskoff, "Pronatalist Policies in Romania," 28 *Economic Development and Cultural Change* 597 (1980), but there were sporadic efforts to revive it. See Chapter 15, note 8.

24. Spengler, note 22 above, at 255. Compare Leslie Whittington, James Alm, and H. Elizabeth Peters, "Fertility and the Personal Exemption: Implicit Pronatalist Policy in the United States," 80 *American Economic Review* 545 (1990).

25. Thomas J. Espenshade and Joseph J. Minarik, "Demographic Implications of the 1986 US Tax Reform," 13 *Population and Development Review* 115 (1987).

population and military power, while the growth of international trade has reduced the significance to a nation's prosperity of having domestic markets large enough to enable producers to realize all possible economies of scale. In addition, the more crowded a country becomes, the greater are the congestion externalities (traffic jams, pollution, and so forth) that it must cope with.

A potential problem for a democracy of having a stagnant or declining population is that it results in a shift of political power to the old, whose limited time horizon may lead them to practice "single-issue" voting, which may not be in the interest of society as a whole. But this tendency may be held in check by the altruism of elderly people toward their children and grandchildren. And solving a problem of underpopulation, if there is one, no longer requires increased fertility. Should a Western country want to have a larger (and younger) population, it need not try to fiddle with the birth rate; it need only relax its barriers to immigration. By screening prospective immigrants for signs of intelligence and character, a nation could actually increase the quality of its population at the same time that it was increasing its size—something it could not feasibly accomplish by measures to increase the birth rate, although in the last chapter we shall examine some suggestions for eugenic breeding of human beings. And the society could, if it wanted, reduce the average age of its population by providing financial incentives for young people to immigrate and discouraging the old from doing so.

As for overpopulation, the birth rate in the West today is so low—in many countries it is well below the replacement level[26]—that active policies to discourage procreation are unnecessary to correct any perceived external costs of additional population. It is true that population can continue to grow, even without immigration, long after the birth rate has dipped below replacement; the birth rate is determined by the number of men and women (particularly the latter) in their fertile years, not by the number of children. But eventually the "birth-dearth" children become the fertile cohort of the population, and if they have no more (or few more) children than their parents did, the population will begin to decline.

I do not mean to suggest that the birth rate has fallen because people are concerned with overpopulation. The objection would be the same as to the suggestion that if France had really been underpopulated, French couples would voluntarily have produced more children. The birth rate has fallen because infant mortality has declined (so fewer births are required for a family to have a high probability of attaining their target number of adult offspring) and the cost of children has risen. This rise is due partly to the fact that the opportunity cost of women's time in the household has risen as their opportunities to work outside the home have improved, partly to a shift in demand

---

26. *Below-Replacement Fertility in Industrial Societies: Causes, Consequences, Policies* (Kingsley Davis et al. eds. 1987).

from quantity to quality of children, and partly to an increase in leisure activities for women.[27] Women's opportunities to work outside the home have improved not only or mainly because such work has become physically less demanding—for women have long done physically demanding work—but also because, with fewer children and more labor-saving devices, the value of women's time in household work has fallen and with it the opportunity costs of working outside the home.

Although anything that reduces the attractiveness of marriage and takes women outside the home can be expected to foster sexual permissiveness, that permissiveness is not itself a cause of declining birth rates. It is another effect, along with declining births, of the change in women's employment opportunities, a change that has increased their opportunity costs of bearing and raising children and reduced their financial dependence on men.

I conclude that at present in wealthy nations there is no strong economic argument for either pronatalist or antinatalist policies, or for pronatalist or antinatalist justifications of policies more commonly debated on other grounds, such as abortion and homosexuality. But insofar as overpopulation *is* a concern of our society, one can see, just as with the ancient Greeks, in whom fear of overpopulation was deeply ingrained (Zeus, for example, was said to have "stirred up the Trojan War to relieve the world of overpopulation"),[28] why we would be more likely to tolerate homosexuality than traditional Jews, with their ingrained fear of underpopulation. And we should be alert to policies that have unintended pronatalist or antinatalist effects. Child-welfare programs aimed at the poor, such as Aid to Families with Dependent Children, may stimulate births among the poor, while policies aimed at facilitating the entry of middle-class women into the labor market may reduce the middle-class birth rate. Such a combination may leave the overall birth rate unchanged and simply make the population as a whole poorer.

Progress

Another macroeconomic effect of sexual mores might be conjectured. One observes that the Western nations have on the whole been enormously productive and innovative compared to the rest of the world—and also far more prudish. Could these attributes be related, and specifically could the second be one of the causes of the first? Maybe people in the West have channeled

27. T. Paul Schultz, *Economics of Population* 160, 166–168 (1981). Note that an increase in the demand for quality could result (in the absence of legal prohibition) in an increased demand for abortion and infanticide, as well as for contraception. The trade-off between quality and quantity of children is emphasized in Becker, note 11 above, ch. 5.

28. L. P. Wilkinson, "Classical Approaches—I. Population & Family Planning," 50 *Encounter*, 22, 23 (April 1978).

energies that would otherwise have been dissipated in polygamy and sexual intrigue into technological invention and economic production; or maybe sexual restraint promotes a personal character more suited to economic activity than a libertine's character is. Yet ordinarily we do not think that cutting down the range of activities in which individuals may engage promotes technological innovation and other sources of economic productivity and growth. On the contrary, as the communist nations learned to their sorrow, the more restricted are people's consumption opportunities, the less incentive they have to work hard to obtain the resources necessary for consumption. The hardest line taken against sexual pleasure—that of the Roman Catholic Church—is correlated not with support for free markets and economic progress but instead with a disdain for material progress that may have slowed, and certainly has not quickened, the pace of economic growth in Catholic countries. Polygamy did not seem to hold back the Mormons, or Puritanism to spur economic progress more than less ascetic versions of Protestantism did.

The most powerful counterexample to the puritanism-is-progressive conjecture is Japan. Judeo-Christian reservations concerning sexual pleasure have never gained a significant following there, yet their absence has not prevented the emergence of a work-and-saving ethic that is stronger even than in the West. Apparently a nation does not need the Christian sexual ethic in order to prosper. It is true that the divorce and illegitimacy rates in Japan are low and that Japanese women in particular are sexually conservative by American standards,[29] but this need not have anything to do with sexual scruples. Because relatively few Japanese women are employed outside the home,[30] they remain dependent on men for support to a greater extent than women in the developed countries of the West; this could explain the low rate of illegitimate births. Abortion (and, until recently, infanticide as well, as I noted in Chapter 5), contraception, male adultery, and pornography flourish in Japan; the birth rate is very low; and homosexuality is tolerated.[31] The parallelism to ancient Greece is apparent.

Unlike Japan, Sweden is at once sexually permissive and economically stagnant. But the causality appears to run in the opposite direction from that claimed by the puritanism-is-progressive school. The elaborate Swedish welfare system, by greatly reducing the dependence of women on men for support, may well be responsible for the extraordinary illegitimacy rate in Sweden. But

29. Samuel H. Preston, "The Decline of Fertility in Non-European Industrialized Countries," in *Below-Replacement Fertility in Industrial Societies,* note 26 above, at 26, 36–37; Shin'ichi Asayama, "Adolescent Sex Development and Adult Sex Behavior in Japan," 11 *Journal of Sex Research* 91 (1975).

30. Preston, note 29 above, at 37.

31. "Japanese males are not only freer sexually compared with their wives but also openly enjoy much more freedom than do American and probably European men." Asayama, note 29 above, at 109. And see references in Chapter 2.

that welfare system is the product of a socialist ethos that has held the country back economically, not of attitudes of sexual permissiveness that may well be a consequence (in part at least) of the social policies designed to reduce the dependence of Swedish women on men.

What has given the puritanism-is-progressive idea such plausibility as it has is not theory or historical evidence but a series of misleading correlations. The first, just noted, is that socialist policies may simultaneously slow economic growth and promote sexual freedom, creating a suggestive but misleading inverse correlation between economic growth and sexual freedom. Second, as we saw in Chapter 5, busy people, in the sense of people whose opportunity costs of time are high, are likely to be sexually rather austere because most forms of sexual activity are time-intensive—certainly those that are most visible, such as a string of affairs—and people tend to be busier in prosperous than in stagnant societies. People are sexually austere because they are prosperous, not prosperous because they are sexually austere. And if we switch focus from prosperity to some more strenuous conception of social achievement, such as intellectual and artistic creativity, political energy, or even military prowess, then we have only to instance ancient Greece to refute any suggestion that Judeo-Christian sexual ethics are a precondition to such achievement. The Swedish example suggests that those ethics are not a precondition to the gentler egalitarian values, either.

Another misleading correlation is between time spent in market activities and *measured* national output. A reallocation of time from a market activity to a leisure activity that does not require substantial market inputs, such as sexual activity, will reduce measured national output, although it may increase that output in real economic terms, which take account of nonmonetized as well as monetized costs and benefits.

Finally, sexual freedom happens often to have been a plank in the platform of left-wing movements, movements that are hostile to free markets and that, if they get into power, adopt policies that retard economic growth—sometimes disastrously so, as recent history demonstrates. The student radicals of the 1960s were opposed to both conventional sexual morality and capitalism. The same was true of the Soviet Union in its initial and most radical phase, before Stalin took over. But the correlation between political radicalism and sexual permissiveness is adventitious. Radicals tend to conflate and then oppose the salient elements of the status quo: conflate and then oppose, under the rubric of "bourgeois morality," what may well be unrelated features of the society against which they are rebelling. Evidence for this conjecture may be found in the Cuban revolution. The Batista regime, which preceded Castro's, was capitalist and libertine; Castro's was (and is) socialist and puritanical. There are other examples. The Maoist regime in China was puritanical, in reaction to the tolerance of prostitution and other vices that had been a conspicuous feature of the Kuomintang regime. The relation in Iran between the regime of the shah and the revolutionary Islamic regime that replaced it—the first capitalist and (by Islamic standards) sexually permissive, the second anticapitalist and sexually repressive—is similar. The left in Canada used to be ambivalent about birth control because the traditional supporters of birth control were neo-Malthusians, and Malthus had the reputation of being a reactionary.[32] Different economic systems are compatible with a variety of positions on the spectrum of sexual permissiveness and repression. Political conservatives need not be sexual conservatives. Not all are.[33]

Incest and Revulsion

Earlier I suggested that there is an economic basis for some concern even with such relative peccadilloes as adultery and fornication, so it will come as a surprise that one of the bedrock prohibitions of sex law, the prohibition against incest, is not quite so easy to defend, at least on economic grounds, as one might have supposed it would be. The problem is not that incest is not a bad thing. Even biologists who believe that some degree of inbreeding is good because it preserves adaptive combinations of genes do not advise marriage between *close* relatives.[34] The incest taboo has the further value of minimizing rivalry within a family and preventing families from growing to a size that would be politically destabilizing. These values presumably explain the frequent extension of the taboo to in-laws, that is, persons who are not genetic relatives.[35] I shall not discuss that extension further.

32. Angus McLaren and Arlene Tigar McLaren, *The Bedroom and the State: The Changing Practice and Politics of Contraception and Abortion in Canada, 1880–1980* 72–73 (1986).

33. See, for example, Ernest van den Haag, "Sodom and Begorrah," *National Review,* April 29, 1991, 35, 36, arguing that "society has no compelling interest that justifies prohibiting or even legislating about homosexuality," and urging the military to drop its policy of excluding homosexuals. Which is not to say that van den Haag is a sexual liberal *tout court.* See his article "Pornography and Censorship," 13 *Policy Review* 73 (Summer 1980), discussed in Chapter 13.

34. William M. Shields, *Philopatry, Inbreeding, and the Evolution of Sex* 196–198 (1982). "Philopatry" refers to the disinclination of most people to adopt a nomadic style of life, a style that minimizes the likelihood of mating with a relative. An additional point, though one somewhat antagonistic to the preservation-of-adaptive-combinations rationale for limited inbreeding, is that assortative mating (the mating of likes), which inbreeding promotes, can create greater variance, hence greater opportunities for natural selection, in subsequent generations. But the qualification "limited" inbreeding must be stressed. Close inbreeding, for example as a result of marriage between siblings or even first cousins, produces a high incidence of genetic defects, although in time they might be weeded out by natural selection. I. Michael Lerner and William J. Libby, *Heredity Evolution and Society* 370–373 (2d ed. 1976); Ernst Caspari, "Sexual Selection in Human Evolution," in *Sexual Selection and the Descent of Man, 1871–1971* 332, 340 (Bernard Campbell ed. 1972); Eliot B. Spiess, *Genes in Populations* 276–278 (1977); Philip W. Hedrick, *Genetics of Populations* 155–160 (1983).

35. On the biological and cultural functions of the incest taboo, see, for example, Nancy

The problem is with *punishing* incest, given natural aversion and overlapping criminal punishments. Taking the second point first, we might want to exclude from the crime of incest cases in which a parent or other adult relative raped or seduced a child, since these cases are within the general prohibition against the use of coercion in sexual as in other relationships. Against this it can be argued that incestuous seduction of a fertile girl is more harmful than ordinary child seduction because of the risk of damaged offspring and also is more difficult to apprehend because of the privacy of the home. Both are good reasons for added punishment, but not necessarily for creating a separate crime.

The residual category of incest after the coercive cases are removed consists largely of sibling incest and of intermarriage among close cousins, although there is also some incest between fathers and their adult daughters and there would be more if it were legal.[36] Sibling incest would be rare even if not prohibited, because persons brought up together from early childhood rarely find each other sexually attractive (see note 36). But some siblings are not brought up together, and others do not possess the avoidance instinct. Once siblings reach adulthood, why should they be forbidden to have sex and marry? The obvious answer is that their children may well be sickly or deformed. It is not a satisfying answer, however, because we do not forbid people who are carrying the same dangerous recessive gene to marry each other. In both cases there is danger to the offspring, but only in the case of incest do law and taboo intervene. Moreover, the prohibition against incest is a prohibition against sexual intercourse, not just against procreation; and even the latter prohibition may be unnecessary, because most sibling couples would be afraid to have children. Improvements in techniques of contraception and abortion thus have weakened the case for prohibiting incest.

Intermarriage among close cousins is treated more leniently than sibling

---

Wilmsen Thornhill, "The Evolutionary Significance of Incest Rules," 11 *Ethology and Sociobiology* 113 (1990); James B. Twitchell, *Forbidden Partners: The Incest Taboo in Modern Culture* (1987), esp. appendix, "A Synopsis of the Biological, Psychological, and Sociological Approaches to Incest," at 243; Carl N. Degler, *In Search of Human Nature: The Decline and Revival of Darwinism in American Social Thought*, ch. 10 (1991). There have been occasional calls for the decriminalizing of incest. See, in particular, Herbert L. Packer, *The Limits of the Criminal Sanction* 314–316 (1968).

36. But probably not much more. Pierre L. van den Berghe, "Human Inbreeding Avoidance: Culture in Nature," 6 *Behavioral and Brain Sciences* 91, 96–98 (1983), offers theory and evidence that children are likely to be "imprinted" in early childhood with a revulsion against sex with the people with whom they are living at the time. This is why sibling incest is rare. Father-daughter incest is more common because only the daughter is imprinted in this way, and she is much weaker than, and is dependent on, her father—as a child. But by the time she is an adult, and often earlier, she can—and will—leave. Indeed, teenage runaways are often fleeing an incestuous relationship with their father.

incest; in many societies, including almost half the states in the United States, it is not prohibited at all. (At a time when the English considered it incest to marry an in-law, a marriage between first cousins was perfectly proper.) This is a puzzle. Although the danger of cousin marriage to offspring is much less than in the case of sibling marriage, the latter form of incest is largely prevented by instinct; the former is not, and is therefore far more common and a larger social problem. As before, it can be argued that since we do not require couples to undergo genetic screening before they are allowed to have sex, it is arbitrary to forbid first cousins to have sex. But there is nothing arbitrary about picking out a class of sexual unions that, if fertile, are likely to produce damaged offspring and prohibiting them without at the same time launching a universal program of genetic screening. The effect of the prohibition is to redirect cousins' procreative activity into channels in which they are much less likely to produce damaged offspring. The result is healthier, and no fewer, infants, with only a slight reduction in the pool of sexual partners available to the cousins.

All this assumes that parents are not perfectly altruistic toward their children and do not bear the full costs of any genetically impaired children that they produce. Without this assumption, incest would not be a source of externalities. But the assumption is realistic.

Our discussion of incest and much that preceded it should make clear that even if sex were a morally indifferent subject, there would still be regulation of sex, and social attitudes that would inspire and back up such regulation. But they would be regulation and attitudes founded on practical, concrete, nonmoralistic concerns with the external effects of sex and with the use of force or fraud to gratify sexual desires. Given both the difficulty (of which more in subsequent chapters) of producing persuasive justifications for forbidding pornography, premarital intercourse, and consensual sodomy, and the high cost of preventing these and other effectively victimless crimes, it is unlikely that the economically optimal system of regulation would be as extensive as what we have today in many parts of the United States. Except that it would try to avoid subsidizing the production of illegitimate children, it would resemble the Swedish system.

Left out of account, however, is what may be the biggest externality: the revulsion that so many people in our society feel at the very idea of promiscuity and of sexual deviance. Revulsion seems a better explanation for why incest has been criminalized than concern with genetic fitness or even with the coercion of minors by persons standing in a fiduciary relationship to them. From *Oedipus Tyrannus* to *Chinatown,* incest has had a rare power to disgust, unlike sex between unrelated persons known to harbor dangerous recessive genes.[37] The disgust that homosexual intercourse arouses among many het-

---

37. The core of the incest taboo—a prohibition against sex with a member of one's nuclear family—appears to be common to all human societies, past and present. George Peter Murdock,

erosexuals explains the survival of sodomy laws better than the external effects of such intercourse do. The fact that the AIDS epidemic has had relatively little effect on attitudes toward homosexuality is evidence of this, although it is possible that one effect has been to increase sympathy for homosexuals as well as fear of them, and the effects could be offsetting.[38]

There is nothing in principle to disqualify disgust, even when irrational (and revulsion at incest is not irrational), from counting as an external cost to which a polity dedicated to economic efficiency should pay heed. There have been plenty of cases in which funeral homes were held to be nuisances because they reduced the value of the residential property in the neighborhood, even though the cause of the loss of value in these cases was a silly, ostrichlike reluctance to be reminded of death.[39] A liberal polity, it can be argued, takes preferences as they come, and if the majority hate homosexuals or fornicators or foot fetishists, so much the worse for them (at least if the disutility to them of being punished or ostracized is less than the utility to the majority of knowing that the law condemns the practices that the majority hates).

Maybe; but John Stuart Mill, the greatest of classical liberals, thought "constructive injury," as he described the feelings of those "who consider as an injury to themselves any conduct which they have a distaste for," a poor basis for public regulation.[40] He pointed out that "in its interferences with personal conduct it [the busybody public] is seldom thinking of anything but the enormity of acting or feeling differently from itself."[41] To allow people to decree that "no person shall enjoy any pleasure which they think wrong," even though that enjoyment is harmless except for the indignation it arouses, is to open the door wide to persecution, the essential spirit of which is

Social Structure 284–285 (1949). A few, however, have permitted royalty or other special people to engage in it. David M. Schneider, "The Meaning of Incest," 85 Journal of the Polynesian Society 149 (1976). For a thorough discussion of the biological basis of the incest taboo, see van den Berghe's article, note 36 above; also commentary thereon, author's response, and bibliography, all in 6 Behavioral and Brain Sciences 102–123 (1983); and Joseph Shepher, Incest: A Biosocial View (1983). I discuss incest further in Chapter 14.

38. The percentage of Gallup Poll respondents who favor legalizing homosexual relations between consenting adults rose from 43 to 45 percent between 1977 and 1982, dipped to 44 percent in 1985, then plunged to 33 percent in 1986 and 1987, but by 1989 had soared to 47 percent. Gallup Report nos. 244–245, January-February 1986, 3; Gallup Report no. 289, October 1989, 13.

39. See, for example, Williams v. Montgomery, 184 Miss. 547, 186 So. 302 (1939); cf. Everett v. Paschal, 61 Wash. 47, 111 Pac. 879 (1910).

40. John Stuart Mill, On Liberty 76, 78 (David Spitz ed. 1975).

41. Id. at 78.

punishment for the affront of thinking or acting differently from the persons doing the punishing.[42]

Even if not persuaded, the reader should remember that I am trying to abstract from the moral dimension of sex. If sex were a morally indifferent subject, it is hard to imagine people wanting to punish homosexual relations conducted in private between consenting adults, any more than they would want to punish people who eat with their fingers or pick their noses when they think no one is looking. I am thus unpersuaded by Thomas Nagel's attempt to make the concept of a sexual perversion—an immoral sexual practice—more perspicuous by proposing the idea of "gastronomical perversion," which he illustrates with the example of a person who eats magazines that contain pictures of food.[43] A person who did such a thing (otherwise than as a joke) would arouse pity, and maybe some disgust or even alarm, but no one would call him immoral or think he should be punished.

For many purposes, it is true, revulsion—whether or not clothed with the epithet *moral*—is a brute fact that the policymaker cannot ignore. It may, for example, affect the psychological impact of sexual abuse on children (greater, presumably, in a society in which people are taught to regard such abuse with revulsion); it may, as we shall see in Chapter 11, affect the decision whether to relax the armed forces' ban on homosexuals even if the decision maker believes that revulsion at homosexuality is irrational. But it should not pretermit examination of what the proper scope of sexual regulation would be if the supposed moral aspects somehow evaporated and we treated sex with the same moral indifference with which we treat eating.

To repeat: if after acquainting himself with all the facts bearing on the sexual perversions, as he may choose to regard them, a person is left with so profound a revulsion that he desires the state to step in and punish the practitioners and is willing to bear his fair share of the public expense of such punishment, I would have nothing further to say to him except that he ought to reread chapter 4 of *On Liberty*. But the qualification beginning "if after" is essential. Much of the revulsion that we feel about sexual behavior different from our own reflects an ignorance about sex and its consequences that is

---

42. Id. at 81. For elucidation of Mill's famous distinction between "self-regarding" and "other-regarding" conduct—only the latter was in his view a proper object of social or legal condemnation, however "immoral" the public considered the self-regarding conduct in question—see C. L. Ten, *Mill on Liberty*, ch. 2 (1980). The extensive critical literature is illustrated by Gertrude Himmelfarb, *On Liberty and Liberalism: The Case of John Stuart Mill*, ch. 4 (1990), and by Harry M. Clor, "Mill and Millians on Liberty and Moral Character," 47 *Review of Politics* 3 (1985). James Fitzjames Stephen's book *Liberty, Equality, Fraternity* (1873), an attack on *On Liberty*, is a central document in the moralistic tradition of sexual regulation, and is examined in the next chapter.

43. "Sexual Perversion," 66 *Journal of Philosophy* 5, 7 (1969).

understandable, even rational, given the taboo character of the subject in our society. (The history of persecution is, in general, a history of ignorance.) Were that ignorance dispelled, we might move rapidly toward the model of morally indifferent sex.

If we ignore moral revulsion, and all population effects, as justifications for regulating sexual behavior, we still are left with complicated factual questions of the sort raised in the discussion of sex education and with equally complicated factual questions, raised in the next section of this chapter, concerning the practical implementation of sexual regulation. Even when simplified as much as I am attempting to do, normative economic analysis of sexual regulation remains a formidable task.

The Efficacy of Sexual Regulations

An optimal system of regulation is a function not only of the social costs of the practices one seeks to regulate but also of the cost of effective regulation (ineffective regulation can be bought cheaply). History and current practice appear to teach that laws regulating sex are inefficacious because most sex crimes are, either de jure or de facto, victimless. By this I mean not that such crimes do no harm—they may or may not—but that the victim, if any, is either unidentifiable or unwilling or unable to play the role of complaining witness. Illicit relations of whatever kind between consenting adults, including fornication, adultery, prostitution, and homosexual and heterosexual sodomy, are traditional examples of "victimless" crime, as is the sale of pornography; they are certainly victimless in the practical sense that both parties are willing participants. Perhaps they are better described as crimes in which not the victim but the fact of victimization is frequently unascertainable. The seduction of children, and many rapes, are victimless in the severely practical sense that the victim is unlikely to complain to the authorities. The victim may not be aware that he or she is a victim; may not be a credible complainant or witness because of youth; may not be able to furnish corroboration (the perennial problem of rapes in which the victim is not injured); may be unwilling for reasons of reputation to complain; or may be dead without anyone but the parties to the crime knowing it—as in the case of illegal abortion, whose main victim, of course, is the fetus. Victimless crimes, in either the de jure or the de facto sense, are not completely beyond the power of government to punish. But, as we should have learned from Prohibition and the "war on drugs," the investigation and prosecution of victimless crimes may require an immense investment of investigatory and prosecutorial resources for distinctly limited returns.

At a time when society was united in fiercely condemning such victimless crimes as sodomy, the technology of law enforcement was too primitive to enable the authorities to catch many offenders. These are two separate reasons for the savage penalties for such crimes. Since the expected cost of punishment to an offender is the product of the probability of punishment and the severity of punishment if he is caught, a low probability of punishment can, to some extent anyway, be offset if we jack up the penalty. But this is no panacea, humanitarian objections to one side. We know that the threat of the death penalty does not drive the murder rate down to zero even at times and in places where the probability of apprehending a murderer is high and the probability of imposing the death penalty if he is apprehended is also high. So we should not be surprised that, for a crime whose perpetrators are apprehended very rarely because it is a victimless crime and society does not have effective techniques for catching the perpetrators of such crimes, the threat of the death penalty may have only a modest deterrent effect. There seems to have been a good deal of homosexual activity even when it was a capital offense.

But probably less than there is today. The inefficacy of sex laws is easily exaggerated. The Connecticut statute that forbade the use of contraceptives, struck down in *Griswold v. Connecticut* (discussed in Chapter 12), was not quite the joke that Robert Bork has said it was.[44] The statute was understood not to apply to the use of devices that prevent disease, so it did not interfere with the sale of condoms, or even of diaphragms, because diaphragms are occasionally used to protect damaged tissues. Nor was any effort made to enforce the statute against private doctors who supplied women with contraceptive advice and devices. But the statute made it impossible to operate birth control clinics in the state, because their activities in violation of the statute could not be concealed or redescribed. There is an analogy to the effect of the Sherman Act in driving cartels underground at a time when the sanctions for violation of the act and the investigatory and prosecutorial resources employed in its enforcement were too feeble to deter covert cartels.[45] All birth control clinics in Connecticut shut down after the state's highest court upheld the constitutionality of the statute in 1940.[46] They did not reopen until the U.S. Supreme Court invalidated the statute in 1965.[47]

44. Robert H. Bork, *The Tempting of America: The Political Seduction of the Law* 95–96 (1990).

45. George J. Stigler, "The Economic Effects of the Antitrust Laws," in Stigler, *The Organization of Industry* 259 (1968).

46. State v. Nelson, 126 Conn. 412, 11 A.2d 856 (1940).

47. On the closing of the clinics after *Nelson*, see Mary L. Dudziak, "Just Say No: Birth Control in the Connecticut Supreme Court before *Griswold v. Connecticut*," 75 *Iowa Law Review* 915 (1990); Comment, "The History and Future of the Legal Battle over Birth Control," 49 *Cornell Law Quarterly* 275, 280 (1964); Alvah W. Sulloway, *Birth Control and Catholic Doctrine* 33 (1959); Brief for Appellants in the U.S. Supreme Court in *Griswold v. Connecticut* at 6 (on this point—that the law had caused the birth control clinics to shut down—the state in

In regard to the efficacy of sexual regulations, the closest analogy to the birth control clinic is the abortion clinic. Laws forbidding abortion will not prevent abortions. But they will—even if few resources are devoted to enforcement (and few resources *were* devoted to enforcing the abortion laws)[48]— make abortion either more dangerous, by driving it underground,[49] or more expensive, by forcing the pregnant woman to travel to a place where abortion is legal (and delay spells danger, too, since abortion is a riskier operation the later in the pregnancy it takes place). Either way, abortion is made more costly, so one can expect fewer abortions than if abortion were legal. How many fewer? In other words, how many abortions can actually be attributed to the Supreme Court's decision in *Roe v. Wade*? No one knows, because the number of illegal abortions before (or for that matter after) *Roe* is not known. What is more, we do not know how many states would have jumped on the "pro-choice" bandwagon, which was gathering momentum in the period leading up to *Roe*: between 1969 and 1973, the year *Roe* was decided, the number of legal abortions performed in the United States increased more than thirtyfold.[50] The legislative trend makes it impossible to determine the incremental effect of *Roe*. But we may be able to say something about the effect of legalization, whether by legislative or by judicial action. Estimates of the number of illegal abortions before *Roe* support the conclusion ("conjecture" would be more accurate) that 70 percent of abortions today would be performed anyway if abortion were illegal.[51] This implies that legalization— besides reducing the cost of and mortality from abortion—increases the number of abortions by more than 40 percent, presumably by making abortion cheaper and safer.

Griswold agreed with the defendants). There appears to be no basis for Bork's contention that "the professors had some difficulty arranging a test case but finally managed to have two doctors who gave birth control information fined $100 as accessories." Bork, note 44 above, at 95. Shortly after the New Haven birth control clinic created to test the validity of the statute opened, the police raided it on the complaint of a citizen that the clinic was breaking the law, and after questioning the director and medical director obtained and executed warrants for their arrest. They were booked, charged, tried, and convicted. Comment at 296; see also Dudziak. The question whether the statute was enforced and the suit genuine was probed extensively in the oral argument of the *Griswold* case. The briefs and the transcript of the argument may be found in *Landmark Briefs and Arguments of the Supreme Court of the United States: Constitutional Law,* vol. 61, 3 (Philip B. Kurland and Gerhard Casper eds. 1975).

48. Kristin Luker, *Abortion and the Politics of Motherhood* 53–54 (1984).

49. The mortality rate for abortion fell very steeply after the Supreme Court invalidated state laws forbidding abortion. Christopher Tietze, *Induced Abortion: A World Review* 106 (4th ed. 1981) (tab. 25).

50. Computed from Gerald Rosenberg, *The Hollow Hope: Can Courts Bring about Social Change?* 180 (1991) (tab. 6.1).

51. Id. at 355.

These figures are based, as I have said, on estimates of the number of illegal abortions before *Roe v. Wade,* and it has been argued that they are vastly overestimated.[52] Even so, with the cat out of the bag, as it were—a large number of abortion clinics, thousands of doctors and nurses skilled in performing abortions, and a militant feminist movement—there would unquestionably be a vast number of illegal abortions if abortion were once again banned. Moreover, many states would not ban abortion even if *Roe v. Wade* were overruled and the issue returned to state control, so the time and travel costs of obtaining a legal abortion to most women living in states in which abortion was illegal would still be low.

Long after the penalties for homosexual relations between consenting adults were moderated, and even though no nation in modern times—not even Nazi Germany or communist Cuba—has made systematic efforts to discover and punish such relations when conducted in private, the existence of criminal penalties must have reduced the amount of homosexual activity somewhat. Unless such penalties are not enforced at all, which has in fact become the norm in those U.S. states that retain them on their books, their existence will impose at least a slight expected punishment cost and, more important, will raise the costs of search for homosexual partners by creating incentives to conduct the search in a clandestine manner. Anything that raises the cost of an activity will reduce its amount—and not only, in the case of homosexuality, on the part of opportunistic homosexuals. Homosexual preference may be unaffected, but a preference for homosexual relations does not dictate the frequency of those relations. The more costly they are, the less frequent they will be. So if there were a compelling reason to want to reduce the amount of homosexual activity in society, the retention of criminal penalties, even mild ones that are but weakly enforced, could be defended, especially since the cost to the taxpayer of retention and weak enforcement is trivial. But it is a big "if." It also ignores a traditional objection to underenforced criminal statutes: they vest enforcement officials with enormous discretion, which invites discriminatory enforcement.

The foregoing analysis may help explain why masturbation (at least when solitary and in private) has never been made a crime, even though both in the early Christian era and in Victorian England (and America) it was regarded—much as illegal drug use is today—as a serious offense against good morals, a crime against unborn generations, a factor predisposing the perpetrator to sex crimes, and a form of attempted suicide, all rolled into one. The cost of detection would be extremely high, so effective deterrence would require savage punishment. Few people have ever thought that such punishment would be commensurate with the actual severity of the offense, especially since the principal offenders are minors. I acknowledge that in making these

---

52. Germain Grisez, *Abortion: The Myth, the Realities, and the Arguments* 42 (1970).

points I am both ceding a role to retributive justice in the design of criminal penalties and ignoring the (presumably modest) behavioral effects of even a radically underenforced law. But the second point may be cancelled by the social costs of such a law when enforced in a discriminatory manner. Discrimination seems of the essence in the enforcement of sex laws. Who can think of one *prominent* homosexual in the century since the trial of Oscar Wilde who, even if he flouted his homosexuality, was prosecuted for engaging in homosexual acts?[53]

An example of a victimless sex crime that the law deters to a large although perhaps deceptive extent—and this despite little investment in enforcement—is bigamy, the crime of being married at the same time to two or more persons. Marriage is a public act, relatively difficult to conceal; having two or more wives is very difficult to conceal. The analogy is to the operations of a birth control clinic, which, unlike the actual use of a contraceptive, are also difficult to conceal. But in a society that does not attempt to forbid adultery or fornication, or attach significant disabilities to illegitimacy, a person who is not a stickler for formality can easily substitute concubinage, which is a kind of informal marriage, for the second and any additional marriages. So bigamy is deterred,[54] but a practice that is a close substitute,[55] and that would seem to create the identical evils (whatever exactly they are), is not. Maybe the evils are not completely identical. Concubinage leaves the wife's status paramount. In bigamy, although only the first marriage is valid, the first wife cannot be confident that she retains the primary commitment of her husband.

The essential porousness of the bigamy prohibition is shown by the fact that there is still open polygamy in Utah. The polygamist avoids committing bigamy by not applying for a license for any of his marriages after the first.[56] The later marriages are technically cohabitations, and this makes him an adulterer; but prosecutions for adultery, even in Utah, are rare. The children of these informal marriages are illegitimate, but there are few remaining disabilities of illegitimacy, as we are about to see. It is true that the wives (all but the first) lose the conventional spousal benefits—medical insurance and

53. Actually there was one, the great English mathematician Alan Turing. Convicted in 1952, he avoided prison by agreeing to submit to female-hormone treatments, designed to reduce male sexual desire, for one year. A year after completing, apparently without incident, the course of treatments, Turing committed suicide; but it is unclear whether there was any connection between the prosecution, or the treatments, and the suicide. He had not lost his job as a result of the legal proceeding or its aftermath, nor had he seemed otherwise affected by it. Andrew Hodges, *Alan Turing: The Enigma*, ch. 8 (1983), esp. 487–488.

54. Not completely, of course. Roderick Phillips, *Putting Asunder: A History of Divorce in Western Society* 296–302 (1988).

55. Jean-Louis Flandrin, *Families in Former Times: Kinship, Household and Sexuality* 181 (1979).

56. Dirk Johnson, "Polygamists Emerge from Secrecy, Seeking Not Just Peace But Respect," *New York Times*, April 9, 1991, A22.

the like. But there is a big difference in deterrent effect between declining to confer the privileges of marriage on members of polygamous unions and punishing polygamists as criminals. The main practical significance of the crime of bigamy today may be to deter the form of fraud that consists of a man's purporting to marry a woman when, unbeknownst to her, he is already married and therefore cannot form a valid marriage with her.

The *New York Times* article on polygamy in Utah (note 56) quotes polygamists as defending their practice by reference to the increasing recourse to cohabitation by Americans, homosexual as well as heterosexual, in lieu of marriage. They make the point that law is relative to public opinion. The more that irregular unions become accepted by public opinion, the more likely prosecutors are to look the other way when people in Utah use a combination of marriage and cohabitation to replicate polygamy.

Although the criminal law is not totally ineffective in the sexual sphere, the cost in the circumstances prevailing in the Western world today of extirpating such victimless crimes as fornication, prostitution, and homosexual sodomy, or even of significantly reducing their incidence, is so high that it seems quixotic to look to the criminal law for help even in dealing with such undoubted externalities of nonmarital sex as venereal disease, in particular AIDS. Criminalization may actually undermine efforts to fight venereal disease. Consensual sexual relations conducted in private are essentially beyond the law's reach; but as soon as the participant in such relations—the prostitute (heterosexual or homosexual), the adulterer, and so forth—surfaces with a complaint or a visit to a doctor or to the hospital, he or she is placed within the law's reach. In addition, criminalization retards the dissemination and circulation of accurate information about the risks involved in an activity.

Along these lines it has long been argued that a licensed prostitute, required to undergo periodic testing for venereal disease, is less dangerous to the community than one who plies her trade free from regulatory supervision. So while a severe law against prostitution, even though difficult to enforce because prostitution is for all practical purposes a victimless crime, would reduce the number of prostitutes, it would also increase the spread of disease by those prostitutes who remained. The licensing of prostitutes is therefore an attractive policy—in principle—but, if we may judge from the European experience, not in practice. The intrusiveness of a scheme that required frequent medical inspections, and that by labeling women as prostitutes precluded them from engaging in prostitution on a part-time basis (as many preferred to do), drove most prostitutes into the illegal market, with the result, for example, that in 1958, the last year in which Italy had such a scheme, only 2,560 prostitutes were registered under it.[57] Most other countries had abandoned similar schemes as futile years earlier.

---

57. Gibson, note 9 above, at 224; see also id. at 106–107, 128. The systems for licensing

The complicated effects of laws pertaining to sex are nowhere better illustrated than in the case of the laws, now much trimmed back as a result of decisions by the Supreme Court cited in Chapter 12, that attach disabilities to being illegitimate. It might seem that such laws would reduce not only the number of illegitimate births but also—and this may be one object of such laws—the amount of nonmarital intercourse, by attaching an extra cost to it. Yet both effects may be doubted. The principal badge of illegitimacy is that the illegitimate child does not have the status of an heir. But in Anglo-American law this status is significant only if the person whose heir you are dies without a will. One is free by will to leave one's property to whomever one pleases—an "heir" is simply a person who inherits if there is no will—and this means that one not only can leave property to an illegitimate child but also can disinherit legitimate children. So the cost of illegitimacy is slight. (It is higher when one includes children's benefits that are not defeasible, for example, social security survivors' benefits.) And while it might nevertheless make a woman somewhat more reluctant to engage in nonmarital intercourse, it might make a man more eager to do so, knowing that the offspring of such a relationship would not be his heirs so he would not have to go to the bother of expressly disinheriting them, as he would want to do if, as is more likely than not, he did not want an illegitimate child to share in his estate. If all Americans had a will, the bother would be trivial; but many do not.

The strongest case for using the concept of legitimacy to discourage nonmarital intercourse came before the Supreme Court in *Michael H. v. Gerald D.*[58] A California statute conclusively presumed that a child born to a married woman was her husband's child as well as her own. A man who had had an affair with a married woman, and who a paternity test showed was almost certainly the father of her child, sued for visitation rights, claiming that the statute was an unconstitutional deprivation of his interest in his natural child. The Supreme Court upheld the constitutionality of the statute, at least as applied to a case (such as that before it) where the married couple

---

prostitutes had some grotesque features. In nineteenth-century Italy, for example, a girl could register as a prostitute at the age of 16, but could not marry without parental consent until she reached 30. Id. at 54. It is no surprise that abolition of the licensing system, and its replacement by a prohibition of solicitation but not of prostitution per se, was a feminist project. Id. at 44–45, 224–227. The licensing of brothels has continued in Germany, however, save for a hiatus between 1927 and 1933. Richard J. Evans, "Prostitution, State and Society in Imperial Germany," 70 *Past & Present* 106, 128–129 (1976). This may attest to the efficiency of the German civil service. And see generally Decker, note 9 above, at 66, 132–141. In this country the sequence was registration, then segregation in red-light districts, then prohibition. Joseph Mayer, *The Regulation of Commercialized Vice: An Analysis of the Transition from Segregation to Repression in the United States* (1922); cf. Walkowitz, note 9 above. Nevada's 36 licensed brothels, however, have managed to keep their employees completely AIDS-free. "Legalised Prostitution," *Economist*, September 7, 1991, 28, 29.

58. 491 U.S. 110 (1989).

wanted to raise the child as their own. I am surprised that the decision was not unanimous—in fact it was only five to four. The idea that the Constitution gives an adulterer rights over the issue of the adultery, an idea that if accepted would require bastardizing the child for the adulterer's sake, carries the idea of a constitutional right to sexual freedom beyond anything we shall encounter in Chapter 12 ("The Sexual Revolution in the Courts").

Designing an Optimal Punishment Scheme for Sex Crimes

The heterogeneity of sex offenders and the substitutability of sexual practices complicate the design of a rational scheme for punishing sexual offenses. Consider the child abuser, the pedophile. There are two types of pedophile (corresponding to the two types of homosexual)—the opportunist, who substitutes a child for an adult sex partner when an adult is temporarily unavailable, and the "true" pedophile, who, being fixated on sex with children, does not consider adults an acceptable, let alone a superior, substitute. The responsiveness of these two types of offender to changes in the severity of response or in the resources devoted to apprehension and punishment is different.[59] Which should be punished more heavily? The committed offender, it might seem, because he derives a larger benefit from the offense and therefore is more difficult to deter. But suppose he is not deterrable at all, so great is the subjective benefit he derives. Then punishment is wasted on him, from a deterrent standpoint. From the standpoint of broader crime control, however, it may not be wasted at all. A person who is not deterrable by threat of punishment can still be prevented by imprisonment from committing crimes for the period that he is in prison; the longer that imprisonment, the more crimes are prevented. So probably, on balance, the committed offender should be punished more heavily than the opportunistic one. This conclusion may grate on our moral sensibilities, which incline us to want to punish less severely the person acting under compulsion than the person making a rational choice. Yet from an economic standpoint, both the opportunistic and the committed offender are acting rationally. The only difference is in their alternatives and hence in their behavior.

The responsiveness of offenses to sanctions is thus a function not only of the offender's preferences but also of his options. It is no surprise that there is more recidivism by homosexuals who break laws against homosexual

---

59. For empirical evidence, see Kevin Howells, "Adult Sexual Interest in Children: Considerations Relevant to Theories of Aetiology," in *Adult Sexual Interest in Children* 55, 80 (Mark Cook and Kevin Howells eds. 1981).

activity than by violators of the rape and incest laws.[60] The average rape or incest violator incurs a lower cost in substituting the lawful version of his act than a homosexual does in substituting a heterosexual act.

There are complex trade-offs in the design of a criminal sex code. If premarital sex is discouraged, the incentives for pederasty are increased; if pederasty is punished severely, the incidence not only of premarital sex but also of rape can be expected to rise, especially since an above-average sex drive has been found to be characteristic of rapists,[61] as economic analysis would predict. It might seem obvious that if premarital sex is not discouraged, the incidence of rape will fall, and perhaps with it the optimal punishment for rape, because the fewer the benefits from rape, the less severe the punishment need be in order to deter it. This line of reasoning would lead us to expect rape to be punished less severely in sexually permissive societies than in sexually repressive ones. But there are additional factors to be considered. In a repressive society girls and even women are sequestered, and this increases the expected cost to the rapist, while in a permissive society men and women mingle freely, and by giving the would-be rapist more access to potential victims this lowers the expected cost of rape. Furthermore, it is more difficult in a permissive society to prove that a rape has occurred, because unchaperoned association between the sexes engenders situations in which the giving of consent is uncertain and contestable. Difficulty of proof is therefore another factor that reduces the expected cost of rape to the rapist in a permissive society.

In summary, both the expected benefits *and* the expected costs of rape are lower in a permissive than in a repressive society, so the optimal penalty might be the same. Two other considerations, however, which happen to be closely related to each other, push in favor of a lower optimal penalty for rape in the permissive society. Without a cult of virginity, the cost of rape to the woman and her family is lower; at the same time, the cost of reporting a rape to the police is lower, and therefore the cost of apprehending the rapist is lower, which tends to offset the difficulty of proving that intercourse was not consented to and was therefore rape. Both factors reduce the optimal severity of punishment, leading one to expect the relative severity with which rape is punished to be less in a permissive society, and this in fact is suggested by the tables in Chapter 3.

We should not be surprised at the abolition of the suit for breach of promise

60. Paul H. Gebhard et al., *Sex Offenders: An Analysis of Types* 711–712 (1965). And this despite the fact that, at the time of the Gebhard study, the probability of apprehension was thought to be slightly higher for homosexual offenders than for incest and rape offenders. Id. at 800 (tab. 137).

61. Ron Langevin, Daniel Paitich, and Anne E. Russon, "Are Rapists Sexually Anomalous, Aggressive, or Both?" in *Erotic Preference, Gender Identity, and Aggression in Men: New Research Studies* 17, 33–34 (Ron Langevin ed. 1985).

(to marry), which served mainly to compensate a woman for the loss of her virginity, a common incident of engagement.[62] The function that the breach of promise suit had performed on the eve of abolition—that of discouraging the man from breaking off the engagement—was taken over by the gift of the diamond engagement ring with the understanding that the woman could retain it if the man broke off the match.[63]

Rationality crops up in some odd places in law. Colonial Americans executed men who had sexual intercourse with animals, fearing that such intercourse would produce dangerous monsters.[64] When this belief waned—and therefore the perceived social costs of the conduct fell—the severity of punishment declined also. It is equally unsurprising that societies which believed that sodomy caused earthquakes should have punished the practice severely.

Pornography can operate both as a substitute for rape and as a complement to it—can operate, in short, either to reduce or to increase the incidence of rape. The net effect remains unknown, as we shall see, and as a result the case for criminalizing the sale of pornography is weak if one takes the mildly libertarian position that voluntary behavior should not be prohibited without a good reason. There is fairly good evidence, however, that pornography is a substitute for (rather than a complement to) exhibitionism, voyeurism, and sexual offenses against minors generally,[65] offenses typically committed by timid persons who do not want direct physical contact with adults and may consider a picture a close substitute for a living sex object. The more we want to prevent these offenses, the less we should try to suppress pornography.

The Political Economy of Sexual Regulation

We have seen that a number of sexual laws, and sexual customs having the force of law, including a variety of apparently senseless, seemingly vestigial sexual laws in this and other Anglo-Saxon societies (culturally, although not ethnically, ours is still an Anglo-Saxon society), make sense—social-functional sense—when analyzed in economic terms. This is not to say that these laws are good; that is a moral issue. It is to say that they are rational means for promoting social ends. For example, we have seen the law of marriage and

---

62. Margaret F. Brinig, "Rings and Promises," 6 *Journal of Law, Economics & Organization* 203, 204–205 (1990). Suits for the tort of seduction are similar, so we should not be surprised that the tort has been abolished in most states.

63. Id. at 213.

64. John D'Emilio and Estelle B. Freedman, *Intimate Matters: A History of Sexuality in America* 17 (1988).

65. Berl Kutschinsky, *Studies on Pornography and Sex Crimes in Denmark* 99–159 (1970), esp. 100 (tab. 1).

divorce (broadly construed to include the regulation of extramarital activity ranging from adultery to pederasty) rationally adapt to changes in the prevalent sexual morality that are themselves adaptive to changes in women's occupational roles, in effective sex ratios, and in other factors singled out as pertinent by economic theory. Later chapters will give additional evidence of such adaptations; no-fault divorce and the abolition of the marriage defense to rape are two examples. Such dramatic lags in adaptation as the retention by half of the U.S. states of laws criminalizing sodomy should not be allowed to conceal the essential rationality of much sex law, over time and across cultures. Even the sodomy laws, though no longer functional, may once have been, as we saw in Chapter 6, although the severity of the traditional punishments seems rooted in irrational fears. The continued retention of those laws by many of our states, deplorable as that may be from a variety of perspectives (see Chapter 11), becomes less anomalous when we remember that the laws are not enforced, and so the pressure for formal repeal is relaxed. In broad terms, though with many exceptions, the historical and cross-cultural pattern of sexual regulation is consistent with studies that find an impress of efficiency on many laws, including the customary laws of ancient and primitive societies.[66]

What is the mechanism, akin to self-interest at the level of individual decision making, by which efficient laws and customs are generated? This question has puzzled economic analysts of law, but in some cases a Darwinian type of answer is plausible. Take a custom such as clitoridectomy. Suppose in some primitive society the role of the clitoris in female orgasm is noticed, and it is also noticed that women with a highly developed capacity for sexual pleasure are more susceptible to the blandishments of seducers. A polygamist, or for that matter the father of a girl, might tumble to the idea that a wife whose clitoris was removed would require less supervision by her husband. Such women would become more valuable in the marriage market—would command higher brideprices or require lower dowries—than other women, and polygamists whose wives were circumcised would prosper more than other polygamists. So the benefits of the practice would be perceived, and eventually it would become generalized and regularized in the form of a custom understood to be normative.

The suggestion that many sexual laws and customs may be efficient is not intended to deny the case for reform. The assumption that efficiency should guide public policy is contestable; not all sexual laws and customs are efficient; and, as we have begun to see in this chapter and will see more clearly in subsequent ones, economic analysis provides a lever—albeit, on the basis of

---

66. See, for example, *Economic Analysis of Law*, note 6 above, esp. pt. 2; William M. Landes and Richard A. Posner, *The Economic Structure of Tort Law* (1987); Posner, *The Economics of Justice*, pts. 2 and 3 (1981).

present knowledge, which is radically incomplete, a modest one—for urging more liberal public policies toward sex upon persons who are open to liberal arguments. (I mean, of course, liberalism in its nineteenth-century, John Stuart Mill sense, rather than in its modern welfare-state sense.) But this raises a question: if we have more regulation of sex than the liberal theory of the state can justify, what is the cause of this overregulation? Is it sheer ignorance, which as a matter of fact is a plausible explanation of the Victorian fear of masturbation? Is it conservative or religious ideology? Maybe so—certainly in part so. But when laws cannot be explained as measures for correcting externalities or otherwise promoting economic efficiency, the economist is inclined to consider next the possibility that they are designed to redistribute wealth, perhaps at the behest of some interest group.[67] Some of our sex laws do seem to be of this kind. An example is the prohibition of bigamy (polygamy), which by limiting competition among men for women increases the sexual and marital opportunities of younger, poorer men. The prohibition is in effect a tax on wealth, for only wealthy men can afford multiple wives. The tax does not generate revenue directly, but, by reducing the cost of a wife, it transfers wealth from the more affluent to the less affluent (and more numerous) men.

Similarly, the gradual decriminalization of homosexual activity may be due less to an exogenous growth of tolerance among the heterosexual population than to the fact that urbanization has increased the number of practicing homosexuals, who, being geographically concentrated, can organize more effectively for political action than if they were dispersed. This is to speak of the supply side of political influence, but the demand side, too, has in recent years encouraged political action by homosexuals: since the advent of AIDS, homosexuals have had more to gain from enlisting government on their side than was formerly the case—massive financial assistance in fighting the scourge.

Finally, the antiabortion movement in the second half of the nineteenth century, which produced the laws struck down in *Roe v. Wade,* was powered to a significant degree by physicians who, wanting a monopoly on medical practice, made abortionists—who were not regular physicians—the symbol of the moral and medical hazards of allowing nonprofessionals to provide medical services.[68]

Since so much sex law seems harmful to women, or at least insensitive to

---

67. See, for example, George J. Stigler, *The Citizen and the State: Essays on Regulation* (1975); Gary S. Becker, "Pressure Groups and Political Behavior," in *Capitalism and Democracy: Schumpeter Revisited* 120 (Richard D. Coe and Charles K. Wilbur eds. 1985); Joseph P. Kalt and Mark A. Zupan, "Capture and Ideology in the Economic Theory of Politics," 74 *American Economic Review* 279 (1984).

68. James C. Mohr, *Abortion in America: The Origins and Evolution of National Policy, 1800–1900,* ch. 6 (1978) ("The Physicians' Crusade against Abortion, 1857–1880"), esp. 160.

their concerns, it is tempting to suppose that a good deal of that law must be a successful effort by men to redistribute wealth (in the broadest sense) from women to themselves. This would make sex law much like other forms of special interest legislation. But there are several problems with the suggestion. The first is that many legally sanctioned or even compelled practices that are superficially misogynistic may actually be in the best interests of women. The most dramatic example is female infanticide in societies in which women's opportunities are severely limited (not necessarily as a result of discrimination). In such societies, infanticide may increase the number and wealth of females who survive to adulthood. The second problem with the suggestion is that neither all men nor all women are identically situated with respect to the benefits and costs of discrimination against the other sex. Fathers of daughters do not benefit from discrimination against women, and we have seen that the Greek and Roman law of dowry sought to protect the interests of such men. Male employees may gain from excluding women from certain employments, but male employers may lose from such exclusion. Some women benefit from sexual freedom, others lose. And women linked financially or through altruism to men (husbands, sons, fathers, brothers) may be harmed by measures that redistribute wealth from men to (other) women. Since men and women have overlapping interests, it is simplistic to attribute a particular law to the interests of men or the interests of women.

Often it is difficult to be confident whether the thrust of a particular law is redistributive or efficient, and of course it could be both. For example, despite what I said just a moment ago, there may *conceivably* be an efficiency justification for the Western world's taboo against polygamy. It is not, however, that a polygamous marriage imposes costs on the first wife or other existing wives; that objection can be met by requiring the consent of the existing wife or wives to any additional marriages by their husband. The most serious third-party effects are on children, and we shall examine them more closely in Chapter 9. For now it is enough to point out that in a society in which fathers play an important role in child care, the reduction in the time and resources that a polygamous father can devote to each of his children, relative to what he would do if monogamous, provides an argument for regulating or even prohibiting the practice. (This again assumes that at least one of the parents is not totally altruistic toward his or her children.) Yet the taboo itself may have nothing to do with this point. It may have everything to do with the fact that polygamy is anomalous in a system of companionate marriage, because a man is unlikely to have the same reciprocal relationship of love and trust with multiple wives; as well as with the fact already noted that it benefits a few men at the expense of the many.

As I noted in the last chapter, in such cultures as that of modern Sweden and that of the American black ghetto, an analogue to a polygamous system is emerging. In both these cultures the male investment in child rearing has declined, to be replaced by investment by the taxpayer and such tax-supported institutions as Sweden's publicly funded day-care centers. Sweden's intrusive regulation of parental performance illustrates governmental paternalism in almost a literal sense. Insofar as public substitutes for the father are adequate from the child's standpoint and cheap, there may be no loss; if they are inadequate or expensive or both, there may be a heavy loss.

It would be heroic to contend that all sex laws can be explained on either efficiency or distributive grounds. Our Christian heritage, and in particular the deeper hold that Christian belief has on Americans than on other Westerners (except perhaps the Irish), may well be an independent factor in our retention of conservative sex laws. And yet Japanese women, for example, have more conservative sexual attitudes than American women,[69] no thanks to Christianity. Moreover, independent does not mean noneconomic. It may be possible to account for the greater tenacity of religious belief in this country on economic grounds, the essential point being that diversity of religious beliefs, a diversity constitutionally guaranteed in this country, stimulates religiosity by providing everyone with a religious niche in which he or she can feel comfortable; while homogeneity, owing, for example, to the existence of an established church, dampens religiosity by discouraging the growth of religious diversity.[70] This point has been anticipated by a study which notes that Sweden, strikingly secular though it is, has an established church to which virtually all Swedes belong, and which concludes that "religious diversity seems to increase the saliency of religion."[71] The causality, however, could run in the reverse direction: interest in religion might simply be too limited in Sweden to support more than one church.

It may be possible to go beyond a diffuse religious heritage in explaining the conservatism of many American legislators with respect to contraception and abortion. The role of the Roman Catholic Church in spearheading the opposition of a large Catholic population to liberalizing the highly restrictive contraceptive laws of Connecticut and Massachusetts (invalidated by the Supreme Court in 1965 and 1972) has been well documented.[72] Corroboration may be found in a statistical study of national policies toward contraception

69. Asayama, note 29 above, at 107–108.

70. Richard A. Posner, "The Law and Economics Movement," 77 *American Economic Review Papers & Proceedings* 1, 9–12 (May 1987); Michael W. McConnell and Richard A. Posner, "An Economic Approach to Issues of Religious Freedom," 56 *University of Chicago Law Review* 1, 54–59 (1989). This "niche" theory has a biological counterpart; remember the discussion in Chapter 4 of the advantages of sexual over asexual reproduction.

71. Richard F. Tomasson, *Sweden: Prototype of Modern Society* 85 (1970).

72. C. Thomas Dienes, *Law, Politics, and Birth Control*, ch. 5 (1972); Comment, note 47 above, at 281–282; Dudziak, note 47 above, at 927–931; Joseph L. Dorsey, "Changing Attitudes toward the Massachusetts Birth-Control Law," 271 *New England Journal of Medicine* 823, 825 (1964).

and abortion in 1962 and 1972. The most powerful explanatory variable was the percentage of the population that was Roman Catholic: the higher the percentage, the less liberal the policies.[73] The independence of women was also found to be positively related to the liberalism of a nation's policies on contraception and abortion, as my theory predicts.[74]

An intriguing possibility that I cannot explore adequately within the compass of this book is that Christian sexual ethics may in their origin have reflected competition both with pagan religions and with Judaism for the support of women.[75] We saw in the preceding chapter that those ethics represented in their time an effort to elevate the economic and social status of women above its level in religions that competed with Christianity. Christian missionaries actively sought to convert both pagan and Jewish women, and early Christian communities offered women positions of power denied them in the rival religions.[76] So Christian sexual ethics, even if dysfunctional in certain modern settings, may reflect an adaptation to the economic opportunities of an earlier era.

And those ethics continue to appeal, on quite practical grounds, to many women—those who are specialized in the mother's role, a role that the sexual freedom sought by many other women undermines.[77] A woman cannot make a binding promise never to have an abortion, and therefore cannot "sell" her reproductive capacity to her husband for as high a "price" as she could in a world in which abortion was forbidden. The clash over abortion is, in part anyway, a clash of interests and not just of ideologies (of course, ideologies can reflect interests).

A final point is that ignorance has undoubtedly played a large role in the public regulation of sex. Because sex and above all sexual deviance are taboo subjects in our society, children and youths do not receive a solid education in them, and as a result they harbor a good deal of misinformation that often

73. Marilyn Jane Field, *The Comparative Politics of Birth Control: Determinants of Policy Variation and Change in the Developed Nations* 100–110 (1983), esp. 100–101 (tabs. 5.1, 5.2).

74. Id. at 187–189.

75. Unlike today, Judaism appears to have been a proselytizing religion in the early Christian era. "Proselytes," *Encyclopaedia Judaica*, vol. 13, 1182–83 (1971).

76. Elisabeth Schüssler Fiorenza, "Word, Spirit and Power: Women in Early Christian Communities," in *Women of Spirit: Female Leadership in the Jewish and Christian Traditions* 29 (Rosemary Ruether and Eleanor McLaughlin eds. 1979). See generally Ben Witherington III, *Women in the Earliest Churches* (1988); also Robin Lane Fox, *Pagans and Christians* 308–310 (1987); Wayne A. Meeks, *The First Urban Christians: The Social World of the Apostle Paul* 81 (1983); Dimitris J. Kyrtatas, *The Social Structure of the Early Christian Communities* 132–133, 183 (1987).

77. McLaren and McLaren, note 32 above, at 68–69; Sandra Harding, "Beneath the Surface of the Abortion Dispute: Are Women Fully Human?" in *Abortion: Understanding Differences* 203 (Sidney Callahan and Daniel Callahan eds. 1984).

persists throughout adult life. Examples were given in Chapter 2. Religiosity and ignorance about sex go hand in hand in Western culture because traditional Christianity is hostile not only to sex but also to public discussion of sex; we saw in examining the controversy over sex education that it is not an irrational hostility. Public ignorance is a pervasive background to political action because individual members of the public rarely have a large stake in a particular governmental policy measure. Such "rational ignorance"—which not only provides a purchase for interest group pressures but also lends a random component to public policy—has played a large role in the public regulation of sexual behavior.

Moral Theories of Sexuality

Are Moral Theories Falsifiable?

The economic analysis of sexual behavior, customs, and regulations is the newest member of a large family of functional theories about sex, by which I mean theories that view sexual phenomena as functional or instrumental to personal or social goals. The functional approach is resolutely secular, scientific in either a broad or narrow sense, and disinclined to view sexual activity in moral terms. Not only the sociobiological theory of sex sketched in Chapter 4 but also Freud's sexual theory (and its inversion by Marcuse, discussed later in this chapter) is functional in this sense. So are the sexual theories of contemporary feminists and a multiplicity of sociobiological and anthropological theories about sex.

These examples should help us toward an awareness of the heterogeneity of functionalism. I could spend a lot of time defending the economic approach, or more broadly the rational-actor approach, against its rivals within functionalism; but the time would not be well spent, because it would suggest the existence of deeper cleavages than there are. Sociological and anthropological approaches to sex are highly compatible with the economic approach, which can indeed be seen as a fruitful relabeling, reinterpretation, reduction, and extension of these theories. As for the evolutionary biology of sex, it is, if not a foundation of my analysis, continuous with it.

Even Freud's theories of sex seem for the most part continuous with the ideas of biology and psychology on which I drew in formulating the economic approach. For example, the emphasis Freud placed on the formation of male homosexual preference in infancy as a result of paternal rejection and an excess of maternal affection can be reinterpreted in modern biological terms by reference to the infant's providing cues that alert his parents to his unfitness for normal masculine development and by doing so help them to shape him for an alternative style of living. One of Freud's theories—the "primal horde" concept, in which law and custom are seen as the product of sons' rebellion against their fathers—resonates well with the economic emphasis on competition for women between older and younger men in a polygamous society, and with the biological emphasis on that competition as well.[1]

Feminism has generated a number of specific hypotheses concerning rape (and sexual molestation generally), pornography, and other sexual topics that can be tested empirically, with results that I discuss in subsequent chapters. Although in detail, tone, and degree of commitment to social constructionism the feminist approach seems remote from the economic, there are affinities. Correctly from an economic standpoint, feminism attributes the traditional view of the woman's social role to women's dependence on men for their protection and that of their offspring. And it correctly predicts that, as that dependence lessens, women's strategy in matters of work, sex, and marriage will change, as the Swedish experience demonstrates. The economic approach thus helps explicate the linkages that make the feminist model a plausible one.

To find a real, no-holds-barred rival to the economic approach, we must look outside functionalism to what I call the moral theories of sex. These theories teach that sex is quintessentially a moral issue; that it is from the principles of morality that we learn what is proper sexual behavior and from those principles as well that we learn the proper role of the state in matters of sex and even what it is that causes people to engage in particular sexual practices. The principles of morality thus provide foundations for both a positive and a normative theory of sex in opposition to economic and other functional theories.

But does this not create an impasse? Two scientific theories can be compared in terms of criteria, such as simplicity and fruitfulness, that scientists accept as relevant to a choice between theories. But there is no accepted metric for comparing two moral theories, let alone a moral theory and a scientific one. The immense literature of moral disputation may seem to belie this assertion, and yet the inability of the disputants to join issue on, let alone to resolve, such deeply contested questions as the morality of abortion or even of divorce or contraception convicts the literature in many minds of futility.

This verdict may be premature. It is true that a moralist can insulate his theories from rational disagreement by stating them in a form that makes them self-sealing, unfalsifiable. If you say you have an unshakable intuition that sodomy is against God's law, there is no reply that will—or ought to—shake you. But most moralists, especially those writing in the Catholic tradition, are not content to stop with faith, intuition, revelation, or like guarantors

---

1. Robin Fox, "In the Beginning: Aspects of Hominid Behavioural Evolution," in *Biosocial Man: Studies Related to the Interaction of Biological and Cultural Factors in Human Populations* 1, 15–16 (Don Brothwell ed. 1977).

against argument or refutation. They want to make factual assertions as well—and falsifiable ones at that—such as that homosexuality leads to earthquakes (a commonplace of medieval thought). When they do, they enter the rational lists, and invite the rational merits of their moral theories to be compared with the merits of functional theories.[2]

This point is obscured because moral philosophers rarely take the time to study factual claims. When a Joel Feinberg or a Ronald Dworkin defends the rights of homosexuals, he does so by finding logical flaws in the views of the attacker rather than by identifying factual errors.[3] But it is often at the level of facts that moral theories are weakest. I begin with an example somewhat distant from my subject: National Socialism. The Nazi ideology is a moral theory—that is, a theory of right and wrong, of good and evil, of imperative duties. Among ideologies familiar to us its closest affinity is with Social Darwinism. If a Nazi says that he has an unshakable intuition that Germans should rule the world and reduce the rest of its inhabitants to helots or corpses, I do not think one can have a rational disagreement. But Nazism, while glorifying intuition and disparaging intellect, was not content to rest on intuition. Integral to its ideology was a series of factual claims, among them:

1. Native speakers of German, unless they are Jews, constitute a biologically distinct race—as do Jews.

2. The German race is greatly superior to other races (stronger, smarter, braver, more steadfast), particularly the Slavic race. So Germany could be expected to conquer Russia easily despite Russia's vastness and its much larger population.

3. Racially heterogeneous nations are markedly inferior to racially homogeneous ones. So Germany would benefit from killing or expelling its Jews, and by the same token had little to fear from the United States, a nation composed of many different European "races" and with many Jews and Negroes thrown in as it were for good (or rather bad) measure, hence thoroughly "mongrelized." The Soviet Union had many Jews too, so this was another reason for setting a low value on its military capability.

4. A powerful will (namely Hitler's) could offset the material superiority of Germany's enemies. Anyway, people in wealthy democratic nations have no fighting spirit.

---

2. Hilary Putnam, *Realism with a Human Face* 175 (James Conant ed. 1990), remarks in a similar vein that the "entanglement" of factual with ethical claims provides purchase for ethical criticism. His example is human sacrifice by the Aztecs, a practice that rested in part on beliefs that have since been falsified.

3. Joel Feinberg, *Harmless Wrongdoing*, chs. 29 and 30 (1988) (vol. 4 of *The Moral Limits of the Criminal Law*); Ronald Dworkin, *Taking Rights Seriously*, ch. 10 (1977) ("Liberty and Moralism"). So Feinberg, for example, appears to take as gospel the plainly exaggerated claim that 10 percent of Americans are homosexuals. *Harmless Wrongdoing* at 75.

5. Scientific theories to which Einstein and other Jews had made important contributions must be false.

6. Persecuting male homosexuals would raise the German birth rate.

Even before the Second World War, it was fairly evident to persons with scientific knowledge that the first five propositions were false; any residual doubts about them were dispelled by the course and outcome of the war. The last is difficult to disprove, but we have seen that it has no basis in theory and that there is no evidence for it either.

What I have done in this example is to recast a moral theory as a scientific one that generates testable hypotheses. Nazism predicted that the Soviet Union would cave in, that the United States would either stay out of the war or be ineffectual militarily if it entered, that an atomic bomb could not be built, and so on. These predictions turned out to be false, and it is their falsification by the course and outcome of the war, rather than the revelation of the Nazis' cruelty, that I suspect dished Nazism as a popular ideology. Had Germany won, the history of moral opinion in the last half of the twentieth century might have been different.

We can use the same approach with moral theories about sex. We can ransack them for their factual implications and then assess the accuracy of those implications, and by that means determine whether these theories provide an adequate positive and normative analysis of our subject. For example, Kant based his view that masturbation, sodomy, and other forms of nonvaginal sex are immoral on the twofold ground that animals never engage in such acts and that, since the only purpose of sex is procreation, nonprocreative sex is against nature.[4] In contrast, he thought drinking liquor in moderation all right because it promotes sociability[5]—but so, as he failed to recognize, may nonprocreative sex. And animals *do* engage in nonprocreative sex—do masturbate and sodomize and so forth. Kant was likewise on false factual ground in arguing that because sexual love is not human love but purely appetitive, sex outside of marriage is immoral per se.[6] Insofar as sex is a bonding element in a mutually supportive, mutually altruistic relationship, it is not purely appetitive, regardless of the legal form of the relationship. Kant's views of sex cohere with his basic ethical philosophy only because they rest on factual assumptions that are false. An austere bachelor, Kant apparently accepted uncritically his community's official position on sex.

Here are two contemporary examples, from Anita Bryant's account of her evangelical Christian crusade against a homosexual rights ordinance in Dade County, Florida, of the entanglement of facts and moral values. "Homosexuals cannot reproduce—so they must recruit." "Although a person may be a

4. *Lectures on Ethics* 170 (Louis Infield trans. 1930).
5. Id. at 159.
6. Id. at 167.

homosexual . . . he can make a deliberate choice to come out of it."[7] The first sentence is a non sequitur. Even if we grant the assumption that homosexuals would be dismayed at the prospect of the disappearance of homosexuality in the next generation, this would drive them to try to recruit boys or men into their ranks only if such efforts were likely to succeed and if without recruitment homosexuality would disappear in a few generations. The second of these conditions is especially implausible. It seems that even without recruitment, there is a fresh crop of homosexuals in every generation. The causality of homosexual preference is not well understood, but the principal factors appear to be genetic, hormonal, or developmental, or some combination of these, rather than recruitment. As for Bryant's contention that a homosexual "can make a deliberate choice to come out of it," it is true that a homosexual may decide not to engage in homosexual acts; but this is not what she means. She means that even a person with a strong homosexual preference can make up his mind to go straight, as it were. And this is certainly false in the vast majority of cases. One piece of evidence is that marriage does not decrease homosexual preference, although many homosexuals who marry do so in the hope that it will.[8] Bryant's proposition may be as false as the proposition that anyone who has a strong heterosexual preference can, by an effort of will, change that preference to a homosexual one.

Christian and Liberal Theories of Sex

Anita Bryant's opposition to homosexual rights has deep Christian roots, which I want now to examine in somewhat greater detail than in Chapter 2. We can confine our inquiry to Roman Catholicism. The reason is not that Protestants, including Puritans and evangelical Protestants (such as Bryant herself), do not have distinctive, and on the whole restrictive, views of sexual morality, but rather that their views do not differ in a fundamental sense from those articulated by the great Catholic theologians, above all Paul, Augustine, and Aquinas. The Protestant assault on monasticism, and on clerical celibacy generally, was motivated less by disagreement over the moral significance of sex than by a belief that these institutions fostered sexual immorality. The Protestants thought, in other words, that they had uncovered contradictions in the Catholic implementation of Christian sexual morality. With the morality

---

7. Anita Bryant, *The Anita Bryant Story: The Survival of Our Nation's Families and the Threat of Militant Homosexuality* 62, 69 (1977). Bryant's book is not a scholarly work, but it reflects widespread beliefs about homosexuality—including beliefs that many intellectuals share but are reluctant to voice for fear of offending homosexuals.

8. Michael W. Ross, *The Married Homosexual Man: A Psychological Study* 121–122 and tab. 12.1 (1983).

itself they had little or no quarrel, except that they did not think marital sex intrinsically shameful, as many Catholic theologians did. Another ground for focusing on the Catholic position is that Catholics are more prone than Protestants to offer *reasons* for religious beliefs and practices.

At the conceptual (as distinct from political or historical) root of Christian sexual morality is the Christian (originally Jewish) concept of deity. Pagan deities are usually personifications of forces in nature, and morality is therefore understood in pagan societies to be a human construct, although already in the work of the Greek tragedians of the fifth century B.C. we can see the emergence of Zeus as an ethical being who prefigures the God of the Christians, though his are not Christian ethics. Plato, too, was reaching for something beyond naturalistic deities. Sex is a strong force in nature, and it was natural therefore for the pagan deities to express themselves sexually. A monotheistic deity is inevitably more abstract, because he is the representative of something larger and vaguer than a specific force in nature such as the sea or thunder and lightning; and the more abstract the deity, the less natural it is for him to express himself sexually.[9] Although abstract, the Christian God is not without attributes. Power, of course, is one; but the others are intellectual and ethical—God is not only all-powerful but also all-knowing and all-good—and reason and morality are precisely what seem to distinguish human beings from animals. The Christian God is thus at the farthest possible remove from animal nature. And we humans, having been created in the image of God, are invited, indeed commanded, to think of ourselves as dramatically different from animals though always in danger of lapsing into the animal state.

Most Western intellectuals no longer believe in God, but many of them continue to believe that the metaphor of man's having been created in God's image captures an important truth: that we are not just animals with large brains but beings of a special worth and dignity, endowed with a moral sense and entitled to respectful treatment by our fellow man. This is the ethics of Kant, and it is influential in modern moral philosophies that in their particulars are remote from Kant, such as the egalitarian moral philosophy of Ronald Dworkin.

Despite having been created in the image of God, man does many things, such as eating, defecating, and ejaculating, that animals do, and they are therefore not things to be proud of. Insofar as they are indispensable to the life of the individual and of the human race, they are okay, although a few saintly people will try to minimize the occasions for them. But carried beyond the indispensable, they become animalistic, and therefore unnatural and disgusting. On this view the only proper human function of the sexual organs is procreation; any contraceptive or extravaginal sexual activity, such as mas-

9. David F. Greenberg, *The Construction of Homosexuality* 183 (1988).

turbation or sodomy, is therefore unnatural—as indeed is stimulating the clitoris, a specialized sexual organ oddly (from the Catholic standpoint) unrelated to procreation.

What is more, women and children are also created in God's image and are therefore also entitled to dignity and respect. Respect for their humanity requires that procreative activity be directed into a channel—monogamous marriage without divorce, at least divorce pagan style, which often, perhaps typically, was tantamount to abandonment of the wife by the husband—that protects women and that gives children a reasonable prospect of being raised in an environment in which they can develop into good Christians. Abortion thus is doubly damned: before or after quickening, as a form of contraception; after quickening (or ensoulment, if, as in the modern Catholic view, this occurs earlier—indeed, at the moment of conception), as a form of infanticide, itself forbidden because it is the killing of an innocent being created in God's image. Even public nudity is a bad thing—and this is one of the striking differences between pagan and Christian attitudes—not only because the wearing of clothes is so salient a difference between people and animals and therefore a mark of man's distinctive dignity, but also because the wearing of clothes signifies our common humanity.[10] There are beautiful and ugly bodies, young and old ones, strong and sickly, sturdy and deformed, but a covering of clothes conceals these differences in our animal endowments, redirecting attention from the animal parts to the divine part, our soul. The concept of clothing as egalitarian and spiritual is difficult to recapture in an age when clothing is used to mark economic differences and to heighten animal charms, yet it lives on in the few schools that still require their pupils to wear uniforms.

The idea that the elaborate set of social conventions, expressive of a moral ideal, that I have described defines what is "natural" for man invites and has received considerable derision,[11] as in the homosexual joke, "If God had intended men to be homosexuals, He would have given them assholes." The derision is misplaced. We really do have specialized reproductive organs, primarily the penis, testes, vagina, uterus, and ovaries. The fact that the urinary tract passes through the penis does not make the penis a dual-purpose organ, because a male can urinate without having a penis. All that he cannot do without a penis—or could not do before the miracles of modern medicine— is inseminate. Insofar as the anus is capable of erotic stimulation, it is a genuine dual-purpose organ, but obviously a man needs an anus even if he is not homosexual. It is not absurd, therefore, to argue that we have been given

10. Peter Brown, *The Body and Society: Men, Women and Sexual Renunciation in Early Christianity* 315–317 (1988).

11. See, for example, John Boswell, *Christianity, Social Tolerance, and Homosexuality: Gay People in Western Europe from the Beginning of the Christian Era to the Fourteenth Century* 11–15 (1980).

a set of organs whose function is procreation and that to use them in some other way, for example in conjunction with organs such as the anus that do not have a procreative function, is contrary to nature's plan. It is not the anus but the clitoris that is an embarrassment to the idea that all sexual organs are specialized to reproduction.

The argument I have been sketching is not an absurd argument even after the existence of masturbatory and sodomitical activities, not to mention promiscuity, infidelity, and infanticide, among animals is acknowledged. For what is natural to an animal is not necessarily natural to man, or even to another animal. It is natural for a cat to hunt mice, but not for a mouse to hunt cats. It may be natural for one baboon to sodomize another; it need not be natural for one man to sodomize another.

But although the traditional objections to the Catholic concept of the natural in sex are shallow, the concept itself reflects an incomplete understanding of the natural functions of human sexuality. The continuous sexual availability of the human female, for example, is not an imperative of procreation, since women are fertile only a few days each month; its biological function, rather, is to bind the male to the female so that he will be more likely to protect her and her offspring (Chapter 4). The result is that most human sexual intercourse is sterile even if no measures to avoid conception are taken—a fact that is, indeed, the foundation of the Catholic endorsement of the rhythm method of avoiding conception. Masturbation and homosexuality are among nature's ways of managing the competition of men for women, and in addition the formation of homosexual preference in some males may foster procreation indirectly by making these males available for the protection of their nieces and nephews. Contraception, and even abortion, may foster the Church's own design of encouraging the production of "quality" children, children sufficiently civilized and educated to become good Christians; and under the social and economic conditions prevailing in modern societies such as that of Sweden, an insistence on compliance with the traditional marriage-centered Christian morality may no longer be necessary for the protection of women and children. And just as the Church, after its austere early beginnings, dropped its objections to cuisinary art, so might it be thought to be required by consistency to drop its objections to *ars erotica,* viewed as a system for transforming animalistic sex into a refined, distinctively human system of pleasure—a system arguably more expressive of *human* nature than the furtive, hurried, and joyless copulations implicitly and sometimes explicitly recommended by the Church Fathers.

Consider the Catholic objection to the surgical-hormonal "reassignment" of a transsexual to the sex to which he feels he "really," although not genitally, belongs. The objection is not to medical intervention designed to change the way we were born. Catholics do not consider human intervention in nature unnatural. The objection is that, since the transsexual will not be fertile in his new sex, the purpose of the reassignment is to facilitate nonprocreative inter-course, believed by Catholics to be unnatural for man.[12] The objection is superficial. The transsexual feels an unbearable discordance between his gen-der and his sex that he is desperate to correct whether or not he intends to become sexually active in his new situation. And even if his motives are sexual, we know that nature has not ordained procreation as the sole aim of human sexual activity, so the desire for nonprocreative intercourse cannot rightly be considered unnatural.

The point is not that the idea of a distinctly human nature is wrong or empty but that it no longer points inexorably to Christian sexual morality. Perhaps, though, all that is necessary is to prune the concept of such inessential details as its making sexual pleasure problematic even in marriage: a pruning that another and closely related religion with an abstract deity, Islam, has done from the beginning, as to a considerable extent have Judaism and most versions of Protestantism. It is done in Elizabeth Anscombe's powerful defense of Pope Paul's 1968 encyclical *Humanae Vitae* and, at greater length, in Roger Scruton's philosophical study of sex.[13]

Superficially the message of these works is that people who channel their sexual energies into marriage lead happier, richer, more fulfilled lives than those who do not. Here is Scruton on what is wrong with homosexuality: "In the heterosexual act, it might be said, I move out *from* my body *towards* the other, whose flesh is unknown to me; while in the homosexual act I remain locked within my own body, narcissistically contemplating in the other an excitement that is the mirror of my own."[14] A like thought is expressed in

12. Oliver O'Donovan, *Begotten or Made?* 18–30 (1984). I want to qualify my frequent references to what Catholics believe by reminding the reader that Catholic thought is not a monolith. For a striking example, see Andrew M. Greeley, *The Catholic Myth: The Behavior and Belief of American Catholics* 93 n. 3 (1990), challenging the proposition that nonprocreative sex is unnatural; the author is a priest and a sociologist. That the Catholic tradition of natural law contains resources for proposing the reform of traditional Catholic doctrines is powerfully argued in John T. Noonan, Jr., "*Tokos* and *Atokion*: An Example of Natural Law Reasoning against Usury and against Contraception," 10 *Natural Law Forum* 215 (1965). See also next footnote.

13. G. E. M. Anscombe, "Contraception and Chastity," in *Ethics and Population* 134 (Mi-chael D. Bayles ed. 1976); Roger Scruton, *Sexual Desire: A Moral Philosophy of the Erotic* (1986). For criticism of the encyclical and of Anscombe, respectively, see Carl Cohen, "Sex, Birth Control, and Human Life," in *Ethics and Population* at 119; Bernard Williams and Michael Tanner, "Comment" (on Anscombe's essay) in *Ethics and Population* at 155. In denying that sexual pleasure in marriage is problematic, Anscombe was following the lead of the Church itself. *Gaudium et Spes* (December 5, 1965), pt. 2, in *Vatican Council II: The Conciliar and Post Conciliar Documents* 948, 952–953 (Austin Flannery ed. 1975).

14. Scruton, note 13 above, at 310. The narcissistic character of homosexuality is a recurrent theme. See, for example, John Simon, "Homosexuals in Life and the Arts," *New Leader*, October 28, 1974, 14; cf. George F. Gilder, *Sexual Suicide* 227 (1973). And not only among sexual conservatives: see Sigmund Freud, "The Sexual Aberrations," in *Three Essays on the Theory of*

this feminist criticism of prostitution: "To be able to purchase a body in the market presupposes the existence of masters. Prostitution is the public recognition of men as sexual masters; it puts submission on sale as a commodity in the market."[15] The common theme is that these nonmarital sexual relationships are intrinsically less satisfying than marital ones.

Why a relationship with someone more rather than less like oneself should be thought intrinsically unfulfilling is unclear, and seems contrary to the ideal of companionate marriage. But suppose Scruton is right that the fact that a male homosexual's preferred sex partner is another man reduces the psychological distance between the partners to the point of making the relationship narcissistic, almost masturbatory. What is a person who has a strong homosexual preference to do? He may be unfortunate, deprived, but why immoral? And while no doubt most prostitutes would prefer to be happily married and many, perhaps most, of their customers would prefer not to have to buy sexual services, we do not usually regard inferior substitutes for preferred goods or services as therefore immoral. A person with a hearing aid does not hear as well as people with normal hearing, but we would not on that account counsel him to throw away the hearing aid.

To read Anscombe or Scruton in this utilitarian light, however, is to miss their essential point, well brought out in Scruton's remark that "in love the other is treated not as means but as end; his desires and pleasures are mine, and mine, I hope, are his."[16] This, of course, is not true in prostitution; or, Scruton would add, in a homosexual encounter, because of what he believes to be its inescapably narcissistic character. Love that, consistent with the quoted passage, is conceived of in altruistic rather than in possessive terms fits nicely the Christian—in modern intellectual circles more likely to be called the Kantian—notion that human beings are entitled to equal dignity and respect: entitled, therefore, to be treated as ends rather than just as means. But it is not true that all sexual encounters must be motivated or accompanied by love in order to satisfy Christian or Kantian criteria. The prostitute who gets her price is obtaining a resource that she deems necessary or useful to attain her ends in life, not the customer's; in this respect a voluntary sexual transaction, however mercenary, is no different from any other market transaction. Not is it plain that altruistic love must be foreign to all homosexual encounters. Part of the Greek rationalization of pederasty was that it helped prepare boys for manhood. That rationalization, which is repeated by modern

---

Sexuality 13, 23 n. 1 (James Strachey trans. 1949), and the discussion of Marcuse's views later in this chapter.

15. Carole Pateman, "Defending Prostitution: Charges against Ericsson," 93 *Ethics* 561, 564 (1983).

16. Scruton, note 13 above, at 159.

pederasts (see Chapter 14), may be unconvincing, but it does suggest that homosexual love is not *necessarily* selfish. Pederasty aside, some adult homosexuals form durable relationships, and more would do so if society provided the same support for such relationships that it does for durable heterosexual relationships through the institution of marriage.

I conclude that the Christian project of "naturalizing" our conventional sexual morality is a failure. But I am no more convinced by the efforts of Feinberg, Dworkin, and other moralists writing in the tradition of the Enlightenment to pitch sexual freedom on Kantian ground, unfazed by Kant's specific views on the subject. Their tactic—it is especially conspicuous in Dworkin's attack on Patrick Devlin[17]—is to insist that moral principles, to be worthy of respect, must be reflective, reasoned; it is impermissible to base legal regulations of sex on prejudices, disgust, superstition, received opinion, personal aversions, anecdote, malice, mere rationalizations, or other unreasoned grounds. Feinberg and Dworkin are both talking about the proper limits of criminal law; and one of the greatest legal writers in the moralistic tradition that culminates in Devlin—I mean James Fitzjames Stephen—would have agreed with them that the criminal law is, in general anyway, an inapt tool for enforcing morality.[18] But Feinberg and Dworkin mean to suggest more: that prejudice, revulsion, and other "irrational" antipathies are not a proper ground for any form of public policy, and probably not even for any moral sentiment. This is implicit, for example, in Dworkin's fierce criticism of a decision that upheld the navy's right to exclude homosexuals from military service, a decision unrelated to criminal law.[19]

Yet, and here I repeat a point introduced in the preceding chapter, disgust and other strong emotions in fact supply the sturdiest foundations for moral feelings. You cannot convince a person by *argument* that infanticide is a bad thing. If he demands an argument—seriously, and not just when playing philosophy—this merely shows that he inhabits a different moral universe from you, and there is no arguing between universes. The revulsion that modern Americans feel against infanticide is deeper than any reason they could give for the revulsion.[20] An even clearer case is sexual intercourse between men and animals. Most people in our society find this a disgusting practice, yet it is hard to give reasons why. We do not scruple to eat lambs or make their skins into clothing; why do we worry about inserting the human

---

17. Dworkin, note 3 above, criticizing Patrick Devlin, *The Enforcement of Morals* (1965).

18. James Fitzjames Stephen, *Liberty, Equality, Fraternity* 135–136 (1873).

19. Ronald Dworkin, "Reagan's Justice," *New York Review of Books,* November 8, 1984, 27.

20. This is an instance of Wittgenstein's point (the theme of *On Certainty* [G. E. M. Anscombe and G. H. von Wright eds. 1969]) that the true foundation of our certitudes is intuition, not proof. For an application to morality, see my book *The Problems of Jurisprudence* 76–77 (1990).

penis into one of their orifices? Does it hurt or degrade them? Does it brutalize a man to copulate with an animal? Such questions are irrelevant, because the disgust we feel is not the product of utilitarian calculation. The fact that the prohibition against human intercourse with animals cannot be derived from the model of morally indifferent sex just shows that that model, attractive as it is to John Stuart Mill's modern followers (among whom I count myself), is at odds with contemporary Western morality—and not merely with the periphery of that morality, but, at least in the case of "bestiality," with its core.

The neglect of this point lends a note of the absurd to Feinberg's agonizing over a hypothetical case put by Irving Kristol.[21] The case is indeed an effective riposte, as it was intended to be, to the kind of rationalistic ethics that Feinberg and Dworkin advocate. A company wishes to sell tickets to a gladiatorial contest in which the contestants will fight to the death. Adult gladiators of sound mind are willing to participate for a suitable compensation, which the audience for the contest is happy to cover together with all the other costs of the event. On what ground could the project be deemed immoral and forbidden? Feinberg mentions a variant of Kristol's case: the sale of a testicle by a willing seller to a willing buyer.[22] The same question arises: what if any ground is there for prohibiting the sale?

Well, one can think of grounds, more easily for the gladiatorial example than for the testicular one (the sale of a testicle by a man who has two to a man who has none does not strike me as absurd or offensive). It is sound social policy to minimize people's firsthand acquaintance with death; it makes them more squeamish, hence easier to control with light threats. "The more peaceful a community has become, the more cowardly the citizens become; the less accustomed they are to standing pain, the more will worldly punishments suffice as deterrents, the faster will religious threats become superfluous . . . In highly civilized peoples, finally, even punishments should become highly superfluous deterrents; the mere fear of shame, the trembling of vanity, is so continually effective that immoral actions are left undone."[23] This analysis may explain the social demand for gentleness. But if we happen to find it an unconvincing bit of political sociology, we will not therefore abandon the taboo against gladiatorial contests. Alternatively, we might assimilate the taboo to the broader taboo against suicide, and defend that on the ground that it is a form of self-insurance designed to protect us from doing ourselves irrevocable harm in a fit of despondency that would pass if we were prevented from acting on it. But this argument, too, is rationalization; the root of the

---

21. Feinberg, note 3 above, at 128–133, 328–331.

22. Id. at 171.

23. Friedrich Nietzsche, "Notes (1880–81)," in *The Portable Nietzsche* 73, 75 (Walter Kaufmann ed. 1954). Would it were so!

horror that most people feel at the idea of suicide lies deeper than the reasons we can give for it.

So if prostitution, homosexuality, fornication, or any other offense against traditional Christian sexual morality evoked as wide and deep an antipathy as infanticide, gladiatorial contests, or suicide, those offenses would *be* immoral. Period. There would be no purchase for critique. Placing the burden of giving justifying reasons on the defender of that morality would be a mere ploy. But since the requisite intensity and unanimity of feeling on these matters no longer exist, their immorality *is* contestable (as, increasingly, is that of suicide)—and the contestants will get nowhere invoking the moral traditions of the West, whether in Catholic or Enlightenment versions. It is true that some fragments of the traditional sexual morality retain their compelling moral authority: the taboos against rape, against certain forms of public nudity, against bigamy, and, as I mentioned, against bestiality. The challenge for the traditional moralist is to derive the remaining tenets of the traditional morality from these taboos, viewed as unshakable moral intuitions and hence as fit premises for moral argument. No one has been able to meet that challenge. The biggest effort has been to build on the infanticide taboo an argument against abortion, but it founders on the inability to establish that human life must be said to begin before quickening, or for that matter before viability or even birth.

The idea of moral feeling as datum rather than inference has played an important role in the defense of traditional sexual morality, being available to those who either are not believing Christians or do not want to confine their message to those who are. As a utilitarian, H. L. A. Hart has felt bound to accept the offensiveness of immoral sexual practices as a ground for punishing them, but he insists on distinguishing between practices that are in some sense public—and therefore are maximally offensive because flaunted—and those that are conducted in private. This is why his criticism of Devlin distinguishes between bigamy—a public status—and mere adultery.[24] By this logic we would expect Hart to make the same distinction between homosexual marriage and homosexual acts conducted in private between consenting adults—prohibiting the former but not the latter.

Considerations of utility to one side, there is an aspect of punishing homosexual acts that grates on the Enlightenment sensibility. Before there was a sharp awareness of homosexual preference, the punishment of homosexual acts conformed to the fundamental principle of the Enlightenment that the law's proper concern is with deeds, not thoughts. But today the real horror of homosexuality, for those who feel it as horror, is the preference itself. A heterosexual who descends as it were to a homosexual act in the absence of a heterosexual opportunity or to demonstrate dominance in a prison setting

---

24. *Law, Liberty and Morality* 41 (1963). Hart was replying to an earlier version of Devlin's book cited in note 17 above.

may disgust, but he does not horrify, because he is not what our society considers a "real" homosexual. A real homosexual is someone who *prefers* his sexual partners to be of his sex. The inclination, not the act, condemns, even though for civil-libertarian reasons no one proposes to punish the inclination, at least criminally (the inclination is enough, however, to keep a homosexual out of the armed forces). If you say that you would like to kill X but of course will not because you are a civilized, law-abiding person, no one is apt to think much worse of you; but if you (being male) say that you'd like to have sex with that nice-looking young man but of course will not because you are law-abiding, afraid of AIDS, or whatever, you will stand condemned in the minds of many as a disgusting faggot. Homosexual acts are punished in an effort, however futile, to destroy the inclination.

If we are followers of John Stuart Mill, we shall be inclined to set up in opposition to the proposition that moral revulsion is elemental, requires no justification, the principle that government has no business regulating beliefs, preferences, or even conduct, as long as it is private. So nudist colonies on private property are all right, but nudists should not be permitted to parade in the public streets. By the accommodation implied in distinguishing public from private behavior, social experiments that are offensive to the majority can be conducted with minimal harm to the majority. Indeed, the only harm is the indignation that some members of the majority will feel at the thought that somewhere, perhaps thousands of miles away, a group of people are acting on preferences that the majority finds disgusting. Since thought, unlike sight and hearing, has no physical bounds, the state's claim to regulate private behavior leaves no zone of protection for experiments in living;[25] and it promotes a meddlesome, intolerant, censorious, and sectarian spirit.

But the idea that law is concerned only with public behavior, the outer man as it were, is only one strand in the liberal tradition. Another (and one not alien to Mill himself) is that it is a proper function of law to make us more civilized. So we come back to the question whether preserving, or, more realistically, restoring, traditional Christian morality will do this. Utilitarian moralists of conservative ethical bent, such as James Fitzjames Stephen and Patrick Devlin, try to show that it will. They do this chiefly by imagining the consequences if immoral activity became extremely common as a result of the relaxation of traditional legal and customary norms. "Let us suppose," says Stephen,

---

25. This implication of the conservative position is well brought out in a passage from Robert H. Bork, *The Tempting of America: The Political Seduction of the Law* 123 (1989): "No activity that society thinks immoral is victimless. Knowledge that an activity is taking place is a harm to those who find it profoundly immoral." This is precisely the type of "harm" that Mill, rightly in my view, rejects as a basis for government action. Mill went further, and disapproved not only of legal regulation based on mere disapproval of self-regarding acts but also of purely social disapprobation of such acts; but we need not follow him that far.

that men and women are made as equal as law can make them, and that public opinion followed the law. Let us suppose that marriage became a mere partnership dissoluble like another; that women were expected to earn their living just like men; that the notion of anything like protection due from the one sex to the other was thoroughly rooted out; that men's manners to women became identical with their manners to men; that the cheerful concessions to acknowledged weakness, the obligation to do for women a thousand things which it would be insulting to offer to do for a man, which we inherit from a different order of ideas, were totally exploded; and what would be the result? The result would be that women would become men's slaves and drudges, that they would be made to feel their weakness and to accept its consequences to the very utmost.[26]

This was written more than a century ago, and we must make allowance for a different moral climate. But Stephen was writing against Mill, who believed that the sky would *not* fall if women were freed from the traditional servitude called freedom by Stephen. Mill was right.[27]

Devlin is worried about the consequences for the family if vices such as alcoholism or homosexuality spread to one-quarter of the population.[28] But the repeal of Prohibition did not create a nation of alcoholics, and there are neither theoretical nor empirical reasons for expecting us to become a nation of homosexuals should the legal and customary barriers to homosexuality be thrown down. Devlin also echoes the old idea that widespread sexual irregularity results in national decline—or worse; "History shows that the loosening of moral bonds is often the first stage of [national] disintegration."[29] He cites no evidence for this proposition, and I do not believe that there is evidence he could cite. It is true that the morals of the Romans were shameful by Christian standards, but it was as true in the glory days of the republic and the early empire as in the period of decline and fall—indeed it is in the latter, not the former, period that we find the Christian sexual outlook anticipated. And in the fourth century the empire *became* Christian, only to collapse in the following century. Devlin's broader point is that "a recognized morality is as necessary to society as, say, a recognized government."[30] If we insert

26. Stephen, note 18 above, at 237; see also id. at 212–219.
27. This is not to deny the kernel of insight in Stephen's prediction. The emancipation of women, as we saw in Chapter 7, can hurt women who are specialized to household production, that is, to producing and raising children. This is the basis, I argued, for the opposition of many women to abortion rights, as well as being a factor in the feminization of poverty.
28. Devlin, note 17 above, at 14.
29. Id. at 13. The view is usually referred to Gibbon, but Gibbon did not list the sexual immorality (as he viewed it) of the Romans among the causes of the collapse of the Roman Empire. Edward Gibbon, *The History of the Decline and Fall of the Roman Empire*, vol. 7, 305 (J. B. Bury ed. 1902). See also A. H. M. Jones, *The Later Roman Empire 284–602: A Social Economic and Administrative Survey*, vol. 2, ch. 25 (1964).
30. Devlin, note 17 above, at 11.

"sexual" between "recognized" and "morality," we shall realize that the proposition is by no means self-evident.

Stephen, in contrast to Devlin, has rather little to say about sexual or other vices. Indeed, one of his most striking passages anticipates the sexual-autonomy decisions of our Supreme Court. "There is a sphere, none the less real because it is impossible to define its limits, within which law and public opinion are intruders likely to do more harm than good. To try to regulate the internal affairs of a family, the relations of love or friendship, or many other things of the same sort, by law or by the coercion of public opinion is like trying to pull an eyelash out of a man's eye with a pair of tongs. They may put out the eye, but they will never get hold of the eyelash."[31] Yet on the next page Stephen "affirms in a singularly emphatic manner a principle which is absolutely inconsistent with and contradictory to Mr. Mill's—the principle, namely, that there are acts of wickedness so gross and outrageous that, self-protection apart, they must be prevented as far as possible at any cost to the offender, and punished, if they occur, with exemplary severity." And it seems from the context that he is referring to sodomy.[32]

The reconciliation of these passages requires that we understand a position that Stephen shares with Devlin but expresses more forcefully; it is the central idea of *Liberty, Equality, Fraternity*: "All experience shows that almost all men require at times both the spur of hope and the bridle of fear, and that religious hope and fear are an effective spur and bridle . . . If, then, virtue is good, it seems to me clear that to promote the belief of the fundamental doctrines of religion is good also, *for I am convinced that in Europe at least the two must stand or fall together.*"[33] I infer that Stephen, a man basically of secular outlook and a strong exponent of Bentham's, though not of Mill's, brand of utilitarianism, thought Christianity an essential part of the system of social control in Europe and therefore believed that the central doctrines of Christianity, regardless of their independent merit, deserved profound respect, and some backing from law. This is different from believing that Christian sex doctrine is good in and of itself—something Devlin does appear to have believed, although, as it seems to me at any rate, on severely deficient evidence.

Is belief in Christianity essential to social order, as Stephen believed? That is too large a question to venture on here. But the superficial evidence, at least, is that it is not. The three nations in which, according to the public opinion poll results mentioned in Chapter 6, religious belief holds the strongest sway are the United States, South Africa, and Ireland (including Northern

---

31. Stephen, note 18 above, at 162.

32. James Fitzjames Stephen, *Liberty, Equality, Fraternity* 154 n. 13 (R. J. White ed. 1967) (editor's note).

33. Stephen, note 18 above, at 70 (emphasis added).

Ireland), all Christian, all with above-average levels of violence. Of the three nations over which, according to the poll, religious belief has the weakest hold, one is not Christian at all (Japan), the others are only nominally Christian (Sweden and Denmark), and all have below-average levels of violence and other social pathologies. The combination in the United States of an extraordinarily high crime rate with an extraordinary degree of allegiance to Christian beliefs must make one question the pacifying effects of Christian zeal. It is possible, of course, that the minority of nonbelievers is committing a greatly disproportionate share of the crimes. In fact, there is some negative correlation between religiosity and criminality in our society,[34] but it is not strong enough to permit us to lay our crime problem at the door of the godless. Moreover, the causal significance of the correlation is uncertain. It would not be surprising if people who had decided not to conform to the commands of temporal law tended also to reject the parallel commands of divine law—and, along with those commands, divinity itself. On this interpretation of the correlation, the same complex of personality traits or of opportunities and constraints that cause people to commit crimes cause them also to reject religion.[35] However that may be, to argue convincingly that a nation should buy into Christian *sexual* morality in order to strengthen Christianity as a means of reducing crime requires the additional step of arguing that Christianity is a package deal, as Stephen apparently believed. The evidence from Scandinavia is that it may well be, so that rejection of Christian sexual ethics may lead to a more general disenchantment with Christian teachings. Yet, to repeat, godless Sweden is a more peaceful country than the United States.

Of course, one can be an enthusiastic Christian without being a good Christian; perhaps that is the American problem. But if so, no solution is in sight.

I said at the beginning of this chapter that the moral approach to sex constitutes a positive theory of sexual behavior, customs, and law, and not just a normative one; yet I have spent all this time without mentioning positive theory. The positive theory seems to come down to this: that our sexual attitudes, and the customs and laws that grow out of them and perhaps reinforce or even alter them by some feedback process, are the product of moral attitudes rooted in religious beliefs rather than in the sort of functional considerations examined in the preceding chapter. In support it can be noted,

---

34. Lee Ellis, "Religiosity and Criminality: Evidence and Explanations surrounding Complex Relationships," 28 *Sociological Perspective* 501 (1985); Kirk W. Elifson, David M. Petersen, and C. Kirk Hadaway, "Religiosity and Delinquency: A Contextual Analysis," 21 *Criminology* 505, 522–524 (1983).

35. Cf. Lee Ellis and Robert Thompson, "Relating Religion, Crime, Arousal and Boredom," 73 *Sociology and Social Research* 132 (1990).

as I have done, that sexual attitudes are correlated with religious affiliation and that a nation's sexual laws are correlated with its religiosity. Belief that God has commanded me to refrain from some act provides a powerful reason for my refraining, a reason that will at times overcome biological and social motivations for doing the act. But religious belief may itself be plastic. Religious doctrine in matters of sex does not emanate clearly from authoritative texts; recall how skimpy are the sexual teachings of the Old Testament and the Gospels. It is created by religious institutions responding to social concerns, such as the concern in the early era of Christianity with the status of women. Doctrine frequently lags behind changes in social practice, but when it does we predict—and observe—a growing refusal to abide by it.

There is another dimension of doctrinal plasticity; it helps to explain the divergence in this country between religiosity and right conduct. I pointed out in Chapter 7 that religious diversity appears to foster religious belief. Here I add that the same diversity may undermine the effectiveness of religion as a form of social control. If there is a great smorgasbord of religious sects to choose from, a person whose inclinations are antisocial can gravitate to whichever is most tolerant, most forgiving, of his particular vice. A competitive religious market will provide consolation for the vicious and prescribe discipline for the strong, even though the vicious need discipline more. The market will give people what they want rather than what they need.

To summarize, we can have no confidence that religiously or for that matter philosophically derived sexual doctrine provides an accurate index to contemporary sexual behavior or an adequate set of reasons for either retaining or overthowing the traditional, and today embattled, morality.

Sexual Radicals

I have thus far kept within the banks of the mainstream of Western thought. I want now to glance at two radical critiques of conventional sexual morality: that of Bertrand Russell, the advocate of morally indifferent sex, and especially that of Herbert Marcuse.[36] Russell was a great philosopher, but *Marriage and Morals* bears no resemblance to *Principia Mathematica*. It is the work of a very intelligent man and brilliant writer but owes nothing as far as I can see to Russell's philosophical thought or methods, unless it be the notion that philosophy "is able to suggest many possibilities which enlarge our thoughts

36. Russell, *Marriage and Morals* (1929); Marcuse, *Eros and Civilization: A Philsophical Inquiry into Freud* (1955). A possible bridge between Russell and Marcuse is Wilhelm Reich, *The Sexual Revolution: Toward a Self-Regulating Character Structure* (1945). A somewhat more up-to-date, and (therefore) sexually more explicit, version of Russell's plea for the "unmoralizing" of sex is Lars Ullerstam, *The Erotic Minorities* (1966). It is, however, less eloquent than Russell's book.

and free them from the tyranny of custom."[37] *Marriage and Morals* is not a sustained argument but a polemic. It treats conventional views of sex as absurd, and religion as despicable. It illustrates a vein of off-the-cuff philosophical advocacy of sexual immorality that can also be found in Plato's *Republic* and in Diderot,[38] and it illustrates my remark in Chapter 1 that the philosophy of sex is a weak field. The value of such works lies in their challenge to the conventional-minded to give reasons for their settled beliefs. But we know that the hurling of such a challenge might reflect the fallacy that only beliefs for which reasons can be given are worthy of being held—when in fact our most firmly grounded beliefs, moral as well as epistemological, are products of intuition rather than reasoning.

For Russell, conventional sexual morality is a gratuitous cruelty inflicted by superstition called religion. This is not a fruitful or interesting position. Marcuse shared Russell's contempt for that morality—recall from Chapter 1 how Marcuse turned Freud on his head by reconceiving repression designed to induct young people into monogamous sexuality as tyranny rather than civilization.[39] But unlike Russell, Marcuse offers arguments. Specifically he argues that Freud's view of sex, and before Freud the Christian view—which in fact Freud's resembles to a surprising degree—is essentially political; that Freud was articulating the sexual norms of capitalist society. Marcuse accepts from Freud and, for that matter, Aquinas the idea that genital sexuality in a monogamous setting is the mature form of sexuality. Anything else is infantile, narcissistic, an escape from reality to fantasy. Economic productivity in a capitalist setting requires sublimation—work *is* sublimation. The genitalization of sex frees up men's energies for work. Procreative intercourse reinforces the capitalist work ethic indirectly as well by making sex itself purposive, instrumental, in fact a form of production—the production of children.[40] The patriarchal family is a little factory (which, we recall from Chapter 1, is just how economists think of it!). Deviant sex—nongenital sex, what Marcuse calls "the perversions"—transports us to a realm of fantasy in which subversive thoughts can germinate. "Against a society which employs sexuality as means for a useful end, the perversions uphold sexuality as an end in itself; they thus place themselves outside the dominion of the performance principle and challenge its very foundation. They establish libidinal relationships which

37. Bertrand Russell, *The Problems of Philosophy* 157 (1912).

38. William F. Edmiston, *Diderot and the Family: A Conflict of Nature and Law*, ch. 3 (1985).

39. Here is Marcuse's incisive summary of Freud's position: "The methodical sacrifice of libido, its rigidly enforced deflection to socially useful activities and expression, *is* culture." Marcuse, note 36 above, at 3.

40. Cf. Max Weber, *The Protestant Ethic and the Spirit of Capitalism* 158–159 (Talcott Parsons trans. 1958).

society must ostracize because they threaten to reverse the process of civilization which turned the organism into an instrument of work."[41]

How then did capitalism survive the sexual revolution of the twentieth century, a revolution already well advanced in the 1950s when *Eros and Civilization* appeared? The answer is that capitalism has co-opted, or in Marxian phraseology "commodified," sex. Erotic advertising and popular culture have made it just another form of consumption, just another of the "thoughtless leisure activities" of a capitalist society.[42]

Although Marcuse would like to see "a decline in genital supremacy" and the "disintegration" of such institutions as the "monogamic and patriarchal family,"[43] he realizes that we cannot have a viable society in which people spend all their time in narcissistic sexual activity. He thinks we could be perfectly happy with a lower standard of living because so many of the things consumed in a rich capitalist society are superfluities, "manipulated comforts."[44] But people would still have to work. He believes, however, that if we abandoned our exclusive focus on genital sexuality, the whole human body and the entire range of human activities, importantly including work, would become eroticized. We would work because we loved to work. It would be fulfilling, rewarding work, not the alienated labor of a capitalist society. Polymorphous perversity would usher us to the threshold of Utopia.

That is absurd; and although the broader proposition—that sex has the potential to be a politically subversive force—is one Marcuse shares with distinguished thinkers as otherwise diverse as Augustine, Freud, Orwell, and Foucault, it too seems false. *Any* political or economic system seems compatible with *any* system of sexual mores—provided that the occupational status of women is held constant; for it is that status which holds the key to a society's sexual mores. Marcuse does not entirely neglect the status of women; he imagines that there once was a matriarchal era characterized by "erotic freedom" and "a low degree of repressive domination."[45] If there ever was such an era, it probably was characterized by erotic freedom—so, at least, the economic analysis of sexuality presented in this book implies. But rising relative incomes for women and shifts in their occupational profile which may indeed have promoted erotic freedom have not destabilized capitalism.

Marcuse's most interesting point is that capitalism has an uncanny ability to defang potentially subversive forces such as sex and art. The argument is

---

41. Marcuse, note 36 above, at 50. The literary counterpart to this vision is Thomas Mann's great novella, *Death in Venice*.
42. Marcuse, note 36 above, at 94.
43. Id. at 201.
44. Id. at 151.
45. Id. at 65.

easier to grasp, and has some undoubted merit, in the case of art. The widespread dissemination of cheap copies of famous artworks can, by creating a "thick layer of familiarity [which] interposes itself, like an esthetic cataract, between the work and ourselves,"[46] turn great works of art into kitsch: the fate of Van Gogh, who is to American undergraduates a Hollywood character who decorates the walls of their rooms with brightly colored pictures of trees, flowers, and peasant cottages; of the *Mona Lisa;* and of Beethoven's *Fifth Symphony.* The counterpart transformation of sex is a little obscure, but I suppose Marcuse had in mind the trivializing of sexual love in American popular culture. Popular culture is culture for trivial minds; it trivializes everything it touches. True enough, but with what effect? Has sex had a subversive thrust in societies not dominated by American popular culture? No examples come to mind. The sexual revolution has continued apace since Marcuse wrote; genital supremacy, monogamy, and patriarchy have all declined; yet we are no nearer Utopia. Late capitalism has paved the way for more capitalism. The idea that polymorphous perversity is the road to Utopia has been shown to be no more convincing than the contrary idea, held by persons with whom Marcuse had much in common at the level of description though not of prescription, including the expositors of Catholic and Victorian sexual doctrine, that a moral conception of sex—a conception as repressive as his was permissive—is vital to civilization.

46. Arthur C. Danto, "Marc Chagall," in Danto, *The State of the Art* 95, 96 (1987).

PART THREE

The Regulation of Sexuality

Marriage and the Channeling of Sex

THE HISTORY of public policy toward sex since the beginning of the Christian era is one of efforts to confine sexual activity to marriage. Even today, such confinement is an ideal to which most Americans subscribe, however much the reality differs. The degree to which the ideal can be attained depends in part on how wide or narrow the authorized channel is. If polygamous or incestuous or homosexual marriages were permitted, the amount of nonmarital sex would decline; if second marriages were forbidden, the amount of nonmarital sex would increase. Therefore the first topic I treat is restrictions on marrying. The treatment is not exhaustive. The prohibition of homosexual marriage, for example, is deferred to Chapter 11. Taboos against incest and miscegenation are ignored. The focus is upon the limitations on remarriage (and hence upon the rules of divorce) and upon the polygamy taboo. After discussing the restrictions on marrying, I turn to the sanctions for nonmarital sex (excluding coercive sex, such as rape and the seduction of children, also the subject of a later chapter). These include punishing adultery, fornication, and prostitution and stigmatizing children born out of wedlock. My emphasis throughout is on seeking functional explanations for rules and practices often thought to be based unreflectively on tradition, superstition, or misogyny.

Restrictions on Marrying

The easier it is to marry, the less nonmarital sex we can expect. Were there no limitations on the age of marriage, on marrying relatives, on divorce (viewed as a license to remarry), or on the number of persons to whom one could be married at the same time, it would be easy for people to channel their sexual activity into marriage. Islam, while punishing adultery severely, facilitates the channeling of male sexual activity into marriage by permitting polygamy and repudiation (divorce at the will of the husband), although repudiation is not costless to the husband because he must compensate the wife.[1] The inverse relationship between restrictions on marrying and the amount of nonmarital sex also lay behind the efforts of the medieval Roman Catholic Church to encourage people to marry young in order to reduce the incidence of masturbation, fornication, and homosexuality. The lower rate of masturbation among young lower-class males than among young middle-class males in modern America, a difference due, as I remarked in Chapter 5, in part to the higher average age of marriage in the middle class, is another example of this inverse relationship.

Obviously there are limits to a policy of removing restrictions on marriage as an antidote to nonmarital sex. Without any restrictions, marriage would be a contract for sex, no different from any other contract: the relationship between a prostitute and her customer would be marriage. Temporary marriage, permitted to Shiite Muslims, approaches this limiting case. The marriage is for whatever length of time the parties agree upon. It could be an hour. The only thing that saves temporary marriage from being a contract for prostitution is that there are restrictions on the frequency with which a woman can enter into such a marriage.[2] It is "real" marriage because the offspring are legitimate; but, especially when entered into by a man who is already married, it will strike Westerners of traditional values as immoral.

Similarly, although ancient Greece and Rome imposed few restrictions on marriage, these were licentious societies by Christian standards in part *because* their rules of marriage were so lax. It may not be an accident that they prescribed no formalities for marriage. The more consequential a contract is, the greater the need for formalities as a means of ensuring that the parties know what they are getting into. This is a familiar point in discussions of the role of the seal and of consideration in the law of contracts.[3] We expect more formalities of marriage the more difficult it is to obtain a divorce.

The essential point is that for the idea of marriage as the only legitimate channel for sexual activity to have substance, marriage must be a legally defined relationship having certain invariant properties, rather than just the name of an infinitely variable contractual relationship. The Catholic Church had, from the beginning, a substantive conception of the marital relationship—that of companionate marriage—which it has bequeathed to modern people in the West regardless of their religious beliefs. So let us consider what

1. Jamal J. Nasir, *The Status of Women under Islamic Law and under Modern Islamic Legislation* 96–98 (1990). Also, the divorced wife will usually retain custody of any children of the marriage. Id. at 131–132.

2. Generally, she must wait two months after the expiration of the temporary marriage before remarrying. Id. at 100.

3. Lon L. Fuller, "Consideration and Form," 41 *Columbia Law Review* 799 (1941).

restrictions on freedom of contract are necessary to make marriages companionate.

One is a minimum age for marriage. The Church wanted people to marry young in order to reduce the amount of nonmarital sexual activity—but not too young, because then the marriage was unlikely to be companionate.[4] If, as is common in societies that have no age of consent, the husband is an adult at the time of marriage but the wife is an adolescent, the difference in ages will reduce the companionability of the marriage. It will do this both directly, because people who are far apart in years tend to have different tastes and interests, and indirectly, because the older a spouse is at marriage, the sooner the marriage can be expected to be cut short by death. Moreover, the younger the spouse or spouses are, the likelier it is that the marriage has been arranged by their families. In that event, there is a substantial probability that they will be poorly matched. Families do not have perfect or even very good information about the intimate preferences of their children. Besides, they have interests that conflict with those of their children—interests, for example, in securing or cementing alliances. The Church tried to place limits on arranged marriages by insisting that both spouses freely consent and by eliminating the traditional requirement that the bride's father consent. I say "place limits on" rather than "forbid" because there is an ambiguity in the concept of an arranged marriage. As long as either prospective spouse can veto the marriage, the parents' role in "arranging" a match becomes like that of marriage brokers, and companionate marriage is possible even though the marriage is in a sense arranged.

The Question of Divorce

A policy of encouraging companionate marriage has complex implications for the rules of divorce. One can argue with almost equal plausibility that such a policy implies the desirability of forbidding divorce altogether or, at the other extreme, of permitting divorce at will,[5] or perhaps of permitting divorce only

---

4. Perhaps because it was trapped between these conflicting desires, the Church did not alter the Roman age of consent, which was 12. W. W. Buckland, *A Textbook of Roman Law from Augustus to Justinian* 114 (2d ed. 1932).

5. "No-fault" divorce, now pretty much the rule in Western nations. Roderick Phillips, *Putting Asunder: A History of Divorce in Western Society* 561–572 (1988); Antony Copley, *Sexual Moralities in France, 1780–1980: New Ideas on the Family, Divorce, and Homosexuality: An Essay on Moral Change* 212–215 (1989). No-fault divorce is not quite divorce at will, because usually a period of separation is required. But either spouse can abandon the other and then, after the prescribed period has elapsed, get a divorce without either obtaining the consent of the abandoned spouse or having to prove that that spouse had violated his or her marital obligations, engaged in other wrongdoing, or otherwise furnished grounds for divorce. For good discussions of the evolution of Western marriage and divorce, see, besides Phillips' book, Martine Segalen, *Historical Anthropology of the Family*, chs. 4–6 (1986). And for a compendium of useful data,

on specified grounds, such as insanity or adultery. In a regime of no divorce, prospective spouses will have incentives to engage in elaborate marital search, because the cost of a mistake is so high. The longer or more intense the search, the likelier it is to produce a good match. And once married, a couple in a regime of no divorce has a strong incentive to invest in the companionability of the marriage, since the cost of substituting another marriage is infinite.

But there is another side to the coin. Since marital search takes time and is more likely to be successful the more mature the searcher is, a regime of no divorce implies a high average age of marriage, hence many unmarried young persons; and the more such persons there are, other things being equal, the more nonmarital sex there will be. Reinforcing this effect is the fact that the high search costs of companionate marriage will have an independent negative impact on the marriage rate. It is true that divorce locks into marriage some people who would otherwise return to the pool of the unmarried, and to this extent it may appear certain to reduce the incidence of nonmarital sex. But the appearance may deceive. The metaphor of imprisonment is significant. Because the limitations of human foresight doom some marriages to fail eventually no matter how strong the incentives of prospective spouses to search carefully before marriage and afterward to invest heavily in marital companionability, a regime of no divorce will condemn some persons to unintended noncompanionate marriages, while if divorce were permitted these same persons might be able to form second marriages that would be companionate. Noncompanionate marriage, we know, is a breeding ground for extramarital sex, as spouses look elsewhere for companionship. The upshot is that the lock-in effect will reduce the amount of fornication because there will be no persons who are unmarried as a result of divorce, but it may increase the amount of adultery. The danger is especially great when women are no longer literally inaccessible to men, no longer imbued with a distaste for sex, no longer—in Bertrand Russell's words—kept stupid and uninteresting by being denied an education.[6] Yet if these methods of preventing female adultery are, therefore, preserved, companionability in marriage will be unattainable.

The fact that noncompanionate marriage is poorly designed for channeling sexual activity into marriage provides another explanation—besides the desire to improve the status of women and children as part of a broader humanitarian and egalitarian ideology—of the Christian preference for companionate marriage, as well as a partial explanation of pagan licentiousness. Perhaps it

---

see Hugh Carter and Paul C. Glick, *Marriage and Divorce: A Social and Economic Study* (rev. ed. 1976).

6. For evidence, see Robert R. Bell, Stanley Turner, and Lawrence Rosen, "A Multivariate Analysis of Female Extramarital Coitus," 37 *Journal of Marriage and the Family* 375, 383 (1975); and see generally Anthony P. Thompson, "Extramarital Sex: A Review of the Research Literature," 19 *Journal of Sex Research* 1, 10 (1983).

also explains why Islam makes marriage so easy for men; otherwise the incentives for men to commit adultery would be overwhelming, given the traditionally noncompanionate character of Muslim marriages.

We can also see how the combination of companionate marriage and a ban on divorce could be thought an effort by the Church to improve the status of women without unduly encouraging nonmarital sex. The ban on divorce protects the woman against abandonment; and while one effect is to encourage adultery in its aspect as a substitute for remarriage, and perhaps also fornication because the average age at marriage will rise, another effect is to discourage adultery and fornication as forms of search in the remarriage market.[7] In a society that allows divorce, a man can begin searching for a new wife while he is still married to the old one; not so in a regime of no divorce. Yet an ideal of marriages that are based on affection creates pressure for the safety valve of divorce when affection between the spouses fades.[8] There is a *closeness* to companionate marriage that can make the relationship unbearable if the spouses lack affection for each other. It is this that makes the marital prospects of the homosexual so poor in a society in which marriages are companionate and that explains why in modern society the religious or educational heterogeneity of the spouses increases the probability that the marriage will fail.[9] And no doubt the heterogeneity of persons increases as authority crumbles and people become more individualistic. We can see with the aid of hindsight that by encouraging companionate marriage, the Church inadvertently helped to create not only a homosexuality problem but also a divorce problem. And we can also see why (with the important exception of England) the Protestant nations of Europe—ever alert, like Islam, to the incentives that religious practices and institutions can inadvertently create to engage in nonmarital sex—decided that marriage required the safety valve of divorce.[10]

Although companionate marriage creates so much pressure for divorce as eventually to make a policy of no divorce untenable, the other extreme— divorce at the will of either party—might on balance undermine companionate marriage just as much. The commitment to a marriage is less the easier the marriage is to dissolve, so prospective spouses will spend less time in marital search if divorce at will is allowed. The result will be a worse match between

7. Gary S. Becker, Elisabeth M. Landes, and Robert T. Michael, "An Economic Analysis of Marital Instability," 85 *Journal of Political Economy* 1141, 1154 (1977).

8. For historical evidence, see Robert L. Griswold, *Family and Divorce in California, 1850–1890: Victorian Illusions and Everyday Realities* 174 (1982).

9. For evidence, see Becker, Landes, and Michael, note 7 above, at 1183.

10. Phillips, note 5 above, ch. 2; E. William Monter, "Women in Calvinist Geneva (1550–1800)," 6 *Signs: Journal of Women in Culture and Society* 189, 195 (1980). So the Puritan influence in America may help explain why the American colonies recognized divorce (Phillips at ch. 4), as the mother country did not.

spouses, which in turn will undermine the companionability of marriage and by doing so increase the likelihood of divorce. And since exit from the relationship is so easy, spouses will spend less time trying to make the marriage a success. The tendency in a regime of divorce at will is, therefore, to substitute for a single, durable companionate marriage a succession of shorter and perhaps no more companionate marriages. Divorce at will also recreates the problem of serial polygyny that existed in medieval Europe as a result of the frequency with which women died in childbirth. With divorce at will, older men compete with younger men for young women, and the younger men are at an economic disadvantage in this competition.

The bad effects of divorce at will would be mitigated if judges took a realistic view of marital assets in deciding the financial consequences of a divorce. To the extent that awards of alimony or of property compensate wives for the career opportunities that they gave up by marrying, women are encouraged to invest in the marriage, notably by having children, for their investment is protected. And men are discouraged from divorcing lightly because the cost is high. On both counts marriage should be more stable. Granted there is another side to this coin: the less the wife has to lose by a divorce, the less incentive she will have to make a success of the marriage. But probably on balance the failure of courts—and it is a common failure in this country[11]—to insist on full compensation for divorced women destabilizes marriage, just as business partnerships would be destabilized if courts systematically undercompensated one of the partners upon the dissolution of the partnership.

Between no divorce and divorce at will lie two other possible regimes. One is consensual divorce; just as a partnership can be dissolved by agreement of the partners, so might a marriage be dissolvable by agreement of the spouses. There are three problems. In a society in which men dominate women, the husband may be able to coerce his wife to "agree" to a divorce.[12] Perhaps in any society a person who wants a divorce can usually badger the other spouse into consenting, if consent is required. In the last resort he (or she) can buy the spouse's consent, in which event the divorce is genuinely consensual; but even genuinely consensual divorce undermines companionate marriage by reducing the cost of failure to achieve companionability.

The other intermediate regime is divorce upon proof of a ground that demonstrates the marriage has failed. What counts as failure depends on the

---

11. See, for example, James B. McLindon, "Separate But Unequal: The Economic Disaster for Women and Children," 21 *Family Law Quarterly* 351 (1987), and studies cited there.

12. Traditionally a problem in Japan, which recognized consensual divorce. Max Rheinstein, *Marriage Stability, Divorce, and the Law* 121–122 (1972). Islam also recognizes consensual divorce. But since the husband can divorce the wife at will, all that this means is that the wife can buy her way out of the marriage. Nasir, note 1 above, at 78–81.

goals of marriage. In noncompanionate marriage the only things likely to frustrate those goals are sterility and female adultery. Conditions that make companionate marriage difficult or impossible to attain are more numerous. They include the insanity of a spouse, a spouse's imprisonment for a lengthy term, substantial physical or mental cruelty by one spouse toward the other, and adultery by either spouse. (Making adultery a ground for divorce has the incidental benefit, in a society hostile to nonmarital sex, of reducing the incidence of such sex. Nonmarital sex is more costly when it entitles one's spouse to a divorce.) In the absence of one or more of these conditions, spouses have some prospects of being able to work out their problems through renewed investment in marital companionship—and a strong incentive to make the investment, since they are stuck with each other.

Within the framework sketched here, the essential presupposition of a regime of divorce on grounds is that courts have the ability to ascertain in particular cases whether the conditions normally necessary for a marriage to be companionate still exist. If the conditions do exist, the spouses should be able to attain the goal of companionability—provided they do not have the easy exit of divorce at will. Note, however, that since the main practical effect of barring divorce is merely to prevent remarriage (because the husband may still have to support his wife after their divorce), the bar will alter the behavior only of a spouse who desires to be free to remarry. Note also that unless steps are taken to prevent collusion, spouses who desire to divorce can do so by manufacturing evidence of the existence of one of the grounds for divorce. Especially in adversarial legal systems such as we find in England and America—systems in which lawyers are responsible for investigation and proof—courts are poorly equipped to prevent collusive litigation. One predicts therefore that, other things being equal, divorce on grounds is likely to give way to no-fault divorce earlier in these countries than in countries that have an inquisitorial system of justice, in which the primary responsibility for ascertaining the facts lies with the judge.

Despite the inherent deficiencies of limiting (but neither forbidding nor allowing at will) divorce in order to preserve companionate marriage, if the only goal of marriage policy were to promote such marriage it would be difficult to understand the choice of either no divorce or divorce at will as regimes to govern the dissolution of marriage. Even if judges operating under a regime of divorce at will fully compensated the wife for the investment she had made in the marriage, that regime would not promote companionate marriage as effectively as a regime of divorce on grounds. The latter might even be the regime that prospective spouses themselves would prefer. Suppose most people want a companionate marriage. They know that achieving this goal depends in part on the investment they make in the marriage as spouses. That investment will be greater the more difficult it is to get out of the marriage. So, ex ante (that is, in advance of the marriage), they may prefer rules that make it difficult to dissolve the marriage. This is an example of efficient precommitment.

If I am correct that divorce on grounds promotes companionate marriage more effectively than divorce at will does, this may explain, wholly apart from any considerations of misogyny or even innocent judicial error, why divorced women tend to receive less compensation under a regime of divorce at will.[13] They will invest less in the marriage, and hence the optimal compensation for the loss of their investment will be lower.

The promotion of companionate marriage was not the only goal of divorce law even in the era of divorce on grounds. Otherwise why was not sterility one of the grounds, since the presence of children encourages companionate marriage by increasing the costs of divorce to the spouses? Not only has marriage policy other goals besides the promotion of companionate marriage; that promotion may be a means to those goals rather than an end in itself. One is the protection of children, and this helps explain why divorce is often made more difficult in societies in which families are large.[14]

Another goal, the protection of women, helps explain not only why divorce was forbidden for so long in Christian societies but also why no exception was made for sterility. Divorce in a society in which women's principal asset is their fertility, and in which the social safety net is porous or nonexistent and the mechanisms for enforcing legal obligations (such as that of support) weak or undeveloped, places the divorced woman who because of age or other causes is no longer fertile, and who lacks independent means, in extreme economic peril. Medieval law recognized both the right of a deserted wife to support from her husband and the right of an abused wife to live apart from her husband yet be supported by him. And, by also forbidding the husband to remarry (the practical meaning of no divorce), the law discouraged desertion and abuse and so minimized the occasions for legal intervention, bound always to be clumsy and often ineffectual. Even in modern America, no-fault divorce has meant a decline in the standard of living of many women.

The point about protection of women may explain why impotence is a ground for divorce although sterility is not. Impotence is a ground on which the wife, not the husband, would be seeking divorce. Even better from the

---

13. H. Elizabeth Peters, "Marriage and Divorce: Informational Constraints and Private Contracting," 76 *American Economic Review* 437, 448–449 (1986); Lenore J. Weitzman, *The Divorce Revolution: The Unexpected Social and Economic Consequences for Women and Children in America* xiv (1985); Lloyd Cohen, "Marriage, Divorce, and Quasi Rents; Or, 'I Gave Him the Best Years of My Life,'" 16 *Journal of Legal Studies* 267, 277 and n. 30 (1987). But see Herbert Jacob, "Another Look at No-Fault Divorce and the Post-Divorce Finances of Women," 23 *Law & Society Review* 95 (1989).

14. Gary S. Becker and Kevin M. Murphy, "The Family and the State," 31 *Journal of Law and Economics* 1, 14 (1988), reprinted in Becker, *A Treatise on the Family* 362, 375–376 (enlarged ed. 1991).

wife's standpoint would be a rule that made male sterility, but not female sterility, a ground for divorce. But the difference in legal treatment between sterility and impotence dates from a time when impotence was pretty much the only recognized symptom of male incapacity to procreate. By denying men the right to divorce on the ground of female sterility, society can give women an insurance policy against the consequences of their turning out to lack the most important female asset in a traditional society.

Impotence is by definition a condition that can afflict only men, but we should note that the actual ground for divorce—what I have been loosely and inaccurately calling impotence—is in fact physical incapacity for intromission, whether that incapacity is due to the male or to the female. Defects in the vagina or surrounding tissues that make penetration impossible are rare, but the symmetry of allowing divorce by reason of either spouse's inability to perform sexual intercourse has significant implications. Despite its frequent disparagement of nonprocreative sex, the Catholic Church consistently recognized the importance of sexual intercourse, even when nonprocreative, to companionate marriage, an institution it wanted to encourage apart from any reproductive goals.[15] An alternative aim to impute to the recognition of impotence as a ground for divorce, however, is the elimination of what would otherwise be a powerful incentive for the wife to commit adultery.

The law's traditional treatment of adultery, whether as a crime, as the tort of "criminal conversation," or as a ground for divorce, reflects a twofold asymmetry between the husband's and the wife's adultery. There is first the familiar point that adultery is a graver wrong to the husband than to the wife. While the wife's adultery can deprive her husband of offspring, the husband's adultery is very unlikely to deprive his wife of offspring because of the vast inseminative capacity of men and because men are unlikely to devote so many resources to the protection of their illegitimate children as to deprive their legitimate children of essential protection. It is consistent with this point that at a time when adultery was criminal, an adulterous wife was punished more severely if she became pregnant as a result of her adultery.[16]

Second, a husband's adulteries are more likely than a wife's to be casual. Evolutionary biology implies that a married man may be attracted to a woman precisely because she is *not* his wife, whereas a married woman may be attracted to a man because he would be a superior protector for her and her children—in other words a better husband;[17] therefore the wife's adultery is

---

15. It is consistent with this point that impotence was not a ground for divorce if the man was elderly at the time of the marriage. Vern L. Bullough and James Brundage, *Sexual Practices & the Medieval Church* 137, 140 (1982).

16. Phillips, note 5 above, at 348–349.

17. Donald Symons, *The Evolution of Human Sexuality* 207–208, 232–252 (1979). Recall the discussion in Chapter 4 of the different optimal sexual strategies of the two sexes.

a graver threat to the marriage. These considerations may explain the "double standard"—which is more than a slogan: there was a time in England when the wife's adultery entitled the husband to divorce, but the husband's adultery entitled the wife only to a judicial separation unless the husband committed bigamy or there were other circumstances of aggravation. Yet the orthodox Christian line, here breaking sharply with pagan antecedents, had long been that male adultery was a serious offense, with or without bigamy or other aggravating circumstances.[18]

How to explain the near-universal movement to divorce at will in a culture (that of the West today) which is more emphatic than ever before that the only kind of worthwhile marriage is companionate? The economic literature on the family emphasizes the declining private value, and hence stability, of marriage in a society in which women have improved job opportunities and a tightly woven social safety net. The improved job opportunities (a function of such things as the increase in service jobs, the decline in child mortality, and the advent of labor-saving household devices) raise the woman's opportunity costs of household work, signally including child rearing, and as a result the couple has fewer children and the wife specializes less in household work.[19] The husband therefore gains less from the marriage, so invests less in trying to preserve it. The wife's increased economic independence, whether owing to greater market income or to greater social income, also reduces her willingness to work at improving a bad match.[20] As a result, the demand for divorce rises to the point where the principal consequence of confining divorce to grounds is that spouses wanting to divorce invest resources in manufacturing them. If an essential value of marriage is companionship, a marriage that loses its companionate value is bound to fail regardless of the legal structure. At this point internal goals of the legal system—the goals of economizing on judicial resources and of reducing perjury—become decisive in favor of allowing either consensual divorce or divorce at will.

18. Leah Lydia Otis, *Prostitution in Medieval Society: The History of an Urban Institution in Languedoc* 105–106 (1985). On legal recognition of the double standard, see Phillips, note 5 above, at 348; Carmel Shalev, *Birth Power: The Case for Surrogacy* 27–28 (1989).

19. The effect of women's job opportunities on fertility is emphasized in Gary S. Becker, "An Economic Analysis of Fertility," in Becker, *The Economic Approach to Human Behavior* 171 (1976). On this view, the post–Second World War "baby boom" can be explained by the fall in women's market opportunities when millions of men returned to the job market from military service, inducing women to reallocate their time to the household—a "market" the principal output of which is children. Michael S. Teitelbaum and Jay M. Winter, *The Fear of Population Decline* 74 (1985).

20. For some evidence that social insurance and welfare programs increase the propensity to divorce, see John McDonald and Zane A. Spindler, "Benefit-Induced Female Sole Parenthood in Australia, 1973–85," 27 *Australian Economic Papers* 1 (1988); Jan H. M. Nelissen and Piet A. M. Van den Akker, "Are Demographic Developments Influenced by Social Security?" 9 *Journal of Economic Psychology* 81, 99–106 (1988).

The Question of Polygamy

The importance of the ideal of companionate marriage in shaping marriage policy in Christian culture may be the key to explaining the hard line which that culture has taken against polygamy (throughout this discussion I use *polygamy* as a synonym for *polygyny*). The prohibition of polygamous marriage may appear to make no sense from the standpoint of protecting women. Polygamy increases the effective demand for women, resulting in a lower average age of marriage for women and a higher percentage of women who are married.[21] Of course, not all women want to marry young, or to be one of several wives of the same man, or indeed to marry at all. But rarely is a person made better off by having an option removed. Forbidding polygamy withdraws one option from a woman, namely that of being a nonexclusive wife. By doing so it reduces competition among men for women and thus reduces the explicit or implicit price that a woman can demand in exchange for becoming a wife—even a sole wife.

But this analysis is incomplete. In most polygamous cultures a woman cannot make an enforceable contract to be a man's only wife,[22] and this limitation on freedom of contract reduces the advantages of polygamy for women. The option of polygamy is given them, but the option of monogamy is withdrawn. Polygamous societies think polygamy a good thing just as monogamous societies think monogamy a good thing. We must consider why this is so and in particular why polygamy seems unnatural in a culture dedicated to companionate marriage.

The taboo against polygamy in Christian societies runs so deep that there is little felt need to justify it and therefore little sensitivity to the contradictions that such efforts to justify it as are made often involve. In *Hyde v. Hyde*[23] the question for an English court was whether to recognize a Mormon marriage made in Utah at a time when polygamy was lawful there. The marriage was not itself polygamous. Both spouses had been single at the time of the marriage, and the husband had not taken any additional wives since; on the contrary, he had renounced the Mormon faith, and he and his wife were living in England. He wanted a divorce on the ground of her adultery. The court refused to give it to him. The ground was that persons united in a Mormon marriage could not be considered "husband" and "wife" within the meaning of English divorce law, since one of the "essential elements and invariable features" of marriage "as understood in Christendom" is monogamy.[24] But

---

21. Becker, *A Treatise on the Family*, note 14 above, ch. 3.
22. There is a trend, however, in modern Muslim societies toward permitting such contracts. Nasir, note 1 above, at 25–26.
23. 1 L.R. 130 (Matrimonial Ct. 1866).
24. Id. at 133.

Mormons are Christian, so the argument from the universality of Christian practice fails. The court added that England had "no law framed on the scale of polygamy, or adjusted to its requirements."[25] A nice point—but inapplicable to the case at hand because the plaintiff had only one wife and he wanted to divorce her on a ground recognized in England as well as in Utah. He was not asking the court to create a law of polygamy to govern his conduct.

In the parallel American case, *Reynolds v. United States*,[26] the issue was whether a federal law forbidding polygamy in the Territory of Utah infringed the right of Mormons, guaranteed by the First Amendment to the Constitution, to exercise their religion freely. The answer was no. "Congress was deprived [by the First Amendment] of all legislative power over mere opinion, but was left free to reach actions which were in violation of social duties or subversive of good order."[27] Polygamy is subversive of good order: not only has it "always been odious among the northern and western nations of Europe, and, until the establishment of the Mormon Church, was almost exclusively a feature of the life of Asiatic and of African people," but "in fact, according as monogamous or polygamous marriages are allowed, do we find the principles on which the government of the people, to a greater or less extent, rests . . . Polygamy leads to the patriarchal principle . . . which, when applied to large communities, fetters the people in stationary despotism, while that principle cannot long exist in connection with monogamy."[28] The opposite would be more accurate. Polygamy conduces to the creation of powerful families, offsetting the power of the center.[29]

The question of polygamy returned to the Supreme Court in *Cleveland v. United States*,[30] a prosecution for violation of the Mann Act, which at the time forbade transporting women across state lines for "immoral" purposes. The defendant—a Mormon who continued to believe in and practice polygamy despite the Mormon Church's abandonment of the practice[31]—had taken

25. Id. at 136.

26. 98 U.S. 145 (1878). Reynolds was Brigham Young's private secretary.

27. Id. at 164.

28. Id. at 164–166.

29. For evidence, see my book *The Economics of Justice* 168 (1981) (tab. 2). According to Richard D. Alexander et al., "Sexual Dimorphism and Breeding Systems in Pinnipeds, Ungulates, Primates, and Humans," in *Evolutionary Biology and Human Social Behavior: An Anthropological Perspective* 402, 432–433 (Napoleon A. Chagnon and William Irons eds. 1979), it is no accident that all great powers have been monogamous societies: no government could effectively control a large, populous nation, the authors argue, if families were allowed to grow as strong as polygamy would enable. On this view, the point of monogamy is precisely to permit political power to be concentrated in the state.

30. 329 U.S. 14 (1946).

31. Thousands of Mormons live openly in polygamous unions in Utah; prosecutions are rare. Dirk Johnson, "Polygamists Emerge from Secrecy, Seeking Not Just Peace But Respect," *New*

one of his wives across a state line. The Court upheld his conviction, remarking without elaboration that "the establishment or maintenance of polygamous households is a notorious example of promiscuity."[32] Yet one defense of polygamy—a defense prominent in Islamic thinking—is that it reduces promiscuity by providing additional lawful outlets for male sexuality.

We thus can get little help in our quest from the courts, but there is a rich literature, which goes back to Hume and indeed to Aquinas, on the relative merits of monogamy and polygamy, Mormon and otherwise.[33] The pro side makes a number of points already touched on: polygamy ensures a husband for every woman and reduces the incidence of adultery, fornication, and prostitution; is accepted as normal in the Old Testament; is permitted already, in the form of remarriage; offsets a shortage of men; and increases the number of children. With regard to Mormon polygamy, the further point is made that by reducing the intensity of the emotional bond between husband and wife, polygamy frees the husband to devote more of his emotional energies to the Church. But this is also a point in the litany of criticisms of polygamy. Polygamy weakens the ties of affection between husband and wife; it is inconsistent, as Aquinas argued, with companionate marriage. The polygamist's wife is one of several, sometimes many, women among whom her husband must divide his time. She is sexually deprived, lonely, jealous, given to intrigue, and (particularly if she is his first wife) degraded. These consequences would be mitigated if a wife could make a contract with her husband that required her consent to his taking additional wives. But such contracts were forbidden in Mormon society, as they are in most polygamous societies.

Polygamy undermines companionate marriage in other ways. The literature harps on the insensitivity, brutality, and tyranny of the polygamous husband; he is the lord and master; he treats his wives like chattels, like slaves. These complaints may be exaggerated, but there are several reasons for believing that they contain a kernel of truth. The first is the frequent disparity in age between the husband and many of his wives (maybe all but the first). An older

---

York Times, April 9, 1991, A22. See also Potter v. Murray City, 585 F. Supp. 1126, 1129 (D. Utah 1984), affirmed, 760 F.2d 1065 (10th Cir. 1985); Ken Driggs, "After the Manifesto: Modern Polygamy and Fundamentalist Mormons," 32 *Journal of Church and State* 367 (1990).

32. 329 U.S. at 19.

33. For examples, see David Hume, "Of Polygamy and Divorces," in *Essays: Moral, Political, and Literary* 181 (Eugene F. Miller ed. 1985); Jessie L. Embry, *Mormon Polygamous Families: Life in the Principle* (1987); Richard S. Van Wagoner, *Mormon Polygamy: A History* (1986); John Cairncross, *After Polygamy Was Made a Sin: The Social History of Christian Polygamy* (1974); Ndabaningi Sithole, *The Polygamist* (1972) (a novel); Irving Wallace, *The Twenty-Seventh Wife* (1961) (another novel); Gunnar Helander, *Must We Introduce Monogamy?* (1958); *The Women of Mormonism* (Jennie Anderson Froiseth ed. 1882); George Q. Cannon, *A Review of the Decision of the Supreme Court of the United States in the Case of Geo. Reynolds v. The United States* (1879); T. B. H. Stenhouse, *Exposé of Polygamy in Utah* (1872); James Campbell, *The History and Philosophy of Marriage* (1869).

man is likelier to have the resources necessary to maintain multiple wives than a younger one, and the older he is relative to the wife, the more likely he is to strike her as tyrannous and she to strike him as naturally inferior.

Second and more interesting, the more wives a man has, the likelier he is to manage his household (or households) on a hierarchical rather than on an egalitarian basis. He may have little choice. The costs of coordination through negotiation are higher the greater the number of activities that have to be coordinated—indeed, those costs rise faster than the number of links necessary to connect all the parties.[34] The higher the costs of transacting, the likelier is a substitution of hierarchical for transactional coordination and direction. And any hierarchical relationship bears a family resemblance to a master-servant relationship; thus we find the law continuing to use the terms "master and servant" to describe the legal relationship between an employer and his employee. Just as prostitution, which in Chapter 5 I called a form of polyandry (many husbands), itself a form of polygamy, tends to create a relationship that is commercial, impersonal—a transaction on the spot market—so polygyny (many wives, the usual form polygamy takes) creates a relationship tending more to the businesslike, the managerial, than to the affective.

A related point is that the lack of companionship implicit in a polygamous marriage gives the wives an incentive to engage in extramarital sex, at the same time that it gives them more opportunities to do so because they perforce spend most of their time away from their husband. Since the benefits of extramarital sex are greater for the polygamist's wife and the costs lower, the polygamous husband has an incentive to maintain intrusive surveillance over his wives, to restrict their activities, and to punish severely any flirtations or other infractions of strict fidelity; and the wives will perceive these measures as tyrannous.

It may not be an accident that the congeries of practices loosely referred to as "female circumcision"[35]—primarily, the removal of the clitoris and (until marriage) the sewing up of the entrance to the vagina (infibulation)—are found only, as far as I am able to determine, in polygamous societies, except that, as we saw in Chapter 5, Victorian doctors used clitoridectomy as a last resort to "cure" female masturbators. (Purdah, an alternative method of exerting close control over wives, also is found only in polygamous societies,

---

34. The formula for the number of links required to connect all members of an n-member set is $n(n-1) / 2$.

35. On which see Janice Boddy, *Wombs and Alien Spirits*, ch. 2 (1989). Chinese foot-binding is analyzed as a method of sequestration of women in Mildred Dickemann, "Paternal Confidence and Dowry Competition: A Biocultural Analysis of Purdah," in *Natural Selection and Social Behavior: Recent Research and New Theory* 417, 428–429 (Richard D. Alexander and Donald W. Tinkle eds. 1981). Dickemann's essay is a veritable catalogue of the ways in which men in polygamous societies try to prevent women from straying. See also Laura Betzig, *Despotism and Differential Reproduction: A Darwinian View of History*, ch. 4 (1986).

for it is a Muslim institution, and Islam permits polygamy.) By reducing the woman's capacity to experience sexual pleasure, the removal of the clitoris reduces the risk of a wife's committing adultery, a more serious risk in a polygamous than in a monogamous culture because the satisfactions of marriage to the wife are fewer. Infibulation is a measure for ensuring virginity until marriage.

In the terminology introduced in Chapter 6, polygamy increases the agency costs of marriage, inciting cost-reducing efforts by the husband-principal that may be costly to the wives-agents and that therefore may make the freedom that wives in a polygamous marriage would otherwise have illusory. Female circumcision is analogous to the medieval chastity belt, a measure for preventing the wife from committing adultery when the husband, being away at war, would face insuperable costs of maintaining surveillance over her by normal methods.

One can see how, at a time when companionate marriage represented a step up the social ladder for most women, polygamy seemed retrograde and even misogynist, despite the fact that it reduced the number of spinsters. Whether this was a correct evaluation is difficult to say. Some women gain from polygamy—those who prefer being the nonexclusive wife of a wealthy man to either being the exclusive wife of a nonwealthy one or remaining unmarried. Other women lose, particularly those who would be the exclusive wife of a wealthy man in a monogamous society. If the costs stemming from the polygamous husband's efforts to police his wives weigh heavily on the wives, the balance may tip against the practice from the women's standpoint. In principle, polygamy with the consent of all of the husband's wives would be the unambiguously best regime for women because it would expand their choice set. But a premodern legal system might be incapable of determining whether consent had been freely given, which may explain, as we have seen, why divorce on grounds was preceded by a stage of no divorce.[36] In these circumstances, the second best choice from the woman's perspective might be no polygamy.

One factor that strongly supports monogamy in a traditional Christian society (and that may explain the confidence with which the judges in *Hyde* and *Reynolds* denounced polygamy), but has no contemporary significance, is that polygamy undermines a system of marriage law in which divorce either is forbidden or is available only on specified grounds. If a man who does not like his wife but has no grounds for divorcing her is free to take another wife, the rule preventing divorce at will is set largely at naught (not entirely, because he may still be required to support the first wife), for we recall that the principal

---

36. The dependence of complex legal rules on the emergence of a legal system capable of overcoming the high information costs that plague primitive societies is a theme in Posner, note 29 above, chs. 6 and 7.

significance of divorce is as a license to remarry. As this point implies, systems of law such as the Islamic and the African tribal, in which polygamy is permitted, make it easy for men to divorce. A society that wants to make divorce difficult has perforce to forbid polygamy, unless the only reason that the society made divorce difficult was to protect the woman in a financial sense; for the taking of additional wives need not reduce a man's obligation to support his present wife or wives.

Other social concerns with polygamy are noted in the literature as well, or can readily be excogitated. It reduces the diversity of the gene pool,[37] and by the same token increases the likelihood of incest. While at the same time it enables the exceptional man to spread his genes more widely, it reduces the opportunity for the exceptional woman to do so, because the average number of children per married woman is smaller under polygamy than under monogamy.[38] Polygamy makes families into little states (this could of course be a good thing in a society that lacked an effective machinery of government). In a society that values marital chastity it promotes fraud: a man will offer marriage to overcome the woman's resistance to having intercourse with him but not tell her he is already married. It aggravates disparities of wealth and power between men; it is almost as if poorer men were emasculated. It reduces a father's per-child investment of time and other resources in the raising of his children, because more children are competing for those resources (a polygamous husband has a much greater reproductive capacity than a monogamous one), and also because men spend time competing with other men for women. Indeed, the male rivalry that polygamy incites can dissipate substantial resources. We can predict that as egalitarian sentiment rises in a society, as a society becomes more peaceable, and as the emphasis in the society shifts from quantity to quality of children—quality being a function in part of the father's investment in the child's upbringing—polygamy will come to seem ever more anomalous and benighted, whether or not it is good or bad for the typical woman in the society.

Finally, to persons acculturated to monogamy, a polygamous culture is bound to seem promiscuous, as it did to the Supreme Court in the *Cleveland* case. Recall the distinction—highly visible in the *Hyde* decision—between a nominalistic and a substantive notion of marriage. Anyone who adheres to a substantive notion, that is, a notion of marriage as a restriction on sexuality, is likely to think of polygamy as a matter of renaming concubines wives, and hence as a condonation of concubinage. Temporary marriage reinforces this impression. And note how it can make the Islamic limit of four wives illusory:

---

37. Ernst Caspari, "Sexual Selection in Human Evolution," in *Sexual Selection and the Descent of Man 1871–1971* 332, 343 (Bernard Campbell ed. 1972).

38. Becker, *A Treatise on the Family*, note 14 above, at 86; Martin Daly and Margo Wilson, *Sex, Evolution, and Behavior: Adaptations for Reproduction* 289 (1978).

since a temporary wife does not count against the limit, a man can, for example by specifying the duration of the temporary marriage at ninety-nine years, obtain a de facto permanent fifth wife. In addition, we have seen that wives in a polygamous system have more incentive to engage in extramarital sex than wives in a monogamous system. A related point is that the legion of young bachelors that a polygamous system creates increases the demand for extramarital sex on the part of men as well as of women and also foments opportunistic homosexuality. From a Christian perspective, then, the sexual practices of a polygamous society are bound to seem highly irregular.

The negative effects of polygamy are mitigated in a society in which women are highly productive of goods besides children, as they were in African tribal society (where polygamy flourished and brideprice was common),[39] and as they are today.[40] A society in which women did all the work, and men's only role was to inseminate them, might well be polygamous (provided the men held on to political power), since one man can inseminate many women. It is only when men provide affective and material support to women and children that companionate marriage—an institution inseparable, I have been arguing, from monogamy—is apt to emerge. It may well be that even when women are liberated from economic dependence on men, children still derive substantial benefits from the presence of a father in the household. But insofar as women are not completely altruistic toward their children, the cost to a child of being without a father will not be fully reflected in the woman's decision whether to become or remain married.

We can expect, then, this pattern: polygamy, de jure or de facto, in a society of noncompanionate marriage; monogamy in a society of companionate marriage; and monogamy with an admixture of de facto polygamy in modern Western nations, where marriage is companionate but many women have

---

39. Jack Goody, *Production and Reproduction: A Comparative Study of the Domestic Domain* 33–34 (1976); Goody, "Bridewealth and Dowry in Africa and Eurasia," in Jack Goody and S. J. Tambiah, *Bridewealth and Dowry* 1 (1973). Brideprice, or bridewealth, is the money or equivalent that a man must pay his bride's family in exchange for their consent to the marriage. The opposite of dowry, it implies that women are highly productive. Posner, note 29 above, at 186–189.

40. So it was not a joke for the wife of a polygamist in Utah to state in 1991, "I see it [polygamy] as an ideal way for a woman to have a career and children." Johnson, note 31 above, at A8. The woman in question is a lawyer and one of nine wives of the mayor of a small town. In light of this example, should polygamy be permitted in our society? Mill thought that for the U.S. government to ban polygamy in Utah was contrary to liberal principles, provided residents of Utah who did not like the system were free to move elsewhere. John Stuart Mill, *On Liberty* 85–86 (David Spitz ed. 1975). He did not canvass all the possible social costs of polygamy, many of which, however, seem rather speculative; but the taboo against polygamy runs too deep to make the suggestion to permit it a feasible one in any state of the U.S. Anyway, most of the benefits can be achieved by contract, without the formality of marriage; in this regard the reader should compare the discussion of the question of homosexual marriage in Chapter 11.

children outside of marriage because they are no longer dependent on men, and where in addition the decline of the traditional morality, and in particular of the limitations on divorce, reduces the felt immorality of polygamy—its conflict with the society's sexual laws and norms.

Greece and Rome represent an intermediate state: formally monogamous but quasi-polygamous by virtue of widespread resort to concubinage as a marriage supplement, not substitute (a distinction noted in Chapter 2). The explanation may be that, on the one hand, companionate marriage was uncommon in these societies, a factor tugging them toward polygamy, but that on the other hand, they were urban societies to a significant extent—at least our information about their sexual and marital customs principally concerns their cities. Until modern times polygamy tended to be prohibitively expensive in cities because urban married women generally did not work, and therefore—unlike, for example, in the agrarian economies of African tribal society—the entire burden of support was thrown on the husband.

I close by noting some parallels to nonhuman primates. Some primate species are monogamous, others polygamous. Monogamy is found in species in which the adult male renders extensive care to offspring and is *not* specialized in a defensive role (which would give him less time and render him less fit to play a big child-rearing role), in which males and females do not differ much in size, and in which there is a close synchrony of all activities between males and females.[41] Polygamy is found in species in which there is strong bonding among females, with some occupying leadership roles; in which males spend some years in all-male groups; and in which the adult male can fairly be characterized as "a somewhat peripheral or socially aloof reproductive male."[42] All these features, except pronounced dimorphism, have counterparts in human societies.[43]

Regulating Nonmarital Sex

A public policy of channeling sex into marriage may seem to imply the desirability of punishing nonmarital sex, or in economic terminology of making a substitute less attractive because more costly. The strategy is apparent

41. Linda Marie Fedigan, *Primate Paradigms: Sex Roles and Social Bonds* 254 (1982); Patricia L. Whitten, "Infants and Adult Males," in *Primate Societies* 343, 345 (Barbara B. Smuts et al. eds. 1986).

42. Fedigan, note 41 above, at 240.

43. A cautionary note with regard to such comparisons, however, is sounded in J. Patrick Gray and Linda D. Wolfe, "Correlates of Monogamy in Human Groups: Tests of Some Sociobiological Hypotheses," 18 *Behavior Science Research* 123 (1984). Richard D. Alexander et al., note 29 above, argues that the mild dimorphism of men and women suggests that human beings have an innate, though mild, tendency to polygamy.

in laws, which remain on the books in a slight majority of U.S. states but are rarely enforced, punishing adultery.[44] But the effects of punishing other forms of nonmarital sex are complex, especially in a regime of companionate marriage. For example, if fornication and homosexuality were punished with sufficient certainty and severity to be significantly deterred, the average age of marriage would fall and the number of married homosexuals would rise, and both phenomena would reduce the fraction of companionate marriages. A related point is that the class of persons who have a proclivity for premarital sex will include a disproportionate number unwilling to make the commitment entailed by companionate marriage; it is better, in a regime dedicated to promoting companionate marriage, to keep these persons out of the marriage market. Furthermore, fornication is bound to seem a more serious offense in a system of arranged than in one of companionate marriage. In but only in the former system it imposes third-party costs, because in that system a daughter is an asset of her family, and is worth less if she is no longer a virgin.

These examples suggest a tension in traditional Christian sexual policy. Fornication is a lesser, not a greater, offense in a system of companionate marriage, which the Church tried to encourage, than in a system of noncompanionate marriage, which it tried to discourage. The general point is that a policy of seeking to close off all avenues of nonmarital sex encourages noncompanionate marriage by forcing people unfit for marriage into the marriage market, contrary to the Church's program of promoting companionate marriage. The tension was recognized by the medieval Church in its overtly condoning prostitution and covertly condoning monastic homosexuality and clerical concubinage. The ideal of companionate marriage in combination with the high cost of marriage ensured a large population of bachelors whose sexual needs had somehow to be accommodated. At the same time companionate marriage was a sufficient novelty, and the practice of noncompanionate marriage sufficiently tenacious, that the patronizing of prostitutes did not seem as anomalous as it came later to seem.

By the last half of the nineteenth century, with the fraction of unmarried men dropping as the rise in incomes placed marriage within the means of almost every man, with companionate marriage becoming more common and

---

44. Although it has been estimated that almost 50 percent of married men commit adultery in the course of their lives and almost as large a fraction of married women (Thompson, note 6 above, at 18), prosecutions have become so rare as to be front-page news: William E. Schmidt, "Treating Adultery as Crime: Wisconsin Dusts Off Old Law," *New York Times,* April 30, 1990, A1. In the case reported in the *Times* article, a husband filed a criminal complaint of adultery against his wife in order to gain leverage in their divorce and custody battle; the charge was later dropped. Active enforcement of Connecticut's adultery statute (Holly English, "Adultery Cases Prod State to Look between the Sheets," *Connecticut Law Tribune,* October 29, 1990, 1) merely doomed the statute. "Bill to Void Adultery Law Goes to Weicker," *New York Times,* April 4, 1991, A12. Governor Lowell Weicker signed the bill, so the adultery law has been repealed.

prostitution therefore a less needed safety valve, and with prostitutes reacting to the shortage of bachelors by marketing their services increasingly to married men, the stage was set for the purity movement, a major goal of which was to extirpate prostitution. The Mann Act, aimed primarily at the interstate traffic in prostitutes, is a legacy of this movement.

A traditional concern with nonmarital sex is that it produces an undesirable by-product—illegitimate children. It might seem that companionate marriage would minimize the problem by making nonmarital sex an inferior substitute for marital sex. Not necessarily. In a regime of noncompanionate marriage with sequestered women, men's extramarital sexual activities are confined to prostitutes, concubines, and other men (or boys); only the second of these is likely to produce children. In a regime of companionate marriage, prospective spouses engage in courting (search), which often includes premarital sex; some fraction of courtships fail but produce offspring, who are illegitimate.[45] It might seem to follow that the higher the average age at which women marry, the more illegitimate children there will be, because the period of premarital sex will be longer.[46] This is possible, but not certain. Delayed marriage implies delayed courtship. The length of courtship may be constant, and likewise the number of children produced during it. The number may actually be smaller if courtship is less likely to fail (that is, not end in marriage) if the woman is older and therefore more mature.

I said that the production of unwanted offspring is perceived as a problem of, an argument against, nonmarital sex. But it could equally well be said, and perhaps with greater historical accuracy, that the offspring are treated as "unwanted"—are stigmatized as bastards—in order to discourage nonmarital sex.[47] More than stigma is involved. In the period of greatest Christian enthusiasm, the illegitimate child had no right to demand support from either parent. And until fairly recently he had no right to inherit from his father unless the father named him in his will, or to obtain survivor's benefits under welfare programs such as social security.

From the standpoint of discouraging fornication, the denial of the illegitimate child's right to support by either parent was perverse; it reduced the cost of fornication. The denial of a right of support from the father alone, however, must have been a potent deterrent to a woman's engaging in non-

45. Peter Laslett, "Introduction: Comparing Illegitimacy over Time and between Cultures," in *Bastardy and Its Comparative History: Studies in the History of Illegitimacy and Marital Nonconformism in Britain, France, Germany, Sweden, North America, Jamaica and Japan* 1, 53–59 (Peter Laslett, Karla Oosterveen, and Richard M. Smith eds. 1980).

46. David Popenoe, *Disturbing the Nest: Family Change and Decline in Modern Societies* 93–94 (1988).

47. Cf. Jo Ann Jones et al., "Nonmarital Childbearing: Divergent Legal and Social Concerns," 11 *Population and Development Review* 677, 678 (1985).

marital sex in the era before a generous social safety net; for it shifted the whole burden of child support to her. The mere denial of a right to equal inheritance with the father's legitimate children must have been a far milder deterrent.

The legal disabilities of illegitimate children could never have been the main deterrent to a woman's engaging in nonmarital sex. The main deterrent must have been the extreme difficulty, before there were paternity tests, of proving who the father was and thereby establishing a claim that he contribute to the support of the child. Today, not only are the legal disabilities of illegitimate children negligible, but it is far easier to establish paternity; on both counts the disincentives for a woman to bear a child out of wedlock have been reduced. When these developments are combined with the growing economic independence of women from men that is due both to women's improved job opportunities and to the existence of a social welfare system that no longer discriminates against illegitimate children, the soaring rate of illegitimate births in this and other countries ceases to surprise.[48]

This discussion illuminates the trade-offs between fornication and adultery, and hence permits predictions of the relative frequency of these two practices under different social conditions. Imagine a society in which female virginity is highly prized, paternity tests are unknown, illegitimacy is penalized, and contraception is imperfect. Men will have a strong incentive to substitute adultery for fornication, because pregnancy is unsuspicious in a married woman and because adultery under the postulated conditions may enable the man to produce a child that he does not have to support; while adultery will be cheap for the woman because her husband will not be able to prove that her child is not his and hence will not be able to escape the duty to support it. It will be all the cheaper for her if divorce is prohibited; the prohibition will also increase wives' demand for adultery, because the option of remarriage will be denied them. Modern social conditions (effective contraception, paternity tests, easy divorce, erosion of the disabilities of illegitimacy and of the cult of virginity) make fornication a more attractive substitute for adultery than it used to be, so we would expect the relative incidence of the two practices to have shifted against adultery.

My discussion has left out stigma. Although I do not deny the possibility

---

48. For U.S. and British statistics, see Daniel Scott Smith, "The Long Cycle in American Illegitimacy and Prenuptial Pregnancy," in *Bastardy and Its Comparative History,* note 45 above, at 362, 366 (tab. 17.1); Peter Laslett, *Family Life and Illicit Love in Earlier Generations: Essays in Historical Sociology* 113, 123 (1977) (figs. 3.1, 3.4); Phillips Cutright, Karen Polonko, and George Bohrnstedt, "Determinants of 1950–1970 Change in Illegitimacy Rates in Developed Populations," 12 *Journal of Comparative Family Studies* 429, 430–431 (1981) (figs. 1, 2); U.S. Commission on Civil Rights, "A Growing Crisis: Disadvantaged Women and Their Children" 10 (May 1983) (tab. 2.4).

that social stigma can affect behavior,[49] the stigma of illegitimacy must have declined years ago for legislatures and courts to have removed most of the disabilities of bastardy. It may have declined as part of the long-term loosening of Christianity's grip on people's thinking here and abroad, but another explanation is, once more, the changing status of women. As women become more independent of men economically, a shift in female sexual and marital strategies occurs that generates among other consequences a higher rate of divorce and, because women do not need to be married in order to be able to support their children, a higher rate of illegitimate births as well.

It might seem that contraception and abortion would neutralize the factors behind the rising fraction of illegitimate births. But they would not do so even if the dramatic increases in the efficacy of contraceptives and in the safety and availability of abortion had made unwanted births a thing of the past (which they have not). "Unwanted child" and "illegitimate child" are not synonymous. A woman may want a child but not a husband; the growing emancipation of women has made this increasingly a viable option.[50]

With divorce at will now the rule in the nations of the West and the legal and social differences between legitimate and illegitimate birth trivial, the groundwork has been laid for the replacement of marriage, a status relationship—that is, a relationship imposing rights and duties that cannot be altered by contract—by contractual cohabitation, the relationship at issue in "palimony" cases.[51] From a practical standpoint, no-fault divorce converts a marriage that produces no children into a contract of marriage terminable at will, while, from that same standpoint, the erasure of the disabilities of illegitimacy equates a cohabitation that produces children to formal marriage. As a result of the virtual elimination of progressive income taxation in this country, even the tax benefits of marriage have largely disappeared. (Depending on the precise amount and distribution of a couple's income, there may be a small tax gain—or loss—from marriage.) Today, spouses who want a really durable

---

49. For an interesting discussion, see Robert Moffitt, "An Economic Model of Welfare Stigma," 73 *American Economic Review* 1023 (1983).

50. For evidence that public welfare induces some unmarried teenage girls to carry their fetus to term rather than to have an abortion, see Arleen Leibowitz, Marvin Eisen, and Winston K. Chow, "An Economic Model of Teenage Pregnancy Decision-Making," 23 *Demography* 67 (1986). See also Robert D. Plotnick, "Welfare and Out-of-Welfare Childbearing: Evidence from the 1980s," 52 *Journal of Marriage and the Family* 735 (1990).

51. Most famously Marvin v. Marvin, 18 Cal. 3d 660, 557 P.2d 106 (1976). See Lenore J. Weitzman, *The Marriage Contract: Spouses, Lovers, and the Law*, ch. 15 (1981); Carol S. Bruch, "Cohabitation in the Common Law Countries a Decade after *Marvin*: Settled in or Moving Ahead?" 22 *U.C. Davis Law Review* 717 (1989). Herma Hill Kay and Carol Amyx, "*Marvin v. Marvin*: Preserving the Options," 65 *California Law Review* 937 (1977). Common law antecedents are discussed in Stephen Parker, *Informal Marriage, Cohabitation and the Law 1750–1989* (1990). A palimony suit is a suit for the breach of an express or implied contract of cohabitation.

relationship must try to create one by contract or by informal commitments, in much the same way that an employer and employee might agree to replace the standard common law regime of employment at will with a contract of employment for a fixed term, or might specify the consequences of termination of the employment relationship, or might take other steps to try to make their relationship a durable one.

In the absence of strong religious scruples against nonmarital sex, it is difficult to find a purchase for resisting this movement from status to contract—incongruous as the movement may seem in a century that has witnessed the opposite movement in so many areas, ranging from retirement to franchising to leasing an apartment. The substitution of cohabitation for marriage is already well advanced in the Scandinavian countries. Sweden, for example, provides in effect a form contract for couples who wish to cohabit without undertaking the commitment traditionally implied by marriage. With cohabitation formalized in this manner, marriage rendered largely contractual in character by divorce at will, and the disabilities of "illegitimate" birth abolished, Sweden has gone far to assimilate marriage, the status relationship, to cohabitation, the contractual relationship.[52] Shiite temporary marriage, the duration of which is a matter of agreement between the parties, is a parallel institution.

African tribal society, in which divorce is easy, uses brideprice to enforce marital duties.[53] If the bride runs away without fault on the part of the husband, he keeps the brideprice; but if he abandons or otherwise mistreats her, she (or her family) is entitled to its return. Dowry played a similar balance-wheel role in Greek and Roman law. We can expect parallel institutions to emerge in our society if marriage gives way to purely contractual arrangements for sexual and procreative activity;[54] a start in this direction is that formal contracts of cohabitation are becoming increasingly common.[55] By this route even polygamy may be making a comeback, at least in Utah (see note 31). It is true that 84 percent of the cohabitation contracts in Lenore Weitzman's sample specify monogamy.[56] But in the remaining 16 percent may be seen possibilities for a revival of polygamy—and not necessarily just in Utah. The more inroads freedom of contract makes on formal marriage, the more diffi-

52. Mary Ann Glendon, *The Transformation of Family Law: State, Law, and Family in the United States and Western Europe* 273–277 (1989), esp. 276.

53. Becker, *A Treatise on the Family,* note 14 above, at 44, 129; Posner, note 29 above, at 186–191. A parallel Islamic institution is dower, which is paid by the husband to the wife (not the wife's father, as is common with brideprice), to be retained by her in the event of divorce. Nasir, note 1 above, ch. 2 and 96.

54. Recall Margaret Brinig's discussion of engagement rings (Chapter 6).

55. Weitzman, note 51 above, ch. 15.

56. Id.

cult it will be for society to withhold legal recognition of unconventional forms of voluntary sexual relationships, including polygamous and homosexual relationships. It just will not let them be called marriage.

The big question in all this is the effect on children of making the nuclear family ever more easily dissolved, and hence fragile, transient. We noted in Chapter 6 that modern cohabitation is (even) less durable than modern marriage, and in Chapter 7 we glanced at the literature on the consequences for children of growing up in fatherless households. We saw that the major consequence may be a diminution in the resources invested in the child, and this could in principle be compensated for by a generous welfare system, as in Sweden. The qualification "in principle" is important. Few countries have the Swedish taste for socialization, and the crushing level of taxation entailed by such a taste is giving even the Swedes second thoughts.

But all this is rather academic. A refusal to give legal recognition to cohabitation will not reverse the tendency toward easy dissolution of the nuclear family. For that, divorce at will would have to be abolished and divorce on grounds restored. That is not a realistic prospect. In a modern society composed of affluent, individualistic people, the law cannot force couples to live together against their will. It is this practical helplessness that powers no-fault divorce. The principal effect of refusing to give legal recognition to cohabitation—an effect entirely perverse from the standpoint of preserving the nuclear family for the sake of the children—will be to make it more difficult for women to obtain contractual protection for themselves and their children against abandonment by the child's father.

The overarching lesson of this chapter is that marriage-related laws regulating sex have been on the whole efficient adaptations to social conditions—even such exotic regulations as the prohibition of polygamy, a prohibition plausibly related to a concern with achieving the socially optimal parental investment, and even such frontal assaults on freedom of contract as the prohibition of divorce, a prohibition that in the particular historical circumstances in which it was created and enforced protected women from exploitation. If this is a correct picture of the law's development in this area, we can expect continued legal change, in particular toward increased recognition of cohabitation.

The Control of Pregnancy

Contraception

For Adults

Surprisingly little is known about the early history of contraception, despite Norman Himes's painstaking research.[1] Coitus interruptus, which requires no money and no technological sophistication, has been known since at least biblical times; it was Onan's technique for avoiding impregnating his brother's widow. It was known, discussed, practiced—and approved—by Islam from the beginning.[2] But the Roman Catholic Church from its inception took a hard line against any method of contraception (as well as against abortion), and made no exception for married persons. Not until the discovery of the rhythm method of contraception in this century did the Church's position bend, and then only to the extent of allowing the use of that method, in practice among the least dependable. Whether, in the face of the Church's strong disapproval, coitus interruptus or any other method of contraception was widely practiced in the West by married couples before the French Revolution is unclear.[3] But, if we may judge from Casanova's *Memoirs* and Malthus' reference to "improper arts to prevent the consequences of irregular

1. Norman E. Himes, *Medical History of Contraception* (1936). See also Angus McLaren, *A History of Contraception: From Antiquity to the Present Day* (1990).
2. B. F. Musallam, *Sex and Society in Islam: Birth Control before the Nineteenth Century* (1983).
3. P. P. A. Biller, "Birth-Control in the West in the Thirteenth and Early Fourteenth Centuries," 94 *Past & Present* 3 (1982); *Popular Attitudes toward Birth Control in Pre-Industrial France and England* (Orest Ranum and Patricia Ranum eds. 1972). By the end of the seventeenth century, however, aristocratic English families were using a combination of abstinence, abortion, and coitus interruptus to limit the number of children. Randolph Trumbach, *The Rise of the Egalitarian Family: Aristocratic Kinship and Domestic Relations in Eighteenth-Century England* 175 (1978).

connexions," contraception was common in nonmarital liaisons, including relations with prostitutes.

Families have always been able, and have often been inclined, to limit fertility by a combination of periodic abstinence and abortion or infanticide, with perhaps some unreliable but not totally inefficacious methods of contraception thrown in.[4] It is the relative importance of contraception in family planning before the modern era that is unknown and may have been small, except in France, where coitus interruptus began to be practiced widely by married couples in the Revolutionary period. To what extent this was due to Revolutionary anticlericalism is another unknown. Angus McLaren suggests, quite in the spirit of my analysis, that the earlier use of contraceptives by married couples in France than in England was related to the higher rate of infant mortality in France,[5] which implied that French parents lacked either the resources or the desire to raise many children and as a result faced a higher cost of noncontraceptive sex than English couples did.

When effective contraceptives appeared on the market and the perceived desirability of large families diminished (in part because the decline in infant mortality meant that a couple did not have to produce many children in order to be reasonably confident that two or three would survive to adulthood), many Catholics began using them in defiance of the Church. Today, in America at any rate, the use of contraceptives is as common among Catholics (other than those of Hispanic ethnicity) as it is among Protestants and Jews.[6]

Effective or not, is the Church's continuing disapproval of contraceptives entailed by Catholic commitment to companionate marriage inconsistent with that commitment or neutral with regard to it? On the one hand, by reducing the number of children, contraception might be thought to reduce the gains from marriage to the husband, and especially to the wife, whose economic dependence on her husband, and hence her desire to remain married, is apt

---

4. See, for example, Warren C. Sanderson, "Quantitative Aspects of Marriage, Fertility and Family Limitation in Nineteenth Century America: Another Application of the Coale Specifications," 16 *Demography* 339 (1979); Paul A. David and Warren C. Sanderson, "The Emergence of a Two-Child Norm among American Birth-Controllers," 13 *Population and Development Review* 1 (1987); also references on infanticide in Chapter 5. David and Sanderson, "Rudimentary Contraceptive Methods and the American Transition to Marital Fertility Control, 1855–1915," in *Long-Term Factors in American Economic Growth* 307 (Stanley L. Engerman and Robert E. Gallman eds. 1986), ascribe the fall in the marital fertility rate in late nineteenth-century America to a combination of reduced levels of marital coitus and a variety of contraceptive devices.

5. McLaren, note 1 above, at 165.

6. This convergence was virtually complete by 1970. Charles F. Westoff and Norman B. Ryder, *The Contraceptive Revolution* 28–29 and tab. II.9 (1977). Possibly reflecting the Church's especially strong stand against sterilization, however, is the fact that contraceptive sterilization remains less common among Catholics. Larry L. Bumpass, "The Risk of an Unwanted Birth: The Changing Context of Contraceptive Sterilization in the U.S.," 41 *Population Studies* 347, 357–358 (1987).

to be greater the more children the couple has. Contraception is therefore one of the factors that has increased the breakup of marriages. On the other hand, contraception encourages and strengthens marriage, especially companionate marriage, by reducing the cost of marital sex and by making the wife more companionable; no longer need she be continually pregnant and preoccupied with children to the exclusion of her husband. The net effect of contraception on companionate marriage is therefore difficult to estimate, but it seems a fair guess that there are fewer marriages, and that a larger fraction of them are companionate. Perhaps the Church's opposition to contraception is best understood as a corollary of its disapproval of nonmarital sex, the cost of which is unequivocally reduced by contraception.[7]

The deeper objection to contraception from a Catholic standpoint is that it divorces sex from reproduction. It makes it instrumental to other ends, such as pleasure and companionship; and the Church, traditionally although not unwaveringly, has disapproved of making sex instrumental to any end other than reproduction—even the end of promoting companionate marriage. The Church's approval of the rhythm method may seem to undermine this and any other ground for disapproval of artificial contraception. It does not. The rhythm method can be characterized as a form of (periodic) abstinence. So it is not nature versus artifice but abstinence from sex versus indulgence in sex that distinguishes the rhythm method, which is approved, from other methods, which are disapproved.

For Teenagers

Notwithstanding Catholic doctrine, the acceptance of contraception within marriage, and for that matter among unmarried adults, is so nearly universal in modern Western nations as to make extended discussion of the merits of permitting it otiose. More controversial is the question of contraception for unmarried teenagers. Analysis resembles that of sex education in Chapter 7. The use of contraceptives increases the frequency of nonmarital sex but reduces the probability that an unwanted birth will result. It also reduces the probability of abortion, a substitute (largely) for contraception. Someone who believes that teenage childbearing and abortion are worse evils than teenage sex should therefore support the provision of contraceptives to teenagers unless he harbors either the unrealistic notion that society can solve all three problems at once by enforcing sexual abstinence on teenagers or the equally unrealistic notion that if contraceptives were banned, teenagers would be scared off sex by the risk of pregnancy. The former notion is unrealistic

7. For evidence that the availability of contraceptives indeed increases the amount of non-marital sex, see, in addition to the references in Chapter 5, Elise F. Jones et al., *Teenage Pregnancy in Industrialized Countries: A Study Sponsored by the Alan Guttmacher Institute* (1986), esp. 8–9 (tab. 1.2), 186–189.

because virginity has lost its value and (a related point) because teenage girls are no longer sequestered. The latter notion is unrealistic because the decline of the cult of virginity has reduced the private cost of giving birth out of wedlock, because abortion (legal or illegal) is increasingly available as a back-up to contraception, and because no ban on contraceptives can prevent a couple from resorting to anal or oral sex, or to coitus interruptus—which as a matter of fact is commonly, and unreliably, used by teenagers.[8]

All this is not to suggest that contraceptives provide a complete solution for those who consider teenage pregnancy a more serious social problem than teenage sex. Their availability increases the frequency of intercourse by teen-agers, and such frequency is a major determinant of pregnancy risk.[9] It would not be if contraceptives were totally effective and always used, but they are neither, especially when the potential users are ignorant about the biology of sex and the relative efficacy of the various contraceptives—as many teenagers are, especially in America.[10] The availability of contraceptives could even *increase* the number of teenage pregnancies. Teenagers might exaggerate the efficacy of contraceptives to the point of perceiving the risk of pregnancy as ·very low, and as a result be induced to engage in far more frequent sexual intercourse than they would have had they understood the risk. Or teenage sex might simply be highly responsive to a fall in price, and the availability of contraceptives does reduce the price of sex.

So the question is empirical, but the answer seems to be that the availability of contraceptives does reduce the incidence of teenage pregnancy. During the 1970s and 1980s, while the amount of teenage nonmarital sexual activity was soaring, the number of illegitimate births to teenagers increased far more slowly than the total number of illegitimate births, and the principal reason appears to have been contraception (rather than abortion).[11] Family-planning clinics, whose stock in trade is dispensing contraceptives and advice on how to use them, are estimated to have averted hundreds of thousands of preg-

8. Maris A. Vinovskis, "An 'Epidemic' of Adolescent Pregnancy? Some Historical Consider-ations," 6 *Journal of Family History* 205, 217 (1981).

9. See, for example, Michael A. Koenig and Melvin Zelnik, "The Risk of Premarital First Pregnancy among Metropolitan-Area Teenagers: 1976 and 1979," 14 *Family Planning Perspec-tives* 239 (1982).

10. Jones et al., note 7 above, at 52. See also the essays in *Adolescents, Sex, and Contraception* (Donn Byrne and William A. Fisher eds. 1983). Why don't parents inform their children about sex? Why should it be a matter for state action? It has been conjectured that the incest taboo inhibits parents and children from discussing sex with one another, the taboo inclining them to regard each other as sexless creatures. A. R. Allgeier, "Informational Barriers to Contraception," id. at 143, 151. But parents and children in Sweden, for example, discuss sex freely; that is an important reason for the greater efficacy of contraception among Swedish than among American teenagers.

11. Vinovskis, note 8 above, at 216–218. For the statistics on teenage versus other illegitimate births, see U.S. Department of Commerce, Bureau of the Census, *Statistical Abstract of the United States 1990* 67 (1989) (tab. 90).

nancies (and abortions) among teenage girls, of whom apparently the vast majority were unmarried.[12]

The Swedish experience suggests that an aggressive program of explicit sex education, coupled with an aggressive program of making contraceptives available to teenagers,[13] can reduce the rate of pregnancy to low levels in a teenage population that is even more active sexually than the corresponding American population—which may of course be a consequence of more effective contraception. One cannot be sure that such programs would work as well in the United States as they do in Sweden, where formal sex education reinforces informal sex education within the home (see note 10) and would be less effective without it. Still, the public programs probably have some incremental effect, for Sweden redoubled its efforts in sex education and in the provision of contraceptives at the same time that it liberalized its abortion laws, and the result was a decline in the number of abortions even though teenage sexual activity increased.[14] The problem in America is that the equilibrium political balance between the supporters of permissive and of restrictive sex policies involves permitting teenagers to buy contraceptives, providing public support for teenage girls and their children if the girl becomes pregnant and decides to carry the fetus to term (whether or not she is married), and even—though this is highly controversial—permitting them to abort, but does not involve requiring schools or other institutions to offer sex education, to include contraceptive methods in the course on sex education if they do offer one, or to dispense contraceptives, along with advice on their proper use. This political balance has contributed to our unique combination of rampant teenage sex, a high rate of teenage pregnancy, a high rate of abortion, and a vast number of births to teenagers, most of them illegitimate and many of those unwanted.[15] A further contributing factor is that in a society such as ours, in which sex is morally problematic, many teenage girls consider planning for sex by taking effective contraceptive measures more immoral (because intentionality is an important factor in our moral judgments) than succumbing on the spot to sexual temptation.[16]

12. Jacqueline Darroch Forrest, "The Impact of U.S. Family Planning Programs on Births, Abortions and Miscarriages, 1970–1979," 18 *Social Science and Medicine* 461, 462, 464 (1984).

13. Swedish law requires pharmacists to sell contraceptives and also requires that contraceptives be available for purchase from vending machines. Jan Stepán and Edmund H. Kellogg, *The World's Laws on Contraceptives* 48 (1974). See also Jones et al., note 7 above, ch. 8.

14. Charles F. Westoff, "Perspectives on Nuptiality and Fertility," in *Below-Replacement Fertility in Industrial Societies: Causes, Consequences, Policies* 155, 167–168 (Kingsley Davis et al. eds. 1987). See also Jones et al., note 7 above, at 181, 187–201. But maybe the parents redoubled their own efforts.

15. Jones et al., note 7 above, ch. 2; also references in Chapter 6 of this book.

16. Id., note 7 above, at 64; Donald L. Strassberg and John M. Mahoney, "Correlates of the Contraceptive Behavior of Adolescents/Young Adults," 25 *Journal of Sex Research* 531 (1988); Meg Gerrard, "Emotional and Cognitive Barriers to Effective Contraception: Are Males and

The idea that puritanism may actually encourage teenage pregnancies and unwanted births is difficult to accept, but that is only because *effective* puritanism, that is, puritanism that induces premarital sexual abstinence, would indeed have the opposite effect. A puritan ethic that has only a modest effect in reducing the amount of teenage sex may produce more teenage pregnancies and unwanted births than moral indifference to such activity would do. So, at least, a comparison of the United States and Sweden suggests.

It is true that even a decisive shift toward the Swedish model would not drive the rate of teenage pregnancy to zero, since in neither country are *unwanted* and *illegitimate* synonyms.[17] But the rate would be lower,[18] and one result would be a decline in the number of abortions—which ought to be an important consideration to those who consider abortion a greater crime than nonmarital sex. It is for some. For example, a distinguished Catholic theologian has called for a relaxation of the Church's ban on contraception in order to reduce the amount of abortion[19]—a subject to which I now turn.

Abortion

Opposition to abortion is concentrated among those who believe it a form of infanticide. This should help us understand why abortion had so little moral resonance in ancient Greece and Rome, provided the father consented.[20] Those

---

Females Really Different?" in *Females, Males, and Sexuality: Theories and Research* 213, 220–224, 233 (Kathryn Kelley ed. 1987); *Adolescents, Sex, and Contraception*, note 9 above, passim.

17. Cf. Sandra L. Hanson, David E. Myers, and Alan L. Ginsburg, "The Role of Responsibility and Knowledge in Reducing Teenage Out-of-Wedlock Childbearing," 49 *Journal of Marriage and the Family* 241 (1987).

18. Laurie Schwab Zabin, "The Impact of Early Use of Prescription Contraceptives on Reducing Premarital Teenage Pregnancies," 13 *Family Planning Perspectives* 72 (1981). Recall from Chapter 6 that the rate of unwanted births is more than twice as high in the United States as in Sweden.

19. Bernard Häring, "A Theological Evaluation," in *The Morality of Abortion: Legal and Historical Perspectives* 123, 134 (John T. Noonan, Jr., ed. 1970). It is noteworthy, too, that Germain Grisez, in his emphatically Catholic book denouncing abortion, *Abortion: The Myth, the Realities, and the Arguments* (1970), supported the decision in *Griswold v. Connecticut*, which invalidated Connecticut's anticontraceptive law. His reason was that "the use of contraceptives does not violate any person's rights nor in any clear or proximate way injure the common purposes of civil society." Grisez at 438. For helpful discussions of the abortion controversy, see *Abortion: Understanding Differences* (Sidney Callahan and Daniel Callahan eds. 1984); Hyman Rodman, Betty Sarvis, and Joy Walker Bonar, *The Abortion Question* (1987); Elizabeth Mensch and Alan Freeman, "The Politics of Virtue: Animals, Theology and Abortion," 25 *Georgia Law Review* 923 (1991).

20. Eva Cantarella, *Pandora's Daughters: The Role and Status of Women in Greek and Roman Antiquity* 165 (1987).

societies did not consider infanticide any sort of crime, let alone a form of murder. In an infanticidal society, abortion might actually be considered a moral advance by those people who did have qualms about infanticide, because abortion is a substitute, and a particularly important one if effective methods of contraception are lacking. The situation is different in a society that considers infanticide a crime, as Christian society did from the start. What is more, if we assume that abortions will be far more common among unmarried than married women because the cost of a child is normally higher to the former than to the latter (an assumption borne out by the statistics, as we shall see), a society that reprobates nonmarital sex will be inclined to view abortion, other than following an unprovoked rape, as an effort by a malefactor to escape the consequences of her malefaction.

It is therefore not surprising that, from the beginning, the Church took a hard line against abortion. Later it became even harder. At first the fetus was not thought to receive the soul until quickening took place—that is, until the motion of the fetus could be felt. Until then, abortion was not infanticide, although it was still condemned as a form of contraception. For both biological and theological reasons, the moment of ensoulment was later pushed back to conception, with the result that since 1869 all abortions have been unlawful for Catholics—with (as we shall see) one narrow, ambiguous exception consisting of a subset of therapeutic abortions called indirect abortion.[21]

In traditional Catholic thought, abortion after ensoulment was even worse than infanticide because it had the terrible consequence of condemning the fetus to limbo—the fate of all unbaptized souls. This provided a compelling argument for refusing to permit even indirect abortion. The argument is no longer encountered in Catholic discussions, because it is now believed that the fetus can be baptized before being aborted. The abandonment of the argument leaves the infanticide taboo as the only strut beneath the Catholic doctrine on abortion. It is true that even without that taboo many, perhaps most, abortions would remain wrong in the eyes of the Church because abortion is a form of birth control, designed, like the use of contraceptives (but, arguably, unlike the rhythm method), to divorce sex from reproduction. This rationale would be weak, however, when the woman seeking the abortion was a victim of rape, and that is not an exception recognized by Catholic doctrine. That is why I say that the assimilation of abortion to infanticide is the *essential* premise of the Catholic view of abortion.

To understand the exception that the Church does recognize, one must understand the Catholic doctrine of double effect. An act that has two effects, one good, one bad, is not culpable if committed for the sake of the good

---

21. On the evolution of Catholic abortion doctrine, see John T. Noonan, Jr., "An Almost Absolute Value in History," in *The Morality of Abortion,* note 19 above, at 1; Roger John Huser, *The Crime of Abortion in Canon Law: An Historical Synopsis and Commentary* (1986).

effect alone. So if you are on a life raft that can hold only one person, and someone tries to climb aboard, you can shove him off without culpability, provided you are doing so only to save yourself and not, in addition or instead, to kill him.

It might appear to follow that abortion would be justified whenever it was necessary to save the life of the mother. But that is not the Catholic position:

> Fetal loss that is in no sense the purpose or intent of the physician, but occurs as a side effect of some very seriously indicated therapy or surgery demanded without delay for the sake of the mother, is indirect and can be justified under the principle of double effect. Direct abortion, however, as one that is intended as an end in itself or as a means to an end, and is undertaken precisely and directly for the purpose of interrupting the pregnancy before viability, clearly includes the malice of a direct attack on innocent human life, *even though this is done in the interest of the mother's health.*[22]

So if a pregnant woman develops cancer of the uterus, fatal unless the womb is removed immediately, the doctrine of double effect permits the removal even though the fetus dies. The act is the removal; it has two effects, and only the good effect is desired. But if the woman is simply too debilitated to survive the birth of her child, abortion is impermissible, because it would not be a mere by-product of a treatment for the debilitation. The only act would be the killing of the fetus, whose death, therefore, would not be the unintended consequence of another act, undertaken for a different purpose. Does this distinction make any sense? I think it does. In the first case the mother is simply defending her life against the disease, much as the man on the raft is defending his life by pushing off—not deliberately drowning—the swimmer. The analogy fails in the second case not only because the act itself is killing (not just shoving, with death an incidental effect), but also, a less casuistic point, because an essential although implicit condition, that of priority of right, is missing. The mother is permitted to defend herself against cancer because the cancerous cells have no rights in her body. The man on the raft is permitted to defend himself against the swimmer because in the contest for the raft, first in time is assumed to be first in right. The assumption could be questioned. Although priority of possession or occupation is a common rule for allocating property rights, in the case of the life raft it has little to commend it except convenience, since it is presumably only luck that determined who would get to the raft first. Why should luck determine who lives? Because it does in so many other cases? However these questions are answered, in the case of debilitation the mother has no claim to have rights superior to the

---

22. "Abortion, II (Moral Aspect)," *New Catholic Encyclopedia*, vol. 1, 28 (1967) (emphasis added). See also Häring, note 19 above, at 125, 135–136; Huser, note 21 above, at 86–88; Noonan, note 21 above, at 26–34, 41–42, 46–50; Hans Lotstra, *Abortion: The Catholic Debate in America* 36–38 (1985).

ensouled fetus. Mother and fetus are on a par. They have an equal right to life. The mother has no right to take the fetus's life to save her own.

The Catholic position thus has an impressive logic,[23] though I shall note possible flaws later. But it is a position that the members of modern Western societies, including our own, reject almost unanimously. At the time of *Roe v. Wade* all but three state abortion statutes made an explicit exception for or embracing the case in which an abortion was necessary to save the life of the mother, and this regardless of whether the abortion was direct or indirect.[24] Only a fringe of the right-to-life movement in this country wants to stop abortions necessary to save the mother's life, or even where the mother's life would merely be endangered by her carrying the fetus to term. The movement's position resembles the traditional Jewish position (though one now likely to be held only by Orthodox Jews), which permitted abortion if the mother's life was in danger and based this permission on an explicit preference for existing over potential life.[25] It is, I am sure, the position of most observant Catholics in this country as well.

Protestants were and are as hostile to infanticide as Catholics. But as they never pushed ensoulment back to conception,[26] they have never had as strong a doctrinal basis for forbidding abortion in the earliest stages of pregnancy, although the original Protestants condemned early abortion as a form of contraception, which they thought inconsistent with God's injunction to be fruitful and multiply.[27] The Catholic backdating of ensoulment reflected, in the first place, the same biological discovery that influenced nineteenth-century lawmakers in forbidding abortion before as well as after quickening: the discovery that conception occurred when the sperm fertilized the ovum.[28] Before then, no one was quite sure when fetal life began. In the second place, the change in the dating of ensoulment reflected the doctrine of Immaculate Conception (that is, that Mary had been born free of original sin), proclaimed shortly before the Church extended its ban on abortion to the unquickened fetus and itself a product in part of the new understanding of conception. It was hardly to be supposed that what had been immaculately conceived had nonetheless lacked a soul for some weeks afterward; and while early ensoul-

23. At least if one ignores, as I shall, its most curious feature: abortion, if direct, is forbidden even if the fetus is not expected to survive to birth, so both mother and fetus will die. Daniel Callahan, *Abortion: Law, Choice and Morality* 424–425 (1970).

24. Rodman, Sarvis, and Bonar, note 19 above, at 173–174.

25. David M. Feldman, *Marital Relations, Birth Control, and Abortion in Jewish Law* 275 (1968).

26. Noonan, note 21 above.

27. Martin Luther, "Lectures on Genesis," in *Luther's Works*, vol. 4, 304 (Jaroslav Pelikan and Walter A. Hansen eds. 1964). See generally Grisez, note 19 above, at 156–165.

28. Joseph W. Dellapenna, "The History of Abortion: Technology, Morality, and Law," 40 *University of Pittsburgh Law Review* 359, 404 (1979).

ment could have been confined to Mary, it was instead imputed to all human fetuses.

The gulf between orthodox Catholic and mainline Protestant thinking on abortion has grown. Two of the three Protestant theologians who contributed to the volume edited by John Noonan (note 19) were quite willing to countenance abortion for reasons unrelated to preserving the mother's life. Reform Jews likewise. But evangelical and fundamentalist Protestants, like most Orthodox Jews, disapprove of any abortion not required to save the mother's life. For them, life begins at conception, regardless of any niceties about ensoulment.

When in the late nineteenth century medical techniques for aborting the fetus improved, and the rate of nonmarital pregnancy rose as a consequence of the loosening grip of Christian sexual morality, the demand for and supply of abortion rose too. But because abortion remained illegal, the most visible consequence of the rise was an increase in deaths among women undergoing abortions, often in illegal "abortion mills."[29] The response of the women's movement of the day, abetted as we know from Chapter 7 by the medical profession,[30] was to press for more effective laws against abortion and for increased educational and family-planning efforts aimed at reducing the incidence of unwanted pregnancy. The response proved inadequate. The rising frequency of nonmarital sex, against a background of imperfect contraception, increased the demand for abortion. The increased demand, together with the growing political power of women, resulted in a progressive liberalization of abortion laws, although in the United States a major assist was required from the Supreme Court. Today abortion is legally available, essentially on demand, in most of the developed world, at least in the early stages of pregnancy (up to twelve or sometimes eighteen weeks); and it is estimated that more than 25 million legal abortions are performed each year, of which more than 1.5 million take place in the United States.[31]

From the statistics for the U.S. we learn that the vast majority of women

29. For disturbing statistics on deaths from illegal abortion in Canada between 1926 and 1947, see Angus McLaren and Arlene Tigar McLaren, *The Bedroom and the State: The Changing Practices and Politics of Contraception and Abortion in Canada, 1880–1980* 51 (1986).

30. And not just in this country. McLaren, note 1 above, at 190.

31. Stanley K. Henshaw, "Induced Abortion: A World Review, 1990," 22 *Family Planning Perspectives* 76, 78 (tab. 2) (1990). The qualification *essentially* on demand is important. Many developed countries place more restrictions on abortion than the United States does under the regime of *Roe v. Wade*. In fact, Mary Ann Glendon, *Abortion and Divorce in Western Law* 151–154 (1987), lists only five western European or North American countries besides the United States in which abortion is available on demand—Austria, Denmark, Greece, Norway, and Sweden. The other twelve that she studied require counseling or physician certification or both (Glendon at 145–150), but "in practice, in most of these . . . countries it now seems quite easy for a woman legally to terminate any unwanted pregnancy in the first trimester." Glendon at 13.

who have abortions are unmarried (83 percent) and a quarter are under the age of 20.[32] Slightly more than 91 percent of the abortions are performed no later than the twelfth week of pregnancy. This is not bad by world standards, but in a number of countries, including Denmark, Sweden, Singapore, and Hungary, the percentage of early abortions is higher. For example, in Denmark it is 97.6 percent. The difference may be related to the fact that in the United States only 13 percent of abortions are performed in hospitals, compared to 100 percent in Denmark, Sweden, and Hungary.[33] Abortion clinics are not as widely dispersed geographically as hospitals, and the higher the search and travel costs of obtaining an abortion, the later in the pregnancy the abortion will be performed.

Although it is difficult to gauge the effect of legalization on the number of abortions, since the number of illegal abortions is not a reported statistic, there is no doubt that the effect is positive (Chapter 7). Search and travel costs are much lower when abortion is legal, and medical risk too. It has been estimated that between 1963 and 1968, a period in which abortion was illegal in most states and the majority of abortions performed in the United States were illegal, 72 out of every 100,000 abortions resulted in the death of the mother; by 1976, after *Roe v. Wade* (1973) had made most abortion legal, that figure had fallen to 0.8 per 100,000.[34] It should not be assumed that all deaths from illegal abortion were due to incompetence on the part of persons performing the operation. Many may have been due instead to the fact that the higher search and travel costs of abortion when the procedure is outlawed delayed abortion, and mortality rises by 30 percent for each week of delay.[35] Since the full price (which includes not only the nominal price but also travel and all other costs, including nonpecuniary costs such as time and medical risk) of abortion fell when it was legalized, the amount of abortion rose, as economic theory predicts it would.

32. The statistics in this paragraph are from Henshaw, note 31 above, at 82–83, 85–86 (tabs. 4–7).

33. There are no figures for Singapore. The reluctance of American hospitals to perform abortions, documented in Gerald Rosenberg, *The Hollow Hope: Can Courts Bring about Social Change?* 189–195 (1991), reflects the controversiality of abortion in this country. In 1985, for example, only 17 percent of public hospitals performed abortions, compared to 23 percent of private non-Catholic hospitals. Id. at 190 (tab. 6.2).

34. Christopher Tietze, *Induced Abortion: 1979* 86 (3d ed. 1979); by 1979 the figure had fallen even further, to 0.5. Christopher Tietze, *Induced Abortion: A World Review 1981* 93–94 (4th ed. 1981) (tab. 21). The fall in deaths from abortion was of course smaller, since there were more abortions, but it was nevertheless dramatic: from 6.9 per million women aged 14 to 44 in 1953–1957 to 0.3 per million in 1973–1977. Tietze (1981) at 106 (tab. 25). The first figure is a rough estimate because the number of illegal abortions is unknown. The mortality (to the mother, that is) is now much lower for abortion than for childbirth. Rodman, Sarvis, and Bonar, note 19 above, at 65.

35. Tietze (1981), note 34 above, at 92.

The determinants of the decision to abort have now to be considered. Studies find that women, even teenagers, base the decision for the most part on rational (which is not to say, necessarily, morally acceptable) factors. Thus, women are more likely to abort if they are unmarried, if they are *not* in the class for which public aid provides an attractive alternative to employment as a source of financial support, if they live in cities (which reduces the search and travel costs of abortion), or if they are enrolled in school: in short, if the costs of having a child relative to the costs of abortion are high.[36] With these economic factors taken into account, Catholicism ceases to be a significant determinant of the decision whether or not to abort[37]—a result that attests to the power of the economic model of human behavior. Most of the factors that increase the costs of having a child affect teenagers more than they affect adult women, for example, interruption of schooling and lack of emotional and material resources for raising a child without the assistance of the father. Consistent with this observation is the fact that the rate of abortion, corrected for differences in frequency of sexual activity and in fertility (which would, for example, predict a very low abortion rate among women over the age of 50), is almost ten times higher for unmarried teenagers than for other women.[38]

Neither concern for the mother's health, the only admissible factor for an observant Catholic (with the further qualifications that the abortion must be indirect and that the mother must be in mortal danger), nor rape, incest, or possible deformities or other health problems of the fetus (which are circumstances influential with many persons who oppose abortion on demand but who do not want to outlaw all nontherapeutic abortions), figure prominently among the factors inducing a decision to abort. Thus, in a recent survey of women who had had an abortion, only 1 percent gave as a reason for deciding to abort that they were victims of rape or incest, 7 percent that they had

36. Arleen Leibowitz, Marvin Eisen, and Winston K. Chow, "An Economic Model of Teenage Pregnancy Decision-Making," 23 *Demography* 67 (1986); Eve Powell-Griner and Katherine Trent, "Sociodemographic Determinants of Abortion in the United States," 24 *Demography* 553 (1987); Robert M. Pierce, "An Ecological Analysis of the Socioeconomic Status of Women Having Abortions in Manhattan," 15D *Social Science and Medicine* 277 (1981).

37. Leibowitz, Eisen, and Chow, note 36 above, at 73–74; Robert Y. Butts and Michael J. Sporakowski, "Unwed Pregnancy Decisions: Some Background Factors," 10 *Journal of Sex Research* 110, 115 (1974); but see Dorie Giles Williams, "Religion, Beliefs about Human Life, and the Abortion Decision," 24 *Review of Religious Research* 40 (1982). These are American statistics, but it is interesting to note that Catholic Italy (or should one say nominally Catholic Italy?) has one of the highest abortion rates in the world—far higher than the United States. Elise F. Jones et al., *Pregnancy, Contraception, and Family Planning Services in Industrialized Countries* 7 (1989) (tab. 2.1). Incidentally, racial as well as religious differences tend to wash out in these studies when the economic factors are controlled for.

38. Jan E. Trost, "Abortions in Relation to Age, Coital Frequency, and Fecundity," 15 *Archives of Sexual Behavior* 505, 508 (1986).

health problems, and 13 percent that the fetus might have a health problem.[39] These percentages actually overstate the influence of such factors because most of the women gave several reasons for having an abortion. The most frequently cited were that the woman "is concerned about how having a baby could change her life" (76 percent), "can't afford baby now" (68 percent), "has problems with relationship or wants to avoid single parenthood" (51 percent), "is unready for responsibility" (31 percent), "doesn't want others to know she has had sex or is pregnant" (31 percent), and "is not mature enough, or is too young to have a child" (30 percent—rising to 81 percent for women under 18 years of age, dropping to 4 percent for women 30 or older). Neither this survey nor any other evidence that I have seen suggests that decisions to abort are commonly made on completely frivolous grounds, such as preference for a child of a particular sex; of course, it has only recently become feasible to ascertain the sex of the fetus in time for an early abortion.

Against this background, which constitutes a summary of the principal data on abortion in this country, let us see whether we can make some progress toward resolving the normative question of what if any restrictions should be placed on a girl's or a woman's right to abort her fetus. At first glance the question seems to depend—given our society's strong taboo against infanticide—on whether or not one believes that an infant's life begins at conception, at quickening, at viability (when the fetus could live outside the mother's body), at some other stage of pregnancy, or at birth; and that is a religious or metaphysical question that defies rational analysis. At least it defies economic or utilitarian analysis, for nothing in economics or utilitarianism determines the boundaries of the community whose welfare is to be maximized. Attempts to use "reason" to fix those boundaries lead merely to such absurd propositions as that "on any fair comparison of morally relevant characteristics . . . the calf, the pig and the much derided chicken comes out well ahead of the fetus at any stage of pregnancy."[40] But the willingness of most right-to-lifers to condone abortion where it is necessary to save the mother's life, and this regardless of the subtleties of double effect, shows that the answer to the question of when human life begins does not necessarily determine, even in a highly charged moral discourse, whether abortion is permissible.

Even the pristine Catholic position has an internal tension. First of all, it usually will be uncertain whether carrying the fetus to term will actually kill the mother; ordinarily one is trading off the certainty of the fetus's immediate

39. Aida Torres and Jacqueline Darroch Forrest, "Why Do Women Have Abortions?" 30 *Family Planning Perspectives* 169, 170 (1988) (tab. 1).

40. Peter Singer, *Practical Ethics* 118 (1979). I particularly like the two "anys," the "well," and the word "practical" in the title of the book. Other examples of the absurdity of appealing to rational principles to determine who is inside and who outside the community are discussed in my book *The Problems of Jurisprudence* 339–340 (1990).

death against at most a high probability of the mother's dying unless the pregnancy is aborted. Cancer is a mysterious disease; some people recover without treatment; so while it is certain that removing the cancerous womb before the fetus reaches viability will kill the fetus, it cannot be (as) certain that the mother will die if the womb is not removed. Therefore, if the aim is to maximize the number of lives saved, a rule that forbids abortions with no exceptions other than for cases where the fetus cannot be saved seems better. Second, the application of the principle of double effect to abortion disregards the reason the woman became pregnant. Suppose, as will usually be the case, that it was as a result of engaging in nonmarital sex, itself a mortal sin in Catholic doctrine. The symmetry between her life and that of her fetus is destroyed. Only the fetus is innocent. We do not allow a person to assert a right of self-defense when his own wrongdoing has placed him in the position in which his life is endangered—as where, for example, a fleeing robber shoots at a pursuing policeman because the robber reasonably believes that his own life is in danger. No more (it might seem) should a woman who was blame-worthy in becoming pregnant be allowed to demand medical treatment that will kill the fetus.

Thus, even the seemingly uncompromising Catholic position may represent a compromise with practical realities—two to be precise. The first is that a rule forbidding a woman to have an abortion even if her life is in danger will not be obeyed: the private benefits of abortion in that case are simply too great. The second (and related) reality is that Catholics as well as non-Catholics today believe that the life of an adult is more valuable than that of a fetus. The second point is particularly significant because it undermines a basic premise of the right-to-life movement, which is that a fetus is indistin-guishable from a child. (That is why the movement will not countenance abortion in the case of rape: it would be monstrous to allow a mother to kill a *child* because it was the product of a rape.) Most people think a child's life is as valuable as an adult's; so if they also think that a fetus's life is not as valuable as an adult's, they must, if they are consistent, believe that a fetus's life is worth less than a child's life and therefore that a fetus is not worthy of the same respect due a child. There is a sense, I am arguing, in which even deeply religious Catholics believe this.

That sense emerges more clearly if we turn from the orthodox Catholic position, itself ignored by most American Catholics, to the mainline right-to-life position, which is that direct as well as indirect abortion is permissible if the mother's life is in danger. That position implicitly sets a much higher value on an adult life than on a fetal life. Suppose the mother has a 10 percent chance of dying unless she has an abortion. A majority of supporters of the right-to-life movement would think abortion permissible in these circum-stances. The implication is that one mother is worth ten fetuses. I do not think these people would think a mother worth more than a child. This implies that one child is also worth ten fetuses. And this, I claim, is what right-to-lifers are committed to believing if they want their beliefs to be consistent.

Another clue to how the fetus is valued is that when abortion was a crime, it was not punished as severely as murder. Deliberately killing an infant was and is murder; deliberately inducing abortion was not. Of course, the consequence of a crime is not the only consideration in determining the severity of punishment. Another is the probability of apprehension and conviction; the lower that probability, other things being equal, the more severely the crime should be punished. By that criterion, abortion should have been punished more severely than killing an infant because it is more difficult to detect. Instead it was punished much less severely.

Many decent, upright people in our society believe that a deformed or severely retarded or otherwise profoundly impaired newborn is less valuable than a healthy newborn, although they would be unlikely to put it so. The existence of this belief is shown by the fact that many babies of the former type are allowed to die (a form of abandonment of the newborn—the traditional method of infanticide) by agreement between the parents and the obstetrician.[41] This is a form of infanticide that is widely if tacitly condoned. Of course, the right-to-life movement emphatically disagrees with this position, but I am suggesting that it has compromised its own position by endorsing what it considers to be another form of infanticide, namely abortion, provided only that it is infanticide for the sake of saving the mother's life.

This discussion has shown that most people in our society are willing to trade a fetus's life for other goods, not necessarily involving the life of another innocent person. The next step on this slippery slope is to note that even when the decision to abort is grounded in some baser consideration, such as the effect on the mother's income of carrying the fetus to term, the consequence of the abortion may be to save a life, albeit not the mother's. For if there were no abortions, and if as a result population grew faster—as almost certainly it would if abortion were effectively repressed[42]—society would reach a condition of perceived overpopulation sooner; the birth rate would fall; and children would not be born who would have been born had abortions been permitted in the earlier period. These children are saved by allowing abortion. Even in the nearer term, abortions do not reduce the number of births by the number of abortions. Abortion is often used to affect the timing rather than (or as well as) the number of births. Moreover, it returns a woman to the population that is at risk of becoming pregnant sooner than if she carried the fetus to term, thereby permitting a larger number of completed pregnancies.

41. See, for example, Anthony M. Shaw and Iris A. Shaw, "Birth Defects: From 'Dilemmas of Informed Consent in Children,'" in *Moral Problems in Medicine* (Samuel Gorovitz et al. eds., 2d ed. 1983).

42. Jones et al., note 7 above, at 8–9 (tab. 1.2).

A related consideration—that an abortion performed on a woman who would otherwise die saves the woman's fertility and thereby allows future births—is one of the justifications offered for applying the doctrine of double effect to indirect abortion.[43]

On the basis of such considerations it has been estimated that it takes 1.83 abortions to reduce the population by one,[44] which in turn suggests—at least to an economist—that an abortion kills, as it were, only half a child. It is true that insofar as infanticide has some replacement effect too—if the parents had kept the baby, they would be less likely to have another—the same argument can be made in favor of infanticide. In fact, infanticide when the infant is horribly deformed or unhealthy is widely tolerated even in our society, as I have just pointed out, and here the replacement effect is maximized. Here it becomes pertinent to the abortion controversy to note that the long-run growth in intolerance of infanticide seems related to a number of eminently practical factors rather than to some sudden burst of moral illumination. (For it appears that infanticide continued on a large scale in Europe long after the Church first condemned it—indeed, until well into the nineteenth century.)[45] The first is the decline in infant mortality. The more infants who die, the less resonance infanticide has: the child killed at birth was quite likely to have died anyway, especially if it was sickly. The second factor is improvements in neonatal medicine that have made it easier to repair a deformed infant and to give a sickly infant reasonable life prospects. The third factor, which is of particular importance given the traditionally higher frequency of female than of male infanticide, is the improvement in women's employment prospects, which reduces the expense of a girl—whether the expense of a dowry or the expense of supporting her in spinsterhood.[46] Fourth is improvements in con-

---

43. Häring, note 19 above, at 135–136. But see note 23 above.

44. Stephen P. Coelen and Robert J. McIntyre, "An Econometric Model of Pronatalist and Abortion Policies," 86 *Journal of Political Economy* 1077, 1097 (1978).

45. William L. Langer, "Infanticide: A Historical Survey," 1 *History of Childhood Quarterly: The Journal of Psychohistory* 353, 355–361 (1974). It is true that John Boswell, in *The Kindness of Strangers: The Abandonment of Children in Western Europe from Late Antiquity to the Renaissance* 111–113 (1988), argues that many abandoned children did not die but were instead "recycled" as slaves or prostitutes. *Quaere* whether this fate implies a delicate consideration for the interests of children.

46. This is not to say that the killing of healthy female infants has everywhere been abandoned. Yoram Ben-Porath and Finis Welch, "Do Sex Preferences Really Matter?" 90 *Quarterly Journal of Economics* 285, 307 (1976), presents evidence that in Bangladesh a girl is more likely to survive to maturity if born into a family that has more boys than girls, while boys' likelihood of survival is unrelated to the number of girls in the family. The evidence of sex-biased infanticide (invariably in favor of killing girls) is summarized in Sarah Blaffer Hrdy and Glenn Hausfater, "Comparative and Evolutionary Perspectives on Infanticide: Introduction and Overview," in *Infanticide: Comparative and Evolutionary Perspectives* xiii, xxxii–xxxiii (Glenn Hausfater and Sarah Blaffer Hrdy eds. 1984).

traception—and abortion—which make it easier for a couple to attain a target number of children (declining infant mortality helps too). And fifth is growing social wealth: the parents can abandon to state-supported or privately supported foster care a child they cannot afford.

Several of these factors are important in what until recently was a parallel trend against abortion, but that trend was reversed when changes in women's occupational pattern altered the traditional female sexual strategy in the direction of more sexual freedom, fewer children, and greater female control over reproduction, and when abortion became a safe and inexpensive procedure. At that point attitudes toward infanticide and abortion diverged, and the infanticide taboo began to lose its grip on thinking about abortion.

If practical considerations are as important in shaping our attitudes toward even such emotion-charged subjects as infanticide and abortion as I am suggesting they are, perhaps we should forge ahead with our cold-blooded examination of the value of the life that is destroyed by abortion. We should note, for example, that abortion enables parents to invest more in their children, thereby increasing the quality of the children at the expense of their quantity,[47] an effect reinforced by the use of abortion to postpone childbearing to a time that may be more opportune for the child as well as for the parents (their interests being intertwined). A study of Swedish children born after their mothers were denied permission to abort showed that as adults they got into an unusual number of criminal scrapes, had a higher-than-average incidence of alcoholism, and in other respects were less well adjusted than the average Swede.[48] And in the conditions of poverty that still obtain in many parts of the world, the decision to forgo abortion could result in the starvation of one or more of a couple's other children.

The problem with all this trading back and forth of lives, and the reason it will not wash under the doctrine of double effect, is that it violates the Christian and Kantian injunction to treat human beings as ends rather than means. We are speaking of deliberately killing the fetus, regarded as a human being on grounds impossible rationally to confute, for the sake of some other

47. For empirical evidence that the availability of contraception and abortion results in healthier infants, see Michael Grossman and Theodore J. Joyce, "Unobservables, Pregnancy Resolutions, and Birth Weight Production Functions in New York City," 98 *Journal of Political Economy* 983 (1990); Joyce, "The Impact of Induced Abortion on Black and White Birth Outcomes in the United States," 24 *Demography* 229, 240 (1987) (tab. 5).

48. Carolyn Teich Adams and Kathryn Teich Winston, *Mothers at Work: Public Policies in the United States, Sweden, and China* 40 (1980). The children had been born in the 1960s, before Sweden (in 1975) modified its abortion law to permit abortion essentially on demand during the first eighteen weeks of pregnancy. Other studies of children born after their mothers' request for abortion was denied have reached similar conclusions. These studies are summarized in Paul K. B. Dagg, "The Psychological Sequelae of Therapeutic Abortion—Denied and Completed," 148 *American Journal of Psychiatry* 578, 583 (1991). See also Natalie Angier, "Longtime Anger Found in Those Denied Abortion," *New York Times*, May 29, 1991, B8.

children. For it is not true that abortion affects only the timing of birth, even if the number of births is unaffected (and it will not be). The aborted fetus is not born later. It is never born. At best, someone else is born instead.[49] Only in a utilitarian analysis do the sorts of trade-offs essayed in the preceding paragraphs invite moral approval. Yet if I am right that we can find even at the heart of Catholic orthodoxy, and a fortiori at the heart of the modern right-to-life movement, a refusal to value a fetus at the full worth of a child, then—if I am right that even our attitudes toward infanticide are contingent rather than absolute—it becomes difficult to deny the relevance of utilitarian considerations to the abortion debate. Even if the major premise of the right-to-life movement is granted and the fetus is counted as a member of the community of persons whose welfare we seek to maximize, it does not follow that the morally correct policy on abortion is likely to differ greatly from what most of the Western world has converged upon.

Once utilitarian considerations are admitted, the figures presented in Chapter 7 concerning the effect of legalization on the number of abortions become highly relevant. If it is true that prohibiting abortion is unlikely to reduce the number of abortions by more than 30 percent, the benefits of such a prohibition are reduced relative to the costs, which include the danger to the life and health of those women—assumed to be 70 percent of the number who now get legal abortions—who would go ahead and have the abortion even if it were illegal. A prohibition of abortion could of course be coupled with a more vigorous effort at enforcing it than was common in the days before *Roe v. Wade*. But the effort would require enormous resources to make a large dent in the number of illegal abortions, especially given the wide dissemination of abortion techniques, the impending "morning-after" pill (a chemical abortifacient), and the fact that more states could be expected to retain liberal abortion laws than had such laws when *Roe v. Wade* was decided.

Let us push on a bit with the utilitarian analysis. On the benefits side of prohibiting abortion, there are those 30 percent of the currently aborted fetuses who would be saved. Or would they? One effect of the additional cost (in travel, delay, health risk, and a premium to compensate the abortion provider for risking punishment) of abortion when it is illegal is to deter some pregnancies by increasing the benefits of contraception and abstinence. So one way in which the number of abortions is reduced by a legal ban on abortions is that the number of pregnancies is reduced. But since some of the fetuses of the 30 percent of the women who are expected to be deterred by the ban from seeking an abortion would not be conceived, neither would they be saved. Then too, as we have seen, abortions do not reduce the number of children born by the full number of abortions. Nevertheless, a prohibition of abortion, even if not enforced with much more vigor than was displayed

49. Cf. Derek Parfit, *Reasons and Persons* 259, 364 (1984).

before *Roe v. Wade,* would result in a net saving of fetuses, although—after the adjustments just suggested are made—the saving would be much less than 30 percent of those who today are aborted.

The natural next step to take in a utilitarian analysis of abortion would be to trade off the benefits to the saved fetuses against the costs to their parents, to the parents' other children, to women (and men) induced to alter at some cost their sexual or contraceptive practices in order to adjust to the higher cost of abortion owing to its being illegal, and to women killed or injured by illegal abortions. But immediately a problem arises: should the fetus be valued as the fetus itself would if conscious value it, or as the society values it? If the former method is used, few if any abortions of healthy fetuses could be defended on utilitarian grounds. But to use that method would commit us to a form of total utilitarianism, in which the aim is not to maximize the happiness, pleasure, preference-satisfaction, or whatever of a defined population but to maximize the sum of happiness, etc. in the universe, of which fetuses are undoubtedly a part. Such an approach would have implications for population policy generally that we saw in Chapter 7 would be unacceptable. If we therefore confine the relevant community whose welfare is to be maximized to the already born, and if I am right that society—and even the Catholic Church—sets a much lower value on fetal life than on the life of a child or an adult, the benefits of prohibiting abortion would have to be discounted, perhaps steeply. At least this is so when the abortion is performed early in the pregnancy. A utilitarian analysis suggests that the later the decision to abort is made, the weaker are the reasons for the law to respect that decision. The benefits to the woman are fewer because she has already borne some of the burdens of the unwanted pregnancy and because the danger and hence the cost of the abortion procedure are higher, while the health and hence the life prospects of the fetus can be better assessed and so the costs of lost life expectancy may be higher too. Thus the medical advances that have made it easier to discover during pregnancy whether the infant will be born with serious deformities or other health problems help explain how hostility to infanticide can coexist with tolerance for abortion:[50] the more feasible abortion is, the more gratuitous infanticide seems. The strongest case for a late abortion is that serious fetal deformities (some quite gruesome) may not be diagnosable till late in pregnancy, but this problem will eventually be overcome. And even today, third-trimester abortions are rare.[51]

It would be wrong to conclude, however, that my utilitarian analysis unequivocally supports the right to an abortion even at the earliest stages of pregnancy. Quantitative analysis, limited as it must necessarily be in this area, underscores

---

50. Cf. Suzanne G. Frayser, *Varieties of Sexual Experience: An Anthropological Perspective on Human Sexuality* 300–301 (1985).

51. Rodman, Sarvis, and Bonar, note 19 above, at 59–60.

(paradoxically) this uncertainty. The principal benefit of prohibiting abortions is the value of each fetus saved times the number saved, the latter being a function of the percentage of abortions that prohibition actually prevents or deters, which we are assuming (probably extravagantly) to be 30 percent, and the number of abortions required to reduce the population by one, which I am assuming to be 1.83. The benefits of the prohibition are therefore v, the value of one fetus saved, times $.16n$ ($.3 / 1.83 = .16$), where n is the average number of abortions that would be performed each year but for the prohibition. The cost of the abortions that the prohibition prevents or deters is also saved. But it is a small number, almost certainly offset by the costs of enforcing the prohibition and by the higher costs of illegal compared to legal abortion—for remember that most abortions would not be prevented but simply shunted to the illegal market.

On the costs side of the calculation, the most dramatic element—the increase in the risk of the mother's death in an illegal compared to a legal abortion—is almost insignificant in quantitative terms. It has been estimated that even in the 1960s, when abortion was illegal in almost all states, the risk that an abortion would kill the patient was only 72 in 100,000, compared to less than 1 per 100,000 after *Roe v. Wade* (see text at note 34). The ratio of 72 to 100,000 is a soft number because it assumes we know how many illegal abortions there were, and we do not; we have only the crudest estimates. (We can have slightly more confidence in the estimate that during the 1960s no more than four hundred American women died each year as a result of undergoing an abortion.)[52] If we accept the 72 per 100,000 figure and assume that 70 percent of today's legal abortions would reappear as illegal abortions if abortion were prohibited, and if we value the mother's life at ten times that of the fetus, the cost to the mother in increased risk of death would be only $.005v$, a number too small to affect that calculation significantly. The mortality risk to women induced by the prohibition in carrying the fetus to term is also too small to affect the calculation significantly.

We can ignore the risk of death to the pregnant woman who elects to have an illegal abortion, because the risk is so small; but not because "it is a strange argument for the unconstitutionality of a law that those who evade it suffer."[53] Whether one is doing constitutional or legislative analysis, the risks that some women are willing to run in order to have an abortion are relevant because they fix a lower-bound estimate of the costs that the law imposes on those women. If the law were enforced so effectively that the option of evasion was closed to them, these costs would be even higher.

52. Christopher Tietze, "Abortion on Request: Its Consequences for Population Trends and Public Health," in *Abortion: Changing Views and Practice* 165 (R. Bruce Sloane ed. 1971).
53. John Hart Ely, "The Wages of Crying Wolf: A Comment on *Roe v. Wade*," 82 *Yale Law Journal* 920, 923 n. 26 (1973).

The trade-off, then, is between v, the value of the fetus, times 16 percent of the current number of abortions (or, equivalently, $.16v$ times that number); and the costs, unrelated to death, to pregnant mothers who would have gotten a legal abortion but would not risk an illegal abortion, and to these women's other children, present or future. If v in an early abortion were estimated to be $100,000, then the average annual social benefit of forbidding abortion would be $16,000 multiplied by the number of abortions now performed in the United States each year, and the question would be whether the social costs of the additional unwanted births would be greater. Note that the women to whom the costs of having a child were highest would tend to substitute an illegal abortion, so the 30 percent representing completed pregnancies would tend to be those in which the costs to the mothers were lowest. But the tendency would be weak, because the poor and the ignorant might have difficulty obtaining an illegal abortion regardless of need.

The critical uncertainties are v (for consider the effect of estimating it at $1 million—or at $10,000), and the nonhealth costs to those women induced by the prohibition to carry the fetus to term. It is difficult to quantify these variables, and it would be a mistake to try to infer the value of a fetus from the damages that courts award in cases brought on behalf of fetuses killed as a result of a defendant's negligence or other wrong,[54] for these are fetuses whom their mothers intended to carry to term, and the injury is to the mother as well as to the fetus.

There are other problems with the cost-benefit analysis:

1. I have ignored both the lower quality of the average unwanted child and the effect of prohibiting abortion on the pregnancy rate.

2. The assumption that a prohibition of abortion would actually reduce the abortion rate by 30 percent seems extravagant, given changed conditions since *Roe v. Wade*—the putative morning-after pill, the vast abortion infrastructure, the strong commitment of many physicians to the right of abortion, the safety and simplicity of modern procedures for abortion even without a morning-after pill.

3. Population externalities, positive or negative, have been ignored.

4. The costs not of the pregnancy itself but of the unwanted child that results from it may be zero or even negative if the child is put up for adoption. This may help explain why viability—the point, currently about twenty-four weeks, at which the fetus might be able to survive outside the mother's body—has seemed to some analysts an attractive point at which to terminate the right of abortion. The killing of the fetus is peculiarly gratuitous if the fetus has developed to the stage where the mother is no longer required to devote her body to nurturing it. What does she lose if the fetus is extracted and

54. *Prosser and Keeton on the Law of Torts* 367–370 (W. Page Keeton et al. eds., 5th ed. 1984).

allowed to live, rather than being killed? The only cost left in the picture is that of raising the child. That cost is not trivial but the mother can avoid it by putting the infant up for adoption or otherwise abandoning it. Not that these are the same solutions economically. Adoption involves no net social cost; the costs to the adoptive parents of raising the child are offset by the benefits to them of raising it—it was because they expected the net benefits to be positive that they adopted the child. Abandonment merely shifts the costs of raising the child from the mother (and possibly the father, if he can be identified) to the taxpayer. Still, where adoption is a realistic alternative to abortion, the case for a right to abort is weakened.

Even on its own terms, then, the economic or utilitarian (these are not synonyms, but they are closely related) analysis of abortion is inconclusive, although it may show that the extreme positions taken by advocates and opponents of abortion rights are untenable. We need a tiebreaker, a method for allocating the risk of nonpersuasion, such as a preference for limited government, for example as embodied in Mill's principle that government should not intervene in private conduct (Chapter 7), which abortion is if—the most controversial move of all—the fetus is considered a nonmember of the community. No impartial tiebreaker suggests itself. And we must be wary of mixing different levels of analysis. Whether the Supreme Court was correct to recognize a constitutional right to an abortion is, in the first instance anyway, a legal rather than a moral or an economic question, and is deferred to Chapter 12. At the moral level, moreover, there are other concerns to be addressed, such as the concern with creating a precedent for using medical techniques and personnel to kill rather than to treat. (It would be as if we used doctors as executioners in order to make the death penalty more humane.) Or the related concern with creating a climate of opinion in which human life is made to seem cheap and the moral repugnance that most of us feel toward infanticide and euthanasia—more broadly, the elimination of inconvenient persons—is undermined. Yet the narrow utilitarian analysis—narrow because the concerns just mentioned could be given a utilitarian form too—was worth conducting. This is not only because utilitarian ethics are influential in our society, but also because, even from a utilitarian perspective, even if we confine our attention to abortions early in pregnancy, and even when the fetus is valued well below the mother—as I think even devout Catholics are required as a matter of logic to do—it is uncertain that permitting abortion on demand is a sound social policy.

Catholicism and utilitarianism do not exhaust the moral universe, and a willingness to consider competing claims does not commit one to cost-benefit analysis.[55] Feminists, building on the common law principle that there is no

---

55. See Hilary Putnam, "Taking Rules Seriously," in Putnam, *Realism with a Human Face* 193 (James Conant ed. 1990), arguing that the approach of making rules but recognizing

duty to rescue a stranger in distress, have argued that to forbid abortion is to conscript women to save fetuses, and that a woman's refusal to save her fetus is no more a "killing" than her refusal to warn a pedestrian that he is about to slip on a banana peel.[56] There are many objections to the argument.[57] The mother is not a stranger. The common law does require a stranger to assist a person whom he is responsible for having placed in peril. The doctor who scrapes the fetus off the wall of the uterus or sucks it out with a vacuum pump kills the fetus in an uncontroversial sense (whether he is killing a human being is another matter), and in doing so he is acting as the woman's agent.

Then there is the analogy of infanticide to be considered. I called it a taboo not because I wanted to denigrate it as a primitive superstition, let alone to deny the influence—which I have stressed in this chapter—of practical considerations upon it, but because it is one of those beliefs, to which I referred in Chapter 8, that is prior to the reasons we can give for it; it is part of the foundation of our morality, not the superstructure. Historically, abortion and infanticide were close substitutes, which makes infanticide in a sense merely delayed abortion.[58] Their practitioners employ similar techniques of rationalization. Infanticidal societies will sometimes date the beginning of human life from the naming of the child, or from when the child is first nursed, or from the child's first or even third birthday, rather than from birth, to create an interval during which the child's destruction will not be deemed the killing of a human being.[59] In much the same way, some defenders of abortion on demand argue that human life does not begin until birth. The analogy of abortion to infanticide makes it particularly difficult to argue for permitting abortions designed to select the sex of one's children; so much infanticide was designed to do just that.

---

exceptions need not collapse into a balancing approach or a sliding-scale standard. Nor should it be assumed that a utilitarian analysis of abortion must take the same form (namely, economic) as mine; utilitarianism is a highly diverse moral philosophy. For a pertinent example of this point, see L. W. Sumner, *Abortion and Moral Theory* (1981).

56. Judith Jarvis Thomson, "A Defense of Abortion," 1 *Philosophy and Public Affairs* 47 (1971). A variant of the argument emphasizes the heavier burden that a law prohibiting abortion places on women than on men. I discuss this variant in Chapter 12.

57. They are sketched in *The Problems of Jurisprudence*, note 40 above, at 350–352.

58. Susan B. Hanley, "The Influence of Economic and Social Variables on Marriage and Fertility in Eighteenth and Nineteenth Century Japanese Villages," in *Population Patterns in the Past* 165 (Ronald Demos Lee ed. 1977); Wulf Schiefenhövel, "Reproduction and Sex-Ratio Manipulation through Preferential Infanticide among the Eipo, in the Highlands of West New Guinea," in *The Sociobiology of Sexual and Reproductive Strategies* 170, 184–186 (Anne E. Rasa, Christian Vogel, and Eckart Voland eds. 1989).

59. Susan C. M. Scrimshaw, "Infanticide in Human Populations: Societal and Individual Concerns," in *Infanticide: Comparative and Evolutionary Perspectives*, note 46 above, at 439, 441.

But how far is the analogy to infanticide to be pressed? There is a difference between being prevented from killing a child and being forced to carry a child (if that is how we choose to regard a fetus) inside your body. The difference becomes slight, it is true, once the fetus reaches the point at which it can live outside the mother's body, for at that point abortion is not just withdrawal of support. But that is just one more argument against late abortion, and there are plenty of arguments already. It is early abortion that is the tough issue, and here the analogy to infanticide weakens. The human fetus is not even an inch in length until about eight weeks, not two inches until twelve weeks. And let us not exaggerate the depth or breadth of the taboo against infanticide. Its core—in our society anyway, today anyway—is solid but its periphery is fuzzy. Is it infanticide in a bad sense to allow a profoundly deformed newborn to die? There is a difference of opinion on that question. Has a newly fertilized ovum a stronger case to be entitled to live than the profoundly deformed newborn? Reflection on infanticide is unlikely to supply the answer to that question.

As we learn more about the fetus—as science makes the womb more transparent to us—we are likely to feel a stronger empathy for it, to see it more as a baby (that two-inch-long fetus is recognizably human), to feel in short the tug of the analogy to infanticide, and hence to rate the fetus's claims higher than when it could be regarded as a formless lump of tissue. And the higher its claims, the less likely it is that the woman's claim of hardship will be thought to trump them. But if one part of science is undermining abortion on demand, another is undermining the opposition to it. I refer to the morning-after pill, which, when perfected, will make the costs of enforcing laws against abortion on demand prohibitive in early pregnancy (the pill could of course be banned, but, given the example of the "war on drugs," the ban would be porous) and render the abortion controversy largely academic. Perhaps morals wait on biology after all.

Homosexuality:
The Policy Questions

The Phenomenon Reconsidered

The history of social policy toward homosexuals in Western culture since Christ is one of strong disapproval, frequent ostracism, social and legal discrimination, and at times ferocious punishment. One aspect of the sexual revolution of the twentieth century has been a gradual amelioration in the political, legal, and social lot of the homosexual. In the countries of northern Europe (other than England and the Irish Republic), particularly Sweden, Denmark, and the Netherlands, homosexuals today are under very few legal, and relatively few social, disabilities; for the most part they are accorded the same rights and even respect as heterosexuals. The situation in the English-speaking countries, especially the United States, is less favorable. In the United States in particular, not only is there a strong residue of hostility toward homosexuals (particularly male homosexuals), but they labor under a series of legal disabilities. About half the states make sodomy, often defined to include oral as well as anal intercourse, a crime. Frequently the laws do not distinguish between homosexual and heterosexual sodomy, and in that sense might be viewed as neutral between the two sexual orientations. But this would be an unrealistic view in two respects. First, it is generally assumed either that these laws, despite their wording, in fact apply only to homosexual sodomy, or that, if applied to heterosexual sodomy, they would be unconstitutional (see Chapter 12). Second, sodomy is a more important practice to homosexuals than to heterosexuals, since vaginal intercourse is a close substitute for sodomy, but one available only to heterosexuals. Even those states that do not criminalize sodomy between consenting adults fix a higher age of consent for homosexual than for heterosexual intercourse. The armed forces have an inflexible policy, albeit erratically enforced, of banning male and female homosexuals, and this is merely illustrative of a host of formal and informal exclusions from government jobs. As a practical matter, known homosexuals are excluded from jobs involving national security, from federal judgeships,[1] and from teaching jobs in many public elementary and secondary schools. Homosexual marriage is not recognized. And federal and most state antidiscrimination laws do not protect homosexuals against discrimination on the basis of their sexual preference, although a number of municipalities do—which is not surprising when we recall that homosexuals tend to be concentrated in cities.

The efficacy of these legal disabilities is a matter of fair debate. The sodomy laws are no more enforced than the equally common laws that make adultery a crime. The armed forces make little effort to exclude discreet homosexuals of either sex. Homosexual couples can by contract create an approximation to modern marriage, though at higher cost because fringe benefits and social insurance are often more generous for married than for single people. While there is discrimination against homosexuals in private job and housing markets as well as in government job markets, it is much less common in the cities in which homosexuals are concentrated than it is elsewhere; and we have seen why homosexuals, for reasons unrelated to discrimination, can be expected to congregate in their own communities—to self-segregate, as it were. And many homosexuals can "pass" quite easily as heterosexual, though again at some cost, particularly psychic. One reason they can do so is that the most ferocious homophobes are typically incapable of spotting any but the most flagrant homosexual, and sometimes not even him. A homophobe is, after all, someone who believes that a homosexual is a diabolical or grotesque figure, and it is among the diabolical and grotesque, therefore, rather than the merely effeminate, let alone the altogether normal appearing, that he expects to encounter one.

The limited significance of the legal disabilities imposed on homosexuals is shown by their increasing political assertiveness. Like other minority groups they have become a political force to be reckoned with, particularly in the cities in which they form a substantial fraction of the population. Few politicians dare nowadays to express outright antagonism to homosexuals; and in the arts world, the academy, the professions, the mass media, and other influential sectors of American society, criticism of homosexuality or homosexuals is almost as taboo as criticism of blacks, women, or Jews. The term *homophobe*, properly reserved for persons with a pathological fear or hatred of homosexuals, is now, like *racist*, an epithet apt to be bestowed on anyone who so much as questions the most extreme claims made on behalf of homosexuals. Homosexuals have persuaded many heterosexuals to refer to them

---

1. In a large survey conducted by the Kinsey Institute in 1970, 77.2 percent of the respondents thought homosexuals should be forbidden to be judges. Albert D. Klassen, Colin J. Williams, and Eugene E. Levitt, *Sex and Morality in the U.S.: An Empirical Inquiry under the Auspices of the Kinsey Institute* 175 (Hubert J. O'Gorman ed. 1989) (tab. 7.5).

by their preferred term, *gay*, a word from the argot of the homosexual subculture. Advocates for homosexuals have also been rather successful in convincing the American people both that homosexuals are far more numerous (10 percent of the adult population) than appears to be the case (probably no more than 3 percent) and that AIDS is a threat to everyone (rather than to discrete classes of the population, prominently including male homosexuals) and therefore that the federal government should lavishly subsidize efforts to discover a cure.

The question I address in this chapter is whether the present legal status of homosexuals in this country should be changed. (Two specialized topics, however—whether the age of consent should be lowered to the point at which pederasty would be lawful and whether homosexuals should be permitted to adopt children—are deferred to later chapters.) The question would be easier to answer if the extent and particularly the causes of homosexuality were known, as well as the effect of the current legal disabilities on the practices of homosexuals. Suppose at one extreme that there is a huge number of "real" homosexuals in the sense used throughout this book of persons who have a strong and basically lifelong preference for sexual relations with persons of their own sex, that this preference is entirely the result of biological endowment, and that were it not for legal oppression, the behavior of homosexuals other than in matters of sex in the narrowest sense (the gender of the sex partners and the difference in sexual practices necessitated by the partners' being of the same gender) would be indistinguishable from that of heterosexuals. Then it would be very difficult to justify laws that make a "statement" of opposition to homosexuality, which is the main contemporary significance of the laws against homosexual sodomy and is justifiable if at all only if young people choose rather than are destined to become homosexuals. It would be equally difficult to justify laws that exclude homosexuals from certain jobs, for these laws are ultimately premised on the assumption that homosexuals are different from heterosexuals in more than sexual preference. Even the failure to include homosexuals among the classes protected by federal anti-discrimination laws would be difficult to defend, for on these same assumptions the fear and distaste that activate discrimination against homosexuals would be irrational, and the discrimination itself therefore irredeemably vicious.

We must try to estimate, on the basis of admittedly inadequate knowledge, how closely those assumptions approximate the truth. The assumptions are, again, that there are many homosexuals, so both legal and private discrimination against them imposes large aggregate costs; that homosexuality is completely biologically determined, so neither recruitment nor any other feature of the social environment affects the number of homosexuals; and that homosexuals are just like the rest of us except for their different sexual preference and behavior (and even some of the differences in sexual behavior may, as we shall see, have social rather than biological causes), so there is no rational basis for excluding them from any places or activities.

Let us begin with extent. Kinsey found that 4 percent of men were more or less exclusively homosexual their whole lives and another 6 percent had been more or less exclusively homosexual for at least three years between the ages of 16 and 55.[2] The sum of these two figures, 4 percent plus 6 percent, is the 10 percent figure promoted by the homosexual rights movement. Kinsey found that the number of men who had had at least one homosexual experience involving orgasm was much higher—37 percent—but we know that an occasional such experience does not a real homosexual make, any more than occasional heterosexual intercourse transforms a person having a strong homosexual preference into a heterosexual. Those 6 percent in the Kinsey sample who had a homosexual phase lasting three or fewer years probably consisted mainly of heterosexuals who in adolescence turned to homosexuality for want of female companionship, and in addition prisoners, who were overrepresented in the sample.

Because we are dealing with a continuous rather than a binary variable, no attempt to classify the entire male population as either heterosexual or homosexual can be satisfactory. But if it must be done, then 4 percent is too low and 10 percent too high. And these figures are for men only. Apparently there are far fewer lesbians. Only 13 percent of the women in the Kinsey sample had had at least one homosexual experience involving orgasm, compared to the 37 percent figure for men.[3] Suppose the best interpretation of the Kinsey statistics is that 6 percent of adult men and 2 percent of adult women are more or less exclusively homosexual in their sexual preferences. Then the percentage of homosexuals in the population as a whole would be 4 percent. But most estimates of male homosexuality are lower than Kinsey's. Even Paul Gebhard, one of Kinsey's successors as head of the Institute for Sex Research, has argued that the Kinsey figures are too high, in part because of the overrepresentation of prisoners. Gebhard's estimate is that 4 percent of men and 1 percent of women are predominantly homosexual, for an average of 2.5 percent.[4] Many estimates of the number of male homosexuals go down to 2

2. The statistics in this paragraph are from Alfred C. Kinsey, Wardell B. Pomeroy, and Clyde E. Martin, *Sexual Behavior in the Human Male* 650–651 (1948).

3. Alfred C. Kinsey et al., *Sexual Behavior in the Human Female* 474–475 (1953). See also F. E. Kenyon, "Female Homosexuality," in *Understanding Homosexuality: Its Biological and Psychological Bases* 83, 85 (J. A. Loraine ed. 1974); Donald Webster Cory, *The Homosexual in America: A Subjective Approach* 88 (1951); Susan M. Essock-Vitale and Michael T. McGuire, "What 70 Million Years Hath Wrought: Sexual Histories and Reproductive Success of a Random Sample of American Women," in *Human Reproductive Behavior: A Darwinian Perspective* 221, 229 (Laura Betzig, Monique Borgerhoff Mulder, and Paul Turke eds. 1988).

4. Paul H. Gebhard, "Incidence of Overt Homosexuality in the United States and Western Europe," in National Institute of Mental Health Task Force on Homosexuality, "Final Report

percent.[5] If the true number of more or less exclusive male homosexuals is only 2 percent and there are far fewer lesbians, the percentage of homosexuals in the population as a whole might be little more than 1 percent, which if then averaged with my recalculated Kinsey figure would produce an estimate of 2.5 percent. Most estimates of the number of male homosexuals are in fact between 2 and 5 percent.[6]

It might seem that the fewer homosexuals there are, the less dangerous they are along whatever dimension there is reason to fear them, and the more, therefore, society can afford to leave them alone. The other side of the coin is that the more of them there are, the more psychological injury we do by placing them under legal disabilities. The second consideration seems weightier than the first—at least given the fact that the advocates for homosexuals consistently press for acceptance of a clear overestimate of the number of homosexuals. But of course they may have other fish to fry. They may want to exaggerate the potential electoral strength of their constituents in order to impress politicians. And they may recognize that in a pluralistic society, morality and public opinion are not sharply distinguishable, so the more people there are who engage in a practice, the more likely the practice is to be morally acceptable.

As to the causes of homosexuality, the polar positions are on the one hand that it is biologically determined and on the other hand that it is, on the part of men, a selfish, hedonistic choice of the promiscuous and the irresponsible—promiscuous because it is easier to find sex among other men than among women, irresponsible because it is a means of avoiding the responsibilities of marriage and parenthood—and, on the part of women, either a second-best choice by "mannish" women who are unattractive to men or a political choice by angry feminists. The intermediate position emphasizes developmental factors, primarily the relationship between the child and its parents. The stakes are plain. The more that homosexuality can be persuasively depicted as a biologically determined condition like sickle-cell anemia or male pattern baldness, the less sense it makes to place it under restrictions designed to protect children from succumbing to its allures. If, however, it is merely a vicious choice of life-styles, it ought to be repressed as firmly as possible.

The theory and evidence reviewed in previous chapters point strongly although not conclusively toward the determined as distinct from the chosen

---

and Background Papers" 22, 27–28 (DHEW Publication no. [ADM] 76-357, 1976; originally published in 1972). Gebhard's paper cites a number of similar estimates of the number of European homosexuals.

5. As Kinsey himself noted. Kinsey, Pomeroy, and Martin, note 2 above, at 618–620. See also Arno Karlen, *Sexuality and Homosexuality: A New View* 456 (1971).

6. Frederick L. Whitam and Robin M. Mathy, *Male Homosexuality in Four Societies: Brazil, Guatemala, the Philippines, and the United States* 29–30 (1986).

end of the spectrum. The evidence is more powerful than the theory. Homosexual preference, especially male homosexual preference, appears to be widespread; perhaps to be innate (the implication of the studies of identical twins and of the recent brain studies); to exist in most, perhaps all, societies, whether they are tolerant of homosexuality or repressive of it; to be almost completely—perhaps completely—resistant to treatment; and to be no more common in tolerant than in repressive societies. The last point is of course a guess, since no one knows the number of homosexuals in any society, and since small variations in percentage can translate into vast differences in numbers: in two societies of equal population, if 1 percent of the population of one of the societies is homosexual and 3 percent of the other, this means that the second society has three times as many homosexuals as the first. Nevertheless the proposition that homosexual preference is stubbornly resistant to social influence—though savage penalties consistently enforced would no doubt reduce homosexual *behavior* greatly—is difficult to reject, especially when to the statistical evidence is added the characteristic pattern in which homosexuality emerges in the individual. Long before social influence could have a plausible impact on a child's development, children with a strong propensity to become homosexuals will usually display pronounced "sissy" qualities (if a boy—tomboy qualities if a girl), although not all sissies and tomboys grow up to be homosexuals, and not all homosexuals were sissies or tomboys as children. Conversely, we saw in Chapter 4 that Sambian boys, though compelled to fellate adult men, rarely are homosexual as adults.

The first stirrings of homosexual attraction are usually felt in adolescence; and in those adolescents destined to become "real" homosexuals (whether or not they engaged in cross-gender behavior as young children) the feelings of homosexual attraction grow stronger, seemingly inexorably, until they come to dominate the individual's erotic life. In societies in which social disapproval of homosexuals is strong—perhaps in all societies, because there may be no society in which homosexuality is not perceived as a disadvantage—the protohomosexual will usually fight his feelings, often indeed to the extent of dating women and even marrying.[7] But these efforts appear to be, in all but the rarest cases, futile in altering homosexual preference.

The picture is of a condition that may well be hereditary or congenital but that even if developmental appears to take root early in life and independently of social attitudes. Given the personal and social disadvantages to which

7. Besides Michael W. Ross, *The Married Homosexual Man: A Psychological Study* (1983), cited in Chapter 5, see Alan P. Bell and Martin S. Weinberg, *Homosexualities: A Study of Diversity among Men and Women* 162 (1978) (20 percent of male homosexuals in a study of homosexuality in San Francisco had been married); Marcel T. Saghir and Eli Robins, *Male and Female Homosexuality: A Comprehensive Investigation* 95 (1973).

homosexuality subjects a person in our society, the idea that millions of young men and women have chosen it or will choose it in the same fashion in which they might choose a career or a place to live or a political party or even a religious faith seems preposterous.

Of course it is possible that although only people with deep-rooted homosexual preference would "choose" homosexuality in a society that makes it a costly choice, were the costs reduced by the repeal of legal disabilities and the growth of social tolerance, a number of young people who were on the borderline between homosexuality and heterosexuality would cross the line, and the population of homosexuals would swell.[8] This, however, does not appear to be the experience in tolerant societies.[9] No one as far as I know has suggested, let alone presented evidence, that the removal of legal disabilities to homosexuality in countries such as Sweden and the Netherlands, and the growth of social tolerance to which that removal must in large part have been due, caused the number of homosexuals to increase. It has been estimated that in the Netherlands in the 1970s, light years more tolerant of homosexuality than the United States in the period covered by Kinsey's study,[10] only 2.5 percent of the male population was exclusively homosexual, compared to Kinsey's 4 percent; and only 5 percent more were homosexual to some degree.[11] Homosexuality is said to be extremely rare in Sweden.[12] In Japan, another society tolerant of homosexuality, a study of college students found that only 1.5 percent of the boys (and 0.9 percent of the girls) had ever had any homosexual contacts.[13] Kinsey found no increase in homosexuality over

---

8. That a climate of tolerance for homosexuality, perhaps in combination with feminist disparagement of masculinity, can tip young men of uncertain masculinity over the edge into homosexuality is argued in George F. Gilder, *Sexual Suicide* 226–228 (1973), and repeated in a subsequent version of that book, *Men and Marriage* 72 (1986). See also A. J. Cooper, "The Aetiology of Homosexuality," in *Understanding Homosexuality*, note 3 above, at 16.

9. Likewise there is no convincing evidence that seduction is a source of homosexual preference. See C. A. Tripp, *The Homosexual Matrix* 91 (1975), and additional references in Chapter 14 of this book.

10. Rob Tielman, "Dutch Gay Emancipation History (1911–1986)," in *Interdisciplinary Research on Homosexuality in the Netherlands* 9, 13–14 (A. X. van Naerssen ed. 1987).

11. R. W. Ramsay, P. M. Heringa, and I. Boorsma, "A Case Study: Homosexuality in the Netherlands," in *Understanding Homosexuality*, note 3 above, at 121, 130. But since there is reason to believe that Kinsey overstated the percentage of homosexuals, it would be perilous to conclude from this comparison that there are fewer homosexuals per capita in the Netherlands than in the United States.

12. David Popenoe, *Disturbing the Nest: Family Change and Decline in Modern Societies* 178 (1988).

13. Shin'ichi Asayama, "Existing State and Future Trend of Sexuality in Japanese Students," in *Medical Sexology* 114, 127 (Romano Forleo and Willy Pasini eds. 1978). Other surveys

the decades covered by his study, even though the social and legal climate was becoming more tolerant.[14]

The evidence that changes in the social environment do not produce changes in homosexual preference suggests that the distribution of homosexual and heterosexual is bimodal rather than proportionate, a point rather obscured by the Kinsey scale, which might lead one to expect that every point on it (0 through 6) marks off an equal number of people. In fact it seems that the vast majority of people have a strong heterosexual preference, and while many of them will substitute same-sex relations when objects of the preferred sex are unavailable, their *preference* will not shift merely because they can make the substitution at lower cost. A small minority have an equally strong homosexual preference, and while they too will substitute heterosexual intercourse when the benefit-cost ratio shifts far enough in favor of those relations, they do not become heterosexuals by doing so; they still prefer homosexual intercourse. There seem to be few genuine bisexuals in the sense of persons who are indifferent to the gender of their sexual partners and therefore will (if male) prefer sex with a good-looking woman to sex with a homely man but sex with a good-looking man to sex with a homely woman.[15] The genuine bisexual is more dissuadable than a true homosexual from engaging in homosexual intercourse, because he has a good substitute; it is presumably from the ranks of the bisexuals that the occasional "cures" of homosexuality that the literature reports are drawn.[16] Whether his preferences are altered is another matter. Recall the analogy to left- and right-handedness. Most people are right-handed (about 93 percent); almost all the rest are left-handed; there are very few genuinely ambidextrous people. But if there are heavy costs to writing with the left hand, then left-handed people will, though with difficulty, force themselves to write with their right hand.

When we consider how difficult—how well-nigh impossible—it appears to be to convert a homosexual into a heterosexual, despite all the personal and

---

discussed in Asayama's article reveal somewhat higher figures but still far below any American estimates I have seen.

14. Kinsey, Pomeroy, and Martin, note 2 above, at 631. Tolerance of homosexuals may have dipped in the 1950s, since they were among the targets of McCarthyism, but the Kinsey report on male sexual behavior was published in 1948.

15. K. W. Freund, "Male Homosexuality: An Analysis of the Pattern," in *Understanding Homosexuality*, note 3 above, at 25, 39; Bell and Weinberg, note 7 above, at 54–55; Ron Langevin, *Sexual Strands: Understanding and Treating Sexual Anomalies in Men*, ch. 5 (1983).

16. Richard Green, *The "Sissy Boy Syndrome" and the Development of Homosexuality* 213–217 (1987); Karlen, note 5 above, at 583–595; Karlen, "Homosexuality: The Scene and Its Students," in *The Sociology of Sex: An Introductory Reader* 223, 247–248 (James M. Henslin and Edward Sagarin eds., rev. ed. 1978); Joyce Price, "'Therapy' for Gays Questioned," *Washington Times*, February 5, 1990, A3.

social advantages to being a heterosexual in this and perhaps in any society, the issue of homosexual seduction, recruitment, or propaganda is placed in perspective. How *much* more difficult it must be for homosexuals to convert a heterosexual into one of themselves! To this one might be moved to reply that there may be borderline homosexuals who could with a smart shove be pushed to the heterosexual side of the line, but who lacking that shove will end up firmly on the homosexual side. One is speaking here not of convinced bisexuals, as it were, but of persons whose sexual identity is uncertain, and perhaps malleable. Maybe if they fall in with homosexuals at an impressionable age, they will become homosexuals. This is an entirely plausible, commonsensical, even intuitive hypothesis; nor can it be refuted on logical or scientific grounds. There just is no evidence for it, although people have been looking for such evidence for a very long time. Such evidence as we do have bearing on the hypothesis—the twin evidence, the comparisons between tolerant and intolerant societies, the child-development evidence, and so forth— is against it. No doubt a careful study is warranted of homosexuality in English university and intellectual circles, almost all of whose members had attended sex-segregated educational institutions from the age of 7 on. The number of homosexuals in those circles (Keynes, Strachey, Pigou, Forster, Turing, Blunt—the list seems endless) does seem disproportionate to their number in the general population; yet English universities have until recently discriminated against married men, thereby making the universities more congenial to homosexuals than would otherwise have been the case.

We might be more concerned about behavior than about preference. This would be true, for example, if the only thing that worried us about homosexuality was that anal intercourse can spread venereal diseases, such as AIDS, more easily than vaginal intercourse can. But the American public's larger concern, I believe, is that if legal and social inhibitors of homosexual activity are relaxed, young men and women will succumb to the blandishments of homosexual sex and the homosexual style of life. This fear seems misplaced, at least in the case of men; it is a little more plausible with respect to women. Men who, though not homosexual, dislike women nevertheless do not spurn them as sex objects. Rather the contrary: for as feminists tirelessly remind us, sexual intercourse is easily viewed by men as an assertion of male dominance. But women who dislike men—perhaps because they were sexually abused as children or subjected to sexual harassment as college students or as workers, or because they work in an occupation such as prostitution which shows men at their worst, or because they have signed on (perhaps for some of these same reasons) to the radical feminist critique of heterosexuality—may turn away from sex with men and become practicing lesbians.[17] This is a form of

17. Kenyon, note 3 above, at 93; Lillian Faderman, "The 'New Gay' Lesbians," 10 *Journal of Homosexuality* 85 (1984). And recall the discussion of lesbianism in Chapter 6, where I

opportunistic rather than "real" homosexuality, but it differs from male op-portunistic homosexuality in not resulting from a scarcity of heterosexual opportunities. It represents a deliberate commitment to a homosexual style of life and love, and thus reflects a greater degree of choice (as distinct from compulsion) than in the case of exclusively male homosexuality. And because it reflects a greater degree of choice, it should be more subject to the influence of the social environment.

The paradox is that although lesbianism seems potentially more responsive to social control, society exerts much less pressure against it than against male homosexuality. It has been made criminal far less often than male homosex-uality has, and when made criminal has usually been punished less severely.[18] Social disapproval of lesbians is also less than that of male homosexuals. The reason may be that (heterosexual) men dominate law, politics, and social codes, and find lesbianism less disgusting than male homosexuality. For while a heterosexual man is apt to consider it in principle unnatural that anyone should be attracted sexually to a person of the same sex, he is hardly disposed to find the idea of a woman's being attractive disgusting. Thus he can imagine himself a woman's lesbian lover more easily than a man's homosexual lover. Pornographic magazines directed at men frequently show women making love to one another.

Mention of disgust brings me to the third general issue in the evaluation of social controls of homosexuality, and that is the effect of those controls on homosexual behavior itself. This effect is connected with the fundamental question of how we should evaluate the life of a homosexual.

If you ask men who are disgusted by homosexuals what it is, precisely, about homosexual men that makes them disgusting, the answer will not be confined to the fact of erotic attraction and expression between two men, although that is part of it. The objection is to an entire homosexual life-style, involving what are believed to be characteristic demeanors, behaviors, atti-tudes, destinies that the heterosexual (and no doubt many a homosexual) abhors: a life-style believed to be pervaded with effeminacy, including physical weakness and cowardice; with promiscuity and intrigue, prominently includ-ing seduction of the young; with concentration in a handful of unmanly occupations centered on fashion, entertainment, decoration, and culture—such occupations as the theater (above all the ballet) and the arts, hairdressing, interior decoration, women's fashions, ladies' shops, library work; with fur-

---

conjectured on different grounds that lesbian preference was more likely than male homosexual preference to be subject to choice.

18. Usually, not always. In colonial Brazil, for example, female as well as male homosexual intercourse was a capital offense. David F. Greenberg, *The Construction of Homosexuality* 342 (1988).

tiveness and concealment; with a bitchy, gossipy, histrionic, finicky, even hysterical manner; with a concern with externals (physical appearance, youth, dress); with bad health, physical and mental, including suicide and alcoholism;[19] with a wretched old age; with a general immorality and unreliability; with an above-average IQ, education, and income (qualities that make homosexuals even more threatening, more insidious, more seductive and manipulative); and, of course, with narcissim.[20]

It is important to try to separate out the elements in this composite picture that are false or exaggerated; the elements that are the consequence of the social and legal disabilities to which homosexuals in this and many other societies are subjected, not to mention the historical legacy of even graver disabilities; and the elements that represent tendencies inherent in homosexual preference. For it is only the elements in the last set that provide a solid basis for social concern with homosexual preference.

The first two sets are related. The social environment can alter not only the way of life of homosexuals but also the appearance of that way of life to heterosexuals. Take effeminacy. I doubt that it is an artifact of social control. Effeminate males, many though not all homosexual, are a feature of tolerant as well as intolerant societies; they are, for example, the berdaches of American Indian cultures. And the frequency of gender nonconformity in the childhood of homosexuals makes it plausible to expect that effeminacy would be more common among homosexual than among heterosexual adults no matter what the state of public opinion or legal regulation concerning homosexuality. The signaling function of an effeminate manner is not an artifact of repression, nor is the preoccupation with youth, good looks, and being well dressed—a preoccupation apt to reinforce (though not create) an impression of effeminacy.[21] What is true is that in a repressive society, where homosexuals have an incentive to conceal their homosexuality, heterosexuals will tend to exaggerate the percentage of homosexuals who are effeminate. (So may homosex-

19. D. J. West, *Homosexuality Re-Examined* 198–208 (1977); Paul Gibson, "Gay Male and Lesbian Youth Suicide," in *Report of the Secretary's Task Force on Youth Suicide,* vol. 3, *Prevention and Intervention in Youth Suicide* 3–110 (Marcia R. Feinleib ed. January 1989); Stephen G. Schneider, Norman L. Farberow, and Gabriel N. Kruks, "Suicidal Behavior in Adolescent and Young Gay Men," 19 *Suicide and Life-Threatening Behavior* 381 (1989); Bell and Weinberg, note 7 above, at 207; Saghir and Robins, note 7 above, at 132–136 (finding the difference in psychopathology between heterosexuals and homosexuals not to be large, however).

20. James D. Weinrich, "On a Relationship between Homosexuality and IQ Test Scores: A Review and Some Hypotheses," in *Medical Sexology,* note 13 above, at 312; Michael Schofield, *Sociological Aspects of Homosexuality: A Comparative Study of Three Types of Homosexuals* 177 (1965); *Alcoholism & Homosexuality* (Thomas O. Ziebold and John E. Mongeon eds. 1982). Several of the elements of the composite picture of the homosexual life-style I have sketched come together in Jean-Paul Sartre's horrific story of homosexual seduction, "The Childhood of a Leader," in Sartre, *The Wall and Other Stories* 157 (1948).

21. Donald Symons, *The Evolution of Human Sexuality* 204 (1979).

uals.)[22] The reason is that since it is more costly for effeminate homosexuals to pass as heterosexuals than for noneffeminate homosexuals to do so, the former will make less effort at concealment and therefore will constitute a larger fraction of the known homosexuals than of all homosexuals.

The deeper question is whether effeminacy is anything to worry about. I said I would use the word without pejorative overtones; the question now is whether the pejorative overtones that the word undoubtedly carries are a product of intolerance or instead are more deeply rooted in a desire, which need not reflect hostility to homosexuality or other sexual "deviance" per se, to sort everyone into one of just two unambiguous gender bins—the "masculine" and the "feminine." I do not know the answer.

Now for examples of how discrimination against homosexuals is apt to alter their behavior. Their exclusion from particular occupations will skew their occupational pattern in favor of "unmanly" occupations, where their presence will not grate on heterosexual sensibilities, just as blacks in servile occupations do not grate on the sensibilities of white bigots. The benefits of concealing homosexuality will encourage skills in concealment—but will in those homosexuals who are deficient in those skills produce a furtive and anxious manner. Forbidden to make same-sex marriages, homosexuals will lack an important device for taming sexual desire, so they will be more promiscuous than heterosexuals. To conceal their sexual relationships, moreover, they will tend to substitute the sex act, which can be performed in a very short time and in private, for courtship, which is public and protracted. This substitution—of, as it were, sex for presex—will reinforce the public impression of homosexuals as a promiscuous lot. (Substitution of sex for presex is one of the things that make some Americans consider Swedish teenagers immoral. See Chapter 5.) And since homosexuality is a taboo subject in most homes and schools,[23] adolescent homosexuals will find it difficult to learn about sex other than by doing it.[24] The sex act will substitute for reading and talking about it. This is still another prod to promiscuity. Concealment also raises homosexual search costs, and one consequence of higher search

22. Michael W. Ross, "Retrospective Distortion in Homosexual Research," 9 *Archives of Sexual Behavior* 523 (1980).

23. This is changing slowly. Gary Putka, "Uncharted Course: Effort to Teach Teens about Homosexuality Advances in Schools," *Wall Street Journal,* June 12, 1990, 1; Eric Rofes, "Opening up the Classroom Closet: Responding to the Educational Needs of Gay and Lesbian Youth," 59 *Harvard Educational Review* 444 (1989).

24. John Gagnon, "Gender Preference in Erotic Relations: The Kinsey Scale and Sexual Scripts," in *Homosexuality/Heterosexuality: Concepts of Sexual Orientation* 175, 197 (David P. McWhirter, Stephanie A. Sanders, and June Machover Reinisch eds. 1990). The concept of learning by doing as an alternative to learning by being instructed is conventional in business economics.

costs is more mismatches.[25] This is another reason to suppose that the instability of homosexual relationships is aggravated by intolerance. Finally, although not all despised minorities suffer deep psychological wounds from the hostility of the majority, there is evidence that homosexuals do.[26]

Despite all these points, it is unlikely that when every legal disability of homosexuality has been dismantled and every heterosexual has been thoroughly schooled in tolerance, the homosexual life-style will cease to be a distinctive and, to a significant degree, an unhappy one.

The homosexual life-style seems fairly invariant to a society's degree of tolerance, legal and social, of homosexuality.[27] Like most of Southeast Asia, the Philippines is (despite the Spanish and American influence) far more tolerant of homosexuals than the United States is. But the occupational pattern is similar.[28] Philippine homosexuals dominate television and monopolize hairdressing. They form a distinctive subculture that appears, in fact, to be universal.[29] Not all homosexuals belong to that subculture. Not all are "creative." But, on average, male homosexuals do seem more drawn to beauty, adornment, decoration, and decor than heterosexuals,[30] and there is no social theory

25. Gary S. Becker, Elisabeth M. Landes, and Robert T. Michael, "An Economic Analysis of Marital Instability," 85 *Journal of Political Economy* 1141, 1147–52 (1977).

26. Michael W. Ross, "Actual and Anticipated Societal Reaction to Homosexuality and Adjustment in Two Societies," 21 *Journal of Sex Research* 40 (1985). The two societies compared are Sweden and Australia; the first is far more tolerant of homosexuality than the second. See also Ken Sinclair and Michael W. Ross, "Consequences of Decriminalization of Homosexuality: A Study of Two Australian States," 12 *Journal of Homosexuality* 119 (1985).

27. Peter Ebbesen, Mads Melbye, and Robert J. Biggar, "Sex Habits, Recent Disease, and Drug Use in Two Groups of Danish Male Homosexuals," 13 *Archives of Sexual Behavior* 291, 299 (1984); Michael Pollak, "Male Homosexuality—or Happiness in the Ghetto," in *Western Sexuality: Practice and Precept in Past and Present Times* 40 (Philippe Ariès and André Béjin eds. 1985). Cf. Karlen, note 5 above, at 243–247; Ramsay, Heringa, and Boorsma, note 11 above, at 137.

28. Whitam and Mathy, note 6 above, at 84–97.

29. The major theme of Whitam and Mathy's book, note 6 above. On the prevalence of cross-gender behavior and other characteristic homosexual behaviors in societies having widely different levels of tolerance for homosexuality, see id., ch. 2. For evidence that interests in such characteristic homosexual occupations as acting and hairdressing are first manifested by (future) homosexuals when they are children, see Frederick L. Whitam and Mary Jo Dizon, "Occupational Choice and Sexual Orientation in Cross-Cultural Perspective," in *Homosexuality in International Perspective* 5 (Joseph Harry and Man Singh Das eds. 1980).

30. George Domino's finding, in "Homosexuality and Creativity," 2 *Journal of Homosexuality* 261 (1977), that homosexuals are less creative than heterosexuals is deeply flawed, even if his psychometric measures of creativity are fully accepted. He matched his sample of homosexuals with a sample of heterosexuals having the same occupational distribution, thus ignoring the possibility that a larger percentage of homosexuals than of heterosexuals are in creative (artistic and so on) occupations—as appears to be the case.

that explains this. Jews used to be excluded from many of the same occupations that homosexuals are excluded from, but few Jews became hairdressers.

The causality may be as follows: pronounced cross-gender behavior in childhood predisposes a boy to homosexuality; it is generally the effeminate homosexuals who have that childhood experience; and it is generally the effeminate homosexuals who are creative, artistic, histrionic,[31] who in short give the homosexual style of life its distinctiveness. This suggests that the distinctive occupational proclivities of many homosexuals lurk far beneath the reach of social influences, and hence that homosexuals will cluster in the artistic and decorative occupations even after tolerance for homosexuality becomes general throughout society. If so, we can also expect, all other considerations to one side, the average homosexual even in a completely tolerant society to be somewhat more neurotic than the average person, for neurosis is the occupational hazard of artistic people.[32]

I emphasize the qualification "average." Not all homosexuals are effeminate; heterosexuals, especially in intolerant societies, tend to exaggerate the fraction that are. Still, for what it is worth, it has been estimated that 40 percent of homosexuals have some effeminate mannerisms.[33]

The tendency for homosexuals to seek careers in the arts may be the kernel of truth in the constant refrain that homosexuals are narcissistic. Insofar as that claim is a deduction from the proposition that for a man, having sex with another man is like having sex with oneself, it is one of the unconvincing sallies in the moral case against homosexuality examined in Chapter 8. Insofar as it is a proposition of Freudian psychology, it seems discredited.[34] But insofar as artists tend to be narcissistic (grandiose, self-absorbed) and homosexuals tend to be artists, the proposition may have some merit.

The suggested linkage between effeminacy and artistic creativity is speculative, I admit. Maybe homosexuals seek refuge against the contempt and hostility of the heterosexual world in fantasy, and an artist is a brilliant fantasist. Or maybe the homosexual's outsider status gives him or her a unique perspective. The fact that lesbians, who are the opposite of effeminate, also seem, like male homosexuals, disproportionately creative (Gertrude Stein and Virginia Woolf are famous examples) is evidence against the effeminacy thesis,

---

31. Green, note 16 above, at 256–258.

32. See Robert Prentky, "Creativity and Psychopathology: Gamboling at the Seat of Madness," in *Handbook of Creativity* 243 (John A. Glover, Royce R. Ronning, and Cecil R. Reynolds eds. 1989), for a thorough review of the literature on the correlation between psychological abnormality and artistic creativity. An illustrative study is Peter G. Cross, Raymond B. Cattell, and H. J. Butcher, "The Personality Pattern of Creative Artists," 37 *British Journal of Educational Psychology* 292 (1967).

33. Saghir and Robins, note 7 above, at 106–107.

34. Richard C. Friedman, *Male Homosexuality: A Contemporary Psychoanalytic Perspective* 183 (1988); cf. id. at 229–236.

although an alternative explanation is that, until recently, married women were unlikely to have a career, and lesbians are presumably a disproportionate fraction of all unmarried women. (But Virginia Woolf, for one, was married.)

However all this may sort out, it is not the worst fate in the world to be condemned to a career in the arts. In fact, being homosexual may increase one's chances of being eminent. The Goertzels studied a sample of eminent persons, defined as ones who had been the subject of two or more biographies published in English since 1962 (one biography if the person was a foreigner rather than an American).[35] The number in the sample was 317, of whom 82 were women.[36] The Goertzels state that of the 317, 21 (14 men and 7 women) were homosexual or bisexual.[37] As it appears from their discussion that all but 2 of the 21 (both men) were predominantly homosexual, and those two were predominantly heterosexual,[38] let us ignore those two. That leaves 12 homosexual men out of 235 men in the sample and 7 lesbians out of 82 women: 5.1 and 8.5 percent, respectively. These percentages exceed the percentages of male homosexuals and (especially) lesbians in the general population. Most of the eminent homosexuals in the Goertzels' sample, by the way, are artists of one sort or another.

The greatest inherent (by which I mean unrelated to a climate of tolerance or intolerance) disadvantage of homosexuality is the impact on family life in a culture of companionate marriage. Homosexuals are not happy being married to women in a culture in which a woman expects her husband to be her closest, most intimate friend rather than merely an occasional inseminator and a financial support. Homosexual marriage is not the answer. A pair of men is inherently less likely to form a companionate marriage-type relationship than a man and a woman. This is not a proposition about male psychology or about the supposedly narcissistic character of homosexuality. It is a proposition about the biology of sex and reproduction. A male couple could, if the law permitted (an issue discussed in the last chapter of this book), adopt children. But the children would not be the couple's biological children; they might be the biological children of one of the men, but it will be a while before technology enables a child to be produced from the genes of two men. Since the demand for one's own children exceeds that for adopted children, the average homosexual marriage would have fewer children than the average heterosexual marriage. Children are the strongest cement of marriage and the

---

35. Mildred George Goertzel, Victor Goertzel, and Ted George Goertzel, *Three Hundred Eminent Personalities: A Psychosocial Analysis of the Famous* 2 (1978). A more refined analysis might weight the results by the number of biographies of each person, to create a measure of relative eminence.

36. Id. at 162.

37. Id. at 161, 202.

38. Id. at 204.

emotional, if no longer the financial, support of old age. But there is more. The male taste for variety in sexual partners makes the prospects for sexual fidelity worse in a homosexual than in a heterosexual marriage. "It is not heterosexuality that contributes stability [to a marriage], but the presence of a female."[39] And the less stable the marriage, the fewer the children it is likely to produce—which will make the marriage still less stable.

Since there is less sexual strain in a lesbian union, the prospects for stable lesbian marriages are better. An additional consideration is that whereas men, whether heterosexual or homosexual, generally find young persons more attractive sexually than older ones, few women have a strong preference for sexual partners younger than themselves. (We considered the biological reasons for this asymmetry in Chapter 4.) A relationship between an older man and a younger woman is stable; between an older man and an older woman stable at least on the woman's side; but between two older men highly unstable, because neither man is apt to find the other sexually attractive. The older homosexual has poor sexual opportunities and generally lacks the consolation of children.

I do not want to paint with too dark a brush. Childlessness is a disappointment for many but not all, a tragedy for few. More and more people of both sexes are forgoing marriage. There are financial and other compensations for lack of family responsibilities. If old homosexuals are apt to have fewer sexual opportunities than old heterosexuals, young homosexuals are apt to have more; the promiscuity of young male homosexuals is surely not entirely an artifact of social repression. The overall picture is definitely brighter for lesbians, for in addition to the factors already mentioned, it is simple for a lesbian to become pregnant through artificial insemination, an option not open to the male homosexual. But there have been some highly durable relationships between male homosexuals, too, even though the marital status is denied them.[40] Indeed, one study finds male homosexual cohabitations to be more stable than heterosexual cohabitations though less stable than marriages.[41] But this is a misleading comparison because heterosexuals who desire a stable relationship are apt to choose marriage over cohabitation, a choice denied the homosexual. If the figures for heterosexual marriage and heterosexual cohabitation were pooled, the average length of relationship would exceed that of homosexual cohabitation (see note 41). Another study finds

39. Cory, note 3 above, at 141.
40. David P. McWhirter and Andrew M. Mattison, *The Male Couple: How Relationships Develop* (1984).
41. Philip Blumstein and Pepper Schwartz, *American Couples: Money, Work, Sex* 594 (1983) (tab. 3). Surprisingly, the male homosexual cohabitations were more durable than the lesbian ones. The average number of years together were as follows: marriage (heterosexual, of course), 13.9; heterosexual cohabitation, 2.5; male homosexual cohabitation, 6.0; lesbian cohabitation, 3.7.

that "relationship quality" among both male and female homosexual couples is higher than that of cohabiting (but unmarried) heterosexual couples and comparable to that of married couples.[42] Not much weight can be placed on this finding, either. None of the heterosexual couples had children living with them, and the average married couple in the study had been living together for only 52 months (compared to 42 months for the male homosexual couples and 43 months for the lesbian couples).[43]

I conclude that even in a tolerant society the life prospects of a homosexual—not in every case, of course, but on average—are, especially for the male homosexual, grimmer than those of an otherwise identical heterosexual, a conclusion that lends an ironic touch to the appropriation of the word *gay* to mean "homosexual"—usually male homosexual.[44] Anyone in doubt should ponder the implications of a letter dated October 3, 1990, from Admiral J. R. Tichelman, the Dutch military attaché in Washington, to Congressman Gerry Studds, responding to Studds' inquiry about Dutch policy on homosexuals in the military. The admiral's letter encloses an official statement by the Dutch Ministry of Defense that begins by stating emphatically and unequivocally: "Military personnel policy does not discriminate on the basis of sexual orientation. Homosexual orientation gives no grounds to be found unfit for service in the Netherlands armed forces . . . During the medical examination and upon entering the Service no questions will be asked relating to the sexual orientation of the conscript/applicant. In the event that the sexual orientation is brought up by the conscript, it will not be recorded." But the letter ends by stating that "although until now there are no known structural problems about the functioning of homosexuals in the armed forces it has to be considered that most of the homosexuals make a secret of their sexual orientation out of fear for reactions." This in a country that is decades ahead of the United States in tolerance of homosexuality.[45]

Granted, all that this may show is that the Netherlands has a long way to go before becoming a society (perhaps the first in the West) completely tolerant of homosexuals. But if decades of official tolerance have not eliminated social intolerance, one may wonder whether the expectation of eventual complete social tolerance may not be utopian.

If I am correct that even in a tolerant society the male homosexual's lot is

---

42. Lawrence A. Kurdek and J. Patrick Schmitt, "Relationship Quality of Partners in Heterosexual Married, Heterosexual Cohabiting, and Gay and Lesbian Relationships," 51 *Journal of Personality and Social Psychology* 711 (1986).

43. Id. at 713, 714 (tab. 1).

44. Karlen, note 5 above, at 526–532, 601–602; Karlen, note 16 above, at 231–232. This usage goes back to the 1920s, and possibly much earlier; it has never connoted gaiety. Cory, note 3 above, at 107–108.

45. For example, the Netherlands stopped discriminating against homosexuals in military service in 1973. Ramsay, Heringa, and Boorsma, note 11 above, at 127.

likely to be a less happy one on average than that of his heterosexual counterpart, still this is no reason in itself to strew legal or other social obstacles
in the path of the homosexual. On the contrary, *in itself* it is a reason to
remove those obstacles in order to alleviate gratuitous suffering. It becomes a
reason for repression only if repression can change homosexual preference,
incipient or settled, into heterosexual preference at acceptable cost and thereby
make persons who would otherwise become or remain homosexuals happier.
There is no reason to think that repression, psychotherapy, behavior modification, or any other technique of law or medicine can do so in a large enough
number of cases to warrant the costs, not least to the "unconverted" homosexual, that legal and social discrimination imposes.

Maybe we should just be patient; science, which has worked so many
wonders, may someday, perhaps someday soon, discover a "cure" for homosexuality. I suspect, however, that most persons who are already homosexual
will not want to be cured, not because they are oblivious to the advantages
of being heterosexual but because being homosexual is part of their identity.
(Was it always thus? Foucault thought it a product of the modern obsession
with sex, which he dated to the Victorian era.[46] Maybe in a society such as
that of ancient Athens in which being homosexual did not much matter,
homosexuals would not have a lively sense of themselves as being "homosexual." Then the cost of "converting" would be less—but so would be the
benefit.) Jews are conscious of the advantages of converting, changing their
name, and otherwise obliterating as far as possible the traces of their ancestry;
and many Jews might if asked say that they would have rather been born into
another group. But most of them do not convert, because (I conjecture) their
being Jewish is part of their identity, so conversion would have a taste of
death to it—like replacing one's body with another, albeit handsomer, one.
But if the hypothetical cure for homosexuality were something that could be
administered—costlessly, risklessly, without side effects—before a child had
become aware of his homosexual propensity, you can be sure that the child's
parents would administer it to him, believing, probably correctly, that he
would be better off, not yet having assumed a homosexual identity.

And speaking of "cures" for homosexuality, it is possible though paradoxical that tolerance might reduce the incidence of homosexual preference,
although probably only slightly. One of the ironies of homosexuality's taboo
status is that parents are poorly informed about the development of homosexual preference. They may warn their boy to avoid the attentions of strange
men yet completely ignore the boy's gender nonconformity in childhood and
dispatch him to an all-boys' school in adolescence without a second thought
(not that there are many such schools any more). There is a bare chance that

46. See, for example, Michel Foucault, *The History of Sexuality*, vol. 1, *An Introduction* 43,
101 (1978).

the formation of homosexual preference can be prevented by discouraging gender-nonconforming behavior *at its outset* (later is too late).[47] By condoning "sissyish" behavior in infancy, a parent may make it difficult for a little boy to become properly boyish in adolescence, and if in addition he is placed in an environment from which girls are excluded, he may find it impossible to develop a style, a personality, attractive to girls. All this is fearfully speculative, though the English experience is suggestive; but it has the paradoxical yet, I think, plausible implication that parents in a society that is tolerant of homosexuality may have more success in guiding their children along the heterosexual path than parents deprived by the homosexual taboo of accurate knowledge of where that path lies. The tolerant society may also, as previous chapters suggested, have greater success than the repressive one in reducing the spread of venereal disease by and among homosexuals.

Relations between Consenting Adults: Sodomy Laws and Homosexual Marriage

The analysis in the preceding section seems to me decisive in favor of repealing laws punishing homosexual acts between consenting adults. Not that repeal will do many homosexuals much good. The enforcement of these laws has become exceedingly rare (see Chapter 12). It is better not to have laws on the books that reflect ignorance and prejudice; but if they are not enforced, they do little harm, despite much lore to the contrary.

A well-known book by Herbert Packer on the criminal sanction lists the reasons for not punishing homosexual behavior between consenting adults:

1. Rarity of enforcement creates a problem of arbitrary police and prosecutorial discretion.

2. The extreme difficulty of detecting such conduct leads to undesirable police practices.

47. Green, note 16 above, at 318–319, 374, 380–381, 388 (1987); cf. John Money, *Gay, Straight, and In-Between: The Sexology of Erotic Orientation* 124 (1988). This is different from suggesting that an adult homosexual can be cured by psychiatric treatment or by a woman with well-developed sexual skills. For those propositions there is no persuasive evidence, Richard Green, "The Immutability of (Homo)sexual Orientation: Behavior Science Implications for a Constitutional (Legal) Analysis," 16 *Journal of Psychiatry & Law* 537, 555–568 (1988); Freund, note 15 above, at 32–33, despite the occasional claims of successful conversion of a homosexual to heterosexuality through psychiatric treatment. Judd Marmor, "Clinical Aspects of Male Homosexuality," in *Homosexual Behavior: A Modern Reappraisal* 267, 276–278 (Marmor ed. 1980). And it is different from suggesting that "we must, if we can, instill in children the feelings of revulsion [for homosexuality] that guide them to the normal path." Roger Scruton, "Sexual Morality and the Liberal Consensus," in Scruton, *The Philosopher on Dover Beach: Essays* 261, 270 (1990).

3. The existence of the proscription tends to create a deviant subculture.

4. Widespread knowledge that the law is violated with impunity by thousands every day creates disrespect for law generally.

5. No secular harm can be shown to result from such conduct.

6. The theoretical availability of criminal sanctions creates a situation in which extortion and, on occasion, police corruption may take place.

7. There is substantial evidence that the moral sense of the community no longer exerts strong pressure for the use of criminal sanctions.

8. No utilitarian goal of criminal punishment is substantially advanced by proscribing private adult consensual sexual conduct.[48]

The list is less impressive than it looks. Points 1, 2, and 6 are the same. A rarely enforced law creates opportunities for law enforcement abuses, including extortion and the invidious exercise of police and prosecutorial discretion. These used to be serious problems in the administration of the sodomy laws,[49] but that was when the laws were being enforced. The level of enforcement has fallen so low that police abuses have become rare, although the facts of *Bowers v. Hardwick*, discussed in the next chapter, may illustrate such abuse. Point 3 seems wrong, for reasons explained earlier; the distinctive homosexual subculture is not an artifact of law, let alone of unenforced law. Points 5 and 8 are again one point, not two: the sodomy laws, unenforced as they are, are not preventing any conduct that we have a good reason to prevent. They almost certainly do not deter much homosexual behavior. Whether they make a "statement" about social attitudes toward homosexuality that might influence people depends in the first place on whether one thinks the presence of laws on the books is more important than the fact that they are not enforced—whether, that is, words speak louder than actions. Even if they do in some cases, it is exceedingly unlikely that they do in this case: that they influence either the formation or retention of homosexual preference, or the amount of homosexual behavior.

Point 7 is of course true; it is no doubt one reason (along with cost, civil liberties concerns, and competing demands on law enforcers) why these laws are not being enforced. But nonenforcement may be an adequate, if parsimonious, response to the moral sense of the community. Point 4 (knowledge that the law is violated creates disrespect for law generally) is the kind of

48. Herbert L. Packer, *The Limits of the Criminal Sanction* 304 (1968). See also American Law Institute, *Model Penal Code and Commentaries (Official Draft and Revised Comments)*, pt. 2, 365–373 (1980).

49. Project, "The Consenting Adult Homosexual and the Law: An Empirical Study of Enforcement and Administration in Los Angeles County," 13 *UCLA Law Review* 643, 690–720, 763–792 (1966).

point that lawyers love to make but that lacks either theoretical or empirical support, as we shall see in the next chapter. It is true that many people in our society disobey many laws; and this is another way of saying that there is widespread disrespect for law in this society, at least if "respect" is more than notional. But whether, as Packer implies, this disrespect feeds on itself is unknown.

A reason he does not mention for repealing the sodomy laws is to give homosexuals more entrée to professions from which they are now largely excluded. There is, for example, a natural reluctance, given the strong (possibly much exaggerated) belief in the effect of "role models" on behavior, to appoint to judicial positions people who have committed hundreds or even thousands of criminal acts simply because they are homosexuals living in states in which sodomy is a crime. The criminal status of homosexuals' characteristic manner of sexual expression provides at least a talking point for all sorts of other exclusions as well. This is not to say that none of these exclusions is justified; that is a question still to be addressed. But repealing the sodomy laws would clear away one bad reason for the exclusions and enable valid concerns to be addressed more cleanly.

If the sodomy laws ought to be repealed, the logical next question is whether homosexual marriage ought to be permitted. The connection between the two questions lies in the fact that both involve homosexual relations between consenting adults. This makes them different from whether homosexuals should be excluded from military or other occupations and whether laws forbidding discrimination should protect homosexuals. The latter are questions about relations between homosexuals and others, primarily employers.

The libertarian places the burden of proof on those who would limit the right to marry, and adds that there are arguments as well as dogma in favor of including homosexuals within this permission. The existence of a right to marry would raise homosexuals' self-esteem. It would contribute, although perhaps only marginally, to the stability of homosexual relationships, and by doing so would not only make homosexuals happier but also reduce the spread of venereal disease in general and of the justly dreaded AIDS in particular. These are the benefits of permitting homosexual marriage; and the costs seem slight, if I am correct that the removal of the legal disabilities of homosexuality is unlikely to increase the amount of homosexual preference. Homosexual acts, as distinct from preference, would actually be reduced if homosexual marriage reduced homosexual promiscuity.

But there are three differences between punishing sodomy and confining the right to marry to heterosexuals. The first is that permitting homosexual marriage would be widely interpreted as placing a stamp of approval on homosexuality, while decriminalizing sodomy would not, at least not to anywhere near the same extent. To say that an act is not a crime is not to commend it; a great deal of behavior that is disgusting or immoral or both is nevertheless not criminal. But marriage, even though considered sacramental only by Catholics, is believed by most people in our society to be not merely a license to reproduce but also a desirable, even a noble, condition in which to live. To permit persons of the same sex to marry is to declare, or more precisely to be understood by many people to be declaring, that homosexual marriage is a desirable, even a noble, condition in which to live. This is not what most people in this society believe; and for reasons stated earlier it would be misleading to suggest that homosexual marriages are likely to be as stable or rewarding as heterosexual marriages, even granting as one must that a sizable fraction of heterosexual marriages in our society are not stable and are not rewarding. I do not suggest that government's pronouncing homosexual marriage a beatific state would cause heterosexuals to rethink their sexual preference. My concern lies elsewhere. It is that permitting homosexual marriage would place government in the dishonest position of propagating a false picture of the reality of homosexuals' lives.

Against this it can be argued that as heterosexual marriage becomes ever more unstable, temporary, and childless, the suggestion that it differs fundamentally from what homosexual marriages could be expected to be like becomes ever more implausible. And this is true. But it is a point in favor not of homosexual marriage but of chucking the whole institution of marriage in favor of an explicitly contractual approach that would make the current realities of marriage transparent.

The second difference between the sodomy and marriage issues will strike many readers as a trivial addendum to the first. It is that the more broadly *marriage* is defined, the less information it and related terms convey. When we read that Mr. X is married or that Ms. Y is married, we know immediately that X's spouse is a woman and Y's a man. If we invite people to a party and ask them to bring their spouses, we know that each man will either come alone or bring a woman and that each woman will either come alone or bring a man. So a homosexual man will come alone and likewise a homosexual woman. If we do not care to limit the additional guests to spouses, we ask the invitees to bring not their spouses but their "guests." If our son or daughter tells us that he or she is getting married, we know the sex of the prospective spouse. All these understandings would be upset by permitting homosexual marriage. This of course is one reason homosexual rights advocates want homosexual marriage to be permitted. All I wish to emphasize is that there is an information cost to the proposal.

But there is also an information benefit. The denial of marriage to homosexuals prevents a homosexual couple from signaling the extent of their commitment. If marriage were abolished, heterosexual cohabitation would denote indifferently the briefest and the most permanent of relationships. If the "freedom to marry" of which the Supreme Court spoke in *Loving v.*

Virginia[50] were taken seriously, the deprivation to the homosexual couple denied the right to marry would carry a heavy weight; but of course the Court was thinking of heterosexual marriage.

The third difference between the sodomy and marriage issues is the most important. Abolishing the sodomy laws would have few collateral effects, though I have suggested that it would have one: it would make it easier for homosexuals to obtain jobs in fields at present closed to them. Authorizing homosexual marriage would have many collateral effects, simply because marriage is a status rich in entitlements. It would have effects on inheritance, social security, income tax, welfare payments, adoption, the division of property upon termination of the relationship, medical benefits, life insurance, immigration, and even testimonial privilege. (The *Commercial-News* of Danville, Ohio, carried an article under the intriguing banner, "Homosexual Loses Court Battle over Use of Mate's Testimony." The mate in question was another man.) These incidents of marriage were designed with heterosexual marriage in mind, more specifically heterosexual marriages resulting in children. They may or may not fit the case of homosexual marriage; they are unlikely to fit it perfectly. Do we want homosexual couples to have the same rights of adoption and custody as heterosexual couples? Should we worry that a homosexual might marry a succession of dying AIDS patients in order to entitle them to spouse's medical benefits? These questions ought to be faced one by one rather than elided by conferring all the rights of marriage in a lump on homosexuals willing to undergo a wedding ceremony.

None of these points is decisive against permitting homosexual marriage. All together may not be. The benefits of such marriage may outweigh the costs. Nonetheless, since the public hostility to homosexuals in this country is too widespread to make homosexual marriage a feasible proposal even if it is on balance cost-justified, maybe the focus should be shifted to an intermediate solution that would give homosexuals most of what they want but at the same time meet the three objections I have advanced.

Denmark and Sweden, not surprisingly, provide the model. What in Denmark is called registered partnership and in Sweden homosexual cohabitation is in effect a form contract that homosexuals can use to create a simulacrum of marriage. The Danish law goes further than the Swedish: it places the registered partners under all the provisions of the marriage code except those relating to children, although a question has arisen whether the registered partner has the same beneficial rights in his (or her) partner's private pension

---

50. 388 U.S. 1, 12 (1967). The decision invalidated a state law forbidding miscegenation. In subsequent decisions the Supreme Court has continued to describe the right to marry as a "fundamental right." See, for example, Zablocki v. Redhail, 434 U.S. 374, 383–386 (1978); Turner v. Safley, 482 U.S. 78, 94–99 (1987).

that a spouse would have.[51] Sweden, which already has defined a quasi-marital status for cohabiting heterosexuals, allows cohabiting homosexuals to elect that status, the main feature of which is an even division, upon the dissolution of the relationship, of what in this country would be called community property.[52] The Danish approach is mechanical in assuming that the presence of children is the only thing that distinguishes heterosexual from homosexual marriage. The Swedish approach assumes, realistically I think, that a homosexual relationship, even when meant to last, is more like heterosexual cohabitation than like heterosexual marriage, so the forms that the Swedes have worked out to regularize what is after all an extremely common relationship in their country provide the appropriate model for homosexuals who want to live together in ours. It may indeed offer an increasingly attractive model for heterosexuals as well.

Discrimination against Homosexuals, with Particular Reference to Military Service

The question whether homosexuals should be permitted to serve in the armed forces is part of the larger question whether discrimination on the basis of sexual preference should be forbidden. The reason for taking the more specific question first is that the arguments for excluding homosexuals from the armed forces are stronger than the arguments for excluding them from most other jobs. Thus, if the former arguments fail, the ground is laid for a comprehensive principle of nondiscrimination.

The principal arguments that are made against homosexuals in the military are fourfold.[53] I list them in ascending order of persuasiveness. First, homo-

51. Michael Elmer and Marianne Lund Larsen, "Explanatory Article on the Legal Consequences Etc., of the Danish Law on Registered Partnership." This article, the English translation of an article that appeared in the Danish law journal *Juristen* in 1990, is available from Landsforeningen for Bøsser og Lesbiske (National [Danish] Organization for Gays and Lesbians) in Copenhagen. Incidentally, in the first nine months in which the law on registered partnerships was in effect, 553 couples were registered, of which 119 were lesbian couples. Letter from Dorthe Jacobsen to John A. Shope, November 14, 1990. This is further evidence that lesbianism is indeed less common than male homosexuality.

52. Ake Saldeen, "Sweden: More Rights for Children and Homosexuals," 27 *Journal of Family Law* 295, 296–297 (1988–89); Mary Ann Glendon, *The Transformation of Family Law: State, Law, and Family in the United States and Western Europe* 276 (1989).

53. The discussion that follows relies in part on a series of consultants' reports, commissioned but when received rejected by the Department of Defense, on the issue of allowing homosexuals to serve in the U.S. military. Theodore R. Sarbin and Kenneth E. Karols, "Nonconforming Sexual Orientations and Military Suitability" (Defense Personnel Security Research and Education Center, Report no. PERS-TR-89-002, December 1988); Michael A. McDaniel, "The Suitability of Homosexuals for Positions of Trust" (Defense Personnel Security Research and Education Center,

sexuals are likely to be blackmailed into giving up military secrets. This is a weak argument. Not only is it inapplicable to persons who acknowledge their homosexuality—and those who conceal it can in fact rise to the highest levels of command in the armed forces, as in government generally—but only a tiny fraction of military personnel have access to military secrets.

The second argument is that homosexuals are on average less stable than heterosexuals. This point may be correct, but its relevance is unclear, and this on several counts. First, the artistic, often effeminate homosexual who is most likely to have a problem of psychological adjustment is least likely to find the military an attractive career—a decisive consideration when, as now, all our service personnel are volunteers rather than conscripts. Second, if male homosexuals are on average less suited psychologically to a military career than male heterosexuals, lesbians are more suited to such a career than heterosexual women.[54] Corresponding to the effeminacy of a male heterosexual, as a trait that distinguishes the average homosexual from the average heterosexual, is the mannishness of a female homosexual, which makes her better soldier material than her feminine sister and which may explain why lesbians are a larger fraction of female soldiers than male homosexuals are of male soldiers.[55] Third and most important, the military does not hire on a first-come, first-served basis. It screens its applicants to determine their fitness for military service. Unless the screen somehow fails to identify the maladjusted homosexual, there is no reason to have a cruder filter that excludes all homosexuals.

Report no. PERS-TR-87-006, September 1987); McDaniel, "Preservice Adjustment of Homosexual and Heterosexual Military Accessions: Implications for Security Clearance Suitability" (Defense Personnel Security Research and Education Center, Report no. PERS-TR-89-004, January 1989). See also the Crittendon report, "Report of the Board Appointed to Prepare and Submit Recommendations to the Secretary of the Navy for the Revision of Policies, Procedures and Directives Dealing with Homosexuals" (December 21, 1956–March 15, 1957). The official position of the Department of Defense on homosexuals in the military is at 32 C.F.R. pt. 41, App. A, ¶H (1989). It is a brief laundry list of concerns, upon which department officials decline to elaborate. These concerns are spelled out at somewhat greater length in a study by the Canadian armed forces that, partly in reliance on the position of the American military, recommends continuing the ban against permitting homosexuals to serve. Charter Task Force, *Final Report* (September 1986). Nevertheless, as we shall see, the Canadian government has since relaxed the ban.

Similar arguments are sometimes made to deny homosexuals the right to work as police officers. Childers v. Dallas Police Dept., 513 F. Supp. 134, 146–147 (N.D. Tex. 1981). This opinion by the way contains the worst argument I have seen for excluding homosexuals from public employment: "It is likely that Plaintiff would have been subject to harassment by his fellow workers." Id. at 142.

54. One newspaper headline tells it all: Jane Gross, "Navy Is Urged to Root Out Lesbians Despite Abilities," *New York Times,* September 2, 1990, 9. And see note 58 below.

55. Joseph Harry, "Homosexual Men and Women Who Served Their Country," in *Bashers, Baiters & Bigots* 117 (John P. De Cecco ed. 1985).

The Crittendon Report (note 53) contains the flat statement, apparently by the chief of naval personnel, that there is no correlation between homosexuality and either ability or attainments.

The third argument against allowing homosexuals to serve in the armed forces is that homosexual superior officers may coerce their subordinates for sexual favors; this is the ground on which the admiral commanding the Atlantic Fleet has urged the rooting out of lesbians.[56] The broader point is that sexual intrigue can reduce operational effectiveness.[57] But this bridge was crossed when the armed forces admitted women over the same objection. Whenever there is sexual interest between a superior and a subordinate employee, there is a potential for sexual harassment. That potential is rarely thought an impressive ground for sexual segregation, and it seems no more impressive as a ground for excluding homosexuals. This is not to deny that there are lesbian cliques in the navy and in the other services, lesbians preying on nonlesbian subordinates, and all the rest. Sexual harassment is a reality. It just is not ordinarily thought a sufficiently serious problem to warrant the blanket exclusion of a whole class of workers, especially when, as in the case of the navy's lesbians, they appear to be of above-average ability.[58] Likewise the fact that sexual interest between co-workers can distract them from their tasks: Marcuse's point about the subversive potential of Eros, writ small.

The fourth argument for excluding homosexuals seems the worst but is the best. It is that the morale of heterosexuals, and hence the effectiveness of the military services, would suffer if homosexuals were allowed to serve. It seems the worst argument because it has the identical form as the argument for racial segregation of the armed forces, which was not ended until 1948. Because whites do not want to serve with blacks, blacks should be confined to all-black units; because heterosexuals do not want to serve with homosexuals, homosexuals should be kept out of the armed forces altogether. One might think that before giving the slightest credence to the argument, we should investigate the basis of the heterosexuals' hostility. Does it rest on

56. Gross, note 54 above. Fear of sexual intrigue is a traditional reason against permitting homosexuals to work in any bureaucratic, hierarchical organization. Greenberg, note 18 above, at 438; Ralph Slovenko, "Homosexuality and the Law: From Condemnation to Celebration," in *Homosexual Behavior,* note 47 above, at 194, 208.

57. On this point Christie Davis, "The Social Origins of Some Sexual Taboos," in *Love and Attraction: An International Conference* 381, 384–386 (Mark Cook and Glenn Wilson eds. 1979), builds an argument that the more powerful the military of a country is, the more likely the government is to try to repress homosexuality throughout the society.

58. The commander of the Atlantic Fleet noted that investigations of suspected lesbianism are often pursued halfheartedly because "experience has also shown that the stereotypical female homosexual in the navy is hard-working, career-oriented, willing to put in long hours on the job and among the command's top professionals." I have quoted from the text of the admiral's communiqué released by the Department of Defense. The *Times* (note 54 above) misquoted it slightly, for example by substituting "performers" for "professionals."

ignorance and prejudice? Do they think that homosexuals cannot or will not fight, or that they will rape or seduce heterosexuals, or that homosexual preference is contagious? There is no reason to believe that homosexuals who want to join the armed forces and who pass all the physical, mental, and psychological tests that the armed forces administer to recruits are militarily less effective than heterosexuals, or cause trouble, or otherwise degrade military performance. Many homosexuals are known to have served in the American military in the Second World War, the Korean War, and the Vietnam War, and studies of their military records show that they did as well on average as the heterosexuals. It may seem that they must have been rather a select group, inasmuch as they were able to conceal their homosexuality. But in fact homosexuals are not required to conceal their homosexuality in order to join or remain in the armed forces; mostly they need only not flaunt it.

Although complete data are not available, it appears on the basis of a study conducted by Congressman Gerry Studds that outside Great Britain and the nations that once were colonies of Great Britain (including the United States, India, Australia, New Zealand, and Canada), a majority of nations do not attempt to exclude homosexuals from their armed forces, including several nations whose armed forces are highly regarded, such as France, Germany, Switzerland, and Sweden.[59] During the Second World War the German army was considered, not despite but because of Nazi persecution of homosexuals, a refuge for them, because the military command was too busy to worry about trying to root out homosexuals; evidently they were not considered a threat to effective military performance. The idea that homosexuals will not or cannot fight seems a canard, on a par with the idea that Jews or blacks will not or cannot fight. And even if the presence of homosexuals did degrade military performance, one would have to ask how much it degraded it before deciding that the costs of allowing homosexuals to serve in the armed forces

59. Other nations that do not exclude homosexuals from their armed forces are Denmark, Norway, Finland, the Netherlands, Belgium, and Spain. I have no information about any other nation except Greece, which excludes them. Some of the nonexcluding nations place restrictions on homosexuals that seem to have no direct parallel with respect to heterosexuals; for example, the Swiss armed forces forbid homosexuals to form "cliques." Canada seems to be moving away from its policy of exclusion. Under an interim policy that it has adopted while studying the matter further, it does not discharge members of the armed forces who are found to be engaging in homosexual activities but imposes certain career restrictions on them. I assume it would not permit a known homosexual to enlist.

The Sacred Band of Thebes—the elite of the Boeotian army, which was one of ancient Greece's best—is not, however, an apt precedent for liberalizing our armed forces' policy on homosexuals, all changes in warfare and society in the last two and a half millennia to one side. The Sacred Band consisted of men and their boy lovers. Christie Davies, "Sexual Taboos and Social Boundaries," 87 *American Journal of Sociology* 1032, 1055–56 (1982). If my analysis of Greek homosexuality is correct, most of these men (and boys) were heterosexual as we use these terms today.

outweighed the benefits. Among the benefits to the military would be saving the cost of administering a policy of excluding homosexuals, expanding the supply of soldiers, reducing the incentives to fake homosexuality when a draft is in force, and bolstering the self-esteem of homosexuals by deeming them fit to serve their country in positions of responsibility and danger.

So why do I say that the argument about the impact on heterosexuals' morale of allowing homosexuals to serve is a good argument for exclusion rather than a despicable argument that should be dismissed out of hand? Because the question of morale is separable from the question of the merits of the exclusion. Suppose American soldiers harbored the irrational but unshakable belief that to attack on Friday the thirteenth would bring disaster. This belief would be a fact that their commander would be obliged to take into account in scheduling attacks. If it was very important to attack on Friday the thirteenth, he might try to educate the soldiers out of their superstition; but if it was not very important or if the superstition was extremely tenacious, he might think it best to yield. It is the same with the homosexual question. By 1981 the percentage of Dutch people who thought homosexuality was dirty, deviant, or abnormal had fallen below 10 percent.[60] It is no surprise that the Dutch do not exclude homosexuals from their armed forces. The corresponding figure for Americans, based on the statistics in Chapter 2, would probably be 70 percent. In one survey 62 percent of the heterosexual veterans in the sample said that homosexuals should not be permitted to serve in our armed forces, and only 12 percent that they should (the rest were uncertain).[61] A principal reason was that heterosexuals were upset at the prospect of being seen in the nude by a homosexual. However silly a reason this may seem, one cannot simply *assume* that declaring homosexuals fit for service in our armed forces would create no morale problems. Remember that the armed forces were integrated only after the blacks had proved themselves

60. Tielman, note 10 above, at 14.

61. Paul Cameron, Kirk Cameron, and Kay Proctor, "Homosexuals in the Armed Forces," 62 *Psychological Reports* 211, 217 (1988) (tab. 4) (the corresponding figures for nonveterans were 41 and 25 percent). The representativeness of the sample has been challenged. David F. Duncan, "Homosexuals in the Armed Forces: A Comment on Generalizability," 62 *Psychological Reports* 489 (1988); Myron Boor, "Homosexuals in the Armed Forces: A Reply to Cameron, Cameron, and Proctor," 62 *Psychological Reports* 488 (1988). And some of the questions asked in the survey were loaded, for example: "If you were nude or your genitals were exposed in a public place (such as a restroom, bathhouse, or shower), what would be your reaction if you noticed someone of your sex watching you and deriving obvious sexual pleasure from your nudity (i.e., they were getting 'turned on' by your body)?" Cameron, Cameron, and Proctor at 212. But as Duncan realistically remarks, "I would not be surprised if the views of the US public were much like those reported by Cameron, Cameron, and Proctor." Duncan at 489. The Canadian study based its recommendation against allowing homosexuals to serve in the Canadian armed forces entirely on considerations of morale, such as the uneasiness of heterosexuals at the thought of being commanded by homosexual officers. Charter Task Force, note 53 above, vol. 1, pt. 4, at 8.

in all-black units during the Second World War, and that women still remain segregated to some extent from men in our armed forces. And there is the larger public to be considered: would it become hysterical at the prospect that some of the soldiers manning our nuclear missile silos might be homosexual?[62]

It is true that not all of the nations that allow homosexuals to serve in their armed forces are as tolerant as the Netherlands, Denmark, and Sweden. Switzerland has a conservative sex ethic, similar to that of the United States. Finland is distinctly less tolerant of homosexuals than Sweden.[63] Spain is sexually conservative in many ways, though contemptuous tolerance of homosexuality is, as we know, a characteristic of Mediterranean cultures. None of these armed forces is anywhere as powerful as ours, however, and maybe that makes a difference (the finger-on-the-nuclear-trigger point). On the whole, it is the more tolerant nations that permit homosexuals to serve and the less tolerant that do not. The United States is among the least tolerant.

Another strut beneath the policy of our armed forces is the anxiety, itself a result in part of the hostility to homosexuality in our society, that many heterosexual men feel concerning their heterosexuality. There is a lurking fear that at bottom one may be one of *them*. The fear is exacerbated in a homosocial setting such as traditionally characterized the military (and still does in combat units, from which women remain excluded). In these settings men develop strong emotional, though generally not erotic, bonds. It is important to them that the line not be crossed. An official policy against retaining any "line crossers" helps to reassure that the line will be maintained.

But there is more to the story. In a 1989 Gallup Poll 60 percent of the respondents opined that homosexuals should be allowed to serve in the military.[64] Police forces are quasi-military, yet the New York City, San Francisco, and Los Angeles police have opened their ranks to overt homosexuals without incident. And the experience with coed dorms and bathrooms in colleges is that sexual desegregation is not eroticizing but often the opposite.

The most important reason for doubting that dropping the ban on homosexuals in the military would cause serious morale problems is simply that a large number of homosexuals already serve without significant difficulties.[65]

62. William P. Snyder and Kenneth L. Nyberg, "Gays and the Military: An Emerging Policy Issue," 8 *Journal of Political and Military Sociology* 71, 81 (1980). Some probably are homosexual, but unofficially, as it were.

63. Thomas Fitzgerald, "Gay Self-Help Groups in Sweden and Finland," 10 *International Review of Modern Sociology* 15 (1980).

64. Michael R. Kagay, "Homosexuals Gain More Acceptance," *New York Times,* October 25, 1989, A24, discussing Gallup Report no. 289, October 1989, 14. Only 47 percent of the respondents thought that homosexuals should be allowed to teach in high school. Gallup Report at 15.

65. Indeed, one study found that the same percentage of male homosexuals as of male heterosexuals served in our armed forces during the Second World War. Harry, note 55 above.

Some of these men and women conceal their homosexuality from their heterosexual comrades and superiors, but many do not. Yet for the most part they are accepted, generally without fuss, unless they get arrested or otherwise misbehave in ways that would land heterosexuals in trouble for corresponding forms of sexual misconduct. It is as if, before 1948, a large number of black soldiers had served in integrated units under the fiction that they really were white men.

So there are good arguments for dropping the ban against homosexuals in the armed forces, but there are also bad arguments, such as the argument that there would be a significant educative effect, which would in time erode heterosexual soldiers' hostility toward homosexuals and indeed public hostility generally. True, the homosexuals would not do as badly as the heterosexuals expected, and might indeed do just as well as the heterosexuals. And there is evidence that working with homosexuals promotes tolerance,[66] though the evidence is difficult to interpret because the causality could run in the opposite direction: the tolerant are more apt to work with them. But what weakens the point is precisely that homosexuals *already* serve in the armed forces in considerable number. The incremental educative effect of formally acknowledging their existence might be slight. And even if it would be large, this would merely pose, not answer, the question whether the armed forces should be required to serve as an agency for public enlightenment at some unknown cost in military effectiveness. Notwithstanding its excellent performance in the Persian Gulf war, the American military has a long history of problems in achieving military effectiveness, and such problems can of course be immensely costly in lives and money. If we give the military social assignments, we also give it an excuse for failing to achieve combat effectiveness, and perhaps we risk giving it a taste for meddling in nonmilitary affairs generally.

That excellent performance, by the way, is a two-edged sword in the debate over whether to continue the prohibition against homosexuals in the armed forces. On the one hand, it allayed many of the concerns about the effectiveness of our armed forces and also demonstrated their ability without loss of effectiveness to integrate large numbers of blacks and other racial and ethnic minorities and women—so why could they not do the same with homosexuals,

---

Apparently any tendency to exclude homosexuals was offset by the reduced eligibility of homosexuals for marital and parental exemptions. In an all-volunteer force we would expect the number of male homosexuals to be lower, and the number of lesbians higher, than in a conscripted force with marital or parental exemptions.

66. Ramsay, Heringa, and Boorsma, note 11 above, at 131. Cf. William Paul, "Social Issues and Homosexual Behavior: A Taxonomy of Categories and Themes in Anti-Gay Argument," in *Homosexuality: Social, Psychological, and Biological Issues* 29, 47 (William Paul et al. eds. 1982).

and with equal success? (And no doubt there were a number of homosexuals in our Persian Gulf expeditionary force, performing unexceptionably.) On the other hand, the better the performance of the armed forces, the stronger the argument for civilian deference to military judgments, one of which is that homosexuals should be barred from military service.

Even though homosexuals *can* serve in the American military, despite the formal bar against them, provided they are discreet, the removal of the bar would do much for their self-esteem—for it is terrible to tell people they are unfit to serve their country, unless they really are unfit, which is not the case here—and would be a step forward in social justice. At what cost? This is impossible to estimate with any confidence, because of the counterfactual character of the analysis. We need an experiment, and this leads me to propose that we adopt Canada's approach and, without relaxing the bar against recruitment of homosexuals to serve in our armed forces, permit them once in to remain (with or without career restrictions), provided of course that they do not engage in the sorts of misconduct that would get them kicked out if they were heterosexuals. Such a difference in treatment between new applicants and existing employees would be analogous to amnesties for illegal immigrants and to the greater scope allowed for random drug testing of job applicants than of the already employed.[67] Experience would show whether military morale or other factors affecting military effectiveness suffered from the acknowledged presence of known homosexuals, and would therefore provide guidance for a definitive resolution of the debate over whether to allow homosexuals to serve.

However we ought to proceed, we should at least drop the weak arguments for excluding homosexuals from the military, for those arguments are used to bar them with even less justification from other jobs. A combination of the blackmail and instability concerns supplies the traditional rationale for excluding homosexuals from positions, whether in the government or in the private sector, requiring a security clearance.[68] The rationale is weak, not only in theory but also in evidence. For when one searches the literature on espionage, sabotage, and other forms of treason, one finds—despite lurid claims,[69]

67. Compare Harmon v. Thornburgh, 878 F.2d 484 (D.C. Cir. 1989), with Willner v. Thornburgh, 928 F.2d 1185 (D.C. Cir. 1991).

68. Gregory M. Herek, "Gay People and Government Security Clearances: A Social Science Perspective," 45 *American Psychologist* 1035 (1990); Note, "Security Clearances for Homosexuals," 25 *Stanford Law Review* 403 (1973).

69. "The usual reason given for the danger of homosexuals in government work is that their perversion makes them vulnerable to blackmail . . . Dr. Schilt, however, sees this risk as far less important than the homosexual's own nature. Citing Mitchell [a National Security Agency employee who had defected to the Soviet Union] as an example, Dr. Schilt points to the pattern of absence of guilt feelings and the sense of belonging to a higher order of mankind above authority and morality." Sanche de Gramont, *The Secret War: The Story of International Espi-*

redolent of the time when homosexuality and treason were thought two sides of the same coin—little evidence that homosexuality is particularly widespread among traitors.[70] It is difficult to make a persuasive argument that a known (hence blackmail-proof) homosexual who satisfies all intellectual, psychological, and other criteria for a security clearance should be denied one.

Whether homosexuals should be allowed to serve in jobs involving close contact with minors, such as school teaching and athletic coaching, is deferred to Chapter 14 on coercive sex and seduction. The main argument against is that even if the homosexual is perfectly well behaved, he is an inappropriate role model for heterosexual youths who may be uncertain about their own sexual identity; his example may tip them to the homosexual side of the ledger.[71] Whether there are many adolescents sitting on this particular razor's edge may be doubted, for reasons I have stated earlier, but is in any event a consideration in the debate over allowing homosexuals to adopt or otherwise obtain custody of children, discussed in the last chapter of this book. Until all these issues are sorted out, a blanket prohibition against job discrimination against homosexuals may be premature.

That brings me to the last issue in this chapter: whether the laws against racial and sexual and related forms of discrimination perceived as invidious, laws such as Title VII of the Civil Rights Act of 1964,[72] should be extended to cover homosexuals. Such an extension is not necessarily inconsistent with a belief that homosexuals may be unsuitable for some jobs; exceptions can be made. Indeed, with respect to all but racial discrimination, Title VII already contains a blanket exception for situations in which a particular sex, ethnicity, religion, and so on (anything but race or color) is a bona fide qualification for the job in question; heterosexual preference might be a bona fide qualification for some jobs.

---

onage since World War II 395 (1962). Senator Joseph McCarthy was an assiduous ferreter out of homosexuals in government service. John D'Emilio, Sexual Politics, Sexual Communities: The Making of a Homosexual Minority in the United States 1940–1970 41–49 (1983).

70. So concludes Chapman Pincher, Traitors: The Anatomy of Treason 103 (1987). Despite this conclusion he speculates that resentment at being branded as deviants and criminals may in fact have predisposed some of the famous British homosexual traitors, such as Anthony Blunt and Guy Burgess, to commit treason. Yet apparently there is reason to believe that it is traditional to employ homosexuals in diplomatic and secret services. Tripp, note 9 above, at 216–221. (A book not at all concerned with this question nevertheless compares "passing" as heterosexual to "play[ing] the double agent." Brian Pronger, The Arena of Homosexuality: Sports, Homosexuality, and the Meaning of Sex 113 [1990].) In that event we would expect a disproportionate number of traitors to be homosexual, not because homosexuals are more traitorous by inclination than heterosexuals but because they are preferred by the secret services.

71. For argument contra, see Dorothy I. Riddle, "Relating to Children: Gays as Role Models," 34 Journal of Social Issues 38 (1978).

72. 42 U.S.C. §2000.

There are two ways to approach the question whether to extend the discrimination laws to cover discrimination against homosexuals. The first is to ask, given Title VII and cognate laws, is there any reason to exclude homosexuals from a protected category that already includes not only racial, religious, and ethnic groups but also women, the physically and mentally handicapped, all workers aged 40 and older, and, in some cases, even young healthy male WASPs?[73] Is there less, or less harmful, or less irrational discrimination against homosexuals than against the members of *any* of these other groups? The answer is no.[74] But the second way to approach this question is to ask whether it is a good idea to have a law forbidding private discrimination in employment. I own to skepticism on this score.[75] To explain the grounds for my skepticism would carry me beyond the proper scope of a book on sexuality, so let me just say that the question whether to provide legal protection to homosexuals against discrimination in employment and other areas of life is part of a much larger question having little to do with anything special to sexual preference. But note that affirmative action policies, which antidiscrimination laws encourage (when they are not interpreted to forbid them!), put the squeeze on white male homosexuals by reducing the job opportunities of white males without giving homosexuals any protection against being made to bear the brunt of the reduction.

73. Since a white can complain about discrimination in favor of a black, provided the discrimination is not pursuant to a bona fide affirmative action plan. McDonald v. Santa Fe Trail Transportation Co., 427 U.S. 273 (1976); Rucker v. Higher Educational Aids Board, 669 F.2d 1179 (7th Cir. 1982).

74. Martin P. Levine, "Employment Discrimination against Gay Men," in *Homosexuality in International Perspective,* note 29 above, at 18.

75. See my article "The Efficiency and the Efficacy of Title VII," 136 *University of Pennsylvania Law Review* 513 (1987).

The Sexual Revolution in the Courts

IN A SERIES of decisions between 1965 and 1977, the Supreme Court created a constitutional right of sexual or reproductive autonomy, which it called privacy. The pattern made by these decisions resembles the model of morally indifferent sex discussed in this book. Later the Court cut back, to the point where, at this writing, the future of the right to privacy is in considerable doubt. In addition to the privacy cases, the Court in its period of sexual libertarianism struck down additional restrictions on sexual freedom under a variety of other constitutional rubrics, such as freedom of speech.

The rise and decline of sexual libertarianism in the Supreme Court has evoked a staggering outpouring of commentary in law reviews and books, commentary concerned primarily with the soundness of the Court's decisions as a matter of constitutional doctrine. I have only a peripheral interest in that question, a question that depends not only on facts and beliefs about sexuality but also on views concerning interpretation, the force of precedent, and the nature of a federal system. My primary interest is in the understanding of sexual issues that is displayed by the Supreme Court and other courts, and in the motives or forces that impelled the Court first to become a standard-bearer in the sexual revolution and then to falter in that role.[1]

From *Griswold v. Connecticut* to *Roe v. Wade*

The first case of note is *Griswold v. Connecticut,* decided in 1965. Connecticut law made it a crime for any person to use "any drug, medicinal article or

---

1. For a helpful introduction to the cases, see Bruce C. Hafen, "The Constitutional Status of Marriage, Kinship, and Sexual Privacy—Balancing the Individual and Social Interests," 81 *Michigan Law Review* 463 (1983).

instrument for the purpose of preventing conception."[2] The law contained no exception for married persons. The two defendants—the executive director of the Planned Parenthood League of Connecticut and the medical director of a birth control clinic that the league had just opened in New Haven in order to test the law's constitutionality—were convicted and fined $100 each for offering advice on contraception to married persons and also for prescribing contraceptive devices for the wives. The Supreme Court held that the law was unconstitutional as applied to married persons. The different opinions (six in all) of the justices debate at length the question whether there is any provision of the Constitution that might entitle married couples to use contraceptives. The much-criticized majority opinion by Justice William O. Douglas is candid in acknowledging the absence of such a provision. But noting that a number of the provisions do protect privacy in one form or another—the Third Amendment, for example, which restricts the quartering of troops in people's houses in peacetime, and the Fourth Amendment, which protects people in their persons, papers, effects, and houses against unreasonable searches and seizures—Douglas finds a "right of marital privacy"[3] to be implicit in the document as a whole.

The opinion is curiously reticent about the purposes of marriage and why a ban on the use of contraceptives might be thought to interfere with those purposes. The analysis in this book should help us see that a statute that limits contraceptive intercourse within marriage may undermine companionate marriage by imposing in effect a tax on marital sex; and today, even more than at the time of the Bill of Rights, companionate marriage is the dominant form of marriage in this country—is virtually what we *mean* by marriage. So the statute plausibly was antimarriage. Douglas hinted at this when, partly to tie the Fourth Amendment more closely to the case, he emphasized the offensiveness of "allow[ing] the police to search the sacred precincts of marital bedrooms for telltale signs of the use of contraceptives."[4] But this is judicial overkill. The Connecticut statute, on the books since 1937 (but a successor to a similar statute passed in 1879), had never been enforced against married persons, or for that matter against any other class of users. The statute did not forbid the manufacture, importation, or sale of contraceptives; and while in principle manufacturers, importers, and sellers of contraceptive devices were aiders and abettors of violations by the users of the devices (save in the case of condoms, considered disease preventives as much as contraceptives), the statute was no more enforced against suppliers than it was against users. Nor was any attempt made to prevent doctors from prescribing diaphragms and other female contraceptives.

2. 381 U.S. 479, 480.
3. The term actually is introduced in a concurring opinion. Id. at 486.
4. Id. at 485–486.

The statute's sole office was, in conjunction with the prohibition of aiding and abetting, to discourage the establishment of birth control clinics. In this respect the statute was, as I noted in Chapter 7, completely effective. The principal clientele of such clinics are women from the lower social classes.[5] Middle-class women prefer to go to private gynecologists for advice on contraception and prescriptions for contraceptive devices. No one has ever suggested that these women were affected by the Connecticut statute in the least. Just the poorer women were affected.

Although most states placed some restrictions on contraceptives, for example by permitting only licensed pharmacies to sell them to the consumer, only Massachusetts had a statute like Connecticut's, attempting to ban the use of contraceptives.[6] These statutes owed their survival to the power of the Catholic Church in Massachusetts and Connecticut. It is true that the statutes were not Catholic in origin. Comstockery was not a Catholic movement; it was in fact anti-Catholic. But by the 1960s most Protestants had swung around from opposition to birth control to support for it. Now, among major sects at any rate, only the Catholic Church and loyal Catholic parishioners supported the Connecticut statute.[7]

Neither the rarity of the Connecticut statute, nor its distributive impact (that it affected only the poor), nor the role of the Church in its survival was mentioned by any of the justices. Most lawyers, it is true, would ascribe no significance to the role of the Church. It is generally thought a bad argument that a statute, just because it embodies Christian morality, should be struck down as an establishment of religion, which the First Amendment forbids: so many unimpeachable laws—the laws against murder, for example—rest on Christian morality. But that is not quite correct. The concept of murder as a moral wrong is not the invention of Christians, or for that matter of the Jewish authors of the Ten Commandments. All known societies have a concept of murder, that is, of impermissible killing of a human being, because no society could function effectively without it. Yet not all societies are Judeo-

---

5. Norman E. Himes, *Medical History of Contraception* 357 (1936) ("American birth-control clinics serve primarily the working classes"); Linda Gordon, *Woman's Body, Woman's Right: A Social History of Birth Control in America* 288–289 (1976); Elise F. Jones et al., *Pregnancy, Contraception, and Family Planning Services in Industrialized Countries* 108 (1989). I am not speaking of abortion clinics; they came later.

6. See Brief (in the U.S. Supreme Court) of Planned Parenthood Federation of America, Inc., as amicus curiae in *Griswold v. Connecticut,* App. A., at 19A–27A, for a complete list of statutes and a summary of their provisions. The Massachusetts statute was struck down in *Eisenstadt v. Baird,* discussed next, as was a New York statute, though it was considerably less restrictive, in *Carey v. Population Services International,* also discussed later in this section.

7. In addition to references in Chapter 7, see C. Thomas Dienes, *Law, Politics, and Birth Control* 142–147 (1972). Dienes also points out, however, that organized Catholic support for legal prohibitions against contraceptives diminished during the 1960s. Id. at 196–197.

Christian. There are differences between Christian morality and the morality of the pagan cultures, for example in the treatment of infanticide. But these are historical differences. Today the prohibition of infanticide is general in civilized societies, not all of which are Christian. The Christians may have been the innovators, but the innovation has diffused and is now the common property of mankind.

It is otherwise with a prohibition on the use of contraceptives *by married people*. By 1965 this was a sectarian position of the Catholic Church, rejected by most Americans and retained as positive law in only two states, where the Church held enough power to block repeal—enough power to block repeal but not enough power to enforce the statute effectively, save against birth control clinics, where minimal enforcement efforts were enough. (Opposition to abortion had and has a strong religious flavor too, but is far more broadly based; it cannot be considered a merely sectarian cause.) So poor people, who arguably needed contraception the most, were impeded in obtaining the information and devices that they required in order to be able to practice contraception effectively.[8] And they were impeded for the sake of religious doctrine rather than for the advancement of any plausibly secular goal. There was no argument that Connecticut was underpopulated, that large families are happier than small ones, or that knowledge of contraceptive methods by married persons promotes adultery. The best argument for the law's amazing breadth was that if it had had an exception for married persons, it could not, as a practical matter, have been enforced against fornicators (and the Court has never questioned the propriety of a state's seeking to prevent nonmarital intercourse). The birth control clinics would be in business ostensibly to serve married couples but in fact serving all comers. The clinics could escape liability as aiders and abettors by formally confining their services to married couples, but by not requiring proof of marriage they could in fact serve unmarried persons as well, and there would be nothing the state could do about it.

This is the best argument for the statute, but not a good one. Not only could birth control clinics be required to demand proof of marriage, just as bars are required to demand proof of age, but the argument imputes to the

8. Birth control clinics produce large increases in successful contraception among the women who patronize them. Himes, note 5 above, at 386 (1936) (increase in success rate from 55 to 90 percent), for there is a strong positive relationship between education and the use of contraceptives. Robert T. Michael, "Education and the Derived Demand for Children," 81 *Journal of Political Economy* S128, S140–S161 (1973); Mark R. Rosenzweig and Daniel A. Seiver, "Education and Contraceptive Choice: A Conditional Demand Framework," 23 *International Economic Review* 171, 197 (1982), and birth control clinics provide in effect remedial education for low-income—and therefore on average poorly educated—women. Were there no such clinics, moreover, this could increase the number of abortions, since abortion and contraception are (mainly) substitutes. Theodore Joyce, "The Impact of Induced Abortion on Black and White Birth Outcomes in the United States," 24 *Demography* 229, 231, 241 (1987).

state a desire for effective enforcement that seems to have been quite lacking. Connecticut prosecutors, perhaps embarrassed by this anachronistic law, were unwilling to enforce it actively. Only birth control clinics, which by their very nature flaunted their status as aiders and abettors, were in peril. The law was largely a statement, a symbol. This is not necessarily a criticism, although it is an argument against trying to justify the law's application to married persons by reference to exigencies of enforcement. Laws that are weakly enforced, or not enforced at all, are sometimes defended as statements of moral principle that have at least a suasive effect. Indeed, the proposition that they have such an effect is an article of faith among lawyers, as we saw in the discussion of sodomy laws in the preceding chapter—although it may well be false.[9] But the point I want to make here is that the only "statement" made by Connecticut's contraception law was that the Catholic Church had enough temporal power in Connecticut to obtain official backing for an unpopular Catholic doctrine. Nor can this power be equated to democratic preference. A passionate minority often can procure the passage of legislation inimical to the majority, and even more often can block the repeal of legislation that may once have commanded majority support but no longer does. Finally, insofar as the statute was more than a statement, it was an oppression of poor people.

I am not suggesting that it would be an appropriate judicial office to root through the state and federal criminal codes for statutes whose enactment or retention can be traced to sectarian pressures and to strike them down as establishments of religion. Nor am I interested in joining the snipe hunt for a convincing legal-doctrinal ground for the *Griswold* decision. I doubt that one exists. But should that be the end of the legal analysis? A constitution that did not invalidate so offensive, oppressive, probably undemocratic, and sectarian a law would stand revealed as containing major gaps. Maybe that is the nature of our, as perhaps of any, written Constitution; but yet, perhaps the courts are authorized to plug at least the more glaring gaps. Does anyone really believe, in his heart of hearts, that the Constitution should be interpreted so literally as to authorize every conceivable law that would not violate a specific constitutional clause? This would mean that a state could require everyone to marry, or to have sexual intercourse at least once a month, or that it could take away every couple's second child and place it in a foster home. Of course no state is likely to do such things; and if it were likely, that would argue such a change of moral outlook in this nation as to make our present intuitions a poor guide. Yet we do find it reassuring to think that the courts stand between us and legislative tyranny even if a particular form of tyranny was not foreseen and expressly forbidden by the framers of the

---

9. Richard A. Posner, *The Problems of Jurisprudence* 213–215 (1990). A striking example of the refusal of people to take their cues from the law is the nonimpact of *Bowers v. Hardwick* on attitudes toward homosexuals. See note 56 below.

Constitution. But this cannot be the end of the analysis either. The subsequent course of the jurisprudence of sexual autonomy shows, as we are about to see, that judicial efforts at plugging holes in the written Constitution tend to break out of the modest limits that such metaphors as filling gaps and plugging holes imply. And if the Court had stayed its hand, it is quite likely that the Connecticut statute would have been repealed in a few years, given the strong national trend against such laws and the fact (which may of course be related) that organized Catholic endeavors to retain such legal prohibitions against contraceptives as remained were losing steam (see note 7).

The generative potential of the *Griswold* decision became clear seven years later with the decision in *Eisenstadt v. Baird*.[10] The defendant had been convicted of aiding and abetting a violation of the Massachusetts contraceptive statute—which since *Griswold* had been confined to the use of contraceptives by unmarried persons—by handing an unmarried woman a package of spermicidal foam at a talk that the defendant was giving on birth control. To determine whether the law's differential treatment of married and unmarried persons was arbitrary, and hence a denial of the equal protection of the laws, the Court first asked whether the difference in treatment might be justified as a way of deterring fornication, a misdemeanor under Massachusetts law. The answer was no. The law permitted the sale of contraceptives to unmarried and married alike for the prevention of disease. Married persons might—indeed, usually would—use contraceptives in adulterous intercourse. And the five-year maximum punishment for violating the statute was disproportionate to the ninety-day maximum for fornication. The Court hinted that pregnancy and the birth of an unwanted child were also a disproportionate punishment for a misdemeanor. It concluded that deterrence of fornication "cannot reasonably be taken as the purpose of the ban on distribution of contraceptives to unmarried persons."[11]

Every one of the Court's points is flawed. First, punishing the provider of an illegal good or service much more heavily than the buyer or user is commonplace. By way of pertinent example, under many statutes forbidding prostitution the prostitute's customer is not guilty of a crime at all, and so the seller's punishment is infinitely heavier than the buyer's. To punish fornication heavily would be absurd, because it is a minor crime, perhaps one best dealt with indirectly. Second, pregnancy and an unwanted child are not the *intended* punishment for fornication; the hope, rather, is that the prospect of pregnancy and of an unwanted child will deter fornication—although a likelier consequence is that it will induce fornicators to use condoms. As for the fact that they can do this without violating the statute and that married persons can use any contraceptive to engage in adultery, this just shows that

10. 405 U.S. 438 (1972).
11. Id. at 450.

the statute, like most statutes, does not pursue its goals to the exclusion of competing values and as a result is not as effective as it would be if it did. And it is not as if the state *wanted* to except married persons; after *Griswold*, it had no choice. Nor is the exception for condoms fatal to the statute's integrity. The state has an interest in preventing disease as well as in preventing fornication, and since adultery is not a victimless offense and is a ground for divorce, perhaps it is more easily deterrable than fornication without any need to impede contraception, in which event the exemption of married persons need not be thought devastating to the statute's goals. Moreover, since condoms obviously are not everyone's first choice for a contraceptive—and this was even truer before the specter of AIDS began to stalk the land—a law that impedes the supply of all other contraceptives will raise the cost of fornication and so reduce its incidence.

The real objection to the Massachusetts statute is not that it cannot deter fornication. It will deter some. Indeed, it will deter a good deal more than a statute, unenforceable as a practical matter, making fornication a misdemeanor—the statute whose constitutionality was not questioned. The Court stripped the state of the only possibly effective weapon it had against fornication. Nor is the real objection to a statute forbidding the use of contraceptives that if it does deter any fornication, it will do so at disproportionate cost, because there will be more pregnancies and more unwanted children. Although a higher percentage of premarital intercourse will result in pregnancy, there will be less such intercourse; for all one knows, the effects may cancel out and the number of pregnancies and unwanted children therefore remain the same, although the Swedish experience suggests otherwise. The real objection to the statute is that there is no good reason to deter premarital sex, a generally harmless source of pleasure and for some people an important stage of marital search. (Yet this is an equal objection to a statute forbidding fornication, and the Court has never questioned the constitutionality of such statutes.) There are good reasons for wanting to deter unwanted pregnancies, but that aim is more likely to be achieved by encouraging than by discouraging the use of contraceptives. A statute forbidding that use thus has few benefits and many costs.

Since the Court could find no rational basis for the withholding of contraceptives from unmarried persons, it concluded that the Massachusetts statute denied the equal protection of the laws. But it must have been bothered by the fact that *Griswold* had been so emphatic about *marital* privacy, implying that unmarried couples had fewer rights. For the Court added: "The marital couple is not an independent entity with a mind and heart of its own, but an association of two individuals each with a separate intellectual and emotional makeup. If the right of privacy means anything, it is the right of the *individual*, married or single, to be free from unwarranted governmental intrusion into matters so fundamentally affecting a person as the decision whether to bear or beget a child."[12] Read literally, all that this hyperbolic passage says is that the government cannot force unmarried persons, any more than it can force married persons, to have children—a proposition few will quarrel with, although its provenance in the text or history of the Constitution is not easy to find. Implied, however, is the further proposition that notwithstanding the unchallenged misdemeanor fornication law (easily overlooked because totally unenforced), unmarried persons have a constitutional right to engage in sexual intercourse. For if they do not, it is an illegal activity; and how can the Constitution be violated by a state's prohibiting the sale of an input (contraception) into that activity? The *realistic* answer is that the antifornication statute was a dead letter, and nothing could bring it to life. The state's real target was contraception; the state wanted, for the same sectarian reasons that had kept the Connecticut statute alive, to prohibit as much contraception as the Supreme Court would allow it to prohibit.

In the next decision in this sequence, *Carey v. Population Services International*,[13] the Supreme Court struck down three restrictions in New York's law regulating the distribution of contraceptives: contraceptives could not be sold or distributed to anyone under the age of 16; they could be sold only by a licensed pharmacist; and they could not be advertised or displayed. The second and third restrictions were end runs not only around *Baird* but also around *Griswold*, because the predictable effects of the restrictions—higher prices for contraceptives and less information about them—would be felt by married as well as unmarried persons. The first restriction is the most interesting. There is a much stronger public feeling against children having sexual intercourse than against fornication between adults. This makes *Population Services International* a more difficult case than *Baird*, but not insuperably so. For one of the reasons for the stronger feeling is that pregnancy is a greater disaster for a teenage girl than for a grown woman, and this observation was the Court's lever for upending the law. The law might deter some girls from engaging in intercourse, but to the extent that deterrence failed, the adverse consequences would be more severe on the whole than under the Massachusetts law. Moreover, deterrence was likely to fail. Teenagers are on average more impulsive, hence on average less responsive to incentives, than adults are (although Chapter 10 presented evidence of rational behavior by teenagers toward abortion). They are less mature, and one badge of maturity or expe-

---

12. Id. at 453 (emphasis in original). The casual equation in this passage of marital with nonmarital relationships jars with the Court's encomia to marriage in the right-to-marriage cases glanced at in the preceding chapter, and in *Griswold* itself. So highly does the Court regard the married state, even in a disembodied form, that it has held that a prison inmate has a constitutional right to marry, albeit not to have a sexual relationship with his or her spouse. Turner v. Safley, 482 U.S. 78, 94–99 (1987).

13. 431 U.S. 678 (1977).

rience is the ability to reckon up the full consequences of a proposed course of action.

The law could not even be defended forcefully as a backup to parental authority. It is true that most American parents do not want their teenage children, especially their daughters, to engage in sexual intercourse. But even among these parents, many think it more prudent to instruct their daughters in contraception than to trust them to refrain from intercourse. The authority of these parents is undermined by a law that forbids the dispensing of contraceptives to teenagers in all circumstances. Oddly, then, the provision of the New York law that at first glance seems the most clearly reasonable—keeping contraceptives away from children—is actually the least reasonable.

Between *Baird* and *Population Services International* came *Roe v. Wade*,[14] which conferred on women an absolute constitutional right against governmental restrictions on abortion in the first trimester of pregnancy, a qualified right in the second, and in the third a right limited to the protection of the mother's life or health.[15] The majority opinion has been much maligned for its long and seemingly irrelevant discourse on the history of attitudes toward and laws regulating abortion since the ancient Persians, for the casualness of its quest for the constitutional source of a right of abortion, and for the mechanical division of the gestation period into three equal segments carrying different legal consequences. The first and third criticisms are misplaced. The history is relevant to show that attitudes and laws concerning abortion have varied greatly over time and across cultures; it is not a history of uniform and severe condemnation. It is also relevant to show that the strict Catholic position not only is of relatively recent origin but also has never been accepted in Anglo-American law.[16] And it is relevant to show that the legal sanctions against abortion were actually weakening until in the nineteenth century concerns were raised about the inherent hazardousness of abortion as a medical procedure—hazards that medical progress has eliminated. The history thus shows that the abortion taboo, if that is what it should be called, is weaker than the taboo on infanticide; and having shown this, the Court is then able to argue with some persuasiveness that the fetus is not in fact regarded as a person—for if it were, abortion like infanticide would have been punished as murder, which it was not.

14. 410 U.S. 113 (1973).

15. The Supreme Court extended these abortion rights to minors in Planned Parenthood v. Danforth, 428 U.S. 52 (1976), a decision the Court then relied on in *Carey v. Population Services International* to bolster that decision. The abortion "right" is formal, in the sense that one must be able to afford the abortion. There is no right to public funding of abortions. Maher v. Roe, 432 U.S. 464 (1977); Harris v. McRae, 448 U.S. 297 (1980). The distinction has considerable practical significance. Among other things it helps explain our high incidence of unwanted births.

16. The Texas statute invalidated in *Roe v. Wade* contained an exception for abortions, whether or not indirect, undertaken with the purpose of saving the mother's life.

Having thus demoted fetal life to a level beneath that of full human life, the Court had cleared the way to balancing the interest of the pregnant woman in aborting the fetus with the undoubted interest of the state in protecting its citizens, including children. These interests have the convenient property of being oppositely related to the stage of the pregnancy in which the abortion is performed. The earlier it is performed, the stronger the mother's interest in abortion because she will be spared more of the risks and inconveniences of pregnancy, and the weaker the state's interest in preventing abortion because the fetus is that much less than a child. The later the abortion is performed, the weaker is the mother's interest, both because she has borne more of the burdens of pregnancy already—they are a sunk cost that abortion could not now restore—and because she presumably could have had the abortion earlier and thus minimized the impact on the state's interest; and the stronger that interest is because the fetus is more nearly a child. The respective interests are therefore best accommodated, or in economic language the joint costs of abortion and of preventing abortion are minimized, by a sliding scale whereby the woman's right to an abortion diminishes with every day of pregnancy. But so refined a standard would be difficult to administer, and a simple trichotomous rule is substituted instead.

Recast in the manner I have just sketched—and it is a recasting faithful to the spirit of Justice Harry Blackmun's opinion if not to its terminology—*Roe v. Wade* emerges as a statement of social policy congruent with the model of morally indifferent sex, though not necessarily entailed by it (see Chapter 10).[17] And when *Roe* is set alongside the case in which the Court later extended the right of abortion to minors (see note 15), the contraceptive cases, and cases decided in the same period limiting the power of government to impose disabilities on illegitimate children,[18] conferring paternity rights on unwed fathers,[19] and confining the prohibition of pornography largely to hard-core pornography,[20] it is possible to argue that by the mid-1970s the Supreme Court had set the United States on a course of convergence with Sweden in matters related to sex. I am sure the Court never dreamed of requiring

17. So viewed, the opinion's most questionable feature is allowing abortion as late as the ninth month if the mother's health requires it without insisting that the hazard to her health be substantial. This and other penetrating criticisms are made in John Hart Ely's classic article "The Wages of Crying Wolf: A Comment on *Roe v. Wade*," 82 *Yale Law Journal* 920 (1973).

18. Such as Weber v. Aetna Casualty & Surety Co., 406 U.S. 164 (1972); Gomez v. Perez, 409 U.S. 535 (1973); Jimenez v. Weinberger, 417 U.S. 628 (1974), and Trimble v. Gordon, 430 U.S. 762 (1977). The Court's emphasis in these cases is on the harshness of making the child pay the penalty for the parent's misconduct. To this it could be replied that if the child prevails, the legitimate heirs of the parent are then likely to pay the penalty for the parent's misconduct, and they are just as innocent.

19. The principal decision is Stanley v. Illinois, 405 U.S. 645 (1972).

20. Miller v. California, 413 U.S. 15 (1973).

government to subsidize nonmarital sex and childbearing, as Sweden has done with its exceptionally generous welfare programs; after all, the Court allowed the states and the federal government to deny public funding of abortions (see note 15), thus making the "right" of abortion rather empty to the indigent. The Court, as it were, left the subsidy side of Swedish sexual policy to Congress and state legislatures. It confined itself to sweeping away legal restrictions on sexual freedom.

Why it got as deeply involved in sex as it did is unclear. I share Thomas Grey's skepticism that the justices actually believe, with Bertrand Russell, that sex ought to be a morally indifferent matter, like eating. Grey believes that the justices regard sex as a great and mysterious force which must be ordered and controlled, and that the sexual privacy decisions that I have been discussing were designed to stabilize sex by enabling people to limit (through contraception and abortion) the costs of pregnancy.[21] Maybe so; but this approach led Grey, writing in 1980, to predict incorrectly that a conservative Supreme Court would invalidate the laws against sodomy and fornication in order to stabilize nonmarital sexual relationships, which were becoming more common. He said, for example, that "the homosexual community is becoming an increasingly public sector of our society. For that community to be governed effectively, it must be recognized as legitimate."[22]

Grey's prediction was falsified in only six years. It is helpful, as we try to understand why, to examine the different textures of the four opinions I have discussed. The most conventional are *Baird* and *Population Services International*. The principle of equal protection of the laws—that government must treat likes alike, or in other words must base differences in treatment on rational distinctions—is uncontroversial. The question was therefore whether the different treatment of married and unmarried, or over 16 and under 16, with regard to the availability of contraceptives was rational, and one could argue with some plausibility that it was not. The gravest objection to the decisions was that they created an irrational distinction of their own in the application of the equal protection clause to sexual regulation and to economic regulation. The Court demanded that sexual regulations make sense; it made no similar demand of economic regulations. Consider the provision of the New York statute invalidated in *Population Services International* reserving to licensed pharmacists the right to sell contraceptives. The Court had upheld a similar restriction on freedom of contract—forbidding opticians to replace eyeglass frames without a prescription from an optometrist or ophthalmolo-

---

21. Thomas C. Grey, "Eros, Civilization and the Burger Court," 43 *Law and Contemporary Problems* 83 (Summer 1980). The Court had actually described sex as a "great and mysterious motive force in human life" in one of its early obscenity decisions. Roth v. United States, 354 U.S. 476, 487 (1977).

22. Grey, note 21 above, at 97.

gist—in an opinion that fairly breathes indifference to such freedom and that, although decided before the sexual freedom cases, exemplifies the Court's consistent policy from the late 1930s to today toward equal protection challenges to economic regulation.[23] Why it should be thought a worse offense against constitutional principle for a state to raise the price of condoms than to raise the price of eyeglasses remains the abiding mystery of the Court's brush with sexual libertarianism. The answer the Court would have given if asked—that sexual and reproductive freedom is a "fundamental" right and economic liberty is not—just relabels the question. One might have thought libertarianism indivisible; that the same arguments which show that people ought to be allowed to make their own choices in matters of sex and procreation, though with due regard for the interests of third parties, also show that they ought to be allowed to make their own choices with regard to nonsexual goods and services. No doubt castration is a greater deprivation of liberty than the denial of a barber's license, but the denial of that license may be a greater deprivation than being forbidden to buy condoms from vending machines.

If the Constitution itself distinguished between sexual markets and other markets, this would be answer enough to a proposal to equate the two types of market. But it does not—or rather it gives *more* protection to property than to liberty (for example, in the contracts and taking clauses). The curious appropriation of the word privacy to describe what is not privacy in the ordinary sense but rather freedom is an attempt by semantic legerdemain to make sexual liberty appear to occupy a different plane of social value from economic liberty.[24] It does not.

That the text of the Constitution does not establish the priority of sexual over nonsexual liberty is, in fact, the lesson of *Griswold* and *Roe*. With refreshing candor Justice Douglas in *Griswold* abandoned the pretense that every constitutional right must have a specific textual provenance. This, together with rhetorical maladroitness,[25] exposed his opinion to pointed professional criticism, because the interpretive method that he employed had (and has) little standing in professional thinking about the Constitution. He used

23. Williamson v. Lee Optical of Oklahoma, Inc., 348 U.S. 483, 488–489 (1955). See also Railway Express Agency, Inc. v. New York, 336 U.S. 106 (1949); Ferguson v. Skrupa, 372 U.S. 726, 729 (1963); City of New Orleans v. Dukes, 427 U.S. 297 (1976) (per curiam); Minnesota v. Clover Leaf Creamery Co., 449 U.S. 456, 464–470 (1981).

24. I protested against this appropriation in *The Economics of Justice* 323–331 (1981). (I shall never cease to be amazed at the Court's assertion in *Baird* that if the right of privacy means *anything*, it means the right to use contraceptives in an illegal relationship.) On the parity of economic and noneconomic markets in classical liberalism, see, for example, Aaron Director, "The Parity of the Economic Market Place," 7 *Journal of Law and Economics* 1 (1964).

25. Henry T. Greely, "A Footnote to 'Penumbra' in Griswold v. Connecticut," 6 *Constitutional Commentary* 251, 263–265 (1989).

the text and history of the document as a source of general values from which to construct a nontextual right, the right of marital privacy. Perhaps this interpretive technique could have been made respectable by further elaboration and application, but the Court did not try to do that and instead switched (notably in Roe v. Wade) to the more conventional, but no more satisfactory, "substantive due process" ground that Justice John Marshall Harlan had urged in his concurring opinion in Griswold.[26] One reason for the switch may have been that the interpretive method of Griswold made more sense in the peculiar circumstances of that case than it would have, for example, in Roe v. Wade. So absurd and repulsive was the Connecticut statute as applied to married persons that a failure to invalidate it would have exposed the Constitution as incomplete, time-bound, and loophole ridden, which is not how Americans like to think of their fundamental charter. The parallel in the abortion setting would be a law that enacted orthodox Catholic doctrine and thus forbade an abortion (unless it was "indirect"—see Chapter 10) even where necessary to save the mother's life. Values of liberty and autonomy fairly to be regarded as immanent in the eighteenth-century document could well be thought an appropriate basis for regarding such a law as contrary to the pervasive spirit of the document. And we know that the letter killeth, but the spirit giveth life—a point that sexual conservatives would quickly recognize if it were argued that marriage statutes which do not specify that the spouses must be of opposite sexes authorize homosexual marriage.[27]

A general right of abortion such as recognized in Roe v. Wade is much more difficult to relate to the spirit of the document, and there is a corresponding desire to find a firmer textual handle. But is there one? The Fifth and Fourteenth Amendments forbid the national government and the states to deprive a person of life, liberty, or property without due process of law. There is no problem with describing a prohibition against abortion as a deprivation of a pregnant woman's liberty; the problem comes in describing it as a denial of due process of law. The history as well as semantics of the term points to procedural rather than to substantive rights. There is also, it is true, some historical warrant both for viewing the due process clause as a requirement that legal sanctions be applied only in accordance with written law, and for viewing the due process clause of the Fourteenth Amendment— or if not the due process clause then the privileges and immunities clause of the same amendment—as making some or even all of the specific guarantees

26. 381 U.S. at 499–502; see also Poe v. Ullman, 367 U.S. 497, 522 (1961) (Harlan, J., dissenting). I explain substantive due process later in this chapter.
27. Baker v. Nelson, 191 N.W.2d 185 (Minn. 1971); Adams v. Howerton, 486 F. Supp. 1119 (C.D. Cal. 1980).

of the Bill of Rights applicable to state action.[28] But neither interpretation would generate a right to sexual freedom. For that one needs the pure concept of substantive due process that the Supreme Court had employed in a series of discredited decisions, most famously Dred Scott's case and *Lochner*.[29] That history may explain the apologetic and perfunctory manner in which Justice Blackmun in *Roe* located "a right of personal privacy, or a guarantee of certain areas or zones of privacy,"[30] encompassing the right to an abortion, in the due process clause.[31]

Blackmun's opinion in *Roe*, like Douglas's in *Griswold*, fails to measure up to professional expectations regarding judicial opinions. The imbalance between the extraordinary care that the opinion in *Roe* lavishes on the history of abortion and the offhand manner in which it treats the constitutional provenance of a right of abortion is jarring to a lawyer, who is bound to think the latter inquiry more important than the former. But the ineptitude of the opinion is more general. The history of abortion, though relevant, as I said earlier, does not deserve the attention that the opinion gives it and that imparts to the opinion an air of antiquarianism and earnest amateurishness. No effort is made to use the statutory exception for abortions necessary for the protection of the mother's life to drive a wedge between fetal life and other human life, along the lines discussed in Chapter 10. No effort is made to dramatize the hardships to a woman forced to carry her fetus to term against her will. The opinion does point out that "maternity, or additional offspring, may force upon the woman a distressful life and future,"[32] and it elaborates on the point for a few more sentences. But there is no mention of the woman who is raped, who is poor, or whose fetus is deformed. There is no reference to the death of women from illegal abortions. No effort is made to relate the right of abortion to the right of marital privacy recognized in *Griswold*—even though the Texas statute made no exception for abortions by married women—or to the right of contraception, for which abortion is a backup, in *Baird*. And the prose of the opinion is lackluster throughout.

As a specimen of rhetoric—the art of persuasion—*Roe v. Wade* is thus a flop. But even a rhetorical masterpiece would not have persuaded the legal

28. For a balanced discussion of what due process means, see John Hart Ely, *Democracy and Distrust: A Theory of Judicial Review* 14–30, 189–201 (1980).

29. Scott v. Sandford, 60 U.S. (19 How.) 393 (1856); Lochner v. New York, 198 U.S. 45 (1905).

30. 410 U.S. at 152.

31. "This right of privacy, whether it be founded in the Fourteenth Amendment's concept of personal liberty and restrictions upon state action, as we feel it is, or, as the District Court determined, in the Ninth Amendment's reservation of rights to the people, is broad enough to encompass a woman's decision whether or not to terminate her pregnancy." Id. at 153.

32. Id.

profession that a right of abortion is firmly anchored in the Constitution, for of course it is not. This is not to say that any of the decisions I have been discussing is "wrong" as a matter of constitutional law; it is to say that the Court was unable to come up with a satisfactory demonstration of their rightness. And since it was unable to do this, the suspicion naturally arose that the justices were voting their personal values and political preferences. Those values and preferences seemed, moreover, oddly—in light of the justices' personal and professional backgrounds—aligned with those of the student radicals of the 1960s, for whom sexual liberty and political liberty were, as they had been to their guru, Herbert Marcuse, two sides of the same coin, while economic liberty they considered a mask for exploitation.

Other decisions by the Supreme Court during the 1970s had a Marcusean cast also. I confine myself to three examples. *Erznoznik v. City of Jacksonville*[33] held that a city had violated the First Amendment by prohibiting the showing of nude scenes on outdoor movie screens visible from the public highway, since not all photographs of nudes are obscene. That was not the point; the point was that drivers could be distracted by such scenes and that parents should be allowed to control the movies that their children see. *Cohen v. California*[34] held that a state could not enforce standards of decorum in its courthouses that would prevent a person from wearing a jacket on which was printed the slogan "Fuck the Draft"—a slogan whose style as well as whose message epitomized the student movement. And in *Cox Broadcasting Corp. v. Cohn*,[35] the Court held that a state could not prevent the media from broadcasting the name of a dead rape victim. These cases have a doctrinaire cast. They subordinate all other values to the value of expression, especially expression related to sex (sex is in the background of all three of my examples), however weak the First Amendment claim is in relation to competing claims of highway safety, parental authority, judicial decorum, and personal privacy—privacy in its original rather than in the Court's Aesopian sense. As I have said elsewhere, "It is as if the Court had become infected with the student radicalism of the late 1960s and early 1970s, with its emphasis on candor at the expense of privacy, its slogans of 'doing your own thing' and 'letting it all hang out,'"[36] and, I would add, its implied equation of sexual and political liberty.

The Court is not immune to the *Zeitgeist*. How else to explain the reversal of constitutional values between the late nineteenth century and *Roe*, from laissez-faire in the economic sphere and repression in the sexual to repression in the economic sphere and laissez-faire in the sexual? Grey might answer

33. 422 U.S. 205 (1975).
34. 403 U.S. 15 (1971).
35. 420 U.S. 469 (1975).
36. *The Economics of Justice*, note 24 above, at 345.

that the Court recognized the need for regulation in both spheres. But this would be a play on words. If permitting nonmarital intercourse is a method of regulating sex, then equally is deregulating the economy and allowing the free market to order our economic affairs a method of regulating the economy. Indeed, the regulative function of the market is frequently remarked.

There is, in any event, a simpler explanation than Grey's for the Supreme Court's inconsistent treatment of the economic and sexual markets. Until the election of Ronald Reagan, liberal social policies commanded the support of both major political parties. The sexual liberty cases were decided in the same period that the Supreme Court was experimenting with outlawing capital punishment, another item on the liberal agenda, while making little effort to promote economic liberty (little, not none, because the Court in this period interpreted the First Amendment to limit government regulation of advertising). The family-planning movement, which inspired the attack on the Connecticut and Massachusetts contraceptive laws, was and is one of the less controversial threads in the liberal tapestry, and by the time of *Roe v. Wade* it had the strong backing of the rapidly growing, and in the modern sense at least certifiably "liberal," feminist movement. The Supreme Court, in its passivity on the economic front, was also faithfully mirroring the modern liberal outlook.

Reagan's election both confirmed the existence of and amplified a strong current of public opinion that rejected the modern liberal position on a variety of issues, including those related to sex. The association, however adventitious, between 1960s-style student radicalism and sexual promiscuity swelled the current still more. *Roe v. Wade* and other decisions in which the Court had gone out on a jurisprudential limb in the pursuit of liberal policies were symbols of that position to conservatives of all hues. The decisions could not be strongly defended as products of legal reasoning; and—in part thanks to those student radicals again—sexual liberalism had become associated in the public mind with welfare-state liberalism, that is, egalitarianism, rather than with economic liberalism, where it belonged. The decisions managed the remarkable feat of simultaneously offending judicial conservatives, social conservatives, and libertarians. That made the decisions particularly vulnerable should the Court's membership change, as it did, but it also made it likelier that some members of the Court would have a change of heart—and at least one did (Chief Justice Warren Burger).

Chapter 10 contains materials for possibly rebuilding *Roe v. Wade* on utilitarian foundations better understood now (owing mainly to empirical work done in the interim) than when the case was decided. This suggestion will leave most lawyers cold, however, not only because the analysis is inconclusive in its own terms but also because the Constitution does not enjoin the states or the federal government to steer by the light of Jeremy Bentham. The focus of the legal defenders of *Roe v. Wade* has therefore shifted to the equal protection clause, and to the argument that forbidding abortion discriminates against women by subjecting them to a burden—that of pregnancy—from which men are free.[37] But one may question whether this approach can fulfill the lawyer's dream of escaping from having to delve into the practical, utilitarian, economic consequences of legal rules. A difference in treatment does not violate the equal protection clause if it is justifiable, and this particular difference in treatment is prima facie justifiable by the fact that men and women are, by virtue of biology, differently situated in relation to fetal life. To show that the difference actually is unjustifiable from a social standpoint requires consideration of the benefits to the fetus and the costs to others, so utilitarian analysis comes in by the back door. Nor can that door be shut by the argument that whatever justifications might be offered for laws forbidding abortion, the support for those laws comes from people who want to keep women down; and an invidious purpose can condemn a law. In fact an individious purpose can invalidate only a trivial law, such as a law imposing a poll tax or a literacy test for prospective voters; courts are not going to deprive people of essential legal protection just because some supporters of the law that confers that protection had bad motives. The principal support for antiabortion laws, moreover, comes not from misogynists or from "macho" men (a Don Juan would favor abortion on demand because it would reduce the cost of sex), but from men and women who, whether or not Roman Catholic (many of them of course are Roman Catholic), believe on religious grounds in the sanctity of fetal life.[38] That is not a discriminatory or invidious belief, even if there is a correlation between that belief and belief in the traditional role of women, a role that feminists, with much support in history, consider subordinate. More than correlation is involved. For many opponents of abortion, opposition to abortion is part and parcel of opposition to a broader set of practices and values—call it feminism. But of course for many abortion supporters, abortion on demand is the very symbol of feminism. Should the Supreme Court take sides between feminism and antifeminism?

Behind ideology and even religious belief, moreover, may lie concrete economic interests. We saw in Chapter 7 that the debate over abortion, and over the sexual and reproductive freedom of women more broadly, is in part a debate between women who lose and women who gain from that freedom. The freer women are sexually, the less interest men have in marriage, and women specialized in household rather than market production are therefore

---

37. The germ of the argument is Judith Jarvis Thomson's article "A Defense of Abortion," discussed in Chapter 10. For amplification, see Sylvia A. Law, "Rethinking Sex and the Constitution," 132 *University of Pennsylvania Law Review* 955, 1016–28 (1984), and Catharine A. MacKinnon, "Reflections on Sex Equality under Law," 100 *Yale Law Journal* 1281, 1309–24 (1991).

38. Kristin Luker, *Abortion and the Politics of Motherhood* 128–132, 146–147, 174, 186–187 (1984).

harmed. Are not legislatures rather than courts the proper arenas in a democratic system for arbitrating a clash of opposed economic interests? Can we rightly call antiabortion laws even prima facie discriminatory against women if in fact they help some women and hurt others?

Bowers v. Hardwick and Beyond

By the time *Bowers v. Hardwick*,[39] a challenge to the constitutionality of Georgia's law criminalizing sodomy, came before the Supreme Court, the political atmosphere that had nourished the concept of sexual privacy had changed. The conservative voice was louder. Justice Sandra Day O'Connor, Reagan's first appointment to the Supreme Court, had replaced Justice Potter Stewart, who had dissented in *Griswold* but had joined *Baird, Population Services International,* and *Roe v. Wade;* and Chief Justice Burger had begun having second thoughts about *Roe v. Wade,* which he had joined. By a vote of five to four, in an opinion by Justice Byron White, the Supreme Court not only rejected Hardwick's challenge to the Georgia statute but also froze the constitutional right of privacy.

Michael Hardwick had been arrested under peculiar circumstances.[40] A police officer had, with the permission of a house guest who was sleeping in the living room of the apartment that Hardwick shared with another man, entered the apartment to serve an arrest warrant on Hardwick for having been drinking in public. The door to the bedroom was ajar, and the police officer opened it and saw Hardwick engaged in fellatio with another man, who was not Hardwick's roommate but was instead a "one-night stand." The officer arrested both men for violating the state's sodomy statute, and Hardwick as well on the drinking offense and also for possession of a small quantity of marijuana that the officer found in the bedroom. (Georgia's statute defines sodomy to include oral as well as anal intercourse.) The two were held in jail for twelve hours and then released without charges being lodged against them, the district attorney's office having decided not to prosecute.

It is unclear whether anyone had been prosecuted in Georgia for a violation

---

39. 478 U.S. 186 (1986).

40. Recounted in Note, "Constitutional Law—An Imposition of the Justices' Own Moral Choices—*Bowers v. Hardwick,*" 9 *Whittier Law Review* 115, 130–134 (1987). See also Art Harris, "The Unintended Battle of Michael Hardwick: After His Georgia Sodomy Case, a Public Right-to-Privacy Crusade," *Washington Post,* August 21, 1986, C1. The "facts" are based on an interview with Hardwick; they are not discussed in the Supreme Court opinions, were not in the court record, and may not be completely accurate. Among things that Hardwick claimed in the interview which may or may not be true were that the police were out to get him because he had been seen leaving a gay bar and that when he and his accomplice were taken to jail, the police told the other inmates that the two had been arrested for sodomy.

of the sodomy law not involving aggravated circumstances for forty years or more. There had been no reported cases during that period, and although the absence of a reported case does not prove the absence of prosecutions or even convictions, no one connected with the case was able to find one. In any event, the district attorney's policy was not to prosecute adult consensual violators of the law.[41] Hardwick nevertheless brought a suit to invalidate the law, arguing that he planned to continue violating it and was afraid of being prosecuted. The fear apparently was groundless. Hardwick claimed, it is true, that he had been harassed for his homosexuality in having been accused in the first place of drinking in public, but he did not try to show that there was a significant probability of his being arrested for sodomy in the future. It was a fluke that the police had seen him commit the crime in the privacy of his own home.

One might in these circumstances have expected the Court, under its precedents,[42] to dismiss the case as moot,[43] especially given the controversiality of the issue—usually a good predictor of the Court's finding a procedural ground for ducking the merits of a case if it is possible to do so. The Court may not have done this because it wanted to cut back on the concept of sexual privacy in a case that some of the justices may have thought an ideal vehicle for doing so—a veritable reductio ad absurdum of the concept. Justice White begins his opinion by reviewing the sexual privacy cases and finding "that none of the rights announced in those cases bears any resemblance to the claimed constitutional right of homosexuals to engage in acts of sodomy that is asserted in this case. No connection between family, marriage, or procreation on the one hand and homosexual activity on the other has been demonstrated."[44] Had he noted that besides being about family, marriage, and procreation, cases such as *Griswold, Baird, Population Services International,* and *Roe v. Wade* had been about sex, he could not have polished them off so easily. Nor if he had remarked the fact that, on its face anyway, the Georgia statute made sodomy illegal even when heterosexual—even, indeed, when practiced by married persons.

Having set precedent to one side, White embarks on an examination of whether, as a matter of first principles, there is "a fundamental right to engage

41. The qualification is important. In Gordon v. State, 257 Ga. 439, 360 S.E.2d 253 (1987), the Supreme Court of Georgia, shortly after the U.S. Supreme Court's decision in *Bowers v. Hardwick,* upheld a ten-year prison sentence for consensual sodomy with a 16-year-old boy. The information about the district attorney's policy is from the *Washington Post* article, note 40 above.

42. Notably City of Los Angeles v. Lyons, 461 U.S. 95 (1983), also written by Justice White.

43. A challenge to the statute by a heterosexual couple *was* dismissed as moot in the lower court. The statute is not in terms limited to homosexual acts, but the heterosexual couple had not even been arrested, so their fears were especially chimerical.

44. 478 U.S. at 190–191.

in homosexual sodomy."[45] He explains that the class of fundamental rights that are not derived from the text of the Constitution should be limited to those deeply rooted in the nation's history and traditions; otherwise judicial creativity will lack an anchor. So, in conscious or unconscious parody of *Roe v. Wade* (from which White had dissented), he proceeds to examine the historical record, noting that "proscriptions against that conduct have ancient roots"[46] and that sodomy was a crime at common law as well as in all thirteen colonies at the time the Bill of Rights was ratified, in all but a handful of states when the Fourteenth Amendment was ratified, and in half of the states today. "Against this background, to claim that a right to engage in such conduct is 'deeply rooted in this Nation's history and tradition' or 'implicit in the concept of ordered liberty' is, at best, facetious."[47] Or in the words of Chief Justice Burger, concurring, "To hold that the act of homosexual sodomy is somehow protected as a fundamental right would be to cast aside millennia of moral teaching."[48]

Overlooked by both opinions is the fact that at common law sodomy did not include fellatio, the specific act for which Hardwick had been arrested; sodomy at common law was limited to anal intercourse. The extension of the proscription to oral sex came late in the nineteenth century, after the Bill of Rights and the Fourteenth Amendment.[49] White is correct nevertheless that the right to engage in homosexual acts is not deeply rooted in America's history and tradition. It would indeed be "facetious" to contend otherwise. But as the same thing could have been said of the rights recognized in the earlier sexual privacy cases (had, indeed, been said by White himself, in his dissent in *Roe v. Wade*), the opinion appears to slam the door on any expansion of the right of sexual privacy beyond the holdings of the previous decisions read as narrowly as possible.

What is true about the four leading sexual privacy cases that White attempts to distinguish is that all four are about pregnancy, actual or probable. All four can, indeed, be viewed as decisions motivated by a concern with the burdens of unwanted pregnancy, a concern that resonates with the women's movement and thus connects with the Court's decisions invalidating sexually discriminatory legislation under the equal protection clause, and that has no

---

45. Id. at 191.
46. Id. at 192.
47. Id. at 194.
48. Id. at 197.
49. Comment, "History, Homosexuality, and Political Values: Searching for the Hidden Determinants of *Bowers v. Hardwick*," 97 *Yale Law Journal* 1073, 1082–86 (1988). The opinion in *Hardwick* does not say which act prohibited by the Georgia statute Hardwick had engaged in. Perhaps the Court assumed that he wished to be free to engage in any of the acts prohibited by it.

counterpart in the sphere of homosexuals' rights. What is also true is that the Court had never questioned the right of the states to forbid particular sexual acts.[50] Only if the sexual privacy cases were interpreted broadly, as standing for the proposition that the state must have a compelling reason to restrict sexual liberty[51]—an interpretation consistent with the cases, certainly, but not compelled by them—would they cover Hardwick's case. (And cover it easily: from a libertarian standpoint, laws forbidding abortion are more easily justified than laws forbidding sodomy, because abortion has palpable third-party effects—on the fetus—and sodomy does not.) Although White can be criticized for having brushed aside the previous cases too summarily, he could have distinguished them as embodying a principle narrower than Hardwick needed in order to prevail.

White would still have had to meet the argument that the criminal punishment of homosexual acts between consenting adults is as offensive to contemporary notions of the proper scope of government as Connecticut's ban on contraceptives, which the Court had invalidated before there was a line of sexual privacy cases that it might have cited as precedent. If the creation of homosexual rights would have been contrary to millennia of moral teachings, so was (at the time of *Griswold*) the creation of a right to use contraceptives; the moral teachers were in fact the same, and in both cases their influence had declined. Half the states had repealed their sodomy laws. In the half that had retained them, the laws were no longer being enforced unless there was evidence of coercion, public indecency, abuse of minors, or other aggravating circumstances, so in these states the laws had been reduced to backing up uncontroversial regulations of sexual behavior.[52] There was a lesson in the

50. On the contrary, it had affirmed that right in Paris Adult Theater I v. Slaton, 413 U.S. 49, 57–59 (1973), difficult as this position may be to square with *Baird*. In contrast, the Supreme Court of New Jersey invalidated the state's fornication statute under a provision of the New Jersey Constitution that is drawn from the Declaration of Independence but has no counterpart in the U.S. Constitution, conferring an inalienable right to the pursuit of happiness. State v. Saunders, 75 N.J. 200, 381 A.2d 333 (1977).

51. The position forcefully argued in David A. J. Richards, "Unnatural Acts and the Constitutional Right to Privacy: A Moral Theory," 45 *Fordham Law Review* 1281 (1977).

52. The most recent reported cases I have found, outside of military cases, in which the defendant was prosecuted for homosexual acts not involving force, abuse of a minor, or any other conspicuously aggravating circumstance, are State v. Walsh, 713 S.W.2d 508 (Mo. 1986), and Canfield v. State, 506 P.2d 987 (Okla. Ct. Crim. App. 1973). And in *Webb*, it appears from the brief statement of facts that the act was committed either on a street corner or in an automobile, while in *Canfield* it was committed in an automobile. In both cases, therefore, there was an aura of public indecency. The most recent case that I have found involving "unnatural" acts between a heterosexual couple, again without aggravating circumstances (in fact the couple was married), is Cotner v. Henry, 394 F.2d 873 (7th Cir. 1968), a habeas corpus case arising from an Indiana prosecution in 1965. The armed forces, however, continue to court-martial soldiers who commit homosexual acts, and occasionally to imprison them if they are convicted. See, for example, United States v. Jones, 30 M.J. 849 (Navy–Marine Corps Court of Military

nonenforcement of the sodomy laws: if it was not that an attempt to challenge the validity of such laws was moot, it was that the laws, viewed as vehicles of criminal law enforcement rather than as reports of public opinion, no longer reflected popular feeling. Not that homosexuality was approved; far from it. But the will to punish homosexuals as criminals had died.

There is, moreover, the curious fact noted earlier that the Georgia statute neither distinguished between homosexual and heterosexual acts nor made an exception for married persons. Insofar as anal and oral intercourse are methods of contraception, the statute could therefore have been thought invalid under *Griswold*. And even if these practices are regarded, more realistically, as being today primarily methods for introducing variety into a married couple's sex life rather than contraceptive methods, an attempt to prohibit them could be thought an infringement of the right of marital privacy of which *Griswold* had spoken, or as a tax on companionate marriage. But these would be arguments merely for limiting the scope of the Georgia statute, as the Court had done in *Griswold* in holding that the law against contraceptives could not be applied to married persons but leaving the statute in other respects intact, and as, in fact, many state courts have done in interpreting statutes similar to Georgia's.[53] The more pertinent consideration is what the breadth of the statute reveals about the legislators' motives. Evidently the Georgia legislature that passed the sodomy law was concerned not about homosexuality as such but about "unnatural" sexual acts by or on whomever committed. Whatever the arguments that might be marshaled in favor of attempts to suppress homosexuality, they are not available as arguments for suppressing "unnatural" sex acts between men and women—except for the theological arguments, by 1986 made only by orthodox Roman Catholics, and not by many of them, and those are a thin reed to support criminal punishment. They also call into question Justice White's assumption that Georgia's sodomy law was based on "majority sentiments about the morality of homosexuality."[54] The sentiments behind the law, not clearly those of a

---

Review 1990); United States v. Baum, 30 M.J. 626 (Navy–Marine Corps Court of Military Review 1990). Note, moreover, that it is for the most part only cases that are appealed that get reported. Not all convicted persons appeal. Defendants who plead guilty have in general no right to appeal, so it is possible despite the absence of reported cases that people still are occasionally being charged with consensual sodomy and pleading guilty in exchange for a promise of light punishment.

53. See Schochet v. Maryland, 320 Md. 714, 580 A.2d 176 (1990), and cases cited there.

54. 478 U.S. at 196. Moreover, before AIDS an argument could be made that oral and anal sex were socially preferable to vaginal intercourse as forms of sexual expression for unmarried heterosexual couples, because they create no risk of pregnancy. With AIDS, the case for regarding anal sex as preferable in these circumstances weakens, because anal sex is more likely to cause infection with the AIDS virus than vaginal sex; but the case for preferring oral sex is strengthened, since it is less likely than either vaginal or anal sex to spread AIDS.

majority, may have less to do with the morality of homosexuality than with the morality of using certain bodily orifices for purposes not ordained or condoned by the Creator: a sectarian morality.

In their possibly inadvertent equation of fellatio to sodomy, and in their ignoring the ideological roots of the Georgia statute, the majority and concurring opinions in *Hardwick* betray a lack of knowledge about the history and character of the regulation of sexuality. There is also a profound lack of empathy for the situation of the male homosexual in America in the age of AIDS. (AIDS is not mentioned in any of the opinions, although it was mentioned in several of the briefs.) In this respect the dissenting opinions, in their bland decorousness and their formulaic generality, do not differ notably from the majority and concurring opinions, but in this they reflect faithfully the tone and emphasis of Hardwick's brief. If *Roe v. Wade* gave too short shrift to legal doctrine, *Bowers v. Hardwick* gave too short shrift to fact and policy.

Perhaps the strongest argument for Michael Hardwick was that statutes which criminalize homosexual behavior express an irrational fear and loathing of a group that has been subjected to discrimination, much like that directed against the Jews, with whom indeed homosexuals—who, like Jews, are despised more for what they are than for what they do—were frequently bracketed in medieval persecutions. The statutes thus have a quality of invidiousness missing from statutes prohibiting abortion or contraception. The position of the homosexual is difficult at best, even in a tolerant society, which our society is not quite; and it is made worse, though probably not much worse, by statutes that condemn the homosexual's characteristic methods of sexual expression as vile crimes (the Georgia statute carried a maximum punishment of twenty years in prison). There is a gratuitousness, an egregiousness, a cruelty, and a meanness about the Georgia statute that could be thought to place it in the same class with Connecticut's anticontraceptive law, notwithstanding the fact that many states have statutes like Georgia's and only one other had a statute like Connecticut's.

But to see the Georgia statute in this light one must know something about the history of homosexuality and of attempts to repress it; and on the evidence of the briefs and opinions in *Bowers v. Hardwick,* what lawyers and judges mainly know is their own prejudices plus what is contained in judicial opinions. It is true that the American Psychological Association and the American Public Health Association filed an amicus curiae brief in *Hardwick* that contains many pertinent data on oral and anal sex, both heterosexual and homosexual, and on homosexuality generally. But it is full of sappy statements—or so at least they would seem to the justices—such as "oral-genital sex leads to better and happier relationships," and it pretends that homosexuals and their relationships are just like heterosexuals and their relationships.

The narrowness of legal learning is an old story but a true one, especially in regard to constitutional adjudication in general and adjudication under the Fourteenth Amendment in particular. The extraordinary heterogeneity of the practices challenged under the due process and equal protection clauses of the Fourteenth Amendment has prevented constitutional lawyers, and judges preoccupied with constitutional issues, from attaining the necessary specialized knowledge of the subjects regulated, which is a different thing from specialization in legal categories. A specialist in the Fourteenth Amendment is expected to know a lot of judicial opinions and legal doctrinal niceties, but is neither expected nor likely to know much about the history, nature, and practice of sexual regulation.[55] It is not helpful, in this regard, that sex remains a taboo subject in our society.

The less that lawyers know about a subject, the less that judges will know; and the less that judges know, the more likely they are to vote their prejudices. Their decision making will then resemble political decision making, although, because the Supreme Court represents a much smaller sample of political opinion than a legislature, we can expect more variance between the Court's views and those of the community at large than between the legislatures' views and those of the community.

Once liberalism had loosened its grip on the thought of educated Americans, homosexuality, never popular,[56] was unlikely to enlist much judicial sympathy, especially since few conservatives even of libertarian bent were arguing the parity of economic and sexual liberty. The changes in the membership of the Court since *Hardwick,* changes already reflected in the repudiation of *Roe v. Wade*'s rationale and in the curtailment of the abortion rights conferred by

55. Of thirty-three works of legal scholarship commenting on the Supreme Court's decision in *Bowers v. Hardwick,* cited in Earl M. Maltz, "The Prospects for a Revival of Conservative Activism in Constitutional Jurisprudence," 24 *Georgia Law Review* 629, 645 n. 95 (1990), as merely illustrative of the vast outpouring of legal commentary on the decision, only a handful, such as the *Whittier Law Review* and *Yale Law Journal* comments cited in notes 40 and 49 above, go beyond legal-doctrinal analysis. For exceptions to my generalization about judges' knowledge, see Gay Rights Coalition v. Georgetown University, 536 A.2d 1 (D.C. Ct. App. 1987), and Jantz v. Muci, 759 F. Supp. 1543 (D. Kan. 1991).

56. The Gallup Poll reported that in 1985, 47 percent of those polled thought homosexual relations between consenting adults should not be legal, up from 39 percent in 1982—the difference presumably reflecting awareness of the AIDS epidemic. The percentage who thought that homosexual relations should be legal fell in the same period from 45 to 44 percent. Gallup Report nos. 244–245, January–February 1986, 3. The Supreme Court's decision in *Bowers v. Hardwick* was approved by 51 percent of the respondents, while 41 percent disapproved. Gallup Report no. 254, November 1966, 26. Yet between 1986 and 1989, the percentage of Gallup Poll respondents who believed that homosexual relations between consenting adults should be illegal fell from 54 to 36 percent, and the percentage thinking they should be legal rose from 33 to 47 percent. Gallup Report no. 289, October 1989, 13. This result casts doubt on the proposition—central to the jurisprudence of Alexander Bickel—that a decision by the Supreme Court upholding the constitutionality of a statute operates to legitimize the policy embodied in the statute in the public's eye. Alexander M. Bickel, *The Least Dangerous Branch* (1962).

Roe, Planned Parenthood v. Danforth, and other decisions rendered in the wake of *Roe,*[57] suggest that it will be many years before the Supreme Court again takes up the cudgels on behalf of sexual liberty. Even liberal judges may hesitate to reenter this thicket, where ignorance of subject matter and lack of guidance in the constitutional text throw judges back on their own resources to an extent with which few prudent judges of any ideological hue can feel comfortable.

Bowers v. Hardwick left open, though, the question whether Georgia's sodomy law might be vulnerable to attack under the equal protection clause. There are three possible angles. The first is to argue that there is no rational basis for treating homosexuals and heterosexuals differently, whether generally or in particular settings such as that of military service. The second, a variant of the first, which persuaded a panel of the Ninth Circuit in a subsequently vacated opinion,[58] is to argue that to discriminate (as do our armed forces, for example)[59] against persons on the basis of their sexual *preference,* as distinct from their sexual acts, is particularly suspect because sexual preference is a largely immutable characteristic and therefore analogous to sex and race, which under the jurisprudence of equal protection are—race especially—highly disfavored grounds for discrimination. This argument collapses into the first. The use of preference rather than acts as the criterion for exclusion is an essential administrative convenience. It is so difficult to prove commission of a particular sexual act that a rule forbidding the armed services to enlist a soldier who flaunted his homosexuality merely because it could not prove that he had actually engaged in a homosexual act would gut the services' policy of excluding (active) homosexuals.

So we must consider whether it is invidious to discriminate against homosexuals. There are powerful arguments that it is, and one can imagine an extreme case in which they would persuade the Supreme Court. Suppose a public university refused as a matter of policy to hire homosexuals to teach in its law school, on the ground that they might corrupt the law students. Such a rule would be too irrational to stand. But having upheld state sodomy laws against a "sexual privacy" challenge (nominally under the due process clause) in *Bowers v. Hardwick,* the Supreme Court would hardly turn around

57. Of particular note in this regard is Webster v. Reproductive Health Service, Inc., 492 U.S. 490 (1989).

58. Watkins v. United States Army, 847 F.2d 1329 (9th Cir. 1988), discussed in Cass R. Sunstein, "Sexual Orientation and the Constitution: A Note on the Relationship between Due Process and Equal Protection," 55 *University of Chicago Law Review* 1161 (1988). Having vacated the panel's opinion, the full court decided the case for Watkins on a technical ground unrelated to the issue of equal protection. Watkins v. United States Army, 875 F.2d 699 (9th Cir. 1989) (en banc).

59. Watkins v. United States Army, 847 F.2d 1329, 1337–39 (9th Cir. 1988).

and strike them down in the name of equal protection, or order the armed services to allow homosexuals to enlist or states to recognize homosexual marriage. The Court is not so enamored of doctrinal niceties. (That is why, if *Roe v. Wade* is overruled, it will not be resuscitated by an equal protection analysis, however cogent.) It has made its lack of sympathy for the claims of homosexuals plain enough.

The third approach begins with the notion that the sodomy laws, whether implicitly or explicitly, whether as interpreted or as enforced, treat heterosexual and homosexual sodomy differently. This is a historical novelty. In the Christian tradition that informs our regulations of sexual behavior, anal intercourse and fellatio are unnatural acts whether homosexual or heterosexual. We might compare two men, each with a strong preference for anal intercourse. One is drawn to the female anus, the other to the male. The male and female anus are, I assume, indistinguishable from a biological standpoint. But the male whose preference is for the male anus is forbidden to serve in the armed forces, and if he gives way to his preference, he is guilty of the crime of sodomy. What sense does this legal distinction make?

It makes the following sense. Consensual sex in whatever form is as we know a method of cementing a relationship. Anal intercourse between a heterosexual couple, whether it is practiced for contraceptive reasons or, more commonly today, to enhance sexual pleasure either by introducing variety or by catering to the special taste of either partner, cements the couple's relationship. Anal intercourse between a homosexual couple likewise cements a homosexual relationship. But the Supreme Court has made clear that it shares the dominant American preference for heterosexual relationships. Its decisions furthering access to contraception and abortion can be seen as protecting and fostering those relationships by reducing their cost. The Court does not want to facilitate the cementing of homosexual relationships, so it cannot be expected to view with sympathy the claim that anal intercourse is more important to homosexual relationships than to heterosexual ones because male homosexuals cannot have vaginal intercourse with each other.

So while it is true historically—and further undermines the historical analysis in *Bowers v. Hardwick*—that the disgust that homosexuality arouses is partly a reflection of disgust at particular acts whether committed by homosexuals or heterosexuals, it is also true that the modern antipathy to homosexuality is primarily an antipathy to homosexual preference. It is, I conjecture, the fact that some men lust after other men, rather than the form in which that lust is expressed, that in the minds of a majority of the justices of the Supreme Court marks homosexuality as being profoundly different from heterosexuality. It is so different that the equal protection clause must allow the states and the federal government a broad scope for treating the two sexual orientations differently even when expressed in physically similar acts.

THE SUPREME COURT has not succeeded in formulating a coherent body of constitutional doctrine to decide issues of sexual autonomy. That is the negative lesson of this chapter. There is also an affirmative lesson, although it should not be applied dogmatically. The theoretical and empirical materials presented in this and previous chapters could provide a persuasive though far from airtight argument for the results in *Griswold v. Connecticut, Eisenstadt v. Baird, Carey v. Population Services International,* and *Roe v. Wade,* and against the result in *Bowers v. Hardwick,* provided—an essential qualification—that the argument was addressed to judges having two particular attitudes or bents. One is an inclination to approach questions of policy in a secular spirit, receptive to utilitarian, pragmatic, and scientific arguments. The other is a willingness to invalidate state or federal laws on constitutional grounds without insisting that the invalidation be firmly grounded in the text of the Constitution. Judges who do not share these attitudes will be inclined to reject the very idea of a constitutional right of sexual autonomy, or at the very least to refuse to extend it beyond the existing precedents, narrowly interpreted.

Erotic Art, Pornography, and Nudity

THE IMMENSE yet strangely lifeless scholarly literature on pornography, and on erotic presentations generally, is preoccupied with two matters: the social consequences of the obscene and the line between it and the nonobscene. Largely ignored is a host of fascinating questions that I seek in this chapter to bring to the fore. These questions involve the uses of pornography and of other erotica; the causes of pornography (in other words, the factors affecting the demand for and supply of it); whether that demand is greater or less in a sexually repressive society than in a sexually permissive one; the social origins and functions of the concept of obscenity; the relationship between that concept and attitudes toward nudity; and why pornography appears to be growing ever more violent and disgusting. They are positive rather than normative questions, in contrast to questions about the consequences and the definition of the obscene, which are questions asked by people who want to regulate, or deregulate, erotic representations. But I shall discuss those questions also.

The Economy of Erotic Representation

Terminology and Goals

The terms *erotic, pornographic,* and *obscene* overlap in confusing ways. I use *erotic* to describe presentations and representations that are, or at least are taken by some viewers to be, in some sense "about" sexual activity. (The distinction between presentation and representation is essentially between a live performance, broadly defined to include a naked person taking a stroll in a nudist camp, and the use of words or pictures to depict or evoke such a performance. I shall sometimes use *representation* to mean both presentations and representations.) By *pornographic* I denote the subset of erotic presentations and representations that by virtue of their frankness or other offensive or disturbing properties shock or embarrass many people. *Obscene* I use to denote the subset of pornographic works that the law seeks to suppress.

My definitions of pornographic and obscene are a selection from a number of meanings in vogue today. Robert Thompson, for example, offers these definitions: *pornographic*—intended to arouse sexually; *obscene*—intended to shock or disgust; *bawdy*—intended to amuse; *erotic*—intended to arouse feelings of love or affection.[1] *Pornographic* is especially rich in meanings. In addition to the sense in which I am using it, it is used to mean erotic, obscene, intended to stimulate and (or) to slake sexual appetite, sexually explicit, and intended to degrade women—the last being the meaning that feminists want to impose on the word. *Obscene* is a portmanteau word of strong disapproval, and thus it is not misused in such sentences, unrelated to sex, as, "The Holocaust was obscene," or "The electric chair is obscene."

The general category, then, is erotic representation, and a useful place to begin is by asking, as I did in Chapter 5 with respect to sexual activity itself, what goals such representation might serve. Once again the analogy of eating is helpful. It helps us see, for example, that one function of erotic representation is metaphoric, figurative, or formal. Just as those famous apples and pears in Cézanne's still lifes seem not to be "about" fruit in a deep sense (in contrast to Dutch genre still lifes of fruit and other food), a fair amount of erotic art seems not to be about sex in a deep sense. I am thinking, for instance, of the sexual episodes in T. S. Eliot's poem *The Waste Land*—the child seduction ("Marie"), the impotence scene ("the hyacinth girl"), the abortion dialogue, the canoe seduction, the rape of Philomela, the clerk's seduction of the typist, the homosexual solicitation ("Mr. Eugenides"). These are metaphors for the decay and desiccation of modern society (in the typist scene, for example, the presence of Tiresias, a figure from Greek legend, reminds us how far we have come from the great mythological seductions), rather than erotic evocations of sexual activity. Likewise the depictions by the contemporary artist Eric Fischl of masturbation, bestiality, and squalid intercourse.[2] Perhaps even a photograph by Robert Mapplethorpe, which most viewers would think pornographic, in which a man is shown performing cunnilingus on a woman clad only in a corset and stockings.[3] The photograph is taken from a point directly above the woman's head, and the couple is so

---

1. *Unfit for Modest Ears: A Study of Pornographic, Obscene and Bawdy Works Written or Published in England in the Second Half of the Seventeenth Century* ix–x (1979). A category of offensiveness that, though nonsexual, is to many people continuous with the sexually obscene is the scatological, illustrated by Andres Serrano's prizewinning work *Piss Christ*, a photograph of a plastic crucifix immersed in a bottle of the artist's urine. See my article "Art for Law's Sake," 58 *American Scholar* 513 (1989). I do not discuss scatological works in this book.

2. Arthur C. Danto, "Eric Fischl," in Danto, *Encounters & Reflections: Art in the Historical Present* 25 (1990).

3. Robert Marshall, *Robert Mapplethorpe*, pl. 107 (1988) (*Marty and Veronica*).

carefully posed that it seems that if the picture were folded in half, the halves would be identical. The geometrical impression that the picture conveys is reinforced by the sphericality of the woman's breasts and by the contrast between their whiteness and smoothness on the one hand and the blackness and texture of the corset on the other. (It is a black and white photo.) The formal properties dominate the erotic; it is as if body parts were being used to create an abstract painting. Thompson's category of the bawdy belongs here, among what I am calling the formal or figurative uses of sexual imagery, because sex used for the ulterior motive of humor is de-eroticized.

The next function of erotic representations is the informational. A recipe, which is not a representation but an algorithm, is one way of conveying information about cooking. Another way is a picture, whether verbal or pictorial: this is what your honey-glazed Cornish game hen should look like if you follow my recipe carefully. Particularly because sex is a private matter in our society, there is a demand for information about it which is met in part by erotic representations that convey information about the variety of naked bodies, the different shapes and dimensions of sexual organs, the different positions in which sexual intercourse can be performed and the different sexual practices themselves, even the gestures and expressions that accompany or are produced by, or that interpret, sexual activity.

Besides merely informing, erotic representations, like other representations, can—not always but sometimes—strengthen, undermine, or change the viewer's thinking—even, perhaps, his values and ultimately, perhaps, his behavior as well—or at least seek, or seem, to do these things.[4] Information can produce such changes too, but my present concern is with persuasion that works emotively rather than through the patient accretion of facts. *The Waste Land* does not convey significant information about sex, but it does make sex seem disgusting, though I have suggested that this was only an intermediate aim; Eliot had other fish to fry. Jean-Paul Sartre's story "The Childhood of a Leader" disparages homosexuality, but again in the metaphoric, nondiscursive fashion of art and literature. Bergère, the seducer, is a surrealist whose objets d'art include a lifelike sculpture of a turd. Lucien, the young man whom Bergère seduces, pees in the washbasin of their hotel room while getting ready for bed. By the piling on of such details Sartre associates homosexuality with disorder, the unnatural, and the unclean. By contrast, Mapplethorpe's photographs of "leather-clad gays" are not "really in the spirit of documentation . . . They are, rather, celebratory of their subjects, acts of artistic will driven

---

4. We owe to the ordinary-language school of philosophers, and particularly J. L. Austin, the insight that language, including nonverbal languages such as art, performs other functions besides communicating information—such functions as commitment, command, persuasion, and incitement. The formal, or one might say aesthetic, dimension of erotic representation is communicative, but not informational in any clear sense.

by moral beliefs and attitudes. He was a participant and a believer . . . We see [the subject of one of the photos, 'Mr. 10½'] from within a homosexual perception, and it is that perception, that vision, that is the true subject of these works."[5] Feminists worry about the impact on men of erotica that depicts women as enjoying, even craving, the experience of being raped or otherwise sexually degraded. The idea that erotic art criticizes, subverts, polemicizes, celebrates, or degrades is, we shall see, common ground between its most vigorous critics and its most vigorous defenders, illustrating again that puzzling merger of Left and Right noted in previous chapters.

One of the performative functions of erotic representations requires separate discussion. That is the stimulation—and sometimes also the slaking—of sexual desire. The food analogy would be a mouth-watering picture of a food product in an advertisement by the producer. (The analogy is to the stimulation of sexual desire, not to its slaking by masturbation.) Some erotic representations merely remind the viewer of sex—get him thinking about it. Others incite a diffuse desire for sex. Others induce an erection and a desire to ejaculate, and those that do this also make masturbation a more pleasurable response than it would otherwise be, by helping the masturbator form a more vivid fantasy image of sexual intercourse and thus making masturbation a closer substitute for intercourse.

To discuss the aphrodisiacal function of erotica in terms of only the male consumer, as I have just done, is deliberate. We recall from Chapter 4 that men are far more avid consumers of pornography than women. This difference makes sense in terms of two biological points discussed in that chapter: the stronger sex drive of men compared to women and the greater importance to men of visual cues to sexual receptivity. But there is a pitfall in the analysis, and that is to construct the category of the pornographic from a male standpoint. Because the sight of female sexual organs, and of people engaged in sexual intercourse, is highly arousing to many men, men—who until recently controlled not only the production of but also the discourse on pornography—regard the description or pictorialization of these sights as the core of pornography. But from a woman's standpoint a more diffuse, less readily visualizable description of erotic activity, perhaps with components of love or affection or promise of a permanent relationship that would (as we shall see) actually reduce the aphrodisiacal effect of the description on men, might be more arousing than a graphic representation of male sexual organs or of sexual intercourse. Much of what men dismissively describe as "romantic" literature aimed at women may have the same effect on women that hardcore pornography has on men.[6] With this correction, it is possible that wom-

---

5. Arthur C. Danto, "Robert Mapplethorpe," in Danto, note 2 above, at 211, 213.

6. Ann Barr Snitow, "Mass Market Romance: Pornography for Women Is Different," in

en's demand for pornography is less than men's only to the degree that women's sexual drive is less than men's.

Last among the functions of erotic representations is the magical, illustrated by fertility dances.[7] Until very recently sex was essential, or at least very important, to the survival of families, nations, and other human communities,[8] so there was a natural desire to propitiate whatever gods might control procreation and therefore sex.

Armed with these distinctions among the functions of erotica—what I shall call its formal, informational, ideological, aphrodisiacal, and magical functions—we can begin to understand the history, causes, and varieties of, and the controversies over, erotic representation.[9]

The History of Erotic, and Pornographic, Representation

The earliest erotica seems, as one would expect, to have served primarily magical functions. But by the time of the Greeks and the Romans, the emphasis had shifted to the polemical and aphrodisiacal. I am looking at a photograph of a fairly typical erotic Greek vase painting (fifth century B.C.), depicting an orgy.[10] There are six naked men and two naked women, all shown in profile. At the far left is a man holding his penis—probably masturbating. At the far right stand two men, both with erections; one is holding his penis with one hand and poking his anus with the other. In the center of the picture is a man with a huge erect penis; it would be about eighteen inches long if the man were drawn life-sized. He is flanked by two couples, both engaged in sodomy,

---

Passion and Power: Sexuality in History 259 (Kathy Peiss and Christina Simmons eds. 1989). This is Thompson's category (different from mine) of the "erotic" (note 1 above).

7. Curt Sachs, *World History of the Dance* 85–104 (1937), describes ancient fertility dances that modern people would consider sexually graphic. The pervasiveness of sexual themes in dancing—whether fertility dances, ballroom dancing, or ballet dancing—is emphasized in Judith Lynne Hanna, *Dance, Sex and Gender: Signs of Identity, Dominance, Defiance, and Desire* (1988), esp. chs. 3, 7–8.

8. Important but not essential because families could in principle survive through adoption, nations through conquest and immigration, other human communities through recruitment.

9. For helpful description, discussion, and illustrations, see Thompson, note 1 above; Peter Webb, *The Erotic Arts* (rev. ed. 1983); Peter Wagner, *Eros Revived: Erotica of the Enlightenment in England and America* (1988); Peter Michelson, *The Aesthetics of Pornography* (1971); Phyllis and Eberhard Kronhausen, *The Complete Book of Erotic Art* (1978); Poul Gerhard, *Pornography in Fine Art from Ancient Times to the Present* (1969); Morse Peckham, *Art and Pornography: An Experiment in Explanation* (1969); Walter Kendrick, *The Secret Museum: Pornography in Modern Culture* (1987); David Foxon, *Libertine Literature in England 1660–1745* (1965); and two books by Charles I. Glicksberg: *The Sexual Revolution in Modern American Literature* (1971), and *The Sexual Revolution in Modern English Literature* (1973).

10. It is plate B51, following p. 118 in K. J. Dover, *Greek Homosexuality* (rev. ed. 1989).

the penises being partly visible. The depictions, though graphic and instantly recognizable, are not highly realistic, even if the grotesque length of the central figure's penis is disregarded. There is little illusion of depth, the draftsmanship is sketchy and seems rushed, and, but for the subject matter, the painting would strike an unsophisticated modern viewer who measures painting by its closeness to photography as the work of a child.

As we would expect, given the Greek attitude toward sex, the figures in the painting are depicted as enjoying their orgy, and there is no hint of censure on the part of the painter. On the contrary, the orgy is presented in a positive light, as a delightful experience, like a feast or a drinking party. Given the general openness of the ancient Greeks in matters of sex and the lack of realistic detail in the painting, it seems unlikely that it is intended to serve a primarily informational function; it seems, rather, to be celebratory (hence ideological in my nomenclature), aphrodisiacal, and even formal. The last suggestion may seem implausible. But consider: in a society in which sex is a morally indifferent subject, or nearly so, an orgy is likely to appeal to the artist for its formal properties, which it shares with a dance or a feast. It is likely to be perceived as a lively, convivial occasion marked by rhythmic motion, repetitive motifs, symmetry (recall the sodomizing couples that flank the central figure). The penises in the painting have among other functions a decorative one, like arabesques.

Recalling the definition of pornography as erotica that offends, I find it difficult to imagine that the category even existed in ancient Greece; likewise the form of the ʋbscene that is offensive merely because of its frankness. Of course there are practices related to sex that shocked the Greeks so deeply as to be obscene. An example is the lopping off, rumored to have been done by Alcibiades, of the phalluses on the statues of Hermes that stood outside every respectable home in ancient Athens. Alcibiades' offense was not excessive candor. On the contrary, most of us would consider the statues less obscene after the mutilation. Unless sex is a subject charged with moral significance, its depiction is unlikely to shock or embarrass anybody, let alone to call for public regulation, any more than a picture of my greedily devouring a turkey breast would shock you or incite a clamor for public regulation.

I do not want to exaggerate the sexual amorality of the Greeks. We recall their disapproval of lesbianism and their sequestration of respectable women (Chapter 5); and despite the warmth of the Mediterranean climate in summertime, Greek men and women did not go about naked or have sex in public.[11] Odysseus is careful to cover himself when, having been washed ashore at Scheria naked, he encounters Nausicaa. (Homer, however, depicts

---

11. L. P. Wilkinson, "Classical Approaches—III. Nudism in Deed & Word," 50 *Encounter* 18 (August 1978); K. J. Dover, *Greek Popular Morality in the Time of Plato and Aristotle* 205–216 (1974).

a society less libertine than that of Athens in the fifth and fourth centuries B.C.) But by Christian standards, especially those of the early Church, the Greeks were exceedingly casual about nudity and the erotic.[12] That Greek men exercised, wrestled, and engaged in public athletic competitions in the nude (the Olympic Games, for example) is the least of the difference. More important are the nude statuary of young men; the cult of the beautiful naked body that it expressed; the veneration of Priapus, god of the phallus, and of Aphrodite, the goddess of sexual love (illustrating the magical function of erotica); the public performances by nude dancers and nude actresses; the bawdy themes and language in the plays of Aristophanes; the symposia (drinking parties) at which revelers engaged in orgies with flute girls; and of course the erotic vase paintings.[13]

All this changed with the coming of Christianity. Nudity became taboo; sexual desire was disparaged, and with it efforts either to stimulate it or to satisfy it through masturbation. The sexual ideology of the Church left no room for erotic representations, and the poverty and illiteracy of the Middle Ages would have limited the production and dissemination of erotic art and literature in the best of circumstances, although there are some famous examples of bawdy medieval literature and a smattering of erotic pictorial art as well, some of it quite explicit.[14]

We must consider whether the decline of erotic representation in the Christian era was, like so many other changes in sexual custom discussed in this book, related to and perhaps even caused by the changing status of women. It is possible. In the Christian view, woman as well as man had been created in the image of the one God, a God who does not express himself sexually. For a woman to appear in public in the nude, exhibiting herself as a sexual object—even to be shown nude in a painting—was to demean her human

12. *Official* Christian standards, that is; for in fact medieval people were quite casual about appearing nude in public, for example en route to the public bath. Norbert Elias, *The History of Manners*, vol. 1, *The Civilizing Process* 164 (1978).

13. Wilkinson, note 11 above, at 23; Vern L. Bullough, *The History of Prostitution* 35 (1964); Fernando Henriques, *Stews and Strumpets: A Survey of Prostitution*, vol. 1, *Primitive, Classical and Oriental*, ch. 2 (1961). On parallel behaviors in the Roman and early Byzantine period, see Henriques, ch. 3, esp. 101–103; Peter Brown, *The Body and Society: Men, Women and Sexual Renunciation in Early Christianity* 315–317 (1988); Carlo Maria Franzero, *The Life and Times of Theodora* 14–15 (1961). The Theodora of the title is the wife of the Byzantine emperor Justinian. The tales about her, which derive from Procopius' scandalous *Secret History*, must be taken with a grain of salt, but there seems little doubt that she was a prostitute and erotic performer—perhaps even a striptease dancer. Even more casual attitudes toward public nudity are found, of course, in many primitive cultures. For a striking example, see T. O. Beidelman, "Some Nuer Notions of Nakedness, Nudity, and Sexuality," 38 *Africa: Journal of the International African Institute* 113 (1968).

14. Webb, note 9 above, at 105–107.

dignity.[15] A form of artistic representation calculated to stimulate, often to celebrate, and at the very least to remind of male sexual desire could, moreover, undermine companionate marriage by causing men to seek sexual pleasure outside the marriage bed. It is true that despite the Church's fulminations against masturbation, the Church Fathers must have known that it posed few dangers to marriage. But they would not have assumed that sexual desires stimulated by erotic representations would always be slaked so harmlessly; and they regarded masturbation as sinful quite apart from any effect it might have on marriage. Moreover, even if pornography did not incite to any sexual act, its existence, like that of homosexuality, was an affront to companionate marriage because it presupposed a sexual interest unrelated to a companionate relationship with a person conceived of as somehow unique. "The obscene discounted itself owing to the fact that it occluded an interest in the person, or more precisely, owing to the exchangeability of the persons involved."[16]

These are only conjectures, and conjectures that, as it happens, cast little light on the revival of erotic art in the Renaissance. Suddenly the depiction of nude women in the guise of the personae of Greek sexual myths, such as Aphrodite, Europa, Daphne, and Danae, became respectable. Sexual intercourse was not depicted, nor (other than in statuary) male genitalia. But not only are voluptuous young women portrayed in a state of near, and sometimes complete, nudity; many paintings unmistakably allude to sexual intercourse. Consider Titian's *Rape of Europa*,[17] in the Gardner Museum in Boston—one of those mythological couplings to which T. S. Eliot may have been alluding in *The Waste Land*. Scantily clad and in a state of considerable dishevelment, Europa is shown being borne away on the back of a bull. If you know the legend, you know that Zeus changed himself into a bull, abducted Europa, and raped her. In Titian's *Venus with a Mirror*,[18] in the National Gallery in Washington, Venus, naked from the navel up, is prettying herself in front of a mirror, attended by two cherubs, one of whom is Cupid—that is, Eros

---

15. Much later, dance halls were to be shut down on this ground. Gayle Gullett, "City Mothers, City Daughters, and the Dance Hall Girls: The Limits of Female Political Power in San Francisco, 1913," in *Women and the Structure of Society: Selected Research from the Fifth Berkshire Conference on the History of Women* 149 (Barbara J. Harris and JoAnn K. McNamara eds. 1984).

16. Niklas Luhmann, *Love as Passion: The Codification of Intimacy* 119 (1986). The same point is made in Ernest van den Haag, "Pornography and Censorship," 13 *Policy Review* 73, 79–80 (Summer 1980).

17. Harold E. Wethey, *The Paintings of Titian: Complete Edition*, vol. 3, *The Mythological and Historical Paintings*, pl. 141 (1975).

18. Also known as *Venus at Her Toilet with Two Cupids*. Id., pl. 127; also color plate before p. 57. Another great painting in this series is *Danaï with Cupid*, id., pl. 181, showing Danae about to be raped by Zeus. And in *Venus and Dog with an Organist*, id., pl. 127, Venus is shown completely nude except for bracelets and a necklace.

himself. (We know because his quiver is at his feet.) The viewer is left with no doubt about what she is getting ready for.

It is as if the newly restored prestige of classical antiquity licensed Renaissance artists to celebrate in their art the sexual mores of antiquity. And so we find many Renaissance paintings and sculptures depicting with apparent approval not only Zeus' rapes of women but also his homosexual rape of Ganymede.[19]

Renaissance depictions of Greek erotic mythology are rich in color, movement, and design; they thus are erotic representations that serve formal, as well as celebratory and aphrodisiacal, functions. Aphrodisiacal? Renaissance nudes are tame stuff by modern standards; I shall consider why shortly. But sexual explicitness in art or literature is not an absolute. It is relative to the expectations created by contemporary social norms. In a society in which people walk about in the nude, the fact of being nude—as nudists tirelessly remind us—is not a signal of erotic intentions.[20] In such a society a painting of a nude woman is not an erotic representation; that is, it is not perceived as being about sex. But in a society such as that of the Renaissance in which women are expected to be fully dressed except on the most intimate occasions, the depiction of even a partially nude woman will be perceived as erotic with only the slightest additional signals (and perhaps even they are unnecessary), such as the Cupid in *Venus with a Mirror*.[21] Given the different mores of ancient Greece and Renaissance Italy, those Botticelli and Giorgione and Titian nudes may have carried as much erotic charge as the Greek vase painting I described, and more than the bare-breasted, but not erotically engaged, Venus de Milo. If this analysis is correct, it would be philistine to deny the label "art" to paintings and other representations that have erotic as well as formal intentions.

Another reason we are apt to underestimate the erotic charge of Renaissance art is that, rather surprisingly from a sociobiological standpoint, the erotic ideal has changed since the Renaissance. "In the erotic imagination of Europe,

19. James M. Saslow, *Ganymede in the Renaissance: Homosexuality in Art and Society* (1986).

20. Howard C. Warren, "Social Nudism and the Body Taboo," in William Hartman, Marilyn Fithian, and Donald Johnson, *Nudist Society: An Authoritative, Complete Study of Nudism in America* 340, 353 (1970). This book is the best work I know on the nudist movement, the spirit of which is nicely captured in a remark of Bertrand Russell's: "[If public nudity in sunshine and water were allowed] our standards of beauty would more nearly coincide with standards of health, since they would concern themselves with the body and its carriage, not only with the face. In this respect the practice of the Greeks was to be commended." *Marriage and Morals* 117 (1929). Mention of the Greeks, and the larger context of Russell's remark—a book on sex—rather undermines the nudist claim that nudism has *nothing* to do with the erotic.

21. For parallel examples from the seventeenth century, see Thompson, note 1 above, at 183–187. One is "rope dancing." Women danced on rope nets raised above the stage to give the audience a glimpse of naked thighs.

it was apparently impossible until the late seventeenth century for a woman to have too big a belly . . . The breasts of all the famous Renaissance and Baroque nudes in art, however fleshy the rest of the body might be, are delicate and minimal. Heavy breasts are shown to be characteristic of ugly old women and witches . . . Heavy bellies, on the other hand, were worn by the tenderest virgins or the most seductive courtesans, whether in the austere works of the Gothic North or in the lushest productions of Venice."[22]

Perhaps, then, Margaret Miles is right that the nude in art has been, throughout the history of art, simply a naked woman as an object of male sexual desire.[23] Miles rejects the view famously articulated by Kenneth Clark in *The Nude: A Study in Ideal Art* (1956) that the art nude sublimates or transcends the erotic. The nudes that Clark criticizes for aesthetic deficiencies are precisely those that lack the proportions that men find sexually attractive. Clark's ideal in artistic nudity is ultimately an erotic ideal. The grittily realistic portrayal of naked women would be de-eroticizing. By emphasizing the erotic component in nude art, Miles demonstrates the continuity between the erotic and the pornographic.

This is not to say that erotica and pornography are the same thing. In fact, norms of modest dress and deportment created in the Renaissance, and afterward, a space—which seems not to have existed in Greek culture—for pornography as a distinct category of expression, consisting of erotic art that is so sexually explicit by contemporary standards that it shocks many people, with the result that it cannot be exhibited in public. Raphael—ironically enough, given the purity of his religious paintings—kicked off a long, semi-secret tradition of pornographic art by famous artists, among them Carracci, Rembrandt, Watteau, Boucher, Greuze, Turner, Courbet, Rodin, Beardsley, Picasso, Klimt, Schiele, Grosz, Delvaux, Balthus, and Oldenburg.[24] The pornographic art of these distinguished artists is not inferior aesthetically to the average of their other work. (I shall give an example later.) This underscores the continuity between the erotic and the pornographic.

One might have expected the nineteenth century to be a period of rapid growth for erotic representation. (Perhaps it was; there are no statistics on the sale of pornography in the nineteenth century.) The spread of literacy to the lower classes, and the invention of photography, greatly reduced the cost of erotic representation, especially when cost is adjusted for quality. Ordinarily

22. Anne Hollander, *Seeing Through Clothes* 98 (1978).

23. Margaret R. Miles, *Carnal Knowing: Female Nakedness and Religious Meaning in the Christian West* 14 (1989). See also Gill Saunders, *The Nude: A New Perspective* (1989). This was true, in the Renaissance, even of figures not taken from classical mythology, as Miles illustrates with a highly erotic Eve painted by Hans Baldung. Miles at 134–136 and fig. 22.

24. See the Webb, Gerhard, and Kronhausen books, note 9 above; also Wagner, note 9 above, ch. 8.

these developments would have brought about an expansion in output. And Victorian prudery must have created a demand for information about sex which erotic representations could in part, and no doubt did, fulfill. Cutting the other way, however, the Victorian fear of masturbation, coupled with the discovery that female sexual pleasure could safely be disparaged since conception did not require that the woman have an orgasm, increased the demand for censorship. This collision of interests drove erotic representation underground—though not entirely. Especially in France, and particularly in sculpture, the tradition of erotic nude representations persisted, for example in the sculpture of Aristide Maillol. Like their Renaissance forbears, respectable nineteenth-century artists used distance to deflect the censors—that is, they used mythical, legendary, or exotic personages and locales to disguise any implication that the artist was depicting the erotic behavior of his own society.[25]

An example of outright pornography from the period is *Cinesias Entreating Myrrhina to Coition*, by Aubrey Beardsley.[26] It is one of several illustrations that Beardsley did in 1896 for an English translation of *Lysistrata*, Aristophanes' comedy in which the Athenian and Spartan women try by means of a sex strike to persuade their men to end the Peloponnesian War. The translation with its illustrations was printed privately; a public printing would have invited prosecution. The picture shows Cinesias, desperate with desire, chasing his wife. He is depicted with an enormous erect penis—it is the length, and almost the thickness, of his torso—and its grotesque size, in combination with the fact that Cinesias is otherwise dressed (which further draws attention to his penis), is an effective symbol of the severity of the sexual deprivation caused by the strike. The penis and testicles are drawn with anatomical accuracy, sprouting from a bed of pubic hair. Cinesias' outstretched arm is clutching Myrrhina's robe and pulling it free, allowing us to see that underneath her robe she is clad only in a pair of fancy black stockings, which merely draw our eye toward her carefully depicted pubic area.

The drawing resembles the Greek vase painting that I discussed because it is done in outline form with little illusion of depth. But it is more detailed and, except for the disproportionate size of Cinesias' sexual organs (although the size of penises is frequently exaggerated in the vase paintings as well), more realistic. The close resemblance between the vase painting and Beardsley's drawing underscores the relativity of pornography. As far as the degree of graphic depiction of sexual organs in a state of excitation is concerned, the two pictures are on a par, but only one was pornographic in the culture in which it was created.

25. Peter Gay, *Education of the Senses* 379–402 (1984) (vol. 1 of *The Bourgeois Experience: Victoria to Freud*); see also the illustrations between pp. 342 and 343 of Gay's book.
26. Simon Wilson, *Beardsley*, pl. 37 (rev. ed. 1983).

The twentieth century has seen an enormous expansion in the production and dissemination of pornography, particularly since the early 1970s. The reasons have to do with both demand and supply, but particularly the latter. On the demand side, the passing of the dread of masturbation and the spread of education and middle-class values may have increased the amount of masturbation (see Chapter 5) and therefore the demand for products that are complementary to masturbation, of which pornography is one;[27] but the falling age of sexual initiation would cut the other way. The continued taboo status of sex in our society could keep up the demand for information about sex that pornography satisfies in part; yet sex is more freely discussed today than it used to be, and there are more specialists and counselors in sexual dysfunction. The demand for information about sex was greater in the Victorian period than it is today, suggesting paradoxically that there might be a greater demand for pornography in a sexually repressive society than in a sexually permissive one.

The major developments affecting the output of pornography in this century have been on the supply rather than the demand side. The cost of pornography has fallen because of the falling away of efforts by law enforcers to suppress it, and the *quality-adjusted* cost has plummeted with the successive advent of fast film (enabling movement to be photographed), color film, motion pictures, television, color television, color television with stereophonic sound, big-screen color television with stereophonic sound, and, above all, home video recorders, which enable people to enjoy pornographic movies in the privacy of their home and even to make their own pornographic movies if they want. On the near horizon is holographic imagery that will enable television to create a much more realistic illusion of three-dimensionality.

It is technological progress, as well as the decline of the nudity taboo (a decline rooted in the waning, which I have attributed to changes in the occupational status of women, of traditional Christian sexual morality), that has made the erotic art of yesteryear come to seem so tame. From all but the formal and possibly the ideological standpoints, which are the least erotic aspects of erotic art, it simply is a poor substitute, like a Model T for a Lexus ES-250. We should therefore expect that any relaxation of the prohibitions against photographic pornography would lead to a reduction in sales of nonillustrated pornographic books. For evidence we turn to Denmark, where the repeal in 1969 of the legal prohibitions against pornographic photos (the

---

27. For example, at many striptease joints the first few rows in the audience are by tacit understanding reserved for spectators who masturbate as they watch the striptease. James K. Skipper, Jr., and Charles H. McCaghy, "Teasing, Flashing and Visual Sex: Stripping for a Living," in *The Sociology of Sex: An Introductory Reader* 171, 180–181 (James M. Henslin and Edward Sagarin eds., rev. ed. 1978).

prohibitions against printed pornography had been repealed two years earlier) destroyed the market for printed pornography.[28]

Striptease

The evolution of striptease dancing provides a vivid example of changing norms in erotic representation.[29] The origins of the striptease are shrouded in mystery. Contrary to popular impression, the Gospels do not describe the dance of Salomé as a striptease or indeed as any kind of erotic dance; the nature of her dance is left wholly unclear.[30] The "Dance of the Seven Veils" was apparently the invention of Oscar Wilde, whose play *Salomé* became in German translation the libretto for Richard Strauss's opera *Salome,* where the dance was first performed. Only recently has it been danced as a striptease, the veils being discarded one by one until, in a performance of *Salome* by the Lyric Opera of Chicago, Salome ends the dance naked (actually in a transparent body stocking). The dance performance in which female dancers display some naked flesh appears to have had its modern beginning in the cancan and music hall chorus line in the nineteenth century, which evolved into the decorous striptease of Broadway and Hollywood musicals such as *Damn Yankees,* in which the stripper strips down to the equivalent of a bathing suit, and finally into the striptease in which the stripper ends in the nude.

The key to understanding the striptease is the ambiguity, already mentioned, of nudity as a signal of intentions. For nudity to be an erotic signal, it must be associated with sex, so the norm of privacy in sexual relations entails the rejection of public nudity, and public nudity in turn implies a transgression of sexual norms.[31] There are of course degrees of nudity. The stronger the nudity taboo, in the sense of the more fully clad the body is expected to be, the smaller is the amount of nudity required to imply a sexual context and therefore to convey an erotic signal. When the nudity taboo was very strong in our society, the decorous striptease—even the bare thighs of the Radio City Music Hall Rockettes—conveyed a distinctly erotic image. Now that the taboo has greatly weakened, and many respectable women go about their everyday business in what would have been considered a state of nudity or the garb of prostitutes a couple of generations ago, a striptease that ended with the

28. Berl Kutschinsky, *Studies on Pornography and Sex Crimes in Denmark* 13 (1970).

29. See generally David F. Cheshire, "Eroticism in the Performing Arts," in Webb, note 9 above, at 297–306.

30. Matthew 14:6; Mark 6:22.

31. "The idea of obscenity tends to be attached to genital exhibitionism in a cultural milieu which demands the careful covering of the body and especially the genitals." John J. Honigmann, "A Cultural Theory of Obscenity," 5 *Journal of Criminal Psychopathology* 715, 733 (1944).

stripper clad in a bathing suit would not convey a strong erotic signal. For that, more is needed: complete nudity, or at least the exposure of the sexual organs.

This analysis should help us understand why so much contemporary pornography is violent, filthy, and grotesque.[32] The more permissive a society's sexual attitudes, the freer its erotic representations, and the weaker its nudity taboo, the more the demand for pornography will shift (not entirely, of course) toward aspects of sexual depiction that remain tabooed. There is a parallel in the shift in the services offered by prostitutes from "normal" to "kinky" sex, remarked in Chapter 5. We should not leap to the conclusion that because prostitution and pornography are becoming more vile, more sordid, sexual behavior on average is becoming more vile, more sordid.

But to return to the striptease, what is its specific erotic representation? Striptease is not, after all, just the exhibition of a naked woman. It is a form of undressing. It is undressing for sex—that, at least, is the impression that the performer seeks to convey by her gestures and facial expression. It is nudity plus an additional signal of erotic intention or disposition, much as *Venus with a Mirror* is nudity plus an additional signal supplied by the presence of Cupid. In both cases there is an implicit narrative which the viewer is left to complete in his imagination. That is why it is important that the striptease not end in a bathing suit, because a bathing suit is for swimming, not for sex. If the striptease performer is an accomplished dancer and the musical accompaniment is of high quality as well, the striptease may, like a work of art, embody formal properties that have an appeal to the nonerotic sensibility—may *be* a work of art. But the erotic signal that I have described imparts to striptease an unmistakably, and ordinarily a dominant, aphrodisiacal effect.

The example of striptease helps show why, even in a post-Christian society, pornography is apt to seem at least somewhat transgressive. Even to persons remote from traditional Catholic dubieties about sex, sex remains a private activity. Pornography, however, is public: it exhibits or implies engaging in sexual activity before strangers. It has impropriety built into it. It challenges society's sexual norms.

---

32. Anyone who doubts this characterization should read the descriptions in Franklin Mark Osanka and Sara Lee Johann, *Sourcebook on Pornography* 19–42 (1989). But it would be a mistake to suppose all, or even most, contemporary pornography to be of this character. Most, for example, is not violent. F. M. Christensen, *Pornography: The Other Side* 59–60 (1990). Actually, there appears to be less violence in X-rated movies (that is, hard-core pornography) than in movies generally. Ira L. Reiss, *Journey into Sexuality: An Exploratory Voyage* 174–175 (1986). And the vast majority of pornographic works depict nondeviant sex. Maurice Yaffé, "The Effects and Uses of Pornography: Recent Research Findings," in *Medical Sexology* 29, 31 (Romano Forleo and Willy Pasini eds. 1978).

The Bearing of the Status of Women

The spread of pornography in recent years has aroused the concern of radical feminists, and I shall address their concern shortly. Yet whatever the effects on women, the spread itself is positively correlated with the rise in the status of women in Western society.[33] Is this a coincidence? Perhaps not. Although the market for pornography has always been primarily a male one, the concerns about sexual activity that power the suppression of pornography are focused on women. Islam, for example, combines a powerful cult of female chastity with a rigorous suppression of erotic representation, the aim perhaps being to avoid imparting to the culture an erotic cast that would encourage increased association between men and women. And at the other extreme, Denmark, where women enjoy a higher status than almost anywhere else in the world, was the first modern Western country to stop trying to restrict the dissemination of pornography.

The hypothesis that female emancipation promotes a tolerant attitude toward pornography may seem undermined by the example of ancient Greece, where uninhibited erotic representation coexisted with the sequestration of respectable females and a misogynistic cultural tone.[34] There are differences among these examples, though. One is that while in Islam, as in Judaism and Christianity, all women are believed to partake of human dignity, which makes problematic their being depicted primarily as sexual objects, in the ideology of ancient Greece and Rome only women of the citizen class—and then only if they had been spared as infants—were considered worthy of any solicitude at all. The more fundamental point, however, which explains why pornography should be unproblematic when the status of women is either very low (ancient Greece) or very high (modern Denmark) but deeply problematic when it is intermediate, as in cultures dominated by the great monotheistic religions, is that only in these cultures is sex a morally charged subject. There cannot be a concept of the obscene, as I am using the term, in a society in which sex is a morally indifferent subject, like eating; erotic representations have no shock value in such a society.

When women's status is very low, prudery can, as we saw in Chapter 6,

---

33. A regression of the circulation of soft-core pornographic magazines (such as *Playboy*) by state of the United States on variables that include an index of the status of women reveals that circulation to be positively related to women's status. Larry Baron, "Pornography and Gender Equality: An Empirical Analysis," 27 *Journal of Sex Research* 363, 375 (1990). To similar effect, see Reiss, note 32 above, at 182–185. Yet the leading feminist crusader against pornography believes that *Playboy* not only is quintessentially pornographic but also is more harmful to women than hard-core pornography. Catharine A. MacKinnon, *Feminism Unmodified: Discourses on Life and Law,* ch. 12 (1987), esp. 269 n. 36.

34. Modern Japan is a somewhat parallel example, as we shall see.

raise that status; the suppression of pornography is then unequivocally to the benefit of women. When women's social status is very high—or would be if the prevailing standards of sexual morality were relaxed—prudery hurts women by restricting their educational and occupational opportunities. The decline of prudery, however, opens the way to graphic sexual representations, which feminists believe has a negative impact on women's status.

The Social Consequences of Pornography

We are ready to consider what I said at the outset were the commonest normative questions that are raised about erotic representation—the social effects of pornography and how to draw the line between permitted and forbidden erotic representation, the latter being the domain of the obscene, as I use the term. I shall end with a glance at the normative questions that arise when the focus of protection shifts from the audience for erotic works to the erotic performers themselves. The consequences that are thought to warrant public intervention to suppress offensive erotic representations are threefold.

Rape

The first and most concrete is that such representations are said to hurt women by inciting men to rape them. This is believed to be due to either the aphrodisiacal effect of pornography or, as feminists emphasize, the ideological effect. Pornography, insofar as it stimulates the male sexual appetite, increases the probability that the consumer will seek sexual gratification, and rape is one route to such gratification—but of course not the only one. Consensual sexual intercourse is another. And the most proximate route is masturbation, which pornography can make more pleasurable. The twin effects of pornography— inciting sexual desire and enabling that desire to be satisfied in solitude—need not be perfectly offsetting. But this means that by facilitating masturbation, pornography may actually reduce the demand for rape: the substitution effect of pornography (that is, its effect in causing the substitution of masturbation for intercourse) may dominate the complementarity effect (its effect in stimulating desire for intercourse, some of which is violent).

Pornography might still increase the demand for rape overall, however, by persuading the consumer that women like to be raped or that a woman's preferences are unworthy of consideration. In fact much, probably most, pornography, even that which eschews deviance and violence, conveys messages of this sort.[35] Since the pornography industry is neither monolithic nor,

35. Don D. Smith, "The Social Content of Pornography," 26 *Journal of Communication* 16

for the most part, owned or operated by ideologues, it may seem strange that it would produce an ideologically highly uniform product. The strangeness is dispelled when we consider the requisites of aphrodisiacal representations directed to a male audience. The audience is interested in sexual stimulation and pleasure in a fantasy setting; it is not interested in the emotional complications involved in obtaining these goods in a relationship with another human being, or in other aspects of gritty reality such as impotence, exhaustion, and homely physique. This is a point I noted in connection with the Renaissance nude. It may be a point central to erotic representation aimed at men. The male image desired in such representation is one of effortless mastery, and the female image desired is one of youth, beauty, adoration, compliance, subordination, and admiration of stereotypical male characteristics such as strength and aggressiveness. The lack of psychological and physical realism in pornography, its character of "pornotopia" (pornographic Utopia), has been repeatedly remarked.[36] It is, I am suggesting, a function of the aphrodisiacal aim of pornography, which, while not deliberately ideological, conveys as a byproduct of that aim a message that can be interpreted as condoning, even encouraging, rape.

Given these conflicting tugs, the question whether the net effect of pornography is to increase the incidence of rape, and if so significantly, is an empirical one. There are various types of evidence bearing on it, each with its own shortcomings.

In the first place, law enforcement officers, most of whom believe that pornography does increase the incidence of rape, are impressed by the fact that rapists appear to be avid consumers of pornography. But it is not at all clear that they are more avid in this respect than otherwise similar men who do not commit rapes, or if they are more avid that this is a cause of their

---

(1976). On the feminist critique of pornography, see MacKinnon, note 33 above, pt. 3; *Take Back the Night: Women on Pornography* (Laura Lederer ed. 1980); Andrea Dworkin, "Against the Male Flood: Censorship, Pornography, and Equality," 8 *Harvard Women's Law Journal* 1 (1985); K. K. Ruthven, *Feminist Literary Studies: An Introduction* 87–90 (1984). For criticism of that critique from a variety of standpoints, see Fred R. Berger, "Pornography, Feminism, and Censorship," in *Philosophy and Sex* 327 (Robert Baker and Frederick Elliston eds. 1984); Gordon Hawkins and Franklin E. Zimring, *Pornography in a Free Society*, ch. 6 (1988); Daphne Read, "(De)Constructing Pornography: Feminisms in Conflict," in *Passion and Power: Sexuality in History*, note 6 above, at 277; Robin West, "The Feminist-Conservative Anti-Pornography Alliance and the 1986 Attorney General's Commission on Pornography Report," 1987 *American Bar Foundation Research Journal* 681; Richard A. Posner, *Law and Literature: A Misunderstood Relation* 334–337 (1988).

36. See, for example, Smith, note 35 above, at 21–23; Michelson, note 9 above, at 29; Steven Marcus, *The Other Victorians: A Study of Sexuality and Pornography in Mid-Nineteenth Century England* (2d ed. 1974); Donald Symons, *The Evolution of Human Sexuality* 170, 177–178 (1979); Susan Griffin, *Pornography and Silence: Culture's Revenge against Nature* 36 (1981).

assaultive behavior rather than an effect of whatever circumstances lead them to engage in such behavior. If, as I have suggested in previous chapters, rapists typically are men who are unappealing to women and therefore face high costs in the market for consensual sex, it would not be surprising if they both committed rape and consumed pornography at a higher rate than other men, for both rape and masturbation are substitutes for consensual intercourse. Or if the typical rapist is hostile to women, it would not be surprising if he consumed pornography that conveyed an ideological message he found congenial. It would not follow that the pornography had created or even exacerbated his hostility. Furthermore, most rapists who are actually caught and punished are members of the criminal class, and they may have easier access to an illegal product.[37]

The second class of evidence consists of laboratory experiments on male college students to determine whether exposure to pornography of various sorts makes them feel more aggressive toward women or less respectful of women's preferences. Most of the studies conclude that *violent* pornography—but only violent pornography—does have the predicted effects.[38] But the effects may be due to the violence per se rather than to the erotic component.[39] And whether the reactions of college students in a laboratory setting can be extrapolated to criminal behavior is unknown—which is not to deny that some college students are rapists (especially "date rapists").

The remaining category of evidence, and the most promising, is comparative evidence. The comparisons can be across time in the same jurisdiction or across jurisdictions.

First, the advent of the video recorder has probably increased vastly the dissemination of high-quality pornography in the United States, so one might have expected the incidence of rape to have risen. But, as I noted in Chapter 1, it has fallen.

Second, the repeal by Denmark of its pornography law in the late 1960s

37. Paul H. Gebhard et al., *Sex Offenders: An Analysis of Types* 677 (1965). This point was more significant when most pornography was illegal.

38. Edward Donnerstein, Daniel Linz, and Steven Penrod, *The Question of Pornography: Research Findings and Policy Implications*, chs. 5–6 (1987); Linz, Donnerstein, and Penrod, "Sexual Violence in the Mass Media: Social Psychological Implications," in *Sex and Gender* 95 (Phillip Shaver and Clyde Hendrick eds. 1987); Attorney General's Commission on Pornography, *Final Report*, vol. 1, 322–351, 938–1035 (Department of Justice, July 1986) (the "Meese Report"); Letitia Anne Peplau and Constance L. Hammen, "Social Psychological Issues in Sexual Behavior: An Overview," 33 *Journal of Social Issues* 1 (1977). For carefully neutral reviews of the data, see Mary R. Murrin and D. R. Laws, "The Influence of Pornography on Sex Crimes," in *Handbook of Sexual Assault: Issues, Theories, and Treatment of the Offender* 73 (W. L. Marshall, D. R. Laws, and H. E. Barbaree eds. 1990) (this article contains, incidentally, an excellent bibliography); Hawkins and Zimring, note 35 above, ch. 4. See also Osanka and Johann, note 32 above, at 81–84.

39. Reiss, note 32 above, at 176–177.

has evoked some empirical scrutiny, beginning with Berl Kutschinsky's studies (see note 28). The repeal was followed by a sharp drop in sex crimes, but the question whether there was any causal relation—whether, that is, the substitution effect of pornography dominates the complementarity effect—has become mired in controversy.[40] As I noted in Chapter 7, the incidence of rape did not fall; it was the incidence of lesser sex crimes, for which pornography-assisted masturbation was more likely to be a close substitute, that fell. John Court argues that rape rates rose after and because pornography laws (in Denmark and elsewhere) were liberalized, but he does not correct for other potentially explanatory factors, such as the overall increase in crime rates.[41]

Third, a cross-state study by Larry Baron and Murray Straus finds a strong positive correlation between the circulation of soft-core pornographic magazines (the only kind for which circulation figures are available) and the incidence of rape. The correlation persists when certain sociological factors are introduced as additional explanatory variables; nevertheless, the authors doubt that the relationship is a causal one.[42] It also persists when economic rather than sociological data are used as explanatory variables, along with the circulation figures—when, in effect, Isaac Ehrlich's rape regressions are rerun using Baron and Straus's circulation rates of pornographic magazines as an additional explanatory variable.[43] But the question remains whether the relationship between the circulation of pornography and the incidence of rape is one of cause and effect. Another possibility is that both masturbation, assisted or enhanced by pornography, and rape are outlets for men lacking good opportunities to engage in consensual sexual relationship.

Fourth, a potentially significant piece of comparative evidence is the Japanese experience. On the one hand, Japan has a very low incidence of rape, as of other crimes. On the other hand, pornography is sold more openly and more widely than in the United States—and most of it is rape or bondage

---

40. For contrasting views, see J. H. Court, "Pornography and Sex-Crimes: A Re-Evaluation in the Light of Recent Trends around the World," 5 *International Journal of Criminology and Penology* 129 (1976); Osanka and Johann, note 32 above, at 185–193; Ernest D. Giglio, "Pornography in Denmark: A Public Policy Model for the United States?" 8 *Comparative Social Research* 281 (1985); Berl Kutschinsky, "Pornography and Its Effects in Denmark and the United States: A Rejoinder and Beyond," 8 *Comparative Social Research* 301 (1985).

41. John H. Court, "Sex and Violence: A Ripple Effect," in *Pornography and Sexual Aggression* 143 (Neil M. Malamuth and Edward Donnerstein eds. 1984).

42. Larry Baron and Murray A. Straus, *Four Theories of Rape in American Society: A State-Level Analysis* 186–187 (1989).

43. I say "in effect" because Ehrlich's data are for 1960 and the circulation figures are for 1979, so Ehrlich's data had to be updated. Unfortunately in doing this I was unable to obtain data for one of the important economic variables—time served (that is, the severity of punishment)—and if that variable happens to be correlated with the circulation figures, the correlation between those figures and the incidence of rape could be spurious.

pornography.[44] Of course, there are other differences between Japan and the United States. But one of the most significant is that Japan, like ancient Greece, is a misogynistic culture by American standards. If pornography increases misogyny—and indirectly rape—why is the incidence of rape so low in Japan? And why do other misogynistic cultures, such as Spain and Portugal, modern Greece and Turkey, and Italy and Argentina, also have low rates of rape rather than high ones, as one might expect if hostility to women were a factor in rape? The fact that the incidence of rape is low in these countries is further evidence of a point made back in Chapter 7, that rape appears to be a substitute for consensual sex rather than an expression of hostility to women.

Denmark and Sweden, while they have low rape rates by American standards, have high rates by Greek and Italian, as well as Japanese, standards.[45] In 1984, there were 35.7 reported rapes per 100,000 persons in the United States, 11.9 and 7.7 in Sweden and Denmark respectively, and only 0.9, 1.8, and 1.6 in Greece, Italy, and Japan. Sweden and Denmark, like the United States, are countries in which pornography circulates freely, unlike most of the misogynist societies—except Japan. To muddy the picture further, sexually conservative Switzerland had a reported rape rate more than twice as high as sexually more liberal England (5.8 versus 2.7), though lower than Denmark, Sweden, or, of course, the United States. England is a country where pornography is widely available, but it has a much lower incidence of rape than either Denmark or Sweden.

The explanation for the low incidence of rape in misogynistic societies may be that women tend to be secluded in those societies, which raises the cost of rape to the rapist. (I shall have more to say about the causality of international differences in rape rates in the next chapter.) This is a more plausible speculation than that the low level of pornography is responsible, since in one of the societies—Japan—pornography that is unusually violent and rape-oriented even by our standards circulates freely. But it is just a speculation. Alternative possibilities are that rape is grossly underreported in misogynistic societies because the authorities are unsympathetic to the victims or that men in those societies are able to discharge their aggressive feelings toward women in ways closed to them in more progressive cultures, or that women are sequestered and the cost of rape therefore prohibitive.

With all these uncertainties admitted, the conclusion concerning the relation between pornography and rape still must be that pornography has not yet

---

44. Reiss, note 32 above, at 188; Ian Buruma, *Behind the Mask: On Sexual Demons, Sacred Mothers, Transvestites, Gangsters, Drifters and Other Japanese Cultural Heroes* 55, 58–62 (1984); Paul R. Abramson and Haruo Hayashi, "Pornography in Japan: Cross-Cultural and Theoretical Considerations," in *Pornography and Sexual Aggression,* note 41 above, at 173.

45. The statistics in this paragraph are taken from U.S. Department of Justice, Bureau of Justice Statistics, "International Crime Rates" 3 (NCJ-110776 May 1988) (tab. 4).

been proved to affect the incidence of rape.[46] No implications for public policy flow directly from such a conclusion, however, since it does not deny the *possibility* that pornography incites to rape, directly or indirectly. The positive correlation, in this country anyway, between the sale of pornography (admittedly soft-core pornography) and rape is statistically robust. Although this does not establish a causal relation, it is suggestive of one. And if the social value of pornography is small enough, even a slight danger that pornography causes rape may tip the scales in favor of outlawing it.[47] May—until we consider the high law enforcement cost of repressing victimless crimes, the difficulty of distinguishing socially valuable from socially valueless expression, the free-speech policy of the First Amendment, and the possibility that pornography actually reduces the incidence of rape by encouraging prospective rapists to substitute masturbation. I shall return to the second and third points, but first I want to consider a closely related rationale for suppressing pornography.

Harassment and Discrimination

Many feminists believe that even if pornography does not actually incite men to rape, it makes them devalue women and thereby contributes to sexual harassment and other forms of sex discrimination and oppression, large and small. This is possible, but it is a suggestion in considerable tension with the aphrodisiacal thrust of pornography. The audience for pornography is interested in sexual stimulation, not in sexual politics. Pornography does present women as sexual objects, but in moments of sexual excitement even egalitarian men conceive of women in this way. It might make a difference how steady a diet of pornography a given man consumed. It seems to me that only a man truly immersed in the stuff would find his ideas about the proper status of women altered; and we must consider whether a man prone to such immersion is, as it were, redeemable for feminism by being denied the bath he seeks.

Reference to immersion may serve to remind us of the sheer variety of messages that create the ambiance in which values and opinions are formed. People who read *Playboy* and other risqué magazines puzzlingly singled out by feminists such as Catharine MacKinnon as especially menacing to women are not pornography addicts. They are modern middle-class American males whose values are shaped by parents, siblings, peers, schoolteachers, television,

46. Richard S. Randall, *Freedom and Taboo: Pornography and the Politics of a Self Divided* 106–114 (1989). Christensen, note 32 above, at 138, goes further, concluding on the basis of a careful review that the evidence, on the whole, is against the hypothesis that pornography causes rape. Murrin and Laws, note 38 above, lean the other way—slightly.

47. As argued in Cass R. Sunstein, "Pornography and the First Amendment," 1986 *Duke Law Journal* 589.

movies, popular music, and much else besides—very little of which is the printed word, or even the still photograph. The male attitudes that MacKinnon denounces were more strongly entrenched before *Playboy* began publication. They permeate Islamic cultures that ban *Playboy*. The lack of a historical and comparative dimension to MacKinnon's investigation of pornography is a striking omission in her work.

The proposition that pornography affects men's conception of women is difficult to square with the decriminalization of pornography by Denmark and Sweden, which are bastions of female emancipation and political power (though it should be noted that a majority of Swedish women favor prohibiting pornography).[48] And if the feminists are right, why are social conservatives, many of whom would like to return women to the condition of subordination that they occupied before the sexual revolution, so fiercely hostile to pornography? Convergence on ends proves little in itself; but many conservatives who want to suppress pornography want to do so because they believe that pornography promotes sexual freedom and its concomitant—the modern "liberated" woman. Furthermore, if the feminists are right, how is one to explain the existence of homosexual pornography? It is difficult to see what it could have to do with a desire by men to intimidate and humiliate women.

Corruption of Morals

A rationale for suppression that is independent of the effects of pornography on women is corruption of morals. Long recognized as the principal ground in fact for such efforts,[49] it holds that "all who view pornography, even for short periods of time, are affected by it"; even "'soft-core' pornography breeds sexual dissatisfaction and helps break up marriages."[50] We can hear in this passage from a book by a Christian conservative an echo of Marcuse's view that nongenital sexuality undermines marriage—and a very good thing that it does, in that view. But there is no evidence that the consumption of pornography disrupts marriages, and it would be a surprise if it did. It is the rare

48. Joyce Gelb, *Feminism and Politics: A Comparative Perspective* 197 (1989). A major thesis of Gelb's book is that the male-dominated Swedish establishment preempted the issue of women's rights and by doing so retarded the emergence of an effective feminist movement. See, for example, 209–211. That might explain why pornography is allowed to circulate freely.

49. Louis Henkin, "Morals and the Constitution: The Sin of Obscenity," 63 *Columbia Law Review* 391, 406 (1963).

50. Donald E. Wildmon, *The Case against Pornography* 21 (1986). "The pornographer persistently and pervasively advertises the potential joys of promiscuity—of unknown but shapely bodies—continuously stimulates primitive male impulses, and subverts the attempt to maintain monogamous ties." George F. Gilder, *Sexual Suicide* 40 (1973). Gilder sees the feminists as working hand in glove with the pornographers to destroy marriage. He should compare notes with Catharine MacKinnon.

person who actually prefers masturbation to intercourse or who, Pygmalion-like, prefers a picture (in his case a statue) of a woman to the real thing if the real thing is not as *zaftig* as the woman in the picture.

We can expose the nerve of the corruption of morals charge by examining Irving Kristol's articulation of it.[51] His argument is in two steps. The first is to prove that pornography has a potential to corrupt, but as to this all he says is that "if you believe that no one was ever corrupted by a book, you have also to believe that no one was ever improved by a book."[52] As a matter of fact that is what I do believe, but I have crossed swords with Kristol over this issue elsewhere and will merely refer the reader to that discussion.[53] Even if I am wrong, and books can edify, it would not follow that they must also have the capacity to corrupt. After all, to consider the converse case, the fact (if it is a fact) that violent movies engender violent behavior does not entail that peaceful movies pacify.

The second step in the argument is to list the bad things that pornography does to the morals of its consumers. Kristol begins by noting that "pornography differs from erotic art in that its whole purpose is to treat human beings obscenely, to deprive human beings of their specifically human dimension."[54] By "pornography" Kristol must be referring to the type of erotic representation in which the aphrodisiacal function is foremost, for he goes on to explain that the objectionable feature of pornography is that it is "a peculiar vision of humanity," one that discards "the sentiments and the ideals" involved in human sexual activity, leaving the mere husk, "animal coupling."[55] Fair enough. But so what? Human sex does resemble animal sex. It differs principally in sometimes being embedded in a richer emotional relationship than we believe to characterize the relations between mates even in the monogamous animal species. Pornography is not interested in relationships. This makes it empty to some, shocking to others, and more erotic to its consumers. But why the separation of human sexual activity into its animal and affective components should have a corrupting effect, in the sense I suppose of changing

51. "Pornography, Obscenity and the Case for Censorship," *New York Times Magazine*, March 28, 1971, 24. (This article, by the way, is the source of the gladiator hypothetical that gave Joel Feinberg such fits. See Chapter 8.) Kristol acknowledges a debt to Walter Berns, "Pornography vs. Democracy: The Case for Censorship," *Public Interest* 3 (Winter 1971).

52. Kristol, note 51 above, at 24. I assume he means *morally* improved, since educated is not the opposite of corrupted.

53. Posner, note 35 above, at 301–303, discussing Irving Kristol, "Reflections of a Neoconservative," 51 *Partisan Review* 856 (1984). I don't mean, of course, that books have no influence. But there is a difference between the ideas in a book—sources of information and persuasion—and the values or attitudes that the book projects. Pornographic works rarely contain ideas but often project favorable attitudes toward socially disapproved sexual conduct.

54. Kristol, note 51 above, at 24.

55. This quotation and those that follow are from id. at 112.

for the worse a person's or a society's behavior or attitudes, is obscure. So Kristol pushes on. He argues that pornography "provokes a kind of sexual regression," a regression in fact to "infantile sexuality," that is, to masturbation; and while masturbation is natural, "it is precisely because it is so perfectly natural that it can be so dangerous to the mature or maturing person, if it is not controlled or sublimated in some way." The specific danger is that, unless controlled or sublimated, masturbation, spurred on by pornography, will render a man "incapable of having an adult sexual relationship with a woman," for his sexuality will remain "fixed in an infantile mode, the prison of his autoerotic fantasies . . . What is at stake is civilization and humanity, nothing less."[56]

Kristol has signed on with Freud and Marcuse (a strange set of bedfellows, this), each of whom believes that the channeling of the sex drive into marriage is fundamental to civilization as we know it. The only difference is that Freud and Kristol want to preserve that civilization and Marcuse wants to overthrow it. These beliefs about the macrosocial effects of sex have little if any basis in fact. No more securely based is the reasoning that links masturbation to the instability of marriages. Marriage has indeed become less stable, but for reasons rooted in changes in the status of women that have mainly to do with better job opportunities for them. Extirpating pornography will not make marriage more stable; nor are stable marriages, however desirable, a precondition of civilization and humanity.

Kristol's argument would be on solider ground if there were a large class of men who found masturbation with the aid of pornography a superior substitute to sexual intercourse. That would be narcissism with a vengeance, and would call to mind the distinction stressed in earlier chapters between emphasizing the sex drive to the exclusion of the sex object and emphasizing the sex object transformed into a participating other and through this transformation transmuting the character of the relationship from selfish ("narcissistic") to empathic.[57] But as far as anyone knows, there is not a large number of such men.

Note how the feminist case against pornography and Kristol's case undermine each other. The feminists fear that pornography causes rape; Kristol that it causes the substitution of masturbation for intercourse. Since rape is a form of intercourse, Kristol must believe that pornography reduces the incidence of rape, while feminists must believe that it reduces the incidence of masturbation.[58]

---

56. Wildmon and Gilder (note 50 above), in contrast, fear that pornography endangers marriage by inciting nonmarital intercourse.

57. William Simon and John H. Gagnon, "Sexual Scripts: Permanence and Change," 15 *Archives of Sexual Behavior* 97, 108 (1986).

58. Randall, note 46 above, at 101, suggests that pornography increases masturbation only

Deciding What—If Anything—to Punish

The issue of obscenity as it is posed in court cases requires the balancing of the offensiveness of the work in question against its social value, or in my terms the balancing of its aphrodisiacal properties against its formal, informational, and ideological ones. The metaphor of balancing is misleading here, however, because it gives an exaggerated impression of the distinctness of the things being compared. In a society such as ours, in which sex retains a taboo status, a work of erotic representation is offensive (shocking, disturbing, outrageous, disgusting) in proportion as it is calculated to excite the sexual appetite of its viewer. The more this thrust is blunted by the admixture of other messages, the less sexually exciting it is and therefore the less offensive. This assumes that the other messages work at cross-purposes with the aphrodisiacal operation of the work, but often they do. If a seemingly pornographic painting contains formal patterns suggestive of a harmony and serenity incongruous with sexual excitement, or provides information concerning the dangers of sex, or treats sex as degrading (as in "The Waste Land"), it loses much of its sexual kick. This is why it is misleading to emphasize[59] the unmistakable sexual innuendo in so many ballets. The formal harmonies of ballet do not deprive it of its erotic character but do prevent its having a powerful aphrodisiacal impact. It is otherwise if the formal patterns imitate the rhythms of sex (as in striptease), if the information conveyed by the work is information concerning new possibilities of sexual pleasure, if its preachment is preachment of the joys of sex. So when an expert witness in an obscenity trial talks about the nonaphrodisiacal dimensions of an erotic work, he is talking about offensiveness and social value simultaneously.

It is important to distinguish between an offensiveness generated by a perception of the aphrodisiacal character of an erotic work and the offensiveness of its ideology. The First Amendment has long been held to protect the right of an author or artist to preach sexual immorality.[60] It was offensiveness of this second type that lay behind the storm over Robert Mapplethorpe's homosexual photographs, a storm that resulted in the criminal prosecution of the director of the Cincinnati Art Museum (the jury acquitted him). As an aside it should be noted that there is a special difficulty in evaluating the

---

on the part of men who lack sex partners; for men who have partners, the aphrodisiacal effect of pornography produces an increase in intercourse.

59. As in Hanna, note 7 above, at 5–6; see also id., chs. 7 and 8.

60. Kingsley International Pictures Corp. v. Regents of the University of the State of New York, 360 U.S. 684 (1959); American Booksellers Association, Inc. v. Hudnut, 771 F.2d 323 (7th Cir. 1985), affirmed without opinion, 475 U.S. 1001 (1986).

aphrodisiacal properties of erotic representations directed at a sexual-preference minority, in Mapplethorpe's case sadomasochistic homosexuals with a particular fondness for leather goods. If you are not one of those people, you are not likely to be turned on by a photograph in which a bullwhip is seen protruding from Mapplethorpe's anus, or in which a man has thrust his fist into the anus of another man, or in which a man is shown dressed in black leather from head to toe, or in which one man is shown urinating into the mouth of another man. One might, though, imagine the counterpart heterosexual scenes, perhaps by just substituting in one's imagination a woman for a man in each photo, and the result of this imaginative exercise would be to make at least some of Mapplethorpe's homosexual photographs hard-core pornography.

But this is to neglect the photographs' formal properties. Mapplethorpe was a photographer of some, perhaps considerable, artistic distinction. Forget about the extravagant testimony given by art critics at the Cincinnati trial. Such testimony is worthless.[61] Art critics will rise as one to defend any artist prosecuted for obscenity, and they will tell the judge or jury whatever they think it takes to get the artist acquitted. The very high prices that Mapplethorpe's photographs commanded in the market even before the efforts to suppress his homosexual photographs gave him a rare notoriety and sent the prices of his work soaring are better evidence—are in fact good evidence— that they are works of artistic merit. And they are that because of formal properties that detract from the single-minded aphrodisiacal thrust that the photographs might otherwise have for viewers sharing Mapplethorpe's sexual preference.

Mapplethorpe's sexual preference. That is the rub, and the spring of the prosecution. As Arthur Danto remarked in the passage on Mapplethorpe that I quoted earlier, Mapplethorpe's homosexual photographs project approval of the sexual conduct that they record. If they projected disapproval, they could be interpreted as portraits of the damned, like the paintings of Hieronymus Bosch; their offensiveness would be sugared by a welcome message. But as the First Amendment does not permit the censorship of disfavored ideologies—and rightly so—we must disregard the ideological message of the photographs.

I said that formal properties can redeem shocking explicitness. But could not the reverse be argued with equal plausibility: that the erotic, at least when carried to pornographic lengths, undermines the formal qualities of a work of art? The answer lies in a comparison between the pornographic and non-pornographic painting of the masters, such as Balthus (Balthasar Klossowski), one of the greatest living painters. Most Americans would consider Balthus'

---

61. *Obscenity and Film Censorship: An Abridgement of the Williams Report* 109–110 (Bernard Williams ed. 1981); Posner, note 35 above, at 333.

Guitar Lesson[62] a pornographic painting. A woman, the guitar teacher, is sitting on a chair. Stretched across her lap is the pupil, a girl of perhaps 12, lying in exactly the same position as Jesus Christ in the Louvre's *Pietà de Villeneuve-les-Avignons*.[63] The girl's dress is hiked up above her navel, leaving her abdomen and pubic area exposed. The teacher is reaching for the girl's pubic area with her left hand, while her right hand grasps a lock of the girl's hair. It is as if the girl were a large guitar that the teacher is about to play. (The guitar itself is lying on the floor in front of the girl, to enforce the suggestion.) The girl's left hand is reaching up and tugging at the teacher's blouse, exposing one of her breasts. The guitar lesson has turned into another kind of lesson.

The sexuality of prepubescent girls is a recurrent, even obsessive, theme in Balthus' paintings and drawings. It marks them as "sick" in much the same way that Mapplethorpe's homosexual photographs are marked by their subject matter and the implicit attitude of the artist. *The Guitar Lesson*, blasphemy and lesbianism to one side, goes further than Balthus' other paintings toward the explicit depiction of a prepubescent girl engaged in a sexual act; we are seeing her just moments before it is to begin. So it is among other things a painting of the sexual abuse of a child, with no tincture of disapproval. Yet *The Guitar Lesson* is one of Balthus' finest paintings. The parallel of body and guitar, the echo of Christian iconography which not only lends a thematic resonance to the painting but also ties it to the classical tradition in Western art, the striking angles of the various limbs, the pattern of light and dark (white flesh and dark clothing),[64] the distinctively Balthusian fusion of movement and repose, of drama and fantasy, the contrasting expressions on the two faces (the girl's detached, enigmatic; the woman's loving, almost maternal—the echo of Mary again), the grace of the bodies: these elements, themselves not erotic, are exactly the elements, wrought to the same pitch of aesthetic intensity, that mark Balthus' other, more famous, and by current standards unequivocally nonpornographic works, such as *The Room*.[65]

The cases of Mapplethorpe and Balthus[66] suggest a rule of thumb for dealing

62. Sabine Rewald, *Balthus* 30 (1984) (fig. 37).

63. Id. at 29–30 and fig. 38. And the woman's head is inclined at the same angle as Mary's in the *Pietà*. I also sense a resemblance between the woman's face and the face of Mary in Leonardo da Vinci's painting of the Holy Family.

64. The plate unfortunately is in black and white. The painting itself is in a private collection (naturally), and I have never seen it.

65. Rewald, note 62 above, at 119 (pl. 32).

66. It may be objected that in bracketing Balthus and Mapplethorpe in this way I am overlooking the difference between a painting of an imaginary scene and a photograph of a real scene. It is not a categorical difference, since artists frequently paint from models and photographic scenes are often simulated (and not just in movies), and since some paintings are more realistic

with one class of pornographic art (or writing—but there is no longer in this country any governmental censorship of obscenity in print as distinct from pictures or speech). If an artist has achieved a reputation for his nonpornographic work, his pornographic work should be conclusively presumed to have artistic merit—hence in all likelihood not even to be offensive, once the public is educated to the existence, nature, and sources of that merit—and the law should leave it alone. This is a step in the right direction, but it has rather a snobbish, elitist cast; it evokes the eighteenth century, when the poverty and illiteracy of the lower classes confined the right to consume pornography as a practical matter to the upper class. If pornography is highbrow art when made by highbrow artists, why should it not be lowbrow art—but still art, still privileged under the First Amendment—when made by lowbrow artists? If there is an answer to this question it is, I think, that what makes art highbrow—an attention to patterns, allusions, tradition, and resonances—dilutes its erotic impact and by doing so reduces its offensiveness.

Two ways of trying to finesse the difficult problems involved in distinguishing between "low-value" and "high-value" expression should be mentioned. One is to define the central value of the First Amendment's clauses guaranteeing freedom of speech and of the press as the protection of political expression and to relegate art, highbrow and lowbrow alike, to the periphery, where the government can be allowed broad regulatory power. I am unhappy to have to admit that there is historical warrant, and more, for this philistine approach. The framers of the Constitution *were* primarily concerned with the protection of political expression, and democracy *is* more endangered by curtailing such expression than by curtailing artistic expression. But comparisons should be made at the margin. It would be worse to forbid criticism of the government than to forbid erotic representations. At the same time, it would be worse to force every museum to place fig leaves and breast coverings on its paintings and statues than to forbid the teaching of Nazi racial theory in a single class in a small private school.

The second method of finessing the problem of determining social value is to shift the focus of concern from the audience's moral welfare to that of the performer. This is a natural shift with respect to child pornography but it is not limited to that. Consider this argument. Prostitution is illegal in all but a few counties in Nevada. A person who performs sex acts for money is a prostitute. Therefore an actor or actress who performs sex acts in a pornographic film is a prostitute and the filmmaker is an accessory in prostitution, like a pimp or a madam.

This reasoning overlooks a principal purpose of punishing prostitution,

---

than some photographs. In fact *The Guitar Lesson* seems as realistic as a typical Mapplethorpe photograph, and appears to have been painted from life.

which is to protect marriage by discouraging men from seeking sexual satisfaction outside of it and from dissipating in that quest resources needed by their family. The male performers in pornographic movies are not purchasing sexual services; they are being paid. Their resources are being augmented, for the use of their families, if they have families. At best prostitution provides an analogy to the activities of pornographic performers, and an analogy is an insecure ground for legal regulation.

There is another oblique approach, sanctioned by the Supreme Court's ruling that the Constitution allows states to deem appearing in the nude in an erotic performance a violation of the ubiquitous statutes and ordinances forbidding public indecency.[67] The term "public indecency," as usually defined, includes appearing nude in a public place, which in turn is sometimes defined to include not only streets and other outdoor locations but also any places open to the public, such as bars and theaters. Even so construed, these enactments seem at first glance to bear no more ominous relation to artistic freedom than a tax on pencils or paper would bear to freedom of the press. We allow inputs into expressive works to be taxed, even though the effect is to raise the cost of producing those works. What is nudity in, say, *Salome* but an input into the artistic performance? But the analogy quickly breaks down. One reason a tax on pencils or paper would be unobjectionable is that it would be an inapt device for punishing expression, since the incidence of the tax would be borne not only by authors and publishers but by all other users of pencils and paper as well. When government is restricted to acting through general measures, pariahs benefit by the fact that respectable elements also feel the law's pinch.[68] A law forbidding all nudity, including, for example, taking a shower in the nude, would be of this character. But a law limited to *public* nudity is not, for the only people hit by the law besides nude performers are flashers, streakers, and drunks who pee in alleys—all pariahs themselves.

Furthermore, whereas paper is paper whether it is bought by a newspaper or by a maker of gift wrapping, the nudity of a flasher and the nudity of an artistic performer are not the same thing (and this apart from the fact that what flashers flash is, often, their erect penis, which makes their conduct a species not just of public nudity but of obscenity, which is a separate ground from public indecency for prohibition). The difference, which is independent of the quality of the artistic performance, is Mill's difference between self-

---

67. Barnes v. Glen Theatre, Inc., 111 S. Ct. 2456 (1991) (see Introduction). Only four of the justices, however, endorsed the approach which I sketch in the text. The fifth whose vote was necessary to the ruling, Justice David Souter, ruled in favor of the state because he believed that the secondary effects of nude dancing, such as the encouragement it gives to prostitution (remember that striptease artists are frequently prostitutes), were, although speculative, sufficient to justify the suppression of what he considered a marginal, low-value expressive activity.

68. This is the ground for the closely related juristic ideas of equal protection and rule of law. Richard A. Posner, *The Problems of Jurisprudence* 319–320 (1990).

regarding and other-regarding conduct. The flasher thrusts his nudity on an unwilling stranger; the artistic performer sells nudity to willing customers. The alleged "secondary effects" of nude dancing, notably the encouragement of prostitution (see note 67), may or may not identify a true externality (= other-regarding act). Prostitution is itself a consensual activity, and while it may have third-party effects, the link between nude dancing and those effects seems tenuous (and was not argued in the *Barnes* case). That link may be the place to look for a utilitarian justification for the Supreme Court's nude-dancing decision; but it would be naive to suppose that concern with the concrete harms, if any, produced by nude dancing, or for that matter by the commonest kind of "public indecency"—a drunk urinating in an alley— are at the heart of the efforts by state and local government to punish these behaviors. They offend because they violate the nudity taboo of our society, and we should consider therefore whether that taboo has social value. On the one hand, the early Christian emphasis on covering the body may have been intended, in part anyway, to discourage cruelty and violence by drawing a sharp line between human beings and animals; on this view it is related to the abolition of gladiatorial contests.[69] On the other hand, modern Swedes are remarkably casual about nudity by American standards,[70] yet Sweden is a less violent society than America. Western Europe today in general is both more casual about nudity and more pacific than the United States.

Even if our nudity taboo no longer serves any intelligible social purpose, states should be free to prohibit displays of nudity, even if not obscene, to unwilling passers-by. Such displays are "other regarding." They impose costs, in an uncontroversial albeit nonpecuniary sense, and if they have any value, they retain it when forced indoors; and indoors they impose no costs— no direct costs, anyway—because no one is forced to watch against his will. Even if we reject Mill's distinction, the offensiveness of "public" nudity is attenuated, though not eliminated, when the display is to a willing audience out of sight of anyone who would be offended to see it, and when, by reason of the formal or other properties of the performance of which the display is a part, the offense falls below the level that society pronounces obscene.[71] Those properties, moreover, may impart to the display of nudity artistic value,[72] and thereby make the cost of suppression higher than in the case of public indecency properly so called. The application of public indecency laws

---

69. Brown, note 13 above, at 315–317.

70. Richard F. Tomasson, *Sweden: Prototype of Modern Society* 167 (1970).

71. So one might think that a society which considered prostitution a form of nuisance because of its offensiveness to passers-by would encourage rather than outlaw brothels.

72. On the role of nudity in modern dance, see Walter Sorrell, *Dance in Its Time* 425–426 (1986).

to indoor performances punishes as if obscene erotic representations that are often neither obscene nor even pornographic. It would require Salome to wear a bathing suit under her veils. A striptease that is obscene can of course be punished without resort to the public indecency laws.

IT IS TIME to gather together the threads of the analysis into a summary conclusion about whether, or to what extent, pornography should be restricted. We may set to one side child pornography that involves the photographing of child models. Here suppression is clearly warranted to protect the participant in the pornographic performance; and so with pornography in which an adult model is physically injured, as well as pornography exhibited to an unwilling audience. The difficult question is whether any other pornography should be illegal. If the domain of the pornographic is limited to works whose predominant appeal is aphrodisiacal—hence works that rank low in the traditional hierarchy of First Amendment values—it is possible to argue that the harms of pornography, conjectural and uncertain as they are, should be enough to justify punishment. This may be right as a matter of constitutional law, but it seems wrong as a matter of sound social policy. The resources that our society is willing to devote to law enforcement are limited in relation to the amount of violence and other serious lawlessness against which they are deployed. We should not dissipate them in efforts—which are bound to fail—to suppress activities that may be as harmless as witchcraft or heresy.

If this recommendation is rejected, then as a fallback I urge that all printed obscenity, "old" pictures, the works of recognized artists, and (to the extent it can be identified) artistically ambitious work by anyone—categories that include art photography, such as Mapplethorpe's sadomasochistic photos, and stripping to the buff in *Salome*—should be exempt from suppression, although not from regulation designed to protect the unwilling, or young children, from inadvertent exposure to them.[73] In our culture, such categories of erotic representation have little aphrodisiacal effect. It is true that works in these categories often express an ideology of patriarchy and misogyny, as Lynda Nead has charged the Renaissance nude with doing,[74] but that is no ground for suppression. Rather the contrary, since ideological representations are at the center of the expression that the First Amendment protects. So while some feminists will regard my attempt to distinguish between "high" and "low" culture and to exempt the former from obscenity prosecutions as merely a last-ditch defense of patriarchy, their rejection of the distinction jeopardizes

73. See Piarowski v. Illinois Community College District 515, 759 F.2d 625 (7th Cir. 1985).
74. "The Female Nude: Pornography, Art, and Sexuality," 15 *Signs: Journal of Women in Culture and Society* 323 (1990).

all obscenity prosecutions. Margaret Miles, in suggesting that all erotica is aphrodisiacal,[75] aestheticizes pornography. If a *Playboy* pinup belongs to the same genre as a Renaissance nude, then since the latter is plainly protected by the First Amendment, so must the former be. Nead, in suggesting that all erotica is political, brings it into the very core of the First Amendment—the protection of political expression. If there are "no sanctuaries from political reality, no aesthetic or fantastic enclaves, no islands for the play of desire,"[76] the vilest pornographic trash is protected. Maybe it should be. If not, the distinction I have proposed would if accepted go some way toward protecting art from the censor's blade.

75. See text at note 23 above.
76. Susanne Kappeler, *The Pornography of Representation* 147 (1986).

Coercive Sex

THE TITLE of this chapter refers to situations in which one of the participants in a sex act either has not consented to the act or, by reason of being mentally immature or retarded, or deceived, or overawed by adult authority, has not given *effective* consent, that is, consent which society honors. So my discussion is in two parts. The first deals with rape and related sexual offenses (such as attempted rape and the noncriminal offense known as sexual harassment) against adults. I confine my discussion to rape of women by men; rape of either men or women by women is exceedingly rare, as is male homosexual rape outside of prisons.[1] The second part of the chapter deals with the sexual abuse of children, mainly girls. Issues pertaining to actual consent dominate the first part, issues pertaining to what I call effective consent the second. Both parts use the model of morally indifferent sex to orient the analysis, while paying some attention to the principal rivals in this area. These are the feminist approach (more accurately approaches) and the approach of civil libertarians, who when discussing sexual as well as other offenses emphasize the rights of the defendant.

Other differences between the two parts of this chapter besides the age of the victims are the sex of the victims and the nature of the offenses. Although rape of men is rare enough to be ignored outside the prison setting, the sexual abuse of male children, while less common than that of female children, is not rare, and therefore requires discussion. And assaults short of rape or attempted rape that would be considered minor crimes when the victim is an adult are a severely reprobated form of sexual abuse of children—for example, fondling a child's genitals. I shall disregard, however, sexual offenses that involve no physical contact at all, even if the victim is a child. The commonest of these is the crime of exposing oneself in public—exhibitionism, as it is called. As noted in Chapter 5, exhibitionists are shy men who get their sexual

---

1. Paul H. Gebhard et al., *Sex Offenders: An Analysis of Types* 791 (1965).

kicks from the sense of shock that they induce by exposing their genitals to women (sometimes children) on the street or in other public places. They are not violent. Their behavior is offensive and, when the victim is a child, disturbing. But there is no evidence that it inflicts lasting psychological damage, even on children, and on the scale of criminal activity in this society it seems distinctly minor.[2] It is generally treated as a form of public indecency, a misdemeanor, and hence punished lightly, as it should be. Indeed, it may be more suitable for psychiatric than for criminal treatment. Voyeurism causes more distress to its victims because it is perceived as a more serious invasion of privacy, and it is correlated with violent behavior. On both counts it should be, and is, punished more heavily than exhibitionism.[3]

Sexual Abuse of Adults

Contrary to a view held by many feminists,[4] rape appears to be primarily a substitute for consensual sexual intercourse rather than a manifestation of male hostility toward women or a method of establishing or maintaining male domination.[5] Donald Symons, for example, points to anthropological evidence that the incidence of rape rises with brideprice; thus, the more expensive it is to obtain marital sex, the more likely men are to resort to force.[6] Granted, the infrequency of resort to force in male homosexual encounters, even encounters between an adult and a minor,[7] lends some credence to the view that

2. Ron Langevin, *Sexual Strands: Understanding and Treating Sexual Anomalies in Men*, ch. 10 (1983).

3. Id., ch. 11. The consumption of photographic pornography—the principal type of pornography today—is voyeurism in a sense, but not the relevant sense. It is not an invasion of privacy, and it does not place the voyeur (the consumer, not the photographer) in physical proximity to his "victim."

4. See, for example, Susan Brownmiller, *Against Our Will: Men, Women and Rape* (1975). For a helpful survey of the subject matter of this chapter from a moderate feminist viewpoint, see Deborah L. Rhode, *Justice and Gender: Sex Discrimination and the Law*, ch. 10 (1989). The best study of rape from that viewpoint is Linda Brookover Bourque, *Defining Rape* (1989), on which I rely heavily. On the handling of rape cases by the criminal justice system, Gary LaFree, *Rape and Criminal Justice: The Social Construction of Sexual Assault* (1989), is particularly good.

5. Leo Ellis, *Theories of Rape: Inquiries into the Causes of Sexual Aggression* (1989), esp. chs. 3, 5; Donald Symons, *The Evolution of Human Sexuality* 278–285 (1979); Edward Shorter, "On Writing the History of Rape," 5 *Signs: Journal of Women in Culture and Society* 471 (1977); Roy Porter, "Rape—Does It Have a Historical Meaning?" in *Rape* 216, 235 (Sylvana Tomaselli and Roy Porter eds. 1986); Randy Thornhill and Nancy Wilmsen Thornhill, "Human Rape: An Evolutionary Analysis," 4 *Ethology and Sociobiology* 137, 163–164 (1983).

6. Symons, note 5 above, at 281.

7. Gebhard, note 1 above, at 791.

misogyny is an element in many rapes, as does the fact that rape is rare among animals and virtually unknown among man's closest relatives, the nonhuman primates.[8] Still, much rape is sexual in motive, as would be clearer were it not a crime, for studies of persons convicted of rape are by definition heavily weighted toward people who have neither been deterred by a threat of heavy punishment nor been able to elude punishment.[9]

What is the next best thing from a scientific standpoint, however, is that rape is an underreported crime.[10] When it is studied from the point of view of the victims of rape (whether women who have filed complaints of rape or women who have filled out crime-victimization questionnaires), thereby bringing into the study many rapists who are not caught, including many who, given the circumstances of the rape, are unlikely to be caught, we get a clearer picture of the nature of the conduct as it might exist in the absence of criminal sanctions; and we find confirmed the impression that most rapists want to have sex, not to make a statement about, or contribute to, the subordination of women.[11] This is not to deny that rape attracts the violent (those prone to use force to achieve their goals) and the sadistic (who may derive an extra

8. Symons, note 5 above, at 277–278; Barbara B. Smuts, "Sexual Competition and Mate Choice," in *Primate Societies* 385, 392–393 (Barbara B. Smuts et al. eds. 1986). Orangutans are the nonhuman primate exception. Smuts at 392. Another example of animal rapists is discussed in Susan Evarts and Christopher J. Williams, "Multiple Paternity in a Wild Population of Mallards," 104 *The Auk: A Quarterly Journal of Ornithology* 597, 600–601 (1987).

9. As emphasized in Bourque, note 4 above, at 74. See also Mary P. Koss et al., "Nonstranger Sexual Aggression: A Discriminant Analysis of the Psychological Characteristics of Undetected Offenders," 12 *Sex Roles* 981 (1985).

10. How underreported is unclear; estimates range up to an improbable 95 percent. For contrasting views, see Allan Griswold Johnson, "On the Prevalence of Rape in the United States," 6 *Signs: Journal of Women in Culture and Society* 136 (1980); Albert E. Gollin, "Comment on Johnson's 'On the Prevalence of Rape in the United States,'" 6 *Signs* 346 (1980); Diana E. H. Russell and Nancy Howell, "The Prevalence of Rape in the United States Revisited," 8 *Signs* 688 (1983); Russell, *Sexual Exploitation: Rape, Child Sexual Abuse, and Workplace Harassment* 35 (1984); Mary P. Koss, Christine A. Gidycz, and Nadine Wisniewski, "The Scope of Rape: Incidence and Prevalence of Sexual Aggression and Victimization in a National Sample of Higher Education Students," 55 *Journal of Consulting and Clinical Psychology* 162 (1987); Neil Gilbert, "The Phantom Epidemic of Sexual Assault," *Public Interest* 54 (Spring 1991). Gilbert mounts a strong assault against what he terms "advocacy numbers" (p. 63). He may well be correct that estimates from private surveys of victims of rape, attempted rape, and child sexual abuse, most of which have been conducted by feminist scholars, who may (like the rest of us) have unconscious biases that influence their results, are too high; but he acknowledges that the official statistics are too low.

11. Ron Langevin and Reuben A. Lang, "The Courtship Disorders," in *Variant Sexuality: Research and Theory* 202, 218–219 (Glenn D. Wilson ed. 1987); Langevin, note 2 above, at 407–408; Bourque, note 4 above, at 74–75; Johnson, note 10 above, at 146. Chapter 12 of Langevin's *Sexual Strands* (note 2 above) is a good review of what is known about the psychological and other characteristics of rapists. See also Thornhill and Thornhill, note 5 above, at 163–164.

filip of pleasure from the rape victim's agony),[12] for those are men to whom, respectively, the costs of rape are lower, and the benefits of rape greater, than they are to men who are neither violent nor sadistic. But it does suggest that a rational model of "normal" human behavior can be used to analyze the behavior of rapists, including their response to punishment. The aptness of the rational model is further supported by Isaac Ehrlich's study of criminal behavior (discussed in Chapter 5), which finds rapists to be approximately as responsive to incentives, and hence as deterrable by threat of punishment, as persons who commit property offenses, such as auto theft and other forms of larceny.[13]

The rational model has been said to imply, however, contrary to our unshakable moral intuitions, that a man who derives a special pleasure, sexual or otherwise, from the coerciveness of rape ought to be permitted to rape, provided only that he derives more pleasure from the act, over and above all substitutes (such as sex with a prostitute who will, for a price, consent to the man's abusing her physically), than the pain suffered by his victim.[14] This example points to a familiar problem of utilitarianism—the problem of the "utility monster," who by virtue of having a capacity for enjoyment vastly greater than that of the average person in the society appears to stake a utilitarian moral claim to engross a disproportionate share of the society's goods. Only here the utility monster really *is* a monster, who by virtue of having a capacity for sadistic pleasure greater than his victims' capacity for pain stakes a moral claim to be allowed to torture, rape, and kill.

The rational model of human behavior is indeed related to utilitarianism, for both approaches are based on the assumption that people act in accordance with the balance of pleasures and pains. But to suppose that the rational model stands or falls with utilitarianism is to confuse positive with normative analysis. In any event it should be plain that licensing utility monsters such as Bluebeard or de Sade to rape would not really be utility-maximizing, if

12. Langevin and Lang, note 11 above, at 219. Since alcoholics have difficulty controlling their impulses, it is no surprise that a sizable fraction of rapists are alcoholics. Langevin, note 2 above, at 410 (estimating one-third).

13. Ehrlich, "Participation in Illegitimate Activities: An Economic Analysis," in *Essays in the Economics of Crime and Punishment* 68, 94–103 (Gary S. Becker and William M. Landes eds. 1974). See also Keith F. Otterbein, "A Cross-Cultural Study of Rape," 5 *Aggressive Behavior* 425 (1979). Other evidence for the "sex theft" theory of rape was presented in Chapters 4 and 7. See pp. 106–107, 182–183 above.

14. Gary T. Schwartz, "Economics, Wealth Distribution, and Justice," 1979 *Wisconsin Law Review* 799, 806; Dorsey D. Ellis, "An Economic Theory of Intentional Torts: A Comment," 3 *International Review of Law and Economics* 45 (1983). The argument is criticized in William M. Landes' and my book *The Economic Structure of Tort Law* 157–158 (1987), as well as in my article "An Economic Theory of the Criminal Law," 85 *Columbia Law Review* 1193, 1198–99 (1985).

only because of the fear that it would engender in the community as a whole and the expense of the self-protective measures that this fear would incite.

Since the degree to which rape is underreported is unknown, a reliable estimate of its magnitude cannot be made, but it appears to be greater in the United States than in any other developed country—perhaps any other country, period. The reported rape rate in the United States is three times higher than in Sweden or Germany, ten to twenty times higher than in Japan, almost twenty times higher than in France, and more than forty times higher than in Belgium[15]—even though it is punished more heavily in this country. But of course most crime rates are higher in the United States than in other developed countries, and the rape rate, at least in this country, is so unreliable a number as to make international comparisons of the incidence of rape relative to that of other violent crimes highly suspect.[16] It is possible to speculate, however, that a country such as the United States, in which permissive and repressive attitudes mingle, would indeed have more rape than a country that was either consistently permissive or consistently repressive.[17] In a permissive society, sexual gratification is widely available to men and the incentive to seek it by force is therefore reduced. Since, moreover, nonmarital intercourse carries no stigma, women are not reluctant to complain to the police if they are raped, and so the probability of apprehension and punishment is high, which increases deterrence. In a repressive society, women are sequestered, or at least do not mingle freely with men. Not only are the opportunities for rape therefore reduced, but so is the number of ambiguous social situations in which rape is difficult to prove and (for that reason, among others) common;

15. Ellis, note 5 above, at 7, 28; Arthur Frederick Schiff, "Rape in Other Countries," 11 *Medicine Science and the Law* 139, 142 (1971); U.S. Department of Justice, Bureau of Justice Statistics, "International Crime Rates" 3 (NCJ-110776, May 1988) (tab. 4).

16. For what it is worth, there does not appear to be a stable relationship between rape and other crimes against the person, such as homicide and robbery. For example, in the United States there are 4.52 rapes for every homicide and 0.17 rape for every robbery (i.e., rape is several times more common than homicide but several times less common than robbery), while in Japan there are only two rapes for every homicide but almost one (0.89 to be precise) rape for every robbery. Computed from "International Crime Rates," note 15 above, at 3 (tab. 4) (1984 figures). So it does not seem feasible to deflate the rape rate by the overall rate of crime against the person in order to permit a more meaningful international comparison.

17. Cf. Kevin Howells, "Coercive Sexual Behavior," in *The Psychology of Sexual Diversity* 110, 114–115 (Howells ed. 1984). For contrary evidence, see Duncan Chappell et al., "Forcible Rape: A Comparative Study of Offenses Known to the Police in Boston and Los Angeles," in *The Sociology of Sex: An Introductory Reader* 107 (James M. Henslin and Edward Sagarin eds., rev. ed. 1978). Evidence of rape rates in earlier times is poor, but Porter, note 5 above, at 220–223, makes a persuasive argument that the rate was low in preindustrial England, a period fairly described as sexually repressive by modern standards. And recall the rape statistics in Chapter 13.

this is the problem of "date rape" discussed later in this chapter. In addition, there are strong incentives not to report a rape to the authorities in a society in which virginity and chastity are prized; this may be the principal reason why, as I noted in the preceding chapter, reported rape rates are higher in permissive than in repressive societies.

But in our society, on the one hand women mingle freely with men both at work and in social settings, which creates opportunities for precisely those rapes that are difficult to prove, and on the other hand nonmarital intercourse carries a stigma in some social strata—including those from which most police officers and many judges are drawn. These enforcement officials are sympathetic to "respectable" women raped by members of the criminal class but often not to sexually active women raped in compromising situations—say, while drunk on a date or while scantily clad—or to women raped by their husbands. In such settings enforcement officials may believe that the woman has hoked up the rape charge for a strategic advantage, such as jockeying for favorable terms of divorce or trying to explain away a pregnancy. The more suspicious of a class of crime victims the law enforcement community is, the more reluctant the victims will be to report the crime—which increases the probability that they will *be* victims by reducing the probability of offenders' being punished, and therefore deterrence. Reluctance to complain will be especially great if failure to prove the offense exposes the victim to suspicion that she is the real offender—the loose woman, the designing wife.

The problem goes deeper than unsympathetic officials. Rape is a crime usually committed in private, away from eyewitnesses, and all that distinguishes it from ordinary sexual intercourse is lack of consent, which may be difficult to prove in the absence of physical injury, especially if the circumstances make an inference of consensual intercourse plausible. One is not surprised that the probability of conviction for rape is increased if there is a witness or if an "unnatural" act is committed, such as sodomy (presumably less likely to be consented to), and decreased if the woman is young and therefore likely to be attractive to "normal" men believed unlikely to commit rape, if she has an arrest record, if she is either unmarried or complaining of having been raped by her husband, if she is acquainted with the defendant, if she invokes a rape-shield law, implying that she has been sexually active, or if the act occurred at night and away from her home.[18] The difficulty of providing satisfactory proof of lack of consent in an "acquaintance rape" case is one reason for the law's traditional refusal to make marital rape a crime.[19]

18. Kristen M. Williams, *The Prosecution of Sexual Assaults* 47 (1978) (tab. A.1); William Simon and John H. Gagnon, "Sexual Scripts: Permanence and Change," 15 *Archives of Sexual Behavior* 97, 113 (1986); LaFree, note 4 above, at 202 (tab. 8.1).

19. The English common law treated marriage as a complete defense to a charge of rape even if the couple had long been separated. Mary Lyndon Shanley, *Feminism, Marriage, and the Law*

There are so many other reasons that it will help to make a list.

1. There is the problem of proof, just mentioned.

2. In a society that prizes premarital virginity and marital chastity, the cardinal harm from rape is the destruction of those goods, and it is not inflicted by marital rape. We should not be surprised that in those societies seducing a married woman is a more serious crime than raping her.[20] It is more likely to involve a continuing relationship and hence more likely to produce children—children who are not the husband's.

3. In such societies, moreover, virtually the only services that a wife contributes to the marriage are sexual and procreative, and if she tries to deprive her husband of these services, she is striking at the heart of the marriage. It is true that to have a right to demand something does not entail a right to take it by force, but it can dilute the felt impropriety of force.

4. In general, though not always, the lower the divorce rate is, the fewer separations there are; and the problem of proving lack of consent is reduced if the married couple is separated. The exception is where, as in Catholic countries until recently, divorce was forbidden but formal separations, often permanent, took their place.

5. A marriage is unlikely to survive a criminal prosecution of the husband for raping his wife. Suspicion therefore arises that a complaint of marital rape is designed to give the wife leverage in divorce negotiations—and hence may have been fabricated. The problem cannot arise if women cannot divorce.

6. Marital rape may be uncommon, since few wives will refuse their husband's demand for sexual intercourse. So maybe when marital rape is made criminal, the main effect is precisely that identified in the preceding point—to increase the wife's bargaining position in a divorce.

---

in Victorian England, 1850–1895 156–159 (1989); Michael D. A. Freeman, "'But If You Can't Rape Your Wife, Who Can You Rape?': The Marital Rape Exemption Re-Examined," 15 *Family Law Quarterly* 1, 8–15 (1981). This position (accepted until recently in most other countries as well, Freeman at 26–27) was adopted in American rape statutes as well, until a wave of reform broke over the states in the 1970s. Some states have abolished the defense outright; others (now England, too) distinguish between married couples that are separated and those that are living together; still others make marital rape a lesser crime than other rapes. Sonya A. Adamo, "The Injustice of the Marital Rape Exemption: A Survey of Common Law Countries," 4 *American University Journal of International Law and Policy* 555 (1989). See also Susan S. M. Edwards, *Female Sexuality and the Law: A Study of Constructs of Female Sexuality as They Inform Statute and Legal Procedure* 34 (1981); Bourque, note 4 above, ch. 5.

20. Roger Just, *Women in Athenian Law and Life* 68 (1989). The common law made the seduction of a wife a twofold tort against the husband—"alienation of affections" and "criminal conversation." The trend toward the abolition of these torts, on which see Fundermann v. Mickelson, 304 N.W.2d 790 (Ia. 1981), reflects the growing independence of women: the husband's right to bring a tort suit against a wife's lover curtails women's opportunities by deterring men from having adulterous relations with them.

7. The nature of the harm to the wife raped by her husband is somewhat obscure. If she is beaten or threatened, these are palpable harms; but they are the harms inflicted by an ordinary assault and battery. Especially since the goods of virginity and of chastity are not endangered, the fact of her having intercourse one more time with a man with whom she has had intercourse many times before seems marginal to the harm actually inflicted, but is essential to making the offense rape.

Most of the listed reasons for not making marital rape a crime have lost force with time. The problem of proof has diminished because courts have become, or at least consider themselves to have become, more adept at making difficult factual determinations.[21] Most of the other problems have diminished with the reduction in the dependence of women on men—points 2 through 4, obviously; points 5 through 7, subtly (and see note 20). Points 5 and 6 are of diminished importance when divorce is available on demand, which is essentially the situation in the United States today. It is true that easy divorce is not an unalloyed boon for women, but as we saw in Chapter 9, the growing independence of women in this century has, by reducing the inherent stability of marriage, made easy divorce inevitable.

Point 7 is the most interesting—for what it leaves out. An important aspect of the increasing independence of women is the control they obtain over their sexual and reproductive capacity. Any form of involuntary intercourse impairs that control. Marital rape can, after all, produce an unwanted pregnancy. That would be of no moment if a wife surrendered the entire control over her reproductive capacity to her husband in exchange for his protective services, as indeed she once did. But as women's economic dependence on men diminishes, the terms of trade between wives and husbands may alter in favor of the wife. In part because she does not need a husband as much, a woman (at least a woman with good opportunities in the job market) no longer is forced to give up control over her sexual and reproductive capacity in order to get one. A corollary is the elimination of the marriage defense to rape—more especially as husbands' diminished economic power over wives might result in a greater likelihood of a husband's resorting to force against his wife to get his way.

Elimination of the defense would be questionable, however, if the incidence of marital rape were in fact slight, for then phony claims might predominate. It appears not to be slight, but rather to be frequent enough to constitute a significant social problem.[22] What is more, contrary to what most men would

---

21. This trend is a major theme in my book *The Economics of Justice*, pt. 2 (1981), discussing primitive and ancient law.

22. Diana E. H. Russell, *Rape in Marriage: Expanded and Revised Edition with New Introduction* (1990); Russell, note 10 above, at 59 (8 percent of rapes in sample were by husband or ex-husband).

suppose, the long-term emotional and psychological effects of marital rape appear to be more rather than less serious than those of rape by a stranger because of the element of betrayal and breach of trust that is present when a woman is raped by her husband.[23]

Another sign of the changing status of women is the increased attention given to date rape. In traditional societies women do not date. Once unchaperoned dating becomes common, date rape is possible but need not be common. On the one hand, prosecution is inherently difficult because the defendant will often be able to claim, with sufficient plausibility to engender a reasonable doubt, that the victim consented or appeared to consent. This might lead us to expect date rape to be common. But on the other hand, dating (in this respect like marriage) is a voluntary relationship, so the woman has an opportunity to screen out potential rapists—to the best of her ability, which may, however, not be great.

We can expect date rape to be frequent in a society, such as ours, in which sexual mores are not uniform—and apparently it is.[24] The reason is not just differences between the mores of sexually active women on the one hand and of police officers and judges on the other, but differences between the mores of men and of their dates. Suppose, as is in fact the case, that some women in our society believe that the courtship ritual requires them to pretend to resist a man's sexual advances, that others are not coy and when they say no they mean it, that still others are coy like the first group but unlike that group do not intend finally to succumb, and that still others dress and desport themselves in a manner that seems provocative but in fact they adhere to traditional values. Insofar as men find it difficult to distinguish among these groups of women (search costs again), they will make mistakes with respect to the existence of consent.[25] The result will be sexual acts perceived as rape by the victim and reported as rape in victim surveys. Whether they are rape

23. Irene Hanson Frieze and Angela Browne, "Violence in Marriage," in *Family Violence* 11, *Crime and Justice: A Research Review* 163, 188–190 (Lloyd Ohlin and Michael Tonry eds. 1989). The comparison is between the rape of a *married* woman by her husband and by a stranger. The rape of a virgin might inflict more serious emotional or psychological damage than the rape of a married, or otherwise sexually experienced, woman.

24. *Violence in Dating Relationships: Emerging Social Issues*, pt. 2 (Maureen A. Pirog-Good and Jan E. Stets eds. 1989) ("Sexual Abuse in Dating Relationships"). This is nothing new; date rape apparently was quite common in the 1950s and 1960s as well. Kingsley Davis, "Sexual Behavior," in *Contemporary Social Problems* 313, 334–335 (Robert K. Merton and Robert Nisbet eds., 3d ed. 1971). Those were periods both of unchaperoned dating and of change and variance in American sexual mores. Date rape tends to be less violent than stranger rape, but, like marital rape, no less harmful to the victim psychologically. Mary P. Koss et al., "Stranger and Acquaintance Rape: Are There Differences in the Victim's Experience?" 12 *Psychology of Women Quarterly* 1 (1988).

25. Ellis, note 5 above, at 29–30; Bourque, note 4 above, at 65; David Lester, *Unusual Sexual Behavior: The Standard Deviations* 29, 35 (1975); cf. Howells, note 17 above, at 125–126.

in the legal sense will depend on whether the man not only honestly but also reasonably believed that he had consent. This point helps explain why rape is considered a highly underreported crime. It also provides an argument for encouraging sex education designed to dispel the misimpressions that men have about women's attitudes toward sexual aggressiveness.[26]

Sexual harassment is the workplace counterpart to date rape. Lack of privacy makes actual rape in the workplace rare, but lesser degrees of sexual aggression are common, particularly by a male superior against a female subordinate. The woman is often afraid to complain for fear of jeopardizing her job; it will be her word against that of a presumptively more valuable employee. Sexual harassment is treated not as a crime but as a common law or statutory tort, and the principal legal controversy is over the degree to which the employer should be liable for the unauthorized harassment of one employee by another who is not her supervisor. The current answer is that the employer is liable if it has reason to believe that there is sexual harassment in its work force and does nothing about it; in other words, if it is negligent with respect to the problem.[27]

Date rape blends into the ambiguous legal category of rape by fraud.[28] The law usually treats force and fraud symmetrically in the sense of punishing both, though the latter more leniently. It is a crime to take money at gunpoint. It is also a crime, though normally a lesser one, to take it by false pretenses. But generally it is not a crime to use false pretenses to entice a person into a sexual relationship.[29] Seduction, even when honeycombed with lies that would convict the man of fraud if he were merely trying to obtain money, is not rape. The thinking may be that if the woman is not averse to having sex with a particular man, the wrong if any is in the lies (and we usually do not think of lying in social settings as a crime) rather than in an invasion of her bodily integrity. It is otherwise if the man is impersonating the woman's husband or

---

26. Howells, note 17 above, at 129. For some evidence that such misimpressions, rather than a criminal or "psychopathic" personality, are a key factor in date rape, see Koss et al., note 9 above.

27. See Guess v. Bethlehem Steel Corp., 913 F.2d 463, 464–465 (7th Cir. 1990), and Shager v. Upjohn Co., 913 F.2d 398, 404–405 (7th Cir. 1990), interpreting Meritor Savings Bank v. Vinson, 477 U.S. 57, 72 (1986). See generally Catharine A. MacKinnon, *Feminism Unmodified: Discourses on Life and Law*, ch. 9 (1987), and further discussion at p. 395 below.

28. Ellis, note 5 above, at 6.

29. Susan Estrich, *Real Rape* 103 (1987), argues that it should be. Seduction was a misdemeanor in the English common law, but it has gone the way of the suit for breach of promise, a civil remedy largely for seduction. Vern L. Bullough and James Brundage, *Sexual Practices & the Medieval Church* 146–148 (1982); Margaret F. Brinig, "Rings and Promises," 6 *Journal of Law, Economics & Organization* 203, 204–205 (1990). About a third of the U.S. states, however, retain a tort (not a crime) of seduction.

claims to be administering medical treatment to the woman rather than to be inserting his penis in her.[30] In both cases the act itself, were the true facts known to the woman, would be disgusting as well as humiliating, rather than merely humiliating as in the case of the common misrepresentations of dating and courtship.

How to explain the difference in offensiveness? Girls are taught by their parents to be suspicious of the blandishments of suitors; and the careful screening of suitors is the essence of the optimal female sexual strategy, a strategy that Chapter 4 suggested is in the genes. Ordinarily, to be sure, the law does not place the burden of preventing fraud on the victim; it is cheaper for the potential injurer not to commit fraud than for the victim to take measures of self-protection against it. Nevertheless, a person who has acted the fool is likely to feel slightly less offended at having been fleeced. The problems of proof of seduction by false pretenses—in particular the problem of distinguishing by the methods of litigation between a false statement of one's feelings and a change in those feelings—are exquisitely difficult and argue for making a difference in degree a difference in legal kind, substituting victim self-protection for legal remedies. It is a plausible substitution in a society such as ours in which (adult) virginity is for the most part no longer a highly valued good. The decline in that value may explain the abolition of the crime of seduction and the tort of breach of promise as well.

The incidence of rape in the United States may not be as high as some believe (see note 10), but it is high enough to warrant serious consideration of possible ways to reduce it. Measures designed to encourage women to report rape, such as assigning more policewomen to rape squads, are relatively unproblematic, although it is always necessary to consider whether the same resources would buy more law enforcement in an alternative use. Rape-shield laws, now in force almost everywhere in this country,[31] which prevent the defendant's lawyer from routinely extracting the rape victim's sexual history, make good sense in a society such as ours in which most women are sexually active. There can be no presumption in such a society that if the rapist's victim is sexually active, she must be promiscuous or provocative and on either ground incapable of withholding consent or at least the appearance of consent.

Other measures for combating rape, however, are deeply problematic.

1. Criminal punishments for rape could be made more severe than they now are. This would reduce the incidence of rape—a conclusion implied by

30. Edwards, note 19 above, at 39; American Law Institute, *Model Penal Code and Commentaries (Official Draft and Revised Comments)*, pt. 2, vol. 1, 275 (§213.1[2][c]), 330–333 (1980); Ernst Wilfred Puttkammer, "Consent in Rape," 19 *Illinois Law Review* 410 (1925).

31. Frank Tuerkheimer, "A Reassessment and Redefinition of Rape Shield Laws," 50 *Ohio State Law Journal* 1245, 1246 (1989).

Ehrlich's study, which shows that rapists, like other criminals, respond to increases in the severity as well as probability of punishment.[32] But that would not be the only effect. Rape victims would be endangered, because the narrower the spread in punishment between rape and murder, the less the rapist has to lose by killing his victim—and he gains by eliminating the key witness against him. There might also be more acquittals if rape were punished more heavily than it is. The heavier the punishment for a particular crime is known to be, the more inclined a jury may be to resolve doubts in the defendant's favor. That was a traditional problem with the prosecution of rape (a capital offense, like all other felonies) under the English common law.[33] The problem is said to have reached scandalous proportions in Pakistan as a result of the reinstitution of Islamic law, which decrees severe penalties (including death) for rape but surrounds the imposition of the penalties with so many procedural safeguards for the defendant that the law is virtually unenforceable.[34]

2. On the basis of present knowledge, reviewed in the preceding chapter, we have no very good reason to think that curtailing the distribution of pornography would increase the amount of rape, but also no good reason to think it would decrease it.

3. Reinvigorating the crime of seduction, which rape by fraud would resemble, would deflect attention from the rapes that women fear most.

4. The most intriguing proposal is to abolish the defense of reasonable mistake as to consent.[35] Under present law, if a man either does not believe that he has the woman's consent to sex or believes it but is unreasonable to do so in the circumstances, he is guilty of rape. He is not guilty if his belief that he has consent is reasonable. The effect of abolishing mistaken but reasonable belief in consent as a defense would be to increase the expected punishment costs of date rape, but perhaps not greatly, because the rapist can always claim to have had the woman's actual consent; it will be his word against hers, and to convict him the jury must be convinced beyond a reasonable doubt that she rather than he is telling the truth. Abolition would also, by making sex with one's date a riskier business from the man's standpoint, reduce, however slightly, the incidence of such sex. This should make the

32. Ehrlich, note 13 above, at 101 (tab. 5).

33. Frank McLynn, *Crime and Punishment in Eighteenth-Century England* 106–109 (1989). On the generally lackluster enforcement of English rape laws during the common law era, see Anna Clark, *Women's Silence, Men's Violence: Sexual Assault in England 1770–1845,* ch. 3 (1987).

34. Rubya Mehdi, "The Offence of Rape in the Islamic Law of Pakistan," 18 *International Journal of the Sociology of Law* 19, 27 (1990).

35. Compare on this question Estrich, note 29 above, at 103, and Lynne N. Henderson, "What Makes Rape a Crime," 3 *Berkeley Women's Law Journal* 193, 216 (1988), with Stephen J. Schulhofer, "The Gender Question in Criminal Law," 7 *Social Philosophy & Policy* 105, 130–135 (1990).

proposal attractive to men and women holding conservative views on sex, as well as to feminists who believe that date rape is a link in a chain of intimidation and subordination of women. But whether the median woman would gain from measures to deter date rape is not certain. By increasing the cost of dating to men, such measures would reduce the amount of dating, and heterosexual women would suffer. A similar objection can be lodged against proposals to strengthen the sanctions for sexual harassment in the workplace. The objections are not decisive. We recall that women's sexual strategies are not fixed, but respond to incentives. If legal changes make men less aggressive in initiating dating, we can expect women to become more aggressive. The amount of dating may not fall significantly.

The bracketing of sexual conservatives with feminists in favor of strong rape laws and in opposition to civil libertarians is more readily understandable than the parallel alignment in regard to pornography. Our word *rape* is derived from the Latin *raptus,* meaning "abduction." Traditionally, rape was the offense of depriving a father or husband of a valuable asset—his wife's chastity or his daughter's virginity.[36] Sexually conservative men and women continue to value these assets. Sexually liberal men value them much less and may therefore be inclined to weigh more heavily the rights of men accused of rape, especially since it is a class that potentially includes themselves. Feminists are unlikely to value virginity or chastity, but they see rape as a threat to their control over their reproductive capacity. So they concur with the conservatives, though for different reasons, in regarding rape with utmost gravity.

Sexual Abuse of Children

The problems of proof that vex the law of rape are magnified when the focus switches to the second broad area of coercive sex, that of sexual abuse of children (including the use of children as models in child pornography). But an anterior question is the harm which that abuse does. The aggregate harm is a product of two factors: how grave the harm that such abuse inflicts is on average; and how widespread the abuse is. The gravity of the harm is relevant not only to determining the optimal severity of punishment and to allocating the risk of error between prosecutor and defendant, but also to fixing the age of consent. The scale of the abuse is relevant to the optimal investment of social resources in dealing with the problem. Especially given well-founded concerns with the danger of false accusations of child sexual abuse, it is vital that we determine whether such abuse does as much harm to its victims, and is as widespread, as many fear it to be.

36. Bullough and Brundage, note 29 above, at 141–142.

Intuitively it is obvious that the sexual abuse of children inflicts deep psychological harm. But there are reasons to distrust this intuition. First of all, it could reflect an irrational taboo about the sexuality of children. The idea that children should be sexually innocent is not universal; in fact, it is relatively modern. Can we be sure that in the Middle Ages—when the idea had not yet taken hold and the sexual abuse of children was both common and, to a degree shocking to the modern sensibility, tolerated[37]—such abuse inflicted substantial psychological harm? A second and subtler point—limited to incestuous sexual abuse of children, but that is a highly common type, as we shall see—is that the psychological or even genetic factors that might impel a family member to commit incest might, if he were deterred, bring about by some other, lawful route the same harm attributed to the incestuous act. Third, contrary to popular impression, very little sexual abuse of children is violent or inflicts lasting physical injury, and in the case of young children it is much more likely to take the form of fondling than of penetration.[38]

That an intuition is unreliable does not make it wrong. It just means that we should not rest on it but should instead seek evidence. In fact a large number of psychological studies of the sexual abuse of children have been conducted, and the general conclusion is that such abuse is psychologically harmful to the child, producing behavior problems and depressing school achievement; that the harm persists into adulthood, where it shows up in anxiety and other neuroses, promiscuity, susceptibility to recruitment into prostitution (male as well as female), substance abuse, depression, difficulty in forming and maintaining close relationships, and diminution in sexual self-esteem; and that the harm is more severe the closer the relationship between the abuser and the abused, the wider the difference in their ages, and the greater the degree of force employed by the abuser.[39] Methodological diffi-

---

37. Lloyd deMause, "The Evolution of Childhood," in *The History of Childhood* 1, 43–49 (deMause ed. 1974). DeMause's evidence is anecdotal, and there is a skeptical literature well illustrated by Jerome Kroll and Bernard Bachrach, "Child Care and Child Abuse in Early Medieval Europe," 25 *Journal of the American Academy of Child Psychiatry* 562 (1986). But there is little doubt that attitudes toward the use of children as sexual objects has changed. For example, until raised by statute in 1885 to 16, the age of consent in the English law of rape was only 10. McLynn, note 33 above, at 107. (Consensual intercourse with a younger child was a misdemeanor, that is, a minor crime.) On the frequency of child sexual abuse in history, see, besides deMause's work, Diane H. Schetky and Arthur H. Green, *Child Sexual Abuse: A Handbook for Health Care and Legal Professionals* 24–29 (1988); Christopher Bagley and Kathleen King, *Child Sexual Abuse: The Search for Healing* 26–27 (1990).

38. D. J. West, "Adult Sexual Interest in Children: Implications for Social Control," in *Adult Sexual Interest in Children* 251 (Mark Cook and Kevin Howells eds. 1981); Kevin Howells, "Adult Sexual Interest in Children: Considerations Relevant to Theories of Aetiology," in *Adult Sexual Interest in Children* at 55, 82; *Sexual Offences against Children: Report of the Committee on Sexual Offences against Children and Youths*, vol. 2, 687–688 (1984).

39. Alison J. Einbender and William N. Friedrich, "Psychological Functioning and Behavior

culties, to be sure, abound.[40] The vast majority of studies are either of adults who are in trouble with the law or have sought psychiatric treatment, and who are asked to recall their childhood; or of children shortly after an incident of abuse has brought them to the attention of law enforcement or child-welfare authorities. The first type of study may depend too heavily on the vagaries of memory and in particular is vulnerable to distortion based on the natural human tendency to externalize the causes of one's failures—and so a prostitute asked about her personal history may offer as a self-satisfying explanation for her following so disreputable a vocation[41] an imagined or (more likely) exaggerated history of sexual abuse as a child. Studies of the abused children themselves do not reveal how often the effects of the abuse are permanent or if not permanent how long they last. Both types of study suffer from the difficulty of constructing a proper control group—a group

of Sexually Abused Girls," 57 *Journal of Consulting and Clinical Psychology* 155 (1989); William N. Friedrich, Robert L. Beilke, and Anthony J. Urquiza, "Children from Sexually Abusive Families: A Behavioral Comparison," 2 *Journal of Interpersonal Violence* 391 (1987); M. Gorcey, J. M. Santiago, and F. McCall-Perez, "Psychological Consequences for Women Sexually Abused in Childhood," 21 *Social Psychiatry* 129 (1986); Shane M. Murphy et al., "Current Psychological Functioning of Child Sexual Assault Survivors: A Community Study," 3 *Journal of Interpersonal Violence* 55 (1988); Joan L. Jackson et al., "Young Adult Women Who Report Childhood Intrafamilial Sexual Abuse: Subsequent Adjustment," 19 *Archives of Sexual Behavior* 211 (1990); Brandt F. Steele and Helen Alexander, "Long-Term Effects of Sexual Abuse in Childhood," in *Sexually Abused Children and Their Families* 223 (Patricia Beezley Mrazek and C. Henry Kempe eds. 1981); Diana E. H. Russell, *The Secret Trauma: Incest in the Lives of Girls and Women* 155–156 (1986); David Finkelhor, *Sexually Victimized Children* 107 (1979); Finkelhor, *Child Sexual Abuse: New Theory and Research* 192–193 (1984); Derek Jehu, "Sexual Inadequacy," in *The Psychology of Sexual Diversity,* note 17 above, at 135, 144–147; Mimi H. Silbert and Ayala M. Pines, "Sexual Child Abuse as an Antecedent to Prostitution," 5 *Child Abuse and Neglect* 407 (1981); Mark-David Janus, Barbara Scanlon, and Virginia Price, "Youth Prostitution," in *Child Pornography and Sex Rings,* ch. 7 (Ann Wolbert Burgess and Marieanne Lindeqvist Clark eds. 1984); Richard Dembo et al., "The Relationship between Physical and Sexual Abuse and Tobacco, Alcohol, and Illicit Drug Use among Youths in a Juvenile Detention Center," 23 *International Journal of the Addictions* 351, 362–363 (1988). This list is a small sample of a vast literature. For a useful review, see Angela Browne and David Finkelhor, "Impact of Child Sexual Abuse: A Review of the Research," 99 *Psychological Bulletin* 66 (1986).

40. Patricia Beezley Mrazek and David A. Mrazek, "The Effects of Child Sexual Abuse: Methodological Considerations," in *Sexually Abused Children and Their Families,* note 39 above, at 235; Jon R. Conte and John R. Schuerman, "The Effects of Sexual Abuse on Children: A Multidimensional View," 2 *Journal of Interpersonal Violence* 380 (1987).

41. Which in our society it doubtless is. Whether prostitution is *inherently* disreputable may be doubted. In a society in which sex was a morally indifferent subject, it probably would not be—and in fact there are plenty of historical examples (such as that of the Greek *hetairai,* mentioned in Chapter 6) of respectable prostitutes. I say "probably" because in many societies, including our own, there is moral opposition to some market transactions, such as the sale of blood and other human organs or even the lending of money at high rates of interest, that have nothing to do with sex.

whose members have the same characteristics as the sexually abused persons in the sample except for not having been sexually abused.

The control-group problem bedevils efforts to determine whether incestuous abuse is more harmful than abuse by nonrelatives. We cannot be certain in the case of incest whether it is the sexual act itself that inflicts harm or the family situation that gave rise to the act. The most ominous form of incest, father-daughter, typically occurs in a setting of "marital discord and a poor sexual relationship between the parents"; "unwillingness of the father to seek sexual relationships outside of the family"; "role reversal between mother and daughter which makes the daughter the central female figure in the home with the responsibility of satisfying the needs of the father"; and "conscious or unconscious condonation on the part of the mother of the relationship between father and daughter."[42] All but the second of these factors argue a distinctly unwholesome family relationship which conceivably might inflict the same psychological harm on the daughter even if the father were deterred from committing incestuous acts.[43]

Yet with all these problems conceded, the heavy preponderance of studies which find that the sexual abuse of children leaves deep and lasting scars makes a cumulatively convincing case. Although it is impossible to create an exactly matching control group, the size and persistence of the differences in a variety of measures of social and psychological adjustment between the experimental and control groups in study after study suggest a regularity that is not just an artifact of sample construction. It is not as if the hypothesis that these studies support is an improbable one. Whatever might be the case in a society that was morally indifferent to sex or treated children like adults, ours is not that society, which means that the adult who abuses a child sexually is likely to feel, and to instill, shame and fear. Here by the way is another example (recall the discussion in Chapter 11 of the possible effect on morale of relaxing the formal exclusion of homosexuals from the military) of moral feeling as brute fact which policy makers must take into account whether or not they personally share the feeling. In the case of incest an added factor is the sense of betrayal and breach of trust that the child is bound to feel, at least in retrospect, making incest to child abuse by a nonrelative as marital rape is to other rapes.

Sexual abuse of boys is facilitated by the fact that boys are not watched as

42. Adele Mayer, *Incest: A Treatment Manual for Therapy with Victims, Spouses and Offenders* 25 (1983). See also Steele and Alexander, note 39 above.

43. For different views on this question, compare Karin C. Meiselman, *Incest: A Psychological Study of Causes and Effects with Treatment Recommendations* 107 (1978), with Denise J. Gelinas, "The Persisting Negative Effects of Incest," 46 *Psychiatry* 312, 330 (1983). I set to one side the problem of the incestuous pregnancy.

closely by their parents as girls are.[44] There is speculation, though no solid evidence, that sexual abuse may be a factor in causing some boys to become homosexual.[45] Nevertheless, the emphasis that I have been placing on the sexual abuse of female children is warranted by the fact that it is by far the more common type. As with rape, only more so, sexual abuse of children is underreported. Much of it takes place within the privacy of the home, and the victims are for the most part timid, inarticulate, and of dubious credibility. A very young child may take years to realize that she has been the victim of a sex crime. Estimates of the incidence of sexual abuse of children must therefore be taken with a grain of salt, and there is a natural tendency to discount the very high estimates offered by some feminists. A careful nation-wide mail survey (with follow-up) conducted by the Canadian government does, however, corroborate the somewhat less systematic American studies, and allows one to offer a rough estimate that 20 percent of American women, and perhaps one-fifth as many men, were sexually abused before the age of 18 and that one-third of this abuse was by a relative, often the father.[46] Of course nowadays one is unlikely to consider a 17-year-old girl or even a 16-year-old girl a child; but when her seducer is her father or some other close older relative, it is proper to classify her among sexually abused children.

44. Gebhard, note 1 above, at 298–299.

45. Frank G. Bolton, Jr., Larry A. Morris, and Ann E. MacEachron, *Males at Risk: The Other Side of Child Sexual Abuse* 86–87 (1989); Adele Mayer, *Sexual Abuse: Causes, Consequences and Treatment of Incestuous and Pedophilic Acts* 61–63 (1985); Finkelhor, *Child Sexual Abuse,* note 39 above, at 195; Browne and Finkelhor, note 39 above, at 71. There is pretty good evidence that it predisposes youths to become male prostitutes. Janus, Scanlon, and Price, note 39 above. And male prostitutes service men, not women. But there is no evidence that being a male prostitute will convert a heterosexual into a homosexual, in the sense not of a person who commits homosexual acts—a male prostitute is that by definition—but of a person whose preferred sex object is of the same sex. The effects of sexual abuse on male children, reviewed in Bolton, Morris, and MacEachron, ch. 3, appear to be similar to the effects on female children. Incidentally, male abusers of male children appear to constitute a distinct subgroup within the homosexual population, as they are generally not interested in males who are not children. Bolton, Morris, and MacEachron at 61.

46. *Sexual Offences against Children,* note 38 above, vol. 1, ch. 6, esp. 175, 181; Russell, note 39 above, at 10, 61, 63–72; Finkelhor, *Child Sexual Abuse,* note 39 above, at 2, 10. Bolton, Morris, and MacEachron, note 45 above, at 35–38, offer a useful summary of the literature which supports my 20 percent estimate. (Gilbert, note 10 above, does not mention the Canadian study—indeed mentions only a handful of the studies.) And a judicious summary by Bagley and King, note 37 above, at 75, concludes that up to 25 percent of girls and up to 10 percent of boys are victims of sexual abuse. See also U.S. Department of Health and Human Services, National Center on Child Abuse and Neglect, "Child Sexual Abuse: Incest, Assault and Sexual Exploitation" 1–3 (DHHS Pub. no. [OHDS] 81-30166, rev. April 1981); James Gabarino, "The Incidence and Prevalence of Child Maltreatment," in *Family Violence,* note 23 above, at 219. Incidentally, the overwhelming majority of child sexual abusers are men, not women. "Child Sexual Abuse" at 3; Bolton, Morris, and MacEachron, note 45 above, at 52–56.

The magnitude of the problem, coupled with the persuasive although not conclusive evidence that sexual abuse of children causes serious and not merely transitory psychic injury, warrants a vigorous search for better methods of prevention. The fact that many offenders have normal sexual preferences—they are not pedophiles in preference but merely in conduct, having substituted a child for the adult sexual partner whom they would prefer but who for one reason or another is unavailable to them[47] (as in the typical case of father-daughter incest)—holds out hope that they are deterrable by the threat of criminal punishment. The problem is that, although the punishments for sexual abuse of children are severe, a large number even of the nonobsessive, opportunistic offenders evidently are not deterred, presumably because the probability of apprehension and punishment is very low. And then there are the obsessive pedophiles, who are difficult to deter.

While in principle the punishments for child sexual abuse could be made ever more severe, this would make it more difficult to maintain a difference in punishment between incestuous and nonincestuous child abuse. We want to punish incestuous abuse more heavily because there is evidence that, quite apart from the danger of inbreeding, it does more harm than abuse by non-relatives. So we want to deflect potential child abusers from their own relatives by, as it were, offering them a lighter punishment for preying on strangers. Also, incestuous abuse is more difficult to detect. (Note that these reasons for punishing incest heavily are independent of moral revulsion against the crime, except insofar as moral revulsion aggravates the psychological harm to the victim through the mechanism suggested earlier—the transfer of a sense of shame and fear from assailant to victim.) If we punish child sexual abuse by strangers too heavily, we cannot punish such abuse by relatives substantially more heavily because there are limits to the severity of punishment.

A further and I suspect more serious problem with making the punishments for child sexual abuse even more severe than they are now is that it would exacerbate the understandable concern with the reliability of evidence. The principal evidence of abuse is likely to be the child's word; and children are not always reliable or credible witnesses. False accusations of abuse, often procured by one of the child's parents as a weapon to use in a custody dispute with the other, are not uncommon.[48] This may be the only area of modern criminal law in which there is a significant danger of "frame-ups." Then too the child may simply be mistaken or confused. The devices used to elicit evidence from young children are of questionable reliability. For example, debate rages over the degree to which evidence elicited from children by

47. See Chapter 4; also Kurt Freund et al., "The Female Child as a Surrogate Object," 2 *Archives of Sexual Behavior* 119 (1972). Cf. Bolton, Morris, and MacEachron, note 45 above, at 47–48; Lester, note 25 above, ch. 16.

48. Schetky and Green, note 37 above, ch. 6.

psychologists using anatomically correct dolls in play therapy should be usable in court.[49] The problem of proof exacerbates the problem of the severity of punishment. The heavier the punishment for a crime is, the heavier the costs of an erroneous conviction are, and hence the more reluctant courts will be to admit evidence of questionable reliability that may, however, be indispensable to persuading the jury to convict. Thus, as with rape, an increase in the severity of punishment may be offset by a reduction in the probability of conviction, leaving expected punishment costs (the product of the probability and the severity of punishment) unchanged or even lower.

A fact that stands out in the studies of child sexual abuse is the substantially greater propensity of stepfathers to abuse their stepdaughters than of fathers to do so—an alarming finding when we consider that the propensity of biological fathers to abuse their daughters sexually is far from negligible.[50] The finding makes biological sense. One expects any genetic aversion to committing incest to be felt primarily by the biological relative; in addition, a man is less likely to be altruistic toward a stepdaughter than toward a biological daughter. My reason for hedging ("primarily," "less likely") is that there may well be an exception for a man who acquires parental rights when the child is an infant; this, as we shall see in the next chapter, may fool the genes. But stepfathers usually appear on the scene after the child has emerged from infancy, the mother having been divorced or widowed.

There is a reason independent of biology for expecting incest to be committed more often by stepfathers than by fathers. A daughter will have a stepfather only if her mother is divorced or widowed, and the break-up of the original family may reflect or create tensions that increase the likelihood of sexual abuse. On both grounds, sexual abuse of children is more likely the higher the incidence of divorce. But the implications for policy are obscure, because it is entirely unclear what feasible steps might be taken to reduce the divorce rate. For example, if women were treated more generously by courts in the event of divorce, they would have more incentive to invest in the marriage, but the costs of divorce to them would be less. The effects might be offsetting and leave the divorce rate unchanged.

49. Daniel Goleman, "Doubts Rise on Children as Witnesses: Researchers Quarrel over the Suggestibility of Young Minds," *New York Times,* November 6, 1990, B5; Nelson v. Farrey, 874 F.2d 1222 (7th Cir. 1989), and studies cited there; Robert J. Levy, "Using 'Scientific' Testing to Prove Child Sexual Abuse," 23 *Family Law Quarterly* 383 (1989).

50. Russell, note 39 above, at 234, found that stepfathers are seven times as likely as fathers to abuse their (step)daughters sexually—and 4.5 percent of the women in her sample had been abused by their fathers, most of whom were biological fathers rather than stepfathers. Id. at 216, 233–234. On the danger of abuse by stepfathers, see also id., ch. 17; Finkelhor, *Child Sexual Abuse,* note 39 above, at 25. Cf. *Sexual Offences against Children,* note 38 above, vol. 1, at 529–532, broadening the canvass of dangerous nonrelatives to include guardians and family friends.

A second fact that stands out from the studies is the variance across ethnic groups in the incidence of sexual abuse of children. Diana Russell found, for example, that the percentage of women in her sample who as children had been sexually abused by their fathers ranged from zero among Jews and Asians, to 4.4 percent among blacks, to 7.5 percent among Hispanics, to an astonishing 36 percent among American Indians.[51] It is unlikely that these differences can be explained by differences in education or income. Chapter 5, discussing the relatively low rate of child sexual abuse by blacks, suggested that the explanation for such differences in the incidence of such abuse might lie in differences in sex ratios across ethnic groups. Whatever their cause, these differences in the incidence of child sexual abuse can help tell us where preventive efforts should be concentrated.

The Age of Consent

At what age should consent to have sex be a defense to criminal charges? And should it vary by the sex of the participants or the nature of the sexual act, or perhaps by other factors instead or as well? The law's sharpest distinction in this area is between incestuous and other forms of abuse. There is no age of consent for incest; incest is illegal for all ages. This makes sense, not only because a teenage girl is unlikely to be as independent in dealing with her father or with other close relatives as she would be with a nonrelative but also, and more important, because the social objections to incest—which are by no means the product merely of a mindless taboo—are not limited to coercive incest (see Chapter 7). In the case of nonincestuous sex, however, the age of consent is critical. The higher it is, the more sexual activity is criminalized; the lower it is, the more potentially coercive sex is encouraged. Where to draw the line is a task for experts. But I would predict that the more permissive the society is, and therefore the better informed girls are about sex, the lower the age of consent should be,[52] not because the permissive society is insensitive to the need of children for protection against coercive sex, but because children in a permissive society are better informed about sex and therefore better able to protect themselves.

A male who has sex with a female who has not reached the age of consent is guilty of statutory rape; but many laws excuse the underage female from all criminal liability even if she is no younger than—she might even be older than—her male partner. The Supreme Court has held that this difference in

---

51. Russell, note 39 above, at 254–255.

52. This prediction is complicated by the fact that sexually repressive societies may set a low age of consent in order either to encourage early marriage or to recognize the right of parents to arrange their children's marriages, which is easier to do the younger the child is.

treatment does not deny males the equal protection of the laws.[53] Since the risk of pregnancy falls on the female, not the male, she has an incentive apart from threat of criminal punishment to avoid seduction, and the male does not.

The most difficult question regarding the age of consent is whether, as is the norm in foreign as well as U.S. jurisdictions that have decriminalized homosexual intercourse between consenting adults (other than the Netherlands), the age of consent for engaging in homosexual intercourse should be higher than that for engaging in heterosexual intercourse. A man who has sex with a 17-year-old boy may be guilty of statutory rape, whereas if his object were a 16-year-old girl he would not be. It can be argued that if we put aside all moral objections to homosexuality, the difference ought to run the other way, since only the girl can become pregnant. The fear that animates the difference in the law's approach is, no doubt, that homosexual seduction of an adolescent may cause him to become a homosexual. The fear seems largely, maybe entirely, baseless. It seems odd, moreover, that seduction of girls by men is expected to impair the girls' prospects for a healthy heterosexual adjustment when they are grown women, while seduction of boys by men is expected to facilitate their making a homosexual adjustment when they are grown men. Nor is there evidence that homosexual relations cause psychological harm to adolescent boys, as distinct from children; remember that pederasty, as distinct from pedophilia, refers to sex with adolescents, not with children.

It is curious to reflect that if the age of consent for homosexual relations were lowered to 15, which is the age of consent for girls in Sweden, most pederasty would be legalized. This might be a sensible reform (though the AIDS epidemic complicates the issue considerably), but do not hold your breath waiting for it. "Pederasty" has an awful sound in American ears; the sense of revulsion that the practice inspires, in all but the pederasts themselves, lies deeper than any reason that could be offered. Most Americans would if asked pronounce it a far worse crime than marital rape. No one could convince them that it probably is less harmful to its victims.

Homosexuals as Teachers

The lack of evidence that homosexuals are created by seduction, example, or recruitment casts doubt not only on the maintenance of a higher age of consent for homosexual than for heterosexual sex but also on the widespread practice of barring homosexuals from jobs that involve working with children and adolescents, such as teaching. I do not think it is an adequate answer to supporters of the exclusion, however, to say that if the homosexual teacher

53. Michael M. v. Superior Court, 450 U.S. 464 (1981).

seduces his students he can be fired, or, if they are under age, punished criminally. For the difficulties of apprehension and proof are acute. Another bad argument for allowing homosexuals to be schoolteachers is that pederasty is a salubrious phase for the boys involved, even if they are heterosexual, to pass through as a stage in the process of maturing. The argument is not made by mainline homosexual rights groups but has had some distinguished modern proponents, notably André Gide and Paul Goodman, the former arguing (in his book *Corydon*) from the Greek example, as did Oscar Wilde in his second trial; and there is an appreciable although far from rigorous advocacy literature.[54] The argument is that the mature lover acts as mentor and guide to the boy, helping him over the rough spots of adolescence and being compensated by sexual favors. Like its Greek original, which it closely resembles, the argument has a strong flavor of rationalization, and there is no substantiation for it. Although the possibility cannot be excluded that an erotic element in a teacher-student relationship may benefit the student's education, this implies that a male homosexual teacher would be a worse teacher of girls while a better one of boys; so the net effect is uncertain.

A better argument for dropping the ban against homosexual teachers is that teaching may be attractive to male homosexuals for reasons unrelated to seduction or recruitment. In this country teaching, especially below the college or university level, has a nonmasculine image, which is therefore less likely to deter homosexuals than heterosexuals. In addition, homosexuals may enjoy working with people too young to despise them as homosexuals. If homosexuals find school teaching a particularly attractive occupation and are unlikely to use their position to inveigle children into the homosexual life, this implies that society can obtain good teachers at lower average cost if it does not attempt to exclude homosexuals (unless the admission of homosexuals triggers "heterosexual flight," as one might describe the sexual equivalent of "white flight"). And America has a shortage of good teachers, in part because of the growth of job opportunities for women outside of teaching. A second reason for allowing homosexuals to teach is that adolescence is a crisis stage for many homosexuals, which homosexual teachers might help them surmount.[55]

---

54. For an illustration, see Robert Ehman, "Adult-Child Sex," in *Philosophy and Sex* 431 (Robert Baker and Frederick Elliston eds. 1984). See generally Parker Rossman, *Sexual Experience between Men and Boys: Exploring the Pederast Underground* (1976).

55. Stephen G. Schneider, Norman L. Farberow, and Garbriel N. Kruks, "Suicidal Behavior in Adolescent and Young Adult Gay Men," 19 *Suicide and Life-Threatening Behavior* 381 (1989); Eric Rofes, "Opening Up the Classroom Closet: Responding to the Educational Needs of Gay and Lesbian Youth," 59 *Harvard Educational Review* 444 (1989).

Separating Reproduction from Sex

MUCH OF THIS book has been concerned with the implications of separating sex from reproduction—of, in other words, nonprocreative sexuality in its many forms. But I have assumed that reproduction could not be separated from sex. Modern technology has made this assumption obsolete by perfecting artificial insemination. Even before modern technology, a partial separation of reproduction from sex was achieved by adoption. From the standpoint of the adoptive parents, adoption is a form of nonsexual reproduction: they acquire children without having produced them through sexual intercourse.

Does a discussion of nonsexual reproduction belong in a book on sexuality? It does. We shall see that it has profound implications for sexual attitudes, customs, and regulations.

Adoption

Adoption is the establishment of a parent-child relationship between an individual or couple, on the one hand, and a person who is not the biological child of the adoptive parent or parents—who need not even be a minor—on the other. It is an institution prominent in the law and practice of an enormous variety of cultures, including Babylonia, ancient Greece and Rome, India, China, and Japan.[1] In ancient Greece and Rome, and in Japan to this day,

---

1. For historical background and cross-cultural perspective, see *Adoption in Worldwide Perspective: A Review of Programs, Policies and Legislation in 14 Countries* (R. A. C. Hoksbergen ed. 1986); Leo Albert Huard, "The Law of Adoption: Ancient and Modern," 9 *Vanderbilt Law Review* 743 (1956); Jack Goody, "Adoption in Cross-Cultural Perspective," 11 *Comparative Studies in Society and History: An International Quarterly* 55 (1969); Stephen B. Presser, "The Historical Background of the American Law of Adoption," 11 *Journal of Family Law* 443 (1971); G. R. Driver and John C. Miles, *The Babylonian Laws*, vol. 1, *Legal Commentary* 383–405 (1952); Roger Just, *Women in Athenian Law and Life* 90–95 (1989); Margaret Sanford, "A

many adoptions were (are) of adults. Adult adoption is an unsentimental exchange: the adopted child obtains inheritance rights in exchange for services such as supporting the adoptive parents in their old age or worshiping them after their death. Such exchanges are remote from the concerns of this book and I shall ignore them, focusing instead on the adoption of infants. So Moses and Oedipus are more to the point than Augustus Caesar.

Although to us it is the natural form of adoption, child adoption presents a puzzle. Why should anyone be interested in raising someone else's child? The desire to have children, when separated from a desire for sexual intercourse, seems driven by the "desire" of the genes to replicate themselves. From that standpoint, adopting a child to whom one is not related makes no sense; better to devote the resources one would expend on an adopted child to a sibling, or to a niece or nephew, or even a cousin. So while adoption of relatives might be consistent with the biological model described in Chapter 4, the adoption of nonrelatives, which is highly common in our society, might seem to falsify the model. Not so. The human infant's need for protection has resulted in natural selection in favor of people who not only find infants cute, adorable, but also will bond with them. Because people find infants lovable, a childless couple may want to acquire a child, and once an infant is introduced into a couple's home the couple will bond with it, just as they would with their "own" child. So the genes are fooled. The younger the child is when it is adopted, the more completely they are fooled; a child obtained shortly after its birth, just as biological children are obtained, is a closer substitute for one's biological child than a child who makes its first appearance years later. This is one reason why the demand for infants is so much greater than that for older children. Other reasons (which equally explain the preference of most people to "adopt" a kitten or a puppy rather than an adult cat or dog) are that it is more difficult to bond with the older child, that the child may have come from a home in which it was abused, and that the trauma of switching parental custodians may injure the child emotionally and thereby make it more difficult to raise.

This analysis is supported by the literature on *alloparenting,* the biologist's term for the provision of care for a member of one's species of whom one is

---

Socialization in Ambiguity: Childlending in a British West Indian Society," 13 *Ethnology: An International Journal of Cultural and Social Anthropology* 393 (1974); John Boswell, *The Kindness of Strangers: The Abandonment of Children in Western Europe from Late Antiquity to the Renaissance* (1988) (index references under "adoption"); Taimie L. Bryant, "Sons and Lovers: Adoption in Japan," 38 *American Journal of Comparative Law* 299 (1990); Susan B. Hanley, "The Influence of Economic and Social Variables on Marriage and Fertility in Eighteenth and Nineteenth Century Japanese Villages," in *Population Patterns in the Past* 165, 173–174 (Ronald Demos Lee ed. 1977).

not the genetic parent.[2] Some alloparenting relationships among animals resemble adoption, although more resemble foster care or wet-nursing. The biological functions of alloparenting are various, and include kinship assistance (the sort of altruism discussed in Chapter 4 in connection with the genetic theory of homosexuality) and reciprocal altruism (exchange); the former puts us in mind of the adoption of a relative, the latter the businesslike form of adoption found in ancient Rome and in Japan. There is also exploitive adoption, which corresponds in human history to taking in abandoned children to serve as domestic servants or (and) sexual playthings,[3] and in modern American society to taking in foster children for purposes of sexual abuse. Some alloparenting is apparently designed to give the alloparent experience that will come in handy when it has its own offspring. But there is also reproductive error as a result of which the parent (usually a female) may become imprinted with the young of another animal.[4] That is the true animal parallel to modern American adoption.

Evidently the genes are not completely fooled by adoption. For we observe that people have a strong preference for their "own" children, although the man's preference in this regard will be weakened in a society in which he cannot be reasonably confident about the paternity of "his" children:[5] why worry too much about having your own rather than some other man's children if you can't be sure that your own children really are your own? This qualification to one side, few people who are able to have their own children would forgo the opportunity in favor of adopting a child even if offered a child superior in every respect to what they were likely to produce. The demand for adoption is limited largely to sterile couples. All homosexual couples are sterile, and therefore we would expect the demand for adoption to be especially strong among them, particularly lesbian couples, because their relationships are likely to be more durable than those of male homosexuals. It is no surprise that recognition of the right of homosexuals to adopt is a major goal of the movement for homosexual rights.

There are two big questions about adoption. The first is why formal adoption—that is, creation of the legal relationship of parent and child even if the child is not the biological child of the parent—is a relative novelty in Anglo-

2. Marianne L. Riedman. "The Evolution of Alloparental Care and Adoption in Mammals and Birds," 57 *Quarterly Review of Biology* 405 (1982).

3. Boswell, note 1 above, at 225, 420–421.

4. Riedman, note 2 above, at 425–426.

5. Suzanne G. Frayser, *Varieties of Sexual Experience: An Anthropological Perspective on Human Sexuality* 323–338 (1985); Steven J. C. Gaulin and Alice Schlegel, "Paternal Confidence and Paternal Investment: A Cross Cultural Test of a Sociobiological Hypothesis," 1 *Ethology and Sociobiology* 301 (1980).

American society. The common law did not recognize adoption. Recognition came in American statutes passed in the middle of the nineteenth century; the first English statute authorizing adoption was not passed until 1926. Why so late? There were plenty of childless couples in the old days, and also plenty of orphans. Yet impediments on both the supply and the demand side of the adoption market may have weakened the pressure for recognizing adoption as a legal form. On the supply side, although orphans were plentiful, they generally were raised by close relatives rather than adopted; this is the case even today, and it was all the more so in the era of extended families. And until the sexual revolution that began around the turn of the century, the number of illegitimate children—today the principal source of children for adoption—was relatively small. Another factor is that high rates of infant mortality (some owing to infanticide) and of child mortality, plus the prevalence of child labor and of apprenticeship, eliminated many children who would today be candidates for adoption or foster care. And manor houses, and in Catholic countries also the Church, absorbed many orphaned and abandoned children.

On the demand side of the market, the strong stigma of illegitimacy would have made many couples hesitate to adopt an illegitimate child; and a principal source of the demand for Roman adoption—ancestor worship—was killed by Christianity. In non-Christian societies polygamy, concubinage, and infanticide were alternative methods to adoption of equilibrating the demand for and supply of infants. The taking of an additional wife or a concubine is a standard remedy for childlessness in such societies, as well as an Old Testament commonplace. As for infanticide, which as we know not only is common in preindustrial societies but persisted in Europe long after the Church banned it, the practice argues a less sentimental view of young children than we have become accustomed to and hence a weaker desire to bond with an infant to whom one is not related.

I have proposed reasons why the political pressures for legal recognition and facilitation of adoption would not have been great even in Christian societies. But in addition there was political or ideological antipathy to adoption, based primarily, though I think not only, on a desire to discourage illegitimacy in order in turn to discourage nonmarital adultery and fornication. Adoption reduces the cost of illegitimacy, and therefore can be expected to increase the amount of nonmarital sexual intercourse.[6] Even today, there might be slightly less nonmarital intercourse if a woman contemplating it knew that carrying her fetus to term and putting up the newborn infant for adoption would not be possible if she became pregnant. Another worrisome aspect of adoption from the standpoint of a policy of channeling sex into marriage is

---

6. Consistent with this point, the Catholic Church traditionally was hostile to adoption. Angus McLaren, *A History of Contraception: From Antiquity to the Present Age* 110 (1990).

the boost it offers to nonmarital cohabitation. By adopting his illegitimate child, the man in a cohabiting couple could nullify one of the major pressures to marry. This concern has little contemporary relevance because modern family law gives both parents of a child born out of wedlock rights over the child—which just shows how far society has strayed from a policy of forcing sex into the marital channel.

Another historically but not currently significant objection to adoption is its potential for destabilizing the politics of a country in which government is weak. Adoption is a method by which great families can strengthen themselves. This was a big element in Roman adoption. Powerful families were a more serious threat in England than in America, and this, together with the freer sexual atmosphere of nineteenth-century America than Victorian England, may explain why adoption was given legal status in America first.

The Question of Sale

The second big question about adoption is, why is it so heavily regulated rather than being left, like other voluntary transactions, to the free market?[7] And heavily regulated it is in this country (to which I confine further discussion)—with the results predicted by economics. In most states, only adoption agencies may lawfully supply children for adoption. The agencies are private organizations, most of them nonprofit (often church-sponsored). Many states limit the fees that agencies may charge to the adoptive parents, but the essential regulation is a prohibition against the agencies' "buying" children. Buying is defined in this context as paying the biological mother more than the medical and maintenance costs (food, housing, and so forth) of pregnancy and childbirth. The nonprofit character of most adoption agencies, coupled with regulatory supervision, has generated a cost-plus system of adoption fees, with the result that the limitation on the payment to the biological mother is passed through to, and holds down, the adoption fee. Adoption agencies screen couples applying for a baby, excluding those couples whom the agency considers unfit to raise a child, for example because in the agency's opinion the couple is too old. Applicants who are not screened out often must wait years before the agency has a baby for them to adopt.

Some states permit independent adoption, that is, adoption not arranged through an adoption agency. Usually the arranger is a lawyer or an obstetri-

---

7. I have discussed the question before in two articles, to which the reader desiring an elaboration of my views and further references is directed. "The Economics of the Baby Shortage," 7 *Journal of Legal Studies* 323 (1978) (coauthored with Elisabeth M. Landes), and "The Regulation of the Market in Adoptions," 67 *Boston University Law Review* 59 (1987). For statistics on the demand for and supply of babies for adoption, see Christine A. Bachrach, "Adoption Plans, Adopted Children, and Adoptive Mothers," 48 *Journal of Marriage and the Family* 243 (1986).

cian. He is forbidden to charge a fee for the adoption beyond his usual professional fee for such incidental services as drawing up the necessary papers, in the case of a lawyer, or checking the health of the infant, in the case of an obstetrician. Thus, like the adoption agency, the arranger of an independent adoption is forbidden to "buy" children for adoption, defined as before. But because independent adoption is difficult to monitor (much more so than agency adoption), it often operates much as a free market in babies for adoption would, with payments to the biological mothers that exceed the mothers' medical and maintenance costs and that are recouped in high fees charged the adoptive parents. Independent adoption is therefore commonly referred to as the "gray market." Just as gray is a mixture of white and black, so independent adoption is a mixture of lawful adoption and "baby selling," the latter constituting an illegal (black) market.

The term *baby selling*, while inevitable, is misleading. A mother who surrenders her parental rights for a fee is not selling her baby; babies are not chattels, and cannot be bought and sold. She is selling her parental rights. Of course in like vein one might speak of a slaveowner's selling his rights over the slave. But those rights are rights of ownership; a parent's rights, in our society anyway, are not. So, sacrificing vividness to accuracy, I hereby rename "baby selling" "parental-right selling."

One of the best-confirmed hypotheses of economics—confirmed daily, in fact, in eastern Europe and the Soviet Union—is that a ceiling on the price that may lawfully be charged for a good or service will create both queues (waiting periods) and a black market, provided, of course, that the ceiling is lower than the free market price (otherwise it is not a real ceiling). This is what we observe in the adoption market today. The price ceiling that results from limiting the amount that may be paid the biological mother to her medical and maintenance expenses has created a shortage of babies for adoption. The consequence is queuing by the clientele of adoption agencies and of other lawful suppliers, and a black market for the bolder demanders.

The imbalance between demand and supply is growing. It is true that advances in the treatment of infertility, which have reduced the number of childless couples, may have offset the rising age of marriage, which has increased the number of childless couples because infertility is a positive function of a woman's age. If so, the demand for children for adoption is not increasing. But the supply is decreasing. For even though the increase in the illegitimacy rate has exceeded the decrease in the birth rate, the resulting net increase in the number of illegitimate births has in turn been exceeded by the increase in the rate at which unmarried mothers decide to retain their child rather than put it up for adoption. There appear to be two reasons for this increase. Women's income has risen, making women less dependent on men to support them and their children and thereby reducing the cost of illegitimacy.

And the availability of abortion has reduced the fraction of accidental pregnancies that result in unwanted births.[8]

The diminished supply of babies for adoption, interacting with a demand that is not declining, has exacerbated the effects of the price ceiling. It has increased the queue for babies, increased the number of independent adoptions—many of them black market adoptions—at the expense of the adoption agencies, driven up the black market price of parental rights (to about $25,000 in the case of a healthy white infant, the type of baby most highly valued by the market), and increased the pressures from the adoption agencies for stronger laws against the sale of parental rights and against independent adoption generally.

The straightforward way to deal with the problems created by a price ceiling is to remove the ceiling. Why has this not been done in the adoption market, now that the declining supply of babies for adoption has made the economic consequences of the price ceiling palpable? Usury laws, which are to lending as adoption law is to adoption, have been phased out for just this reason. The answer most students of adoption would give is that the social costs of a free market in babies for adoption would exceed those of the existing regulated market. All the arguments made in support of this proposition, however, either are bad ones or could easily be met by placing minor restrictions on an otherwise free market.

1. *The rich will snap up all the good babies, and the cost of acquisition will deprive those few middle-income couples fortunate enough to obtain a good baby of the resources they require to raise it properly.* Actually the rich do better under the present system than they would in a free market. The rich have connections, and connections are vital in maneuvering in a regulated system. Wealthy couples always manage to jump to the head of the adoption queue, thereby paying a lower real price—a price that includes the cost of waiting as well as the adoption fee—than the couple of modest means, who must wait years for their baby. (Granted this comparison ignores the cost to a wealthy person of using his connections.)

It is true that black market prices for adoption are high, though they are

---

8. On the supply of babies for adoption, see, besides Bachrach's article, note 7 above, Beth Berkov and June Sklar, "Does Illegitimacy Make a Difference? A Study of the Life Chances of Illegitimate Children in California," 2 *Population and Development Review* 201, 209–211 (1976). Bachrach, emphasizing that the drop in the supply was concentrated in the period 1971–1976—the period during which the availability of legal abortion in the United States exploded—ascribes that drop primarily to the increased availability of abortion. The sporadic efforts of the Ceausescu regime in Romania to prevent abortions are credited with producing a glut of foundlings—whom foreigners, in turn, consistent with the economic model, endeavor to purchase at the presumably depressed market price. "Romania Acts on Baby Trade," *Wall Street Journal,* May 17, 1991, A10.

only a small fraction of the total cost of raising a child. But they are not a good predictor of what the price would be in a free, unregulated market. For they are high because the seller has to be compensated for bearing the risk of punishment and because illegal sellers incur high costs of operation by virtue of having to conceal their activities from the authorities. Competition among pregnant women to sell their parental rights would drive the price of those rights down to a level only slightly above the medical and maintenance costs of pregnancy. Since those costs are saved by a woman who does not become pregnant, the net additional cost of buying parental rights over an existing baby, versus making a baby, would be slight or even negative—as where a woman having high opportunity costs of pregnancy (maybe she has a high income) buys the parental rights of a woman whose opportunity costs of pregnancy are low.

What is probably true is that most women who sold their parental rights would be less prosperous than the women who bought them. But this means that parental-rights selling would be wealth-equalizing.

2. *The sale of parental rights may be value-maximizing from the standpoint of pregnant women and infertile couples, but it is bad from the standpoint of the children.* Of course the welfare of children as well as that of their natural and adoptive parents should be considered in the design of public policy, since neither set of parents can be relied on in their decision making to weight the child's welfare as highly as the child itself would do, if it could be consulted. Adoption agencies screen adoptive parents in the interest of the children, and this screening would not be an inherent feature of a market in parental rights, just as it is not a feature, at least a systematic feature, of independent adoption. But adoption agencies lack good information about the relative fitness of competing couples seeking children, and many of the rules that such agencies have employed—such as requiring that the adoptive parents be of the same religion as the infant's parents (for it is unrealistic to speak of the infant's religion), or automatically excluding all couples over 40 years of age—make a poor fit with the interests of the child. There is no evidence that children adopted independently—even those obtained through the black market—are less happy or successful or well adjusted than children adopted through agencies, though admittedly the question appears not to have been studied.

3. *What about the danger that pedophiles will buy parental rights over children in order to abuse the children sexually?* Given the problems discussed in the preceding chapter of controlling sexual abuse of children, and the high incidence of such abuse especially by stepfathers, this danger cannot be dismissed out of hand. But it can be minimized, perhaps even eliminated, by forbidding the sale of rights over children who are no longer infants—say children more than six months old. Very few child abusers have a sexual interest in infants; very few would acquire an infant for the purpose of being able to abuse it five or ten or fifteen years later; and whereas a stepfather

usually first encounters his stepchild after the latter has emerged from infancy, when it is too late for the stepfather to be expected to form a parental-type bond that will inhibit incest with the child, the adoptive father ordinarily meets his adopted child when the latter is an infant, and would do so only then if the sale of rights over noninfants was prohibited. The suggested restriction on sale would be a minor curtailment of the market because for reasons discussed earlier there is little demand—little legitimate demand, at any rate—to adopt children past infancy. Moreover, persons with a criminal record of child abuse, or even all men not living as part of a heterosexual couple, could be forbidden to buy parental rights.

4. *The sale of a human being in any circumstances and for any reasons is morally repulsive, and if permitted could undermine the taboo against slavery.* A variant of this argument, made by Margaret Jane Radin,[9] is that what she naturally terms baby selling promotes "commodification," which—we recall from the discussion of Marcuse in previous chapters—is the tendency, characteristic of capitalist societies, to view goods and services as things that can be exchanged in a market. Fair enough, but some of us believe that this and most societies could use more, not less, commodification and a more complete diffusion of the market-oriented ethical values that it promotes. If, for example, clean air were commodified, we would have less air pollution than we do.

A better answer, though, is that baby selling, when viewed as a method of adoption, is not at all like the sale of a person into slavery. The "purchasers" get no more power over the baby than natural parents have over their children. What is sold, in fact, is not the baby but the natural mother's right to keep the baby—which is why I said that "baby selling" is misnamed. The term misled Radin.

5. *The sale of parental rights will encourage eugenic breeding, altering the human gene pool in potentially harmful ways.* Markets foster innovation; so should we not be concerned that eugenic entrepreneurs will try to breed a race of supermen and superwomen? Too great a disparity among human beings, owing to selective breeding of some, could create differences among persons in physical appearance and in physical and mental ability that would undermine cooperation and foment conflict, exploitation, even genocide, and, much like selective breeding of domestic animals, could introduce harmful mutations or, like incest, reduce genetic diversity. There are three reasons to discount these dangers. The first is that the market is unlikely to attract fertile couples. The second (and related) reason is that most people want their baby, biological or adopted, to be like them, so only Superman and Superwoman will want to have Superbaby. There is a genetic explanation for this preference (which is gene-fooling when the baby is adopted)—the similarity increases

9. "Market-Inalienability," 100 *Harvard Law Review* 1849, 1925–28 (1987).

confidence that it is *your* baby, not someone else's—and in addition it reduces the potential for conflicts between parents and child. Third, long before the eugenicists create a master race, biological parents will be improving their babies by surgical intervention in the fertilized ovum.

The more plausible concern with the genetic effects of parental-rights selling is the opposite. The mothers are likely to be drawn from the lower strata of society; and, if poverty and intelligence are negatively related, the IQs of these mothers will be below average, and the average IQ in society will therefore fall, with possible detrimental effects—higher costs of public education, more crime, and so on. But the danger that IQs will fall hardly seems a serious one, even if there is a strong, and genetic rather than environmental, positive correlation between income and IQ. It is not so much that if infertile couples were willing to pay for rights over high-IQ babies, a supply would be forthcoming, for demand would be limited by price. It is that most of the babies who would be obtained in a free market in parental rights are not babies who would be aborted; they are babies who would be retained by unmarried mothers. There probably will be a net increase in the number of babies from this class of mothers (I will return to this point), but a small one.

6. *How would parental-rights selling work? Could the buyer return the baby if it was not as healthy and intelligent as the seller had warranted it to be? Does this question not show that such a market is simply too bizarre an intellectual construct to deserve serious consideration?* Contracts in which the thing contracted over is a human being do present unique difficulties in matters of remedy, although the usual response is to require modification of the remedy rather than abolition of the market. A contract for the exclusive services of a person for a specified period of time is lawful and enforceable—but not by deeming the person a slave of the other party or even by issuing an injunction commanding him to continue working for that party, as distinct from an injunction forbidding him to work for anyone else. Similar adjustments in the normal principles of contract remedies would be necessary if adoption were left to the market. Adjustments are necessary already for cases in which adoptive parents sue the adoption agency or the independent-adoption middleman because the baby turns out to be defective. Maybe for the baby's sake the purchaser of parental rights should not be allowed the usual privilege of returning defective merchandise, any more than he should be allowed to destroy it, but should be limited to a remedy in damages against the seller for the breach of whatever warranty of quality the seller may have given. Intermediaries—successors to today's adoption agencies—would spring into existence to guarantee quality to buyers.

What is true is that this program *sounds* fantastic and weird, just as it seems fantastic to imagine these literal "bonus babies" bragging when they grow up of the tremendous prices their parents paid in the baby market, and just as it seems fantastic and sad to imagine what would undoubtedly be the pronounced racial element in baby pricing. The demand for babies for adoption is weaker among blacks than among whites, while the supply of such babies is vastly greater; so the price of acquiring parental rights over black babies would be lower unless white couples considered black babies a close substitute for white ones, which most white couples probably would not, even if white demand for black babies were not artificially depressed by opposition within the black community.[10]

One might expect sexual conservatives to favor parental-rights selling because, by increasing the effective demand for children for adoption, it would increase the opportunity costs of abortion. They don't, however, and they may be right (from their standpoint) not to. The greater the demand for children for adoption, the lower the cost of sex, so the more sex there will be; specifically, the more *nonmarital* sex there will be, for married couples rarely consider giving up a child for adoption. Sexual conservatives do not like nonmarital sex. Moreover, the abortion rate may not decline, since that rate is a function in part of the amount of nonmarital sex, which will rise if adoption becomes a more attractive option for pregnant women.

I have left for last Gary Becker and Kevin Murphy's criticism of parental-rights selling, a criticism of particular importance because it comes from within economics rather than from persons hostile to a market system or ignorant of its workings. They argue that "the universal ban on this practice strongly suggests that the sale of children lowers social utility. Young unmarried women and poor parents who need money are the two groups most likely to sell their children. Some children sold to prosperous families who want them may consider themselves better off than if they had remained with their parents. But even children who would suffer greatly might be sold because they have no way to compensate their parents for keeping them."[11] There actually are two arguments here rather than one. The argument from the universal ban on the practice is logically independent of the argument from the adverse effect on children. For one might think the existence of a universal ban against a practice a good reason for suspecting on Darwinian grounds that the practice was a bad one, even if one could not think of a convincing hypothesis as to why it was bad.

Neither of the arguments persuades me. First, the ban is not universal, even if we ignore Roman and Japanese adult adoptions—straightforward commercial exchanges—on the ground that an adult can protect his interests better

10. "A strong statement in 1972 by the National Association of Black Social Workers describing transracial adoption as a form of genocide helped to generate a reconsideration of transracial placements." Arnold R. Silverman, "Nonrelative Adoption in the United States: A Brief Survey," in *Adoption in Worldwide Perspective*, note 1 above, at 1, 8.

11. Gary S. Becker and Kevin M. Murphy, "The Family and the State," 31 *Journal of Law and Economics* 1, 14 (1988), reprinted in Becker, *A Treatise on the Family* 362, 376 (enlarged ed. 1991).

than a child can. Not only was there adoption of children as well as adults among the Romans, but money changed hands frequently.[12] And until the seventh century A.D. an Anglo-Saxon father was permitted to sell his child in a case of necessity, provided the child had not yet turned 7.[13] What is true is that the sale of parental rights appears to be rare outside of the United States today (which is one reason the United States is the major importer of babies—from Romania, Korea, and elsewhere). But then adoption is rare outside of the United States, for reasons presumably independent of legal sanctions. As for the ban on such sales in the United States, it is extraordinarily porous, and parental-rights selling is therefore in fact common, to the despair of its critics. Do words speak louder than actions, or actions louder than words? Little effort is made to stamp out the sale of parental rights, so one may question the social commitment to the ban.

Becker and Murphy's second argument appears to envisage the sale of rights over children who are no longer infants. The picture is of parents who have decided they cannot afford to raise their child after all and therefore abandon it, to its intense distress, to strangers. In these circumstances the sale certainly has a serious third-party effect—that is, an effect on the child—that the parties to the sale may not take fully into account. This is another reason for forbidding the sale of rights over children who are no longer infants, but it does not touch the sale of rights over infants. Here the only sellers are single mothers; and who can say whether the average infant would (if fully informed) prefer to be raised by an unmarried woman eager to unload it rather than by a couple from a higher social and economic stratum eager to raise it? Any loss of welfare to the child, moreover, would have to be compared to the gain to the transacting parties.

If there are no convincing arguments for forbidding the sale of parental rights over infants, why is it forbidden? Three possibilities occur to me. The first is that adoption agencies, which emerged before conditions of demand and supply created attractive entrepreneurial opportunities in parental-rights selling, have a selfish interest in preventing a competing service from emerging; and they have made the label "baby selling" stick. Second, the persisting influence of collectivist ideologies in all modern Western states, including the United States, creates ideological resistance to allowing the "commodification" of a good or service heretofore forbidden to be bought and sold. And third,

12. Boswell, note 1 above, at 65–69, 115–116; A. H. M. Jones, *The Later Roman Empire 284–602: A Social Economic and Administrative Survey*, vol. 2, 1043–44 (1964). This was also true of child adoption in Japan before the twentieth century. J. Mark Ramseyer, "Indentured Prostitution in Japan: Credible Commitments in the Commercial Sex Industry," 7 *Journal of Law, Economics & Organization* 89 (1991).

13. Frederick Pollock and Frederic William Maitland, *The History of English Law before the Time of Edward I*, vol. 2, 436 (2d ed. 1899). I assume that by "necessity" they mean having insufficient resources to raise the child.

by increasing the demand for illegitimate births, a market in babies would reward extramarital sex, a practice still widely disapproved by influential groups in the society.

Homosexual Adoption

The last question I want to discuss under the rubric of adoption is whether homosexual couples should be allowed to buy parental rights. Despite its form, the question is independent of the issue of parental-rights selling. One could retain the ban on such selling but permit homosexuals to adopt children, or one could allow the selling but disqualify homosexuals as buyers. But putting the question in market terms helps to make transparent the trade-offs in a proper social cost-benefit analysis. The homosexual couple must benefit—more precisely must expect to benefit—from the purchase of parental rights over the child, or it would not make the purchase; and the natural mother must expect to benefit too, or she would not make the sale. So if the child is better off, no worse off, or even slightly worse off than it would be in a regime that forbade homosexual couples to adopt, they should be allowed to do so. The analysis becomes more complicated if we admit the possibility of competition between heterosexual and homosexual couples to adopt. This is one reason why a child might be worse off if adoption by homosexuals were allowed. As for the impact on the heterosexual couple that is outbid for the child, that couple's loss is balanced by the gain to the homosexual couple and to the natural mother; she will receive a higher price if there is competition among buyers. The net gain to the adopting couple and the natural mother must be compared with the loss, if any, to the child.

Most adoption agencies, and most domestic relations courts (which must approve adoptions), try to prevent homosexuals from adopting children. Not all do, though. And anyway a ban on adoption by homosexuals does not guarantee that no child will have a homosexual parent. Many homosexuals, especially female homosexuals, have been married[14] and have had children; and a male homosexual who is not married could arrange for a woman to bear his child and abandon it to him. It is impossible as a practical matter to prevent a lesbian couple from having a child, either by artificial insemination or by intercourse with a man willing to give up his paternal rights. Moreover, since the mother is usually given custody of children in the event of divorce, a lesbian who is married, has children, divorces, and is awarded custody of the children may thereafter bring up the children in a lesbian household.

There is thus a fair amount of experience with the raising of children in

14. Twenty percent of male—but more than a third of female—homosexuals in a sample of San Francisco homosexuals in the 1970s. Alan P. Bell and Martin S. Weinberg, *Homosexualities: A Study of Diversity among Men and Women* 162, 166 (1978).

homosexual (principally lesbian) households, and though much of the literature on it is quite worthless, such as a mail survey in which homosexual and
lesbian parents were asked to evaluate their relationships with their children,[15]
there have been several careful studies. In one, British psychiatrists compared
the children in twenty-seven lesbian households with the children in an equal
number of households headed by an unmarried heterosexual woman.[16] Most
of the mothers in both groups were divorced. Some of the lesbians lived alone,
others in lesbian couples. All the lesbians were openly so. The children ranged
up to the age of 17, but most were prepubertal; all, however, were of school
age. The study revealed no differences in either the sexual orientation of the
children in the two groups or their mental health or social adjustment—except
that there was some evidence that the children raised in the households headed
by an unmarried heterosexual woman had *more* psychiatric problems. The
authors acknowledged, however, that most of the children in the study were
too young to exhibit a pronounced sexual orientation and that the study did
not compare children being raised by a lesbian couple with children being
raised by a heterosexual couple. Moreover, almost all the children in the
lesbian households had had a father in the household for at least the first two
years of the child's life.

With these limitations, such a study cannot shed much light on the suitability of lesbians as adoptive couples, let alone of male homosexuals, about
whose abilities as parents almost nothing is known.[17] But it does cast doubt
on confident judicial assertions that a homosexual parent is bound to influence
a child's sexual orientation or impair a child's psychological health or well-
being. Here is a representative quotation:

15. Mary B. Harris and Pauline H. Turner, "Gay and Lesbian Parents," 12 *Journal of
Homosexuality* 101 (1986).

16. Susan Golombok, Ann Spencer, and Michael Rutter, "Children in Lesbian and Single-
Parent Households: Psychosexual and Psychiatric Appraisal," 24 *Journal of Child Psychology
and Psychiatry* 551 (1983). Similar studies with similar results are Martha Kirkpatrick, Catherine
Smith, and Ron Roy, "Lesbian Mothers and Their Children: A Comparative Survey," 51 *American
Journal of Orthopsychiatry* 545 (1981); Beverly Hoeffer, "Children's Acquisition of Sex-Role
Behavior in Lesbian-Mother Families," 51 *American Journal of Orthopsychiatry* 536 (1981);
Richard Green, "Sexual Identity of 37 Children Raised by Homosexual or Transsexual Parents,"
135 *American Journal of Psychiatry* 692 (1978), and Green et al., "Lesbian Mothers and Their
Children: A Comparison with Solo Parent Heterosexual Mothers and Their Children," 15 *Ar-
chives of Sexual Behavior* 167 (1986). See also David J. Kleber, Robert J. Howell, and Alta Lura
Tibbits-Kleber, "The Impact of Parental Homosexuality in Child Custody Cases: A Review of
the Literature," 14 *Bulletin of the American Academy of Psychiatry and Law* 81 (1986).

17. Terry S. Stein, "Homosexuality and New Family Forms: Issues in Psychotherapy," 18
Psychiatric Annals 12, 15 (1988). Although such studies as have been conducted of children
living with homosexual fathers indicate no effect on the children beyond occasional embarrassment at having a homosexual father, Frederick W. Bozett, "Children of Gay Fathers," in *Gay
and Lesbian Parents* 39 (Bozett ed. 1987), I am troubled by the strong tone of advocacy in
Bozett's article, as in *Gay and Lesbian Parents* (in which the studies are collected) generally.

Allowing that homosexuality is a permissible life style—an "alternate life style," as it is termed these days—if voluntarily chosen, yet who would place a child in a milieu where she may be inclined toward it? She may thereby be condemned, in one degree or another, to sexual disorientation, to social ostracism, contempt and unhappiness. Appellant Kathy stresses Dr. Buchanan's testimony that the child at this time—age 10—shows no ill effects from her present environment. Dr. Buchanan finds the child to be normal and well adjusted. The court does not need to wait, though, till the damage is done.[18]

This is not an impressive specimen of reasoning, but that does not mean it is wrong. We do not have enough scientific evidence on the consequences of allowing homosexuals to raise children to be able to scoff confidently at the widespread intuition that it is a bad thing. We therefore should not reject out of hand a decision such as *J.L.P.(H.) v. D.J.P.*,[19] which upheld a limitation on the visitation rights of a divorced father who, the court found, was in the habit of taking his 11-year-old son to homosexual social gatherings and a "gay church," and who testified that he thought it would be "desirable" for the boy to be homosexual. A school of lesbian thought rejects the proposition that a lesbian mother should be neutral with regard to the sexual orientation of her daughters,[20] arguing that "our children are the daughters of women who love women over men. Daughters of lesbians, like freedom fighters everywhere, need to be enlisted in infancy, and protected against heterofemininity by words and actions."[21] A woman who believes this and acts on the belief cannot automatically be assumed to be a fit parent.

All this said, it is undesirable to have a flat rule against permitting homosexuals to have custody of children or even to adopt them. Often the issue of homosexual custody or adoption arises after a parental or parental-style relationship has been created between a homosexual and a child. The child might be the homosexual's own child, and the other parent might be for one reason or another a totally unsuitable custodian. Or the child might have bounced around from one foster home to another, and homosexual adoption

18. N.K.M. v. L.E.M., 606 S.W.2d 179, 186 (Mo. App. 1980). For similar statements see In re Appeal in Pima County Juvenile Action, 151 Ariz. 335, 727 P.2d 830 (Ct. App. 1986); Roberts v. Roberts, 22 Ohio App. 3d 127, 489 N.E.2d 1067 (1985); M.J.P. v. J.G.P., 640 P.2d 966 (Okla. 1982), and cases cited there. Unusual awareness of the scholarly literature on homosexual parents is evident, however, in In re Opinion of the Justices, 530 A.2d 21 (N.H. 1987). For a thorough discussion of the cases and the issue, see Nancy D. Polikoff, "This Child Does Have Two Mothers: Redefining Parenthood to Meet the Needs of Children in Lesbian-Mother and Other Nontraditional Families," 78 *Georgetown Law Journal* 459 (1990).

19. 643 S.W.2d 865 (Mo. App. 1982).

20. Baba Copper, "The Radical Potential in Lesbian Parenting of Daughters," in *Politics of Mothering: A Lesbian Parenting Anthology* 233, 239 (Sandra Pollock and Jeanne Vaughn eds. 1987).

21. Id. at 240. Not all lesbians hold this view. See, for example, Kate Hill, "Mothers by Insemination: Interviews," id. at 111.

might be the child's only prospect for any sort of home life. Considerations such as these have led many courts to reject strict rules forbidding or permitting homosexual adoption in favor of taking a case-by-case approach,[22] which has the further advantage of generating more information about the effects, as yet poorly understood, of homosexual custody on children.

Artificial Insemination and the Issue of Surrogate Motherhood

First used in this country to fertilize a human being in 1884, artificial insemination is not only the oldest and the best known but also the most frequently employed member of a rapidly growing family of technological responses to problems of fertility that are incurable in the sense that the couple cannot be made capable of conceiving through sexual intercourse.[23] Other responses, which employ artificial insemination only as the first stage of the procreative procedure, include in vitro fertilization, in which the woman's egg is fertilized outside the womb, then implanted in the womb and carried to term in the usual way, and the form of surrogate motherhood in which the woman's egg is fertilized outside the body and then implanted in the uterus of another woman—a living incubator. The more common form of surrogate motherhood involves the artificial insemination of a woman who agrees to give up the baby when it is born to the father and his wife. Here the only novelty, compared to unadorned artificial insemination, is contractual, not technological: the arrangement with the surrogate mother. The "surrogate" mother is of course the "real" mother from the biological standpoint, although she is the surrogate for the father's wife. Feminists dislike the "decentering" of the biological mother implied by this terminology, but this is odd because, in opposing abortion, they reject the "privileging" of biological over social categories.

22. See, for example, In re Adoption of Charles B., 50 Ohio St. 3d 88, 552 N.E.2d 884 (1990) (per curiam); Bezio v. Patenaude, 381 Mass. 563, 410 N.E.2d 1207 (1980); M.A.B. v. R.B., 134 Misc. 2d 317, 510 N.Y.S.2d 960 (S. Ct. 1986). In like vein, the Utah Supreme Court has held that polygamists are not automatically disqualified from adopting. In re Adoption of W.A.T., 808 P.2d 1083 (Utah 1991).

23. Helpful discussions of the technologies, and of the issues of law and public policy that they raise, include George P. Smith II, *The New Biology: Law, Ethics, and Biotechnology,* ch. 9 (1989); Sherman Elias and George J. Annas, *Reproductive Genetics and the Law,* ch. 9 (1987) ("Noncoital Reproduction"); Walter Wadlington, "Artificial Conception: The Challenge for Family Law," 69 *Virginia Law Review* 465 (1983); Developments in the Law, "Medical Technology and the Law," 103 *Harvard Law Review* 1519 (1990). A book-length treatment in article form is William Joseph Wagner, "The Contractual Reallocation of Procreative Resources and Parental Rights: The Natural Endowment Critique," 41 *Case Western Reserve Law Review* 1 (1990). The demand for fertility treatments is carefully examined in Debra S. Kalmuss, "The Use of Infertility Services among Fertility-Impaired Couples," 24 *Demography* 575 (1987). I shall use *fertility* broadly to mean capacity for producing a healthy child; thus the possession of recessive genes that would create a serious danger of producing a deformed child is a fertility problem.

Artificial insemination, even of the old-fashioned sort, is rich with social implications. We have seen that, as a practical matter, it places lesbian custody of children beyond the reach of governmental regulation. Beyond that, it allows women to escape having to share parental rights with men, since the sperm donor, whether provided through the woman's physician or through a sperm bank, is anonymous.[24] It therefore accelerates the shift of economic power from men to women, discussed in Chapter 6. And it invites, through the medium of competition among sperm banks, more experimentation with eugenic breeding of human beings. In 1980 several Nobel scientists agreed to contribute sperm to a sperm bank, founded by the physicist Robert Graham, which then advertised the superior genetic properties of its product. The couples who patronized the bank did not want the Nobel laureates' sperm, however, because of the advanced age of the laureates; for the older the male (as well as the female) parent, the greater the risk of birth defects. So the bank no longer has any Nobel donors. But it is thriving, using sperm donated by well-regarded but younger scientists; and its customers appear to be well satisfied with their offspring.[25]

Surrogate motherhood in the form, at once more common and more problematic from a social standpoint, in which the surrogate is the child's biological mother in the fullest sense rather than merely a living incubator contributing nothing to the genetic makeup of the child, expands artificial insemination from a method of coping with male fertility problems to one of coping with female fertility problems as well. This form of surrogate motherhood has stirred a fierce debate to which the economic analysis of adoption has much to contribute.[26]

24. On the institutional arrangements for artificial insemination, see Martin Curie-Cohen, Lesleigh Luttrell, and Sander Shapiro, "Current Practice of Artificial Insemination by Donor in the United States," 300 *New England Journal of Medicine* 585 (1979); Comment, "The Need for Regulation of Artificial Insemination by Donor," 22 *San Diego Law Review* 1193 (1985). Some sense of the magnitudes involved may be helpful. About 65,000 babies are created by artificial insemination every year, almost half from donor sperm and the rest from sperm contributed by the woman's husband or other known sexual partner. In vitro fertilization accounts for 600 of these babies, surrogate motherhood for only 100. Gregory Byrne, "Artificial Insemination Report Prompts Call for Regulation," 241 *Science* 895 (1988).

25. Wadlington, note 23 above, at 468 n. 14; Note, "Eugenic Artificial Insemination: A Cure for Mediocrity?" 94 *Harvard Law Review* 1850 (1981); Katharine Lowry, "The Designer Babies Are Growing Up: At Home with the First Children of the 'Genius' Sperm Bank," *Los Angeles Times,* November 1, 1987, 7 (magazine section). By 1987, the bank had produced forty-one children, but they had not been systematically studied. Indeed I have found no systematic studies of the children of artificially inseminated women. R. Snowden and G. D. Mitchell, *The Artificial Family* 80 (1983); Burton Z. Sokoloff, "Alternative Methods of Reproduction: Effects on the Child," 26 *Clinical Pediatrics* 11 (1987).

26. Further elucidation of my views, and supporting documentation, may be found in my article "The Ethics and Economics of Enforcing Contracts of Surrogate Motherhood," 5 *Journal of Contemporary Health Law and Policy* 21 (1989). A collection of essays pro and con (mostly con) surrogate motherhood is *Surrogate Motherhood: Politics and Privacy* (Larry Gostin ed.

The demand for surrogate motherhood is easy to understand. It is a substitute for adoption, and governmental regulation of adoption has, by reducing the supply of babies for adoption below the level it would reach if the price system were allowed to operate unhindered, increased the demand for substitutes. (Hence critics of surrogate motherhood ought to support the reform of adoption law.) Surrogate motherhood may well be a superior substitute, moreover, both because it enables one member of the couple, at least, the man, to satisfy his desire to replicate his genes, and because genetic overlap between parents and child may reduce intrafamilial conflict. It is criticized, in comparison to adoption, as creating a disadvantaged child—that is, a child who is not to be brought up by both of its biological parents—whereas adoption provides a home for an already existent disadvantaged child.[27] Ignored is the fact that the availability of adoption, by reducing the cost of noncontraceptive sex, increases the probability that children will be born who are put up for adoption—who are, in the eyes of this school of critics, disadvantaged.

Critics of surrogate motherhood focus their ire on the surrogate mother's being allowed to make a *legally enforceable* contract to give up the child to the father and his wife upon the child's birth. Yet without such a contract, the father and his wife have no assurance that they will actually get a baby out of the deal. If, because the surrogate mother reneges, they do not, it means that they have lost a year or more in their quest for a baby—nine months of gestation plus however long it takes before then for the surrogate mother to conceive. And they have no assurance that the next surrogate mother, and the next, will not renege also. Even if the surrogate mother does not renege, she has an incentive to threaten to do so in order to obtain a higher price than the one she agreed to accept back when the contract was signed. In other words, if the law refuses to enforce contracts of surrogate motherhood, it empowers surrogate mothers to commit extortion.

True, that refusal will also cause the couple to screen each prospective surrogate mother more carefully for the genuineness of her expressed willingness to give up the child when it is born; and the result of this more careful screening will be fewer surrogates who decide either that they cannot bear to part with it or that they should try to extort a higher price.[28] But such screening is bound to be costly and of limited efficacy, which means that the benefits of

1990). The practice is strongly defended in Carmel Shalev, *Birth Power: The Case for Surrogacy* (1989); Lori Andrews, *Between Strangers: Surrogate Mothers, Expectant Fathers, and Brave New Babies* (1989); and Peter H. Schuck, "Some Reflections on the Baby M Case," 76 *Georgetown Law Journal* 1793 (1988).

27. Rosalind Hursthouse, *Beginning Lives* 322 (1987).

28. Michael J. Trebilcock, "Commodification" 57 (University of Toronto Faculty of Law, January 28, 1991).

surrogate motherhood will be reduced to both sides of the transaction. The surrogate mother, for example, will receive a lower price because her performance is uncertain. So in the long run surrogate mothers will lose, not gain, from a rule designed to strengthen their bargaining position by allowing them to repudiate their contracts.

Because surrogate motherhood is a frankly commercial arrangement for the production of a baby (although some surrogate mothers offer altruistic reasons for their participation),[29] it invites many of the same criticisms that are leveled against the sale of parental rights. These criticisms are undermined in the setting of surrogate motherhood, however, by the fact that one of the buyers is the baby's biological father. The situation is much like that where a father, having divorced (or been divorced by) the child's mother, remarries and obtains custody of the child and his new wife adopts the child, terminating the natural mother's custodial claims. That last step in the case of divorce followed by remarriage—terminating the natural mother's rights over the child—is harsh from the standpoint of both the mother and the child, since presumably they have bonded. The problem is less serious when the natural mother gives up her rights to the child at birth, as in surrogate motherhood.

Of course we must consider the effect of surrogate motherhood on the child as well as on the transacting parties. But here the effect is even more likely to be positive than in the case of selling parental rights. There the alternative is that the natural mother retains the child, while in the case of surrogate motherhood the child would probably not have been born at all had its mother-to-be not signed a contract to bear a child. Most people derive a net positive utility from living—including adopted children, who seem on average to be about as happy and well adjusted and successful as other children.[30] And the children of surrogate mothers are only half adopted. I grant that the psychological impact of surrogate motherhood on the surrogate mother's other children—the children whose baby brother or sister the mother gives away—must also be considered.[31] But the psychic costs, if any, to those children must be balanced against the possible gains to them from their mother's having a higher income, as well as against the gains to the father of the surrogacy child, to his wife, and to the child.

Concern has been expressed that the typical surrogate mother is exploited and deceived. The evidence does not bear this out.[32] There have been well

29. Philip J. Parker, "Motivation of Surrogate Mothers: Initial Findings," 140 *American Journal of Psychiatry* 117 (1983).

30. Lori B. Andrews, "Surrogate Motherhood: The Challenge for Feminists," 16 *Law, Medicine & Health Care* 72, 77 (1988).

31. Michelle Harrison, "Psychological Ramifications of 'Surrogate' Motherhood," in *Psychiatric Aspects of Reproductive Technology* 97, 103–105 (Nada L. Stotland ed. 1990).

32. Andrews, note 26 above, chs. 16–17.

publicized cases in which the surrogate mother felt intense regret at having to give up "her" child—the *Baby M* case, to which I shall return in a moment, being the most famous—but these appear to be only a small fraction of the total number of surrogate-motherhood transactions. Most surrogate mothers are at least 20 years old and already have children,[33] and few are poor people, because the couple seeking to acquire a child would worry about the health of a poor woman and hence about the prospects for a successful pregnancy and a healthy baby.

The concern with exploitation blends into a more diffuse feminist concern with the symbolic significance of surrogate motherhood as the sale of the surrogate mother's sexuality, a characterization that makes surrogate motherhood reminiscent of prostitution. Not all feminists want to outlaw prostitution, and not all want to outlaw surrogate motherhood, either. All but a few, however, want to permit abortion on demand, and so it is odd that they should think it all right to kill a fetus but immoral to allow rights over it to be sold to a couple who want it to live. The point I want particularly to emphasize, however, is the distinction between sex and reproduction. The prostitute sells sex; the surrogate mother sells reproduction. The reception of sperm into the womb by means of artificial insemination is no more a sexual experience than a Pap test. What is at stake is an infertile woman's right to compensate a fertile woman for the cost (because the tendency in a competitive market is to bid price down to cost) of assisting the former to overcome the consequences of her infertility. I do not see how regulation of that right could be inimical to women's interests as a whole.

I said that artificial insemination, the technology that is basic to surrogate motherhood, further emancipates women from dependence on men. Some feminists agree,[34] but others argue the reverse and extend the argument to surrogate motherhood. "The surrogacy contract enables a man to present his wife with the ultimate gift—a child."[35] It makes the surrogate mothers "patriarchal subordinates" because they have no rights over the children, and even the wife's rights are insecure because "in the last analysis, the child is the father's."[36] If an unmarried man made a surrogate contract, he would not have to share his child with any woman.[37]

33. Martha A. Field, *Surrogate Motherhood* 6 (1988).

34. For example, Shulamith Firestone, in *The Dialectic of Sex: The Case for Feminist Revolution* 10–11 (1970).

35. Carole Pateman, *The Sexual Contract* 214 (1988).

36. Id. at 215–216.

37. The fear that reproductive technology will make motherhood obsolete is made explicit in Barbara Katz Rothman, *Recreating Motherhood: Ideology and Technology in a Patriarchal Society* (1989). On the feminist view of such technology generally, see Isabel Marcus, "A Sexy New Twist: Reproductive Technologies and Feminism," 15 *Law and Social Inquiry* 247 (1990), a helpful review article; also *Reproductive Technologies: Gender, Motherhood and Medicine*

The argument that artificial insemination and the procreative forms, such as surrogate motherhood, that it makes possible emancipate women from dependence on men, and the argument that these things emancipate men from dependence on women, are not contradictory, as they might seem to be; for anything that severs reproduction from sexual intercourse reduces the dependence of each sex on the other. But probably the net shift in the balance of power between men and women is in favor of women. It will be a long time before single men or male couples will be as comfortable raising children as single women or female couples. And even a surrogate mother under contract to an unmarried man would be paid much more than a sperm donor, though admittedly her costs are higher. Nor should we overlook the possibility that single women could use surrogate motherhood to further their emancipation from men. A woman who produces ova but cannot or does not want to carry a fetus to term can freeze her fertilized ova (fertilized by artificial insemination) for implantation in another woman. This is a form of surrogate motherhood that could enable a busy professional woman to have her own biological children without ever being pregnant. My conclusion is that the technological revolution in reproduction has increased and will continue to increase the full income of women relative to men.

It may seem ironic that feminists should worry about a decline in mothering, since feminism has long been understood to aim at liberating women from traditional roles. But again there is no contradiction. Fertility is just another asset, like a professional degree or other job-market human capital. Bottle-feeding reduces the demand for women as wet nurses. Cloning, if it ever develops to the point where a human being can be duplicated, will reduce the demand for women as mothers—as would the development of an artificial womb. In all of these cases the result is (or will be) a reduction in the full income of women. But in the foreseeable future, the net effect of technological and contractual innovations in reproduction will probably be to increase women's full income. Surrogate motherhood raises the demand for women's services; in vitro fertilization cures a female fertility problem; artificial insemination allows women to have children without having sex with a man.

We can trace the judicial reaction to surrogate motherhood by marshaling some quotations from the opinion of the Supreme Court of New Jersey in the *Baby M* case.[38] The surrogate mother in that case, Mary Beth Whitehead, was married, with children, and was not poor. The contract was for $10,000. The couple on the other side of the contract, William and Elizabeth Stern, were professional people, better educated and more prosperous than the White-

---

(Michelle Stanworth ed. 1987), and Patricia Spallone, *Beyond Conception: The New Politics of Reproduction* (1989).

38. In re Baby M, 109 N.J. 396, 537 A.2d 1227 (1988).

heads but not wealthy. Mrs. Stern was thought to have multiple sclerosis, and her doctors had advised her about the possible, although unlikely, complications (some rather gruesome) of pregnancy for a woman with that disease. Upon giving birth, Mrs. Whitehead reneged and decided to keep the child. The lower court enforced the contract and awarded custody to the Sterns. The supreme court reversed, holding that contracts of surrogate motherhood are unenforceable under New Jersey law. It allowed the Sterns to retain custody of the child, in part because Mrs. Whitehead had exhibited symptoms of emotional instability. But it gave Mrs. Whitehead extensive visitation rights rather than extinguishing her parental rights altogether, as the Sterns had desired.

Whether the decision is right or wrong as a matter of law, with regard either to the enforceability of contracts of surrogate motherhood under New Jersey law or to the custody arrangements best for Baby M's welfare (arrangements that recall the judgment of Solomon but not his wisdom),[39] the opinion is rich in illogical and poorly informed statements. "A child, instead of starting off its life with as much peace and security as possible, finds itself immediately in a tug-of-war between contending mother and father."[40] But this tug-of-war is an artifact of legal uncertainty. If the enforceability of surrogate contracts were settled, Mrs. Whitehead would have had no grounds for challenging the Sterns' custody. "The whole purpose and effect of the surrogacy contract was to give the father the exclusive right to the child by destroying the rights of the mother."[41] An obvious point is overlooked: no contract, no child. It is not as if there had been a baby in being when the contract was signed and the mother agreed to give up her parental rights. The purpose of the contract was not to extinguish a mother's rights but to induce a woman to become a mother for the sake of another woman. "Here there is no counseling, independent or otherwise, of the natural mother, no evaluation, no warning."[42] This is patronizing. We do not make people undergo counseling either before signing a contract or before becoming pregnant. The surrogate mother "never makes a totally voluntary, informed decision, for quite clearly any decision prior to the baby's birth is, in the most important sense, uninformed."[43] But as contracts always are made before rather than after they are performed, the court is implying that no contract should ever be enforceable. "Worst of all, however, is the contract's total disregard of the best interests of the child."[44]

39. George P. Smith II, "The Case of Baby M: Love's Labor Lost," 16 *Law, Medicine & Health Care* 121 (1988).
40. 109 N.J. at 435, 537 A.2d at 1247.
41. 109 N.J. at 436, 537 A.2d at 1247.
42. Id.
43. 109 N.J. at 437, 537 A.2d at 1248.
44. Id.

Again the court overlooks the elementary fact that without the contract there would in all likelihood not be a child. The court does not understand the productive function of contracts. It mistakenly believes that they merely rearrange the consequences of accomplished facts, as the court regards the birth of Baby M.

"In surrogacy, the highest bidders will presumably become the adoptive parents regardless of suitability."[45] The implication is of a fixed supply, such as the paintings of Van Gogh, being auctioned off. But the supply is not fixed, and competition among would-be surrogate mothers can be expected to force price down to cost, placing surrogacy within the reach of infertile couples of modest means. In fact the cost of surrogate contracts has been falling in real terms, for the price of $10,000 that the Sterns were charged has been constant for a decade, yet inflation during that decade considerably reduced the purchasing power of $10,000.

The court is worried about "the highest paying, ill-suited adoptive parents."[46] But as wealthy people invariably jump to the head of the queue in a system of regulated adoption, surrogate motherhood will improve the prospects for infertile couples of limited financial means. "The demand for children is great and the supply small. The availability of contraception, abortion, and the greater willingness of single mothers to bring up their children has led to a shortage of babies offered for adoption. The situation is ripe for the entry of the middleman who will bring some equilibrium into the market by increasing the supply through the use of money."[47] Precisely. But this is an argument for, not against, middlemen. The person who does something about an imbalance between demand and supply should not be blamed just because his motivation is financial. The idea that middlemen are parasites reflects the kind of primitive ignorance of economics that we expect to encounter in the Soviet Union, not in New Jersey. "It is unlikely that surrogacy will survive without money . . . That conclusion contrasts with adoption; for obvious reasons, there remains a steady supply, albeit insufficient, despite the prohibitions against payment."[48] That "albeit insufficient" is the giveaway that the court does not understand the market system. The supply is insufficient *because* of the prohibitions against payment, and its insufficiency induces infertile couples to turn to market alternatives, such as surrogate motherhood. The market failure is in adoption, not in surrogate motherhood. Supply is not redeemed from insufficiency by being "steady."

"We doubt that infertile couples in the low-income bracket will find upper

45. 109 N.J. at 438, 537 A.2d at 1248.
46. Id.
47. 109 N.J. at 439, 537 A.2d at 1249 (citation omitted).
48. 109 N.J. at 438, 537 A.2d at 1248.

income surrogates."[49] This is the jurisprudence of envy. Infertile low-income couples, even if one supposes incorrectly that they could never afford the price of a surrogate-motherhood contract, are not helped by policies that limit the options of infertile high-income couples. "There are, in short, values that society deems more important than granting to wealth whatever it can buy, be it labor, love, or life."[50] How those values are served by refusing to enforce contracts of surrogate motherhood the court does not explain.

So deficient is the court's reasoning that the explanation for its result must be sought elsewhere than in its stated reasons. The elsewhere may lie in that hostility to markets that is a staple of the thinking of modern liberal intellectuals,[51] some of whom are judges, and in fear of novelty, a common characteristic of the middle-aged and elderly, from whose ranks judges are drawn. We should therefore not be surprised to find similar concerns expressed by social conservatives, who dislike change and who are less friendly to markets than are classical liberals—the followers of John Stuart Mill and Milton Friedman. George Gilder is representative of this group. He writes, for example, that in vitro fertilization "circumvents the act of love . . . Intercourse is demoted from its pinnacle as both the paramount act of love and the only act of procreation. The trend toward regarding it as just another mode of transmitting and receiving pleasure is thereby somewhat reinforced."[52] This is true; by severing reproduction from sex, any form of artificial insemination highlights the fact that human beings invest sex with other purposes in addition to that of reproduction. But that people do this is a fact, and a good fact unless you are a Roman Catholic who missed *Gaudium et Spes* (see Chapter 8).

Gilder is also concerned lest in vitro fertilization (here he is talking about what I called the first form of surrogate motherhood) attenuate the mother's role because "the fertilized ovum does not have to be placed in the womb of the real 'mother.' Any womb will do."[53] He has got it backward. Artificial insemination—the basis of surrogate motherhood in any form—increases the power of women as mothers by reducing the mother's dependence on the father. But Gilder's real concern, it soon emerges, is with the technological

49. 109 N.J. at 440, 537 A.2d at 1249.

50. 109 N.J. at 440–441, 537 A.2d at 1249.

51. A famous example is the denunciation of the market in blood by Richard M. Titmuss, in his book *The Gift Relationship: From Human Blood to Social Policy* (1971). This is the same Titmuss who many years earlier had coauthored the book that I quoted from in Chapter 1 predicting that capitalist societies would die because people would stop reproducing. "Capitalism is a biological failure." Richard Titmuss and Kathleen Titmuss, *Parents Revolt: A Study of the Declining Birth-Rate in Acquisitive Societies* 116 (1942).

52. George F. Gilder, *Sexual Suicide* 255 (1973). See also Gilder, *Men and Marriage*, ch. 16 (1986).

53. *Sexual Suicide*, note 52 above, at 256.

steps beyond artificial insemination, such as cloning, which could indeed spell
finis to the family. "Individuals no longer so closely tied to mother, family,
and sexuality become more open to a totalitarian state."[54] How so? Liberated
by the power to clone from dependence on women for offspring, men will
become excessively masculine. They will be liberated, in fact, "to celebrate,
like the ancient Spartans, a violent, misogynistic, and narcissistic eroticism"—
epitomized by a Marine Corps boot camp![55]

Leon Kass expresses another concern with the implications of reproductive
technology: "Without the family, we would have little incentive to take an
interest in anything after our own deaths."[56] We can hear the faint, unintended
echo of the traditional belief in the narcissism of homosexuals; having no
progeny, they must have only selfish concerns. But many childless people,
from Elizabeth I to Henry James, from Isaac Newton to Franz Kafka, from
Oliver Wendell Holmes, Jr., to T. S. Eliot, have seemed to care greatly about
the durability of their achievements and the judgment of posterity. And anyway, a person who reproduces by cloning is not childless.

The convergence of socially conservative with radical feminist opinion in
regard to pornography and rape, and now also in regard to reproductive
technology, is not adventitious. Social conservatives want to preserve the
traditional sex roles and therefore oppose the social and scientific changes
that jeopardize those roles. Radical feminists believe that men are so firmly
in control of society, including its technology, that virtually any changes,
whether increased distribution of pornographic materials or advances in reproductive technology, merely entrench female subordination.[57] But not all
radical feminists believe this. Shulamith Firestone looks forward to the time
when artificial reproduction will free women from the experience of childbirth,
which she compares to "shitting a pumpkin."[58]

Eugenics and Population

The greatest worry about technological innovation in the sphere of human
reproduction is that it might allow the selective breeding of human beings.

54. Id. at 257.
55. Id. at 258.
56. Leon R. Kass, "The New Biology: What Price Relieving Man's Estate?" in *Biosocial Man:
Studies Related to the Interaction of Biological and Cultural Factors in Human Populations* 273,
287 (Don Brothwell ed. 1977).
57. Recall from Chapter 1 that Catharine MacKinnon believes that the condition of women
in this country is not only not improving but deteriorating. *Feminism Unmodified: Discourses
on Life and Law* 1–2 (1987).
58. Firestone, note 34 above, at 227.

Hitler, with his zeal for eugenic sterilization,[59] gave human eugenics a bad name. Before him it was a popular cause, perhaps especially among intellectuals, such as Justice Holmes and Bertrand Russell. Much of the fuel for the planned parenthood movement was eugenic.[60] The distinguished English geneticist R. A. Fisher expressed profound concern with the infertility of the upper classes, believing that it portended a significant diminution in the quality of the human gene pool.[61] It seems so *logical* that biology should be enlisted in the drive to make a better world. (It certainly seemed so to Plato.) Yet there are serious objections both empirical and theoretical.

The empirical objections have to do with the history of thinking about and practicing human eugenics, a history that from ancient Greece to modern Singapore is to a surprising degree racist, genocidal, generally nasty, and downright incompetent. Some examples:

1. "Negative eugenics" is most easily practiced by infanticide. In Sparta, "new-born babies were brought by their parents to the elders of their tribe; and if these judged them unpromising, they were thrown into a chasm near the foot of Mount Taÿgetus."[62]

2. Holmes's famous opinion in *Buck v. Bell* ("three generations of imbeciles are enough")[63] upheld a state statute authorizing the sterilization of persons suffering from hereditary insanity or feeblemindedness, but apparently neither Carrie Buck nor her mother nor her daughter (the three generations) *was* feebleminded.[64] Later—in the time of Hitler—the Supreme Court took a dimmer view of sterilization statutes, writing that "strict scrutiny of the classification which a State makes in a sterilization law is essential,"[65] while invalidating the statute before it, which authorized the sterilization of convicted larcenists, on the narrow ground that it arbitrarily excluded embezzlers.

3. When Bertrand Russell in his brilliant polemic for what I have been

59. Robert Proctor, *Racial Hygiene under the Nazis* (1988), passim; "Sterilization Law in Germany: Statistical Survey Concerning Obligatory Sterilization in Germany," 95 *Ecclesiastical Review* 50 (1936).

60. Linda Gordon, *Woman's Body, Woman's Right: A Social History of Birth Control in America* 274–290 (1976). On the history of human eugenics generally, see Daniel J. Kevles, *In the Name of Eugenics: Genetics and the Uses of Human Heredity* (1985).

61. *The Genetical Theory of Natural Selection*, chs. 10–12 (1929). Additional examples of this type of eugenics talk in the interwar period are quoted in Michael S. Teitelbaum and Jay M. Winter, *The Fear of Population Decline* 49–54 (1985).

62. L. P. Wilkinson, "Classical Approaches—I. Population & Family Planning," 50 *Encounter* 22, 26 (April 1978). See generally Emile Eyben, "Family Planning in Graeco-Roman Antiquity," 11/12 *Ancient Society* 5 (1980–81).

63. 274 U.S. 200, 207 (1927).

64. Paul A. Lombardo, "Three Generations, No Imbeciles: New Light on *Buck v. Bell*," 60 *New York University Law Review* 30 (1985).

65. Skinner v. Oklahoma, 316 U.S. 535, 541 (1942).

calling the model of morally indifferent sex turns to eugenics, this famously if erratically progressive thinker and brilliant philosopher turns monster, saying that since blacks are inferior to whites, there is a case to be made that they should not be permitted to reproduce, but concluding that, humane considerations to one side, the proposal should be rejected because blacks are better workers than whites in tropical climes.[66] Of course one must make allowances for the different attitudes about racial matters that prevailed when Russell wrote. It is noteworthy that Russell did not, as most of his European and North American contemporaries would have done, pronounce the white race superior to the yellow.

4. Troubled by the low birth rate of educated couples, and believing that the genes are responsible for 80 percent of a person's life prospects, in 1983 Prime Minister Lee Kuan Yew of Singapore inaugurated a program of encouraging college graduates to increase their birth rate while discouraging—by means of generous grants for voluntary sterilization—low-income and poorly educated persons from reproducing.[67] There was considerable resistance, but in any event the program was overtaken in a few years by a decision that Singapore's overall population was much too small and that even the poor and the uneducated should be encouraged to breed; so the eugenic thrust of Singapore's population policy was blunted.[68] Commentators believe that the decision to encourage all segments of the population to reproduce more was a face-saving device to cover the government's retreat from a eugenic policy that had proved highly unpopular. Among the objectors were well-educated civil servants whose own parents had been neither affluent nor educated.[69]

The main theoretical objections to eugenic breeding of human beings are that it would reduce the diversity of the gene pool (this is a clear effect of cloning) and that it would exacerbate human conflict by making human races, nations, classes, or families as different from one another as breeds of dogs are different from one another. These two points—reduced genetic diversity and increased differentiation among human beings—are only superficially inconsistent. People could become more alike save in one or two salient dimensions, such as intelligence. Note that since the rich are likely to have earlier and fuller access to the technology of eugenic breeding than the poor, differences in wealth might become permanent by being translated into genetic differences in the next generation.

---

66. *Marriage and Morals,* ch. 18 (1929).

67. J. John Palen, "Fertility and Eugenics: Singapore's Population Policies," 5 *Population Research and Policy Review* 3, 5–9 (1986).

68. Id. at 9–10.

69. See, besides Palen's article (note 67 above), V. G. Kulkarni, "Rethinking on Mums," *Far Eastern Economic Review,* June 13, 1985, 25.

If George Gilder is right, we are on a slippery slope if we permit *any* departure from natural procreation by persons ignorant of their genetic makeup, save perhaps the departure implied by the prohibition of incest. But the cat is out of the bag. Companionate marriage encourages assortative mating—likes choosing likes in order to minimize conflict, which is more destructive the closer the association between mates—and assortative mating is a form of selective breeding. Gilder's concern with artificial reproduction is also one-sided. He considers the possible costs, but not the possible benefits, of making the human race healthier and more intelligent. One must not be so timorous about change, about the future. It would surely be wrong to become hysterical over such modest forms of selective breeding as genetic screening followed by surgical intervention to remove or neutralize dangerous recessive genes. Noninfanticidal negative eugenics of this sort is far less problematic than positive eugenics. Genetic screening of sperm donors is routine, and is much more often criticized for not being done thoroughly than for being done at all.[70]

Positive eugenics is more ominous. But since its macrosocial effects lie many decades, perhaps centuries, in the future, and since we do not know whether those effects are likely to be on balance good or bad, it seems idle to worry about them now. Gilder misses this point because he fails to distinguish between a governmental policy of encouraging selective breeding—a policy difficult to implement in a democratic society if only because people do not care much about the genetic composition of the population generations hence, and therefore not something to fear—and allowing the free market to respond to the widely varying preferences of private individuals. If the only eugenic breeding is by customers of sperm banks, the impact on the human gene pool, whether for good or for ill, will be trivial.[71]

My principal concern is with the impact of artificial reproduction on sexuality. And here the main point is that by strengthening the bargaining position of women vis-à-vis men, such reproduction presages a further shift in sexual attitudes and behavior toward the Swedish model. Gilder is therefore right to associate artificial reproduction with women's liberation, although he goes overboard.[72] The Swedish model implies a low birth rate, and thus invites us to consider the possibility that, eugenics to one side, artificial reproduction could affect social welfare by affecting the size of the population. Not that

70. As in Comment, note 24 above, at 1201–4.

71. Hans Moser, "Population Genetics and AID," in *Human Artificial Insemination and Semen Preservation* 379 (Georges David and Wendel S. Price eds. 1980).

72. "Will the scientists and women's liberationists be able to unleash on the world a generation of kinless children to serve as the Red Guards of a totalitarian state?" *Sexual Suicide*, note 52 above, at 262. Radical feminists believe the alliance is between the scientists and the social conservatives—like Gilder!

eugenics and population can be neatly separated. Becker and Murphy argue, for example, that poor people have too few, not too many, children because a child of poor parents cannot compensate his parents for the expense of raising him, something a child of wealthy parents can be made to do by receiving a smaller bequest, the size of the bequest being within the parents' control.[73] But if poor people tend to have worse genes than rich, as R. A. Fisher and Prime Minister Lee, among others, have thought, and if a reduction in the quality of a society's gene pool inflicts an aggregate harm on the society greater than the benefit to the additional poor children who are born, a policy of subsidizing the poor to produce more children would not be optimal. And this is apart from the cost—including the disincentive effects of higher taxes— of financing and administering such a subsidy scheme. Moreover, Becker and Murphy are talking about the supply of poor children in a hypothetical laissez-faire economy. The welfare system already subsidizes the production of children by poor people, and there is no reason to think a higher subsidy is necessary to correct the distortion that Becker and Murphy argue would exist were there no subsidy at all. A further point is that the poor are already having more children than they want because uneducated people (who disproportionately are poor people) find it difficult to use contraception effectively.[74]

This discussion underscores the complexity of the issue of optimal population,[75] optimality being a function of the quality as well as of the size of the population. The difficulty of resolving the issue even in principle, coupled with the dismal record of government interventions designed to influence the birth rate in either direction, the self-correcting tendencies at work in societies afflicted by either gross overpopulation or gross underpopulation,[76] the availability of immigration and emigration to buffer imbalances between actual and optimal population, and the general fatuity of futuristic social planning, suggest that population policy should not be in the forefront of the debate over optimal policies toward sexuality, especially since it is unlikely that artificial reproduction will influence to an appreciable degree either the size

73. Becker and Murphy, note 11 above, at 15–16 (p. 377 of Becker's *Treatise,* also note 11 above).

74. Robert T. Michael and Robert J. Willis, "Contraception and Fertility: Household Production under Uncertainty," in *Household Production and Consumption* 27, 74 (Nestor E. Terleckyj ed. 1976), find a higher percentage of unwanted births to uneducated people than to educated people. But Becker and Murphy might reply that poor people do not want the children only because the children cannot compensate them for the cost of their rearing.

75. Complexity well brought out by the philosophical minuette danced around the issue by Derek Parfit in his book *Reasons and Persons,* ch. 17 (1984).

76. For a case study, see John Knodel, Aphichat Chamratrithirong, and Nibhon Debavalya, *Thailand's Reproductive Revolution: Rapid Fertility Decline in a Third-World Setting,* ch. 10 (1987).

or quality of the population of this or any other society in the foreseeable future. People who are fertile—the vast majority—will, with the exception of the small minority that has serious genetic defects, continue to prefer (be)getting children the old-fashioned way.[77] So I end on a recurrent note in this book: in sex as in other areas of life, beware governmental regulation.

77. Mrs. Stern was an intermediate case. She was not infertile, or the carrier of a dangerous recessive gene, but was worried about the impact of pregnancy on her health.

Conclusion

I HAVE TRIED to take a broad multidisciplinary approach to the related tasks of, first, explaining the variety of sexual behaviors, customs, attitudes, and regulations that we encounter in history and across cultures, and, second, evaluating proposals to change the laws and social policies that concern sexuality. By treating sexual behavior as rational behavior, I was able to use economics, the science of that behavior, to provide a common vocabulary and unifying perspective for my study. Economic analysis, with its useful concepts of substitution and complementarity, search costs and signaling, inferior goods and externalities, and much else besides, not only can explain a great deal of the variance in sexual behavior and regulation over time and across cultures with a minimum of assumptions, and can integrate a bewildering variety of scholarly literatures on sex; it also can generate a range of hypotheses that have the scientifically appealing property of being at once intellectually interesting, theoretically important, socially relevant, counterintuitive, and refutable (hence testable). We saw that a handful of social variables, such as the sex ratio, the degree of urbanization, and, above all, the occupational pattern and economic dependence of women—and all these variables are interrelated—explain much of the variation in, and many of the puzzles and peculiarities of, human sexual behavior and customs, ancient and modern, Western and non-Western, though not all.

In part these conditions affect sexuality through their effect on the type of marriage—whether companionate or noncompanionate, a distinction emphasized throughout this study—that is dominant in a society. Companionate marriage, the normal form in Western nations today, is, we recall, marriage in which the husband and wife are best friends, social and emotional intimates, close companions. The older form of marriage, noncompanionate marriage, is marriage in which the husband provides the wife with occasional insemination and financial support in exchange for her pledge of sexual fidelity, but there is no expectation of an intimate bond. I have emphasized that there are important sexual differences between companionate and noncompanionate marriage. Let me recall just one here. In noncompanionate marriage, since the spouses are virtual strangers in an emotional sense, extramarital sex is a close substitute for marital sex. So we can expect the husband to patronize concubines and prostitutes, and the wife to be susceptible to the blandishments of lovers—except that this means that the husband will have an incentive to sequester her, as in ancient Greece and modern Saudi Arabia. In companionate marriage, marital sex acquires the additional function of cementing the marital relationship. Extramarital sex therefore becomes a poorer substitute, and consequently there is less adultery by the husband and less need to sequester the wife to prevent her from committing adultery. My single most audacious claim is that the sexual differences between companionate and noncompanionate marriage furnish the key to understanding the evolution of sexual morality from the ancient Greeks to the modern Swedes, although the ultimate causal factor in that evolution is the changing occupational roles of women, for it is those roles that determine whether the dominant (or at least most valued) form of marriage in a society will be companionate or noncompanionate.

By deeming sexual behavior rational, I do not commit myself to denying the importance of emotion and of prerational preference, or to exaggerating the degree of conscious calculation. From the genes, and perhaps from early childhood development as well, we obtain our basic sexual drive and preferences. But how we translate these into actual behavior depends on social factors—including opportunities, resources, and constraints. Sex is a means to human ends, and the efficient fitting of means to ends, whether done consciously or unconsciously, is the economist's notion of rationality.

The interface between determined and chosen is illustrated by homosexuality. In this country when we speak of a homosexual we usually mean a person of strong homosexual preference, rather than merely a person who happens to engage in homosexual acts, perhaps when women are unavailable, as in prisons and on naval vessels. I do not consider homosexual preference something that is chosen, any more than one chooses to prefer vanilla to chocolate ice cream. Evidence from twin studies, child-development studies, international statistical studies, and other sources indicates that in all likelihood homosexual preference is an innate rather than an acquired trait. But all that the existence of homosexual preference does is determine the price—not necessarily or primarily a monetary price—that a person is willing to pay for a homosexual versus a heterosexual act or relationship. If the price of vanilla skyrockets, you may decide to substitute chocolate even though you have a strong preference for vanilla; and it is a similar choice, I contend, for either a homosexual or a heterosexual to engage in homosexual or heterosexual acts: choice is influenced not only by preference but also by the costs of indulging a preference. There is much substitutability in the domain of sexuality—one sexual practice for another, one sexual object for another, presex for sex, one sexual transactional form (for example, concubinage) for another (for example, marriage), and nonsexual for sexual activities. And this means that there is much explanatory work for the economist to do.

Economic analysis, and more broadly the scientific attitude that underlies positive economics and emphasizes respect for fact and for clear thinking, has the further value of exposing the shallowness of much moralizing in Western culture generally, and in American culture particularly, about sexuality. Such a critique can clear the ground for a normative analysis in which sexual regulations are evaluated by their practical consequences rather than by their conformity to moral, political, or religious ideas. Clear thinking about sexuality is obstructed by layers of ignorance, ideology, superstition, and prejudice that the acid bath of economics can help us peel away.

In so saying I may seem to be conceding an inevitable shortcoming of an economic approach to sex. If our sexual attitudes are a tissue of ignorance, superstition, prejudice, tradition, and ideology, how likely is it that those attitudes, and the behavior they generate, can be explained as products of rational maximization? The answer is that while I do not question the role of religious and other ideological thought, and of sheer ignorance, in the shaping of sexual attitudes, customs, law, and behavior, the ideologies—and even the ignorance—are themselves, to a significant extent, rational adaptations to the social circumstances in which powerful institutions, such as the Catholic Church, have found themselves at various points in their history.

Despite the emphasis I place on economics, my study is antispecialist[1] in its refusal to limit its method to that of economics. I have drawn heavily on research in other fields, especially biology (to such an extent indeed that my approach might be described as bioeconomic rather than economic) but also philosophy, psychology, sociology, anthropology, women's studies, history, and of course law. There is no fundamental incompatibility either among the fields I have named or between them and economics. If this is an age of specialization, it is also an age in which the lines separating academic disciplines are increasingly frayed, so one can hardly do justice to a subject like sexuality if one is afraid to consult scholarly literatures outside of one's own discipline. I have long believed that law, my primary discipline, could not be understood or improved without a healthy dose of economics. This belief animates the interdisciplinary field known as law and economics in which I

---

1. This places me in jeopardy of violating Weber's dictum that "limitation to specialized work, with a renunciation of the Faustian universality of man which it involves, is a condition of any valuable work in the modern world." Max Weber, *The Protestant Ethic and the Spirit of Capitalism* 180 (Talcott Parsons trans. 1958).

have worked for many years. More than law and economics is needed in order to do justice even to the legal aspects of a subject such as sex; but economics can retain the baton of the multidisciplinary orchestra. Obviously, though, I do not accept all of the findings in the other pertinent scholarly literatures; I am particularly reluctant to embrace extremes of social constructionism that are urged by radical feminists and other strong believers in the plasticity of human nature.[2] Yet the concept of companionate marriage, which figures so prominently in my analysis, is a sociological and historical rather than an economic concept, though it can be given an economic meaning and integrated into an economic framework for understanding sexuality.

If this study brings out the strength of economics, it also highlights its limitations. I have rejected the suggestion that sexual preference is itself chosen; I believe it is for the most part immutable. I have pointed out that economics does not delimit the community whose welfare is to be maximized, and therefore does not tell us whether we must consider the welfare of the unborn in evaluating policies that affect them. And economics does not draw a satisfactory line between self-regarding and other-regarding conduct, that is, between conduct that is personal, and not a fit subject for public regulation, and conduct that is public—that affects strangers palpably—and that therefore is a fit subject for regulation. To make a satisfactory distinction between these two sorts of conduct requires the kind of practical, historically informed, and commonsensical, although unrigorous, analysis that Mill undertook in chapter 4 of *On Liberty*.

Given the vastness of the subject of sex, the novelty of the economic perspective on it, and the inevitable shortcomings of multidisciplinary inquiry (I do not claim competence across the full range of disciplines that I have tried to bring to bear on my subject), there can be no pretense that this book is definitive. And for other reasons as well. One is the lack of logical rigor inherent in a nonformalized theory. Another is the relative paucity of *reliable* data on sex,[3] owing to the necessarily heavy reliance that empirical researchers in this field have placed on "convenience" samples (that is, samples made up of volunteers) and on unverified statements, some concerning events in the distant past (for example, early childhood), and owing as well to lack of observer independence and to the ideological and personal commitments of many of the researchers. Last is the inherent limitations of theorizing, a point that may bear elaboration. Any set of observations can be fitted to an indefinite

---

2. So I run a second risk—that of being lumped with those reactionary essentialists who believe "that individuals cannot be molded to fit into socialist societies such as the Soviet Union without a tremendous loss of efficiency." John M. Gowdy, "Bio-Economics: Social Economy versus the Chicago School," 14 *International Journal of Social Economics* 32, 34 (1987), quoting derisively—just two years before the collapse of communism—the economist Jack Hirshleifer.

3. On which see the careful discussion in Heather G. Miller et al., *AIDS: The Second Decade* 393–419 (1990).

number of theories. The choice among theories is determined by criteria such as simplicity ("elegance"), imaginativeness, scope, integrative power, richness of empirical implications, and clarity that are not themselves criteria of truth. The economic theory of sexuality scores high on these criteria, but this does not prove that it is correct. So this book cannot be an end but only a beginning. My hope is that it will stimulate further exploration of the applicability of the economic model to sexual behavior and regulation.

I want to close, therefore, by indicating a few promising directions for further research. The first concerns the index of punishment severity presented in Chapter 3. By dividing the maximum punishments for sex crimes by the maximum punishments for nonsex crimes against the person, I constructed an index of the relative severity with which a nation, or a state of the United States, punishes sex crimes. The index was found to vary significantly across nations and states. The variance has yet to be explained in a rigorous fashion. It seems related to differences in the intensity of religious belief, but a multivariate analysis might reveal that the economic variables emphasized in my model of rational sexual behavior play a larger explanatory role. Perhaps they explain religious belief as well as sexual behavior and sexual laws. Recall my point about the cafeteria-style character of American religion: Americans may choose a religion to fit their values rather than take their values from their religion.

A richer study of sex-crime law would examine actual punishments rather than the punishments on the books. The divergence may be large, and since actual punishments matter more from a practical standpoint, they may be more likely to exhibit functional or political coherence than the law on the books.

Other studies could be conducted to explore the significance of variables singled out by the economic analysis of sexuality. For example, it should be possible to determine whether, as I suggested in Chapter 5, the incidence of polygamy is a significant predictor of tolerance for homosexuality once other variables, such as the sex ratio and the incidence of companionate marriage, are introduced into the analysis. And likewise whether black males in this country are indeed less prone than white males to abuse children sexually; whether clitoridectomy is—other things the same—indeed more common in polygamous than in monogamous societies; and whether the AIDS epidemic has indeed resulted in a drop in illegitimate births.

Rather broader studies are necessary as well if the promise of the economic approach is to be fulfilled. I have argued that women's occupational structure is a principal determinant of sexual behavior and attitudes, but my supporting evidence was limited to a handful of case studies. Much more could be done to explore the issue. For example, the sexual mores of the Scandinavian nations could be compared (my analysis of Scandinavian mores was essentially limited to Sweden), and related to differences in women's occupational structure, holding constant other economic variables. Norway both is sexually more conservative than Sweden and has a lower percentage of women employed outside the home, while Finland, though also sexually more conservative than Sweden, has at least as high a percentage of women employed outside the home. So here is one apparently confirming and one apparently disconfirming instance, and these ought to be sorted out and the situations in the remaining Scandinavian states, Denmark and Iceland, also factored into the comparison. Other contiguous or otherwise comparable communities should also be compared—the nations of southern Europe, for example, or of Latin America, or of Southeast Asia. Or the tribes of the New Guinea highlands, which differ in their attitudes toward pederasty—and can the differences really be explained, as I conjectured, by differences in young men's access to women?

The history of prostitution is another rich area for study from an economic perspective. I touched on prostitution at many different points in the book, citing some of the many useful monographs and articles on the subject and proposing a number of hypotheses—for example, that a fall in the percentage of bachelors in a society alters the sexual services that prostitutes offer, that prostitution may not be common in polygamous societies despite the high effective sex ratio in such societies, and that prostitutes are becoming more like other women. But I did not attempt a systematic analysis. Such an analysis might focus not only on the effective sex ratio—the higher it is, other things being equal (they are not equal, in the case of polygamy), the greater the demand for prostitutes—but also on the prevalence and lethality of venereal disease, and the degree of urbanization (which reduces the costs of search and of detection), as critical variables determining the extent of prostitution in a society. Another variable—the nature of marriage, namely whether companionate or noncompanionate—is potentially important, but also ambiguous. On the one hand, if marriage is not companionate, then sex with a prostitute is a closer substitute for marital sex; but on the other hand, if marriage is companionate, then relations with a prostitute are less threatening to marriage than keeping a mistress or having relations with another man's wife. A model of the private and social costs and benefits of prostitution that would capture all the key variables would thus require careful thought.

Much work remains to be done on the normative as well as on the positive side of the economic analysis of sex. The indecision that I expressed on such highly charged normative issues as whether to permit homosexual marriage, end the formal exclusion of homosexuals from the armed forces, and eliminate all restrictions on pornography that does not use child models or otherwise abuse its subjects and is not exhibited to an unwilling audience, was not the product of coyness or timidity; it reflected a belief that not enough is known about the likely consequences of such changes in existing law to permit responsible recommendations in a work that aspires to be scholarly rather than polemical. On the issue of homosexual marriage, for example, someone should not only study carefully the experience of Denmark, with its simulacrum of marriage for homosexuals, but also enumerate all the legal incidents of marriage in this country (relating to taxes, fringe benefits including both private and social insurance, testimonial privilege, immigration, and child custody) with a view to estimating the consequences of making them incidents of homosexual relationships at the election of the participants. The effect on military morale and performance (in both tolerant and intolerant societies) of allowing homosexuals to serve requires further study, and I have suggested an experiment for obtaining more data on the question. With respect to the consequences of pornography, additional statistical research is needed concerning the effects, if any, and whether direct or indirect, of pornography on the incidence of rape, with other variables that probably affect that incidence held constant, such as the likelihood and severity of punishment and the ratio of young males to young females.

Although it would be irresponsible to propose sweeping changes in our sex laws on the basis of research as incomplete and frequently equivocal as I have marshaled in this book, it should be apparent that the implications of my analysis are for the most part "liberal" in the classical sense of supporting a diminished role for government. The case for forbidding abortion in the early months of pregnancy, for criminalizing homosexual acts between consenting adults, for banning homosexuals from teaching jobs, for flatly forbidding them to have custody of children, for discouraging contraception and premarital sex, for seeking to alter the birth rate in the United States (in either direction), for refusing to enforce contracts of surrogate motherhood, for regulating adoption as strictly as we do, for trying to stamp out prostitution, and for banning pornography by recognized artists is unpersuasive on the basis of present knowledge. So, however, is the case for subsidizing the production of children out of wedlock, as our welfare program—and Sweden's to a much larger extent—do. But an economic case can be made for publicly subsidizing the dissemination of contraceptive advice and devices to teenagers and for stepping up efforts to prevent the sexual abuse of children, so the implications of the analysis are not entirely laissez-faire. And recall that the case for abortion rights cannot be shown to be stronger than the case against it, so we need a tie-breaker, such as a presumption against government regulation. Public policy tie-breakers are politically controversial. Nevertheless, a fair implication of my analysis is that we should have less government intervention, especially of the prohibitory sort, in the sexual arena.

Despite my occasional criticisms of Swedish welfare policies, I believe that we have much to learn from the Swedish approach to sex, considered as a whole. Some combination of aggressive and explicit sex education from an early age, provision of contraceptives to teenagers, conditioning generous maternity and child-welfare benefits on the mother's having established herself in the job market, solicitous attention to fetal and neonatal health needs, and an end to discrimination against homosexuals may be the essential elements of a realistic (and inexpensive) program for dealing with our national blights of teenage pregnancy, teenage parenthood, and sexually transmitted AIDS. The restoration of Puritan sex ethics is not realistic, and those who preach it are merely evading the difficult questions of policy.

We should of course be wary about embracing Swedish sexual policy uncritically. Apart from the fact that the subsidy elements of that policy may make childbearing out of wedlock too cheap, the effectiveness of public sex eduction may depend on attitudes within the home; indeed, I am told that by far the most effective sex education in Sweden is that which parents impart to their teenage children. Americans do not have the same attitudes—which from a political standpoint is why it will remain impossible for the foreseeable future to take more than a few tentative steps toward the Swedish model. I would very much like to see us take those steps.

Although much remains unclear about the proper scope and direction of public policy in the area of sex, one thing that should be clear from such judicial decisions as *Roe v. Wade, Bowers v. Hardwick,* and *In re Baby M* is that efforts to steer by the light of legal reasoning are doomed to fail. Legal reform, like social reform—like human action generally—requires more than prejudice, tradition, and ideology. It requires knowledge. In this connection we should recall that the ultimate object of theorizing is not to test theories, but to enlarge our knowledge in order to improve our ability to predict and control. In the words of Auguste Comte, "Savoir pour prévoir, prévoir pour pouvoir."[4] Theorizing enlarges our knowledge in part by proposing new causal relationships and by making suggestions for how to go about conforming or refuting them. It is in that sense that this is a book of theory.

Nevertheless, it is not a book for scholars only. The initial motivation for this study was not to propose a new theory of sexuality but to inform myself in my role as a judge and to dispel some of the clouds of ignorance, prejudice, shame, and hypocrisy that befog the public discussion of sex in America generally and in the American legal system in particular. (So, more than is common in a work of theory, the book has summarized a large amount of information about its subject.) If the book succeeds in this negative aim—as it might do, for example, just by convincing the reader that sex, even in its social, ideological, and legal dimensions, can be analyzed in a disinterested and dispassionate fashion—I shall be reasonably content.

4. "To know in order to foresee, to foresee in order to control."

Acknowledgments
Index

Acknowledgments

Dean Robert Bennett of the Northwestern University School of Law invited me to give the 1991 Rosenthal Lectures and by doing so incited the search for a topic that ended in this book. Gary Becker, David Cohen, William Eskridge, David Friedman, Daniel Klerman, Lawrence Lessig, John Noonan, and John Shope made especially important contributions through their extensive comments on a previous draft. Other extremely helpful suggestions came from Lori Andrews, Michael Aronson, John Beckstrom, Ashutosh Bhagwat, Jonathan Cohen, Lloyd Cohen, James Coleman, Harold Demsetz, Ronald Dworkin, Frank Easterbrook, Alan Freeman, Andrew Greeley, William Landes, Jane Larson, Edward Laumann, Hans Linde, Michael McConnell, Elizabeth Mensch, Robert Michael, Guity Nashat, Tomas Philipson, Charlene Posner, Eric Posner, Deborah Rhode, Stephen Schulhofer, George Stigler, Cass Sunstein, Roman Weil, and two anonymous readers for the Harvard University Press.

The staff of the University of Chicago's D'Angelo Law Library, and in particular Paul Bryan and William Schwesig of that staff, rendered exceptional bibliographical assistance. Jonathan Cohen, Mary Jane DeWeese, Lynne Engel, Kevin Esterling, Lawrence Gold, Erick Kaardal, Susan Pacholski, Alison Roberts, Alison Scott, John Shope, and Jeannie Yim provided invaluable research assistance. Amanda Heller did an expert job of copyediting and made a number of helpful substantive suggestions also.

Besides the Rosenthal Lectures themselves, I gave talks based on my research for the book at the National Law Center of George Washington University (as a lecture in the Center's Enrichment Program); at the Law and Economics Workshop of Harvard Law School; at faculty workshops at the Georgetown, Stanford, and University of Chicago law schools; at the Seminar on Rational Models in the Social Sciences, sponsored by the economics and sociology departments of the University of Chicago; as a Wirszup Lecture in the University of Chicago's Woodward Court lecture series; and at the Colloquium in Law, Philosophy and Political Theory at New York University School of Law. In all of these sessions, participants made helpful suggestions.

To all of the above, named and unnamed, I extend my warmest thanks, while absolving them of any errors—of fact, tact, tone, interpretation, whatever—that remain.

Index

Abortion, 34–36, 41, 44, 46, 55, 57, 71, 143–145, 151, 187–188, 196n, 217–218, 264, 268, 271–290, 327, 332–334, 424; relation to adoption, 415; Catholic position on, 226, 273–284 passim; in classical antiquity, 272; clinics, 206; in communist countries, 59; constitutional issue, 286, 288, 332–334, 336–341; costs of obtaining, 277; as crime, 281, 332; and doctrine of double effect, 273–275, 282; feminist position on, 288–289; illegal, 206, 276–277, 284–286; indirect, 273–275, 282, 336; relation of to infanticide, 144; role of interest groups, 172n; in Japan, 69; mortality from, 206, 276n, 277, 286; in Muslim societies, 67; political economy of, 215, 218; politics of, 340–341; and population, 281–282; Protestant and Jewish positions on, 275–276; public funding of, 332n, 334; and quality of children, 283; reasons for, 278–279; religious faith of women having, 278; restrictions on in other countries, 276n; in Romania, 411n; in Scandinavia, 72; statistics of, 276–277; in Sweden, 166, 277, 283; in United States, 166. *See also* Roe v. Wade.
Abstinence, 48, 118–119, 151, 165, 267, 269, 272; clerical, 153. *See also* Celibacy; Sublimation
Acquaintance rape. *See* Date rape
Addiction, 105, 119
Adolescents, 148, 150
Adoption, 287–288, 405–420; of adults, 405–406; in Anglo-American law, 407–409; in other countries, 416; of noninfant children, 412–413, 416; demand and supply, 410–411; genetic basis, 406–407; by homosexuals and lesbians, 407, 417–420; independent, 409–410; interracial, 415; politics of, 408–409, 416–417; by polygamists, 420n; in ancient Rome, 44, 405–409; regulation of, 409–420; welfare of adopted children, 412–413, 416

Adultery, 39, 51, 71, 78, 81–82, 97–98, 119, 134, 158–160, 169, 177, 208, 256–257, 329; as crime, 251, 261; differential punishment of male and female, 184–186, 251–252; as source of externalities, 184–186; as ground for divorce, 249; in marriage law, 252; trade-offs with fornication, 263. *See also* Double standard; Illegitimacy
Aeschylus, 20
Africa; sexual mores in, 148n, 265
Age of consent, 71, 77, 396, 402–403; for homosexual relations, 403; in Sweden, 72, 403
Agency costs, 173, 256–257
Aid to Families with Dependent Children, 115, 168, 196
AIDS, 114–115, 122, 124, 127, 163–165, 186, 209, 215, 313, 345n, 346; incidence among blacks, 139n; incidence among priests, 155n
Alienation of affections, 81, 389n
Alimony, 171–172, 248
Alloparenting, 406–407
Altruism, 216, 407; reciprocal, 407; within family, 189. *See also* Children